The Book of
OLD SILVER

The Book of OLD SILVER

English ～ American ～ Foreign

BY SEYMOUR B. WYLER

WITH
ALL AVAILABLE HALLMARKS
INCLUDING
SHEFFIELD PLATE MARKS

PROFUSELY ILLUSTRATED

CROWN PUBLISHERS
NEW YORK

PRINTED IN THE UNITED STATES OF AMERICA

To

MY MOTHER AND
MY FATHER

AUTHOR'S NOTE

In the preparation of this book I was fortunate in having the counsel and assistance of many friends and the co-operation of many fellow-dealers. I want to thank them all, and especially Mr. Nathan Nathanson of the U. S. Customs; Mr. Ivan Shortt of Ellis & Co. Ltd. of London and New York, from whose great collection of photographs of silver many of the illustrations in this book were made; Mr. Stephen G. C. Ensko and Mr. James Graham, Jr., for permission to incorporate in my tables of American Silversmiths' Marks, their respective compilations of American marks.

SEYMOUR B. WYLER

CONTENTS

LIST OF ILLUSTRATIONS

The Book of
OLD SILVER

I

OLD ENGLISH SILVER

SILVER has always been the most favored of the precious metals for articles of personal or ceremonial ornament and use. Gold, though equal or superior in beauty, malleability, polish and suitability to fine effects, is twice as heavy and therefore much less practical. But the workers in one of these metals almost invariably worked in the other and goldsmithing and silversmithing really constitute one craft. Until recently goldsmith meant a worker in gold and silver.

From the earliest times, and all over the world, this craft of goldsmithing has attracted the best of artists and artisans. The value of the metals compelled a high standard of workmanship and automatically eliminated the inferior producers.

The history of ancient silversmiths is obscured in the fog of time, but since practically none of their silver is available it is not important in the understanding and appreciation of the Old Silver that exists today. It is only when we get to the history of the Art in England, the early customs, regulations and laws, that there is meaning for the amateur or connoisseur of Old Silver.

England produced more fine silver than any other country and the craft had its greatest flowering there. The customs, practices and methods originating in England influenced all other silver producers as English culture and influence spread throughout the world. The "Sterling" standard is an indication of this, though this word owes its origin to a band of immigrant Germans. They called themselves the Easterlings because of the direction in which they lived, and they were first called by King John in approximately 1300 to refine some silver to purity for coinage purposes. In a statute of 1343 the first two letters were dropped from the word "Easterling" and the application of the word "Sterling" to silver commenced.

Silver design, like architecture, followed the great movements and influences of culture and domination. And the periods and styles of silver are on the whole the same as of architecture and furniture.

At the time of the smithing of the first pieces in England, the Church reigned supreme, and the majority of the pieces made were for religious institutions. They were great rarities because of the prohibitive price of the metal in those days. But the shrines, chalices and magnificent altar frontals made for wealthy abbeys were not always the work of monks who worked at goldsmithing. Rather, in many instances, goldsmiths who had reached a high position in their field were admitted to the better abbeys and rapidly promoted because of their artistic skill. The ordinary goldsmith was not a monk vowed to a life relieving him of the normal cares in the struggle for existence, but rather a layman following a highly skilled profession of economic importance and accounted remuneration. Probably at no time during the history of goldsmithing were these men better paid for their labors, and a great number of new craftsmen joined the ranks of this little known industry and apprenticed themselves to the early masters.

The styles of the pieces made then showed a surprising gracefulness of line and proportion, for in those days a silversmith might work on one piece several months in order to complete an object of great beauty. During the Middle Ages goldsmithing was ranked among the highest of the arts, and the work of the various smiths of the time were indeed pieces of great artistic merit. During this period, goldsmiths apprenticed themselves for many years before entering the trade as finished workers. Medieval goldsmiths, however, did not confine themselves only to the production of plate but dabbled as well in many lucrative side-lines. Some were members of the other richer crafts, some often acted as pawnbrokers and they were often especially useful to the Crown. During the twelfth and thirteenth centuries, the machinery of government was becoming steadily more complicated and there were many instances where goldsmiths were called upon to aid in the construction and decoration of royal buildings, as well as the administering of the mints and exchanges.

As time passed and commerce with foreign countries developed, greater quantities of raw silver were brought to England. The English people took largely to the new luxury, and the demand for it increased rapidly. Goldsmiths in the tenancy of the monasteries found they could no longer meet the increased demands for pieces in the precious metals. They wisely took the precaution of forming themselves into guilds or fraternities. The first mention of a goldsmith's company is in the year of 1180, but it appears that this was a voluntary association and carried but little power. As early as the year 1238, many inferior silversmiths immediately took advantage of the trade to make silver of a very much lower standard than was used for government coins, and sold it for the same price as a piece of the correct alloy. With the formation of the first silver guilds in England, a Law of Parliament stated that no silver should be melted unless it had first been assayed by an appointed committee and proved to contain the correct amounts of silver and alloy. In 1335, a second "statutum de Moneta" decreed that each gold- or silversmith must punch on his wares a particular mark of his own, assigned to him by the King. In 1423, an act by Henry VI fixed the price of silver at a definite valuation of twenty-two shillings to the pound. In the succeeding years, this valuation was changed several times. In 1477 a very important law was passed by the London gold-smiths' company, compelling stamping of the leopard's head or crowned leopard's head on every piece of silver of the accepted standard.

In the year 1479, the use of the date letter was first inaugurated. The year of manufacture was to be indicated by stamping a specified letter of the alphabet in a distinctive type of lettering. Thus in the following years we find silver pieces punched with a complete set of hallmarks: the leopard's head, the date letter, the maker's mark.

Although by far the greater portion of silver made during the Gothic period was used and produced for the Church, by no means is it to be thought that plate for use in the private home was over-looked. The birth of secular plate may be said to have been caused by the desires of medieval monarchs to flaunt their power and wealth by displays of magnificent silver and gold objects within their castles. From this arose the inspiration for what is termed domestic silver, as distinguished from that made by the craftsmen of the religious fraternities for use in their ecclesiastical buildings. As we have seen, by the thirteenth century the secular silversmiths had established the foundations of their craft and had developed styles and traditions of distinctly original design. During the thirteenth and fourteenth centuries, silver plate had come into general use in the homes of royalty, and no restrictions were ever placed on the number of articles made for the table. The most popular pieces produced were basins and ewers, ceremonial salts, large dishes, chargers and drink-ing cups of many varieties. A greater number of drinking articles existed than other pieces, for each man reserved the right to his personal cup. This tradition is found not only among the wealthy but even in the peasant classes, but their drinking cups were made of wood.

Gradually foreign influences entered. During the sixteenth cen-tury, domestic plate was greatly influenced in design and style by the influx of foreign silversmiths who came from Italy, France and Germany, in which countries the Italian Renaissance had been fully accepted. The Gothic waned and the Renaissance styles took hold.

Nevertheless there are so few pieces in existence made prior to the sixteenth century that the study of the early goldsmiths can be accurately made only from the libraries of the first silver guilds, and the diaries of prominent persons of the day. The long and bloody Wars of the Roses were undoubtedly responsible for the melting of many magnificent pieces scheduled in ancient inventories. It is for this reason that secular plate from this time is practically unknown. The few remaining examples which unfortunately are not always the representative workings of the better type, are to be found only in private collections and museums. Whenever a piece dating before 1600 is offered at public sale, the price realized is almost fantastic.

This explains the scarcity of secular plate, but what of the pieces carefully stored in the Churches and produced in so much greater profusion? These art treasures carefully protected by the Abbeys were to undergo a fate similar to that of the plate in the homes of royalty and nobility. During the Reformation, the pillage and destruction of practically the whole of the treasures of the Church was effected. However, a further cause for the scarcity of ecclesiastical plate is found in the forced loans which the Tudor and succeeding monarchs commanded from the corporate bodies of the City of London. Many a highly prized specimen was regretfully sacrificed in order to meet the imperious requests of the Sovereign.

During the reign of Elizabeth, internal prosperity resulted in an era of far flung luxury. The stream of art diverted from the Reformation, and from the ecclesiastical channels turned toward domestic and civic comfort and splendor. Wealthy patrons of colleges and universities abundantly endowed their respective Alma Maters with magnificent plate. But the destruction of the majority of this plate was caused by Charles I directly after the Civil War. He borrowed as much money and plate as he could obtain from the leading universities. He promised to repay them for these treasures but did not, and the money was dissipated by this luxury loving monarch. During the Cromwellian era, similar proceedings took place, but during the reign of Charles II the silver business flourished.

Much of the plate had been made from the silver coin of the realm, and in order to prevent the resulting scarcity of coin, the Act of 1696 fixed the standard for plate above that of the silver coinage. The mint had offered a high price for all plate and large quantities were melted down to the ore state.

Laws regulating the silver trade were enacted and especially drastic was the penalty for fraud. In two instances, the penalty for marking inferior silver with the sterling hallmark, was punished by death. It is because of these stringent laws of the English government, upheld today as well as in early times, that practically no forged antique silver is found in Great Britain, for as quickly as the government punished the offender, so it destroyed his wares.

Moreover, the governmental influence on the craft in other ways was so great, that the reasons for many of the features of the craft cannot be understood without a knowledge of the important laws and regulations.

II

LAWS AND REGULATIONS AFFECTING
ENGLISH HALLMARKS

A COMPREHENSIVE study of the complete legislation with regard to the ancient art of goldsmithing and silversmithing might well fill several volumes. The laws passed are many, and invariably written in great detail. Here we will attempt merely to give in a very concise form the high-lights or most important acts and laws that influenced the production of old silver.

The year 1180 commemorates the earliest mention of a guild or fraternity with regard to silversmithing. However, little importance is attached to it as the association was purely a voluntary one and had but few laws to govern it. After its inauguration, the founders were fined for being irregularly established without a proper license from the King.

As early as the year 1238, many inferior goldsmiths took advantage of their trade and produced silver of a very much lower standard than was used for government coins. These pieces were marketed for the same price as those of the correct alloy. Because of these numerous frauds, Henry III ordered the Mayor and aldermen of the City of London to choose six of the most discreet goldsmiths to superintend the craft. This order was duly obeyed and in the succeeding years these men were in turn followed by others in the so-called offices of superintendents or wardens.

The wardens were given more and more power as time went on and in 1300 were authorized to assay every silver vessel produced, to ascertain whether or not it contained the correct proportion of silver and alloy. They became known as "gardiens."

In the year 1327 the Guild of London Goldsmiths became regularly incorporated by Royal Charter, under the title of "The Wardens and Commonalty of the Mystery of Goldsmiths of the City of London." The most important legislation enacted by this Congress was that requiring every silversmith to use a particular hallmark of his own.

The second "Statutum de Moneta" in 1335 declared that inasmuch as counterfeit money had been imported by foreigners, plate was not to be exported without official license in order to protect the coin within the realm of the people. It is interesting to note here that the only means of exit from England officially allowed was from

Dover, at which place foreigners were searched and then permitted to depart from England.

A Statute passed in 1363 commanded that no goldsmith should work gold or silver into a wrought article unless it was of the alloy of good sterling. In the succeeding years, numerous by-laws were enacted in regard to the trade, all of varying importance.

The Guild was reincorporated by charter in 1392 with vastly extended powers. In the provinces there is also evidence of the existence of similar guilds. These, however, will be discussed in detail in their proper place.

During the reigns of Henry VIII and Edward VI the silver coinage in England had been scandalously debased to the extent that in 1551, the coin minted consisted of only three ounces of silver to every pound weight of coins. But in 1560, an act of Elizabeth definitely established the Sterling Standard of 11 ounces 2 dwt. This is the equivalent of 92.5 per cent pure silver and this standard has remained until the present time (with the exception of one period from 1697 to 1720). In order to correct the existing evil state of the coinage at this time, all existing base money was recalled by Royal proclamation on February 19, 1560.

In order to stop the melting of coins for use in silverware, a law was passed in 1696 raising the silverware standard above the coin standard to 11 ounces 10 dwt. (95.8%). Pieces made of this standard were to be stamped with a new mark known as Britannia.

But in 1719 the old standard of 11 ounces 2 dwt. was revived since wares of this content were proven to be more durable than the softer Britannia ware and the higher standard did not accomplish its purpose. Silversmiths merely added pure silver to coin silver to increase the standard. The higher or Britannia standard was not abolished but left to the discretion of individual silversmiths. It is interesting to note that the silver standard of 1719 has never changed since. This same act, which was one of the most important recorded in the annals of the Guild, also imposed a tax of sixpence per ounce on all silver made in Great Britain. This is the first known mention of any duty on plate, but because of the ineffectuality of collecting the duty, this act was repealed in 1757. In its place a law was passed which required a license to be purchased by every goldsmith and silversmith, for which a nominal fee was charged.

The duty on plate was reimposed in 1784 and continued until 1890. The head of the reigning sovereign was punched on the piece in order to denote that the full duty had been paid.

In 1890 the duty on silver was repealed, and the use of the sovereign's head was discontinued.

HALLMARKS

Because of the correct and continued use of hallmarks on English silver, the collector and research student of today is enabled to trace the complete ancestry of nearly any piece made subsequent to 1300. However, let it not be thought that hallmarks were ever originally used for any other purpose than to prevent fraud. On all pieces made from the beginning of the fourteenth century, a series of hallmarks was to be impressed denoting the quality of the piece made, and indicative of the individual maker.

The Leopard's Head mark was first established in 1300 and may be said to be the earliest known hallmark on English silver. In 1363 the name was changed and this particular mark was called a King's mark. Through an error in translation from the French, the name leopard was applied to the head as depicted in the hallmark, but actually the figure used was that of the head of a lion. From 1478 to the George II era there was a crown on the leopard's head. After this time, however, the size of the head was diminished and again through an error in reading the original laws of the guild, the crown was omitted.

MAKER'S MARK

This mark is next in chronological order to the leopard's head. The act of 1363 ordained that every Master Goldsmith should have a mark of his own which was to be impressed on each piece after it had been assayed. The first maker's marks were generally flowers, animals, hearts, crosses, or other symbols generally selected in allusion to the maker's name. It is probably because most of the population at this time was illiterate that this form of mark was used. Shops in London of this period were rarely advertised by name since so few people were able to read. Therefore, we may assume that the earliest silversmiths aped the styles of shopkeepers in advertising or hallmarking their own products. This system fell into disuse in the seventeenth century and by the time of Charles II, initials and letters were used. During the years of the Britannia standard many makers used two individual marks, in order to distinguish silver made of one standard from the other. This caused so much confusion that in 1739 a statute decreed that all silversmiths should use the first initials of their Christian name and surname. At this time all previous marks were discontinued.

DATE LETTERS

Although there has been definite proof of the use of the date letter on silver as early as 1500, the first actual mention is in 1629. From this time on, date letters were used with sufficient frequency to enable one to fill in the missing years, and so be able to determine the exact year in which a piece was made. The use of the date letter was arranged in cycles of twenty years using the letters A to U or V, but excluding J. At the end of each twenty years, a different type of letter was used and the cartouche was changed. It must be mentioned here that dates that one often finds engraved on a piece of silver are of but little help in determining the actual year in which a piece was created, as many pieces were given or bequeathed and the date inscribed signified the time of the presentation, not the time of making.

LION PASSANT

This mark was adopted as the official stamp at the Goldsmiths Hall in London in 1544. All London silver made since then must have this mark.

LION'S HEAD ERASED AND "BRITANNIA"

The only importance to be attached to these two marks is that they denoted pieces made of the higher standard and were used for only 23 years, from 1697 to 1720. It is because of the short term of use of these marks that pieces bearing the Britannia are rare and always sought after by collectors.

SOVEREIGN'S HEAD

This mark should be found on all plate assayed in England from 1784 to 1890 as it was required to be used to denote the payment of duty by the silversmith to the Crown. This mark is actually the head in profile of the reigning King or Queen.

Thus the use of these marks enables us to identify the place, year, and maker of old silverware. Complete tables and the method of using them will be found in a separate section of this book.

III

FRAUDS

WE have seen the great and complicated efforts to maintain the regularity and genuineness of silverware. That was because the continued growth of an industry not only produces craftsmen of merit and ability but also individuals who are not content to deal fairly and earn the rewards of honest labor. The establishing of silversmithing as a permanent and lucrative business was the loophole for many dishonest workers to seek unethical methods by which to prosper. The English, being a keen and farsighted people, took precautions as early as 1327 to try and stop any forms of malpractice. In this year, which marks the incorporation of the Goldsmiths Company, the first measures were taken to guard against the counterfeiting of silver. With the passing years, the Goldsmiths Company grew more powerful and for the last five centuries their word has been law in England. Even today, they assay and hallmark all pieces of English origin, and for this reason very little forged silver is to be found there today. Not only did the Company have the right to punish an offender, but they were privileged to confiscate and destroy his wares as well. In early days, the penalties for forging silver were very severe.

There are many ways in which deception may be practiced in the silver trade, and an attempt will be made here to simplify and explain the various means. However, it must be remembered that the actual contact with a fraudulent piece is the most certain way of detecting the deception.

The earliest known fraud was the sale of plated ware, represented to be of the silver standard. The maker hallmarked the pieces himself and thus the payment of duty and all contacts with the Goldsmith Company were avoided. However, legislation and supervision did away with this type of deception. The quality of the silver in a piece may be proved by the application of acid, the resulting reaction on the metal being definite proof of its fineness. This method is used commonly by tradesmen today in dealing with unmarked pieces.

One of the frequently practiced frauds today is that of subtraction which is in effect the removal of a part or parts of an article after it has been hallmarked. For example, let us say that a silver cup of a certain type is wanted, and the nearest thing available is an urn of similar proportion. By removing the spout, the urn becomes a cup and the order is filled. Also, trays are often found which were originally patens. The feet having been removed and the abrasions carefully erased, a more valuable piece has been created. It is safe to say the fraud of subtraction is usually perpetrated only to create a piece of greater saleability.

A similar fraud is that of addition. This is the adding on of a part to an original piece after it has been hallmarked. The law provides that permission must be obtained from the authorities before making an addition, and that if the additional piece increases the weight of the article by more than a third of its original weight, the added silver must be hallmarked. However, it also decreed that an addition could not be performed if it in any way changed the character of the original article. In other words, a foot, a handle or a spout might be put on, but a coffee pot could not be made from a tankard.

Another type of forgery is that of transformation and this is done to turn an original into a piece of greater worth and more character. A tray might be created from a meat platter, as it is far more saleable from the standpoint of the dealer, and definitely more valuable. Although in this type of fraud the hallmark is left untouched, it often becomes twisted and frequently appears upside down or in the wrong place.

More frequent than these frauds is the transposition of the marks from an article that is old into a piece of modern manufacture. As a rule the marks are taken from an old piece of little value and put into an article which if it were old would command a high price. For example, the part of a handle of a teaspoon on which the marks are impressed is removed and transposed on to the side of a coffee pot that is a good reproduction. In this way, new pieces of apparently antique silver are created.

The counterfeiting of marks constitutes the marking of a piece by other than the Goldsmiths Company and the reasons for this deception are easily discerned. Because of the extreme similarity of some new marks to some old ones, this type of fraud is sometimes found. For instance, the fact that the Britannia standard mark is in use today if the piece is of the recognized quality, is reason enough to promote this fraud. As the old standard mark and the new are alike, all the unscrupulous dealer has to do is to have the date letter omitted, and the piece might well be a fine original from the Queen Anne period.

From all the preceding indictment and explanation of fraudulent practices, the innocent bystander might easily remark that with so many varied types of forgery being practiced, it is impossible to purchase a fine original and be completely certain of its authenticity. However, by no means does the author intend to convey the impression that the majority of these frauds cannot be detected. It is a safe practice though, when in doubt to consult an expert, and if necessary pay him for his advice, for in the long run it will be the cheapest investment.

There are many ways in which to detect the forgeries on pieces of silver. Silver can be tested, hallmarks should be properly placed, and the piece must not antedate its introduction. What is meant by the latter is that if tea caddies were introduced during the reign of Queen Anne, one bearing the hallmark of say 1640 must obviously be a spurious piece. It is well also, to consider carefully the period in which the piece was made. More than often it is just such errors as these that lead to the eventual detection of fraudulent pieces. Even the cleverest forger will slip up somewhere, and as a rule it is the lack of knowledge of the history of silver that defeats the counterfeiter.

To an expert, the easiest method of judging the age of a piece is by its color, and although this rule is not infallible, it generally proves true. Silver over a period of years becomes oxidized many times, and this continued action of the elements on the metal gives it a certain softness of texture and color that is known as patina. Frequent cleaning and use in service mellow the piece, and it assumes a certain smoothness that time alone can produce. One often revels in the beauty of old silver, because of its soft bluish color. This is an integral part of the make-up of the patina.

The insertion of an old set of hallmarks in a modern piece, has been said to be the forgery most in use today. This malpractice entails a great deal of labor such as filing, fitting and soldering the marks into place. The heat of the hard soldering discolors the silver, and necessitates the polishing of the piece to hide the defect. After a time, the solder marks will be visible, and it is for this reason that dealers so often blow their breath on the hallmarks. In this way they can sometimes see signs of the transposition. An excellent test is to put the piece in fire and after a few minutes if the marks have been soldered in, the outline will become visible.

Hallmarks on silver are punched in separately and if one finds a set of four salts or a dozen service plates with all the marks perfectly aligned, there is just cause for suspicion.

IV

THE COLLECTION AND CARE
OF OLD SILVER

IN purchasing pieces of silver from those who are not absolutely reliable, it is well to beware of these so-called bargains. It is a fairly safe axiom to remember that good things are never too cheap. The reason for this may be explained if one considers that the market for silver is very steady, and purchasers, whether dealers or private people, are almost always ready to increase their collections.

Pieces that have additions such as later chasing or engraving, or badly eradicated hallmarks, can be purchased for very little. However, their worth is little more than that of modern silver, for old means antique, and that in turn may be translated into meaning original.

It is best to buy your silver from an unquestionably reliable dealer. He is more likely to detect a fraud than you and if it is not genuine he won't sell it to you except for what it is. If, however, you are acquiring silverware in one way or another not from a reputable dealer, be careful. First, determine what the piece is supposed to be. Look for the hallmarks. Are they complete, consistent and genuine? The marks must not be too regular. They must not be upside down and each detachable piece must be hallmarked. Then determine where it was made, when and by whom. Consider whether the style of the piece is consistent with the period and whether it has the proper patina for its alleged age. If you are at all uncertain give it the acid test to determine whether it is really silver. Then look for abrasions, rough edges, etc., to see if there has been any subtraction. Look carefully to determine whether by irregular joining, welds, curves, solderings you can detect transformation or addition. And most important check the hallmarking to see whether genuine antique hallmarks have been soldered into a more recent article. The extent of your testing and verification will naturally vary with the price and the importance of the ware.

If the hallmarks are not genuine or not genuinely of the piece, then the ware will not have value as an antique. If the fault is in subtraction or transformation, the piece will have value as an antique, but much less than its apparent value. If the fault is in addition, its value as an antique will be that of a piece without the addition.

The absence or incompleteness of hallmarks does not in itself mean that a piece is worthless as an antique. It merely raises that presumption and makes identification and proof very difficult. In the case of incomplete marks, first be sure that the reading is accurate. The absence of the leopard's head or date letter may mean merely that the piece is not London silver but American or French or the ware of some other country. If the marks that are on the silver do however indicate its origin there may be good and interesting reasons for the omission of the other marks. And the least likely of these reasons would be fraud, because a forger taking the trouble to fake an antique would probably be sure to have his hallmarks complete.

If a piece can be positively identified and proven of standard it will have the same value whether or not the hallmarks are complete because the entire purpose of hallmarks is merely to certify when and by whom a piece of standard silver was made.

Worn, badly erased or eradicated hallmarks are a definite fault. Old silverware, to be worth its true value, must be in good condition and a worn mark besides being an indication of a worn piece makes exact identification impossible.

The relative importance of the imperfection can best be gauged by understanding the factors that determine the value of old silver. First and by far the most important is age or scarcity value. Second is size. As a general principle all other things being equal the bigger the piece the more its worth. But this is not absolutely true. The third factor might be considered to be supply and demand, which is another facet of the scarcity factor. For example, there is very little eighteenth century silver available. Therefore, whatever there is, is very valuable. Of course, a large tray will be worth more than a small tray. But a small coffee pot might be worth more if it happened to be a rare example, or if someone needed it to complete a set. Style, workmanship, the intrinsic beauty of the piece, the maker are other factors that have effect upon the value of the silver.

Nevertheless silver other than antique pieces may have considerable value and may be worthy of collection. Careful selection of low and moderate priced pieces today will probably also bring dividends, in time, to the collector.

Authentic reproductions, any hand wrought ware that is genuine will have in the ordinary course of events important and increasing value. The craft now, as a handcraft is almost non-existent. With the passage of time the absorption into private hands of more and more of this later silverware and the inevitable loss and destruction of pieces, the scarcity and therefore the value will increase. The demand also will increase as the custom and fancy of collecting increases and the standards of living improve.

Silverware has always been a premier investment with ever increasing values and it will continue to be so because the supply of it cannot increase, it must decrease.

Machine made silverware may have a collector's value in time, but only in a limited degree. After all, the chief determining factor is scarcity and machines are used to produce quantities.

However, Jubilee Silver made during 1934-1935 and impressed with the mark of the double sovereigns-head (King George V and Queen Mary) has already risen in value.

THE CARE AND CLEANING OF SILVER

The possession of old silver carries with it a responsibility, as pieces of such rarity must be given great care. Old silver should be cleaned regularly with an accepted standard polish or paste, which will in no way be harmful to the texture of the metal. Inasmuch as the great beauty of antique silver lies in its soft color, it is heartily recommended that all cleaning be done by hand rather than by machine. At no time should silver be left to tarnish to such a degree that it makes it necessary to have it buffed, as in doing this, the hallmarks may be eradicated.

With regard to storage of fine pieces, it is suggested that they be wrapped individually in anti-tarnish flannel bags, which will serve as a means of protection. The author has found from practical experience that many people attempt to have their silver lacquered so as to save work in the house. This is definitely not approved of as the lacquer imparts to the old patina a glaring finish which detracts from the beauty of the piece.

FAMOUS ENGLISH GOLDSMITHS

THROUGHOUT the history of silversmithing in England, a few smiths are outstanding for the quality of the work they produced. An attempt is made only to give the highlights in the careers of the most brilliant of these craftsmen.

PAUL LAMERIE

Paul Lamerie was born in Holland April 14, 1688. His family had settled there after escaping from religious persecution in France, one of many of the Huguenots who fled to foreign lands. Because of these family ties of Lamerie which were distinctly French, he is often erroneously thought to have been a French silversmith.

In 1691 Lamerie's father arrived in England and having been of the French aristocracy, would not permit himself to work in a trade. The only profession which embraced manual labor that was acceptable was that of the goldsmith.

At the age of fifteen the young Paul was apprenticed to Peter Platel and it is to this celebrated craftsman that he owes all of his early knowledge of the trade. Very few students were given better opportunity, as Platel's works had been accepted as having reached the zenith of the goldsmith's art. Seven years after his apprenticeship, Lamerie was admitted as a freeman and opened up his first shop. Within a short time his instant success was evidenced by the establishing of a second place of business. In 1717, he was admitted to the livery of the Goldsmiths' Company, and eventually was within reach of the Prime Wardenship of the Guild. During his lifetime he connected himself with the army, and in 1743 attained the rank of Major.

He died in 1751 after a very colorful career. No silversmith throughout English history attained such world-wide fame as did Lamerie, for the quality of his work was distinctly superior to any previously known. As a craftsman, he had a distinct genius for creation and brought many new forms of decoration to the public eye for the first time. It is indeed strange, however, considering his great popularity and success, that he was never appointed as a goldsmith to the crown. Not one article made by Lamerie is to be found in the collection of Royal Plate at Buckingham Palace or Windsor Castle.

Throughout the study of the life of Lamerie, one is apt to be confused by the various spellings of his name. No serious notice need be taken of this if one realizes that that age in which he lived was an illiterate one and people spelled mainly phonetically.

MATTHEW BOULTON

The city of Birmingham is justly proud of Matthew Boulton. Throughout his entire life he was associated with his home city and was one of the earliest of the provincial silversmiths to achieve more than a local reputation. His talents were not confined to silversmithing. During his lifetime he was connected with several other industries, in each of which he left a name well to be remembered. In his younger days, he engaged in the manufacture of hardware and then went into the trade of artistic productions which included articles of Sheffield plate, silver, ormolu and paintings.

Later on he devoted his entire time to the development of Watt's steam engine and made great strides in the field of engineering. In the final stages of his life he brought about numerous improvements in the coining of money, several of which were accepted by the Treasury of England for practical use.

The Boulton family was typical of many known in the seventeenth century, the landed gentry engaged in the manufacturing pursuits. Matthew was born in 1728 and attended school in a suburb of Birmingham. At the age of fourteen he was apprenticed to a trade which he left a short time later to enter business with his father, who was a toy manufacturer. The toy business, as it was then known, was not one in which children's playthings were made, but rather a shop wherein all sorts of trinkets, buckles, seals, boxes and articles of hardware for household purposes were sold. The young Matthew applied himself diligently to this business and before long was entrusted with the entire management of his father's interests. Boulton was married at an early age, but was widowed a short time after. Scarcely a year had elapsed, when his father died and it was this occurrence that brought him into greater prominence than ever before. As his business grew, he became a combined manufacturer and retailer, and was compelled to take in a partner, John Fothergill. Unfortunately, he turned out to be more of a detriment than a help.

Shortly after the discovery of the process known as Sheffield plating, Boulton went to the city of Sheffield better to acquaint himself with this new technique. He realized the tremendous future in store for this new industry and spent several weeks in the work shops of Richard Morton, one of the ablest of the early makers. The ear-

liest mention of a piece of plate by Boulton is in 1762, and he carried
the distinction of having the only foundry outside of Sheffield where
plate was made. He was one of the first craftsmen to adopt the
sterling silver thread edge in place of the plated wire, as he was
convinced that this newer process would protect the pieces at the
points of hardest wear. Many of the Boulton pieces are stamped
with the words: "Silver Borders," in conjunction with his own mark
of a sun which he registered in 1784.

After his success in the production of Sheffield plate his thoughts
naturally turned to the industry of solid silver making. However,
he was faced here with a very serious obstacle, as the silver had to
be hallmarked and the nearest assay office was at Chester, seventy-
two miles away. The only alternative was to send the pieces to the
London assay office, but as this was even further distant, the cost
was too great and the likelihood of damage was ever-present. Boulton gave a great deal of thought to this difficulty and soon became
determined to appeal to Parliament for the establishment of an assay
office at Birmingham. He voiced his opinions on this subject most
intelligently and was given a great deal of publicity. Before long,
his fellow workmen in the city of Sheffield gave him their whole-
hearted support and the two towns requested individual assay offices
at the same time. After a great deal of argument, on the part of the
Goldsmiths of London, against this measure, permission was granted
in 1773, and offices were opened at Birmingham and Sheffield.

Matthew Boulton died in 1809, and conclusive proof of the tremendous success he enjoyed may be gleaned from his will. This
provided for the disposition of close to three quarters of a million
dollars which in those days was considered a huge fortune. Truly, it
may be said that he was successful in every enterprise he undertook,
but that in the production of Sheffield plate he achieved a prominence never since equalled by any other craftsman. He produced
plate of rare quality, and his works are eagerly sought after today
as they are considered among the best specimens of the period in
which he lived.

PAUL STORR

Paul Storr was the most celebrated of the late George III silversmiths, and his works showed a degree of skill equalled previously
only by Paul Lamerie. Throughout his career he enjoyed the distinction of royal and artistic patronage and executed many important
dinner services to special order. He was a great artist and developed
many new modes of decoration in his work. During the last ten years

his skill has become more appreciated than ever—and today many collectors are specializing in the acquisition of pieces by him.

Paul Storr first entered his name at Goldsmiths Hall in 1792, at which time he was a partner in the firm of Rundell and Bridge. In 1821, in conjunction with John Mortimer, he opened the shop of Storr and Mortimer, which has been carried on to the present time in London under the name of Hunt and Roskell.

ANTHONY NELME

Nelme was one of the earliest smiths to achieve prominence and was extensively patronized throughout his career. He entered his mark in the Hall in 1697. Upon his death in 1722, he was succeeded by Francis Nelme, who adopted Anthony's mark and continued his work in the same style.

PETER PLATEL

Platel was one of the Huguenots who escaped to England where he enjoyed a large and extensive patronage. He produced many magnificent pieces for royalty, but he is probably better known as the tutor of Paul Lamerie.

BATEMAN

The members of the Bateman family, which included Anne, Hester, Jonathan, Peter, and William, were all prominent as silversmiths in the George III era. They were among the most popular smiths of their time and their work portrays clearly the exacting apprenticeship to which each was subjected. The name of Hester Bateman is by far the best known of the five, and the work by this celebrated lady smith is greatly in demand. The delicate craftsmanship which was characteristic of her has influenced greatly present popularity. As only a few pieces bearing her hallmark are available, higher prices are paid than ever before.

Among many other craftsmen who achieved fame were: Simon Pantin, Peter Archambo, David Willaume, Richard Gurney, John Cafe, Henry Chawner, and John Emes.

VI

TEA SERVICES

THE spirit of the tea hour seems to be indelibly associated with England, for in no other corner of the world is this simple function still preserved with such dignity and care.

Tea was originally introduced to the English people through an advertisement that appeared in a London newspaper in 1658. "That excellent and by all Physicians approved China Drink called by the Chinese Tcha, by other nations Tay, alias Tee, is sold at the Sultaness Head, a coffee-house in Sweeting's Rents, by the Royal Exchange, London." It was mentioned again in the diary of Samuel Pepys, who in 1660 wrote of having tasted a new beverage from the East and having found it to his liking. However, it was not until 1664 that tea came to be better known. In that year, the East India Company, one of the largest trading establishments of its day, presented two pounds of this new luxury to His Majesty Charles II. Tea cost over one hundred shillings a pound at that time so that the mention of a gift of two pounds of tea to the reigning king of England, need not seem strange.

Although tea was first considered to be expressly for medicinal purposes, it soon grew to be better known as a refreshment. It is recorded that tea found instant favor with the ladies and gentlemen of the court, and it was not long before it was imported in larger quantity. As the importation increased, so the price was lessened and in about 1720, tea had reached a price level where it could be enjoyed by others than just the select and wealthier classes. Leading figures of the day with sufficient funds to indulge themselves, consumed as many as twenty to twenty-five cups daily.

The introduction of tea into England is responsible for the production of many beautiful silver vessels for use in service, and were it not for the instant popularity which greeted its importation into England, the world might well have lost these splendid examples of superb craftsmanship displayed by the silversmiths in the making of silver tea ware.

TEA POTS

The earliest known silver tea pot was made in 1670, this priceless treasure now being in the possession of the Victoria and Albert Museum in London. The pot bears the arms of the East India Company, and is engraved with an inscription of presentation as follows: "This Silver Tea-Pott was presented to ye Comtte of ye East India Cumpany be Ye Honoue George Lord Berkeley Castle A member of that Honourable and Worthy Society and a True Hearty Lover of Them 1670." Were it not for this inscription it might well have been thought to have been a coffee pot, for its shape and size were very similar to the accepted style of coffee pot produced since about 1700. Very few silver tea pots of contemporary date are known. During the reign of Queen Anne many fine specimens of pots were executed to special order of the nobility, but in small sizes only for tea was still very expensive. Not until the reign of George II, 1727-1759, were tea pots made of larger size or in greater profusion.

The early tea pots were severely simple in style, but as the demand brought more and more activity to the silversmiths of the day, many of the early masters indulged in fine chasing and gave full expression to their creative ability. Many of the silver pots made were copied from the exquisite Chinese masterpieces fashioned in porcelain by the potters from the East.

Since the time of George I, tea pots have constantly changed in shape and decoration, as silversmiths all over Europe tried to create pieces expressing the individual tastes of their clients.

Tea pots with characteristic spouts first began to appear in the last quarter of the seventeenth century. The Chinese custom of preparing tea differed from that of the English, and this greatly influenced the change in the shape of the pots. The Chinese poured hot water out of the pot on the leaves, while the English infused the tea in the pot. Tea pots of the Queen Anne and George Ist period were very beautiful, as a rule being of a pear shaped body with a domed lid, the outline being either rounded or polygonal. The popular type with the inverted pear shaped body was introduced about 1730. As the demand for silver tea pots increased to the point where practically every home of good standing owned one, styles repeatedly changed. The Adam period was extremely prolific in designs for tea pots. Typical specimens of the time were made with a circular, oval or octagonal drum shape body, usually with a straight spout. Many in this period had stands to match, as the bottoms were constantly burning and scratching the highly polished wood surfaces of the tea table. It is not unusual, however, to find a tea pot by one maker, and a stand to match by a different smith of a few years later date. This was because people did not realize at first how essential the stands were if their fine tables were to be preserved. The tea pot so popular in Scotland for many years, of a globular shape on a tall

foot, remained purely local, and never found much favor south of
the Tweed.

TEA CUPS AND SAUCERS

Silver tea cups and saucers are among the rarest known objects
in silver, but a few specimens dating from 1684 to 1700 have survived. These, it may be added, are nearly entirely in private collections or on display in leading museums. Both cups and saucers were
of the convex fluted style, later copied by leading porcelain factories.
All were made without handles, proving beyond doubt that the
earliest vessels connected with this beverage were influenced by the
Chinese forms.

COFFEE POTS

Coffee first found its way into England during the Commonwealth, 1649 to 1660, so as a beverage, it antedates tea in England.
However, it was greatly frowned upon at first, as many thought it
to be a drug, and that its constant use would cause the men of the
nation to "dwindle into a succession of apes and pygmies." So radical
was the feeling against coffee that many bills were introduced into
Parliament to prohibit its sale.

The earliest known uses of coffee are traced to Abyssinia, where
it was consumed as early as the fifteenth century. Coffee was also
used in early Mohammedan religious ceremonies as an antisoporific.
However, it was later excluded from these services, as many thought
it to be intoxicating, and contrary to the teachings of the Koran.

Eventually, coffee became popular in England and in 1651 the
earliest known coffee house was opened by a Syrian, Cirques Jobson,
Oxford. However, these places did not meet with the favor of the
King, as he considered them a meeting place for political agitators.
Years later, after much legislation concerning them, coffee houses
were firmly established throughout England. Even today one may
find some that are a few centuries old.

The first silver coffee pot is dated 1681, and was less than 10
inches high, being considerably shorter in height than the "tea-pott"
of 1670. However, the general shape resembled that of the tea pot,
the main difference being that the handle was opposite the spout.
The next examples known had the handles placed at right angles
to the spout, and this style remained unchanged until the beginning
of the George II period. Shortly before 1700, the spout was curved,
and as the Queen Anne period progressed a style of coffee pot of
octagonal shape was very popular. This was merely an alternative
to the regular tapering cylinder. During the George Ist period, the

silversmiths created an object of more beauty, by modifying the tapering cylindrical shape, and curving the base into the spout. The lid became flatter and more deeply moulded, and gradually as the years passed, the accepted style of pot was decidedly dissimilar to the first creations of the earliest craftsmen.

SUGAR BOWLS

Little sugar was imported into England before its use in tea, and consequently the first silver sugar basins were not introduced until the reign of William III, 1695 to 1702. These were originally made with a rounded base, with a saucerlike cover, so very similar to the Chinese tea cup. However, the style was later discarded for a type set on three feet, and many years later were made to match tea pots. Sugar baskets were first made at the time of Queen Anne and reappeared again at the end of the eighteenth century with colored glass linings. About this time, the flair for pierced work found great favor with the silversmiths of the day, and it is for this reason that so many pierced as well as richly embossed sugar bowls are known.

At the time of the production of the first tea services, sugar bowls were decidedly out of proportion in size to the balance of the service. Frequently, they were fully as large as the tea pot. This was because at that time only unrefined sugar was known, the pieces were large and bulky and it was necessary to have a vessel of ample size to contain them.

CREAMERS

The Chinese did not use cream in their tea so that no cream pitchers in silver are known earlier than the time of Queen Anne, when the English adopted their own method of tea drinking, which involved cream and sugar.

The earliest specimens of creamers were made with simple round feet, but this style changed as the shapes of tea pots varied. In later years, as a rule, creamers resembled the general style of the tea pot. The popular type of helmet-shaped creamer was introduced during the George III era and the oval forms of the nineteenth century that followed were called squat creamers.

Various curious shapes were adapted to small creamers. Many eccentric forms are known today, the best known of which is in the shape of a cow. (Such specimens are exceedingly rare and may be confused with the modern Dutch ones that have flooded the market for years.) This was originally a creation of Nicholas Sprimont, a silversmith connected with the Chelsea porcelain factory.

TEA CADDIES

Tea caddies were introduced during the reign of Queen Anne, and specimens from this era are very rare. They were made in greater numbers during the George Ist period. The word caddy is derived from the Malay "kate," which means a weight equivalent to 1 1/15th of a pound. As tea was always sold by the "kate," the name became by transference applied to the case in which it was contained. The word canister, sometimes used instead of caddy, antedated the English adoption of caddy. Its use has been found in an advertisement of 1711.

Caddies were originally made in sets of three and later two, as different blends of tea were used, according to taste preference. It has been suggested that many times the center caddy of a set of three was originally made to be used as a sugar bowl, but this can only be surmised. The earliest known caddies were small, because of the prohibitive prices of tea, but as the beverage became more generally consumed and the price lessened, they were made of a more substantial size. The first caddies were made with a sliding panel and a domed top. The object of the panel was to prevent waste in transferring the tea from the original package, since it was much simpler to insert the tea through the larger opening at the base. Later, caddies were almost invariably made with hinge covers like regular boxes. It is perhaps because of this that so many have been adapted to present day use for cigarette containers.

As a general rule, caddies were placed in an outer case of beautifully decorated wood or shagreen and fitted with a lock and key. However, it is rare to find an original case in use today, as through hard wear and constant usage they were discarded or replaced. Not only were the cases of the caddies supplied with locks and keys but the pieces were, also. Tea was so expensive at that time, that people feared unless it were fully protected, servants might be tempted to steal some of it.

Some of the finest works of celebrated silversmiths are represented in caddies, as specimens of Lamerie and other famous smiths prove. However, the demand for elaborate decoration that came many years later was also transferred to tea caddies. Some of the fantastic and ornate creations applied to caddies are almost unimaginable.

TEA KETTLES

The tea kettle was the natural outcome of the tea pot, for in style it is little more than a tea pot mounted on a base with a spirit lamp for purposes of heating. However, it was not until twenty years after the introduction of tea pots that kettles were made in silver. The earliest known mention of one is in a Royal Warrant of 1687, but no example from that date is known to exist. The earliest one known today is the work of David Willaume executed in 1706, and the next in order, 1709, is the work of the celebrated Anthony Nelme, now owned by the Duke of Portland.

Tea kettles of the first quarter of the eighteenth century follow the lines of the early pear-shaped tea pots, and are circular or polygonal in plan. Later, a globular form was introduced and finally the popular inverted pear shaped type. As a general rule the stands were of delicately pierced work and contained in the center a lamp used for purposes of heating. During the George II era, many richly embossed pieces were created to harmonize with the changing trend towards decorative silver. Kettles of this period were often made with a small triangular stand, which prevented the tea table from being scorched by the heat of the flame of the lamp. In the latter part of the Queen Anne period, occasional mention is made of a huge stand sometimes three feet high on which conveniently to place the kettle next to the table, but only one or two such specimens are extant.

Because of the high cost of tea, the beverage was infused right at the table to prevent waste, and this readily explains the introduction of the tea pot with the lamp. It is very important in purchasing antique silver kettles to note that the hall marks on the bodies and stands match, for over a period of years stands were lost, and replaced by ones of later date. Also, many of the first owners of tea pots had stands made to fit them, to avoid the cost of an extra new piece. These, naturally, are not so desirable nor of value equal to those that are completely hallmarked in stand, body and lamp, and of uniform design as originally made.

URNS

The demand for a larger vessel to be used at social functions caused the silver tea urn to be made. It was usually of immense size and used to contain hot water. Many people actually tried to brew the tea inside these urns, but found upon experiment that the resulting beverage was far from palatable.

Tea urns were introduced about 1760, and at first were made similar to a kettle with a spirit lamp. This was soon altered, and urns were made with a compartment on the inside to hold a heated iron. This was heated in the kitchen and dropped in the compartment. It actually kept the beverage hot for hours. The iron heaters were connected on the inside to the handles.

The styles and shapes were influenced along with other pieces of the day by the contemporary styles. Rarely were they made to match tea services, though, as were kettles.

CHOCOLATE POTS

Although the chocolate pot is not actually a part of the tea service, its history in silversmithing is so closely allied to the coffee pot, it must be mentioned.

Chocolate originated from the West Indies, and was first heard of in England in 1657. As a beverage it grew rapidly in popularity, but being too rich for constant use, vessels for its service were not created in great numbers.

The main difference between a chocolate pot and a coffee pot, is that in the top of the former there is an opening covered by a small hinged lid, rather than a spout. Through this lid, a circular wooden stick was placed to aid in crushing and mixing the chocolate. This was known as a swizzle stick.

As for the changing style and decoration of the chocolate pot, it can only be said that it followed the coffee pot very closely, and was only distinguished by its lack of spout. In later years, as even today, chocolate pots were made with the handle at right angles to the spout.

COFFEE BIGGINS

A biggin, or coffee biggin, is a particular type of coffee pot, conceived by a man of that name. It was in reality a percolator. The coffee was first placed in a separate compartment fitted into a larger vessel, and this larger vessel contained water which was heated from below by an alcohol lamp as used in the kettle.

TEA SERVICES

The first complete tea service incorporated a tea pot, a sugar and a creamer. These three-piece services were made about 1790. A few specimens of prior date are known but are very rare. During the latter part of the George III era, coffee pots to match were added. However, it was not until years later that the complete tea service of six pieces with a kettle and a waste bowl of uniform design was introduced. It may be noted that the waste bowl is comparatively a new note in silversmithing. Judging from the varying styles and profusion of tea services dating later than 1850, it may be safely assumed that afternoon tea was at the height of its popularity during the reign of Queen Victoria. Many of the styles, so popular during the latter part of the Georgian era were reproduced, and are greatly in demand today. It is unfortunate, though, that so many of the earlier models were richly chased and embossed to suit the taste of the hour, for more than often the application of too much ornamentation detracted from the original shapes. It is difficult to realize the tremendous quantity of tea services produced during this era, unless one has viewed the countless different styles copied from the art motifs of foreign countries.

The collection of an antique silver tea service may entail much searching and a great difficulty in matching pieces. However, since no complete services were ever executed, it is within the full right of any collector to own a service of assembled pieces. Many times, makers are asked to make modern matching pieces to an original service of three units. However, a true lover of antique silver will never object to a service that does not match exactly. Rather, it is much more interesting to spend months searching for just that particular coffee or kettle to use with your own service, and finally realize that if you have been fortunate, you have succeeded in accomplishing what every silver dealer is continually trying to do.

VII

MAZER BOWLS

MAZER bowls are among the earliest examples of English domestic silver. They were turned from bird's eye maple wood, which being of a fibrous texture, permitted the bowl to contain liquid without cracking or warping. Frequently the rims were ornamented with precious metals, although many mazers were executed for the poorer classes and were without silver embellishments. Mazer bowls were commonly in use during the thirteenth, fourteenth, and fifteenth centuries. During the reign of Queen Elizabeth they ceased to be made, as other creations of the silversmiths were found to be more useful.

The name "mazer" was probably derived from the German word "mazo," which means a spot. This referred to the speckled nature of the wood; however, the word may have derived from the Dutch "maeser" which means "knot of wood."

Some examples have a silver collar around the rim, which was probably used to conceal the marks of the turning lathe. They may have been copied from the early Roman pottery pieces which had a similar design. Occasionally a mazer was raised on a silver trumpet-shaped stem with a deep foot, ornamented with an open crest for use as a standing cup. In this way, the importance of the piece was often increased.

The usual silver mounts of a mazer were a band around the lip and a circular medallion in the bottom of the inside of the bowl, which was referred to as a "print" or "boss." The early examples are usually deep with narrow lip bands, while the later specimens are shallower with wider bands and an increased capacity. The band was generally used for the purpose of bearing an inscription of presentation or ownership.

Prints on the inside of a mazer were decorated in many varied fashions, although for the most part they consisted of a medallion depicting a religious device, a coat of arms, or a floral motif. Another name occasionally used to describe this medallion is "frounce." Covers for mazer bowls were not unusual although of the sixty examples which have survived to the present day, none is known with its original cover. Although so few mazers have survived the years, at the time of their introduction to English society they were

28

very popular and were made in great profusion. However, by far the greatest number were made of solid wood as each man reserved the right to his personal drinking cup and only a few could afford the luxury of the increased cost of the addition of silver mounts.

The popularity of the mazer may be gathered from the fact that in 1328 there were 182 in the refectory of Christ Church in Canterbury. But eventually silver mounted mazers lost their popularity as pure silver gained in favor.

Mazers were used as early as the twelfth century by the rollicking monks to drink what they called "celestial nectar." One of the most famous is the masterpiece of 1398 in Yorkminster. A most unusual type is John Northwode's mazer of the late fourteenth century at Corpus Christi College, Cambridge. Fixed inside the center of the bowl is a hexagonal pillar with a battlemented top, upon which rests a swan. On the inside of this pillar is a hollow tube, open at both ends and so adapted that the bowl cannot be filled with wine above the top of the tube. Upon reaching that height, the wine begins to flow out, escaping through the end in the bottom of the bowl until empty. A few important mazers are owned by the Harbledown Hospital, one dating from the reign of Edward II.

An interesting allusion is made by Samuel Pepys, in his diary, wherein he describes drinking "In a brown bowl, tip't with silver which I drank off and at the bottom was a picture of the Virgin with the Child in her arms." He refers to the medallion of the sacred subjects found at the bottom of so many mazers.

Mazers were frequently engraved on the silver rims with appropriate inscriptions in Latin and occasionally in English. Many of the early specimens were converted into standing cups by ingenious silversmiths who followed the demand by the wealthy classes for pieces of more importance.

The value of a mazer cannot be measured except by its rarity, and the fact that it is probably the first piece of English domestic plate. The work on them is certainly not representative of first class silversmithing.

DRINKING HORNS

The use of horns for drinking vessels has been recognized from early times, and the medieval silversmiths were quick in adding to their beauty by the addition of fine mountings of silver gilt. Although very few of these early specimens have survived, much curious data has been handed down regarding their use. From remote antiquity comes the superstition and belief in horns as an antidote for poison.

The horn was supposed to vibrate as it came into contact with a substance containing poison. This superstition prevailed as late as the sixteenth century. The medieval member of royalty who possessed a small piece of this horn would attach it to a chain and dip it into the wine before partaking of it, thus reassuring himself. The most prized and theoretically most effective horns were those of the unicorn, an animal which never existed. But the horns of other animals such as the "narwhal" and the rhinoceros were sold by unscrupulous people as genuine unicorn. The form of this fabulous animal of India is well-known as the sinister supporter of the Royal Arms of England.

The influence of the early horn never quite disappeared as many tankards of later years and even of the present day retain the original horn shape. The use of horns, which was widespread in Anglo-Saxon times, steadily decreased and reference to them in later medieval documents is relatively uncommon. The later types of horns were equipped with feet so that they could be set down on the table. Another use of horns was for the purpose of serving as a charter for lands during the middle ages. Accurate proof of this is found in the horn presented to Pusey by King Knute with an inscription confirming the grant of property.

Medieval drinking horns are so rare as to be of little interest to collectors. Actually only five specimens are known. Among these, three important examples are herewith described. The first, now in the possession of Queen's College, Oxford, is engraved with Latin letters on each of three silver gilt bands mounted on the buffalo horn. The second, dating from the first half of the fourteenth century is less ornate, and became the property of Corpus Christi College, Cambridge, in 1352. Another treasure of its type dates from the reign of Henry VII, and is in possession of Christ's Hospital, Horsham.

STEEPLE CUPS, STANDING CUPS AND COVERS

These articles are sequels to the mazer bowl, and they carry certain rites and ceremonies that have been retained to the present time by corporations and fraternities that have rituals dating from the past. Among them is the age-old observance of the taking of wine from a loving cup as a token of friendship. Inasmuch as there were innumerable instances when a foe stabbed an enemy while in the act of drinking, it was not unusual for a guest in a strange house to have a comrade standing by his side while he drank. With dagger drawn, his ally stood ready to defend him in case an attack were made on the drinker. From this sequence we have inherited our present day manner of toasting with regard to loving cups. There are always three people standing; two facing each other and the third behind the person drinking as a safeguard against perfidy.

The standing cup was usually tumbler shaped, resting on a baluster or vase-shaped stem. The cover was slightly domed and surmounted in the usual way by a human figure. Some examples were plain, while others were repoussée with fruits and masks. Sometimes, cups of the early part of the seventeenth century assumed the conical shape with a dome-like cover, surmounted by a high finial, obviously copied from the spires of a church. These so-called steeple cups are generally found in sets of three, one being slightly taller than the other two. They are distinctly peculiar to the reign of James I. Among the many magnificent examples of standing cups and covers that have been handed down to the present time is the "Anathema cup" dating from 1481, and now in the possession of Pembroke College, Cambridge. This is the earliest known hallmarked cup. The second earliest surviving cup is the magnificent Leigh standing cup and cover, dated 1499.

The majority of cups of this type were highly chased with figures in relief and delicate piercings, such as demonstrated in the "Foundress" cup of Christ College, Cambridge. One of the few plain examples is the previously mentioned "Anathema cup." Although simple in form and practically void of decoration, it is by no means lacking in beauty.

Probably more fine specimens of standing cups and covers were executed in Germany than in any other part of the continent. The surviving examples clearly illustrate the importance of the German silversmith of the day. It may be assumed that many of the English cups were the work of German silversmiths who migrated to London.

Two of the finest known cups were sold at the disbursement of the Swaythling collection; one being the Rodney cup and cover of the late fifteenth century which fetched the sum of $38,000, and the other, the Tudor cup bearing the London hallmark of 1500, which was sold for $15,000. These prices readily indicate the appreciation and rarity of these masterpieces of early silversmithing.

COCOANUT CUPS AND OSTRICH CUPS

Many standing cups of the fifteenth and sixteenth centuries were formed of a cocoanut or an ostrich egg mounted in silver and raised on a tall stem. Few early specimens have survived, as the brittle texture of these pieces caused many to be damaged and discarded throughout the years of service. In effect, they were a variation of the standing cup and cover and may be definitely assumed to have been copied from workings of European silversmiths. As a general rule the work was very elaborate and covered a section of the top of the shelf and a part of the base.

Probably the main reason for the use of the cocoanut cup was its great rarity. By owning a specimen of this type, a definite display of wealth could be shown. However, some thought was given to the idea that wine imbibed from these shells contained medicinal properties. In a volume of 1640 they were accredited with having protective powers against colic, rheumatism, and epilepsy.

As early as 1259 a cocoanut cup was mentioned in a will, but no surviving example antedates the middle of the fifteenth century. Evidence of their popularity at the time of their inception may be judged by the inventory plate of Winchester College, in which eleven specimens occurred.

London silversmiths ceased to regard cocoanut shells as curiosities worthy of their skill after the reign of James I. However, for some unexplained reason the fashion was revived about 1770 when large numbers of shells were mounted as cups and goblets with silver lips, linings, and feet. This fashion continued until the early years of the nineteenth century.

Far rarer than the cocoanut cup in England is the ostrich egg cup. A notable example is dated 1592 and is in the possession of Corpus Christi College, Canterbury. The silver garnishings comprise a stem fashioned like the twisted trunk of a tree in the manner of many German cups. The egg of the Ostrich was definitely regarded as worthy of the skill of the greatest silversmiths, as evidenced by the large number of articles such as tankards, cups, ewers and pots fashioned from silver and the egg. Ostrich egg cups appear frequently, although they were usually described as being griffins' egg cups.

The nautilus shell cup, so popular with the silversmiths in Germany in the sixteenth and seventeenth centuries, found little favor in England. Only one specimen has survived, although the delicate character of the shell may account for the destruction of the other examples. This cup is in the form of a melon shell, mounted as a monster of the sea. It was the work of a London silversmith in 1577.

One finds during the medieval times and the Renaissance, numerous objects of little intrinsic value mounted as cups by English silversmiths. It may be, that coming from parts of the earth then little known, these shells were invested with much mystery which enhanced their value and importance. Probably the only reason that any of the early specimens has survived is, that having a small quantity of silver in the mountings, they were hardly of sufficient importance to melt down.

FONT SHAPED CUPS

Another type of cup originating at the beginning of the sixteenth century had a shallow bowl with straight, vertical sides, resting on a wider splayed circular foot, the diameter of the bowl being approximately equal to the height of the cup. These are known as font-shaped cups. The earliest known examples are in the Victoria and Albert Museum and were executed in 1500. Probably the best type known of the few that have survived, is the one owned by the Goldsmiths' Company, which bears the London hallmark of 1503.

As a general rule, font cups are thick and heavy and void of decoration. However, some specimens were embossed as evidenced by the cup of 1515 now in the possession of Corpus Christi College, Oxford. Occasionally these pieces had covers which were almost flat with a knob, and a top suitable for a coat of arms.

BEAKERS

The form of most drinking vessels in use during the middle ages may be classed roughly into two stages: those derived from the beaker and those from the bowl. In all probability the beaker originated from the use of a straight section of ox-horn with one end stopped up. However, it has been impossible to trace either the name or the shape further back than the fourteenth century. It has been suggested that the introduction of the beaker was probably due to traders between England and the Low Country, or to the Protestant refugees, who sought escape from England in the seventeenth century.

Silver beakers were popular as long ago as the Elizabethan era and continued to be made and developed. During the reign of Charles II they were sometimes embossed or ornamented with a band of Acanthus chasing. Otherwise, the majority of these examples differ very little from the early Elizabethan types. They are usually about six inches in height, spread toward the top and made with a molded base. Very few beakers were made in the eighteenth century. A type more popular and differing distinctly from the early examples was that shaped and engraved as a beer barrel. It is curious that so few examples of standing beakers are known with English hallmarks, for on the continent they were by far the most popular type.

By the seventeenth century the original straight table beakers developed a flare in form, and although they remained in use, there is little doubt that they were for the most part replaced by individual cups for drinking. Beakers of the Elizabethan and James I periods were usually embossed in low relief and engraved with foliage. The earliest types were originally made of horn and date back to the middle ages. These shapes were later reproduced by the silversmiths.

Although beakers were reserved for personal use, specimens in silver were indulged in only by the wealthy, and it is for this reason that early examples are very rare and command huge prices. However, as the specimens of the eighteenth and nineteenth centuries were produced in far-flung profusion, they have not yet come to be known as rarities among pieces of Old English silver.

TANKARDS AND MUGS

Certain names applied to silver objects have more or less romantic origins, and such a survival occurs in the word "tankard." Although long since forgotten, the word originally indicated the clumsy hollowed logs bound with iron and used to carry water from city conduits. In later years the name was applied to great wooden mugs bound with metal.

No English silver tankards are known prior to the sixteenth century and generally speaking, many of the earliest specimens displayed some tendency to the natural taper of the early ox-horn. Although made in a vast variety of sizes and shapes, they were all generally of the same tapered type. The exceptions were the few straight cylindrical bodied ones, reproduced from continental models. Many of the earliest tankards were made with bodies of horn or bone which were then mounted with silver covers, neck bands and feet. It was believed that with the bone or horn substance contained therein, the presence of any poisonous substance in the beverage could be immediately detected. Some tankards are found with a body of crystal, for it was generally believed that if the liquid contained any poison it would cloud the crystal on coming in contact with it.

During the James I period the in-curving taper of the horn disappeared in the shape of the tankard, and was replaced by straight sides. During the reign of Charles II, many tankards were produced and while the ornamentation was retained for a short time, molded lips disappeared, covers were made of much simpler style; and the finials of the early types were discarded. Later on in the century, a shorter type of a plain cylindrical body with a flat projecting rim became fashionable. Although tankards were originally made in pint sizes in the beginning of the seventeenth century, they were later made of much larger proportion. Tankards were generally of a uniform shape with an "S" shaped handle. Many are found with encircling bands of silver and these may be said to have survived from the early metal bands on the original wooden receptacles.

Among the types of tankard most sought after by collectors, is "peg" tankard. This type contained a vertical row of pegs fitted on the inside of the body at equivalent distances, and was used to mark the quantity of wine or beer permitted to each man at the passing of the cup. An interesting feature of many of the early tankards was a slot on the under side of the handle. The idea has been suggested that this was used to summon an attendant when a vessel was empty, but whether it was designed for that purpose or rather as a vent to allow the hot air to escape, can only be surmised.

Tankards were made in great profusion throughout England as well as Europe, and the continental influence is easily detected, particularly in those mounted on feet.

During the late 17th century, an offspring of the tankard known as the mug, was introduced. This, in effect, was actually a tankard on a smaller scale, but lacking the cover. These mugs were tremendously popular as beer drinking vessels at the leading universities throughout England.

GOBLETS

Although there is a slight difference between a goblet and a wine cup, they may be classified together as they grew in popularity in the late Tudor period, at which time they replaced the earlier beakers. These were actually vessels made for individual service and numerous examples from the 17th century are available. Goblets date back to very early times and have practically never ceased to be made. After the general adoption of silver wine goblets, the silversmiths lost many of their opportunities for producing varied pieces, as these replaced practically all of the earlier types of drinking equipments. However, with the general importation and use of crystal at the dinner table, wine cups and goblets fell into disuse. It is interesting to note though, that the modern adaptation in crystal for individual service carries out almost perfectly the original design of the goblet or wine cup. Goblets were used for other purposes besides drinking as frequently specimens are found that were made as presentation cups.

TUMBLER CUPS

Originally known as a "bolle," the tumbler cup was introduced during the middle ages for use as a wine vessel. However, no surviving specimen earlier than the end of the 17th century is available. A tumbler cup is quite different from all other drinking vessels in the manner of its construction. It was usually of very heavy silver, the lower part of the bowl being hemispherical and hammered in such a way as to leave a thick bottom. When filled with wine, the round bottom caused the bowl to tumble from side to side, but it was prevented from toppling over by the extra weight of the metal on the under side. Sets of these tumbler cups are found complete rather often because they were usually nested one inside the other. They were quite small in size, being designed, as a rule, to contain only a single drink.

POSSET CUPS, CAUDLE CUPS AND PORRINGERS

The little two-handled cups with covers which came into general use during the second half of the seventeenth century were intended to hold caudle and posset. The squat pear shaped vessels were doubtlessly inspired by objects imported from the Orient. Caudle was made largely of wine, or some alcoholic liquor, to which sugar, spice, and crumbled bread were added. Posset, on the other hand, was somewhat similar to what is known today as porridge, and was composed of bread or oat cakes mixed with curdled milk, combined with wine or beer, and flavored with spice.

These little cups and those referred to as porringers were used for wine and hot drinks. However, from the name porringer which is doubtless a corruption of the word "porridger," it is safe to assume that they were used to serve stews and similar refreshment as well. Porridge, at the time of the making of the little silver containers, was actually a thick soup, while the now obsolete word "pottenger" indicated a maker of pottage, which was a stew of vegetables and meat.

Porringers, as a rule, were made without covers, the bowl usually being less than four inches deep, while caudle and posset cups invariably had lids and were both larger and deeper. Caudle and posset cups, as well as porringers, all appear as early as in sixteenth century inventories, but no examples have survived from this date. Caudle cups were generally decorated in relief with the large animals and fruits characteristic of this period, and sometimes the wide rim of the saucer-like stand in which they were placed, was ornamented, too. Porringers were introduced about 1680 and were popular until about 1715. It is indeed curious that these little vessels have become the most popular of all christening presents as their long association with intoxicating foods and drinks scarcely seems to be congruous with the partaking of nourishment by a child.

BEER JUGS AND CLARET JUGS

Silver beer jugs were made as early as the time of George I, but did not come into general use until the period of about 1770. It is very rare to find original beer jugs as many of the ones sold today have been fashioned from chocolate pots and tankards. Beer jugs resembled in style the water pitcher as known today, while claret jugs were similar to hot water jugs introduced during the early Georgian period.

PILGRIM BOTTLES

Huge pilgrim bottles appeared late in the seventeenth century and continued until the early years of the eighteenth century. As a rule, they were beautifully ornamented, although on many, an over-profusion of decoration is found. The original use of pilgrim bottles was to hold wine for use at large dinners, although they were also made as ornaments for sideboards. There is little doubt but what these massive silver bottles were designed after the outlines of the ancient pilgrim bottles. Earl Spencer owns one of the earliest known pairs, made in 1701, and probably the work of John Goode.

FLAGONS, STONEWARE JUGS AND BLACKJACKS

The word Flagon was definitely derived from the early French "flacon," which denoted a bottle-shaped vessel of leather, having a narrow neck and a plain ovoid body. Closely allied to these flagons were stoneware jugs and blackjacks, which were in use about the middle of the 17th century. Stoneware jugs were popular during the latter half of the sixteenth century, at which time they were imported from Germany and fitted with silver or gold neck bands, feet, and covers, by the English silversmiths. Stoneware is exceptionally hard and non-porous, the surface being glazed by throwing salt into the furnaces while the clay vessels are being baked. The jugs followed the form of the early flagons with the bulbous bodies and narrow necks. The color of the ware varied from a dull gray to a common spotted surface from which was derived the name "tiger Ware." Other rare examples of this type of jug were made of blue glazed earthenware, in the old Lambeth potteries, while occasionally specimens of Rhodian faience come into the market. Examples of these pieces with Elizabethan mounts are extremely rare and fetch high prices at auction.

Blackjacks were vessels of waxed leather used for centuries for carrying and storing liquors. The larger ones became known as bombards, the name being derived from their resemblance to the old cannons of that name. This type was used exclusively for the purpose of storing fine liquors. A smaller type intended for use as a drinking vessel was sometimes mounted with silver and engraved with a coat of arms. The dates of these articles can only be estimated as the silver mounts rarely, if ever, bear any hallmarks.

During the first half of the 17th century, flagons retained the style of decoration which characterized the work of silversmiths of the previous century. The pieces were tall and cylindrical, with feet splayed out into a handle formed by an "S" scroll. Fruits and fishes were commonly the motifs of the design, alternating with other delicately engraved ornamentation. Flagons and stoneware jugs were commonly in use by the churches of England as early as Elizabethan times. They were employed when it was necessary to bring wine to the communion table. Before the middle of the seventeenth century, flagons had developed into vessels of great size and capacity and were frequently made in pairs. As a rule, they were plain and without gilding. The churches of London were particularly rich in such vessels, and a group covering nearly every successive year from 1605 to 1660 is available.

COASTERS AND DECANTER STANDS

The wide use of crystal decanters led to the making of coasters, the commonest type having a wood turned bottom and a solid or pierced silver side. They were introduced during the Adam period while decanter stands were first made during the George I era. However, they were not produced in quantities until nearly forty years later.

Many decanter stands were doubled or tripled, and joined together by a bar and mounted on wheels. These pieces had a small silver handle and resembled the general shape of a cart on wheels, hence the applied name of wine wagon.

A coaster or decanter stand is a clear illustration of the outcome of changing social customs which caused the introduction of many new pieces in silver. As the fashion prevailed to remove the cloth from the dining table for dessert, someone probably conceived the idea of placing the bottle in a stand and coasting it along the table. This explains why the base is covered with baize on the bottom, to prevent any markings on the polished mahogany tables. It is also probable that after the bottles had been refilled several times and the guests had become slightly inebriated, the decanters did not always reach their intended destinations while being passed.

Coasters were made in a wide variety of designs and included examples of delicately pierced work as well as richly embossed specimens. Many were ornamented with a band of grapes and leaves which was appropriate to the wine decanter which it contained. As a rule, coasters were made in pairs or sets of four, six or eight.

EWERS

Many articles in use today were made for entirely different purposes at the time of their conception. These changes are to a large extent due to the refinements which gradually appeared in the social observances connected with the dining table. The common instance, is our practice of washing the hands before sitting down to dinner, which, in effect, is actually a perpetuation of washing the hands at the table. This custom instituted many centuries ago, was symbolized by the use of basins and ewers among the noble families, from the middle ages to the seventeenth century.

Ewers were introduced originally from Italy and quickly rendered the medieval finger bowl obsolete. As a rule they were gilded, and many displayed the graceful forms of the Italian Renaissance. Probably the outstanding creation of the Tudor silversmiths with regard to splendor and magnificence, were their rosewater ewers.

Until the introduction of the fork, the washing ceremony was an essential part of dining, as in those days it was the custom to hold the food in one hand, cut it with the knife, and then lift it to the mouth with the fingers. It was customary for a servant to hold a silver basin in front of each guest. The water was then supplied from a ewer carried by another servant who poured it over the hands of the guest into the basin. At the conclusion of this ceremony, the servant produced a towel with which he dried the hands of the diner. This was recognized as a part of the general etiquette of the dining table, and guests received attention in accordance with their rank.

The custom of using a ewer and basin at the table was not restricted to the wealthy classes as those in more moderate circumstances used specimens made of brass. Although silver ewers and basins were mentioned frequently in wills and inventories, very few have survived to the present day. The amount of precious metal expended on their manufacture rendered them extremely liable to be consigned to the melting pot in time of financial difficulties.

There were three distinct types of ewers made and they are clearly demonstrated by the following examples. An early specimen is that presented to Corpus Christi College, Cambridge, in 1570. This piece has a rounded foot and a swelling octagonal body, the sides of which were alternately engraved with arabesques. Two of the remaining sides were plain and occupied by the angular handle and spout which was attached to the whole of the length of the body.

The second known variety had a vase shaped body and a narrow neck with a spout and scroll handle. It was richly chased and the handle was in the form of a demi-lion. This type is exemplified by one made by Robert Signall, in 1583, which may now be seen in the Victoria and Albert Museum. The third, which appeared during the reign of James I, was, as a rule, undecorated except for heraldic achievements.

The ewers resembled a straight sided goblet with scroll handle and curved spout. The introduction of a vessel so conspicuously lacking in aesthetic charm is typical of a period when silversmiths were seeking originality at all costs. Just previous to 1700 appeared the last standard pattern of ewer. This was known as the helmet shape and was a magnificent example of the proper combination of a good shape with restrained ornamentation. About the middle of the George I period, ewers and basins were discarded and used only as ornaments.

Ewers are very rare and fine specimens fetch fantastic prices. Some are known to have reached a figure at auction of $100,000.

MONTEITH BOWLS, PUNCH BOWLS, AND ACCESSORIES

The magnificence which prevailed in the production of so many silver vessels connected with the ceremony of drinking, is often present in punch bowls. Punch, which was of Oriental origin, consisted of five ingredients: spirits, water, lemon juice, sugar and spice. Thus the assumption is made that the word punch was probably derived from the Hindustani "panch" which meant five. Although the brewing of punch was introduced into England during the reign of Charles I, silver bowls for service do not seem to have been made until after the Restoration.

The earliest known punch bowls were small and of simple design, while those wrought in the later Georgian era were of far greater capacity and generally with a wealth of ornamentation. As early as the Stuart period examples are found with notched rims. However, the type with the removable rim known as the monteith bowl was not introduced until nearly the end of the seventeenth century. The introduction of this type of bowl was attributed to a Scotchman named Monteith, who gained considerable reputation from his ability to brew punch of excellent character. Because of the fact that he wore a cloth coat scalloped in the bottom, much in the same style as were the punch bowls of this time, his name was applied to them. From this time on, all bowls with removable rims were known as monteiths. Many explanations have been advanced regarding the addition of the removable rim, and the most probable of these is that the glasses were placed in the notches to prevent their breakage, when being brought into the dining room by the footman. Another theory advanced was that the bowl was filled with water and the glasses hung from the notches to keep cool.

There seems to be no limit to the sizes of punch bowls, and many were used at important functions. The majority of them have fluted bodies with lion's head ring handles. Monteiths were very popular and a great number were made until the end of the eighteenth century, and may be found today among the plate of most of the corporate bodies who would quite naturally have had frequent opportunities to use them.

Several small accessories necessary to the brewing of punch were introduced by the silversmiths of this time. However, the only one that has survived in any degree is the long handled ladle used for transporting the liquid to the jugs. Occasionally one finds a circular strainer with two wrought handles, which was placed across the jug to strain the punch. Punch ladles were made in a variety of designs and were hammered out of Spanish silver dollars or crown pieces in such a way that the marginal description still appeared on the lip of the ladle. The placing of a coin at the bottom of the bowl was also a common trick.

With the return of entertainment on a larger scale, Georgian drinking accessories have once again come into demand. Because of their low price, punch ladles make ideal items for those interested in old silver.

WINE FOUNTAINS, WINE CISTERNS

These two articles reflect beyond a doubt the indulgence used to achieve the sumptuous display of magnificence in silver but very few examples of wine fountains or cisterns exist now. Wine fountains were actually massive upright vase-shaped covered vessels, fitted with an ice chamber and a small tap from which the wine was drawn into the glasses. Cisterns, on the other hand, were enormous oval bowls, intended to hold water and ice, in which the bottles of wine were placed to cool. Although these pieces were of huge proportions and more than extravagantly covered with ornamentation, they still retained the basic form suggestive of the work of the early silversmiths. The detail of the embossing, usually suggested mermaids, dolphins, or figures of Neptune, and was of the highest quality. Wine fountains are known to have weighed more than 1000 ounces and measured close to four feet in height, while wine cisterns were usually about four feet long and weighed close to 2000 ounces.

The largest piece of English plate known, is an enormous wine cistern made in 1734 by Charles Kandler for the Czar of Russia. The immense proportions will be immediately realized if one notes the excessive weight of nearly 8000 ounces contained in the piece. The actual dimensions of it are five and one half feet long, three and one half feet deep, and three and one half feet wide. In 1672 Charles II presented his mistress with a massive creation weighing over 1000 ounces, but this unfortunately has not survived. The earliest example known today was made two years later, and is now in the collection of the Earl of Rosebery. Although wine cisterns in silver were not made until after the Restoration, specimens of base metal were definitely used during the early part of the seventeenth century.

The wine fountains made during the early part of the eighteenth century were greatly reduced in size and were much more usable. As a general rule they were urn-shaped with a tap at the front and had two or four handles. Shortly after the introduction of silver wine cisterns, practically every home of importance owned one. Further proof of their constant use and even earlier introduction than is originally credited, may be found in many of the early pictures painted by Dutch artists.

WINE COOLERS AND ICE PAILS

The eventual outcome of the early wine cisterns was the smaller and more graceful wine cooler made to contain but a single bottle of wine. The interior was fitted with a removable jacket which held the wine, while the space between the jacket and the wall of the vase formed the ice chamber. These were generally of a vase shape in a single foot and invariably made with two handles. At first wine coolers were very simple in design, but the increasing flair for vessels of excessive ornamentation and richness of design caused the smiths to yield to popular demand. Although most wine coolers were not over twelve inches in height, a few enormous specimens are known. However, as the demand for huge pieces waned, the purchase price was lowered and wine coolers became more and more popular. By the beginning of the nineteenth century, literally thousands of pairs of silver and Sheffield plate had been produced. Also occasionally wine coolers were made with linings of base metal.

The wine cooler was probably an importation from France, as vessels of similar style and shape made in other metals than silver were known there.

Ice pails which were similar in shape to the coolers are known during the eighteenth and nineteenth centuries, and the ornamentation on them was similar to that found on the wine cistern and fountain of a century previous. The main distinction between an ice pail and a wine cooler is that the former was made without an inner jacket and the bottle was not placed in it to cool.

WINE LABELS, WINE FUNNELS, WINE TASTERS

During the reign of George III, the use of small silver labels pierced or engraved with the name of a particular wine, became increasingly popular. These labels were attached to a hanging chain and fitted around the neck of the bottle. It is not unusual to find a complete set of these little gadgets with as many as forty varieties of liquid refreshment included. It is actually necessary to study in detail the various types of wine consumed throughout England, to comprehend the vast number of labels produced. It is rather interesting that only of recent date have labels attracted the attention of the collector. Inasmuch as they require but a small investment, and since many are examples of exquisite workmanship, it is difficult to understand why they have never been appreciated heretofore.

The earliest known funnel for decanting wine is the example of 1661 in the Victoria and Albert Museum. Although these little silver articles were made extensively during the Georgian periods, early examples are scarce. But little attention has been given them, since from the artistic standpoint they are of no great interest. No home in England was considered fully equipped for the service of wine unless it had a funnel and strainer, and for this reason hundreds of later specimens are known today. Inasmuch as funnels are fitted at the base with a detachable strainer many collectors, unable to find suitable tea strainers, have purchased these funnels and retained only the strainer part for use.

The original purpose of the wine taster may be traced back to the time of the middle ages, where it was used on ceremonial occasions by deputised tasters, to see if the beverage contained any poison. In this way the important people who were at the dinner were protected from evil intent. Another use of the wine taster was to aid the vintner in sampling the wine which he was proposing to purchase. For this purpose it was necessary to have a small shallow bowl which would show the clear color of the wine. The vintner's silver taster was a well-known feature in late medieval times, and an example of 1383 appears in the inventory of the owner of a Norwich tavern. The earliest wine tasters were mostly plain saucer shaped articles with a raised dome in the center, the purpose of which was to prove that if the liquid was clear, it could be determined as it passed over the plain surface of the silver. The sides of these tasters were usually embossed with various floral designs or punched with flutes. In the latter half of the sixteenth century, a new type of wine taster was introduced. This was in the shape of a small bowl with a sloping side and a dome bottom, which showed the wine to great advantage. One of the earliest known examples of this type bears the Norwich hall mark of 1573. The next earliest known tasters were the shallow two-handled bowls, about three inches in diameter with wire handles. The early cups used for sipping were generally straight sided on short trumpet shaped feet. There is little doubt that many other vessels of similar type were employed in the tasting of wine, and among these may be mentioned the porringer, or, as it was sometimes called in England, the bleeding bowl. Their use as wine tasters can only be assumed from the few known examples which bear engraving suggestive of that particular service.

Although wine tasters have long since lost their original use, they are popular today for use as ash trays. However, it is most rare to find originals.

VIII

CONDIMENT SETS

THE standing salt was introduced during the middle ages. At the time of its use it was a symbol of social distinction because only a family of great wealth could afford it.

In medieval times, salt was very expensive, it was among the rarest of all table condiments, and for this reason important silver holders were used for it.

Salt has always been regarded with superstition as is evidenced by its uses at rituals among the ancient peoples to whom the "eating of salt" and the "breaking of bread" signified brotherhood. It was the belief that salt was a protection against the evils of witches and today many of us still adhere to the legend that the spilling of salt brings misfortune unless a pinch is thrown over the shoulder. The name saltceller is actually a corruption of the old French "saliere," meaning salt holder.

Originally the master saltcellar was placed in the center of the table at which the master of the house was seated. This particular table was denoted as the high table and distinguished from the others in that it was raised on a dais above the floor level. The position of each person in relation to the master salt was dictated by his social rank and until the seventeenth century, the entire household, from master to servant, ate together in a commonhall. The normal use of salts in the fifteenth and sixteenth centuries may be gathered from the books of "Curtesy" and "Nurture," published in 1508, wherein the passage is quoted: "set your salts on the ryght side where your soverayne shall sytte . . . and at every ende of ye table set a salte sellar . . . and when your soverayne's table, thus arrayed, cover all other bordes with salts, trenchours, and cuppes."

Those sitting at other than the high table were designated as being "below the salt," often causing much ill feeling because of the distinction. In addition to the ceremonial salt were smaller holders known as trencher salts to be placed at varied intervals around the table. The name was derived from the custom of lifting salt from the holder to a wooden trencher with the end of the knife. From descriptions in inventories we note that some of the early salts were often cast of solid gold, beset with jewels. An example of this is known from the diary of Charles I, wherein it is recorded that when he came to the throne in 1625, he sold a gold salt weighing one hundred and fifty ounces that was studded with sapphires, rubies, pearls and emeralds. One of the earliest English standing salts is the Huntsman salt which definitely portrays the Gothic influence in its ornamentation. Although the earliest salts were pieces of great importance in meaning, they were but slight in stature in comparison to the later types, as those known as early as 1313 weighed between six and eleven ounces.

The coming of the Renaissance styles influenced the shapes of standing salts for then they began to assume greater splendor. The early Gothic forms in the sixteenth century were replaced by those known as pedestal salts. In the Tudor period the bodies were rectangular or cylindrical, richly chased or embossed with foliage, fruit and figures. The cover was generally surmounted by a vase which supported a modeled figure. Such ceremonial salts frequently measured sixteen inches in height. Although popular for a considerable time, they were later replaced by the far simpler bell-shaped salt which appeared about 1590. These were made in three sections comprising two salt cellars and a pepper caster, and could be either joined together on ceremonial occasions or used separately. This type which was about eleven inches high was finally superseded by the steeple salts which assumed a greater proportion than ever previously known. Not infrequently steeple salts were made with two bowls.

During the latter part of the seventeenth century the custom of fitting a removable cover to the great salts was discontinued and in its place a bracket was fitted to the rim to support a napkin or plate which protected the salt from dust. These brackets are often mistaken for handles although only rarely does one find examples made with them. During the latter part of the fifteenth century and the first quarter of the sixteenth century standing salts were made in the shape of an hour-glass; ten examples of this type are extant. The finest of this collection is the one given by Walter Hill to New College, Oxford, of which he was Warden from 1475 to 1494. It is one of the unusual types combining beauty in silver work with richly engraved crystal. The use of salts in fancy shapes was very popular during the latter part of the 16th century, and much knowledge of them has been gleaned from the inventories of the royal plate wherein several are mentioned.

One was in the form of a dragon issuing from a shell; another had the shape of a crown falcon, and others were made in the form of men and women holding the receptacles for salt in their hands. These quaint forms of decoration although no longer familiar to us, suggest the fertility of the imagination of the early silversmith. In the will of Edmund, Earl of March, two unique specimens in the shape of dogs are listed. Another interesting example which has survived is known as the Monkey salt and is now in the New College, Oxford.

An early piece which shows the Renaissance influence is an hour glass salt made in 1522, belonging to the Goldsmiths' Company. It is of extreme interest because it is considerably ahead of most of the work of the first fifteen years of the English Renaissance with regard to form. Although the silversmiths in Germany and France greatly influenced the workers in England on much of the domestic plate, the designs for standing salts were original.

During the reign of Queen Elizabeth there was a definite increase in the production of small salts, although some of these are merely reproductions in miniature of the contemporary standing salts. Others which were of circular or triangular shapes were the forerunners of the great variety made in the later periods. The disappearance of the large standing salt is a direct result of the increasing popularity of the individual type. During the Charles II and Queen Anne periods a considerable number were produced which were either faceted or moulded, while those of a few years later assumed more elaborate decoration. From about 1720 to 1740 a salt with a circular bowl and a round foot was much in evidence, many examples of these being attractively decorated with applied leaf work. Towards the middle of the century the prevailing type consisted of a small bowl on three or four feet. Many of these were embossed with floral swage and lion masks above the feet, while others were pierced with rococo designs and fitted with glass liners.

During the Adam period the continued use of pierced work was much in evidence and the use of a blue crystal liner was seen much more frequently. These later salts were made in a wide variety of forms, all of which can be traced back directly in shape and feeling to the trenchers.

Sets of four early Georgian salts are very rare although greatly in demand. However, those of the later period can usually be purchased in their entirety as originally produced.

SALT AND MUSTARD SPOONS

Salt spoons are unknown before the end of the seventeenth century, at which time those made resembled miniature table spoons. The familiar ladle shape appeared at a slightly later date, while those varieties with a shovel shape bowl in use during the George III period as well as a number of eccentric types do not require much description. Mustard spoons, formed like small sauce ladles, date well into the eighteenth century. However, one is mentioned in an advertisement as early as 1678.

CASTERS AND MUFFINEERS

Although white pepper was known for use in England as early as the twelfth century, no form of caster appears among English silver previous to the reign of Elizabeth.

At this time they consisted of a small perforated section attached to bell shaped salts, but as individual articles they were not found earlier than the late Stuart period. The name muffineer was derived from the use of sprinkling salt on buttered muffins and, although, similar in form to casters they were somewhat smaller in size. Those known in the time of Charles II are cylindrical, the top being attached to the body by an elbow joint which consisted of two projection lugs soldered to the lower part of the top. The ears passed two notches in the grooved moulding around the rim of the body, which after being turned slightly, engaged firmly with the top.

Muffineers were made as a rule, in sets of three, one being considerably larger than the other two. The smaller pair were used for pepper, one being for Jamaica and the other for cayenne; while the large one was used for sugar. Casters were made in a variety of shapes and it is not difficult to estimate their approximate date from the form and style of ornamentation. During the Queen Anne period the pear shape, or pyriform, copied from Oriental vases, replaced the cylindrical bodies. This evidently was superseded by an undulating pyriform, with a tapering cover. As a rule, the ornamentation was restricted to bands or engraving around the edge of the cover, the bulging part of the body and the foot. The high domed covers of casters afforded the early silversmiths an opportunity to exercise a branch of their skill soon to become a feature of great importance. This intricate piercing found on so many Georgian casters plus the simplicity of the bodies made them objects of great beauty.

During the first half of the eighteenth century, a small type of caster with a handle, generally known as a kitchen pepper, was introduced. Later in the Georgian era smaller casters in sets of four or six were used to contain pepper and salt for individual service.

CRUET STANDS

Although cruet stands may have existed prior to 1700, the series of surviving pieces seems to begin with the latter part of the reign of Queen Anne. Undoubtedly owing to the difficulty of replacing the fragile contents large numbers were allowed to perish. Cruet stands are important examples of silver work because the finest smiths devoted their full talents to their production. During the medieval times they consisted of glass bottles which were used for vinegar and other flavors, while in the first quarter of the eighteenth century, a combination of bottles and casters fitting into a silver frame was introduced. This type was used on the table and known as a Warwick cruet. Good examples fetch high prices as the rare casters in them increased their value many times. The glass bottles were invariably made with small silver caps which could be placed in the small holes fastened on the sides of the stand. During the eighteenth and nineteenth centuries many varied styles were made among which one of the most popular consisted of a boat shaped stand with handles. In the early part of the nineteenth century, a circular type was introduced and at the same time individual bottles were supplied with the little labels similar to those used on decanters to identify the casters.

MUSTARD POTS

Although mustard was used in England much earlier, there is no evidence of silver containers for it prior to the reign of George I. Specimens from this time are very, very rare and most types obtainable now date from the latter part of the eighteenth century. These were generally made with a cylindrical body and a hinged flat lid, or oval body with domical lid, the sides often pierced and the body fitted with blue glass liners. The earliest known reference to a silver mustard pot appears to be in 1670 in a bill for plate made by Alderman Backwell for Prince Rupert, while the next earliest mention is four years later. One of the most beautiful known examples was executed in 1724 by Paul Lamerie in the shape of a barrel with a scroll handle and domed lid.

FLAT SILVER

FLATWARE SERVICES

GENERALLY speaking, the service of flat silver occupies the throne of honor in the home today, for what bride does not thrill to the thought of possessing her own table silver. In most cases, it is the first purchase in the assembling of the trousseau, and usually the most cherished.

The demand for services in antique silver far exceeds the supply, for flat silver in complete services is distinctly a modern note. However, fine matching services can be collected over a period of time, and for the amateur collector this presents the ideal field of endeavor. A large initial investment is unnecessary, as the chances are that after one has selected a pattern, only a few pieces at a time will be available to purchase. Dealers in old silver are continually buying as much flat silver as possible, for it can be purchased most reasonably in oddments, and yet commands a high price when assembled in a complete service. A few years ago an important collector, well able to indulge herself in the luxuries she wished, wanted to assemble a matched service, all dated prior to the reign of George III. The forks were to be three pronged, the spoons "rattail," and the knives pistol handled. Although she allowed "carte blanche" as regards price, it took over four years of diligent searching all over the world in order to complete the set.

For those who are as well pleased by authentic reproductions, the finest patterns have been copied by contemporary silversmiths with great skill.

SPOONS

The spoon was probably suggested by the shells used in prehistoric times for eating liquid foods. In the Middle Ages spoons were made of bone, horn, crystal, and wood. There is also indication that some were fashioned from metals such as pewter and brass, but the earliest silver spoons in England date no further back than the end of the fourteenth century. The first known mention of a spoon made of a precious metal is in the Bible, wherein the Lord instructed Moses to make golden spoons for the Tabernacle. The age old custom of using a spoon for anointing a sovereign at a coronation is also noted in the Bible. It records how Nathan the Prophet anointed Solomon as King of Israel.

The first known English spoons are really only reproductions of the original ones made in bronze by the Romans and Greeks. However, the word spoon was doubtlessly derived from the fact that in early English times spoons were made of wood and the old English word for a splinter of wood is "spon."

The characteristics of these medieval spoons are a long slender polygonal stem tapering towards the head, and an elongated pear-shape shallow bowl. This definitely suggests that they were not used for thin liquids, but for thicker foods such as cream, custard or posset.

During the 250 years that followed the making of the first silver specimens, the basic form of the spoon remained the same, only the ornamentation or shaping being changed or modified. Such variations as occur are restricted to the ornamental knops at the end of the stems, but the oval or fig shape of the bowl was constant until the reign of Charles I.

A further development is noticed in the style of the stem which was changed from a thin round taper to the more robust hexagonal. The flat stem was not introduced until the Commonwealth.

From the latter part of the fourteenth century until the arrival of the flattened stem, different types of knops distinguished more or less definitely the individual periods. The earliest known was the acorn top, while during the fifteenth and sixteenth centuries, the diamond point and maidenhead predominated. With regard to the last mentioned type, it is interesting to note the variation in the style of headdress in the figure depicted, according to the prevailing fashion of coiffure at the time of the making. During the Tudor period, the knop resembled an inverted bunch of grapes, and sometimes was in the shape of a bird. Seal tops and those with the lion sejant are also known and the influence of the continental silversmiths is noticeable in the series of figures at the end of the stems.

A spoon that became common in the seventeenth century, was an absolutely plain type with a flat handle. It became very popular with the Roundheads, and hence was given the name Puritan spoon.

Apostle spoons are interesting. These were originally made in sets of thirteen, comprising a figure of the Lord and twelve disciples. Complete units of Apostle spoons are perhaps among the rarest known articles in silver, as evidenced by the fact that only a few years ago, a set of thirteen dated 1536 was purchased at auction for a sum in excess of $25,000. Other religious types of spoons de-

picted the figures of saints, cherubs and angels. Apostle spoons are
more plentiful today than these other types, due to the custom of
presenting one to each child on the occasion of his baptism.

At the time of Charles I, the bowls of spoons became egg shaped,
and the stems took on a flat broad rectangular form, the ornamental
knops being discarded. After the Restoration in 1660, the stem was
flattened with the top cleft in two places to suggest a trifid. Also, at
this time, the triangular tongue at the back that covered part of the
bowl, appeared. This style was known as the "rat-tail," and enjoyed much popularity.

By the end of the seventeenth century, the spoon began to assume the shape that is commonly accepted and used today. The
clefts disappeared from the handle, and were replaced by a rounded
end that widened in a concave curve to form the handle. At this
time, the bowl was broad and elliptical, although later it took on a
more pointed shape. In the following years, the handle was turned
upwards towards the face of the bowl and formed a distinct hook.
About the middle of the eighteenth century, the more convenient
down turn superseded the earlier type, and is the accepted style of
handle today.

All manner of engraving and chasing was incised on spoons during various periods, and in some instances the bowls were ornamented with scrolls, foliations and shells. These were often symbolic
of either the use of the spoon or else the person for whom it was
intended. During the last hundred years or so, other styles have
evolved, the most popular being the fiddle-back. This in turn was
changed into the fiddle and thread, sometimes surmounted by a
shell.

Teaspoons were introduced in the late seventeenth century, and
were so small they resembled our present day after dinner coffee
spoons. By the time of George I, the proportions had grown though,
until they were of similar style to those used now.

The dessert spoon was not popular until after the Restoration,
and from then on closely followed the style and shape of the table
spoon.

FORKS

Comparatively speaking, forks are very recent to civilization,
for although knives and spoons are known to have existed in crude
forms, since ancient times, the general use of forks is not found
until the end of the fifteenth century. At this period in history,
forks were known only in Italy, although a few scattered continental

DINNER SERVICE

Paul Storr, London, 1818

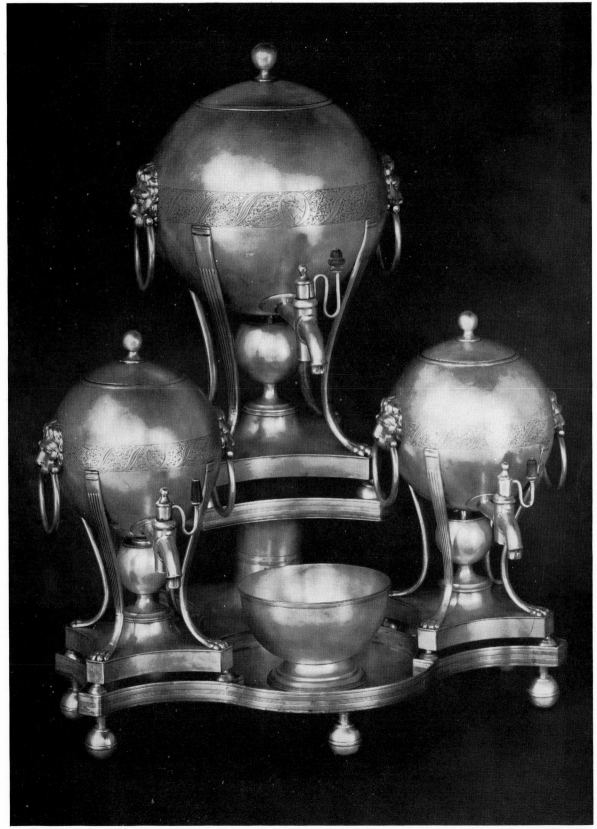

SHEFFIELD TEA MACHINE

Daniel Holy-Wilkinson and Co., London, 1798

ROSEWATER
DISH
London, 1569

ROSEWATER DISH

London, 1680

SILVERGILT MONSTRANCE   German, 16th Century   COVERED CUP   Salzburg, 16th Century

BRANDY SAUCE PAN   John Boddington, London, 1708

PORRINGER

Courtesy J. E. Caldwell & Co.

London, 1683

Courtesy J. E. Caldwell & Co.

GOBLET   London, 1654

CANDLESTICKS   Wm. Denny and John Barnard, London, 1697-1703

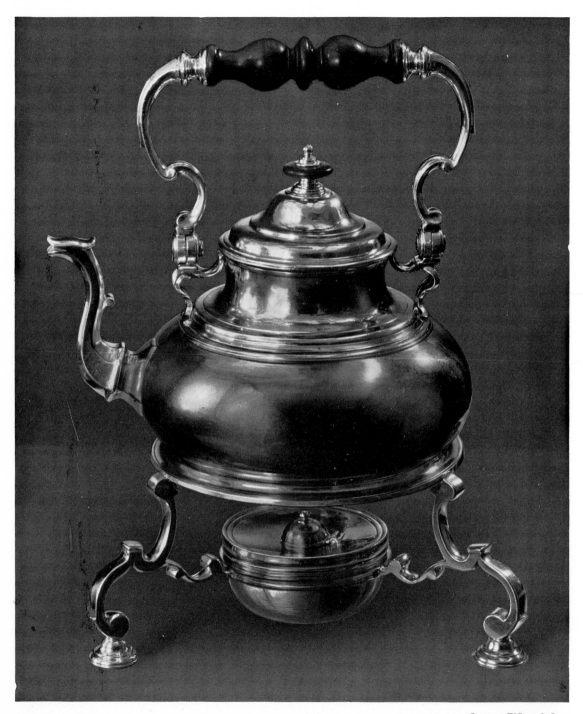

KETTLE AND STAND

Francis Garthorne, London, 1716

CENTERPIECE

Courtesy Marshall Field & Co.

Paul Storr, London, 1820

CANDLESTICKS

Anthony Nelme, London, 1723

Courtesy Metropolitan Museum of Art

Edward Winslow

CHOCOLATE POT

Courtesy Metropolitan Museum of Art

John Burt, Boston, 1712

COFFEE POT

TAZZA   Paul Lamerie, London, 1722   *Courtesy Tiffany & Co.*

COVERED CUP

Paul Storr, London, 1813

BACHELOR TEA SET

William Kingdon, London, 1821

TEA AND COFFEE SET

London, 1784-1795

Gabriel Sleath, London, 1714

CHOCOLATE POT ON STAND

TEA CADDY

London,
1752

Courtesy J. E. Caldwell & Co.

Hester Bateman, London, 1787

COFFEE POT

Courtesy Marshall Field & Co.

Peter and Anne Bateman, London, 1791

COFFEE POT

KETTLE

Ed. Fennell, London, 1767

KETTLE AND STAND

Thomas Whipman and Charles Wright, London, 1762

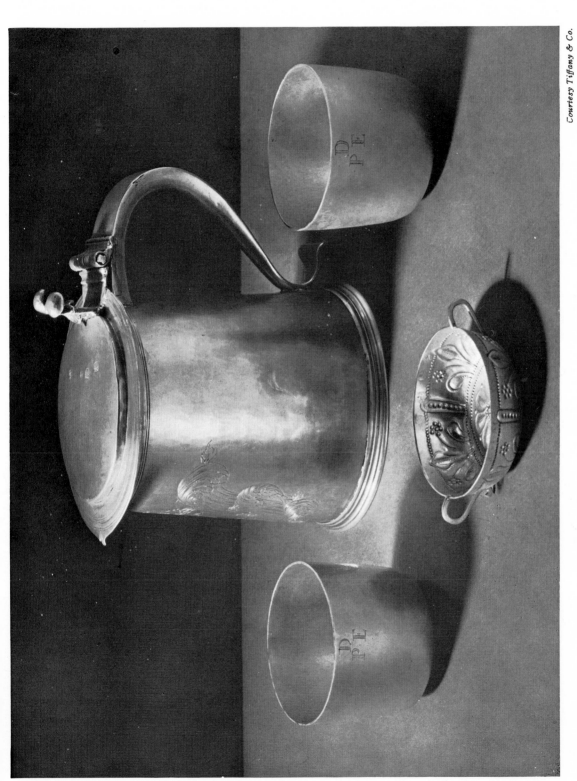

TANKARD   London, 1677   PAIR OF TUMBLER CUPS   London, 1686   WINE TASTER   London, 1649

CAUDLE CUP AND COVER
Gerrit Onkelbag, New York, 1670-1733

Courtesy James Graham, Jr.
Mabel Brady Garvan Collection, Yale Museum

John Coney, Boston   Samuel Vernon, Newport   Adrian Bancker, New York   *Courtesy James Graham,*

pieces have survived. They were eventually introduced into England about two centuries later, after having been noticed by English travelers in Italy.

An interesting reference to forks was published in a book called "Crudities," written at the beginning of the seventeenth century. The allusion is the expression of the author, Thomas Coryate, an Englishman traveling in Italy in 1620. "I observed a custom in all those Italian cities and towns through which I passed that is not used in any other country that I saw in my travels, neither do I think that any other nation of Christendom doth use it, but only Italy. The Italian, and also most strangers that are commorant in Italy, do always at their meals use a little fork when they cut their meat . . . their forks being for the most part made on iron or steel, and some of silver, but these are used only by gentlemen. The reason of this their curiosity is because the Italian cannot endure by any means to have his dish touched by fingers, seeing that all men's fingers are not alike clean. Hereupon I myself thought to imitate the Italian fashion by this fork cutting of meat, not only while I was in Italy, but also in Germany, and often-times in England since I came home."

It seems incredible that in a period of English history so famed for its extravagance and luxury, that forks were rarely used. This new display of refinement was indeed slow in being generally accepted, as evidenced by the few specimens made. However, their use may have been retarded somewhat, because ministers contended it was an insult to God not to touch meat with one's fingers. As more and more travelers noted their use and general advantages in the consumption of food, silversmiths produced forks in greater quantities. It was not until late in the eighteenth century, however, that they were in common use.

The earliest forks made were probably used only for serving pieces, as one in the inventory of the Royal Plate of 1399 weighed fifteen and one-half ounces. Another in a will of 1463, was listed as being used for "grene Gynger." Early in the Tudor period, a type of fork which was really a rudely wrought piece of silver with two prongs at one end, and a small spoon bowl at the other, was known. This was used for lifting "suckets" such as plums or other fruits preserved in syrup.

Even after the introduction of forks, it remained customary for dinner guests to provide their own utensils for eating. This undoubtedly explains the ingenious one-piece combinations which were made to serve the purpose of a spoon and fork. The three pronged fork would serve as the handle for a spoon bowl, by fitting the prongs in two loops and fastening it to the back. The handle hinged back to permit folding for convenience when carrying in the pouch. Surviving examples of these of English origin are very rare, and the few known today are all of continental make.

The earliest forks made were for the most part of iron and steel, with a few in silver owned by families of great wealth. Until the early part of the eighteenth century, a gentleman who traveled carried a knife and fork of his own, as the inns were not likely to have them. Visitors to England were continually criticizing the lack of forks, as they thought the English custom most unsanitary. Even after forks attained a fair amount of popularity, rich people did not possess many of them. Hence it has been suggested that the custom of serving a sherbet in the middle of the meal was introduced in order to permit the servants time to wash the forks for the next course.

The introduction of forks caused silver ewers and basins to fall into disuse completely. The earliest known fully hallmarked English fork is dated 1632. It is 7 inches long, two pronged, and bears the interesting crest of the Earl of Rutland. It remains today on exhibition at the Victoria and Albert Museum in London.

There was very little change in the style of the forks made from the beginning, until nearly the middle of the seventeenth century. At this time, a three pronged type with a flat rectangular handle appeared that closely resembled the Puritan spoon. This was probably copied from a contemporary French specimen, as forks are known to have existed in France as early as 1300. Until about 1730, English forks are found having two, three or four prongs. Thus the number of prongs cannot indicate any particular period. While during the Commonwealth, three prongs are common, after the Restoration three or four prongs were in use and dating from the reigns of William III and Queen Anne, many have only two tines.

With the passing of the Puritan austerity, more refined stems began to appear following the design of contemporary spoons. At first, the flat stem had the wide trifid end, but this soon developed into the more graceful trifid shape, although for some time it retained the notches. From then on, the fork was made similar to the spoon, until the introduction of the plain Old English type with the curved back, which has been generally accepted today, as the most useable and graceful. During the Georgian period stems of forks were ornamented with bright cut engraving or feather edging, although retaining the Old English pattern.

Mention must be made of the pistol handled forks, which were made to match the knives of the period. And there was also a type with a steel prong and a handle of thinly stamped silver filled with a resinous substance.

KNIVES

Knives are known in history a great deal earlier than forks, although ones with silver handles were not made prior to the eighteenth century. The origin of the knife may be traced to prehistoric times, at which time those executed were hardly more than pieces of flint. However, as time progressed, they were made of stone, and later of bronze, iron and steel.

The original use of the knife was of course in hunting and as a means of protection, but evidence exists to prove that the early Greeks used knives in the service of food. This was actually only a large serving knife, employed to cut the meat into smaller pieces, but it definitely laid the foundation for the making of individual table knives in later years.

There is no actual date which can be recorded for the introduction of the knife into England. However, Chaucer who died in 1400, speaks of a Sheffield whittle, the English term for knife. Thus, we may assume that they were used from this time on. Before the introduction of the fork, the diner held his food with one hand on the trencher, and cut it with his knife. In early English times, men carried a knife in a sheath. This type often had an ornamented silver handle, and we know it was used both at meal times and for defense. The custom of carrying a sheathed knife continued until the seventeenth century, and by the end of that age, a knife and a fork were encased in a single sheath. These coverings were exemplary of the beautiful silver work of the period, and many were studded with precious stones. By the beginning of the eighteenth century, the use of the sheathed knife at meal times fell into disuse, and the rich man's table at that time was set with silver handled knives.

One of the most popular types of knife was the pistol handled shape, many of which are reproduced today in modern silver. Other types are the "pied-de-biche," and later on the reeded and plain forms with the shell. While Georgian silver table knives are very rare and sought after by collectors, they are not too desirable for present day service, as they are somewhat too heavy and cumbersome.

Much interest is found in the shapes of the blades fitted to various silver handles during the eighteenth century. Many retain influences of former centuries, and these in turn can be traced back to flint instruments of prehistoric times. As silver blades were only introduced at a much later date, all early knives are hallmarked on the handles. However, many times, only a few out of a set were marked, so the collector need not feel discouraged if he cannot obtain a completely marked lot.

In the early part of the George III era, 1760-1820, dessert knives were introduced, usually with a silver blade and an ivory handle. Often the ivory was colored, purely for decorative purposes, and complete sets in good condition are practically unknown.

SKEWERS

Among the late Georgian table plate is the long pointed skewer used to hold joints of meat in shape. Apart from those having ornamental rings or tops, they vary little in style, and are not attractive as examples of the silversmith's art. In present times, they have been adapted for use as letter openers, in which capacity they are more presentable.

MARROW SCOOPS

The marrow scoop was originally a variation of the bowl of a spoon moulded into a long narrow gulley, which would enable one to dig into the inside of a bone in order to remove the marrow. Marrow now being extinct as a delicacy, their use has been given a distinctly modern note, and they are now employed as highball mixers, and drink stirrers. They were introduced at the time of Queen Anne and made in great profusion, because marrow was the epitome of the fastidious diner's art.

SERVING PIECES, LADLES AND SPOONS

A great variety of spoons suitable for serving and stuffing were made during the Georgian eras. Some, such as sauce ladles are rarely found earlier than the George II period, while long handled tasting spoons are known as early as the time of Queen Anne. Fish slicers, introduced about 1735 were very popular and a great variety with delicately pierced bowls were executed.

TABLEWARE

EPERGNES AND CENTERPIECES

EPERGNES and centerpieces were introduced during the latter part of the George I era, replacing to a large extent the standing salts which had gone out of use. The word epergne was doubtlessly derived from the French "epaigner," meaning to be thrifty. Inasmuch as the small baskets on the epergnes were used to contain condiments, fruits, nuts and similar luxuries from the Far East, the use of these large objects in the center of the table avoided waste. Each person helped himself from the one main epergne, and in this way, those delicacies not used were left on the table and not extravagantly thrown away with the leavings on the plate.

The first epergne fashioned was long and low with a bowl in the center and sweetmeat dishes on either end. In some instances they contained candle holders as well as casters, although such examples are rare. However, the later models were pieces of great height, elaborately decorated and generally consisted of a fruit or flower dish in the center surrounded by any number of small hanging baskets. Later in the century delicate piercing was introduced, and no article of domestic plate illustrated more clearly the height to which that phase of ability had risen. The hanging baskets were often replaced by small dishes on flat stands which could be adapted to individual use. One of the most popular types during the eighteenth century was made in the shape of a pagoda, the Chinese influence also being discernible in the styles of the pierced lattice work and series of semicircular shapes. In the latter part of the century boat shaped center pieces with smaller ones to match were greatly in demand. Epergnes are also found without the side embellishments and resemble huge flower vases with heavy crystal liners.

The extreme popularity of epergnes is readily understood when one realizes that the leading smiths of the period exerted their full efforts to produce masterful creations in silver. Paul Lamerie produced several of great beauty. They afforded him the opportunity for the lavish display and magnificent ornamentation in which he took so much delight. There was an extraordinary one made by him in 1734 for Count Bobrinsky of Russia, and the electroplated reproduction now in the Victoria and Albert Museum affords ample opportunity for inspection. It was a large piece, fitted with casters,

candle brackets and cruet frames surrounding the center body. Because it was impossible to use the entire equipment at one time, the
pieces were all removable and could be replaced by ornamental
knobs. Another important epergne by the same maker is the specimen executed for the Newdegate family.

The epergne was probably copied from pieces of similar plate
made in France at an earlier date. In the nineteenth century crystal
dishes were used in place of the silver bowls because of the lower
cost. For this same reason many more examples were produced in
Sheffield plate than in solid silver. Epergnes, unfortunately are not
in great demand today, as the massive proportions hardly blend with
the present small dining rooms. It was not unusual for some to weigh
as much as one thousand ounces, and specimens of that character
are recorded in the inventory of royal plate as early as 1725.

Before the middle of the eighteenth century actual silver centerpieces were introduced in place of epergnes. Many of these large
covered fruit bowls were made, but very few escaped the melting pot.

DINNER PLATES AND PLATTERS

Although silver dishes and plates were used as early as the middle
ages by royal families but few examples have survived. The predecessors of the modern platter, known as chargers, were used previous
to the Tudor period for carrying the joint of meat to the table. Another piece of similar design known as a Voyder was used for collecting the broken food that remained on the trenchers so that it might
be distributed for charitable purposes. But enormous quantities of
this plate were melted down during the Civil Wars in England and
very few examples antedate the Restoration in 1660. However, a
magnificent set of twelve bearing the London hallmark of 1567 has
survived. The plates were parcel gilt and finely engraved with
scenes depicting Hercules performing feats of strength. They were
eight inches in diameter with a side rim, and although the center
depression was somewhat smaller than in the later plates, they
clearly show the evolution from wooden trenchers. The continuation
of this shape has remained with silver plates. After the Restoration,
plates were produced in great quantity and the former types which
had been quite plain with simple moulded edges assumed ornamental
mounts for the first time.

The French craftsmen who migrated to England were directly
responsible for this new style and for many years rococo shells and
elaborate scrolls were applied to the borders. However, with the

gradual return to pieces of simpler design, the gadroon or bead edge replaced the more elaborate borders. Some of the early dishes of the latter half of the seventeenth century clearly illustrate again the definite influence of the Orient on English crafts. With the importation and continued popularity of Chinese porcelain in England, the silversmiths were soon reproducing the band of decorations by engraving quaint Oriental scenes and figures on the plain surfaces. Early plates command huge prices today as it is indeed rare to assemble a set of twelve or eighteen with the same date letter and by the same maker. For a time plates were so common that they fetched but little above the silver value, but today they have grown exceedingly scarce and are in constant demand.

With the introduction of the large silver dinner service, oval meat dishes of varied sizes appeared. They measured from the small types of ten inches to the venison dishes often as long as twenty-six inches. Those pieces used to hold the meat were equipped with what is now known as the "well and tree" which was, in effect, a series of small channels which allowed the gravy to run through into a large depression at one end of the dish. In the latter half of the nineteenth century porcelain services for dinner plates had come into general use and silver services of this type were no longer made except upon special occasions.

Soup plates as well as dessert plates closely followed the designs of dinner plates although they generally appear at a slightly later date.

SOUP TUREENS

The name tureen as applied to the containers for soup is said to be derived from the fact that Marshal Turenne of France, on one occasion, used his helmet to hold soup.

The tureen was introduced from France, from whence so much English domestic silver has been taken. During the time that Charles II lived in exile he learned many new customs from the French, among which was the custom of serving soup from a large bowl placed on the dining table or sideboard.

Soup tureens are pieces of large proportion, frequently being 22 inches in height including the cover and that they were considered pieces of notable importance is evidenced from the fine display of ornamentation so perfectly executed by the smiths of the period. Those made in the early Georgian period were large oval bowls generally ornamented in the rococo style and set on massive feet, while those produced a short time later displayed the more dignified forms of the Neo-classic era. Tureens were sometimes accompanied by a standing plateau which was placed directly underneath with the intention of protecting the table from the heat of the tureen containing the hot soup.

The earliest known specimen was made in 1703 by the celebrated Anthony Nelme, and formerly was in the possession of Lord Bateman. Further evidence of the popularity of the silver soup tureen or "soupiere," as it was known, is seen at Windsor Castle where numerous examples include thirteen pairs. Many of these were executed by Paul Storr who probably produced more fine specimens than any other maker. During the George III and George IV periods, soup tureens were considered inseparable adjuncts to the dining table, and during the last few years the old custom of serving soup at the table has been revived.

SAUCE BOATS, SAUCE TUREENS AND ARGYLES

The earliest known sauce boat was made in 1698 by William Scarlett. It was of a type directly copied from the French goldsmiths with a low, plain, oval body with double spouts and handles set on a low molded foot. In the second part of the eighteenth century, these types were discarded for boats on three feet with a single spout directly opposite to the handle. In general they followed the prevailing fashions in decoration and were produced in great quantities until the introduction of sauce tureens which were executed as exact replicas in small size, of the soup tureens. The sauce boat is a natural accompaniment to the dinner table and large services often have as many as four pairs with them.

An unusual type of small vessel used for gravy was introduced about 1750 and was called "argyle." These vessels are supposed to have been named after John, the fifth Duke of Argyll. Actually they were gravy tureens with spouts fitted on either side to hold a piece of hot iron which maintained the heat of the gravy. This style was greatly improved a short time later when a jacket was introduced which contained boiling water. Argyles are very rare and only a limited number were produced.

A curious form was made with a bulbous body and a small foot that served as a special compartment for the hot water, in this way offering a greater capacity for the gravy. Many of the early argyles were later converted into coffee and tea pots for which purpose they were admirably suited.

ENTRÉE DISHES, BACON DISHES, CHAFING DISHES, REVOLVING DISHES, DISH COVERS AND HEATERS

Entree dishes were introduced from France and originally called cover dishes or second course dishes. Similar articles generally referred to as sweetmeat dishes, although they were used to hold hot foods, were in use as early as the reign of Charles II. The custom of using the cover as a second dish was introduced during the Georgian era when the dishes were supplied with a removable handle. The dishes made in the Stuart period were restricted to oval shapes and circular domes with molded borders, while those of the later period were oval, circular, or oblong and generally ornamented with a gadroon, thread or bead or similar mount. Many entree dishes which are found in sets of four, six or eight were furnished with so-called heaters in which hot charcoal or boiling water was placed. Some were made with a heater as a combined part and these generally had a small opening with a screw cap at one end into which the water could be poured.

Another type of dish which was originally used for the serving of marrow was known as a second course dish and these are rarely found with covers. An article known as a bacon dish was furnished with a hot water base directly under the dish. It was generally fashioned with a long wooden handle which screwed into a socket at the back of the dish, the socket serving as the opening through which the hot water could be poured into the base. These were used in the service of eggs and bacon and other breakfast foods and during the past few years have become most popular at cocktail parties to hold hors d'oeuvres. Of little interest are the massive domical shaped, deep covers which have now fallen into complete disuse.

Inasmuch as the kitchens of all large houses were quite a distance from the dining rooms, it was necessary to use these covers to keep the food hot while being carried. The problem of heating food at the table was eventually solved by the introduction of the chafing dish which was, in effect, an entree dish fitted into a stand which contained an alcohol lamp in the center. The earliest known types of these were called braziers and were originally introduced by the colonial silversmiths of America. The bodies were pierced with scrollings and ornamental designs and appear to follow the style of a similar object more commonly used in France than in England.

During the Victorian era, another article known as the revolving tureen was first made. It was in the nature of a vegetable dish with a strainer fitted into a large deep oval stand which contained hot water, and also fitted with a corresponding cover which could be rolled back when the food was ready to be served or else left closed in order to retain the heat and keep the food clean.

As prosperity increased in the second half of the eighteenth century, plate was made heavier and heavier and large dinner services were produced for the first time. Soup tureens, sauce tureens, entree dishes, plates, and platters were incorporated into an enormous set containing hundreds of pieces. Complete services are now very rare as upon the settlement of estates in England, they were usually divided among the heirs. However, now and then a magnificent creation practically in its entirety is seen. Unfortunately many of the large pieces in them are too large, useless and obsolete. Throughout history these massive pieces have, as a rule, been converted into other articles.

XI

LIGHTING APPLIANCES

CANDLESTICKS

THE Bible mentions candlesticks, but these solid gold articles were actually for lamps and not candles. The Romans used a crude sort of candle which resembled a modern torch, but it was not until the third century that candles as they are known today were in use. At first these were used exclusively in churches, and the institution of Candlemas Day by Pope Gelasius in the fifth century, was probably the legal adoption of the candlestick. The large number of candles used is an important feature of the ceremony, and the need of some receptacle in which to place the candles was the cause of the origin of the candlestick. The earliest candlesticks were probably made of wood, but later on precious metals were used.

In the description of gifts given by Bishop Aethalwald to the monastery of Peterborough, in 963, candlesticks are mentioned. During the eleventh century, the Abbot Robert sent as a gift to his fellow countryman, Pope Adrian IV, two wonderful candlesticks of gold and silver, which the Pope admired so much that he had them placed in St. Peter's. During the Tudor period mention is made of a banquet given by Cardinal Wolsey to the French embassy and retinue at Hampton Court. As an example of lavish magnificence and splendor by those nearest the throne, the dinner was outstanding. Candlesticks are noted in the following manner: "and upon the nethermost dish garnished all with plate of clear gold, having two great candlesticks of silver and gilt, most curiously wrought, the workmanship thereof, with the silver, cost three hundred marks, and lights of wax as big as torches burning upon the same."

The earliest candlesticks were the type known as prickets. The pricket was actually a sharp point in the top of the shaft to hold the candle, and usually surrounded by a saucer to catch the wax. Although many of the English cathedrals used pricket candlesticks in the Middle Ages, in the sixteenth century they came to be considered monuments of superstition and were destroyed. The pricket was replaced by the socket which held the candle firmly in place.

Although it is accepted as fairly definite that the date of introduction of the socket candlestick was after the sixteenth century, proof of an earlier existence is found in a German picture of 1560, in which a pair is depicted.

Mention is found in wills and inventories of candlesticks which must have been of enormous value. One extremely important example is the pair of sticks given by Henry VI to Cardinal Beaufort in 1439 which were wrought of solid gold, and set with pearls, rubies, sapphires and emeralds.

Very few candlesticks from before the Restoration have survived. An unusual example of the Elizabethan period formed of silver and rock crystal is known, as well as a pair made in 1618, formerly in the possession of Lord Swaythling. They were of curious design, being set on a tripod base. An important set of four bearing the London hallmark of 1637 actually represent in the fuller sense candlesticks as we know them today. Each had a cylindrical stem and a base in the form of an inverted wine glass, with a wide circular disk in the middle to serve as a grease pan. These were probably inspired by a continental model. A magnificent pair from the Restoration period bearing the London hallmark of 1663 was formerly in the Treasury of the Kremlin, Moscow. They were richly ornate with large floral and animal decorations characteristic of the Charles II period, and were no less than 17½ inches in height.

Candlesticks of the Charles II and Queen Anne periods are found in considerable numbers and of varying design. An early form was of square plate throughout while a variation doubtless suggested by French work was octagonal in design. Closely akin to this was another type which had a round fluted column with a square plinth and abacus rising from a square plain moulded foot. Variations giving way to octagonal members with either plain or gadrooned borders are known. These sticks were generally of hammered silver and varied in height from seven to twelve inches.

The law compelling the use of a higher standard attracted the attention of the craftsman to cast work, the softer metal not lending itself to the hammer. Consequently from 1700 on, numerous sets of cast candlesticks are known. This new type was shorter in height than its predecessor and the form had much in common with the standing cup of the period, with the foot generally enriched with mouldings of gadrooned ornamentation. The whole surfaces of the candlesticks were at first left very plain, so that the reflecting light from the candle would be most brilliant. However, the demand for pieces of increased ornamentation which dominated the George II period, had its effect on candlesticks. With the introduction of the rococo style, a new and heavier type of candlestick, sadly lacking in the simplicity and beauty of the earlier type was wrought. Towards the middle of the century, a return to simplicity is noted, and many new varieties in style were produced. One of the popular types was in the form of a column, copied from the early Greek architecture. By now decanters of unusual design were applied, among the most popular being ram's heads, rosettes, medallions and festoons.

About the year 1760, a great change took place in the production of candlesticks, the pieces being made of thin stamped metal loaded with pitch to give them strength. Although this style would undoubtedly have been repugnant to goldsmiths of the Renaissance, the increased economy over cast sticks was found to be most practical.

Cast candlesticks are very much in demand, as a feature was the unusual weight which was quite natural in view of the larger quantity of silver used. The general practice of preparing a model of the candlestick in wax, and then pouring the molten metal into the mold, continued for many years. This same method was employed in making the more elaborate rococo styles. Here the work was in relief, and the separate ornamentations were cast in molds and soldered to the candlestick.

Sets of four early candlesticks are rare and for this reason many people who need four to complete a formal dinner table, have to be satisfied with owning two similar pairs. This situation is true throughout the collection of old silver, for complete services as needed today are rarely found.

CANDELABRA

In ancient Roman times candelabra were known, but at that time candelabra meant, in most cases, a support for a lamp. They were wrought in many different materials including the precious metals, but most of those that have been excavated were in bronze. Some fifty or sixty years ago, parts of a Roman silver candelabrum were found near the city of Hanover. The piece was probably made about the first century or earlier. The general form of early metal candelabra was similar throughout, the base being composed of three spreading feet with the lamps suspended from the arms. On top of the shaft there was usually a figurine or statuette, and the height ran anywhere from twelve inches to ten feet. The early churches possessed many examples patterned after the early Roman form, but there are no examples known today.

Silver candelabra dating prior to the reign of George III are rare. As prosperity increased during the second half of the eighteenth century, the silver was made heavier and heavier and massive candelabra were not uncommon in the great houses throughout the land. The nineteenth century produced many magnificent specimens with three or five lights, and occasionally one finds an important pair made for a large dining hall with as many as twelve lights.

Candelabra for the most part followed the designs used in candlesticks during the Queen Anne period. The prevailing patterns had three branches radiating from a center stem which was surmounted by a molded finial. During the rococo period, twisted branches were not uncommon and the finial center was frequently replaced by a socket. No doubt because of the excessive cost of silver candelabra many more pairs were made in Sheffield plate. For this reason the most representative work of the silversmiths who specialized in the production of candelabra is found in the plate examples.

CHANDELIERS

Chandeliers are known to have existed as early as the twelfth century when they reposed in churches, and although very common among the more important English families, practically none have survived to this date.

One of the most famous executed in silver is the specimen at Hampton Court. It is a massive piece with twelve branches richly decorated with laurel leaf bands and bosses. The upper part is ornamented with four cartouches containing a rose, thistle, harp and fleur-de-lis, each surmounted by a crown. It dates from the reign of William III. Earlier types combining the acanthus decoration of the Charles II period are also known as well as an important pair with eight branches now at Knole Park, Kent. Perhaps the most magnificent English silver chandeliers are found in Russia and outstanding among those is the pair, made by Paul Lamerie in 1734, which formerly hung in the Treasury of the Kremlin. They were in the best style of Lamerie, combining a wealth of decoration and strap work surmounted by a Russian imperial crown. Each was wrought with sixteen individual branches, so an idea of the immensity may be surmised. During the invasion of Napoleon's troops important pieces made in 1630 for the Cathedral of the Assumption in Moscow were melted down. Although chandeliers are recorded among the pieces of larger plate belonging to Charles II, none from his reign have survived in the world's collection.

SCONCES

During the exile of Charles II in the Low Country, he became familiar with many silver vessels previously unknown in England. Among these were silver sconces and shortly after the introduction of these sconces into England, they became very popular and fashionable. A large number have survived from the late seventeenth century and also from the eighteenth century, and handsome specimens make their appearance quite frequently. It appears that they were known as early as the time of Henry VIII as there is mention of them in the account given by George Cavendish of the reception given by Cardinal Wolsey to the French ambassador in 1527. Further references to their use are found in the inventories of royal plate during the Tudor period. From 1660 until the time of Queen Anne, wall sconces were extremely popular and the scarcity of the early examples can be blamed on the wholesale destruction of plate in later years. From an artistic point of view, sconces are representative of the better work of the silversmith and clearly illustrate the high degree of excellence attained by workers in the late seventeenth century. They were made in a variety of patterns generally with the back plates richly embossed. Three principal types are known, among them being one made in 1665 with a single socket attached to the oblong back plate with a rounded top. It was engraved and embossed with elaborate floral designs. Another type which is somewhat less common has an enriched truss in place of a back plate, and a scroll branch with a socket. However, the most standardized pattern consisted of a richly embossed back plate with either one or two branches with sockets. Among the many variations executed, is one which has in the center of the back plate a human arm, grasping in its hand the branch. Silver-framed, mirrored sconces were once very popular but they are seldom encountered today.

The fashion of lighting rooms by means of sconces was generally known throughout England after the accession of Queen Anne. Illustrative of the type most in demand at that time are a pair made in 1703, now in the Victoria and Albert Museum, and a magnificent set of six by the celebrated Peter Archambo. A splendid collection of early sconces is owned by the royal family, and includes two lovely sets bearing the monogram of William and Mary, surmounted by a royal crown. These were all in high relief with strongly defined ornamentation, the craftsman's intention being to reflect as much light as possible.

CHAMBERSTICKS

Throughout the eighteenth century many types of portable chamber candlesticks were used for lighting the way to one's bedroom through the long dark halls, and also to illuminate the chamber itself. In the royal plate of 1438 mention is made of a "hond candilstikke" which may be considered the ancestor of all chamber candlesticks. Although examples prior to 1700 are very rare, an outstanding chamberstick with a circular pan to match, made in 1688, may now be seen at Exeter College. Also, they are rarely found complete, because over a period of years the snuffers have generally been lost.

An ancient custom which descended from medieval times was an auction sale conducted "by inch of candle." A small piece of candle was lighted and allowed to burn itself out and the final bidder before the flame expired was the successful purchaser of whatever was offered for sale. For this purpose special silver holders were made.

TAPER STICKS

A taper stick is actually a reproduction of a candlestick in miniature and was used for melting wax to seal letters, or when impressing a seal to accompany a signature on a document. Tapersticks date back to the time of William and Mary in 1688 and were in use only until the introduction of the gummed envelope. They were intended for use on the writing desk, but later in the century became an actual part of the silver inkstand. Their development followed closely that of the candlestick.

WAX JACKS

Another implement made in silver and used on the writing desk during the eighteenth century was an article called a wax jack. This was actually a wax taper coiled around a spindle. It passed through a socket enclosed in a sort of openwork bird cage. The earliest specimens which date as far back as 1698, were enclosed in a cylindrical box which had a hole in the center of the lid for the wax to protrude. Although often found in completely enclosed silver units the loveliest types were usually pierced.

SNUFFERS

Requisite to early candlesticks were the small snuffers on trays which were evidently in use as early as the sixteenth century. As candles in the early days burned more slowly and the wax ran down the sides of the candlestick, it was frequently necessary to clip the charred pieces of wick. Snuffers were a household essential before the invention of candle wicks which could be entirely consumed by the flame.

Snuffers resemble in shape a pair of scissors, but differ in that one blade is broad, the solid piece set perpendicularly at the end. Those of the post-Restoration period were generally fitted with a box on one blade and a pressing plate on the other which fitted inside. At this time many were equipped with little pans shaped to the form of the snuffers, but later on these gave way to attractive stands made with little handles so that they could be carried about.

The earliest known reference to a snuffer is in the list of plate at All Souls' College at Oxford in 1448. Several examples are known from the sixteenth century, including the specimen in the British Museum which bears the arms of Henry the Eighth.

XII

BOXES

UNFORTUNATELY silver boxes are not representative, as a whole, of the better workmanship of the English and Irish silversmiths. The finest specimens were executed in European countries. Although hallmarked silver boxes are known to exist from as early a time as the reign of James I, 1603 to 1625, they are far from plentiful, few having survived throughout the years. They were rarely made in great profusion, being almost exclusively for royalty and those in court circles.

They were very small in size and consequently many were lost or buried. But it is just because of this scarcity that early silver boxes are so much in demand. Well-marked specimens of authentic date fetch fantastic prices in sale rooms, and collectors and dealers all over the world are always in the market for the better types.

Nearly all small boxes were originally parts of elaborate toilet services, although a few spice and sweetmeat boxes are known to have existed prior to the making of these handsome toilet sets. It may be said, without a doubt, that silver boxes were considered a luxury, and as a rule, were only made to special order for a chosen few.

FREEDOM BOXES

Among the many styles of silver boxes known in England, were small shallow receptacles known as freedom boxes. In shape they were similar to tobacco boxes. They were originally made to hold the vellum certificate used at the presentation of the freedom of a borough to some important personage. As a general rule, the lid was engraved or embossed with the arms of the borough to which the freeman had been admitted.

Freedom boxes are very rare. However, they are not greatly in demand as they are a poor representation of the work of the English silversmiths. Outstanding among freedom boxes were the two executed in solid gold and given with the freedom of certain Irish towns to the fourth Duke of Devonshire and the fourth Duke of Rutland, both holding the same office of Lord Lieutenant of Ireland. Both examples being unmarked, one can only surmise as to their origin, but data that have been handed down concerning the lives of these two prominent men prove fairly conclusively that they were the work of Dublin goldsmiths. Unfortunately, these two fine examples are no longer in their original state, having been melted down. In 1801 and 1813 the gold in them was made into a salver and a platter by the celebrated Paul Storr.

Cork silversmiths in the eighteenth century were busily engaged in making gold and silver freedom boxes. Outstanding among the fine examples extant today, are the ones originally belonging to the Earl of Shelbourne and Admiral Lord Redding, both the work of the famed Irish silversmith, William Reynolds. An earlier example was made in Cork in 1737, and carried with it the freedom of that city. This box is now in the collection of Dean Swift.

POMANDERS

Pomanders were in general use among the wealthier classes as early as the fourteenth century, but examples from this period are no longer obtainable. Such few as have survived from the sixteenth and seventeenth centuries are now in museums and private collections only.

The pomander is a curious corruption of the French word "pomme d'ambre," which means apple of amber. The amber referred to the ambergris, which, when worn, diffused a pleasant odor. A small bar of ambergris, or musk, was enclosed in a silver container and worn around the neck or hung from a girdle. The original "pomme d'ambre" eventually came to be spelled "pomander" and, as such these little boxes are known today.

Pomanders were originally carried to counteract fever and to protect the olfactory nerves from offensive smells prevalent in the Middle Ages. These small boxes which were originally relics of old silver toilet services were practically a necessity for those who wished, and could afford the luxury of protecting themselves against the existing unsanitary conditions. It is said that the pomander owes its general use to Cardinal Wolsey, who filled an orange with a sponge soaked in vinegar, worm wood, rosemary and spices, and carried it with him everywhere. The silversmiths of the day quickly perceived the need for such an article and produced them profusely.

TOILET SETS

In the study of the history of silver, mention is made of small silver boxes, perfume flasks, and other toilet accessories that were used by Queen Elizabeth, but no complete English toilet service dated prior to the seventeenth century is known. However, it is probable that they were in use many years before that as they are noted in the luxurious domestic appointments which appeared in Spain after she began to obtain quantities of silver from her American colonies.

Full credit, however, must be given to France for the general popularity of the toilet set. They were widely used by the court of Louis XIV, and from there the use spread to England; for the court of Charles II used only typically French ornaments in the gold and silver appointments. The only complete English toilet sets which have survived are all dated after the Restoration, 1660.

These services often comprised as many as from 20 to 35 pieces, including all the toilet implements, table mirrors, silver candlesticks, powder and page boxes, precious salvers, pin-cushions, flasks, and innumerable other small articles which help to complete the lady's toilet.

Probably the finest known toilet service in the world today is the one presented by Charles II to Frances Stuart, Duchess of Richmond, and hallmarked Paris, 1672 and 1680. The King himself paid close to ten thousand pounds for this service when it was made, so one can readily imagine the fantastic value placed on it today by collectors.

Although Irish silver toilet sets are very rare, one made by a Dublin silversmith in 1791 is known. Several noted English silversmiths are regarded as the makers of beautiful and elaborate toilet sets. Among these are: David Willaume, Anthony Nelme, and Paul Lamerie.

Toilet sets are very rare. Recently a partially complete set by Paul Lamerie reached a price close to thirty thousand dollars.

TOBACCO BOXES

Tobacco was originally introduced into England by Ralph Lane, the first governor of Virginia, during the reign of Queen Elizabeth. It was carried in small boxes of either base metal or silver, although the latter were not in general use until the following century. No tobacco box antedating the Restoration is known, and the few remaining examples of the period are merely plain, shallow containers of little beauty and no great importance as examples of the silversmith's art in England.

MULLS

Scotch mulls were large or small horns frequently mounted in silver and used for snuff boxes. They are generally found bearing presentation inscriptions and are in demand today, as Scotch silver of early date is always desirable. One of great historic interest is a five-compartment box which was given to the Perthshire Regiment of Gentlemen and Yeomenry Cavalry by James Hay, Esq., captain of the Cassé troup in 1804.

NUTMEG GRATERS

Small boxes suitable for carrying in the pocket, and used to contain nutmeg were particularly popular during the eighteenth century. At this time nutmeg and other flavors had been introduced from the East and were in great favor throughout England. A nutmeg grater was actually a small silver container fitted with an inner grate attached to the cover on the inside. This permitted the dust to fall through into the box. The graters were made in a great variety of styles and shapes, but the general purpose of all was alike. It is interesting to note that they were in use throughout the first half of the Victorian era.

SPICE AND SNUFF BOXES

Spice and sweetmeat boxes appear to have been fashionable during the sixteenth century, and there is direct evidence of their popularity in court circles in the latter half of the following century. However, few English snuff boxes can compare in detail and workmanship with the masterpieces executed by the French craftsmen. One of the earliest known spice boxes dated 1598, survived from the Elizabethan era. It was recently sold at Christie's for upwards of six thousand dollars. It was in the form of a cockle-shell on four feet, the sides ornamented with arabesque on a matted ground and the handles molded with an egg and tongue border.

Another specimen, an oval box made in 1677, was sold at auction for nearly three thousand dollars. These prices are mentioned merely to indicate the great rarity of such articles.

Probably the best known of all snuff boxes are those associated with the Russian silversmiths. In very few countries in Europe were these superb creations so fully appreciated or expertly conceived as there. Many magnificent specimens in gold and enamel date from the nineteenth century and their popularity today for use as table cigarette boxes is wide. These Russian boxes were covered with niello which was a metallic alloy of sulphur and silver having a deep black color. Pieces were decorated with inside designs filled with niello.

It is interesting to note here the collaboration between makers and decorators of English silver pieces. Conclusive proof that articles were often executed by more than one maker is found in the historic gold tobacco box of 1741, made by Humphrey Payne in London. The piece bears his makers' mark as well as the signature on the inside cover of the engraver, John Ellis. Therefore, it is not unusual to find that, although pieces were often completed by one maker, heraldic devices and other ornamentations were often added by contemporary or later craftsmen.

In the past decade, prices of antique silver snuff boxes have risen tremendously, chiefly because many of these early snuff boxes were of a sufficient size to fit cigarettes used today. In this way a person wishing to assemble a well-appointed table of completely original silver might find the necessary containers for a modern note.

VINAIGRETTES

Silver vinaigrettes were regarded as indispensable until the middle of the nineteenth century, and were carried by as great a number of ladies as might outfit themselves today with compacts. These little silver boxes varied greatly in size and style, but being made exclusively for the feminine interest were all of a pretty and pleasing design. The general construction of all vinaigrettes was generally the same. A perforated inner lid permitted the choice aromatic scents to escape, and diffuse a very pleasant scent. Actually, they are a modern adaptation of the sixteenth century pomander, as their original use was much the same.

Vinaigrettes, as a rule were hallmarked under the lid, and the majority of them are of Birmingham origin. In glancing over a collection of possibly a hundred varied types, one would probably find that over 75 per cent were made there, and that in all probability, not more than seven or eight different makers would be represented in the entire lot.

Vinaigrettes are often found with a ring attachment through which a chain was passed, as very often they were worn as lockets.

Vinaigrettes in general exhibited a finer type of workmanship in the fine piercing of the inner lids and delicate repoussée work, than any other of the small silver boxes. Today they are greatly in demand by collectors the world over and in the past ten years their value has increased many fold. One of the most recent adaptations of the vinaigrette is for use as a pill-box or else as a container for saccharine tablets.

XIII

MISCELLANEOUS PIECES

TRAYS, SALVERS AND PATENS

IN the last half of the seventeenth century, small circular trays were used as stands for large silver tankards, but specimens of these are far from plentiful. The earliest known mention of such a piece is in 1661, wherein it is described as follows: "salver . . . is a new fashioned piece of wrought plate, broad and flat, with a foot under neath, and is used in giving beer, or other liquid thing to save the Carpit or Cloathes from drops."

As a general rule the earliest salvers, now referred to as card trays, were simple in design and void of decoration, as opposed to the later types which combined molded or cast borders with engraving, or heraldic insignia in the center. Occasionally small engraved trays of early date are found, and they are by far the most valuable because of their extreme rarity. The introduction and continued use of the circular salver, many of which assumed massive proportions, was undoubtedly influenced by the early rose water dishes. Although many of the larger salvers weighed as much as 200 ounces, largely because of the heavy rococo mounts, examples displaying the full ability of the silversmith's skill may be seen. These excelled particularly in the manner of the engraved and flat shaped work. Perhaps no other article of domestic plate retained the quiet dignity of Queen Anne's time as fully as the salver. During the George II period when the flair for over-ornamentation was prevalent everywhere, a simple style of tray was introduced known as the "Chippendale." The name was applied to them because the borders were reproduced from the rims of tables designed by that great furniture designer. "Chippendale" as well as other salvers were made in a great variety of styles and shapes, including square, circular, oblong and shaped specimens.

Dating from the beginning, the tea service was placed on what is now known as a tea tray. They were almost indispensable to the serving of tea, and increased in size as more pieces were added to form a service. Although made in a wide variety of sizes and shapes, generally supported on four feet, their beauty was not confined to the work on the borders, for the finest decorative engraving was lavished on the plain surfaces. The ordinary tea tray as we know it measured anywhere in length from eighteen inches to twenty-four inches, and was placed on a large table at tea time. However, in the middle of the eighteenth century, a wooden stand was devised with a top of the same size as the silver tray with sockets to hold the feet. These never attained great popularity though, for the regulation tray with its two easily grasped handles was found to be more convenient.

At the time of the neo-classic vogue, a complete change in ornamentation is noted. The craftsmen used flat chased motifs, generally in a wide band around the edge, with the center left plain for an engraved coat of arms. Other variations noted at this time were the introduction of large oval and oblong waiters with high pierced gallery borders, as well as some with wooden or papier mache bases. Waiters for use in large houses were often made in pairs or sets of three, but are rarely found today.

During the Queen Anne and George I periods the paten was introduced. This was in the nature of a circular waiter standing on a low trumpet mouth foot, the joint of which was frequently masked by a circle of cut-card work. Although generally used by the church for sacred purposes, patens were employed in ordinary life to serve as containers for fruit.

INKSTANDS AND STANDISHES

Inkstands or standishes, as they were called at first, were introduced in the first half of the seventeenth century. As a matter of record, the earliest known hallmarked specimen was made in London in 1630.

Within a short time, silversmiths were producing inkstands of great beauty, and also at all times during the history of their production, simplicity was the keynote. Hardly ever did they assume the fantastic forms and over-ornamentation that influenced the other domestic plate during the rococo period. In time they became essentials of the well-appointed writing table and their popularity never waned during the history of silversmithing in England.

The inkstands or standishes made during the reign of Charles II were fashioned like large plain rectangular boxes with two flat covers and a handle in the middle. A specimen of this rare type dated 1685 is now in the Treasury. As time progressed, inkstands were greatly altered in style, and by the eighteenth century the casket type was introduced. Occasionally, these were fitted with a slide drawer below, to hold the sealing wax. This general style of a rectangular tray with receptacles for ink, sand and wafers prevailed during the century. Slight variations occur in some specimens wherein the wafer box in the center was covered by a hand bell which was used to summon the servant when the letter was ready to be sent. In later years, the bell was replaced by a taperstick which previously had been a separate unit. During the George III era, the silver fitments were replaced by glass receptacles with silver tops fitted on to the tray base. One top was pierced with holes in which to place the quills when not in use, another had finer perforations for use as a sandcaster, while the third well contained the ink. The trays were somewhat larger than the earlier examples, the border being ornamented with a concave depression on either side to hold the wax. Steel pens were introduced in 1805, but were not generally used until many years later. For this reason it is not unusual to find inkstands fitted with sandboxes and quill holders, dating well into the nineteenth century.

There was an early mention of an inkstand in the inventory of the plate of Henry VIII, where two are recorded in 1520. One was of Spanish origin, while the other was probably of English make. The specimen of 1630 belonging to Sir John Noble appears to be the only surviving inkstand of those made before the Civil War. One of the most magnificent and largest inkstands ever made, is the one executed by Paul Lamerie for the Duke of Cumberland. One famous inkstand was used by Sir Joshua Reynolds in many of his portraits.

In the collection and purchase of old inkstands, it is essential to make sure that each individual piece is marked, for over a period of years parts may have been lost and replaced. Also many of the early snuffer stands have been converted into inkstands by the addition of wells. It is well to remember that when parts have been added or alterations made, the value of the piece has been greatly lessened.

BREAD, CAKE, AND SWEETMEAT BASKETS

Oval pierced baskets with handles were introduced during the reign of George II at which time they were used for bread, thereby accounting for the decorative wheat sheaves often noted. The earliest examples were low and very heavy, while the later types were generally pierced and much lighter in feeling. However, towards the end of the eighteenth century the piercing was abandoned and baskets were again made with stands that followed the circular or oblong shapes then in vogue.

Baskets were made in a wide variety of shapes which changed with each successive period. Originally the basket was made with a small handle at either end, but this was replaced later by the large swinging handle. Among the interesting examples known of unusual baskets is a George III specimen with a pierced separation in the center, one side of which was marked "fresh" and the other "stale" to indicate the place for each kind of bread. A very rare type, beautifully pierced with an original wicker work pattern typified the unusual designs created by Paul Lamerie. It was made in 1733 and formed part of the collection of Lord Swaythling. In the George II reign, baskets were often made in the form of a large shell on dolphin feet, an example of 1751 being in the collection of Royal plate at Windsor Castle.

The middle of the eighteenth century showed the popularity of delicately pierced sweetmeat baskets. They were actually reproductions in miniature of the larger cake baskets and carried out to the minutest detail the same character of workmanship found in the larger pieces. A variation of the candy dish was in the shape of an escalloped shell, examples of which are very rare. A magnificent pair, formerly in the possession of Sir Montague, were made by Paul Lamerie in 1732, which date is the earliest known reference to a shell. Shells are among the most desirable pieces of old silver as they fit in perfectly with the table appointments of today.

DISH RINGS

Dish rings are peculiar to the work of Irish silversmiths, in whose country they seem to have first come into use about 1750. From this time on they remained as one of the principal articles of table plate until the latter part of the nineteenth century. The dish ring, as made in Ireland, was always circular and resembled in shape an enlarged napkin ring, while English examples of oval body are known. The dish ring was probably introduced in the attempt to avoid the damaging results of standing hot dishes directly on the table. The ring remained on the table throughout the meal to support in turn the soup bowl, the potato bowl, the dessert bowl, and occasionally the punch bowl. Inasmuch as the fashion in Ireland was to serve potatoes in a large wooden bowl which was placed on top of the silver stand, it is not strange that for years these silver articles have been erroneously termed potato rings.

The earliest type of dish ring made is very shallow, the sides of some being less than three inches deep, and the diameter at the rim being generally identical with that of the base. As a rule, the sides were ornamented with shaped and pierced scrolls and flowers, with chased cartouches framed by scrolls for the armorial insignia. Dish rings often portrayed pastoral and farm scenes. Many rings bore the Oriental influence in the Chinese architecture and native figures, these subjects often being combined with European hunting scenes. Dish rings of this character are greatly in demand as specimens of unusual creation by silversmiths in piercing. The later type of dish ring does not have the same amount of appeal since it lacks the charming decoration of the preceding style.

The earliest known reference to a dish ring is in an anonymous inventory of plate dating from 1697, wherein two are mentioned. An advertisement of the same year refers to two rings for the table, although it can only be assumed that dish rings were meant. However, an example as early as 1704 has survived and it is thought most probable that some specimens may have existed a few years earlier. It is interesting to note that the Irish dish rings retained the elaborate ornamentation of the rococo period long after that style had gone out of fashion in England. Reproductions of these rings are made today and have been improved upon by the addition of a blue glass liner which enables them to serve as attractive flower bowls and centerpieces.

DISH CROSSES

As dish rings fell into disuse, dish crosses were introduced to serve the same purpose. They were a great deal more practical than their predecessors because the supports and the feet were made to slide along the rods of the cross in order to contain various dishes. They were introduced during the time of George II and used extensively throughout England. However, they never grew in popularity in Ireland and the dish ring remained there for many years. Dish crosses were sometimes fitted with spirit lamps which helped to keep the food hot.

SILVER FURNITURE

Previous to the Restoration, nearly all plate made was for domestic use, but with the accession to the throne of Charles II many fantastic objects such as silver furniture were introduced. All of these silver pieces are symbolic of the waste of money fostered by the Merry Monarch, who sought to emulate the costly furnishings he had known at the French court. The prevailing extravagance is noted as early as 1674 when a silver bed was made for Nell Gwyn. Although the bed was the work of a foreigner, John Cooqus, it started a vogue among English smiths. A true picture of the lavish splendor of the period is best recorded by the Duchess of Portsmouth, in 1683, on her return from a visit to the apartment of the king's mistress—"great vases of wrought plate, tables, stands, chimney furniture, sconces, branches, braseras, etc.; all of massive silver and out of number."

However, previous references to silver furniture are noted as early as 1508, when a silver weaving stool appeared in the list of Princess Mary's trousseau and again in 1520 at which time Henry VIII possessed a silver mounting block.

In the Royal collection at Windsor Castle, the remains of three magnificent sets of silver furniture are found. Two of them were presents to Charles II and William III from the city of London, and from descriptions, one table alone weighed over eight thousand ounces. In this furniture, as well as in similarly made pieces, only a minimum of wood and iron were used in the construction. Among the numerous other pieces which reflected the wild orgy of spending, are silver mirrors, andirons, and candlestick stands. Mention must also be made of the existence of silver clocks which are known since the latter half of the sixteenth century. Huge silver vases, specimens of which are very, very rare, were made in these times. As a rule they consisted of a garniture of three pieces which included a vase flanked by two enormous flasks.

There is little likelihood that any of the silver mounted furniture will ever come into the market as most of it is preserved at Windsor Castle, Knole House, Seven Oakes, and Ham House.

BUTTER DISHES

Made in great number chiefly in Ireland butter dishes typified the Celtic love of figures and pastoral scenes. They were usually in the shape of a deep oval box, about seven inches long with a high cover surmounted by the figure of a cow which formed the handle. Butter dishes and dish rings show a decided resemblance in treatment, although the former are by no means as fine.

TABLE BELLS

Silver bells were introduced about the time of Queen Anne, and later accompanied inkstands as the center ornament. They are rarities.

SERVING PIECES

Grape shears and asparagus tongs were introduced during the reign of George II. The former were generally made with a wealth of ornamentation while the latter were, as a rule, very simple in design. Cheese scoops were not made in profusion until the late Georgian periods although a few examples of earlier date have survived. They were often combined with ivory and agate handles and are attractive as well as useful.

XIV

THE ENGLISH PROVINCES

SILVERSMITHING IN YORK

YORK was by far the most important provincial city in England in the Middle Ages and was the first town to receive a touch mark by the Act of 1423. However, it was not until twelve years later that statutory recognition was given to it, according to the ordinance of its Mayor. The law provided that no goldsmith anywhere in England should make silver of lower alloy than sterling, nor offer any article for sale without first impressing it with his own mark. In the following years of the fifteenth century, many references to York goldsmiths are found in wills and inventories. In 1560 it was ordained that all work should be "towched with the pownce of the citie, called the halfe leopard head and halfe flowre-de-luyce," that no silver should be worked of "worse alaye than sterlyng" and any-one working gold or silver below these standards should forfeit double the value of the article.

At the time that the city mark and maker's mark were compulsory, a date letter was introduced, so that all York plate made from about 1560 to 1698 should bear three hallmarks. Upon the reestablishment of the York Assay Office in 1700, the town mark was changed and the arms of the city, a cross charged with five lions passant, were thenceforward used in addition. Pursuant to the terms of the Act of 1700, the lion's head was erased, and the figure of Britannia was struck, thereby increasing the number of compulsory marks to five. It was also decreed at this time that the maker's mark should be formed from the first two letters of the surname, as in the case of London. In 1717 the assaying of plate at York was discontinued, as the two principal goldsmiths of the town entered into an agreement with the Newcastle Goldsmiths Company to have plate assayed there upon payment of an annual fee. For this reason no York-marked plate is known between the years of 1714 and 1779. Many variations occur in date letters as shown in the table of marks. In 1858 the office was finally closed and it is likely that it will never be reopened.

SILVERSMITHING IN NORWICH

It is probable that Norwich plate approaches more closely the date of York work than that found in other provinces. The work of the sixteenth century goldsmiths of Norwich is entitled to the highest rank in all of the English provinces, and many of their Elizabethan pieces are fully equal to those produced in London at that time.

Norwich records show a great many goldsmiths working from the end of the thirteenth century and with few intervals names of prominent makers are known down to the end of the seventeenth century. Norwich was one of the seven cities appointed in 1423 to have a "touch." The town mark consisted of a castle and lion and was practically unchanged from 1565 to 1575. No plate was officially marked before 1565, but from that date on, the compulsory assaying and marking with the arms of the city took effect. Although no mention is made of a date letter, it seems clear from the earliest examples that this practice was also begun in 1565, but no date letter mark between the years 1585 and 1624 has appeared, and in all probability, none was used.

The use of the date letter was again resumed in 1624 but discontinued between 1643 and 1688. Finally in this last year, an effort was made to institute a regular system of hallmarking and, with but few variations, marks show a consistency not previously found. The Act of 1697 prevented the Norwich goldsmiths from continuing to work under the old regime, and it appears that only a few survived to take advantage of the legislation in 1701 which permitted them to reestablish an assay office.

Peter Peterson was the one outstanding Norwich silversmith but towards the end of the seventeenth century the craft of Norwich goldsmiths dwindled and disappeared.

SILVERSMITHING IN EXETER

Judging from the examples of plate which have survived to the present time, the goldsmiths of Exeter were probably next to those of Norwich in order of antiquity. But apparently Exeter did not have an official "touch." No assay office was established until 1701, and consequently no records are available prior to this time. Exeter was too far removed from London, it was not convenient for its goldsmiths to send their plate there to have it assayed, and therefore, we may infer that the goldsmiths of Exeter worked under the privileges of a royal charter, although its existence has never been discovered.

During the sixteenth and seventeenth centuries the Exeter town mark was the Roman letter "X." In some early Elizabethan pieces, the mark varied from that of an "x" with a crown over the letter and a pellet on either side, to an "x" in a circular stamp without surrounding dots. In 1701 the Exeter town mark officially used was composed of the arms of the city which consisted of a triple towered castle.

Although only an inference can be drawn due to the lack of records, it seems most probable that the small letters found on early pieces of about the year 1600, were date letters. With the passing of the Act of 1700, date letters were uniformly incorporated into the marking of silver, and thenceforward were changed annually. Their use continued until 1883, at which time the office was closed.

In the absence of records it is impossible to say what plan was used in testing and assaying Exeter plate prior to 1701. However, as it is likely that masters and wardens were used, each was probably entrusted with the punch for striking the town mark. In those instances where a mark occurs which is neither the town mark nor the maker's mark, it may be safely assumed that it was struck by the master or the warden.

SILVERSMITHING IN NEWCASTLE

The earliest known reference to a Newcastle goldsmith occurs in an ordinance of 1248, wherein two goldsmiths were appointed to be in complete charge of assaying the money coined. In 1423, Newcastle was given a touch mark of its own. No further reference to these smiths appears until 1536 when they were incorporated in a common company with freemen of many other trades. Although no Newcastle plate of earlier date than the middle of the seventeenth century has survived, it is known that the art of the goldsmith flourished during the sixteenth century, and in all probability those pieces made were melted down in the troublous times of Charles I.

The Act of William III, which conferred on the Goldsmiths Company of England the sole rights of assaying, reflected great hardship and inconvenience on the goldsmiths of Newcastle, who were put to great expense, risk and delay in sending their plate to London. This hardship was remedied in 1700, when assay offices were established at Exeter, York, Chester, Norwich and Bristol, but Newcastle was not one of the places where mints had been established to recoin money and it was not included. However, there is little doubt that although it was illegal, much plate was made during this time. After many petitions and entreaties set forth by the goldsmiths of Newcastle, royal assent to reestablish the assay office of Newcastle was granted in 1702. This same act provided that all smiths who were freemen of Newcastle should be incorporated and known as the Company of Goldsmiths of New-castle-upon-Tyne. At this time it was compulsory for all plate of the required standard to be struck with the maker's mark, which consisted of the first two letters of his surname, the lion's head erased, the Britannia mark, the town mark, and a variable date letter.

Although the goldsmiths of Newcastle had been constituted as an independent corporation, they continued in association with other tradesmen until 1716. In 1844 the Goldsmiths Company of London endeavored to obtain jurisdiction over all the provincial offices, claiming that great illegalities existed in these places with regard to the correct assaying of plate. Through dint of pressure brought to bear by the London Company, silversmithing at Newcastle finally simmered to nothing, and in 1884 it was finally resolved to discontinue the assay office there.

The town mark of Newcastle, which was probably derived from the original arms of the borough, consisted of a single castle, and was used until about the middle of the seventeenth century. In 1670 the mark was changed and the entire coat of arms of Newcastle, which consisted of three castles in a plain heraldic shield, was struck. About ten years later the shape of the shield was altered and it assumed a more elaborate form. However, the only distinguishing mark is the often repeated use there of the lion passant, "to sinister."

SILVERSMITHING IN CHESTER

The silversmiths of Chester are really entitled to a preference over those of the other provincial guilds, as they are the only ones who still maintain an assay office today. It is fully alive and in constant competition with those of the other large cities in England. It is known that the goldsmiths and money coiners of Chester are recorded as early as 925, which gives them further distinction. From the twelfth to the fifteenth century there is occasional mention of prominent goldsmiths in Chester, but it is not until 1540 that any amount of data is available. From this time on Chester goldsmiths are recorded in a fairly continuous line down to the present day.

Chester was not appointed along with the other provinces in 1423 to have a touch, the reason for it being, that the smiths already had this privilege and had been enjoying it for almost 200 years. Coins were minted in this city as early as the time of Athelestan. Prior to 1573 a maker's mark was not struck, nor was the mark of the assayer used. From this time on, however, all goldsmiths were re-

Bowl (Pair) W. Fountain. London, 1802

Pair of Mugs Henry Cowper, London, 1774

Bowl Fuller White, London, 1765

Tobacco Box Henry Cowper, London, 1792

SHEFFIELD PLATE BOWL   c. 1800   *Courtesy Black, Starr & Frost-Gorham, Inc.*

ONE OF PAIR OF SHEFFIELD SOUP TUREENS   *Courtesy Black, Starr & Frost-Gorham, Inc.*   T. & J. Creswick, c. 1800

TRAY WITH ARMS OF LORD MACKENZIE

Jno. Crouch, London, 1810

CRUET   J. Delmester, London, 1758

CRUET   Andrew Fogelberg, London, 1772

Peter de Riemer, New York, 1769

Daniel Van Voorhis, New York, 1779

John Coney, Boston

TEAPOT

John Jackson, New York, 1736

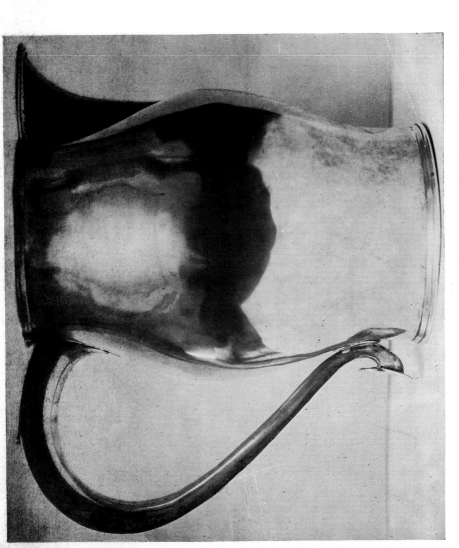

Robert Evans, Boston, 1770

PITCHER

RATTAIL SPOONS

John Ladyman, London, 1715

EUROPEAN SPOONS

Courtesy J. E. Caldwell & Co.

SKEWERS   1770-1792

Paul Revere   Hester Bateman   John Coney

EPERGNE James Young, London, 1792

SOUP TUREEN   Wm. Fountain, London, 1

ENTRÉE DISHES   Wm. Bateman, London, 1

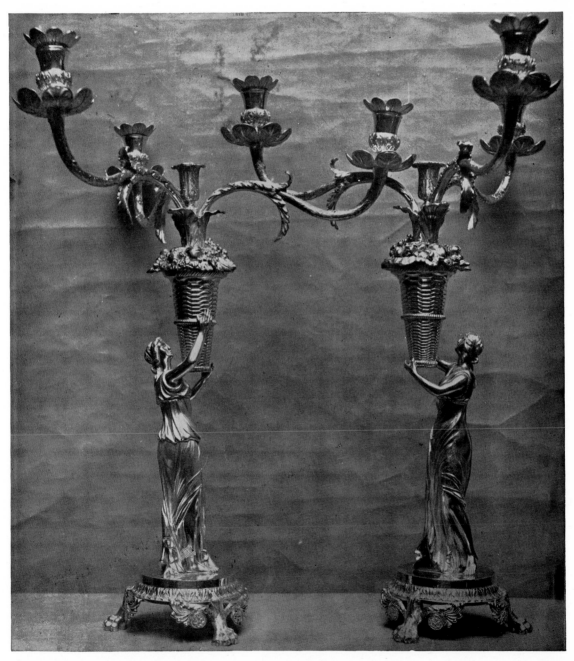

CANDELABRA   W. Pitts, London, 1808

CHAMBER CANDLESTICKS   Matthew Boulton

Top: Nathaniel Smith & Co., Sheffield, 1799-1801
Bottom: J. Parsons, Sheffield, 1783

BOULTON AND FOTHERGILL   Birmingham, 1773

OLD SHEFFIELD TEA TRAY   Circa, 1810

SHEFFIELD INKSTAND   *Courtesy S. Wyler, Inc.*   Watson and Bradbury, London, 1812

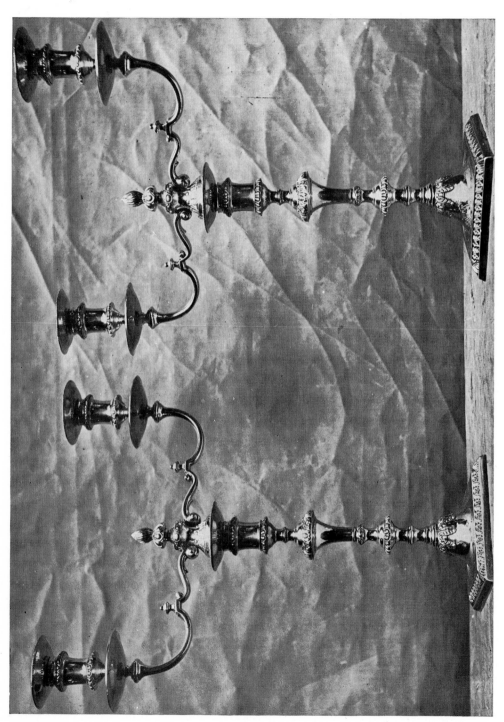

CANDELABRA

E. Capper, London, 1767

Newcastle, 1800

Cup   Shrewsbury, 1560

Courtesy J. E. Caldwell & Co.

COVERED CUP   Sam. James, Newcastle, 1759

quired to punch their wares and guarantee them to be of the required standard.

In 1685 the city of Chester was granted a charter by James II, and although a diligent search has been made, no evidence has been found to indicate that a town mark or date letter was used before this time. Although much plate disappeared from Chester during the reign of Charles I, it must not be imagined that none remains. It is far more probable that much of it is in private collections today and, unfortunately, cannot be accurately identified, as only a maker's mark was used. The operation of the charter granted by James II was suspended by the Act of 1695. However, in 1701, Chester, being one of the principal cities where mints had been erected, was reestablished as an assay office. Until the present time it has continued to flourish, the work executed there in recent years being greatly in excess of that done in past history.

The word, "sterling," found quite frequently on pieces of Chester plate, was probably used as the maker's guarantee that the piece was of a legal alloy. Date letters are known as early as 1688, but one date letter was often used for two to three years. When, in 1701, the assay office was reestablished, the marks followed those used in all the other English provincial towns—the lion's head erased and Britannia. In addition a new form of the town mark, composed of three lions of England dimidiating the three garbs of the Earldom of Chester in a plain shield, plus the date letter and the maker's mark was used. In 1779, an entirely new set of punches was instituted and the town mark was changed accurately to represent the arms of the city, as formerly used from 1687 to 1692. At this time, two new stamps were obtained for the leopard's head and lion passant, and these continued in use until 1784 when the King's head was impressed. In 1823 the leopard's head first appears uncrowned and a new set of date letters was inaugurated.

SILVERSMITHING IN BIRMINGHAM

The establishment of an assay office at Birmingham in 1773 was mainly due to the efforts of one of the great silversmiths. Matthew Boulton, who was by far the outstanding Birmingham smith of all time, personally prepared, on behalf of himself and the other goldsmiths, a petition which was submitted to the London Goldsmiths Company. In the petition was stated the extreme difficulties suffered by the plate workers in the exercise of their trade because no assay offices were conveniently located. The result was the granting of a charter to both Birmingham and Sheffield, and both offices are now in existence. The Act of 1773 provided that all plate should bear the town mark of an anchor, a distinct variable date letter to be changed annually, the lion passant, the figure of Britannia for plate of the standard of eleven ounces, ten dwt., and the mark of the maker, which should be the first letters of his Christian and surname. Very small wares, incapable of being fully marked without injury being done to them, were excepted. For this reason, one often finds vinaigrettes and the like, struck with only a maker's mark and the anchor. There is no particular reason why the anchor should have been chosen as the town mark for Birmingham except that a great deal of overseas commerce was transacted there.

SILVERSMITHING IN SHEFFIELD

As previously mentioned, the assay office in Sheffield was established in 1773, when this right was conferred on Birmingham. The silversmiths of Sheffield lost no time after the Act was passed to proceed in business, and production flourished on a great scale. The marks required to be stamped on all wrought silver assayed at Sheffield, are the town mark of a crown, a date letter, the standard mark which is either a lion passant or Britannia, according to the alloy, and the maker's mark.

From 1784 to 1890 the duty mark was added, as on London plate. In the marking of many pieces the date letter and town mark were combined in one stamp to save space, but this was discontinued many years ago and never again resumed. From 1815 to 1819 the town mark of the crown was struck upside down and the only reason for this can be to differentiate between similar marks of a few years earlier date. It is curious that Sheffield was one of the few places where gold was never assayed until 1904, though in the other provinces both silver and gold objects were wrought.

SILVERSMITHING IN HULL

The goldsmiths of Hull are mentioned as early as the fifteenth century, but they were never incorporated by statute or charter.

Several examples of the plate have been found in and around Hull, stamped with the letter "h" to indicate the town of manufacture. During the seventeenth century the arms of the borough, "three ducal coronets in pale," were adopted as the town mark. Although there is no evidence of any regular assay office having been established, several attempts were made to introduce a system of marking with date letters. Those examples which have survived, however, clearly indicate that this practice was never continued. Although goldsmiths' names are recorded in the archives of the borough as late as 1774, not more than one example of Hull plate of the Queen Anne period is known. It is most probable that those names listed were of dealers in goldsmiths' work, and not manufacturers.

SILVERSMITHING IN LINCOLN

Practically no information regarding the workings of the goldsmiths in Lincoln has ever been found, outside of the fact that it was one of the seven towns appointed by the Act of 1423 to have a touch. However, records and inventories allude to goldsmiths from the twelfth century onwards, and these references appear down to the year 1708. The arms of the city were used as the distinguishing town mark, and were adopted from the coat of arms of the city which consisted of "argent, on a cross gules, a fleur-de-lys or." Pieces bearing the Lincoln mark are very rare and consist mostly of church plate, or an occasional drinking vessel.

SILVERSMITHING IN SHREWSBURY

Although Shrewsbury was not one of the appointed towns in 1423, goldsmithing is known to have been in practice there during the Middle Ages. The provisions of the Statute of 1300, decreeing that "no manner of vessel or other work of silver should be set to sale without having the mark of a leopard's head upon it," were an aid rather than a hindrance to the Shrewsbury silversmiths because the arms of the town were "azure, three leopards' heads, or." One of these heads would naturally be the mark adopted by the Shrewsbury goldsmiths. Many examples of plate marked solely with an uncrowned leopard's head are wrongly ascribed to London. Some of these pieces are undoubtedly the work of Shrewsbury silversmiths.

SILVERSMITHING IN LEWES

The only information relative to this town is the mark adopted by the goldsmiths in the late fourteenth century. It consisted of "Checky (or and azure) on a conton sinister gules a lion rampant or," and pieces of plate bearing this mark are only rarely found.

SILVERSMITHING IN BARNSTAPLE

The most celebrated of all goldsmiths known to have worked in Barnstaple is Thomas Mathew, examples of whose work have been found in many parishes. Much of the plate wrought by him bears, in addition to his name stamp, the mark of a flower or fruit on a slipped and leaved stalk, which is intended to be a representation of a pomegranate. This device is portrayed in the Tregoney arms and it has been suggested that Mathew used this to denote that he was a native of that place. The town mark of Barnstaple was taken from the borough shield and used until 1624. The shield consisted of a bird in a circular stamp, but in 1625 the mark of a triple-turreted tower was granted to Barnstaple as its arms, and this was used until the end of the seventeenth century.

SILVERSMITHING IN PLYMOUTH

A few pieces of plate impressed with a representation of the arms of the borough of Plymouth are known as early as the beginning of the seventeenth century. The arms are composed of "a saltire between four castles." Certain examples bear the sterling mark indicating the legal standard. A curious form of the Britannia standard mark is known on a lighthouse salt made in 1698, on which the standard is described by the technical term "Britan." This mark suggests, therefore, that the piece was probably made about 1698 immediately after the introduction of the new standard, and it became technically represented by the Britannia mark.

SILVERSMITHING OF BRISTOL

It seems most unusual that no record of any assay office has ever been found in Bristol, nor any allusion to a guild of goldsmiths in a town of such importance. Although mentioned in the Act of 1423 as one of the seven towns appointed to have a touch mark, and again in the Act of 1701 as a place where an assay office could be legally established, no trace of any reference to goldsmithing has appeared. A few pieces of Bristol plate are struck with an oblong punch mark bearing the arms of the city, which consist of a ship issuing from a castle.

SILVERSMITHING IN OTHER PROVINCIAL TOWNS

Examples of the work of medieval goldsmiths are known in many outlying communities. As a general rule only a town mark was impressed and but little data of the history of goldsmiths in these provinces is available.

Dorchester	Salisbury	Coventry	King's Lynn
Sherborne	Colchester	Poole	Taunton
Rochester	Channel Islands	Carlisle	Gateshead
Sandwich	Leicester	Leeds	

CALCUTTA

Gold and silver wares have been wrought in India for cen
turies, but it was not until the eighteenth century that articles made
by workers of British origin are noted. In 1808 the firm of Hamilton
and Company was established in Calcutta and numerous fine examples of their work are known. The mark used was that of an
elephant.

XV

IRELAND

SILVERSMITHING IN IRELAND

SILVERSMITHING was practically the only art developed to any high degree in Ireland. There were skilled goldsmiths there prior to the date of the Norman Conquest. The Ardagh Chalice found by a peasant while digging near Limerick indicates the high merit of the craftsmanship of this time. Although several other examples of plate have survived to the present time, by far the majority are lost forever to posterity. Ireland then as now was turbulent, constant political upheavals took heavy toll of family silver, and the enthusiastic champions of the various causes cheerfully surrendered their plate in order to finance their parties.

The similarity of basic forms as compared with English silver is always to be noted, but the decorative scheme was for the most part original, rather than copied from the arts of continental Europe. The silversmiths in Ireland were greatly influenced by their environment, and their native whimsicality is reflected in the original designs found in so many pieces of Irish plate. Of particular notice are the pastoral scenes taken from the every-day farm life and its environs so dear to the hearts of the Celtic race. The chasing on pieces of Irish plate is always to be recognized, because the silversmiths apparently did not care to risk the process of flat hammering on the chased articles. Pieces of this particular style are to be found nowhere but in Ireland.

By the middle of the eighteenth century the prevailing rococo styles waned, and the classic influence introduced by the Adam brothers grew in favor. For many years, however, the delicate embossing enclosing escutcheons for crests and coats of arms, was distinctly reminiscent of the earlier elaborate designs.

The craft of the great Irish silversmith was not confined to Dublin. The city of Cork, with its natural silver mines, became a large center for silversmithing, and examples from the seventeenth century are known. Among other provincial towns producing silver in Ireland may be mentioned Limerick, Galway and Youghal. The curious practice of impressing the word, "dollar" on many provincial pieces is noted, thus bearing witness to the custom, prevalent also in America, of melting Spanish dollars for use in the silver craft. Another variation of hallmark often found on pieces of Cork manufacture is the word, "Sterling." In 1710 this mark was often inscribed to indicate that the pieces were equal in quality to that of the English silversmiths. The story of silversmithing in the provinces may be said to end with the year 1848. Very little silver was made from then on, and today practically all Irish plate is Dublin-made.

Irish silver is regarded by collectors throughout the world as most desirable. Because of the loss of so much of the early plate, very few pieces dating from the seventeenth century are encountered, nor are examples prior to the reign of George III plentiful. Many famous silversmiths are known who worked in the leading cities of Ireland, and examples by them fetch tremendous prices today. However, with the steadily decreasing supply of pieces of Celtic origin, it is safe to assume that within a few years all fine specimens will be in private collections or museums.

SILVERSMITHS OF DUBLIN

The earliest known reference to a guild of goldsmiths in Ireland is recorded in the archives of the Dublin Corporation. The guild is mentioned in the reference to the festival of Corpus Christi in 1498, wherein the town goldsmiths were represented. In 1555 the Dublin Goldsmiths presented a petition to the City Corporation stating that the charter which had been previously given to them had been accidentally burned. They wished to enjoy the privileges to which they were entitled, so they applied to the City Assembly for leave to enter a copy of their charter. In 1557 the application was granted.

Throughout the next fifty years, there appears to have been no entry in the records with reference to any marks to be impressed on gold or silver articles. Because of the continued fraudulent practices and abuses, it was resolved in 1605 by the Dublin City Council that henceforth certain marks should be stamped on all wrought plate, which, in quality, had to be equal to the silver standard coin then current. The above legislation, which is the earliest known reference to the marking of Dublin plate, required the use of the figure of a lion, a harp, and a castle, in addition to the goldsmith's own punch. However, not a single example appears to be known bearing these marks, which were supposed to have been used until 1637. At this time the Dublin goldsmiths became dissatisfied with their status under the domination of the City Corporation. They probably felt their inferiority to the London goldsmiths who had full control of all matters pertaining to the assaying and marking of pieces, without interference by civil authorities. A petition to the King was presented, in which they asked to be incorporated by Royal charter. Their petition was favorably received and in 1637 Charles I granted it.

The archives of the Dublin Goldsmiths Company refer to various articles which were brought in to be assayed. These included ewers and basins, caudle cups, sugar boxes, porringers, trencher salts, spoons and candlesticks. The entries of plate continued until 1649 when a break occurs owing to the loss of records and no further entry appears until 1694. Mention must be made of the strict vigilance shown by the Company in the detection of fraudulent pieces. The punishment for these offenses was severe, and Irish goldsmithing was raised to a high plane. Although we know of the use of hallmarks prior to 1637, no example is known bearing them. The charter of 1637 described the use of the crown harp, which was the king's stamp, as well as the standard mark, plus the makers' marks. The first article made under the new law was dated April 6, 1683, and from that time to the present day no article in silver or gold of Dublin make can be legally sold without being so distinguished. The use of the date letter was adopted at this time, in addition to the crown harp and the maker's mark. A fourth mark, the figure of Hibernia was incorporated in 1730 and was used to denote the payment of duty as ordered by the Commissioner of Excise. From 1807 to 1890, a fifth mark, consisting of a representation of the head of the Sovereign was impressed. This superseded the Hibernia stamp, and was applied to all plate wrought in Ireland, as in every other assay office then open in the United Kingdom.

SILVERSMITHS OF CORK

There is good reason to believe that goldsmithing of high merit was practiced in Cork as early as the Middle Ages. Some of the exquisite chalices, patens, and other church pieces are confidently ascribed to this city, although very little is known of the early history, and the records of the guild date no further back than 1656. In 1631, by a charter of Charles II, the Corporation of Cork was granted privileges which included the power to appoint a Clerk of Assay. His duties combined the testing of weights and measures, rather than the assaying of precious metals.

There being no regular assay at Cork, it seems probable that the only test used was that of the touchstone, except when an assay by cupel was required, which necessitated sending the plate to Dublin. Cork was situated in a direct line with the Spanish peninsula

and the west of France. This afforded increased advantages of inter-
course with these countries, whence the city received not only its
supply of silver, but innumerable emigrant craftsmen who brought
with them knowledge of designs applied by European smiths. This
accounts for the frequent examples known which resembled the
contemporary styles that prevailed on the continent.

The earliest known example of the Cork town mark consists of
a ship duplicated, or a ship between two castles; adopted from the
arms of the city. There were many variations of this mark and it
would appear that each goldsmith adopted his own peculiar town-
mark stamp. Early in the eighteenth century the use of this mark
was discontinued, and between 1710 and 1719 the word "STER-
LING" was introduced as a mark for Cork plate. This mark is also
found in various forms including abbreviations to STER and
STERG. The spelling also varied and specimens are known with
impressions as follows: STARLING, STIRLING, STARLIN,
and STERLIN. As previously mentioned, indication of the plate
having been wrought from Spanish dollars is found in the use of
the word, "dollar," just as the sterling stamp indicated the fineness
of eleven ounces, two dwt.

Makers' marks in Cork, used in the seventeenth and early part
of the eighteenth century, were generally composed of the initials
of the maker combined with a heraldic device. These combinations
disappeared shortly after 1731 when the Dublin Goldsmiths Company prohibited the use of such ornaments. Here may be seen the
complete power of the Dublin Goldsmiths Company to regulate the
production of plate throughout all of Ireland. No date letter was
ever used on pieces of Cork plate, except those assayed at Dublin,
and it is difficult to ascertain the exact year in which a piece was
produced. However, a study of the makers' marks plus the style in
vogue at the time, helps to approximate the date within a score of
years.

SILVERSMITHS OF YOUGHAL

By virtue of a charter granted in 1608 by James I, the Corporation of Youghal was empowered to arrange the various craftsmen
into appropriate guilds. But probably never more than a dozen
goldsmiths were working in the town at any one time. The mark of
a small single masted sail boat by common adoption of the goldsmiths is approximated at about 1620. The boat was commonly
known as a yawl, but heraldically speaking, as a lymphad. Several

names of prominent goldsmiths have been gleaned from the records and the few marks are reproduced.

SILVERSMITHS OF GALWAY

The goldsmiths of Galway adopted the mark of an anchor, generally found in a shaped cartouche. Only rarely is the name of a Galway silversmith apparent as no plate earlier than 1648 or later than 1730 is known. In the George III era, the names of nine goldsmiths are recorded in the books of the Dublin Goldsmiths Company as required by the Act of 1783.

SILVERSMITHS OF LIMERICK

As in the case of the silversmiths of Galway, many Limerick craftsmen are registered with the Company of Goldsmiths in Dublin. The Limerick marks closely resemble those used in Cork, being a triple towered castle plus the maker's initials. For many years these marks remained unidentified, until the discovery of an old Limerick toll-stamp, bearing a castle of similar form.

The word, Sterling, is often found on pieces made in and around Limerick, and these are frequently confused with plate produced in Cork. No records of the existence of a goldsmiths' guild are known in Limerick, but it may be assumed that associations were formed for protective purposes.

SILVERSMITHS OF OTHER PROVINCIAL TOWNS

Pieces have appeared which indicate clearly the production of plate in many smaller communities throughout Ireland. It is commonly supposed that the mark of a hand erect was the town mark for Belfast. Names of goldsmiths are recorded in Dublin which give sufficient evidence that some plate was wrought there.

References to the existence of guilds which included goldsmiths and silversmiths are known in the records of the towns of Kinsale, Derry, Kilkenny, Tipperary, Newry, and Drogheda. Unfortunately no ascribed marks identifying these towns or their goldsmiths are known.

XVI

SCOTLAND

SILVERSMITHING IN SCOTLAND

THE characteristic traits of a people are often reflected in the quality of their art, and so it is with the history of the early Scotch silversmiths. The austerity and simple tastes of the Scotchman are brought to notice by the work of the earliest craftsmen. The majority of silver articles made were definitely for practical use, rather than for purposes of decoration. Most of the early Scotch silver was used in churches, or else in the gentle art of drinking.

Perhaps the most definitely Scotch of all articles made of silver was the quaich, which was originally a small two-handled bowl, made of wood with silver stripings and used for drinking brandy. However, a few of the more affluent Scotchmen had these quaiches especially made to order in solid silver. Only a limited quantity of these are available, hence they have come to be recognized as the most valuable pieces of Scotch silver to be had. Among the other articles definitely attributed to these silversmiths were mulls which were made of large or small horns mounted in silver and used as snuff boxes. Tankards, caudle cups, flagons, jugs, and mazer bowls are all found among the earliest examples, and to a Scotch silversmith named Monteith, we are indebted for the introduction of what is now called a monteith bowl.

Unfortunately, there is very little early Scotch silver available to the collector today, as even the wealthy lairds and chieftains did not indulge in lavish appointments for the home. Also, due to the fact that much plate was melted during the seventeenth century to foster political causes, but little remains today. Since the early smiths could not find sufficient work in any one town, they led a nomadic existence, making small pieces here and there to order. The careful attitude towards spending money, so often characteristic of the Scotch as a people, had its effect on silversmithing. Complete tea services are practically non-existent because families would add but one piece at a time every few years to their sets. Consequently, to find a Scotch tea service of similar date and maker is almost an impossibility. It is interesting to note that in the earliest days of silversmithing in Scotland, it was the general custom for the client to bring his own silver or gold to the craftsman to be wrought at his order. It appears that dishonest workmen diluted and adulterated the metal, and outrageously cheated the customers. Because of this the amount of alloy permissible was regulated by law. Perhaps in no country was stricter adherence to the legislation of the silver craft demanded, and for this reason nearly all Scotch silver found today is of legal standard. The same laws conceived as early as 1483, regulating the quality of the metal, are still in use today.

From the standpoint of the collector or dealer, the original marks used by deacons in Scotland have been invaluable in determining the approximate dates of the earliest pieces, as date letters were not inaugurated until a much later time. Frequently in the provincial towns as well as Edinburgh and Glasgow, just the name of the city was impressed and therefore dates can only be surmised.

Scotch silver presents a field of high endeavor to the collector, not only because of the rarity of pieces, but also because there is a ready market at all times for good specimens regardless of price.

SILVERSMITHING IN EDINBURGH

Previous to the year 1483, silversmiths in Edinburgh were associated with other hammer-wielding trades under the general description of "Hammermen." At this time they presented a petition to the town council asking for certain privileges which would give them more freedom in the furthering of their craft. Before fifty years had elapsed from the time of this grant, they became an independent corporation, as recorded in the records of the oldest minute book, dated 1525.

A statute of the year 1485 decreed a Deacon and searcher were to be appointed to regulate the marking of all pieces of plate. In 1555, a further act of Parliament ordained that each goldsmith was to use his own mark, and that every piece must bear, in addition to this, a deacon's mark and a town mark. It is important to note that the introduction of the deacon's mark was instituted in order to regulate quality of the wrought metal. In 1586 the "Craft," which included the deacon and the masters of the goldsmiths, was empowered to seize any pieces deficient in the required fineness. Finally, in 1687, the first charter was granted to the silversmiths of Edinburgh, and all privileges previously enjoyed were confirmed in addition to more extensive powers.

With the issuance of this charter, notice was given to the smiths of other Scottish towns directing their attention to the necessity of maintaining their gold and silver work up to the required standard.

At the time of the adoption of the Britannia standard in England, all wrought plate was raised to a fineness of eleven ounces, ten dwt., but this was never operative in Scotland. However, with the union of the English and Scotch Parliaments, the Scotch standard for plate was raised in 1720 to conform with that of the English. This same act imposed a duty of sixpence per ounce on all plate manufactured in, or imported into Great Britain. In 1757 the duty on plate was repealed and in its place a license tax was levied which required every person dealing in gold and silver wares to pay a sum each year for the privilege of trading. The former duty was reimposed in 1784 and twenty-three years later the duty on plate was increased from sixpence to one shilling.

It is probable that no marks were used in Scotland before 1457 when the statute of that year provided for the use of a deacon's mark. These requirements with respect to the marking of plate have enabled us to approximate quite clearly the date of their manufacture. A further aid in identifying silver was the adoption of the town mark which was taken from the arms of the burgh which are "Argent, on a rock proper, a castle, triple towered and embattled, sable." In 1681 a variable annual date letter was adopted mainly for the reason that any manufacturer of plate in fraudulent practice might more easily be detected. From 1681 on it is possible to determine the exact year of any marked piece of Edinburgh plate. With the adoption of the date letter the Edinburgh goldsmiths abolished the deacon's mark and in its place substituted the mark of the assay master, which originally consisted of the initials of the assayer. A further alteration in the marking of plate was instituted in 1759 when the use of the assay master's initials was discontinued, and in their place the mark of a thistle was substituted. With the reimposition of the duty on plate in 1784, a fifth mark which consisted of the sovereign's head was struck on all plate to indicate the payment of the duty. As found in England, this mark continued in use until 1890, when all duties on plate were repealed.

SILVERSMITHING IN GLASGOW

The city of Glasgow, although not always as it is now, the largest and most densely populated town in all Scotland, may well lay claim to the premier place among Scottish provinces in importance as the center of the goldsmiths' craft. As found in Edinburgh the goldsmiths were originally incorporated in a large group under the designation of "Hammermen." But the earliest minute books have been mislaid, and little information is available regarding the progress of the guild. However, no Glasgow plate of earlier date than 1681 is known. At this time a date letter was adopted, but its use was discontinued about 1710, and not found again until 1819. For this reason it is necessary to approximate all pieces made during the interval. Between the years 1730 and 1800, a curious punch which consisted of the letter "s" in various shapes, was generally used. Although no definite explanation of this mark has ever been ascertained, it is probable that it was meant to indicate the word "sterling," to guarantee the piece to be of the accepted standard.

The Glasgow town mark adopted from the arms of the burgh is commonly known as the "fish, tree and bell." The actual heraldic description of it being "Argent, on a mount in base an oak tree proper, the trunk surmounted by a salmon proper with a signet ring in its mouth, or, on the top of the tree a red breast, and on the sinister fesse-point a hand-bell both proper."

There appears to be no evidence of the existence of a regular assay office at Glasgow before 1819, proof of which is derived from the variety in the form of the town mark used by the different makers at the same time. The 1819 statute incorporated the Glasgow Goldsmiths Company, empowered it and placed it under similar regulations to those ascribed to Edinburgh.

SILVERSMITHING IN ABERDEEN

It appears that in early times Aberdeen was divided into two distinct towns, known as Old Aberdeen and New Aberdeen. Each maintained its own distinct guilds and trade privileges, the only similarity being the incorporation of the smiths again under the common title of "Hammermen." In neither burgh was the town mark taken from the arms of the city but it was composed of the first two letters; AB or the first two and fifth letters; ABD. It has been suggested that this curious departure in the adoption of a town mark was taken mainly because the arms of the burgh resembled those of Dundee so much.

New Aberdeen, as it was called, until the extension of its boundaries into the adjoining burgh, records at least two goldsmiths as early as the fifteenth century. We have seen that the town mark was varied from AB to ABD and occasionally the Roman capital A was found struck three times instead. Early in the eighteenth century a new stamp composed of three castles in a shaped shell was used by one silversmith who was, in turn, followed by many others in this respect.

SILVERSMITHING IN DUNDEE

A reference in the year 1550 mentioning one David Stevenson as a goldsmith gives credence to the thought that plate was produced as early as this time. The arms of the town were adopted as the mark and consisted of "azure a pot of growing lillies argent." Further variations were adopted by smiths in the seventeenth and eighteenth centuries and in some instances the word Dundee was impressed as well as a thistle mark.

SILVERSMITHING IN ELGIN

The town mark of this burgh was contracted into ELG or ELN, and is sometimes spelled out. A variation is found on some of the earlier pieces which consisted of the representation of a mother and child in an upright, oblong cartouche. Here, again, a supposed town mark is sometimes noted, as well as a thistle as seen on Dundee plate. There does not seem to have been any incorporation of goldsmiths at Elgin, and the earliest record of any smith is 1701.

SILVERSMITHING IN OTHER PROVINCIAL TOWNS

Throughout Scotland many of the smaller provinces are recognized as having produced plate. These include Arbroath, Banff, Greenock, Inverness, Montrose, Perth, St. Andrews, Stirling, Wick and Tain.

XVII

SHEFFIELD PLATE

THE history of the trade known as Sheffield Plating reads like fiction, for its discovery was purely accidental, and its rise as an industry phenomenal.

In the 18th century silver, as an essential part of the well appointed home, was recognized in England as well as abroad, and workmen were busily engaged in creating new ideas. But the price of silver was still too prohibitive to permit any but the noble and wealthy to indulge themselves. It was the discovery of Sheffield Plate that enabled people of moderate means to own exact replicas of the solid silver domestic articles at a fraction of their cost.

The discovery of plating was an accident, but one of sufficient importance to revolutionize the trade life of a city. In time it became a leading industry in England, and the growth of the city of Sheffield from a London suburb, so to speak, to a great manufacturing center, is attributed to it.

It is unfortunate that so little data on the subject of combining metals is available, for there is evidence to show that many centuries earlier, the Jews and Egyptians worked along these lines with a fair amount of success. The Romans as well keenly appreciated the beautiful gold and silver objects which were produced, but so few have survived, that their methods of plating and gilding are practically unknown. There is no doubt though, that none of the early processes resembled plating as discovered and perfected in England.

In 1742, in the garret of a small building known as Tudor House, a mechanic, one Thomas Boulsover, was repairing the blade of a broken knife. He accidentally fused silver and copper during this operation, and discovered that when these two metals were heated to a certain degree they became inseparable. He immediately realized that this strange occurrence might be turned to good purpose, and upon further experimentation found he was able to manufacture small bits such as buttons, boxes and buckles. These are the earliest known specimens of Sheffield Plate.

However, Thomas Boulsover can hardly be called the father of Sheffield Plate, for although he discovered the process and produced a few pieces, he was soon forced to abandon it. The man he employed to travel on the road to introduce his new product, cheated him outrageously, and before long he was left without sufficient funds to continue.

But during the first few months of Boulsover's experimenting, he apprenticed a young man named Josiah Hancock. This young employee was a lad of great vision, and soon realized that the new industry might grow to huge proportions if properly managed. After diligent work he began to progress rapidly, and within a few years Sheffield Plating became a recognized industry largely because of his efforts. New pieces were created, faithful reproductions of sterling pieces were made and there was an increased demand for them, especially because excessive government taxation had forced the price of wrought silver articles to higher levels. The goldsmiths tried to combat the new industry by burdens of taxation and bothersome regulation but it prospered.

Although the city of Sheffield fostered the production of nearly all the Plate made in England for many years, very few pieces can be found in homes or collections there today. Most of the articles made were marketed in the larger cities and in foreign countries.

The first pieces of Sheffield Plate produced were probably purchased by royalty and families of wealth, as evidenced by the number of old pieces found today bearing original crests and coats of arms. It is for this reason that pieces have survived until today in such fine condition, for it was necessary to plate the articles made with an increasing amount of silver, in order that they might not be ruined by the inscriptions and arms being engraved upon them. The better quality pieces were invariably made with a circular, oval or shaped inset of pure silver, designed expressly for the purpose of cresting. As the industry grew and pieces could be produced for lower prices, the so-called middle class families quickly purchased articles for domestic use and the industry enlarged rapidly.

Plate was produced in foreign countries as well, but the English craftsmen so far excelled their neighbors in workmanship and originality, that they received more than 90% of the business. Ireland was one of the largest consumers of Sheffield Plate and today many outstanding collections are to be found in Dublin and other important cities, though there is no evidence of Irish plating.

During the first twenty years of Sheffield Plating, many beautiful articles were produced, which in design and workmanship often equalled the originals in solid silver. The first manufacturers of Plate quickly sensing the opportunities for deception, impressed hallmarks similar to those on silver articles. Examples showing these are extremely rare. The silver manufacturers immediately protested

to the Guild, and the hallmarking of Sheffield Plate was for-
bidden. But in 1773 Sheffield was granted its own assay office and
in 1784 smiths were allowed the privilege of using a maker's mark
of their own, providing it had been approved by the Guild.

The history of Sheffield Plating may be divided into two periods.
During the years from 1750 to 1780, pieces were made of entirely
different style from those which followed in the later period. It
is not rare to find many embossed objects, for the original manufacturers knew that with a wealth of design and ornamentation
they could easily conceal those defects which so often appeared on
the earliest pieces of Plate. This was due solely to their inability
to turn out a perfect product, for the corresponding pieces produced
in solid silver of that period, were of a much simpler style. But as
the years progressed, the ability of the platers reached a higher
degree, and for ten years or so delicately pierced objects were made.
These, while not so graceful as the contemporary pieces in solid
silver, met with much favor. During the first period which might
be called probationary, Dish Rings, Baskets, Cups and Covers, Water
Jugs, Epergnes, Cream Pails, etc., were produced. And it is easy
to recognize pieces from this period by their lack of applied borders,
and silver rims. It is practically impossible to find pieces from the
first period in fine condition, for the process of plating whereby the
silver would not wear through to the copper, had not yet been
perfected.

From 1780 until 1820 the finest Sheffield Plate was produced in
large quantities. By this time, the majority of leading cutlers in Sheffield had begun to manufacture Plate, and the industry was at its
height. With the advent of the Adam Brothers in England, the
demand for pieces of extreme simplicity was so pronounced it influenced the designs of Sheffield Plate objects. Many important
pieces such as Tea Services, Cruets, Candelabra, Trays and various
other household appointments were manufactured in quantity for the
first time. As the years passed, the influence of the master silversmiths in vogue in England at the time caused the designs and
shapes of Sheffield Plate objects to follow in the footsteps of their
creations.

During this, the second period, we find the introduction of a
white metal known as German silver, first used as a base. This new
process was much favored, as the lasting qualities of Sheffield Plate
objects were doubled. This new base would not show through when
the silver was worn off, as did the copper. However, German silver
was not fully accepted until about 1835. It derived its name from

a Mr. Guitike of Berlin, who came over to Sheffield with the first examples of this new compound of nickel, copper, and zinc. The metal itself is of Chinese origin, and was used for centuries in the East before its introduction into England from Germany. The first English smith to avail himself of the new base product was Samuel Roberts. In 1830 he applied for a patent to plate silver on a German silver base.

The process of Sheffield Plating was definitely terminated in 1838, in which year electroplating was discovered by Elkington. Actually, the term Sheffield Plate was the name applied to articles made of copper and coated with silver by fusion. It is not to be confused with the modern silver plate as produced today by means of electrolysis.

Sheffield Plate from the collector's viewpoint, presents an admirable field of endeavor, for as yet prices have not risen to the heights commanded by solid silver articles. However, when one considers the limited supply available and the short period in which it was produced, it seems probable that as time goes on, prices will reach those paid for solid silver articles of similar date. In the past five years, the values of Old Sheffield Plate have doubled, and the farseeing buyer of today will guard carefully those pieces he is fortunate to possess today.

The buyer of Sheffield Plate must be a careful and critical purchaser, as the markets are flooded with semi-old and reproduction pieces that are represented to be genuine. Many brand new pieces are being made now with silver edges and tinned backs that at first seem to be Sheffield Plate. But the connoisseur may detect the fraud mainly by the color of the silver, as the old pieces have a bluish tinge caused by the use of alloy, while pieces that have been electroplated are much whiter. Old Sheffield Plate like old silver should be purchased only from reliable dealers, for even connoisseurs are often misled. Many pieces have worn through over a period of years, and have been replated in order to increase their salability. These pieces should be definitely avoided, as any repairing or replating done to an old piece destroys its value as an original.

XVIII

SILVERSMITHING IN AMERICA

IN direct contrast to silversmithing in England and Europe, the trade in America at the beginning was far from profitable. The early New Englanders were hardy people facing arduous tasks in their struggle for existence and they had little use for the luxury of ornamental silver. At no time was any attempt made to imitate the magnificent baronial silver of England and only pieces for particular use were produced. However, the market was considerably bolstered by the needs of the churches. The Pilgrims of course, were very religious and took great pride in their houses of worship so that much of the early American fine plate was for church use.

It was natural that the first pieces should be reproductions of English pieces which the Colonists had brought with them and from this start a natural evolution took place along the lines of the development of the character of the people.

The simplicity and austerity of their lives caused them to prefer in all things purity of form and a fine sense of proportion to elaboration and bulk. This is true of colonial architecture and furniture as well as of silver.

Much of this early American silver was made in New England but New York and Philadelphia were other important centers of silversmithing. Paralleling the English influence on New England silver, New York silver clearly bore a Dutch influence. Whatever there was of Southern silver perished during the Civil War.

In New England, Newburyport harbored some silversmiths but the city of Boston was the real center for the trade in America. It had the advantage of the first start and was the home of the first known American silversmith.

Boston had built up a flourishing trade with England and the colonial possessions in the West Indies. It was the haven of the wealth and the social life of early America and it was quite natural that the greatest market should harbor also the greatest center of production. It is worthy of note that almost no fraudulent practices prevailed among the colonial silversmiths. Also, living conditions being very stable, very little of the plate was destroyed. Practically the only New England pieces that were melted down were those which were in the hands of Southern families during the Civil War.

An Englishman, John Hull, is generally conceded to be the earliest silversmith in America. He was appointed the first master of the first mint in America. This mint was established in Boston in 1652 by the general court of Massachusetts which disregarded the decision of the higher court in London. Colonists had experienced excessive difficulty in securing a sufficient supply of money to carry on local trade. Their complaints and agitation resulted in this decision of the court which in later years was frequently cited as being a deed of defiance against the Crown.

The Colonists had to do with paper currency and the instability of value of this currency stimulated the demand for silver which was a far better investment than paper money of uncertain value. With this stimulated demand, the establishment of the mint and the availability of English and Scotch artisans who had studied the trade abroad, the craft of silversmithing flowered and produced many outstanding silversmiths and a wealth of fine silverware.

The majority of pieces are a vivid reminder of the fact that early Americans did indulge in tippling. Beer and hard liquor accompanied the Pilgrims from England. No business transaction was consummated, no marriage celebrated and no funeral ceremony performed without the company or spirits. This furthered the production of silver, and tankards, mugs and other drinking accessories are numbered among the best efforts of the Colonial silversmiths. However, the earliest domestic utensil was the spoon, the shape of which underwent many changes from the early "Puritan" types to the early 19th century "Fiddleback." Tea and coffee pots were unknown until the end of the 17th century and few are found antedating 1750. Previous to this though, spout cups are known which were copied from early Chinese models and were undoubtedly the forerunners of tea pots.

Practically the only form of decoration used by American silversmiths was engraving. Chasing and gadrooning are rarely found. The craft flourished until about 1840 when the factories with their machinery for stamping and spinning silver came into general use and the silversmith as a craftsman disappeared.

Many of the early smiths held important civic positions in the community and were generally men of good financial standing. Among the outstanding men who developed the silver trade from its infancy were Jeremiah Dummer, John Coney, John Edwards, and Edward Winslow. They created new styles and pieces, and their fame as superior craftsmen is indelibly associated with Colonial silversmithing. As time went on, the trade became more or less concentrated in the hands of three families: the Burts, the Hurds, and the Reveres. John Burt came to Boston as a young man and was enormously successful, as evidenced by the great value of his inventory. Two sons, Samuel and Benjamin, succeeded him in business, and carried on the traditions of the father in creating many splendid examples. Jacob Hurd, well-known for his military service, enjoyed a brisk business and was finally succeeded by his son, Nathaniel, who eventually became more famous as an engraver of copper plates than as a silversmith.

The most famous American silversmith was Paul Revere, whose works are cherished for their exquisite beauty as well as for the historic association connected with this patriot. His father, originally of French birth, migrated to America where he was apprenticed to John Coney. In 1723, he went into business for himself in Boston, and was so successful that he was able to support a wife and a family of twelve children. Young Paul entered his father's shop at the age of 19, and in the few years that he was connected there, acquired sufficient knowledge and acumen successfully to carry on the business which came to him with the death of his father. Paul Revere, jr., developed great ability as an engraver, which is evidenced by the beautiful crests and armorial designs which adorned many of his pieces. This training enabled him to venture into the realm of copper plating, and eventually this talent caused a great deal of trouble to the Colonies. He frequently published political cartoons in which he derided the British Ministry and these caused no little consternation on the part of the English authorities. One of the most famous pieces of American silver is the magnificent punch bowl ordered by the "Fifteen Sons of Liberty." In this work, Revere reached a degree of excellence rarely attained by any silversmith. The inscription on the side of the bowl is plain-spoken and clearly indicated the feelings of the community at this time: "To the Memory of the Glorious NINETY-TWO Members of the Honorable House of Representatives of the Massachusetts Bay, who, undaunted by the insolent Menaces of Villains in Power, from a strict Regard to Conscience and the LIBERTIES of their Constituents, on the 30th day of June, 1768, voted NOT TO RESCIND."

It has always been difficult to distinguish between the wares of Paul Revere, Sr., and his illustrious son, because in many instances the same maker's marks were used by both.

The Federal, Colonial and state governments did not regulate the craft, set up standards or require date letters. But New York and

Boston each had Societies or Guilds by which the silversmiths themselves regulated their craft and probably other cities also had similar organizations. Baltimore had an assay office with careful supervision by elected silversmiths.

Marks on American silverware consist of the maker's mark which is almost invariably the initials or full name of the maker and occasionally a standard mark. No date letters were used and the dates of pieces can be determined only by other factors, such as engraving, style, etc.

In the collection of American silver one must be careful accurately to identify makers' marks because in many instances English and Irish pieces are misrepresented as American by the removal of all marks except the makers' marks.

XIX

SILVERSMITHING IN EUROPE

AN extensive study of European silver reveals one similarly striking fact with regard to nearly all countries; very little of the early plate remains, even though silversmithing on the continent may be traced back as early as the fifth century. The continual struggle for power and existence, plus the dire need for money caused many art treasures to be consigned to the melting pot. Again, the fact that so much of the early plate was made for use in the churches which were in constant fear of destruction, made it necessary to bury a great deal of the silver in the ground for preservation. Sometimes these pieces were not excavated or brought to light for centuries. However, the amount that has been found in this way is so minute compared to the great quantities that were buried, that one stops to wonder why so much more has not been discovered. The book records of the various townships speak of the large quantities of plate made, and yet very little remains to be viewed today.

Unfortunately, there is but little data available regarding the earliest pieces. This is due to the fact that only a few records have survived, and those that have are generally in such a state of decay that they are practically illegible. Although only a little early plate may now be seen in museums, it definitely proves that many magnificent pieces were wrought as early as the eighth century.

SILVERSMITHING IN AUSTRIA

Although it is known that several small towns in Austria had their goldsmiths, Vienna was by far the most important center wherein the art of the metal worker flourished. From the time of Rudolph IV, this city was the permanent residence of the German emperors, and Court Goldsmiths were appointed. It was thought that these smiths were exempt from guild regulations, and consequently, were not compelled to hallmark their wares. Therefore many pieces which were thought to be of Viennese origin cannot be definitely so assigned.

Wenzel Jamnitzer, one of the most famous goldsmiths of the sixteenth century was born in Vienna, but migrated to Nuremberg in 1534. It is here that he built up his reputation for excellent craftsmanship. Many other great silversmiths were apprenticed in

Vienna and surrounding cities, but for the most part they produced their best work in other countries. A few Austrian silversmiths who achieved recognition in their native country are known, including Erhard Efferdinger, identified from his important Gothic monstrance made in 1524, and Marx Kornblum, whose fame results from a few specimens of enamel and metal combination.

Vienna developed rapidly as the social center of the country, particularly during the brilliant reigns of Charles VI (1712-1740) and Maria Theresa (1740-1780). That period brought work that was definitely under the influence of the French craftsmen, as is proved by the many pieces in the Louis XIV style. A specific example of this work is seen in the magnificent gold toilet services made for the Empress by Anton Mathias Domanek. During the eighteenth century a taste for the pieces of English design was noted by the advertisements of a few London goldsmiths in Austria who carried on an enjoyable and rather brisk trade.

SILVERSMITHING IN THE BALTIC STATES

There is definite proof that plate was wrought for several centuries in the Baltic States. But Reval, the capital of Esthonia, and Riga, the capital of Latvia, were the only towns of importance where gold and silver were worked. Hans Ryssenback, who worked in the last quarter of the 15th century, achieved the greatest prominence as a goldsmith. Although it is supposed that many workers resided in Riga during the sixteenth century, only two names have descended to the present time; Hans Urma and Thomas Smallde. Silver made in Riga is easily distinguished from that made elsewhere in the Baltic States because Riga used a town mark as early as the sixteenth century.

No secular plate has survived from Finland although goldsmiths worked there in medieval times. The national museum at Helsingfors has a few pieces of plate from the late eighteenth century which prove the charming quality of the work of the Finnish silversmiths.

SILVERSMITHING IN BELGIUM

At the beginning of the sixteenth century, Antwerp was at the height of its commercial prosperity. Naturally, it was invaded by many of the greatest artists and an enormous quantity of plate was produced there. However, by the end of the seventeenth century, the era of vast wealth was over and Belgium fell victim to a prolonged depression. During the period of 1466 to 1695, many important pieces were created, and as many of the early records are still available, the student of Belgian silver is enabled to get a clear insight to the workings of the smiths and their craft.

Although Antwerp was the center of prosperity, the city of Bruges was by far the most important as the center of artistic activity. Flemish art reached its zenith during the reign of Charles the Bold when many of the world's most famous craftsmen worked in Bruges, but none of the splendid secular plate for which the Flemish goldsmiths were noted remains today. However, some pieces used by the church for daily and festival services have been preserved.

Although there was no definite legislation with regard to silver previous to 1814, many of the early makers used date letters, which have been an invaluable aid in tracing the exact year in which a particular piece was made. Silver in Belgium was made in two qualities; that of 900 fine being shown by the block letter "A" in an irregular shield, and that of 800 fine being denoted by the same letter in a square shield.

It is interesting to note that many of the early Flemish pictures depict objects of silver, and from them we have gleaned much knowledge. In the National Gallery of London hangs the world-famous picture "Taste" done so beautifully by Gonzales Cozues in 1618. The picture shows a cylindrical caster, definitely proving that this article was known in Flanders earlier than in England.

In the city of Antwerp there was one outstanding silversmith, called Hans of Antwerp, but as his maker's mark has never been positively identified, not one actual piece can be said to have been definitely wrought by him.

As early as the fifteenth century, a guild of goldsmiths was organized in Ghent, and this is the earliest note of any such association in Belgium. An outstanding master in this romantic city was Corneille de Bont, who worked in the 15th century.

Many other cities in Belgium produced silver and gold objects at an early date, and among them were the towns of Mons, Liege, and Tournai.

CZECHOSLOVAKIA

The city of Prague was outstanding as the center of art in Czechoslovakia. Under the encouragement and fostering of Premysl Otakar II, the "gold king of the thirteenth century," the art of the silversmith and goldsmith flourished to a high degree. Even to the present time many pieces have been preserved which are recognized as the work of masters, and from which many later artists on the continent copied their designs. However, the silversmiths of Prague were themselves influenced by craftsmen of foreign lands.

Prague was the center for the carving of semi-precious stones and beautiful ornaments and many of these were surmounted by bands of magnificently chased gold and silver. They reveal the highest degree of workmanship, and a limited number of specimens may be seen today in museums.

The only other city in Czechoslovakia noted as a center for goldsmithing, was Olomuc, known today as Olmutz. Pieces have been traced from here as early as 1575, as the workers registered their marks with a town corporation. Although it is definitely known that many smiths wrought their wares previous to this time, no definite marks or pieces are available.

SILVERSMITHING IN DENMARK

No Scandinavian silver dated previous to the thirteenth century has survived, although pieces were made as early as the eighth century. The demand was mostly for pieces of practical use and so artists from other European countries did not settle there to work. The creators of luxurious silver from other countries could find no ready market for their wares in Denmark, and for this reason the majority of articles found pertain to the necessities of life. Much data regarding the life of the silversmith has been obtained from early records, and as early as 1685 the first ordinances governing the production of silver were introduced. During the Thirty Years War vast quantities of plate were buried in the earth for protection against invading enemies, and only recently have numerous pieces been found, thus making the present day collection of early Danish silver more comprehensive.

A distinctly Danish article was the drinking horn. These horns, originally made of whalebone or some other hardy substance by the early settlers in Iceland, were introduced by fur traders and travellers coming to Denmark to purchase their winter supplies. The Danish silversmiths mounted these horns with bands of plain silver, and an object which had theretofore been purely useful became ornamental.

Shortly after the inauguration of horns and other silver drinking vessels, the demand for pieces of more florid taste is noted. From this time silver was executed only of a heavily embossed nature, as the Danish smiths did not possess the skill necessary to indulge in flat chasing. Therefore, Danish silver with contemporary chasing dated prior to 1700 is most valuable. Perhaps ninety per cent of all silver made in Denmark was wrought into drinking vessels, and extravagant ornaments had little vogue.

The name of Magnus Berg is outstanding, as he gained the greatest recognition throughout Europe in his special field of beautifully carved ivory pieces.

Copenhagen was the center of silversmithing in Denmark and pieces from there bear the town mark "in an ellipse, three towers or minarets above the date." The only other town in Denmark where silver was produced was Odense which registered the town mark of "a fleur-de-lys, joined to two spreading leaves in an ellipse."

SILVERSMITHING IN FRANCE

The earliest known French silver dates back to the time of the Roman invasion when silver and gold were used as decorations on horsetrappings. From 588 to 659 a silversmith known as St. Eloi did more to promote the industry than any other man and he is the patron saint of the French goldsmiths. He organized the first guild and secured from the French government permission for this organization to be its own lawmaking body with full privileges. In no other country in the world was a guild formed as early as in France. The French were the first in Europe by several centuries fully to understand and accept the craft of precious metal working. At the time of St. Eloi the craft was practiced only by the priesthood, and it was not until the beginning of the twelfth century that the craft of silversmithing was secularized.

The first statute that required the use of a town mark was enacted in 1275. And in 1313 the first punch of guarantee was introduced, and was denoted by a fleur de lys in a lozenge. The use of the date letter in conjunction with the town mark was introduced in 1416.

With the introduction of the town mark, definite importance was accorded to the industry. When in 1313 the guarantee mark was used, plus the date letter one hundred years later, the actual system of hallmarking silver in France was established. The mark of guarantee was very similar to that used in other countries to denote the actual fine silver content of a piece. During the reign of Louis XII a new office of Farmer of the Reserve was created. This appointee was required to impress his mark next to the maker's mark to show that duty had been charged on the piece. Then, the law required that this Farmer stamp another symbol as proof of the payment of duty. These peculiar punches were used until the duty was abolished. In 1797 the tax was reimposed, but was levied at the time of the imposition of the first stamp, so the discharge mark was eliminated. Inasmuch as the standard of the silver was proved by the same mark, French silver from that date on was only impressed with the symbol of the maker, the town mark and the duty mark.

A splendid piece of early French silver extant today is the beautiful cup of the Kings of France and England. Originally the work of French silversmiths, it was sent as a gift to the King of England, and later returned to France. It was then sent to Spain but was finally shipped to England where it reposes today in the British Museum. It depicts the life of St. Agnes, and is worked in beautifully executed relief.

In recent times the outstanding name in French silver history is that of Odiot who is credited with being the creator of the style known as Empire. Rivalled in excellence only by the Brothers Adam in England, Odiot's designs spread like wildfire throughout Europe and few styles of any period have enjoyed the lasting compliment as did the Empire. Royalty throughout Europe commissioned Odiot to make magnificent services, and much of his silver is known today.

The finest collections of French plate are not to be found in France. The Royalty of Europe and England, eager to own these fine treasures, collected them carefully, and today the most comprehensive collection of French silver in the world is in the possession of Great Britain's Royal family. French silver is ardently sought after by collectors and its value is great. The pieces are beautifully made, finely proportioned and delicately designed. France is second only to England in the excellence of its silversmithing.

SILVERSMITHING IN GERMANY

Today in Germany there is a wealth of early ecclesiastical plate to be seen, dating back to the twelfth century. Although this nation produced gold and silver objects as early as the fifth century, few of these very early efforts have survived. Among the first known pieces of secular plate are the Ewer of Goslin produced in 1477, and the celebrated Luneburg Horn of silver and ivory, made in 1486. These two historical works of art exemplify the characteristic traits of the German silversmith, wherein a wealth of detail and almost an over-profusion of ornamentation are to be observed. Hardly ever is a definite note of simplicity found, and this includes the silver made in Germany today. The influence of the Renaissance is apparent in the goldsmith's art earlier than in any other craft.

This influence was introduced in 1490, and was firmly established by 1520.

The inheritance by the present generation of a great quantity of old German silver can be laid to the fact that this country suffered practically no great losses of plate. The only noticeable disappearance occurred during the Thirty Years War, when hundreds of magnificent pieces were the target for those who invaded to pillage and plunder.

Until 1884, all legislation governing the production of silver was enacted by each separate state of the empire, and hundreds of minor statutes were passed. It is almost impossible to enumerate the individual ordinances, as over five score towns were producing silver in Germany.

Augsburg and Nuremberg were the chief centers of silversmithing. Here the craft of the goldsmith was stimulated by the opulence of the people, as well as by the patronage of ecclesiastics, princes and nobles. The town mark used for Augsburg was "a pineapple erect." Date letters were impressed which have been most helpful in aiding the collector to arrange a chronological list of pieces.

The city of Nuremberg was second only to Augsburg in the quantities of plate produced, and its silver wares were denoted by the letter "N." At first a capital Roman "N" was used, and during the nineteenth century a capital script "N" in a circle was substituted. After 1760 date letters are noted.

Silver in Germany was made of many different standards and each piece was registered and marked accordingly. Today most of the silver manufactured is 800 fine, which is a lesser degree than our own or the English sterling.

Gold and silver tipped horns were used for drinking as early as the days of Caesar. In the years that followed, these are closely identified with the work of the German silversmiths who took the horns of the bison or ulus for these objects. Later on many of the early specimens were bound with silver worked in beautiful detail.

Beakers were very popular during the sixteenth, seventeenth and eighteenth centuries when they were employed as guild cups. Many examples depict Scriptural and classical scenes in high relief.

Among the most unusual articles produced were the ivory, stoneware, amber, and serpentine tankards, invariably mounted with silver. The use of the metal wherever possible clearly proves the definite flair for silver in the Reich.

Double cups, as well as hunting cups in sets of from six to twenty were also made. The double cups with their familiar bosses are distinctly German and were made nowhere else in Europe. They served as household objects as well as things of beauty, for the smaller tops were reserved exclusively for the ladies of the house, while the master consumed his fill from the three-quarter bottoms. These pieces are often referred to as bridal cups, and were the subject of much wagering and amusement in their usage.

Silver objects of every known description are credited to German smiths during the seventeenth and eighteenth centuries. Germany stands alone as the only country in Europe where pieces for purely decorative purposes were produced. The silversmiths frequently modeled animals of massive proportion and it is not unusual to find a replica of a life sized eagle or a small beast. Nautilus shells and ostrich cups met with great favor in Germany, and a few examples which have been carefully preserved may be seen today. Tea services, vases, candelabra, etc., are all products of this age of silversmithing, and probably more plate was exported from Germany than from all the rest of Europe.

In the study of silversmithing in Nuremberg, the name of Wenzel Jamnitzer is preeminent. Often called the Cellini of Germany, he migrated from Vienna in 1534, and continued to produce pieces of rare quality until his death in 1585. He was one of five sons, each of whom lived to create a reputation in the field of art. Jamnitzer often specialized in the production of silver pieces combined with fine enamel, and his works were purchased by collectors throughout Europe. Today, if an example of his work is sold in the open market, the true appreciation of his ability is found in the huge prices realized.

SILVERSMITHING IN HUNGARY

Judging from the number of magnificent vessels unearthed from graves, it is likely that silver was made in Hungary as early as the Middle Ages. The records also tell of rich endowments of plate given to wealthy brides of the day. However, as most of that has perished, the real history of silversmithing in Hungary may be said to start about 1600. As early as the thirteenth century, goldsmiths held important positions in the realm of power, and under the reign of the Anjou kings, they were even granted arms of their own. Today the churches are filled with objects of costly precious metals, showing the early appreciation of beautiful things in Hungary. The goldsmiths' guilds which were formed in each town greatly encouraged the craft, and today the museums are rich in the art that was produced many centuries before.

As evidenced almost everywhere, drinking articles were made in great profusion. However, the most proficient workmen specialized in the production of unusual enamel and gold pieces often combined with colored crystal. Some of the later pieces have been preserved and a visit to the churches in Hungary will quickly prove the high quality of this work.

Goldsmiths were greatly influenced in their designs by the craftsmen of surrounding countries. In the sixteenth century the German trend is noticed, while in Transylvania the silversmiths who were in constant touch with the East displayed definite traits of Oriental artistry. In the South, a definite Turkish manner is found, which combined with the above gives a varied trend in design to the silver of Hungary.

Silver legislation in Hungary commenced at the beginning of the sixteenth century when an ordinance decreed that no maker should sell an unmarked piece. Not only was it necessary for each article to be impressed with the maker's private mark, but after being subjected to a test of quality, it had to be further marked by two fellow workers who would swear under oath as to the silver content. During the seventeenth and eighteenth centuries the hallmark regularly in use was "a castle with central tower, above the numeral 13 in ellipse or irregular outline." In 1836 the word "PESTH" was introduced, and followed in 1866 by the capital Roman "P" which served as a date letter.

SILVERSMITHING IN HOLLAND

Silver was not particularly in general use in Dutch households until about 1850, when a mild wave of prosperity allowed this extravagance. At this time, as in former days, Holland silversmiths specialized in the production of drinking vessels, ewers and basins and a little ecclesiastical plate. It is indeed strange though that tankards were rarely included among domestic pieces.

Early examples of Dutch silver fetch tremendous prices as very few specimens earlier than the fifteenth century have survived. Amsterdam was the center of silversmithing although examples of work are known from the smaller towns, such as Breda, Dakkum, The Hague, Haarlem, Hertagenbisch, Leeuwarden, Rotterdam, Utrecht and Zwolle.

Van Viamen stands out in Holland as the most prominent silversmith. He came from a family famed all over Europe for their accomplishments in art, and a number of beautiful pieces are attributed to this great craftsman. The only other name of prominence

Dublin, 1822

Courtesy S. Wyler, Inc.

TEA SET

Dublin, c. 1730

BOWL

Dublin, 1715

Courtesy S. Wyler, Inc.

PAIR OF BEAKERS

SUGAR   John Irish, Cork, 1750

JUG   Thos. Walker, Dublin, 1718

SALTS   J. Johnson, Dublin, 180

PAIR OF CUPS   *Courtesy S. Wyler, Inc.*   Dublin, 1736, Robert Calder

R. Gray & Son, Glasgow, 1819

J. McKay, Edinburgh, 1810

SALTS

CREAM JUG   James Dempster, Edinburgh, 1790

TEA SET

SUGAR BOWL   Edinburgh, 1784

Edinburgh, 1776

PAIR OF BEAKERS

SHEFFIELD SUPPER DISH

Nathaniel Smith, 1

TEA POT   Paul Revere   Detroit Museum   *Courtesy James Graham, Jr.*

SUGAR BOWL AND CREAM JUG   Paul Revere, Boston   *Courtesy Metropolitan Museum of Art*

Courtesy James Graham, Jr.

HEBREW CANDLESTICK

Myer Myers, New York, 1760

Courtesy Metropolitan Museum of Art

COFFEE POT   Made by F. T. Germain, Paris, (Louis XV) for the King of Portugal

PEG TANKARD   Stavanger, 1812

ITALIAN   16th Century

DANISH BEAKER   17th Cent.

SILVER-GILT CASKET by Vianen Flemish,
17th Century

PORTUGUESE PERFUME BURNER   18th Cent.

PORTUGUESE EWER AND BASIN   18th Century

Tobacco Box
Amsterdam, 1796

Chalice
Antwerp, 16th Century

One of Set of Four Candlesticks Representing
Four Continents
Paris, 1790

Snuffers and Stand
Italian, 17th Century

Knife, Fork, and Spoon in Traveling Case
Spanish, 17th Century

Standing Cup
Niels Jonson, Copenhagen, c. 1720

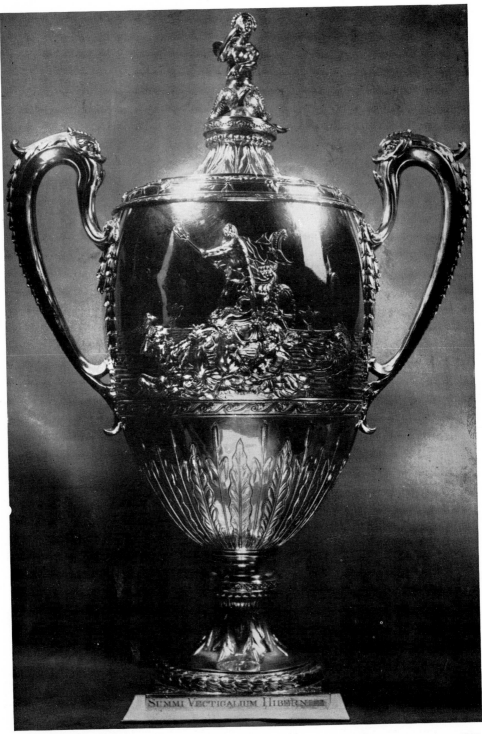

COVERED CUP   Fred Kandler, London, 1778

CANDELABRA SUITE   Matthew Boulton, c. 1800

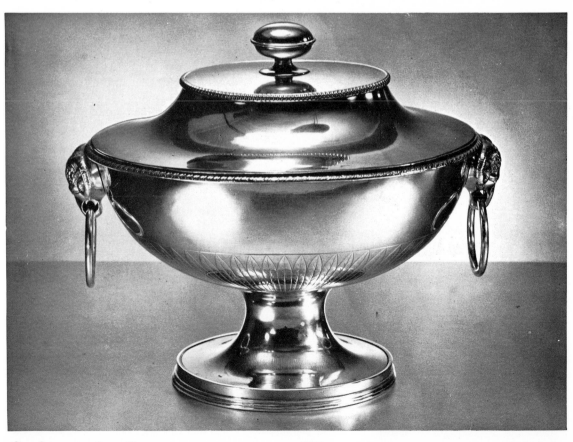

OLD SHEFFIELD SOUP TUREEN   c. 1790   *Courtesy Marshall Field & Co.*

Matthew Boulton, c. 1800

VENISON DISH

c. 1785, Coll. Lord Amherst

SHEFFIELD KETTLE

Courtesy S. Wyler, Inc.

c. 1810

c. 1770

Sheffield Wine Cooler on Plateau

Old Sheffield Globe Ink Stand

c. 1765

c. 1760

Rare Sheffield Goblet

Rare Sheffield Mace

OLD SHEFFIELD EPERGNE AND PLATEAU   c. 1810   *Courtesy S. Wyler, Inc.*

CASTER
John Coney, Boston

TEAPOT Josiah Austin, Charlestown

PLATE Keonraet Ten Eyck, Albany, 1716

SNUFFER

Cornelius Kierstaede, N.Y.

CANDLESTICKS   Jacob Hurd, Boston, 1702-1758   *Courtesy Metropolitan Museum*

SAUCE BOAT   Joseph Richardson, Philadelphia   *Courtesy Metropolitan Mu*

associated with early Dutch silver is that of Johans Lutma, who was the devoted friend of the great Rembrandt. His portrait done by this celebrated artist is well known.

The town mark used by the city of Amsterdam was "a narrow shield, charged with three saltires in pale, and surmounted by an arch bow." The silver standard was indicated by the "head of Perseus," with the letter "a" on his cap, in a circle. All Holland silver bore the duty mark as well as the stamp of the maker.

SILVERSMITHING IN ITALY

No country in all of Europe was richer in ecclesiastical plate than Italy, but in direct contrast it suffered the greatest losses in secular plate. This was not alone due to the results of conflict and invasion but also to intentional destruction. Many of the later artists, lacking a sufficient quantity of metal were forced to remake earlier pieces.

The Renaissance began and had its first flowering in Italy. The city of Florence was the world's center of art, and students from all over the continent came there to be apprenticed. They had to submit a finished work as an example of their skill, and if accepted, they were then known as full-fledged masters. Some of the most beautiful gold and silver work in the world was made in Italy at this time and goldsmithing was raised to a higher standard than ever known before. Royalty from all of Europe sent to Italy for services to be made to special order, and since time was not an important element, the most magnificent results were achieved. As time progressed, the love of luxury, the desire for elegance and splendor so increased that one finds very few pieces of church plate during the sixteenth century. Rather, the finished articles were pieces of wondrous beauty which graced the halls of those so well able to afford extravagances. Much work in the combination of gold and crystal was produced and the most noted of workers who specialized in this field was Valerio Belli, 1468 to 1546. Of course, the most famous goldsmith of all time—Benvenuto Cellini was an Italian. Very rarely has any artist in his field achieved such a high degree of perfection as was displayed in the works of Cellini. Unfortunately less than a dozen pieces of his work exist today, but it is significant that articles wrought by him command higher prices than those of any other silversmith in the world, regardless of date.

Under the pontificate of Nicholas V, 1447 to 1455, the patronage of the arts really commenced, yet, unfortunately, nothing of the work of the period remains. A decided flair for the improvement of original pieces caused the destruction of many. Many of the world's famous painters and sculptors occasionally tried their hands at goldsmithing, but nothing remains of their efforts.

The first goldsmiths' association in Italy is recorded as early as 1035, while in 1314 the city of Florence introduced legislation protecting the industry. Prior to the consolidation of the numerous small Italian states, each section used its own particular markings. The general laws passed which definitely legalized the production of silver in Italy were not introduced and adopted until 1873.

SILVERSMITHING IN NORWAY

The only silver known in Norway prior to 1400 consisted of a few odd pieces of jewelry and seals, and an occasional silver tipped drinking horn. However, from the year 1425, the craft assumed a real importance and until the end of the fifteenth century it was recognized as a major industry among the arts. The two outstanding centers of silversmithing were Christiania and Bergen, the latter being of far greater importance. A few prominent silversmiths are known from each of these places, from examples of their work which have survived. In Christiania, Romanus Moller and Berendt Platt are noteworthy as the two silversmiths who specialized in the production of pieces reproduced along the styles of the English masters. These pieces are unusual for their extreme simplicity, as most of the early Norwegian silver was rather ornate. In Bergen, the most proficient craftsmen known were Martin Finchenberger and Albert Grath.

The silversmith in Norway specialized for the most part in the production of drinking accessories. Beakers of typical Scandinavian design were made in great profusion and were invariably modeled after the Danish pieces made from horn years previously. Of extreme interest to the student of Norwegian silver is a small two-handled bowl called the "oreskall." This article was made exclusively in Norway and only rarely are examples obtainable. Tankards were by far the most popular pieces fashioned from silver. However, the majority of them were of wood, as only a limited number of inhabitants were wealthy enough to indulge in the luxury of silver. This situation is comparable to the one existing in Scotland, when silver quaiches were made for the prosperous and wooden ones for the peasants.

The city of Stavanger was also a thriving silver center after 1593. Here there was a rather unusual procedure in regard to the legislation on silver. Anders Hansen, a local worker built up a reputation as the outstanding silversmith of the town and ruled the industry for years. However, he accomplished this by political influence, rather than by dint of the quality of the work he produced. In this way he was able to create a monopoly, and in 1789, the records list his name as the only smith known in Stavanger. He even went so far as to disallow the practicing of any other silversmith in the town. He himself introduced the fraudulent practice of impressing his maker's mark on all pieces brought to his shop for repair. The competition offered by Jacob Campbell, a smith who finally secured permission to work in Stavanger, caused the exposure of Hansen.

All Norwegian silver was required to be marked with a maker's mark and a standard stamp. The town mark for Bergen, by far the most flourishing silver center of Norway, was a "mosque or domed building, above seven pellets, in outline."

SILVERSMITHING IN POLAND

The general destruction of art in Poland was deplorable, particularly after the invasions of the Mongols in 1241, 1259, and again in 1287. They effected the wholesale slaughter of the efforts of the earliest Polish artists, to the extent that practically no pieces remain. Poland was producing beautiful silver as early as the year 1000, but, unfortunately, all that has been left to posterity are two silver chalices. One of these bears the date 1166, and is considered to be the finest example of early silver known today. For many years after the Mongolian invasions, art suffered a great depression and very few efforts in any artistic direction were attempted. However, under Casimir the Great, the country again evinced a new interest in silversmithing and many unusual statues and reliquaries were made. The forms of monstrances made during the fifteenth century were dominated by the styles of the Gothic architecture, and this lack of originality is found throughout Polish smithing. Until the middle of the fifteenth century, Bohemian influences are noted, but from that time on the characteristics of the Nuremberg craftsmen were predominant. The dynastic connection between Hungary and Poland may be quickly detected in the similarity of their art, and often when pieces of unmarked silver appeared, it was impossible to distinguish the country of origin.

The Stwasz family in Poland exerted great influence on the decoration of ecclesiastical and secular plate, and their ability as masters of their art was finally recognized when they were appointed as goldsmiths to the Polish court. Krakow, the old capital of Poland, attracted many rich merchants and it became widely known as an important gem center. This naturally caused great prosperity among those displaying artistic talents, and it was in this city that Polish silversmithing reached its greatest heights. Nearly all the plate remaining from these times is ecclesiastical as only those pieces stored in churches escaped destruction in the horrible siege of the city of Krakow in 1655 by the Swedes. Lemberg and Vilna are also known as towns where silver was produced, but neither attained the fame of Krakow. Throughout the political history of Poland and its everchanging government, the influence of foreign artists on the designs in silversmithing is recognized.

SILVERSMITHING IN PORTUGAL

After the rise of Portugal in the fifteenth century to one of the foremost colonizing powers in Europe, a marked development in the taste of the people is noted. The demand for personal luxuries grew by leaps and bounds and before long a ready market for fine gold and silver was established. Likewise, the churches benefited by this cultural ascent, and houses of worship were filled with beautiful pieces fashioned from costly metals. During the reign of Emanual I, the call for plate increased as Portugal enjoyed greater and greater wealth, and during this time some of the most magnificent objets d'art in all of Europe were produced.

During the Portuguese Empire, 1499-1580, social life in Lisbon is said to have equalled that of Rome. This Golden Age of silversmithing was accompanied by the most intensive appreciation of fine art in the history of the country. Shortly after this, a style of architecture, known as the Arte Manuelina, was introduced which influenced the work of the goldsmiths greatly. Unfortunately, this new trend lacked beauty and the pieces of plate can hardly be called artistic.

No native metal could be mined in Portugal so importation was the only means of supply. Eventually trading became more difficult and this resulted in a natural shortage of silver. As the metal became scarcer, pieces were made of a much thinner gauge, and their appearance also suffered. During the sixteenth century, Portuguese plate was prone to over-ornamentation and resembled the work of the Spanish smiths to such a degree that it was impossible to distinguish between the two in the absence of marks.

The beautiful creations of the two previous centuries were replaced by pieces which bore the influence of foreign silversmiths. However, in 1703, the date of the Methuen treaty with England, the styles of the British silversmiths were reproduced almost exclusively. In Lisbon and Oporto, the two main centers of silversmithing in Portugal, the demand for pieces in the English style progressed to the degree where many of the fraudulent workers punched English hallmarks on their wares.

During the reign of John V, 1706-1750, the most serious destruction of plate in the history of Portugal commenced. His extravagances led to enormous debts and he was forced to melt large quantities of plate to pay for these indulgences. In 1755, the earthquake and resulting fires completed the loss.

The earliest record of the legislation for silver in Lisbon is noted in 1460, while in Oporto the mention of assayers occurs as early as 1570. However, a complete system of hallmarking silver was not established in Portugal until the eighteenth century. The national mark used on gold and silver wares was "A capital Roman 'P' beneath a pellet in arched outline." In Lisbon the town mark adopted was "A capital Roman 'L' beneath a crown, in regular outline." Several other towns in Portugal are known for silversmithing and among these Beja, Broga, Setubal, and Evara are to be remembered.

SILVERSMITHING IN RUSSIA

The Russian art is said to date from the time of Vladimir, 956 to 1015. Although the names of no Russian silversmiths survived from the Middle Ages, that of the famous icon painter, Rublev, is remembered from this period. During the sixteenth and seventeenth centuries the splendor of the Czar's plate was the envy and talk of every visitor to the palace, although most of it was executed by foreign smiths. It was said that although the Russian silversmiths were great copyists they could not create originals. Therefore, most of the designs found in Russia were not the work of their own countrymen. The westernization of Russia by Peter the Great created new tastes in art, so that before long the majority of the typically domestic pieces were discarded. The introduction in 1700 of a system of compulsory hallmarking had a great effect on the industry, particularly in Moscow and St. Petersburg, which were the main silver production centers.

The Russian silversmiths created pieces for practical use which were to be found no place else in the world. The most conspicuous of these was the bratma, which was used as a toasting glass at funerals, for blessings, and at every imaginable function. Often the remains of the deceased were cremated, and the ashes put into the bratma to be buried in the grave. They were fashioned from gold, silver, or precious stones and no wealthy home in Russia was without one. Another typically Russian creation in silver was the kaush, which was a small boat shaped vessel with one handle, used for ladling daily drinks. A small brandy cup, known as a charka was also introduced about the year 1800. The discovery of a product known as niello caused great alteration in the general appearance of the silver pieces. Niello was a variety of black inlay enamel which was used on silver either as a form of decoration or as a means of lettering. The popularity of this alloy has never waned. It is still used at the present time.

Russia contributed the icon to the world of art. This was a beautiful painted piece depicting a Scriptural scene, surmounted by a casing of gold or silver. Icons were made in several styles varying from the rich ones encrusted with precious gems to the peasant icons mounted in copper or some other inexpensive metal.

Although Moscow and St. Petersburg are outstanding as silver centers, other places such as Kaluga, Kazan and Kiow, are known. The town marks used by the main cities are as follows:

Moscow—"A double-headed eagle displayed, holding in his dexter claw a sword, and in his sinister a ball, above the letters MOCK above B.A. in outline."

St. Petersburg—"A double-head eagle displayed, holding in his dexter claw a dagger and in his sinister an orb in outline."

SILVERSMITHING IN SPAIN

Conquest in the New World brought vast wealth to Spain, and again from 1556 to 1590, under the rule of Phillip II, the prosperity of the country increased. Phillip, who was one of the chief monarchs of Christendom, adorned the great Escorial with vast quantities of plate and finely jeweled objects, executed by the leading silversmiths of foreign countries as well as by Spanish craftsmen. Never before had the patronage of the goldsmith in Spain increased so materially. The glory of the Spanish Renaissance was surpassed only by Italy's. But this era, although the most scintillating in Spanish history, has left no traces of its magnificence, though ecclesiastical silver from this time has survived.

The defeat of the Armada in 1588 was a stirring blow to material prosperity, and the art of the goldsmith declined. With the accession to the throne of Phillip III, Spanish power began to wane, and the arts in general deteriorated to the lowest point in the history of the country. The practice of looting treasures of a country by invading enemies is evidenced by the amount of Spanish plate found today in France and England. The soldiers of those countries being sufficiently educated to appreciate fine art, realized that these pieces were more valuable in their original form than if melted down. It is interesting to note that during the eighteenth century, although the Spanish silversmiths were influenced by the influx of French art, the demand was great for typically English table appointments, and so we find cruets, inkstands, candelabra, and other articles of domestic plate made at this time.

In the study of Spanish silver notice must be taken of the huge monstrances used to decorate many of the fine buildings. These custodia, as they were termed in Spain, contained beautifully executed silver and gold statuettes and are of importance for the high quality of the work. Two of the outstanding examples known today were created by Enrique d'Arphe, one for Cordoba in 1513, and the other for Toledo in 1524. His son Antonia, greatly influenced by the style of the Renaissance, produced a most unusual type in 1544 at Santiago. Juan d'Arphe who was the best known of this illustrious family is remembered for the great and important custodia created at Valladolid.

Spanish silver from the fifteenth to the seventeenth century was prone to over-elaboration because the silversmiths worked to special order of the wealthy and noble classes.

Peculiar to Spanish silver history was a shallow dish with a short foot, the shape of which was derived from early Valencian pottery.

As early as the thirteenth century, silversmiths were working at Toledo, Saville, and Burgos, while in the fourteenth century the craft spread to Valencia, Valladolid, Guadalupe, Genoa, and other small towns. The most important center of silver production was Madrid, with Barcelona a close second in the quality and quantity of pieces produced. The filigree work closely related to the Spanish silversmiths was conceived in Barcelona, and work in this design was done later at Cordova and Salamanca. Very little data relative to early Spanish hallmarks is available and it is only through book records that have been preserved, that pieces can be accurately dated or identified.

SILVERSMITHING IN SWEDEN

Silversmithing in Sweden first achieved prominence as an art under the patronage of Charles X and Gustavus Adolphus. It was not until the seventeenth century that the smiths produced pieces of any great importance, and then most of them bear the mark of

German influence. Only the few pieces in filigree design are definitely Swedish. It has been very difficult to date the few early pieces which have survived, since no hallmarks were used until the seventeenth century. Pieces were reproduced from century to century, so one can only surmise the time of their creation. Among the most typically Swedish pieces produced were unusual bridal crowns of silver and gold which held great favor throughout the small villages.

The cities of Gothenburg and Stockholm were the only important centers of silversmithing. The mark adopted by the city of Stockholm was "a maiden's head, affronte, in irregular shield." In 1759 a state control mark which consisted of the arms of Sweden was adopted. This was represented by "three crowns, two and one, in ellipse or inverted trefoil."

SILVERSMITHING IN SWITZERLAND

Swiss domestic silver fell victim to the melting pot in time of war, as did the plate in nearly every other country in Europe. Unfortunately, there is no silver left today that illustrated the important art movement that occurred from 1430 to 1530. Drinking articles were produced here in great quantities as well as many other pieces directly copied from the work of the German silversmiths. Not only were German objects reproduced, but all pieces definitely show the Teutonic influence in design. In 1880 the control of silver was regulated by law, and pieces were made with either of the following standards: the standard of 875 fine was represented by a "bear rampant," while those made of the consistency of 800 bore the mark of a "hen contourne, in ellipse." Zurich, the most prosperous city in Switzerland, was easily the main center of silver production, although seventeen other towns were recorded.

HOW TO IDENTIFY HALLMARKS

Bear in mind that the marks must be exact. There is often great similarity between marks of widely differing times, places and makers. The marks must also be complete to insure certainty of identification.

FIRST, DETERMINE THE PLACE OF ORIGIN.

If you know this, refer below to the special instructions for that locality and then to the Tables of Hallmarks for that locality. But if you do not know the origin the following *probabilities* may be helpful.

LEOPARD'S HEAD, LEOPARD'S HEAD ERASED: London.

Other possibilities: Leopard's head erased also used by Provinces, 1697-1719. Also Chester used similar markings to London but Chester is noted chiefly for small pieces.

LION PASSANT: English.

THISTLE: Edinburgh.

HARP: Dublin.

FISH AND TREE: Glasgow.

ONE OR TWO MARKS ONLY: American.

Especially if the marks are names or initials. Possibly English Provincial, Scotch or Irish.

"STERLING"; Irish or American.

"COIN," "DOLLAR," "STANDARD," ETC.: American. Possibly Irish.

ORNATE CAPITAL LETTERS WITH CROWN OR FLEUR DE LIS: French.

HAND: Antwerp. Possibly Belfast.

SPREAD EAGLE: German though there are many other possibilities.

If the marks do not indicate the origin perhaps the character, style or workmanship of the piece may give a clue. If not, a process of elimination must be used.

IF YOU KNOW THAT THE ORIGIN OF THE PIECE IS
LONDON. Look for the date letter. Consult the "Marks on London Plate" tables and you will determine the year of manufacture. These tables will also indicate the standard and show what other marks were necessary. The remaining mark will be the maker's mark. Consult the "Index of English, Scotch and Irish Marks" and this will indicate the page on which the maker's mark is listed. Names will be shown for 1697 or later. But maker's names before 1697 cannot be identified though the marks can be verified. Maker's marks may also be found by consulting the "London Goldsmiths Marks" tables for a number of years before and after the date of the piece.

ENGLISH Provincial, Scotch or Irish. If town is known consult the tables for that locality to identify date letter. Then consult "Index of English, Scotch and Irish Marks" for the maker. If town is not known the maker's identification will probably indicate the town. Otherwise a process of elimination is necessary.

SHEFFIELD PLATE. Consult Tables.

AMERICAN. Consult tables which are alphabetically listed according to last names. If mark consists of initials the last letter probably is the initial of the last name.

FRENCH. Consult "French Hallmarks" tables which are arranged according to the character of the marks (Letters, Flowers, etc.)

GERMAN. Consult "German Marks" tables which are in three sections arranged alphabetically by towns (according to the character of the marks). This will give the number of the mark which will be identified in the "Index of German Marks." If you know the town, refer to the proper section. Otherwise, try each section until the mark is found.

OTHER COUNTRIES. Consult "Hallmarks of Other Countries Tables" (arranged according to the character of the marks). This will provide a number which will be identified in the "Index of Hallmarks of Other Countries."

	Leopard's Head Crowned.	Date Letter.
EDW. IV 1478-9		
1479-80	●	B
1480-1		
1481-2	●	D
1482-3		
RICH. III. 1483-4		
1484-5		
HEN. VII. 1485-6	●	h
1486-7		
1487-8		
1488-9	●	ll
1489-90		
1490-1	,,	n
1491-2	●	O
1492-3		
1493-4	,,	Q
1494-5	,,	R
1495-6		
1496-7	●	T
1497-8		

	Leopard's Head Crowned.	Date Letter.
1498-9	●	a
1499 1500	,,	b
1500-1	,,	c
1501-2	,,	d
1502-3		
1503-4	,,	f
1504-5	,,	h
1505-6		
1506-7	●	i
1507-8	,,	kk
1508-9	●	l
HEN. VIII 1509-10	●	m
1510-1	,,	n
1511-2	,,	o
1512-3	,,	p
1513-4	,,	q
1514-5	,,	r
1515-6	●	s
1516-7	,,	t
1517-8	,,	u

	Leopard's Head Crowned.	Date Letter.
1518-9	●	A
1519-20	●	B
1520-1	,,	C
1521-2	●	D
1522-3	,,	E
1523-4	,,	F
1524-5	,,	G
1525-6	,,	h
1526-7		
1527-8	,,	K
1528-9	,,	L
1529-30	,,	M
1530-1	,,	N
1531-2	●	O
1532-3	,,	P
1533-4	,,	Q
1534-5	,,	R
1535-6	,,	S
1536-7	,,	T
1537-8	,,	V

	Leopard's Head Crowned.	Date Letter.	Lion Passant from 1544.
1538-9	●	A	
1539-40	●	B	
1540-1	,,	C	
1541-2	,,	D	
1542-3			
1543-4	,,	F	
1544-5	●	G	●
1545-6	●	H	●
1546-7	,,	I	,,
EDW. VI. 1547-8		K	
1548-9	,,	L	●
1549-50	,,	M	,,
1550-1	,,	N	●
1551-2	●	O	●
1552-3	,,	P	●
MARY. 1553-4	,,	Q	,,
1554-5	,,	R	,,
1555-6	,,	S	,,
1556-7	,,	T	,,
1557-8	,,	V	●

	Leopard's Head Crowned.	Date Letter.	Lion Passant		Leopard's Head Crowned.	Date Letter.	Lion Passant.		Leopard's Head Crowned.	Date Letter	Lion Passant
ELIZ. 1558-9	🦁	a	🦁	1578-9	🦁	A	🦁	1598-9	🦁	A	🦁
1559-60	,,	b	x ,,	1579-80	,,	B	,,	1599 1600	,,	B	🦁
1560-1	,,	c c	,,	1580-1	,,	C	,,	1600-1	,,	C	,,
1561-2	,,	d	🦁	1581-2	,,	D	,,	1601-2	,,	D	🦁
1562-3	🦁	e	,,	1582-3	,,	E	,,	1602-3	,,	E	,,
1563-4	,,	f f	,,	1583-4	,,	F F	,,	JAS. I. 1603-4	,,	F	,,
1564-5	,,	g	,,	1584-5	,,	G	,,	1604-5	,,	G	🦁
1565-6	,,	h	,,	1585-6	,,	H	,,	1605-6	,,	h	,,
1566-7	,,	i	,,	1586-7	,,	I	,,	1606-7	,,	I	🦁
1567-8	,,	k k	,,	1587-8	,,	K	,,	1607-8	,,	K	,,
1568-9	,,	l	,,	1588-9	,,	L	,,	1608-9	,,	L	,,
1569-70	,,	m m	,,	1589-90	,,	M	,,	1609-10	,,	M	,,
1570-1	,,	n	,,	1590-1	,,	N	,,	1610-1	,,	N	🦁
1571-2	,,	o	,,	1591-2	,,	O	,,	1611-2	,,	O	,,
1572-3	,,	p	,,	1592-3	🦁	P	🦁	1612-3	,,	P	,,
1573-4	,,	q	🦁	1593-4	,,	Q	,,	1613-4	,,	Q	,,
1574-5	,,	r	,,	1594-5	,,	R	🦁	1614-5	,,	R	,,
1575-6	,,	s s	,,	1595-6	,,	S	,,	1615-6	,,	S	,,
1576-7	,,	t	,,	1596-7	,,	T	,,	1616-7	,,	T	,,
1577-8	,,	u	,,	1597-8	,,	V	,,	1617-8	,,	V	,,

	LEOPARD'S HEAD CROWNED.	DATE LETTER.	LION PASSANT.		LEOPARD'S HEAD CROWNED.	DATE LETTER.	LION PASSANT.		LEOPARD'S HEAD CROWNED.	DATE LETTER.	LION PASSANT.
*1618-9		a		1638-9		b		1658-9		A	
1619-20	,,	b	,,	*1639-40	,,	B	,,	1659-60	,,	B	,,
1620-1	,,	c	,,	1640-1	,,	C	,,	CHAS. II. 1660-1	,,	C	,,
1621-2	,,	d	,,	1641-2	,,	D	,,	1661-2	,,	D	,,
1622-3	,,	e	,,	1642-3	,,	E	,,	1662-3	,,	E	
1623-4	,,	f	,,	1643-4	,,	ff	,,	1663-4	,,	F	,,
1624-5	,,	g	,,	1644-5	,,	G	,,	1664-5	,,	G	,,
CHAS. I. 1625-6	,,	h	,,	1645-6	,,	H	,,	1665-6	,,	H	,,
1626-7	,,	i	,,	1646-7	,,	I	,,	1666-7	,,	I	,,
1627-8	,,	k	,,	1647-8		K		1667-8	,,	K	,,
1628-9	,,	l	,,	1648-9	,,	L	,,	1668-9		L	
1629-30	,,	m	,,	COMWTH. 1649-50	,,	M	,,	1669-70	,,	M	,,
1630-1	,,	n	,,	1650-1	,,	N	,,	1670-1	,,	N	,,
1631-2	,,	o	,,	1651-2	,,	O	,,	1671-2	,,	O	,,
1632-3	,,	p	,,	1652-3	,,	P	,,	1672-3	,,	P	,,
1633-4	,,	q	,,	1653-4	,,	Q	,,	1673-4	,,	Q	,,
1634-5	,,	r	,,	1654-5	,,	R	,,	1674-5	,,	R	,,
1635-6	,,	s	,,	1655-6	,,	S	,,	1675-6	,,	S	,,
1636-7	,,	t	,,	1656-7	,,	T	,,	1676-7	,,	T	,,
1637-8	,,	v	,,	1657-8	,,	V	,,	1677-8	,,	U	,,

Year	Leopard's Head Crowned	Date Letter	Lion Passant
1678-9	(crowned leopard's head)	a	(lion)
*1679-80	,,	b	(lion)
1680-1	(crowned leopard's head)	c	(lion)
1681-2	,,	d	,,
1682-3	,,	e	,,
1683-4	,,	f	,,
1684-5	,,	g	,,
JAS. II. 1685-6	,,	h	,,
1686-7	,,	i	,,
1687-8	,,	k	,,
1688-9	,,	l	,,
WM. & MY. 1689-90	(crowned leopard's head)	m	(lion)
1690-1	,,	n	,,
1691-2	,,	o	,,
1692-3	,,	p	,,
1693-4	,,	q	,,
1694-5	,,	r	,,
WM. III. 1695-6	,,	s	,,
MAY 29, 1696, TO MCH. 27, 1697.	,,	t	,,

Year	Britannia	Datl. Letter	Lion's Head Erased
*1697 MCH. 27 TO MAY 29	(britannia)	a	(head)
1697-8	,,	b	,,
1698-9	,,	c	,,
1699 1700	(britannia)	d	(head)
1700-1	,,	e	,,
1701-2	,,	f	,,
ANNE. 1702-3	,,	g	,,
1703-4	,,	h	,,
1704-5	,,	i	,,
1705-6	,,	k	,,
1706-7	,,	l	,,
1707-8	,,	m	,,
1708-9	,,	n	,,
1709-10	,,	o	,,
1710-11	,,	p	,,
1711-2	,,	q	,,
1712-3	,,	r	,,
1713-4	,,	s	,,
GEO. I. 1714-5	,,	t	,,
1715-6	,,	u	,,

Year	Britannia	Date Letter	Lion's Head Erased
1716-7	(britannia)	A	(head)
1717-8	,,	B	,,
1718-9	,, LEOPARD'S HEAD CROWNED	C	,, LION PASSANT
*1719-20	(crowned leopard's head)	D	(lion)
†1720-1	,,	E	,,
1721-2	(leopard's head)	F	(lion)
‡1722-3	,,	G	,,
1723-4	,,	H	,,
§1724-5	(head)	I	(lion)
1725-6	,,	K	,,
1726-7	(head)	L	(lion)
GEO. II. 1727-8	,,	M	,,
1728-9	,,	N	,,
1729-30	(head)	O	(lion)
1730-1	,,	P	,,
1731-2	,,	Q	,,
1732-3	,,	R	,,
1733-4	,,	S	,,
1734-5	,,	T	,,
1735-6	,,	V	,,

Year	Leopard's Head Crowned	Date Letter	Lion Passant
1736-7	(crowned leopard's head)	a	(lion)
1737-8	,,	b	,,
*1738-9	,,	c	,,
1739-40	(crowned leopard's head)	d	(lion)
1740-1	,,	e	,,
1741-2	,,	f	,,
1742-3	,,	g	,,
1743-4	,,	h	,,
1744-5	,,	i	,,
1745-6	,,	k	,,
1746-7	,,	l	,,
1747-8	,,	m	,,
1748-9	,,	n	,,
1749-50	,,	o	,,
1750-1	,,	p	,,
†1751-2	(crowned leopard's head)	q	(lion)
1752-3	,,	r	,,
1753-4	,,	r	,,
‡1754-5	,,	t	,,
1755-6	,,	u	,,

	LEOPARD'S HEAD CROWNED.	DATE LETTER.	LION PASSANT.		LEOPARD'S HEAD CROWNED.	DATE LETTER.	LION PASSANT.			LEOPARD'S HEAD CROWNED.	DATE LETTER.	LION PASSANT.	KING'S HEAD.
1756-7	🦁	A	🦁	1776-7	🦁	a	🦁		1796-7	🦁	A	🦁	👤
1757-8	,,	B	,,	1777-8	,,	b	,,		1797-8	,,	B	,,	,,
1758-9	,,	C	,,	1778-9	,,	c	,,		*1798-9	,,	C	,,	,,
1759-60	,,	D	,,	1779-80	,,	d	,,		1799 1800	,,	D	,,	,,
GEO. III 1760-1	,,	E	,,	1780-1	,,	e	,,		1800-1	,,	E	,,	,,
1761-2	,,	F	,,	1781-2	,,	f	,,		1801-2	,,	F	,,	,,
1762-3	,,	G	,,	1782-3	,,	g	,,		1802-3	,,	G	,,	,,
†1763-4	,,	H	,,	1783-4	,,	h	,,	KING'S HEAD.	1803-4	,,	H	,,	,,
1764-5	,,	I	,,	†1784-5	,,	i	,,	👤	†1804-5	,,	I	,,	,,
1765-6	,,	K	,,	1785-6	,,	k	,,	,,	1805-6	,,	K	,,	,,
1766-7	,,	L	,,	1786-7	,,	l	,,	👤	1806-7	,,	L	,,	,,
1767-8	,,	M	,,	1787-8	,,	m	,,	,,	1807-8	,,	M	,,	,,
†1768-9	,,	N	,,	1788-9	,,	n	,,	,,	†1808-9	,,	N	,,	,,
1769-70	,,	O	,,	1789-90	,,	o	,,	,,	1809-10	,,	O	,,	,,
1770-1	,,	P	,,	1790-1	,,	p	,,	,,	1810-1	,,	P	,,	,,
†1771-2	,,	Q	,,	1791-2	,,	q	,,	,,	1811-2	,,	Q	,,	,,
1772-3	,,	R	,,	1792-3	,,	r	,,	,,	1812-3	,,	R	,,	,,
1773-4	,,	S	,,	1793-4	,,	s	,,	,,	1813-4	,,	S	,,	,,
1774-5	,,	T	,,	1794-5	,,	t	,,	,,	1814-5	,,	T	,,	,,
1775-6	,,	U	,,	1795-6	,,	u	,,	,,	1815-6	,,	U	,,	,,

Date	Leopard's Head	Date Letter	Lion Passant	King's Head
1816-7	(leopard's head)	a	(lion)	(king's head)
1817-8	,,	b	,,	,,
1818-9	,,	c	,,	,,
1819-20	,,	d	,,	,,
GEO. IV. 1820-1	,,	e	,,	(king's head)
1821-2	(leopard's head)	f	(lion)	,,
1822-3	,,	g	,,	,,
1823-4	,,	h	,,	,,
1824-5	,,	i	,,	,,
1825-6	,,	k	,,	,,
1826-7	,,	l	,,	,,
1827-8	,,	m	,,	,,
1828-9	,,	n	,,	,,
1829-30	,,	o	,,	,,
WM. IV. 1830-1	,,	p	,,	,,
1831-2	,,	q	,,	(king's head)
1832-3	,,	r	,,	,,
1833-4	,,	s	,,	,,
1834-5	,,	t	,,	,,
1835-6	,,	u	,,	,,

Date	Leopard's Head	Date Letter	Lion Passant	King's Head
1836-7	(leopard's head)	A	(lion)	(king's head)
VICT. 1837-8	,,	B	,,	(queen's head)
1838-9	,,	C	,,	,,
1839-40	,,	D	,,	,,
1840-1	,,	E	,,	,,
1841-2	,,	F	,,	,,
1842-3	,,	G	,,	,,
1843-4	,,	H	,,	,,
*1844-5	,,	I	,,	,,
1845-6	,,	K	,,	,,
1846-7	,,	L	,,	,,
1847-8	,,	M	,,	,,
1848-9	,,	N	,,	,,
1849-50	,,	O	,,	,,
1850-1	,,	P	,,	,,
1851-2	,,	Q	,,	,,
1852-3	,,	R	,,	,,
1853-4	,,	S	,,	,,
†1854-5	,,	T	,,	,,
1855-6	,,	U	,,	,,

Date	Leopard's Head	Date Letter	Lion Passant	Queen's Head
1856-7	(leopard's head)	a	(lion)	(queen's head)
1857-8	,,	b	,,	,,
1858-9	,,	c	,,	,,
1859-60	,,	d	,,	,,
1860-1	,,	e	,,	,,
1861-2	,,	f	,,	,,
1862-3	,,	g	,,	,,
*1863-4	(leopard's head) *Leopard's head as above*	h	(lion) *Lion passant as above*	,,
1864-5		i		,,
1865-6	,,	k	,,	,,
1866-7	,,	l	,,	,,
1867-8	,,	m	,,	,,
1868-9	,,	n	,,	,,
1869-70	,,	o	,,	,,
1870-1	,,	p	,,	,,
1871-2	,,	q	,,	,,
1872-3	,,	r	,,	,,
1873-4	,,	s	,,	,,
1874-5	,,	t	,,	,,
1875-6	,,	u	,,	,,

	LEOPARD'S HEAD	DATE LETTER	LION PASSANT	QUEEN'S HEAD		LEOPARD'S HEAD	DATE LETTER	LION PASSANT
1876-7	🦁	A	🦁	👑	1896-7	🦁	a	🦁
1877-8	,,	B	,,	,,	1897-8	,,	b	,,
1878-9	,,	C	,,	,,	1898-9	,,	c	,,
1879-80	,,	D	,,	,,	1899 1900	,,	d	,,
1880-1	,,	E	,,	,,	1900-1	,,	e	,,
1881-2	,,	F	,,	,,	EDW. VII. 1901-2	,,	f	,,
1882-3	,,	G	,,	,,	1902-3	,,	g	.
1883-4	,,	H	,,	,,	1903-4	,,	h	,,
1884-5	,,	I	,,	,,	1904-5	,,	i	,,
1885-6	,,	K	,,	,,	1905-6	,,	k	,,
1886-7	,,	L	,,	,,	1906-7	,,	l	,,
1887-8	,,	M	,,	,,	1907-8	,,	m	,,
1888-9	,,	N	,,	,,	1908-9	,,	n	,,
1889-90	,,	O	,,	,,	1909-10	,,	o	,,
1890-1	,,	P	,,		1910-1	,,	p	,,
1891-2	,,	Q	,,		1911-2	,,	q	,,
1892-3	,,	R	,,		1912-3	,,	r	,,
1893-4	,,	S	,,		1913-4	,,	s	,,
1894-5	,,	T	,,		1914-5	,,	t	,,
1895-6	,,	U	,,		1915-6	,,	u	,,

1916	a
1917	b
1918	c
1919	d
1920	e
1921	f
1922	g
1923	h
1924	i
1925	k
1926	l
1927	m
1928	n
1929	o
1930	p
1931	q
1932	r
1933	s
1934	t
1935	u
1936	A
1937	B

DATE.	MAKER'S MARK.	DATE.	MAKER'S MARK.	DATE.	MAKER'S MARK.	DATE.	MAKER'S MARK.	DATE.	MAKER'S MARK.	DATE.	MAKER'S MARK.	DATE.	MAKER'S MARK
1479-80		1500-1		1516-7		1527-8		1536-7		1551-2		1561-2	
1481-2		1501-2		1517-8		,,		1537-8		,,		,,	
1488-9		1503-4		1518-9		1528-9		1538-9		,,		,,	
1490-1		1504-5		,,		,,		1539-40		,,		,,	
1491-2		,,		,,		,,		1540-1		1552-3		,,	
1493-4		1506-7		1519-20		1529-30		,,		1553-4		,,	
1494-5		,,		,,		1530-1		1541-2		,,		1562-3	
,,		1507-8		,,		1531-2		1543-4		1554-5		,,	
,,		,,		1520-1		,,		,,		,,		,,	
1496-7		,,		1521-2		1532-3		,,		1555-6		,,	
,,		,,		,,		,,		,,		1556-7		,,	
,,		,,		,,		,,		1514-5		,,		,,	
1498-9		1508-9		,,		1533-4		1545-6		1557-8		,,	
1499-1500		,,		1522-3		,,		,,		,,		,,	
		1509-10		,,		,,		,,		,,		,,	
		1510-1		1523-4		1534-5		,,		1558-9		,,	
		,,		,,		,,		1546-7		,,		,,	
		1511-2		,,		,,		1547-8		1559-60		,,	
		1512-3		1524-5		,,		1548-9		,,		,,	
		1513-4		,,		,,		,,		,,		,,	
		1514-5		1525-6		,,		,,		,,		,,	
		,,		,,		1535-6		1549-50		,,		1563-4	
		,,		,,		,,		,,		,,		,,	
		,,		-,,		,,		,,		,,		,,	
		,,		1527-8		,,		,,		,,		,,	
		1515-6		,,		,,		1550-1		1560-1		,,	
		,,		,,		,,		,,		,,		,,	

Date.	Maker's Mark.	Date.	Maker's Mark.	Date	Maker's Mark.	Date.	Maker's Mark.	Date.	Maker's Mark.	Date.	Maker's Mark.	Date.	Maker's Mark.
1563-4	K	1567-8		1569-70		1571-2	TL	1575-6		1577-8		1581-2	HW
"	RD	"	L	"	RV	"		"	AS	"		1582-3	
1564-5		"		"		"	AB	"	M	"		"	
"		"		1570-1		"	NR	"	TB	"		"	
"		"	CF	"		1572-3		"	M	"		"	IF
"	IC	"	RD	"		"		"		"	RP	"	G
"		"		"		"	HB	"		1578-9	tb	1583-4	RS
"		"	B	"		"	HR	1576-7		"		"	
"	R	"	B	"		"		"		"		"	IF
1565-6		"		"		1573-4	B	"		"		"	IH
"	I·P	1568-9	IF	"	HB	"	IF	"	IH	"	B	1584-5	IC
"		"	M	"	M	"	N	"	H	"		"	W
"		"	N	"		"	IP	"		1579-80	HC	"	
"	HW	"		"	IH	"		"	RI	"		"	
"	RK	"	R	"		"	X	"		c. 1580	H	"	RW
1566-7		"	IH	1571-2	F	"		"	IH	1580-1	SB	1585-6	
"	A	"		"		"		"	WC	"		"	
"		"		"		"	HR	"		"		"	
"		"		"	TA	"		"	tb	1581 2		1586-7	M
"		"	RA	"	J	"		"	A	"		"	
"		"		1574-5		"		"	LR	1577-8	HW	"	T
"		1569-70	F	"		"	VS	"	LR	"	RW	"	T
"	T	"		"		1575-6	HC	"	m	"	B	"	
"	WH	"		"	CF								

Date.	Maker's Mark.	Date.	Maker's Mark.	Date.	Maker's Mark.	Date	Maker's Mark.	Date.	Maker's Mark.	Date.	Maker's Mark.	Date.	Maker's Mark.	Date.	Maker's Mark.
1587-8		1593-4		1597-8		1601-2		1605-6		1608-9		1610-11			
,,		,,		1598-9		,,		,,		,,		,,			
,,		1594-5		,,		1602-3		,,		,,		,,			
,,		,,		,,		,,		,,		,,		,,			
,,		,,		,,		,,		1606-7		,,		,,			
1588-9		,,		1599-1600		,,		,,		,,		,,			
,,		,,		,,		,,		,,		,,		1611-12			
,,		1595-6		,,		,,		,,		,,		,,			
,,		,,		,,		,,		,,		,,		,,			
,,		,,		,,		,,		,,		,,		,,			
1589-90		,,		,,		1603-4		,,		1609-10		,,			
,,		,,		,,		,,		,,		,,		,,			
,,		,,		1600-1		,,		,,		,,		1612-13			
1590-1		,,		,,		,,		,,		,,		,,			
,,		1596-7		,,		,,		,,		,,		,,			
,,		,,		,,		,,		1607-8		,,		,,			
,,		,,		,,		,,		,,		,,		,,			
1591-2		,,		,,		1604-5		,,		,,		,,			
,,		,,		,,		,,		,,		1610-11		,,			
,,		,,		1601-2		,,		,,		,,		,,			
,,		1597-8		,,		,,		,,		,,		,,			
1592-3		,,		,,		,,		1608-9		,,		,,			
,,		,,		,,		,,		,,		,,		,,			
,,		,,		,,		1605-6		,,		,,					
,,		,,		,,				1608-9							

Date.	Maker's Mark.	Date.	Maker's Mark.	Date.	Maker's Mark.	Date.	Maker's Mark.	Date.	Maker's Mark.	Date.	Maker's Mark.	Date.	Maker's Mark.
1613-14	TC	1615-16	(eagle)	1618-19	A	1622-3	ER	1625-6	CB	1629-30	BP	1632-3	D
"	MH	"	WF	"	IC	"	ED	1626-7	PH	"	RC	"	IM
"	WZ	1616-17	IA	"	ID	"	H	"	IX	"	IT	"	(owl)
"	N	"	RN	"	C	"	IF	"	HS	"	CG	"	GB
"	HB	"	IP	"	RC	1623-4	(flower)	"	HB	"	PG	"	IG
"	RS	"	IA	"	RW	"	WC	"	RB	1630-1	TD	"	IH
"	IM	"	(crown)	"	WC	"	IM	"	AH WW	"	WM	1633-4	IB
1614-15	RB	"	RW	"	RC	"	RC	"	BY	"	RS	"	WM
"	RC	"	RC	"	IS	"	EH	"	WS	"	↓	"	JE
"	BF	1619-20	E	1619-20	E	"	RS	"	WS	"	IM	"	(shell)
"	IMFB	"	(face)	"	FM	1627-8	TB	1627-8	SW	"	IA	"	ES
"	SO	"	E	"	AB	"	RS	"	RI	"	WC	"	HB
"	ID	"	IC	"	RK	"	IF	"	WS	1634-5	RS	"	RC
"	HM	1617-18	RW	"	RG	1624-5	IH	"	TB	"	RS	"	RS
1615-16	CR	"	HB	1620-1	IC	"	(eagle)	"	TE	"	B	"	M
"	IR	"	IV	"	II	"	O	1628-9	TV	"	HM	"	PG
"	MH	"	RS	"	IS	"	A	"	RM	"	WC	"	RW
"	HS	"	IC	"	IWT	"	J	"	(shell)	"	DW	"	DW
"	IS	1621-2	RP	1621-2	EL	"	BY	"	(monogram)	"	WR	"	RC
"	(anchor)	"	WC	"	α	1625-6	LE	"	(lion)	1635-6	U	"	PB
"	IW	"	IF	"	H	"	IV	"	BY	"	C-B	1635-6	JF
"	(flower)	"	H	"	B	"	HS	"	WS	"	VS	"	LI
"	RD	"	CC	"	RW	"	SW	"	C	"	EH	"	RS
1618-19	(bear)	1618-19	IP	"	C	"	HS	1629-30	DG	1632-3	PB	"	RH
		"	WR	1622-3	RD	1629-30	WS	"	RB	"	TE	"	RO
						"	TB					"	RS

Date.	Maker's Mark.	Date.	Maker's Mark.	Date.	Maker's Mark	Date.	Maker's Mark.	Date.	Maker's Mark.	Date.	Maker's Mark.	Date.	Maker's Mark.
1635-6		1637-8		1640-1		1643-4		1649-50		1653-4		1657-8	
"		"		"		"		1650-1		1654-5		"	
"		1638-9		"		1644-5		"		"		"	
"		"		"		1645-6		"		"		"	
"		"		"		"		"		"		"	
"		"		"		"		"		1655-6		"	
1636-7		"		"		1646-7		"		"		1658-9	
"		"		"		"		1651-2		"		"	
"		"		1641-2		"		"		"		"	
"		"		"		"		"		"		"	
"		"		"		"		"		"		"	
"		"		"		1647-8		1652-3		"		"	
"		"		"		"		"		"		"	
"		"		"		"		"		"		"	
"		"		"		"		"		"		"	
1637-8		"		"		"		"		"		"	
"		"		"		1648-9		"		1656-7		1659-60	
"		"		"		"		"		"		"	
"		"		"		"		"		"		"	
"		1639-40		1642-3		"		1653-4		"		"	
"		"		"		"		"		"		"	
"		"		"		1649-50		"		"		"	
"		"		"		"		"		1657-8		"	
"		"		"		"		"		"		"	
"		"		1643-4		"		"				"	
"		1640-1											

Date.	Maker's Mark.	Date.	Maker's Mark.	Date.	Maker's Mark.	Date.	Maker's Mark.	Date.	Maker's Mark.	Date.	Maker's Mark.	Date.	Maker's Mark.
1660-1		1662-3		1664-5		1665-6		1668-9		1670-1		1671-2	
"		"		"		"		"		"		"	
"		"		"		"		"		"		"	
"		"		"		1666-7		"		"		"	
"		"		"		"		1669-70		"		"	
"		"		"		"		"		"		"	
"		"		"		"		"		"		"	
"		"		"		"		"		"		"	
"		"		"		1667-8		"		"		"	
"		"		"		"		"		"		1672-3	
"		"		"		"		"		"		"	
"		"		"		"		"		"		"	
1661-2		"		"		"		"		"		"	
"		"		"		"		"		"		"	
"		1663-4		"		"		"		1671-2		"	
"		"		1665-6		1668-9		"		"		"	
"		"		"		"		"		"		"	
"		"		"		"		"		"		"	
"		"		"		"		"		"		"	
"		"		"		"		"		"		"	
"		"		"		"		"		"		"	
"		"		"		"		"		"		"	
"		"		"		"		"		"		"	
"		"		"		"		"		"		1673-4	
"		"		"		"		"		"		"	
1662-3		1664-5		"		"		"		"			

Date.	Maker's Mark	Date	Maker's Mark	Date.	Maker's Mark	Date.	Maker's Mark	Date.	Maker's Mark	Date.	Maker's Mark	Date.	Maker's Mark	Date.	Maker's Mark
1673-4		1674-5		1676-7		1677-8		1678-9		1680-1		1681-2		1683-4	
,,				,,		,,		1679-80		,,		,,		,,	
,,		1675-6		,,		,,		,,		,,		,,		,,	
,,		,,		,,		1678-9		,,		,,		,,		,,	
,,		,,		,,		,,		,,		,,		,,		,,	
,,		,,		,,		,,		,,		,,		,,		,,	
,,		,,		,,		,,		,,		,,		1682-3		,,	
,,		,,		,,		,,		,,		,,		,,		,,	
,,		,,		,,		,,		,,		,,		,,		,,	
,,		,,		,,		,,		,,		,,		,,		,,	
1674-5		,,		1677-8		,,		,,		,,		,,		,,	
,,		,,		,,		,,		,,		,,		,,		,,	
,,		,,		,,		,,		,,		1681-2		,,		,,	
,,		,,		,,		,,		,,		,,		c. 1682		,,	
,,		,,		,,		,,		,,		,,		1682-3		,,	
,,		,,		,,		,,		c. 1680		,,		1683-4		,,	
,,		,,		,,		,,		,,		,,		,,		,,	
,,		,,		,,		,,		1680-1		,,		,,		,,	
,,		1676-7		,,		,,		,,		,,		,,		1684-5	
,,		,,		,,		,,		,,		,,		,,		,,	
,,		,,		,,		,,		,,		,,		,,		,,	
,,		,,		,,		,,		,,		,,		,,		,,	
,,		,,		,,		,,		,,		,,		,,		,,	
,,		,,		,,		,,		,,		,,		,,		,,	

Date.	Maker's Mark	Date.	Maker's Mark	Date.	Maker's Mark	Date.	Maker's Mark	Date.	Maker's Mark	Date.	Maker's Mark	Date.	Maker's Mark
1684-5		1685-6		1686-7		1688-9		1689-90		1690-1		1692-3	
,,		,,		,,		,,		,,		,,		,,	
,,		,,		,,		,,		,,		,,		,,	
,,		,,		,,		,,		,,		,,		,,	
,,		,,		,,		,,		,,		,,		,,	
,,		,,		,,		,,		,,		,,		,,	
,,		,,		,,		,,		,,		,,		,,	
,,		,,		,,		,,		c. 1690		,,		,,	
,,		,,		,,		,,		1690-1		1691		,,	
,,		,,		,,		,,		,,		,,		,,	
,,		,,		,,		,,		,,		,,		,,	
,,		,,		1687-8		,,		,,		,,		,,	
,,		,,		,,		,,		,,		,,		,,	
,,		,,		,,		,,		,,		,,		,,	
,,		,,		1689-90		,,		,,		,,		,,	
,,		,,		,,		,,		,,		,,		,,	
,,		,,		,,		,,		,,		,,		,,	
,,		,,		,,		,,		,,		,,		1693-4	
,,		,,		,,		,,		,,		,,		,,	
,,		,,		,,		,,		,,		,,		,,	
,,		,,		,,		,,		,,		,,		,,	
,,		,,		,,		,,		,,		,,		,,	
1685-6		1686-7		,,		,,		,,		,,		,,	
,,		,,		,,		,,		,,		1692-3		,,	
,,		,,		,,		,,		,,				,,	
,,													

Date.	Maker's Mark	Date.	Maker's Mark	Date.	Maker's Mark
1693-4	H·P	1695-6	I·S	1696-7	T·B
,,	R	,,	P·M	,,	I·B
,,	T·K	,,	I·H	,,	R·W
,,	E·T	,,	M·B	,,	F·O·H
,,	W·S	,,	W	,,	F
,,	R·M	,,	S	,,	C
,,	I·G	,,	A·G	,,	R·C
1694-5	E·M	,,	M·M	,,	S
,,	S	,,	I·K	,,	T·B
,,	S·T	,,	I·D	c. 1696-8	Ga
,,	A·N	,,	E·S		
,,	R·I	,,	I·S		
,,	P	,,	S·W		
,,	F·H	,,	M·E		
,,	H·B	,,	I·S		
,,	H·V	1696-7	W		
,,	S·I	,,	G·M		
,,	I	,,	I·Z		
,,	I·R	,,	T·O		
,,	T·A	,,	T·B		
,,	M·G	,,	I·C		
,,	W·H	,,	I·Z		
,,	I·F	,,	T·B		
1695-6	R·G	,,	L·I		
,,	H				

Date	Goldsmiths' Marks and Names			Date	Goldsmiths' Marks and Names			Date	Goldsmiths' Marks and Names		
1697	[CO]	Lawrence Coles	ent. 1697	1697	[CH]	Jas. Chadwick	ent. 1697	1697-8	[BI]	Jos. Bird	ent. 1697.
"	[TH]	——— Thriscross	" "	"	[Gi]	Wm. Gibson	" "	"	[DV]	Chas. Overing	" "
"	[RO]	Alexr. Roode	" "	"	[Ba]	Name not traced.		"	[BR]	Thos. Brydon	" "
"	[WE]	Mathew West	" "	"	[AL]	Thos. Allen	" "	"	[IS]	Thos. Issod	" "
"	[ED]	Jas. Edgar	" "	"	[BR]	Moses Brown	" "	"	[PE]	Robt. Peake	" "
"	[M]	Andrew Moore	" "	"	[GA]	Danl. Garnier	" "	"	[SC]	Wm. Scarlett	" "
"	[TO]	Edmd. Townsend	" "	"	[Ash]	Thos. Ash	" "	"	[ST]	Jos. Stokes	" "
"	[WI]	C. Williams	" "	"	[AS]	" "	" "	"	[Ro]	Philip Rolles	" "
"	[MA]	Mathew Madden	" "	"	[AS]	" "	" "	"	[FA]	John Fawdery	" "
"	[Jo]	Lawrence Jones	" "	"	[AR]	Fras. Archbold	" "	"	[AS]	Thos. Ash	" "
"	[FR]	Wm. Francis	" "	"	[BR]	Benj. Bradford	" "	"	[ED]	James Edgar	" "
"	[H]	John Hodson	" "	"	[BA]	Wm. Bainbridge	" "	"	[Sp]	Richard Syngin	" "
"	[IR]	Edward Ironside	" "	"	[SM]	Jno. Smithsend	" "	"	[BI]	Joseph Bird	" "
"	[AS]	? Thos. Ash	" "	"	[WI]	——— Wimans	" "	"	[M]	Andrew Moore	" "
"	[GA]	Geo. Garthorne (probably)	" "	"	[Py]	Benj. Pyne	" "	"	[IS]	Joyce Issod	" "
"	[GA]	Daniel Garnier (see p. 153)	" "	"	[SH]	Jno. Shepherd	" "	"	[DI]	Isaac Dighton	" "
"	[DI]	Isaac Dighton (see p. 155)	" "	"	[HO]	Frances Hoyte	" "	"	[WI]	——— Wimans	" "
"	[GI]	Wm. Gimber	" "	"	[RO]	Hugh Roberts	" "	"	[Ne]	Anthy. Nelme	" "
"	[CO]	Edwd. Courthope	" "	"	[Jo]	Ed. Jones	" "	"	[Co]	Geo. Cox	" 1698
"	[HO]	Sam. Hood	" "	"	[Br]	Wm. Brett	" "	"	[Co]	John Cove	" "
"	[CA]	Christr. Canner	" "	"	[GR]	Dorothy Grant	" "	"	[BV]	Wm Bull	" "
"	[GA]	Fras. Garthorne	" "	"	[Co]	Stephen Coleman	" "	1698-9	[GA]	Geo. Garthorne	" 1697.
"	[PA]	Thos. Parr	" "	"	[BR]	Jno. Brassey	" "	"	[MA]	Wm. Mathew	" "
"	[DB]	Wm. Denny & John Backe }	" "	"	[NI]	Rich. Nightingale	" "	"	[BR]	Jonath'n Bradley	" "
				"	[Ti]	Geo. Titterton	" "	"	[JO]	Edwd. Yorke	" 1705.
				"	[LA]	Jn'th'n Lambe	" "				

Date.	Goldsmiths' Marks and Names.	Date.	Goldsmiths' Marks and Names.	Date.	Goldsmiths' Marks and Names.
1698-9	Henry Collins? ent. 1698.	1699 1700	Fras. Singleton ent. 1697.	1700-1	Phillip Roker ent. 169
,,	Richard Nightingale? ,, 1697.	,,	Sam. Thorne ,, ,,	,,	Mat. Madden ,, ,,
,,	Isaac Dighton ,, ,, (see pp. 152 and 154)	,,	Isaac Davenport ,, ,,	,,	George Lewis ,, 169
,,	Name not traced.	,,	Jno. Chartier ,, 1698.	,,	Henry Aubin ,, 170
,,	,, ,, ,,	,,	Sam Dell ,, 1697.	,,	Rich. Biggs ,, ,,
,,	Jos. Sheene.	,,	Pierre Platel ,, 1699.	,,	Steph. Edmonds ,, ,,
,,	Benj. Bentley ,, 1698.	,,	John Downes? ,, 1697.	,,	Wm. Gossen ,, ,
,,	Wm. Matthew ,, 1697.	,,	Isaac Davenport ,, ,,	,,	Edm. Proctor ,, ,,
,,	Wm. Fawdery ,, 1698.	,,	? Gould.	,,	John Tiffin ,, 170
,,	John Ruslèn ,, 1697.	,,	John Leach ent. 1697.	,,	Alex. Roode? ,, 169
,,	Wm. Scarlett ,, ,,	,,	Joseph Ward ,, ,,	1701-2	Frans. Singleton (see 156).
,,	Jno. Ladyman ,, ,,	,,	John Cory ,, ,,	,,	Ed. Gibson ent. 16
,,	Robt. Cooper ,, ,,	,,	Richd. Syngin ,, ,,	,,	Pierre Harache ,, ,
,,	Lawrence Coles ,, ,,	,,	Andrew Raven ,, ,,	,,	Benj. Watts ,, 16
,,	John Sutton ,, ,,	,,	John Laughton ,, ,,	,,	Sam Hood ,, 16
,,	John Hely ,, 1699.	,,	Alex. Roode ,, ,,	,,	Sam Jefferys ,, ,,
,,	Job Hanks ,, ,,	,,	Philip Oyle ,, 1699.	,,	Henry Green ,, 17
,,	Jno. Porter ,, 1698.	,,	John Broake ,, ,,	,,	Wm. Andrews ,, 16
,,	White Walsh ,, ,,	1700-1	Wm. Fawdery ,, 1700.	,,	Thos. Brydon ,, ,,
,,	Benj. Bentley ,, ,,	,,	Jos. Stokes as 1697.	,,	Wm. Keatt ,, ,,
1699 1700	Wm. Lukin ,, 1699.	,,	Sam Wastell ent. 1701.	,,	Willo'by Masham ,, 17
,,	Benj. Traherne ,, 1687.	,,	Jno. Jackson ,, 1697.	,,	Name not traced.
,,	John Cory ,, 1697.	,,	Name not traced	,,	Wm. Keatt ,, 16
,,	John Diggle ,, ,,	,,	Thos. Jenkins ,, ,,	,,	Sam Hawkes ,,
		,,	David Willaume ,, ,,	,,	Fras. Archbold ,, ,,
		,,	Ralph Leeke ,, ,,	,,	Josh. Field ,, 17

Date.	Goldsmiths' Marks and Names.	Date.	Goldsmiths' Marks and Names.	Date.	Goldsmiths' Marks and Names.
1701-2	John Goode ent. 1700.	1702-3	Jonathan Madden ent. 1702.	1704-5	Thos. Saddler ent. 1701.
"	Ralph Leeke „ 1697.	"	Robt. Lovell „ „	"	Henry Penstone „ 1697.
"	John Danl. Read & Sleamaker } „ 1701.	"	Matt. Cooper „ „	"	Jno. Cole „ „
"	Alexr. Hudson „ „	1703-4	Jno. Rand „ 1704.	"	Jno. East „ „
"	Stepn. Coleman „ 1697.	"	Thos. Jenkins „ 1697.	"	Jno. Gibbon „ 1700.
1702-3	Henry Greene „ 1700.	"	Ed. Gibson „ „	"	Chas. Adam „ 1702.
"	Richd. Syngin „ 1697.	"	Wm. Andrews „ „	"	Geo. Havers „ 1697.
"	John Eckfourd „ 1698.	"	Name not traced.	"	Wm. Middleton „ „
"	Wm. Gamble „ 1697.	"	J. Broake.	"	Alex. Hudson „ 1704.
"	Jonath'n Crutchfield „ „	"	Soane or Soame.	"	Wm. Spring „ 1701.
"	Humph. Payne „ 1701.	"	Jonah Kirke „ „	"	Jno. Cooke „ 1699.
"	Name not traced.	"	Gabl. Player „ 1700.	"	Ishml. Bone „ „
"	Thos. Sadler „ „	"	Saml. Smith „ „	"	Jno. Fletcher „ 1700.
"	Jos. Ward „ 1697.	"	Chas. Williams „ 1697.	1705-6	Robt. Timbrell „ 1697.
"	Jno. Downes „ „	"	Jno. Snelling „ „	"	Wm. Fawdery „ „
"	Jno. Cope „ 1701.	"	Nat. Greene „ 1698.	"	Samuel Pantin „ 1701.
"	Thos. Waterhouse „ 1702.	"	Name not traced.	"	Jon. Madden „ 1702. (see 1702)
"	Wm. Barnes „ „	"	Wm. Warham „ 1703.	"	Isaac Liger „ 1704. (see below)
"	Abm. Russell „ „	"	Wm. Charnelhouse „ „	"	Matthew Pickering „ 1703.
"	Jas. Chadwick as 1697.	"	Andr. Archer „ „	"	Wm. Fleming „ „
"	Matt. Cooper ent. 1702.	"	Thos. Peele „ 1704.	"	Thos. Spackman „ 1700.
"	Hy. Greene „ 1700.	"	Wm. Petley „ 1699.	"	Mathw. Lofthouse „ 1705.
"	Name not traced.	1704-5	Robert Stokes ?	"	Saml. Wastell „ 1701.
"	Henry Aubin, see 1700. (earliest ment. 1700).	"	Wm. Denny „ 1697.	"	Josh. Readshaw „ 1697.
"	? Fraillon.	"	Geo. Lewis „ 1699.	"	Isaac Liger „ 1704.
"	Name not traced.				

LONDON GOLDSMITHS' MARKS

Date.	Goldsmiths' Marks and Names.		Date.	Goldsmiths' Marks and Names.		Date.	Goldsmiths' Marks and Names.	
1705-6	[mark]	Jonah Clifton ent. 1703.	1707-8	[mark]	Pierre Le Cheaube ent. 1707.	1708-9	[mark]	Thos. Wall ent. 1708.
"	[mark]	Jno. Corosey " 1701.	"	[mark]	Richard Hutchinson " 1699.	"	[mark]	Jno. Clifton " "
"	[mark]	Wm. Warham " 1705.	"	[mark]	Philip Roker " 1697.	"	[mark]	Richard Clarke " "
"	[mark]	Thos. Corbet " 1699.	"	[mark]	Benj. Harris " "	"	[mark]	John Chartier " 1698.
"	[mark]	Natl. Lock " 1698.	"	[mark]	Chr. Atkinson " 1707.	1709-10	[mark]	Jno. W. & Edw. Stocker & Peacock } " 1705.
"	[mark]	John Barnard " 1702.	"	[mark]	Phil. Rainaud " "	"	[mark]	Jno. Clifton (?)
1706-7	[mark]	Jos. Barbitt " 1703.	"	[mark]	Thos. Fawler " "	"	[mark]	Thos. Allen " 1697.
"	[mark]	Wm. Matthew " 1700.	"	[mark]	Jos. Smith " "	"	[mark]	Fras. Turner " 1709.
"	[mark]	Wm. Juson " 1704.	"	[mark]	Samuel Lee " 1701.	"	[mark]	Isr'l. Pincking " 1697.
"	[mark]	Timothy Ley " 1697.	"	[mark]	Benj. Pyne " 1697.	"	[mark]	Hy. Greene " 1700.
"	[mark]	John Backe " 1700.	"	[mark]	Saml. Wastell " 1701.	"	[mark]	Laun. Keatt " 1701.
"	[mark]	Launcelot Keatt " 1701.	"	[mark]	John Backe " 1700.	"	[mark]	Jno. Rand " 1704.
"	[mark]	Benj. Pyne " 1697.	1708-9	[mark]	Mary Matthew " "	"	[mark]	Simon Pantin " 1701.
"	[mark]	Jacob Margas " 1706.	"	[mark]	Jos. Bird " 1697.	"	[mark]	Phil. Rolles " 1705
"	[mark]	Jno. Ladyman " 1697.	"	[mark]	Thos. Farren " 1707.	"	[mark]	See 1702.
"	[mark]	Louys Cuny " 1703.	"	[mark]	Philip Rolles, Jr. " 1705.	"	[mark]	Wm. Francis " 1697.
"	[mark]	Jno. Abbot " 1706.	"	[mark]	Wm. Warham " 1703	"	[mark]	Andrw. Dalton " 1708.
"	[mark]	Wm. Spring " 1701.	"	[mark]	Lawrence Jones " 1697.	"	[mark]	Ebenezr. Roe " 1709.
"	[mark]	Jno. Crutcher " 1706.	"	[mark]	Chris. Riley " "	"	[mark]	Thos. Prichard " "
"	[mark]	Wm. Fordham " "	"	[mark]	Alice Sheene " 1700.	"	[mark]	Hen. Clarke " "
"	[mark]	Name not traced.	"	[mark]	Jno. Read " 1704.	"	[mark]	Jas. Wethered " "
1707-8	[mark]	Danl. Sleath " 1704.	"	[mark]	Jno. Bodington " 1697.	"	[mark]	Richd. Watts " 1710.
"	[mark]	Wm. Fleming " 1697.	"	[mark]	Wm. Fawdery " 1698.	1710-1	[mark]	Thos. Folkingham " 1706.
"	[mark]	Thos. Burridge " 1706.	"	[mark]	Henry Greene. " 1700.	"	[mark]	Jno. Smith " 1710.
"	[mark]	John Leach " 1697.	"	[mark]	Anty. Blackford " 1702.	"	[mark]	Wm. Hinton " 1704.
"	[mark]	Anthy. Nelme " "				"	[mark]	Geo. Gillingham " 1703.

Date.	Goldsmiths' Marks and Names.		Date.	Goldsmiths' Marks and Names.		Date.	Goldsmiths' Marks and Names.	
1710-1		Lewis Mettayer ent. 1700.	1711-2		John Porter ent. 1698.	1712-3		Thos. Bevault ent. 1712.
"		Ed. Cornock „ 1707.	"		Richard Williams „ 1712.	"		Jno. M. Stockar „ 1710.
"		Jno. Wisdom „ 1704.	"		Wm. Penstone „ „	1713-4		Samuel Margas „ 1706.
"		Wm. Pearson „ 1710.	"		Ed. Jennings „ 1709.	"		Ambrose Stevenson „ „
"		Wm. Twell „ 1709.	"		Jno. Read „ 1704.	"		Natl. Locke 1698.
"		Jas. Beschefer „ 1704.	"		Lewis Mettayer (probably).	"		Hugh Roberts „ 1697.
"		Jacob Margas . 1706.	"		Nich. Clausen ent. 1709.	"		Gabriel Sleath „ 1706.
"		Jas. Rood „ 1710.	"		Ed. Holaday „ „	"		Mark Paillet „ 1698.
"		Jno. Keigwin „ „	"		Aug. Courtauld „ 1708.	"		Henry Collins „
"		Gabriel Sleath „ 1706.	"		Hen. Greene „ 1700.	"		Edw. Vincent (?)
"		Name not traced.	"		Jno. Chamberlen „ 1704.	"		Jno. Ludlow „ 1713.
"		Jacob Margas „ „	"		Isaac Dalton „ 1711.	"		Gundry Roode „ 1709.
"		Jas. Goodwin „ „	"		Wm. Matthew „ „	"		Thos. Mann „ 1713.
"		Abm. Russell (?) „ 1702.	"		Jonthn. Newton „ „	"		Thos. Ewesdin „ „
"		Robt. Keble „ „	1712-3		Thos. Sutton „ „	"		Wm. Looker „ „
"		Jos. Sheene „ „	"		Jno. Rand „ 1704.	"		John Bathe „ 1700.
"		Jno. Stoskar „ „	"		Seth Lofthouse „ 1697.	"		Wm. Juson „ 1704.
"		Wm. Truss „ „	"		Isaac Dalton „ 1711.	"		Seth Lofthouse „ 1697.
"		Hezk. Mountfort „ 1711.	"		Ed. Gibson „ 1697.	1714-5		Robt. Timbrell & Benj. Bentley } „ „
"		Isaac Malyn „ 1710.	"		Wm. Lukin „ 1699.	"		David Tanqueray „ 1713.
"		Jno. Flight „ „	"		Richd. Bayley „ 1708.	"		Joseph Fainell „ 1710.
1711-2		Edmd. Pearce „ 1704.	"		Richd. Raine „ 1712.	"		Thomas Bevault „ 1712.
"		Dorothy Grant „ 1697.	"		John Hobson „ 1697.	"		Glover Johnson „ „
"		John East „ „	"		Glover Johnson „ 1712.	"		Mich'l Boult „ „
"		Joseph Barbitt „ 1703.	"		Wm. Turbitt „ 1710.	"		Name not traced.
			"		Richd. Williams „ 1712.			

Date.	Goldsmiths' Marks and Names.	Date.	Goldsmiths' Marks and Names.	Date.	Goldsmiths' Marks and Names.
1714-5	Wm. John — England & Vane } ent. 1714.	1715-6	Robt. Hill — ent. 1716.	1717-8	Joseph Ward — ent. 171
,,	Sam Welder — ,, ,,	,,	Thos. Holland — ,, 1707.	,,	Edward Barnet — ,, 171
,,	Rich'd Green — ,, 1703.	1716-7	John Holland — ,, 1711.	,,	Chas. Jackson — ,, 171 (see 1718 below)
,,	Jno. Holland — ,, 1711.	,,	Nat. Roe — ,, 1710.	,,	William Pearson — ,, 171 (see 1716)
,,	Saml. Hitchcock — ,, 1712.	,,	Jos. Clare — ,, 1713.	,,	Isaac Riboulau — ,, 171
,,	Saml. Welder — ,, 1714.	,,	Thos. Mason — ,, 1716.	,,	Edw. Barnet — ,, 171
,,	Philip Brush — ,, 1707.	,,	Paul Lamerie — ,, 1712.	,,	Phil. Robinson — ,, 171
,,	Josiah Daniel — ,, 1714.	,,	Thos. Ewesdin — ,, 1713.	,,	Thos. Holland — ,, 170
,,	Nathl. Bland — ,, ,,	,,	Jas. Seabrook — ,, 1714.	,,	Jno. Harris — ,, 1710
,,	Richd. Gines — ,, ,,	,,	Petley Ley — ,, 1715.	,,	Wm. Street — ,, 171
,,	Henry Beesley — ,, ,,	,,	Phillip Robinson — ,, 1713.	,,	Jas. Smith — ,, 1718
,,	Henry Miller — ,, ,,	,,	Joseph Clare (see above and 1719) ,, ,,	,,	Thos. Shermer — ,, 171
1715-6	Thos. Allen — ,, 1697.	,,	Anty. Nelme — ,, 1697.	,,	Starling Wilford — ,, ,,
,,	David Killmaine — ,, 1715.	,,	Geo. Lambe — ,, 1713.	1717-8	Paul Hanet — ,, ,,
,,	Fras. Plymley — ,, ,,	,,	Wm. Bellassyse — ,, 1716.	,,	Thos. Burridge — ,, ,,
,,	John Corporon — ,, 1716.	,,	David Green — ,, 1701.	,,	Wm. Bellamy — ,, ,,
,,	Danl. Sleamaker — ,, 1704.	,,	Jno. Guerrie — ,, 1717.	,,	Sam. Welder — ,, ,,
,,	Humph. Payne — ,, 1701.	,,	Danl. Cunningham — ,, 1716.	1718-9	Ambrose Stevenson — ,, 1706
,,	Petley Ley — ,, 1715.	,,	Jos. Bell — ,, ,,	,,	Wm. Petley — ,, 171
,,	Thos. Port — ,, 1713.	,,	Richd. Edwards — ,, ,,	,,	Paul Hanet — ,, 1715
,,	Richard Greene — ,, 1703.	,,	Jas. Morson — ,, ,,	,,	John Farnell — ,, 1714
,,	Edward Jones — ,, 1697.	,,	Wm. Pearson — ,, 1717.	,,	Chas. Jackson — ,, ,,
,,	Josiah Daniel (see 1714) — ,, 1714.	1717-8	Jas. (?) Fraillon — ,, 1710.	,,	Thos. Parr — ,, 1697
,,	Jas. Goodwin — ,, 1710.	,,	Robt. Kempton — ,, ,,	,,	Geo. Beale — ,, 1713
,,	Danl. Yerbury — ,, 1715.	,,	Wm. Penstone — ,, 1717.	,,	Ed. Holaday — ,, 1709
,,	Geo. Lambe — ,, 1713.				

TE.	Goldsmiths' Marks and Names.	Date.	Goldsmiths' Marks and Names.	Date.	Goldsmiths' Marks and Names.
	David Tanqueray ent. 1713. (see 1714)	1719-20	John Gibbons ent. 1700.	1719-20	Joseph Fainell ent. 1710.
	Henry Clarke ,, 1709. (see 1709)	,,	Thomas Shermer ,, 1717.	,,	Phyllis Phillip ,, 1720.
	Thomas Mason ,, 1716.	,,	Wm. Darkeratt ,, 1718. (see 1718)	,,	Richard Gines ,, ,,
	Thomas Tearle ,, 1719. (see 1719 below)	,,	Edw. Barrett ,, 1715.	,,	Wm. Scarlett ,, ,, (O.S. as before 1697)
	John Keigwin ,, 1710.	,,	James Smith ,, 1718.	,,	Mary Rood ,, ,,
	John Sanders ,, 1717.	,,	Gabriel Sleath ,, 1706.	1720-1	Christr. Gerrard ,, ,,
	Wm. Fawdery ,, 1697. (as 1705)	,,	Thos. Allen ,, 1697. (2nd Mark)	,,	John Edwards ,, 1697.
	Wm. Darkeratt ,, 1718.	,,	Thos. Morse ,, 1718.	,,	Thos. Evesdon ,, 1713. (see 1721-2)
	Hugh Saunders ,, ,,	,,	Edw. Gibbon ,, 1719.	,,	William Looker ,, ,,
	John Bignell ,, ,,	,,	Saml. Smith ,, ,,	,,	Paul Lamerie ,, 1712.
	Geo. Gillingham ,, ,,	,,	Jos. Steward ,, ,,	,,	Paul Crespin ,, 1720.
	Jno. Millington ,, ,,		Jos. Clare, as 1716-7.	,,	Geo. Lambe ,, 1713. (widow of)
	Jno. Lingard ,, ,,	,,	Chris. Gerrard ent. 1719.	,,	William Fawdery ,, 1720.
	Do. do. (for O.S.) ,, 1719.	,,	Edmd. Hickman ,, ,,	,,	Henry Millar ,, ,,
	Thos. Tearle ,, ,, (see 1718-9)	-20	Wm. Pearson ,, ,,	,,	Thomas Folkingham ,, ,,
	Thos. Langford ,, 1715.		Geo. Brydon ,, 1720.	,,	Petley Ley ,, 1715. (see 1716)
	Réné Hudell ,, 1718.	,,	Thos Gladwin ,, 1719.	,,	John Fawdery ,, 1697.
	Wm. Spackman , 1714.		Starling Wilford ,, 1720.	,,	Matt. Cooper ,, ,,
	Geo. Boothby ,, 1720.		John Lingard ,, 1719.	,,	Ann Tanqueray ,, 1720.
	John White ,, 1719.		John Jones ,, ,,	,,	Chas. Jackson ,, 1714.
	John le Sage ,, 1718.	,,	Paul Hanet ,, 1717.	,,	Sarah Holaday ,, 1719.
	Benj. Blakeley ,, 1715	,,	Edwd. Hall ,, 1720.	,,	Hugh Arnett & } ,, ,, Ed. Pocock }
	Wm. Paradise ,, 1718.		Bowles Nash ,, ,,	,,	Name not traced.
	Lawrence (?) Jones ,, 1697.	,,	——— Hodgkis ,, 1719.	,,	Thos Bamford ,, ,,
		,,	Phyllis Phillip ,, 1720.		

Date.	Goldsmiths' Marks and Names.			Date.	Goldsmiths' Marks and Names.			Date.	Goldsmiths' Marks and Names.		
1720-1	IB	Jno.	Bromley ent. 1720.	1720-1	Fe	Edw.	Feline ent. 1720.	1721-2	SP	Simon	Pantin ent. 171
,,	BW	Benj.	Watts ,, ,,	,,	IS	Jas.	Seabrook ,, ,,	,,	IW	John	Wisdome ,, 172 (probably)
,,	IB	John	Bignell ,, ,,	,,	IS	Jos.	Steward ,, ,,	,,	IL	Jane	Lambe ,, 171
,,	IB	John	Betts ,, ,,	,,	HM	Henry	Miller ,, ,,	,,	Tu	Ed.	Turner ,, 172
,,	MB	Michl.	Boult. ,, ,,	,,	SQ	Geo.	Squire ,, ,,	,,	BV	Abm.	Buteux ,, 172
,,	SH	Saml.	Hitchcock ,, ,,	,,	GS	Gabl.	Sleath ,, ,,	,,	SL	Saml.	Lee ,, ,,
,,	TS	Thos.	Sadler ,, ,,	,,	RO	Phil.	Roker (N.S.) ,, ,,	,,	WI	Geo.	Wickes ,, ,,
,,	GB	Geo.	Boothby ,, ,,	,,	PR	Do.	do. (O.S.) ,, ,,	,,	SP	Hugh	Spring ,, ,,
,,	PR	Phil.	Rolles ,, ,,	,,	GB	Geo.	Brydon ,, ,,	,,	MR	Mary	Rood ,, ,,
,,	HO	Jno.	Hopkins ,, ,,	,,	HG	Hen.	Greene ,, ,,	,,	GR	Gundry	Roode ,, ,,
,,	IH	Do.	do. ,, ,,	,,	EP	Edwd.	Pearce ,, ,,	,,	TR	Wm.	Truss ,, ,,
,,	SW	Saml.	Welder ,, ,,	,,	BR	Jno.	Brumhall ,, 1721.	,,	WT	Do.	do. ,, ,,
,,	JP	*John	Penfold ,, ,, (probably)	,,	IN	Jno.	Newton ,, 1720.	,,	OB	Name not traced.	
,,	FT	Fras.	Turner ,, ,,	,,	WM	Wm.	Matthew ,, ,,	,,	HO	Sarah	Holaday ,, 1719 (see 1720-1)
,,	IM	Jas.	Morson ,, ,,	,,	SL	Saml.	Lee ,, ,,				
,,	IM	Jno.	Millington ,, ,,	,,	HC	Henry	Clarke ,, ,,	,,	BE	Joseph	Bell ? ,, 1716
,,	TF	Thos.	Folkingham ,, ,,	,,	IC	Jno.	Corosey ,, ,,	,,	EV	Thos.	Evesdon ,, 1713 (see 1720-1)
,,	IL	John	Ludlow ,, ,,	,,	IF	Jno.	Farnell ,, ,,	,,	Pe	Edmund Pearce ,, 1720	
,,	TM	Thos.	Mann ,, ,,	,,	GI	Glover	Johnson ,, ,,	,,	SP	Simon	Pantin ,, 1717 (see above)
,,	IE	Ed.	Jennings ,, ,,	,,	WL	Wm.	Looker ,, ,,	1722-3	BN	Bowles	Nash ,, 1721
,,	EI	Do.	do. (O.S.) ,, ,,	,,	PR	Phil.	Rainaud ,, ,,	,,	Fe	Edward	Feline ,, 1720 (see 1720)
,,	RW	Richd.	Watts ,, ,,	1721-2	EV	Ed.	Vincent ,, ,, (probably)	,,	IS	Jno. le	Sage ,, 1718
,,	BB	Name not traced.		,,	IL	Isaac	Liger ,, ,,	,,	WO	Ed.	Wood ,, ,,
,,	IB	J.	Burridge ,, ,,	,,	IA	Henry	Jay ,, ,,	,,		Benj.	Pyne as 1706
,,	BB	Jno.	Barnard ,, ,,	,,	IC	Jos.	Clare ,, ,,	,,	RB	Name not traced.	
,,	AS	A'brose Stevenson ,, ,,		,,	AMEP	M. Arnett &		,,	NE	Anth.	Nelme as 1716
						Ed. Pocock }		,,	EI	Edw.	Jennings ent. 1720

Date	Name	Entered		Date	Name	Entered		Date	Name	Entered
1722-3	Jno. Bignell	ent. 1720.		1722-3	Richard Watts	ent. 1720.		1723-4	John Bignell (see 1720 and 1722)	ent. 1718.
,,	Natl. Gulliver	,, 1722.		,,	Ed. Dymond	,, 1722.		,,	Geo. Squire	,, 1720.
,,	David Willaume	,, 1720.		,,	Jeremiah King	,, 1723.		,,	Thos. Wall (?)	,, 1708.
,,	Jno. Eckford	,, ,,		,,	Do. do.	,, ,,		,,	Arte Dicken? or / John Diggle	,, 1720. / ,, 1697.
,,	Isaac Riboulau	,, ,,		,,	Wm. Soame	,, ,,		,,	John Motherby (?)	,, 1718.
,,	Pere Pilleau	,, ,,		,,	Do. do.	,, ,,		,,	Sam Hitchcock	,, 1712.
,,	Edw. Wood	,, ,,		,,	John Jones	,, ,,		,,	Wm. Fawdery?	,, 1720.
,,	Jas. Gould	,, 1722.		,,	Do. do.	,, ,,		,,	Jnthn. Robinson	,, 1723.
,,	Nich. Clausen	,, 1720.		,,	Henry Dell	,, 1722.		,,	Richd. Edwards	,, ,,
,,	Phil. Robinson	,, 1723.		,,	Wm. Owen	,, 1723.		,,	John Owing	,, 1724.
,,	Phil. Goddard	,, ,,		,,	John Gibbons	,, ,,		,,	John Edwards & / Geo. Pitches	,, 1723.
,,	Do. do.	,, ,,		,,	Meshach Godwin	,, 1722.		1724-5	Richd. Bigge (probably)	,, 1700.
,,	Natl. Gulliver	,, ,,		1723-4	John East	,, 1721.		,,	Richd. Scarlett	,, 1719.
,,	Isaac Cornasseau	,, 1722.		,,	Thos. Farrer	,, 1720.		,,	David Tanqueray	,, 1720.
,,	Do. do.	,, ,,		,,	Thos. Morse	,, ,,		,,	Abm. Buteux	,, 1721.
,,	Michl. Nicholl	,, 1723.		,,	Aug. Courtauld	,, 1708.		,,	Meshach Godwin	, 1722.
,,	John Clarke	,, 1722.		,,	Jnthn. Madden	,, 1702.		,,	Humphy. Payne	,, 1720.
,,	Geo. Young	,, ,,		,,	Edw. Peacock	,, 1710.		,,	Paul Crespin	,, ,,
,,	Jno. Clarke	,, ,,		,,	Richd. Scarlett	,, 1723.		,,	Jacob Margas	,, ,,
,,	Jas. Fraillon	,, 1723		,,	John Chartier	,, ,,		,,	Fleurant David	,, 1724.
,,	Ed. Dymond	,, 1722.		,,	Arte Dicken	,, 1720.		,,	Do. do.	,, ,,
,,	Joseph Adams?	,, ,,		,,	Paul Lamerie	,, 1712.		,,	Mathw. Lofthouse	,, 1721.
,,	John le Sage	,, 1718.		,,	John Jones	,, 1719.		,,	John Edwards	, 1724.
,,	Philip Brush?	,, 1707.		,,	Edw. Gibbons	,, 1723.		,,	Edw. Conen	,,
,,	Isaac Cornasseau	,, 1722.		,,	Wm. Spackman	,, 1720.		,,	John Jones	,, 1723.
				,,	Jnthn. Robinson	,, 1723.		,,	W'sc'mbe Drake	,, 1724.
								,,	John White	,, ,,

Date.	Goldsmiths' Marks and Names.		Date.	Goldsmiths' Marks and Names.		Date.	Goldsmiths' Marks and Names.	
1724-5		Jas. Burne ent. 1724.	1725-6		Jacob Margas ent. 1720. (see 1724)	1726-7		Robt. Lucas ent. 1726 (variant of mark of)
"		Do. do. " "	"		Starling Wilford (?) " " (see 1728 and 1737).	"		Thos. Evesdon " 1713 (see 1720 and 1721)
"		Saml. Hutton " "	"		Edward Feline " " (see also 1722-1729)	"		Fras. Nelme " 1722
"		Do. do. " "	"		John Gibbons " 1723	"		Bern'd. Fletcher " 172
"		Ed. Peacock " "	"		Edw. Vincent " " (see 1729)	"		Thos. Bamford " 172
"		John Owing " "	"		Thos. Mason " 1720.	"		Robt. Williams " 1726
"		Peter Simon " 1725.	"		Jas. Gould " 1722.	"		Do. do. " "
"		John Gibbons " 1723.	"		John Edwards " 1724.	"		Gawen Nash " "
"		Aug. Courtauld " 1708.	"		Geo. Wickes " 1721.	"		Chas. Perier " 172
"		Josiah Daniel " 1714.	"		Thos. Clark " 1725.	"		Do. do. " "
"		Peter Simon " 1725.	"		Thos. England " "	"		Geo. Brome " 172
"		John Motherby " 1718.	"		Wm. Scarlett " "	"		Peter le Chaube " "
"		John Pero " 1717.	"		Peter Tabart " "	1727-8		Isaac Ribouleau " 172
"		Jnthn. Newton " 1718.	"		Do. do. " "	"		* Jas. Smith " "
1725-6		Abm. de Oliveyra " 1725.	"		Mathew Cooper " "	"		Edw. Wood " 172
"		John Eckfourd " "	"		Do. do. " "	"		Ed. Cornock " 170
"		Josh. Healy " "	"		Louis Laroche " "	"		Saml. Bates " 172
"		Do. do. " "	"		John Flavill " 1726.	"		Thomas England " 172
"		Robt. Lucas " 1726.	1726-7		Name not traced.	"		Richard Pargeter " 173
"		Harvey Price " "	"		Wm. Darkeratt " 1724.	"		Matt. Cooper " 172 (see 1725)
"		John Gorsuch " "	"		Richd. Green " 1726.	"		?Andrew Raven " 170
"		Wm. Toone " 1725.	"		Benj. Pyne (as before 1697).	"		Jno. le Sage " 172
"		Jos. Bird " 1724.	"		Peter Archambo ent. 1722.	"		Name not traced.
"		Hugh Saunders " 1718.	"		Wm. Fawdery " 1720.	"		Sarah Holaday " 172
"		Paul Hanet " 1721.	"		Wm. Atkinson " 1725.	"		John East " 172
"		Fras. Garthorne " "				"		Jonah Clifton " 172

DATE.	Goldsmiths' Marks and Names.	DATE.	Goldsmiths' Marks and Names.	DATE.	Goldsmiths' Marks and Names.
27-8	Saml. Laundry ent. 1727.	1727-8	Saml. Green ent. 1721.	1729-30	Anthony Nelme ent. 1722.
,,	Edmd. Bodington ,, ,,	,,	Wm. Shaw ,, 1728.	,,	Chas. Martin ,, 1729.
,,	Chas. Kandler & Jas. Murray ,, ,,	1728-9	Wm. Darkeratt ,, 1720.	,,	Edwd. Feline ,, 1720. (see 1722 and 1725)
,,	Do. do. ,, ,,	,,	James Goodwin ,, 1721.	,,	Abel Brokesby ,, 1727. (see 1727)
,,	Edw. Bennett ,, ,,	,,	Tim. Ley (as before 1697)	,,	Simon Pantin ,, 1717. (see 1728)
,,	Hester Fawdery ,, ,,	,,	Blanche Fraillon ent. 1727.	,,	George Jones ,, 1724. (see 1735-6)
,,	Thos. Cooke ,, ,,	,,	Isaac Callard ,, 1726.	,,	Name not traced.
,,	Richd. Hutchinson ,, ,,	,,	Name not traced.	,,	Paul Lamerie ,, ,,
,,	Chas. Kandler ,, ,,	,,	James Wilkes ,, 1722.	,,	Ralph Maidman ,, 1730.
,,	Geo. Weir ,, ,,	,,	Peter Archambo ,, 1720.	,,	Richd. Scarlett ,, 1720. (see 1723)
,,	Do. do. ,, ,,	,,	Josh. Holland ,, ,,	,,	Name not traced.
,,	Name not traced. ,,	,,	Simon Pantin (see 1729) ,, ,,	,,	John Jones ,, 1729.
,,	Abel Brokesby ,, ,,	,,	John Millington ,, 1728.	,,	Saml. Margas ,, 1720.
,,	Dike Impey (probably) ,, ,,	,,	Edward Bennett ,, 1727.	,,	Chas. Alchorne ,, 1729.
,,	Benj. Bentley ,, 1728.	,,	Ralph Frith ,, 1728.	,,	Sam. Welder ,, ,,
,,	Mary Johnson ,, 1727.	,,	Do. do. ,, ,,	,,	Benj. Goodwin ,, ,,
,,	I. Wichaller ,, 1728.	,,	Geo. Hodges ,, ,,	,,	Name not traced.
,,	Chas. Hatfield ,, 1727.	,,	Do. do. ,, ,,	,,	Edith Fletcher ,, ,,
,,	Sam. Laundry ,, ,,	,,	John Fawdery ,, ,,	,,	Eliz. Goodwin ,, ,,
,,	Matw. Cooper ,, 1725.	,,	John Montgomery ,, ,,	,,	Jas. Maitland ,, 1728. of the "Grasshopper," Suffolk Street.
,,	David Willaume ,, 1728.	,,	? John Richardson ,, 1723.	,,	Aug. Courtauld ent. 1729.
,,	Danl. Cunningham ,, 1720.	,,	? Wm. Fordham ,, 1706.	,,	Paul Lamerie ,, 1712.
,,	Richd. Gines ,, ,,	,,	Starling Wilford (see 1725 and 1737) ,, 1729.	1730-1	Saml. Jefferys ,, 1697.
,,	Geo. Gillingham ,, 1721.	1729-30	John Tuite * ,, 1721.	,,	Gabl. Sleath ,, 1720.
,,	Chas. Hatfield ,, 1727.	,,	Thos. Tearle ,, 1720.	,,	
,,	Jacob Foster ,, 1726.	,,	Ed. Vincent (see 1725) ,, ,,	,,	

Date	Goldsmiths' Marks and Names	Date	Goldsmiths' Marks and Names	Date	Goldsmiths' Marks and Names
1730-1	Richd. Bayley ent. 1720.	1731-2	Sarah Parr ent. 1720.	1733-4	Aug. Courtauld ent. 1729
,,	Wm. Belassyse ,, 1723.	,,	Robt. Geo. Abercromby & Hindmarsh ,, 1731.	,,	Jas. Slater ,, 1732
,,	Isaac Callard ,, 1726.	,,	Wm. Woodward ,, ,,	,,	Richd. Bayley ,, 1720
,,	Wm. Petley ,, 1720.	,,	Thos. Causton ,, 1730.	,,	* Henry Herbert (of the "Three Crowns") ,, 1734
,,	Perè Pilleau ,, ,,	,,	Etienne Rongent ,, 1731.	,,	Wm. Soame ,, 1732
,,	Chas. Kandler ,, 1727.	,,	Wm. Darker (see 1731) ,, ,,	,,	Eliz. Buteux ,, 1731
,,	John White ,, 1719.	1732-3	Richd. Beale ,, ,,	,,	Danl. Chapman ,, 1729
,,	Anne Tanqueray ,, 1720.	,,	Sam Jeffy Laundry & Griffith ,, ,,	,,	Lewis Pantin ,, 1733
,,	? Saml. Laundry ,, 1727. (see also 1727)	,,	Joseph Smith ,, 1728.	,,	Chas. Sprage ,, 1734
,,	John Chapman ,, 1730. (see 1737)	,,	Edw. Pocock ,, ,,	,,	Robt. Abercromby ,, 1731 (see 1734)
,,	Samuel Hitchcock ,, ,,	,,	John Sanders ,, 1720.	,,	Geo. Braithwaite ? earliest ment. 1728.
,,	Jas. Jenkins ,, 1731.	,,	John Fawdery (see 1728) ,, 1728.	1734-5	Ralph Maidman ent. 1731.
,,	Wm. Justus ,, ,,	,,	Fras. Pages ,, 1729.	,,	Caleb Hill ,, 1728.
,,	Wm. Reeve ,, ,,	,,	? Matt. Lofthouse ,, 1705.	,,	Lewis Mettayer ,, 1720.
,,	Aaron Bates ,, 1730.	,,	Name not traced.	,,	Wm. Gould ,, 1732
,,	Aug. Courtauld ,, 1708.	,,	Wm. Lukin ,, 1725.	,,	Robt. Abercromby ,, 1731. (see 1733)
1731-2	John Gamon ,, 1728.	,,	Fras. Spilsbury ,, 1729. (same mark found in square stamp).	,,	John Newton ,, 1726.
,,	Edwd. Yorke ,, 1730.	,,	Thos. Parr ent. 1732.	,,	Mary Pantin ,, 1733
,,	Geo. Hindmarsh ,, 1731.	,,	Wm. Matthews ,, 1728.	,,	Richd. Pargeter ,, 1730.
,,	David Willaume ,, 1728.	,,	Jas. Savage ,, ,,	,,	Hugh Arnell ,, 1734
,,	Wm. Darker ,, 1731.	,,	John Pero ,, 1732.	,,	Alex. Edw. Coates & French ,, ,,
,,	Thos. England ,, 1725.	,,	Jas. Gould ,, ,,	,,	John Taylor ,, ,,
,,	Jane Lambe ,, 1729.	,,	Geo. Smith R. W. (as 1696).	,,	Wm. Gould ,, ,,
,,	Mary Lofthouse ,, 1731.	,,	Wm. Soame ,, ,,	,,	John Jacob ,, ,,
,,	Thos. Merry ,, ,,	,,	Chas. Gibbons ,, ,,	,,	John Pollock ,, ,,
,,	Jeffrey Griffith ,, ,,	,,	Wm. Shaw ,, 1728.	,,	Jas. Manners ,, ,,
		1733-4	John Eckfourd, jr. ,, 1725.		

First column group

	Mark	Goldsmiths' Marks and Names			Date
4·5	EF	Edw.	French	ent. 1734.	1736-7
	IB	Jas.	Brooker	" "	"
	SH	Sam.	Hutton	" "	"
	WK	Wm.	Kidney	" "	"
5-6	G·I	Geo.	Jones	" 1724.	"
	T·G R·C	Richd. Thos.	Gurney & Cook }	" 1734.	"
	EB	Edw.	Bennett	" 1731.	"
	KA	Fred	Kandler	" 1735.	"
	B·G	Benj.	Godfrey (see 1739)	" 1732.	"
	GE	Grif.	Edwards	" "	"
	WS	Wm.	Shaw	" 1727.	"
	PB	Peter	Bennett	" 1731.	"
	IW	John	White	" 1724.	"
	AT	Wm.	Atkinson	" 1725.	1737-8
	WY	Wm.	Young	" 1735.	
	EI	Name not traced, (see 1729-30)			"
	FN	Francis Nelme		" "	"
	I·B	John	Barbe	" "	"
	GH	Geo	Hindmarsh	" "	"
	CH	Christn.	Hilland	" 1736.	"
	D·L	Name not traced			"
	H·H	Henry	Herbert (of the "Three Crowns")	" 1734.	"
	LH	Lewis	Hamon	" 1735.	"
6-7	NY	Name not traced.			"
	WG	Wm.	Garrard	" 1735.	"
	SW	Sam.	Wood	" 1733-7.	"

Second column group

Mark	Goldsmiths' Marks and Names			Date
BW	Benj.	West	ent. 1737.	1737-8
RB	Robt.	Brown	" 1736.	"
AH	Ann	Hill	" 1734.	"
TM	Thos.	Mason	" 1733.	"
JJ	John	Jones	" "	"
I·F	John	Fossey	" / "	"
B·T	Bennet R.	Bradshaw & Tyrill }	" 1737.	"
IK	Jerem.	King	" 1736.	"
TM	Thos.	Mann	" "	"
DH	David	Hennell	" "	"
BW	Benj.	West	" 1737.	1738-9
H·H	Henry	Herbert	" 1734.	"
HP	? Harvey	Price	" 1726.	"
LA MF	Joseph	Allen & Co.	" 1729.	"
GW	Geo.	Weekes	" 1735.	"
JS	Jos.	Sanders	" 1730.	"
SB	Saml.	Blackborrow	" 1720.	"
TW	Thos.	Whipham	" 1737.	"
G·H	Geo.	Hindmarsh (see 1735-6)	" 1735.	"
S·W	Starling	Wilford	" 1729.	"
IC	John	Chapman (see 1730)	" 1730.	"
R·W	Robt.	Williams	" 1726.	"
RB	Richd.	Beale	" 1731.	"
S·I	Simon	Jouet	" 1723.	1739-40
T·I	Thos.	Jackson	" 1736.	"
TG	Thos.	Gladwin	" 1737.	"

Third column group

Mark	Goldsmiths' Marks and Names		
IB	John	Barrett	ent. 1737.
GB	Geo.	Baskerville	" 1738.
PP	Philip	Platel	" 1737.
I·I	Jas.	Jenkins	" 1738.
GR	Gundry Roode		" 1737.
IR	John)	Robinson	" 1738.
I·S	Jas.	Schruder	" 1737.
WS	Wm.	Soame	" 1738.
SW	Sam.	Wood	" 1737.
DW	Denis	Wilks	., "
R·Z	Richd.	Zouch	" 1735.
IW	Thos.	Whipham	" 1739
FK	Fred	Kandler	" 1735.
I·R	Jno.	Robinson	" 1738.
L·D	Louis	Dupont	" 1736.
T·R	Thos.	Rush	" 1724.
BB	Benj.	Blakeley	., 1738.
HB	Henry	Bates	" "
PB	Philip	Brugier	. "
WW	Wm.	West	" "
FP	Fras.	Pages	" 1739.
RH	Robt.	Hill	" "
IL	James	Langlois	" 1738.
FK	Fred	Kandler	" 1735.
RB	? Richd. Bayler		" 1739.
IP	John	Pero (see 1732)	" "

Date.	Goldsmiths' Marks and Names.*	Date.	Goldsmiths' Marks and Names.	Date.	Goldsmiths' Marks and Names.
1739-40	Humphrey Payne ent. 1739.	1739-40	Thos. England ent. 1739.	1739-40	Jessie McFarlane ent. 1739
,,	Sarah Holaday ,, 1719.	,,	Robt. Lucas ,, ,,	,,	Wm. Justus ,, ,,
,,	Benj. Godfrey ,, 1732. (see 1735)	,,	Ben. Godfrey ,, ,,	,,	Wm. Young ,, ,,
,,	Thos. Whipham ,, 1737.	,,	Do. do. ,, ,,	,,	Jas. Manners ,, ,,
,,	Chas. Hillan ,, 1741.	,,	Gawen Nash ,, ,,	,,	John Harvey ,, ,,
,,	Wm. Kidney ,, 1739.	,,	John Bryan ,, ,,	,,	Chas. Jackson ,, ,,
..	Paul Lamerie ,, ,,	,,	Richard Beale ,, ,,	,,	Thos. Rush ,, ,,
,,	Ben. Blakeley ,, ,,	,,	John Cam ,, 1740.	,,	Thos. Gilpin ,, ,,
,,	Isaac Callerd ,, ,,	,,	J. Barbitt ,, 1739.	,,	Danl. Chartier ,, 1740
,,	Jeff. Griffith ,, ,,	,,	Richd. Pargeter ,, ,,	,,	Wm. Shaw ,, 1739
,,	Thos. Tearle ,, ,,	,,	Marmdk. Daintry ,, ,,	,,	Richd. Gosling ,, ,,
,,	Jnthn. Fossy ,, ,,	,,	Ed. Bennett ,, ,,	,,	Fras. Spilsbury ‡ ,, ,,
,,	Paul Crespin ,, ,,	,,	Do. do. ,, ,,	,,	Louis Hamon ,, ,,
,,	John Harwood ,, ,,	,,	Bennett Bradshaw & Co. ,, ,,	,,	Sam. Hutton ,, 1740
,,	Richd. Bayley ,, ,,	,,	Thos. Bamford ,, ,,	,,	John Gamon ,, 1739
,,	Robt. Abercromby ,, ,,	,,	John Eckford ,, ,,	,,	Fras. Nelme ,, ,,
,,	Lewis Dupont ,, ,,	,,	Wm. Shaw ,, ,,	,,	Henry Morris ,, ,,
,,	Wm. Hunter ,, ,,	,,	John Jacobs (see 1750) ,, ,,	,,	Thos. Pye ,, ,,
,,	Wm. Gwillim ,, ,,	,,	John Pero (see p. 190) ,, ,,	,,	Jas. West ,, ,,
,,	Geo. Boothby ,, ,,	,,	John White ,, ,,	,,	Jas. Paltro ,, ,,
,,	Edw. Aldridge ,, ,,	,,	Henry Herbert ,, ,,	,,	John Harwood ,, ,,
,,	Wm. Soame ,, ,,	,,	Richd. Zouch ,, ,,	,,	Denis Wilks ,, ,,
,,	Peter Bennett ,, ,,	,,	Susan'h Hatfield ,, ,,	,,	Philip Roker ,, ,,
,,	Henry Bates ,, ,,	,,	J. McFarlane ,, ,,	,,	Simon Jouet ,, ,,
,,	John Tuite ,, ,,	,,	Henry Morris ,, ,,	,,	Chas. Clark ,, ,,
			John Luff ,, ,,	,,	John le Sage ,, ,,

Date.	Goldsmiths' Marks and Names.	Date.	Goldsmiths' Marks and Names.	Date.	Goldsmiths' Marks and Names.
9-40	BS — Benj. Sanders ent. 1739.	1740-1	JO — ? John Owing ent. 1724.	1742-3	PC — Paul Crespin ent. 1739.
	AO — Abm. de Oliveyra ,, ,,		RC (bird) — Name not traced.	,,	JA MF — Jos. Allen & M'decai Fox } ,, ,,
	TM — Thos. Mason ,, ,,	,,	CS — Do. do.	,,	RB — Robt. Brown ,, ,,
	CM — Chas. Martin ,, 1740.	,,	JR — John Roker ,, 1740.	,,	FS — Fras. Spilsbury ,, ,,
	JS — Jos. Steward ,, 1739.	,,	AL — Abm. le Francis ,, ,,	,,	ET — Eliz. Tuite ,, 1741.
	GS — Geo. Smith ,, ,,	,,	BG — Benj. Gurdon ,, ,,	,,	AC JN — Anne Craig & John . Neville } ,, 1740. (see 1745)
	LL — Louis Laroche ,, ,,	,,	DH — David Hennell ,, 1739.	,,	SW — Saml. Wells ,, ,,
0-1	JR — John Robinson ,, ,,	1741-2	JS — James Shruder ,, ,,	,,	RA — Robt. Abercromby ,, 1739.
	GE — Griff. Edwards ,, ,,	,,	EG — Eliza Godfrey ,, 1741.	,,	JM — Jas. Montgomery ,, 1742.
	JP — John Pollock ,, ,,	,,	SR — Saml. Roby ,, 1740.	,,	IT — Jos. Timberlake ,, 1743.
	IS — Jos. Sanders ,, ,,	,,	GW — Geo. Wickes ,, 1739.	,,	PG — Phillips Garden ,, 1739.
	BS — Benj. Sanders ,, 1737.	,,	TF — Thos. Farren ,, ,,	,,	CR — Paul Crespin ,, ,,
	WG — Wm. Garrard , 1735.	,,	DG — Dinah Gamon ,, 1740.	,,	IC — John Cam ,, 1740.
	GS — Gabl. Sleath ,, ,,	,,	JN — John Newton ,, 1739.	1743-4	DW — Dd. Williams ,, 1739.
	RG&Co — Richd. Gurney & Co ,, 1739.	,,	TG — Thos Gilpin ,, ,,	,,	BS — Benj. Sanders ,, ,,
	EW — Ed. Wood ,, 1740.	,,	CH — Chas Hillan ,, 1741.	,,	RA — ? Robt. Abercromby ,, ,,
	CB — Chas Bellassyse ,, ,,	,,	JS — John Stewart (?)	,,	WH — Wm. Hunter ,, ,,
	SH — Sarah Hutton ,, ,,	,,	PA — Peter Archambo ,, 1739.	,,	WG — Wm. Gould ,, ,,
	EL — Ed. Lambe ,, ,,	,,	JW — Jas. Willmott ,, 1741.	,,	JW — Jas. Wilks ,, ,,
	TM — Thos. Mercer ,, ,,	,,	IS — John Spackman ,, ,,	,,	EF — Ed. Feline ,, ,,
	JB — John Barbe ,, 1739.	,,	CL — Chas Laughton ,, 1739.	,,	AC — Aug. Courtauld ,, ,,
	GR — Paul Crespin ,, 1740.	,,	TL — Thos Lawrence ,, 1742.	,,	GJ — Geo. Jones ,, ,,
	IP — Isabel Pero ,, ,,	,,	JK — Jer'mi'h King ,, 1739.	,,	JA — Jer'mi'h Ashley ,, 1740.
	LO — Lewis Ouvry ,, ,,	,,	BG — Benj. Gurdon ,, 1740.	,,	HB — Henry Brind ,, 1742.
	IG — Jas. Gould ,, 1741.	,,	RT — Robt. Tyrrill ,, 1742.	,,	RA — Robt. Abercromby ,, 1739.
arl	EA — Edwd. Aldridge ,, 1739. (see 1744)	1742-3	JG — Jno. Gould ,, 1739.	,,	PP — Pere Pilleau ,, ,,

Date.	Goldsmiths' Marks and Names.			Date.	Goldsmiths' Marks and Names.			Date.	Goldsmiths' Marks and Names.		
1743-4	TW	Thos.	Whipham ent. 1737.	1744-5	IM	Jas.	Morrison ent. 1740.	1746-7	ES	Ernest	Sieber ent. 1746.
"		Name not traced.		1745-6	BW	Benj.	West „ 1739.	"	GY	Geo.	Young „ „
"	ID	Isaac	Duke „ 1743.	"	TW WW	Thos. Wm.	Whipham & Williams } „ 1740.	"	SM	Saml.	Meriton „ „
"	EM	Ed.	Malluson „ „	"	AC IN	Ann John	Craig & Neville } (see 1742) „ „	"	HH	Henry	Herbert „ 1747.
"	GM	Geo	Methuen „ „	"	IH	John	Holland „ 1739.	"	HH	Do.	do. „ „
"	CI	Chas.	Johnson „ „	"	BC	Ben.	Cartwright „ „	"	SJ	Simon	Jouet „ „
"	AF	Ann	Farren „ „	"	FK	Fred.	Kandler „ „	"	BC	Benj.	Cartwright „ 1739.
"	GR	Geo.	Ridout „ „	"	WC	Wm.	Cripps „ 1743.	1747-8	IS	Jno.	Sanders „ „
"	R·S	Robt.	Swanson „ „	"	FC	Fras.	Crump „ 1741.	"	WG	Wm.	Gould „ „
1744-5	W.S	Wm. Wm.	Soame or „ 1723. } Shaw „ 1727.	"	IH	John	Higginbotham „ 1745.	"	RK	Richd.	Kersill „ 1744.
"	EA	Edwd.	Aldridge „ 1739. (see 1740)	"	GB	Geo.	Baskerville „ „	"	WW	Wm.	Williams „ 1742.
"	EF	Ed.	Feline „ „	"	IM	Jas.	Manners, Jr. „ „	"	S·C	Saml.	Courtauld „ 1746. (see 1750).
"	LP	Lewis	Pantin „ „	"	IK	? Jer'mi'h King „ „		"	IOM	Jacob	Marsh „ 1744.
"	Rp	Robt.	Pilkington „ „	"	IS	John	Swift „ 1739. (probably, see 1754-5)	"	ITC	Thos.	Carlton „ „
"	CH	Chas.	Hatfield „ „	"	IK	Sam	Key „ 1745.	"	I·E	? John	Eckfourd „ 1739.
"	PA	Peter	Archambo „ „	"	RA	Robt.	Andrews „ „	"	BG	? Benj. Benj.	Griffin or „ 1742. Gignac „ 1744.
"	J2	John	Quantock „ „	"	IH	John	Harvey „ „	"	IR	John	Richardson „ 1743.
"	AV	Aymé	Videau „ „	1746-7	SW	Sam	Wood „ 1739.	"	IP	Thos.	Parr „ 1739.
"	JB	John	Barbe „ „	"	IG	Jas.	Gould „ 1743.	"	MD	M'duke	Daintry „ „
"	IE	John	Edwards „ „	"	WH	Wm.	Hunter „ 1739.	"	WS	Wm	Solomon „ 1747.
"	WB	Wm	Bagnall „ 1744.	"	WP	Wm.	Peaston „ 1746.	"	SH	Saml.	Herbert „ „
"	P·C G	Wm Peter	Gwillim & Castle } „ „	"	IM	Jas.	Morrison „ 1744.	"	I·F	John	Fray „ 1748.
"	JS	Jas.	Smith „ „	"	HM	Henry	Morris „ 1739.	"	B·C	Ben.	Cooper „ „
"	INe	John	Neville „ 1745.	"	IB	Jos.	Barker „ 1746.	1748-9	EM	Edwd.	Medlycott „ „
"	FI	Thos.	Jackson „ 1739.	"	EV	Ed.	Vincent „ 1739.	"	IW	John	Wirgman „ 1745.
"	NS	Nich's	Sprimont „ 1742.	"	AK	Ann	Kersill „ 1747.	"	HP	Hmphy.	Payne „ 1739. (see 1739)
								"	EC	Elias	Cachart „ 1742.

Date.	Goldsmiths' Marks and Names.	Date.	Goldsmiths' Marks and Names.	Date.	Goldsmiths' Marks and Names.
1748-9	M'decai Fox — ent. 1746.	1749-50	Geo. Bindon — ent. 1749.	1750-1	John Berthelot — ent. 1750.
"	Wm. Grundy " 1748.	"	Thos. Mann " 1739.	"	L'r'nce Johnson " 1751.
"	John Carman " "	"	John Alderhead " 1750.	"	Phillips Garden " "
"	Geo. Young " 1746.	"	Jas. Tookey " "	"	Math. Brodier " "
"	John Barbe " 1739.	"	Wm. Wooler " "	"	Fras. Crump " 1750.
"	Geo. Hunter " 1748.	"	Geo. Morris " "	"	Do. do. " "
"	Phillips Garden " "	"	Thos. Jeannes " "	c. 1750-60	Name not traced.
"	Wm. Shaw " 1749.	1750-1	John Priest " 1748.	1751-2	? John Wetherell " 1743.
"	Eliz. Hartley " 1748.	"	Chas. Chesterman " 1741.	"	John Payne " 1750.
"	Eliz. Jackson " "	"	Eben. Coker " 1739.	"	Denis Wilks " 1747.
"	Eliz. Oldfield " "	"	John Rowe " 1749.	"	Fred Knopfell " 1752.
"	Ed. Dowdall " "	"	Richd. Gurney & Co. " 1750.	"	Saml. Taylor " 1744.
"	Danl. Shaw " "	"	S. Herbert & Co. " "	"	P. Werritzer " 1750.
"	Walter Brind " 1749.	"	Louis Guichard " 1748.	"	Thos. Moore " "
1749-50	Wm. Grundy " 1743.	"	Geo. Campar " 1749.	"	Wm. Woodward " 1743.
"	Dan. Piers " 1746.	"	Fuller White & John Fray } " 1750.	"	G. & S. Smith " 1751.
"	Benj. Cartwright " 1739.	"	Henry Bayley " "	"	Geo. Morris " "
"	Paul Crespin " "	"	John Jacobs " 1739. (see 1739)	"	Nicks Winkins " "
"	Name not traced.	"	Saml. Courtauld " 1746. (see 1747 and 1755)	"	Paul Pinard " "
"	Jerem'h King " "	"	Paul Lamerie " 1732. (see 1729 and 1730)	"	Ed. Doweal " "
"	Abm. Portal " 1749.	"	A. Montgomery " 1750.	"	Thos. Beere " "
"	Abm. le Francis " 1746.	"	Michl. Ward " "	"	Phil. Bruguier " 1752.
"	Jabez Daniel " 1749.	"	Geo. Bindon " 1749.	1752-3	Robt. Cox " "
"	Wm. MacKenzie " 1748.	"	John Harvey " 1750.	"	Lewis Haman " 1739.
"	Wm. Kersill " 1749.	"	Thos. Smith " "	"	Robt. Cox " 1752. (see above)
"	Andrew Killick " "			"	Wm. Alexander " 1742.
"	Henry Haynes " "			"	John Payne " 1751.

Date.	Mark	Goldsmiths' Names.	Date.	Mark	Goldsmiths' Names.	Date.	Mark	Goldsmiths' Names.
1752-3	WH	Wm. Homer ent. 1750.	1753-4	TR	Thos. Rowe ent. 1753.	1755-6	WS	Wm. Sanden ent. 1755.
,,	W·WS·P	Wm. Shaw & / Wm. Priest } ,, 1749.	,,	SS	Saml. Smith ,, 1754.	,,	LS	Simon Le Sage ,, 1754.
,,	JB	John Berthelot ,, 1741.	,,	LL	Simon Le Sage ,, ,,	,,	MF	Magd'n Feline ,, 1753.
,,	JR	John Richardson ,, 1752.	,,	HC	Henry Corry ,, ,,	,,	TW	? Thos. Wright ,, 1754.
,,	DP	Danl. Piers ,, 1746.	,,	BC	* Benj. Cartwright ,, ,,	,,	S·C	Saml. Courtauld ,, 1746. (see 1750)
,,	CC	Chas. Chesterman ,, 1752.	,,	SB	Sarah Buttall ,, ,,	,,	PC	Paul Crespin ,, 1739. (see 1749)
,,	I·C	John Carman ,, ,,	1754-5	P·A·P·M	Peter Archambo & / Peter Meure } ,, 1749.	,,	W·B·I·P	Wm. Bond & / John Phipps } ,, 1754.
,·	RG	Richd. Goldwire ,, 1753.	,,	RP	? Robt. Perth.	,,	WT	Wm. Turner ,, ,,
,,	PG	Phillips Garden ,, 1751.	,,	WC	Wm. Cripps ,, 1743.	,·	WB	Wm. Bond ,, 1753.
1753-4	GH	Geo. Hunter ,, 1748.	,,	IQ	John Quantock ,, 1754.	,,	JJ	Jas. Jones ,, 1755.
,,	DP	Danl. Piers ,, ,,	,,	I·A·S	Ed. Aldridge & / John Stamper } ,, 1753.	,,	PT	Peter Taylor ,, 1740.
,,	T&W	Turner & Williams ,, 1753.	,,	PG	Phillips Garden ,, ,,	,,	FV	Fred Vonham ,, 1752.
,,	R·G	Richd. Gosling ,, 1739.	,,	IM	John Munns ,, ,,	,,	SS	Saml. Siervent ,, 1755.
,,	RH	Robt. Hennell ,, 1753.	,,	DM	Do'thy Mills ,, 1752.	,,	J·W	John Wirgman ,, 1745.
,·	JC	John Cafe ,, 1742.	,,	JH	John Holland ,, 1739.	,,	RM	Richd. Mills ,, 1755.
,,	AJ	Alex. Johnston ,, 1747.	,,	IS	John Steward ,, 1755.	,,	BB	Benj: Brewood ,, ,,
,,	FW	Fuller White ,, 1744.	,,	TC	Thos. Collier ,, 1754.	,,	ED	Ed. Doweal ,, 1751.
,,	DW·IF	Denis Wilks & / John Fray } ,, 1753.	,,	HD	Henry Dutton ,, ,,	,,	RCox	Robt. Cox ,, 1755.
,,	WB	Wm. Bond ,, ,,	,,	W·B	Walter Brind ,, 1749.	,,	R·G	Do. do. ,, ,,
,,	TT	Thos. Towman ,, ,,	,,	GB·WS	Geo. Baskerville & / Wm. Sampel } ,, 1755.	,,	TB	Thos. Beezley ,, ,,
,,	I·E	John Edwards ,, ,,	,,	DPW	Dobson Prior / & Williams } ,, ,,	,,	AS	Albert Schurman ,, 1756.
,,	G·S·C	Gabl. Sleath & / Fras. Crump } ,, ,,	,,	D	John Delmester ,, ,,	,,	JR	John Robinson ,, 1739.
,,	DCF	D. C Fueter ,, ,,	,,	W·I	? Wm. Justus ,, 1739.	1756-7	SW	Saml. Wheat ,, 1756.
,·	DS	Dorothy Sarbit ,, ,,	,,	IS	John Swift (see 1745 and below) ,, ,,	,,	P·G	Pierre Gillois ,, 1754.
,,	EA	Edward Aldridge ,, 1743. (see 1740 and 1744)	,,	HM	Henry Miller ent. 1740.	,,	WR	Wm. Robertson ,, 1753
,,	E·I·S·A	Edwd. Aldridge & / John Stamper } ,, 1753.	1755-6	IS	John Swift ,, 1739.	,,	WC	Wm. Caldecott ,, 1756

Date.	Goldsmiths' Marks and Names.			Date.	Goldsmiths' Marks and Names.		
1756-7		? Thos.	Gilpin	ent. 1739.	1757-8		John	Schuppe	ent. 1753.
,,		Thos.	Heming	,, 1745.	,,		Wm.	Cafe	,, 1757.
,,		Name not traced.			1758-9		Fras.	Nelme	,, 1722.
,,		Mathew	Roker	,, 1755.	,,		Saml.	Taylor	,, 1744.
,,		Paul	Callard	,, 1751.	,,		Wm.	Cripps	,, 1743.
,,		John	Edwards	,, 1753.	,,		Name not traced.	
,,		Wm.	Gould	,, ,,	,,		Wm. Shaw & Wm. Priest	} ,, 1749.
,,		T. & W.	Devonshire Watkins	} ,, 1756.	,,		Name not traced.	
,,		Ben.	Cartwright	,, ,,	,,		John	Hague	,, 1758.
,,		Edw.	Jay	,, 1757.	,,		Wm.	Bell	,, 1759.
1757-8		David	Hennell	,, 1736.	,,		Lewis Francis	Herne & Butty	} ,, 1757.
,,		Joseph	Clare (see 1716)	,, 1713.	,,		Jos.	Bell	,, 1756.
,,		Eliza	Godfrey	,, 1741.	,,		Name not traced.	
,,		John	Jacobs	,, 1739.	1759-60		S.	Herbert & Co.	,, 1750.
,,		W. & R. Peaston		,, 1756.	,,		Fred.	Kandler	,, 1739.
,,		Ed.	Darvill	,, 1757.	,,		John	Delmester	,, 1755.
,,		Robert	Innes	,. 1742.	,,		John	Perry	,, 1757.
,,		Stephen Ardesoif		,, 1756.	,,		Saml.	Wood, 2nd mk.	,, 1739.
,,		Ed.	Bennett	,. 1739.	,,		Geo.	Ibbott	,, 1753.
,,		John Thos.	Kentenber & Groves	} 1757	,,		John	Perry	,, 1757.
,,		John	Frost	,, ,,	,,		Simon	Le Sage	,, 1754.
,,		Do.	do.	,, ,,	,,		? Walter Brind		,, 1749.
,,		John Chas.	Hyatt & Semore	} ,, ,,	,,		Wm.	Cripps	,, 1743.
,,		Arthur	Annesley (see 1761)	,, 1758.	,,		John	Hyatt	,, 1748.
,,		Robt.	Burton	,, ,,	,,		Henry	Bayley (probably).

DATE.		GOLDSMITHS' MARKS AND NAMES.	DATE.		GOLDSMITHS' MARKS AND NAMES.	DATE.		GOLDSMITHS' MARKS AND NAMES.
1759-60		? Saml. Wheat ent. 1756.	1761-2		John Horsley.	1763-4		Danl. Smith & Robt. Sharp }
,,		Stephen Abdy & Wm. Jury } ,, 1759.	,,		John Gorham ent. 1757.	,,		T. & W. Chawner (probably).
,,		Alex. Barnett ,, ,,	,,		Arthur Annesley ,, 1758. (see 1757)	,,		Ebenezer Coker ,,
,,		Thos. Congreve ,, 1756.	,,		Geo. Hunter ,, 1748.	,,		Phil. Vincent ent. 1757
,,		Thos. Doxsey ,, ,,	,,		Magdalen Feline ,, 1753.	,,		Wm. King ,, 1761
,,		Wm. Moody ,, ,,	,,		Thomas Heming ,, 1745. (see 1756)	,,		John Buckett.
,,		Wm. Day ,, 1759.	,,		Mary Piers ,, 1758.	,,		John Aspinshaw ,, 1763
,,		Saml. Eaton ,, ,,	,,		Thos. Powell ,, ,,	,,		John Lamfert ,, 1748
,,		? Jno. Kentenber	1762-3		Jas. Jones ,, 1755.	c. 1763-4		Name not traced.
1760-1		Robt. Rew ,, 1754.	,,		Wm. Tant ,, 1773. (probably)	,,		Do. do.
,,		Edwd. Wakelin ,, 1747.	,,		Wm. Sampel ,, 1755.	1764-5		D. & R. Hennell ,, 1768
,,		Name not traced.	,,		Louis Black ,, 1761.	,,		? Thos. Hannam Rich. Mills }
,,		Fuller White ,, 1758.	,,		Thos. Whipham & Cnas. Wright } ,, 1757.	,,		Name not traced.
,,		Alex. Saunders ,, 1757.	,,		Geo. Ibbott ,, 1753.	,,		W. & R. Peaston (probably).
,,		John Moore ,, 1758.	,,		Saml. Delamy ,, 1762.	,,		Names not traced.
,,		C'nst'ne Teulings ,, 1755.	,,		W. & J. Deane ,, ,,	,,		John Hyatt & C. Semore } ent. 1757
,,		Wm. Howard ,, 1760.	,,		Jos. Bell ,, 1756.	,,		Aug. Le Sage ,, 1767
,,		Geo. Methuen ,, 1743.	,,		Edwd. Aldridge & Co.	,,		Thos. Freeman & J. Marshall } ,, 1764
,,		John Eaton ,, 1760.	,,		Wm. Day ,, 1759.	,,		Anthy. Calame ,, ,,
c. 1760-1		Name not traced.	,,		Wm. Watkins ,, 1756.	,,		J. A. Calame ,, ,,
,,		Jeremy Lee ,, 1739.	,,		Edward Aldridge ,, 1739.	,,		John Innocent (probably).
1761-2		Richd. Rugg ,, 1754.	,,		R Peaston ,, 1756.	,,		W. & R. Peaston ,, (see above)
,,		Wm. Plummer ,, 1755.	1763-4		Richd. Thomas ,, 1755.	,,		Wm. Cafe ent. 1757
,,		Louis Herne & Fras. Butty } ,, 1757.	,,		Tmpsn. Davis ,, 1757.	,,		Name not traced.
,,		Fras. Butty & Nicks. Dumee } ,, ,,	,,		Edward Aldridge ,, 1739.	,,		Do. do.
,,		Wm. Shaw ,, 1749.	,,		Thos. Whipham & Chas. Wright } ,, 1758.	,,		Thos. Whipham & Chas. Wright } ,, 1758

DATE.	GOLDSMITHS' MARKS AND NAMES.	DATE.	GOLDSMITHS' MARKS AND NAMES.	DATE.	GOLDSMITHS' MARKS AND NAMES.
1765-6	Names not traced.	1767-8	Thos. Bumfries & Orlando Jackson } ent. 1766.	1769-70	John Kentenber ent. 1757.
"	Do. do.	"	S. Herbert & Co. " 1750.	"	Aug. Le Sage " 1767.
"	Wm. Caldecott ent. 1756.	"	Name not traced.	"	Edwd. Lowe " 1777.
"	Eben. Coker (probably).	"	Wm. Abdy " 1767.	"	Walter Brind " 1757.
"	Name not traced.	"	Geo. Fayle " "	"	Wm. Grundy " 1748.
"	Emick Romer "	"	Wm. Tuite (probably).	"	Septimus & James Crespell }
"	Name not traced.	"	Name not traced.	"	Thos. Jackson " 1769.
"	? R. Peaston.	1768-9	John Parker & Edwd. Wakelin }	"	Louisa Courtauld & Geo. Cowles. }
"	John Allen ent. 1761.	"	James Hunt ent. 1760.	"	Robt. Rogers " 1773.
"	Sam. Howland " 1760.	"	T. & W. Chawner (probably).	"	John Baker " 1770.
"	Geo. Hunter " 1765.	"	Dan. Smith & Robt. Sharp }	1770-1	Benj. Gignac " 1744.
"	T. & W. Chawner (probably).	"	Name not traced.	"	Thos. Heming " "
1766-7	Name not traced.	"	Fras. Spilsbury, Jr.	"	Jas. Allen " 1766.
"	Louisa Courtauld.	"	? Eliz. Tuite ent. 1741. (see 1742)	"	Septimus & James Crespell } see 1769.
"	John Lampfert ent. 1748.	"	Name not traced.	"	? Thos. Powell ent. 1756.
"	John Langford & John Sebille }	"	Edward Capper (probably).	"	Thos. Arnold " 1770.
"	Matthew Ferris " 1759.	"	Fras. Crump ent. 1756.	"	John Baxter " 1773.
"	Thos. Hannam & John Crouch }	"	W. & J. Priest.	"	Chas. Wright.
"	Fras. Crump " 1756.	"	John Lamfert " 1748.	"	? John Buckett " 1770.
"	Geo. Andrews " 1763.	"	Benj. Blakeley " 1739.	"	John Langford & John Sebille }
"	Thos. Dealtry " 1765.	"	John Darwall " 1768.	"	Name not traced.
"	Chas. Miegg " 1767.	1769-70	John Neville (probably).	"	E. Romer (probably).
"	Dorothy Mills (probably).	"	Chas. Aldridge & Henry Green }	"	Orlando Jackson ent. 1759.
"	Thos. Wynne ent. 1754.	"	Fras. Crump ent. 1756.	"	Sam. Wheat " 1756.
1767-8	Jno. Richardson " 1752.	"	Geo. Seatoun.	"	John Gimblett & Wm. Vale } " 1770.
"	Names not traced.	"	Chas. Woodward.	"	J. Bassingwhite " "
				1771-2	John Crouch & Thos. Hannam }

Date.	Goldsmiths' Marks and Names.		Date.	Goldsmiths' Marks and Names.		Date.	Goldsmiths' Marks and Names.	
1771-2	TF	Thos. Foster ent. 1769.	1772-3	HH	Henry Hallsworth.	1774-5	PF	P. Freeman ent. 1774.
,,	DB	David Bell ,, 1756.	,,	A·F	Name not traced.	,,	WF	Wm. Fennell.
,,	I·S	? Robt. & Jno. Schofield } ,, 1776.	,,	I·F	John Fayle ent. 1772.	,,	IY	Jas. Young 1775·
,,	T·D D	Thos. & Jabez Daniel }	,,	WE	Wm. Eley (probably).	,,	IS	Jas. Stamp ,, 1774.
,,	S·B	? Sarah Buttall ,, 1754.	1773-4	R·S D·S	Dan. Smith & Robt. Sharp } ent. before 1773.	1775-6	W·T	Walter Tweedie ent. before 1773.
,,	JA	Jonathan Alleine.	,,	OI	Orlando Jackson ,, 1759.	,,	E C	? Ed. Capper (see 1776.)
,,	WP	Wm. Penstone.	,,	IH	John Harvey ,, 1739.	,,	W C	? Wm. Cox.
,,	W·S	Wm. Sheen ,, 1755.	,,	TS	Thos. Smith ,, 1750.	,,	IK	? John Kentish Jas. King or Jas. Kingman } ent. 1773·
,,	T·C	Thos. Chawner.	,,	LV	Name not traced.	,,	WS RC	Wm. Sumner & Richd. Crossley } ,, 1775·
,,	S·H	Saml. Howland ,, 1760.	,,	AB LD	Abr'm Barrier & Lewis Ducornieu }	,,	IY	Jas. Young ,, ,,
,,	AU	A. Underwood.	,,	WS	Wm. Sheen ,, 1775.	,,	TL	Thos. Langford (probably).
,,	CC	Chas. Chesterman ,, 1771.	,,	T·D J·D	Jabez & Thos. Daniel } see 1771.	,,	I·E W·F	? John Easton & Wm. Fearn or Wm. Fennell, etc. }
,,	EI	Edwd. Jay ,, 1757.	,,	BD	Burrage Davenport.	,,	RR	Robt. Ross ent. 1774·
,,	T·T	Thos. Towman (probably).	,,	SW	Saml. Wood (probably).	,,	MC	Mark Cripps ,, 1767.
,,	WT	Wm. Tuite ent. 1756.	,,	PF	P. Freeman ent. 1773.	,,	CW	Chris. Woods ,, 1775.
,,	IR	John Romer ent before 1773.	,,	MM	Mary Makemeid ,, ,,	,,	RR	Richd. Rugg ,, ,,
1772-3	I·C	John Carter ,, ,,	,,	TT	Thos. Tookey ,, ,,	,,	RI	Robt. Jones ,, 1776.
,,	TC	Thos. Chawner ,, ,,	,,	LD	Louis de Lisle ,, ,,	,,	T·G B·M	Geo. Baskerville & T Morley } ,, 1775.
,,	ET	Eliz Tookey ,, ,,	,,	WLB	Wm. Le Bas ,, ,,	,,	RP	Robt. Piercy ,, ,,
,,	WF	Wm. Fearn ,, ,,	1774-5	IS	Jas. Stamp ,, 1774.	,,	LD	Louis Ducomieu
,,	BD	Burrage Davenport ,, ,,	,,	WP	Wm. Penstone ,, ,,	,,	BS	Ben Stephenson ,, ,,
,,	I·A	John Arnell ,, ,,	,,	ET	Eliz. Tookey ,, 1773.	1776-7	CH	Name not traced.
,,	J·S	John Swift ,, ,,	,,	T·E	Thos. Evans ,, 1774.	,,	HS	Henry Sardet,
,,	P·N	Philip Norman ,, ,,	,,	IY OI	Jas. Young & Orlando Jackson } ,, ,,	,,	RP	Robt. Piercy ,, ,,
,,	CW	Chas. Wright ,, ,,	,,	I·D	John Deacon ,, 1773.	,,	AB	Alexr. Barnet ,, 1759.
,,	P·D	Peter Desergnes or Peter Devese. }	,,	TD	Thomas Daniel (probably).	,,	N·D	Nich. Dumee ,, 1776.
,,	Wa	? Wm. Watkins ,, 1756.				,,	W·C G·H	Geo. Heming & Wm. Chawner } ,, 1774.

Date.	Goldsmiths' Marks and Names.		Date.	Goldsmiths' Marks and Names.		Date.	Goldsmiths' Marks and Names.	
776-7	I·L	John Lautier ent. 1773	1778-9	NH	Nichs. Hearnden ent. 1773.	1780-1	H·P	Name not traced.
"	LW WT	John Wakelin & Wm. Taylor } " 1776.	"	ED	Ed. Dobson " 1778.	"	I·P	Joseph Preedy.
"	HCAG	Chas. Aldridge & Henry Green } " 1775.	"	RC DS RS	Rich. Carter, Danl. Smith & Robt. Sharp } " "	"	I·K	John Kidder ent. 1780.
"	A·C	A. Calame " 1764.	"	WE GP	Wm. Eley & Geo. Pierpoint } " 1778.	1781-2	TP AH	T. B. Pratt & Arthur Humphreys } " 1773.
"	EC	Edwd. Capper or Edwd. Cooke } " 1773.	"	I·D	John Deacon " 1776.	"	C·W	Chas. Wright " 1775.
"	A·L	Aug. Le Sage " 1767.	"	CK	Chas. Kandler " 1778.	"	RC	Robt. Cruickshank " 1773.
"	P·R	Phil. Roker " 1776.	"	EL	Ed. Lowe " 1777.	"	IC TH	John Crouch & Thos. Hannam } " "
"	E·R	Eliz. Roker " "	"	GR	Geo. Rodenbostel " 1778.	"	I·L	Josh. Lejeune " "
777-8	HG	Henry Greenway " 1775.	"	TW	Thos. Wallis " 1773.	"	LK	Luke Kendall " 1772.
"	JA	Jon'th'n Alleine.	1779-80	I·S	John Schofield " 1778.	"	GH WC	Geo. Heming & Wm. Chawner } " 1781.
"	RM RC	Robt. Makepeace & Richd. Carter } " 1777.	"	EF d	Edith Fennell " 1780.	"	WP WW	Wm. Playfair & Wm. Wilson } " 1782.
"	I·H	Joseph Heriot " 1750.	"	WGHC	Geo. Heming & Wm. Chawner } " 1774. (see also 1781)	"	TD IW	Thos. Daniel & John Wall } " 1781.
"	WH	Wm. Holmes " 1776.	"	HB	Hester Bateman " 1774.	1782-3	GS	Geo. Smith " 1782.
"	WP	Wm. Potter " 1777.	"	T·S	Thos. Satchwell " 1773.	"	IW	John Wren " 1777.
"	WH WC	Wm. Howe & Wm. Clark } " "	"	TP RP	Thos. & Richd. Payne } " 1777.	"	GG	George Giles (probably).
"	WG	Wm. Grundy " "	"	WF	W. L. Foster " 1775.	"	AF SG	Andr. Fogelberg & Steph. Gilbert } ent. 1780.
"	GN	Geo. Natter " 1773.	"	EWGF	Wm. Grundy & Ed. Fernell } " 1779.	"	RH	Robt. Hennell " 1773.
"	RI IS	Robt. Jones & John Schofield } " 1776.	"	LC SC	Louisa & Samuel Courtauld } " 1777.	"	WB	Wm. Bayley.
"	GN	Name not traced.	"	FS	Fras. Stamp " 1780.	"	NAA	This mark is A N S A. Name not traced.
"	TD	T. Daniel " 1774.	1780-1	WG	Wm. Garrard (probably).	"	AP PP	Abm. Peterson & Peter Podie } " 1783.
778-9	HCAG	Name not traced.	"	RJDM	Jane Dorrell & Rich. May } ent. 1771.	1783-4	I·L	John Lamb " "
"	AF	Andrew Fogelberg.	"	I·S	Jas. Sutton " 1780.	"	IS IB	Jas. Sutton & Jos. Bult } " 1782.
"	JD	J. Denzilow.	"	WV	Wm. Vincent " 1773.	"	WT	Wm. Tant " 1773.
"	W·E	Wm. Eley.	"	IM WH	Jas. Mince & Wm. Hodgkins } " 1780.	"	W·B	Wm. Brown (probably).
"	HB	Hester Bateman. " 1774.	"	TB AH	T. P. Boulton & Arthur Humphreys } " "	"	SB	? Saml. Bradley.
"	WH ND	Wm. Holmes & Nichs. Dumee } " 1773.	"	IL IR	John Langlands & John Robertson } " " of Newcastle	"	A·F SG	Name not traced.

Date.	Goldsmiths' Marks and Names.		Date.	Goldsmiths' Marks and Names.		Date.	Goldsmiths' Marks and Names.	
1783-4	E·F	Ed. Fennell ent. 1780.	1786-7	SG/EW	Saml. & Edwd. Godbehere Wigan } ent. 1786.	1789-90	TW	Thos. Willmore ent. »
„	SW	Saml. Wintle „ 1783.	„	TP·AH	T. Arth. Pratt & Humphreys } „ 1780.	„	PC	Name not traced.
„	WS	Wm. Sumner „ 1782.	„	W·S	Wm. Sutton „ 1784.	1790-1	P·P	Peter Podie „ »
„	(script)	Name not traced.	„	WR	Wm. Reynolds „ 1773.	„	TP/ER	T. E. Phipps & Robinson }
„	IT	John Townshend „ 1783.	„		Robt. Hennell as 1782.	„	GS/WF	Geo. Wm. Smith & Fearn } „ »
„	TC	Thos. Chawner „ 1773.	„	HC	Henry Chawner ent. 1786.	„	RH	Robt. Hennell
„	IT	John Tayleur „ 1775.	„	GG	Name not traced.	„	PB/IB	Peter & Jonath'n Bateman } „ »
„	IS	John Schofield „ 1778.	„	CA	Chas. Aldridge „ 1786.	„	SD	Saml. Davenport „ »
1784-5	LI	Name not traced.	„	TD	Thos. Daniel „ 1774.	„	WA	Wm. Abdy
„	BM	Do. do.	„	DD	Danl. Denny „ 1782.	„	AP	Abm. Peterson
„	CH	Chas. Hougham „ 1785.	„	WP	Wm. Pitts „ 1786.	1791-2	WP/JP	Wm. Jos. Pitts & Preedy }
„	HG	Hen. Greenway „ 1775.	1787-8	SM	Saml. Massey (probably).	„	GB	Geo. Baskerville (proba...
„	SA	Stephen Adams „ 1760.	„	JH	Name not traced.	„	GS	Geo. Smith ent. »
„	SG	Saml. Godbehère „ 1784.	„	WE	Wm. Eley.	„	RS	Robt. Salmon »
„	WS	Wm. Simmons „ 1776.	„	T·M	Thos. Mallison ent. 1773.	„	WF/DP	Wm. Danl. Fountain & Pontifex } „ »
„	PG	Peter Gillois „ 1782.	„	DS/RS	Danl. Robt. Smith & Sharp } „ 1780.	„	IB/EB	Jas. & Eliz. Bland } „ »
„	RI	Robt. Jones „ 1778.	1788-9	EI	Edwd. Jay „ 1773.	„	JL	John Lamb „ »
1785-6	WA	Wm. Abdy „ 1784.	„	IC	John Carter before „	„	TS	Thos. Streetin „ »
„	I·MF	Name not traced.	„	IP	Tho Powell, probably 1770.	„	EB	Name not traced.
„	HV	Do. do.	„	GB	Geo Baskerville (probably).	„	SG/RW	Do. do.
„	B·L	Ben. Laver „ 1781.	„	HC	Henry Cowper ent 1782.	1792-3	W·L	Do. do.
„	W·T	Walter Tweedie „ 1775.	„	CB	Cornls. Bland „ 1788.	„	WP/IP	Wm. Jos. Pitts & Preedy (see above
„	TW	Thos. Wallis „ 1778.	„	TO	Thos. Ollivant „ 1789.	„	HC	Henry Chawner ent. »
„	TD	Thos. Daniel „ 1774.	1789-90	HB	Hester Bateman „ 1774.	„	TH	Thos. Howell „ »
„	I·K	John Kidder „ 1780.	„	HG	Henry Greenway „ 1775.	„	TN	Thos. Northcote.
„	TS	Thos. Shepherd „ 1785.	„	IT	John Thompson „ 1785.	„	GS/TH	Geo. Thos. Smith & Hayter } ent.
„	A·B	Abm. Barrier „ 1775.	„	I·Æ	John Edwards „ 1788.			

Date	Mark	Name	Note
792-3	WF PS	Wm. Paul. Frisbee & Storr	ent. 1792
"	IF	John Fountain	" "
"	TG	Thos. Graham	" "
"	EI	Edwd. Jay	" "
793-4	IW RG	J. Robt. Wakelin & Garrard	" "
"	IM	John Moore	" 1778
"	IS	John Schofield	" "
"	PB AB	Peter & Ann Bateman	" 1791
"	RM TM	Robt. & Thos. Makepeace	" 1794
"	DU NH	Duncan Urquhart & Naphtäli Hart	" 1791
"	IF IB	John Fountain & John Beadnall	" 1793
"	WF IF	Wm. & John Fisher	" "
794-5	WF	Wm. Frisbee	" 1792
"	IK	John King	" 1785
"	MB	? Mark Bock (see 1798)	
"	FT	? Francis Thurkle	
"	IR	John Robins	ent. 1774
"	JW	John Wren	" 1777
"	MP	Michl. Plummer	" 1791
"	WF	W. Fountain	" 1794
"	TN GB	Thos. Northcote & Geo. Bourne	" "
795-6	RG	Richd. Gardner or Robt. Gaze	" 1773 " 1795
"	TE	Thos. Ellis	" 1780
"	RM	Robt. Makepeace	" 1795
"	PB AB	Peter & Ann Bateman	" 1791
"	TP AH	T. B. Pratt & Arthur Humphreys	" 1780
"	WE	Wm. Eley	

Date	Mark	Name	Note
1795-6	SH	Name not traced	
"	IP IP	J. & J. Perkins	ent. 1795
"	HN	Henry Nutting	" 1796
1796-7	SP	Name not traced	
"	RH DH	Robt. & David Hennell	" 1795
"	IM	John Mewburn	" 1793
"	IBO	Jos. B. Orme	" 1796
"	WEH	Wm. Hall	" 1795
"	HC IE	Hy. Chawner & Jno. Eames	" 1796
1797-8	RC	Richd. Crossley	" 1782
"	HC IE	Henry Chawner & John Emes	" 1796
"	GC	Geo. Cowles	" 1797
1798-9	EM	E. Morley	
"	IP	Jos. Preedy	" 1777
"	IB	John Beldon	" 1784
"	WE WF	Wm. Eley & Wm. Fearn	" 1797
"	GS	Geo. Smith	
"	IH TL	Jos. Hardy & Thos. Lowndes	" 1798
"	M·B	? Mark Bock	
"	JE	John Emes	
"	TD	Thos. Dealtry	" 1765
1799/1800	WP	Wm. Pitts	" 1781
"	WB	Wm. Bennett	" 1796
"	WP	Wm. Pitts	" 1799
"	RC	Richd. Cooke	" "
"	AF	Andrew Fogelberg	" 1776
"	IH	John Hutson	" 1784
"	WS	Name not traced	

Date	Mark	Name	Note
1799/1800	IP	Jos. Preedy	ent. 1800
1800-1	PS	Paul Storr	" 1793
"	IW RG	J. Robt. Wakelin & Garrard	" 1792
"	WH	Wm. Hall	" 1795
"	SG EW IB	Saml. Godbehere, Ed Wigan & J. Bult	" 1800
"	TH IC	Thos. Hannam & John Crouch	" 1799
1801-2	RG	Robt. Garrard	" 1801
"	I·P	John Parker	
"	JE	John Emes	" 1796
"	PB AB WB	Peter, Ann & Wm. Bateman	" 18co
"	GS TH	Geo. Thos. Smith & Hayter	" 1792
"	RH DH SH	Robert, David & Saml. Hennell	
1802-3	IH	John Harris	" 1786
"	DS BS	Digby Scott & Benj. Smith	" 1802
"	HB	Wm. Burwash	" "
"	PB AB WB	Peter, Ann & Wm. Bateman	" 1800
"	AB GB	Alice & George Burrows	" 1802
"	CB TB	Christr. & T. W. Barker	" 1800
1803-4	B·L	Benj. Laver	" 1781
"	TH	Thos. Holland	" 1798
"	GB TB	G. & T. Burrows	
"	SG W	Saml. & George Whitford	" 1802
"	AJ	Name not traced	
"	IR	John Robins (probably)	
"	TR	? Timothy Renou	
"	JA	John Austin	
1804-5	W·P	Wm. Purse	

Date.	Goldsmiths' Marks and Names.	Date.	Goldsmiths' Marks and Names.	Date.	Goldsmiths' Marks and Names.
1804-5	**S·B** Name not traced.	1808-9	**TM** ? T. W. Matthews.	1812-3	**TB** ? T. Barker.
"	**RB&R** Rundell, Bridge & Rundell.	"	**I·C** John Crouch ent. 1808.	"	**JS** ? John Sanders.
"	**GW** Geo. Wintle ent. 1804.	"	**E·M** E. Morley.	"	**TI** Thos. Jenkinson (probably).
"	**RG** Robt. Garrard " 1802.	"	**WE WF WC** Wm. Eley, Wm. Fearn & Wm. Chawner } " "	"	**RE EB** Rebecca Emes & Edwd. Barnard } ent. 1808.
"	**I·H** Jos. Hardy " 1799.	"	**HN RH** Henry Nutting & Robt. Hennell } " "	"	**GS** Geo. Smith " 1812.
"	**HN** Hannah Northcote " 1798.	"	**RC GS** Richard Crossley & Geo. Smith } " 1807.	"	**MS ES** Mary & Eliz. Sumner " 1809.
1805-6	**DP** Danl. Pontifex " 1794.	"	**W·S** Wm. Sumner " 1802.	1813-4	**IC WR** Jos. Craddock & Wm. Reid } " 1812.
"	**J·E** John Emes.	"	**JC** John Crouch " 1808.	"	**P·S** BRITANNIA Paul Storr " 1793.
"	**TA** ? T. Ash.	1809-10	**CH** Chas. Hougham " 1785.	"	**IWS WE** J. W. Story & W. Elliott } " 1809.
"	**W·B R·S** Wm. Burwash & Richd. Sibley } " 1805.	"	**TW** Thos. Wallis " 1792.	1814-5	**SH** Saml. Hennell " 1811.
"	**TS** Name not traced.	"	**DW** David Windsor (probably).	"	**RE EB** Emes & Barnard " 1808.
1806-7	**RH SH** R. & S. Hennell " 1802.	"	**TJ** Thomas Jenkinson "	"	**SA** Stephen Adams, junr.
"	**PB WB** Peter & Wm. Bateman " 1805.	"	**SJ** Name not traced.	"	**W·B** Wm. Bell (probably).
"	**JS** John Sanders (probably).	1810-1	**TH SH** Do. do.	"	**W·E** Wm. Elliott ent. 1810.
"	**CF** Crespin Fuller "	"	**RC** ? Richd. Cooke ent. 1799.	"	**IL WA** Name not traced.
"	**IS** John Salkeld "	"	**BS IS** Benj. Smith & Jas. Smith. }	"	**SH IT** S. Hennell & J. Taylor } (probably).
"	**T·R** Thos. Robins "	"	**TP ER** T Phipps & E. Robinson }	1815-6	**TP ER JP** Name not traced.
"	**WF** Wm. Fountain ent. 1794.	"	**SB IB** Name not traced.	"	**JE EF** Do. do.
1807-8	**TG IC** T. & J. Guest & Josh. Cradock } " 1806.	"	**TW JH** Thos. Wallis & Jonath'n Hayne } " 1810.	"	**I·P G·P** Do. do.
"	**PB WB** P. & W. Bateman " 1805.	"	**IC TH** John Cotton & Thos. Head } " 1809.	"	Emes & Barnard as above.
"	**SW** Saml. Whitford " 1807.	"	**JB** James Beebe " 1811.	"	**RG** Robt Garrard ent. 1801.
"	**T·H** Thos. Halford " "	1811-2	**BS** Benj. & Jas. Smith.	"	**CR DR** Christ'n Reid & ano'r of Newcastle " 1815.
"	**BS** Name not traced.	"	**WK** Wm. Kingdon (probably).	1816-7	**WB** Wm. Burwash " 1813.
"	**TR** T Robins " "	"	**RR** Robt. Rutland ent. 1811.	"	**IL** Jas. Lloyd.
"	**IWS** ? J. W. Storey.	"	**SH** Saml. Hennell " "	1817-8	**S SR ILD** Name not traced.
1808-9	**I·C** John Crouch " 1808.	"	**DS BS IS** Digby Scott, Benj. Smith, Jas. Smith } (probably).		
"	**RE WE** Name not traced.				

Date.	Goldsmiths' Marks and Names.	Date.	Goldsmiths' Marks and Names.	Date.	Goldsmiths' Marks and Names.
1817-8	WB Wm. Bateman ent. 1815.	1823-4	I·B John Bridge ent. 1823.	1830-1	T·D Thos. Dexter (probably).
,,	M·S Name not traced.	,,	ES Benj. Smith.	,,	RA WS Name not traced.
,,	WC Wm. Chawner ,, ,,	1824-5	TH GH Thos. & Geo. Hayter ,, 1816.	1831-2	W·H ,, ,,
,,	TR T. Robins (probably).	,,	SC Name not traced.	,,	R·H R. Hennell.
,,	WC Wm. Chawner ent. 1815.	,,	R·H Robt. Hennell.	1833-4	PS Paul Storr ent. 1793.
,,	GP Geo. Purse.	,,	FB Name not traced.	,,	AS JS AS Adey, Joseph & Albert } Savory ,, 1833.
1818-9	GW Geo. Wintle ,, 1813.	,,	WE CE IE Do. do.	1834-5	N·M N. Morrison (probably).
,,	IW Joseph Wilson.	,,	G·K Geo. Knight (probably).	,,	I·F Jas. Franklin ,,
,,	RG Robt. Garrard ,, 1801.	,,	WE Wm. Edwards (,,).	,,	WB W. Bellchambers ,,
1819-20	SR ID Name not traced.	1825-6	TC James Collins (,,).	,,	RP CP Name not traced.
,,	A·H Do. do.	,,	IB John Bridge ent. 1823.	,,	T·E T. Eley.
,,	HN Henry Nutting ,, 1809.	,,	RP R. Peppin (probably).	1835-6	CF Chas. Fox ent. 1822.
,,	WS Wm. Stevenson (probably).	,,	C·E C. Eley (,,).	,,	JCE J. Chas. Edington ,, 1828.
,,	TI See 1812-3 above.	,,	FH Fras. Higgins (,,).	,,	CR GS Reily & Storer (probably).
,,	PR Philip Rundell ent. 1819.	1826-7	IL HL CL John, Henry & Chas. } Lias ent. 1823.	1836-7	CF See 1835-6.
1820-1	WB Wm. Bateman ,, 1815.	,,	A·B·S A. B. Savory ,, 1826.	,,	EB EB IW WB Edwd. Barnard, Edwd. Barnard, jr., John Barnard & Wm. Barnard } ent. 1829.
,,	IL HL John & Henry Lias ,, 1819.	,,	RC Randall Chatterton ,, 1825.	1837-8	WE Wm. Eaton.
1821-2	TB Thos. Baker ,, 1815. or Thos. Balliston ,, 1819.	1827-8	BP Name not traced.	,,	RS Richard Sibley (probably).
,,	IET ? J. E. Terry & Co. ,, 1818.	,,	T·C·S T. Cox Savory ,, 1827.	,,	GW George Webb ,,
,,	ICF ? John Foligno.	,,	JW Jacob Wintle ,, 1826.	,,	RG Robert Garrard ent. 1821.
,,	CoCo An Exeter maker (probably).	,,	ME Moses Emmanuel (probably).	,,	MC Mary Chawner.
,,	JA IA J. & J. Aldous ,,	1828-9	WS Wm. Schofield (,,).	1838-9	WT RA Wm. Theobalds & Robt. Atkinson. } ,, 1838.
1822-3	PS Paul Storr ,,	,,	ES E. S. Sampson (,,).	,,	CR GS Rawlins & Sumner.
,,	WA William Abdy ,,	1829-30	JH Jas. Hobbs (,,).	1839-40	WB DB Wm. Bateman & Danl. Ball } ,, 1839.
,,	WT Wm. Trayes ent. 1822.	,,	EE Edward Edwards.	,,	FD Francis Dexter ,, ,,
1823-4	IS Name not traced.	,,	RG Robt. Garrard ent. 1801.	,,	WC Wm. Cooper (probably).
,,	JA John Angell (probably).	1830-1	C·P Chas. Plumley (probably).	,,	I·T Jos. Taylor ,,

Date.	Marks & Names		Date.	Marks & Names		Date.	Marks & Names	
1839-40	EE	Ed. Edwards (probably).	1847-8	EE	Eliz. Eaton.	1864-5	EKR	
1840-1	GL	Name not traced.	1848-9	EJ BW	E. J. & W. Barnard. }	1865-6	IJK	I. J. Keith.
"	TC	Thos. Cording "	"	RH	R. Hennell.	"	R·H	Richd. Hennell.
"	GA	Geo. W. Adams ent. 1840.	"	JW	Jacob Wintle (probably).	1866-7	GE GF	
"	JA JA	J. & J. Aldous.*	1849-50	CTF GF	Chas. T. Fox & Geo. Fox }	1867-8	GM HD	Macaire & Dewar.
"	MC GA	Mary Chawner & Geo. W. Adams } " "	"	F D	Frans. Douglas.	"	ML HL	
1841-2	JS AS	Jos. & Albert Savory " "	"	WRS	W. R. Smily.	1868-9	AS	
"	J·L	John John Lacy or Law } (probably).	1850-1	IK	John Keith.	"	CSH	Chas. Stuart Harris.
1842-3	JCE	J. Chas. Edington ent. 1828.	"	GI	George Ivory.	1869-70	J EBW J	J., E., W., & J. Barnard.
"	R·H	R. Hennell.	1851-2	EB JB	E. & J. Barnard.	1870-1	WS	Wm. Smiley.
"	WB WS	Brown & Somersall (probably).	1852-3	JE	James Edwards (probably).	1871-2	HE W	H. E. Willis.
1843-4	W·K·R	Wm. K. Reid.	"	IF	I. Foligno.	1872-3	RS	Richd. Sibley.
"	WB	Wm. Brown (possibly).	1853-4	EB&JB	E. & J. Barnard.	1873-4	RM EH	Martin Hall & Co. of Sheffield.
"	JA JA	Joseph & John Angel see 1844.	1854-5	WRS	W. R. Smily.	1874-5	JEM GW	Mappin & Webb.
"	RS	Richd. Sibley ent. 1837.	1855-6	GA	George Angell.	1875-6	W	
1844-5	R·G	R. Garrard " 1801.	1856-7	CTF GF	Chas. T Fox & Geo. Fox }	1876-7	C.F.H	Messrs. Hancock.
"	J&A J&A	Joseph & John Angel.	1857-8	HW	Henry Wilkinson of Sheffield.	1877-8	"	" "
"	RGH	R. G. Hennell.	1858-9	JA	Joseph Angell.	"	RJL	
"	BS	Benj. Smith (probably).	"	W·M	W. Mann.	"	TJ	
1845-6	ISH	John S. Hunt ent. 1844.	"	GP EB	Roberts & Briggs.	1878-9	SS	Stephen Smith.
"	CTF GF	Chas. T. Fox & Geo. Fox. }	1859-60	GA	George Angell.	1879-80	DH CH	Hands & Son.
1846-7	GFP	G. F. Pinnell.	1860-1	EE JE	Messrs. Eady.	1880-1	JWD	J. W Dobson.
"	H·H	Hyam Hyams.	"	CR WS	Rawlins & Sumner.	"	EYI	
"	EJ &W B	E. J. & W. Barnard.	1861-2	RH	Robt. Harper.	"	WIS	
1847-8	IL HL	John & Henry Lias.	1862-3	R·H	Richard Hennell.	1881-2	FH	Francis Higgins.
"	RP GB	R. G. Pearce & Burrows. }	1863-4	GF	Geo. Fox.	1882-3	CSH	Chas. Stuart Harris.
			1864-5	GA	Geo. Angell.			

Date.	Goldsmiths' Marks and Names.			Date.	Goldsmiths' Marks and Names.			
1882-3	JA JS			1900-1	CCP	C. C.	Pilling.	
1883-4	JNM			1901-2	C.K	C.	Krall.	
"	J ASM F			1902-3	WC	W.	Comyns & Sons.	
"	PW			1903-4	WB&S Mr D	Edward	Barnard & Sons, Ltd.	
1884-5	JBH	J. R.	Hennell.	"	HL	H.	Lambert.	
1885-6	J W J			"	J W			
"	CFH	Messrs.	Hancock.	"	J W EC W			
"	J.W. F.C.W	J. F. C.	Wakeley & Wheeler.	1904-5	WJ			
1888-9	D&C			1905-6	TB	Thos.	Bradbury of Sheffield.	
"	WD			"	A & H	Alstons &	Hallam.	
1889-90	CFH	Messrs.	Hancock.	1906-7	C&Cº	Carrington & Co.		
1891-2	EH			1907-8	J&S			
1892 3	E·H			"	LG			
"	WC	W.	Comyns.	1908-9	Tᴴ &S	Thos. Sheffield.	Bradbury & Son of	
1893-4	SWS	S. W.	Smith & Co. (of Birmingham).,	"	HSP Lᴰ			
"	ST			"	&W W	Wakeley & Wheeler.		
1894-5	LG CL			1909-10	IMS	John	Marshall.	
"	JB ER	Brownell & Rose.		1910-1	SJP	S. J.	Phillips.	
"	WBJ	Messrs.	Barnard.	1911-2	CTH JW	Thomas &	Co., Bond Street.	
1895-6	J.S			1912-3	H&C Lᵗᴰ	Heming & Co., Ltd.		
"	JNN			1913-4	AP FP	A. & F.	Parsons, (of Edward Tessier).	
1896 7	SₕHₐ &	W.	Hutton & Sons, Ltd.	"	SG			
1897-8	JBC	Messrs.	Carrington.	1914-5	D&J W	D. & J.	Welby.	
1898-9	GG			1915-6	PDH C W	Dobson &	Sons.	
1899 1900	ℰℭ P	E. C.	Purdee.	"	SJP	S. J.	Phillips.	
"	RP			1916-7	LAC	Crichton	Bros.	
				1917-8	HSP			
				1918-9	C&R C	Chas. & Richard	Comyns.	

Date	Town Mark	Date Letter	Maker's Mark	Maker's Name		Date	Town Mark	Date Letter	Maker's Mark	Maker's Name
ELIZ. 1559-60		A		... .		1583-4	[town]	B	WR	Wm. Rawnson.
1560-1		B		. . ..		1584-5	[town]	b	"	" "
1561-2		C		... ...		1585-6		c		... ...
*1562-3	[town]	D	RG	Robert Gylmyn.		1586-7		d		... ...
1563-4		E		... ...		1587-8	"	e	GK	Geo. Kitchen.
1564-5	[town]	F	M	... ...		1588-9		f		... ...
1565-6		G		... ...		1589-90		g		... ...
1566-7	[town]	H	[mark]	Christopher Hunton.		1590-1	"	h	CK	Geo. Kitchen.
1567-8		I		... ...		1591-2		i		... ...
1568-9	[town]	K	RB / TS	Robert Beckwith. / Thomas Symson.		1592-3	[town]	k	WR / RG	Wm. Rawnson. / Robt. Gylmyn.
1569-70	[town]	L	RG	Robert Gylmyn.		1593-4	"	l	WH	? Wm. Hutchinson.
1570-1		M	♡	Name not traced.		1594-5	"	m	CK	Geo. Kitchen.
1571-2		N		... ...		1595-6		n		... ...
1572-3	[town]	O		John Lund. / William Foster.		1596-7		o		... ...
1573-4		P		... .		1597-8	"	p	CH	Chris. Harrington.
1574-5	"	Q	GK	George Kitchen.		1598-9		q		... ...
1575-6	[town]	R	"	" "		1599/1600	"	r	ET	Fras. Tempest.
1576-7		S	TW	Thomas Waddie.		1600-1		s		. ...
1577-8	"	T		Indistinguishable.		1601-2	"	t	"	" "
1578-9		V		... ...		1602-3		u		... ...
1579-80		W		... ...		JAS. I. 1603-4		w		... .
1580-1		X		... ...		1604-5	"	v	CH	Chris. Harrington.
1581-2		Y		... ...		1605-6		y		... ...
1582-3	"	Z	WR	William Rawnson.		1606-7		z		... ...

	TOWN MARK.	DATE LETTER.	MAKER'S MARK.	MAKER'S NAME.			TOWN MARK.	DATE LETTER.	MAKER'S MARK.	MAKER'S NAME.	
1607-8		𝕷	ℌ	John	Moody ?	1631-2		𝕒	SC	Sem.	Casson.
1608-9		B	RC PP	Robt. Peter	Casson. Pearson.	1632-3		𝕓	,,	,,	,,
1609-10	,,	𝕮	FT	Fras.	Tempest.	1633-4	,,	𝕔	RH	Robt.	Harrington.
1610-1	,,	𝕯	PP ,,	Peter	Pearson.	1634-5	,,	𝕕	TH	Thos.	Harrington.
1611-2	,,	𝕰	CH	,, Chris.	,, Harrington.	1635-6	,,	𝕖	I·T	John { Thomason or Thompson.
1612-3	,,	F	FT	Fras.	Tempest.	1636-7		𝕗	RH	Robt.	Harrington.
1613-4		𝕲	PP	Peter	Pearson.	1637-8		𝕘	TH	Thos.	Harrington.
1614-5	,,	𝕳	,,	,,	,,	1638-9	,,	𝕙	RW	Robt. or Richd.	Williamson, Senr. Waite.
1615-6		𝕴	CM FT	Chris.	Mangy.	1639-40	,,	𝕚	FB	Francis	Bryce.
1616-7	,,	𝕶	,,	Fras.	Tempest.	1640-1		j		...	... ...
1617-8		𝕷		...	... ...	1641-2	,,	𝕜	I·T	John	Thomason.
1618-9	,,	𝕸	SC	Sem.	Casson.	1642-3	,,	𝕝	TH	Thos.	Harrington.
1619-20	,,	𝕹	PP	Peter	Pearson.	1643-4	,,	𝕞	I·T	John	Thomason.
1620-1	,,	𝕺	SC	Sem.	Casson.	1644-5		𝕟		...	... ...
1621-2	,,	P	PP	Peter	Pearson.	1645-6	,,	𝕠	CM	Chris.	Mangy.
1622-3		𝕼	,,	,,	,,	1646-7		𝕡		...	... ...
1623-4		𝕽	RW D	Robt.	Williamson.	1647-8		𝕢		...	... ...
1624-5 CHAS. I		𝕾	TH	...	... ...	1648-9 COMWTH.		𝕣		...	... ...
1625-6		𝕿	RH	Thos.	Harrington.	1649-50		𝕤	P	James	Plummer.
1626-7	,,	𝖀	W	Robt.	Harrington.	1650-1		𝕥	,,	,,	,,
1627-8	,,	𝖁	IP	? James	Plummer	1651-2	,,	𝕦	,,	,,	,,
1628-9		𝖃		...	... ...	1652-3	,,	𝕧	,,	,,	,,
1629-30	,,	𝖄	CM	Chris.	Mangy.	1653-4		w		...	... ...
1630-1	,,	𝖅	W	Thomas	Waite.	1654-5	,,	𝕩	TW	Thomas	Waite.
						1655-6	,,	𝕪	,,	,,	,,
						1656-7	,,	𝕫	PM	Philemon	Marsh.

	TOWN MARK.	DATE LETTER	MAKER'S MARK	MAKER'S NAME.		TOWN MARK.	DATE LETTER.	MAKER'S MARK	MAKER'S NAME.
1657-8		A	IP	John Plummer.	1682-3		A	GG	George Gibson.
1658-9		B	,,	,, ,,	*1683-4	,,	B	WB	Wm. Busfield.
1659-60		C	WW TT	Wm. Waite. John Thomason.	1684-5 JAS. II.		C	IP	John Camidge. John Plummer.
1660-1	,,	D	IP	John Plummer.	1685-6		D	RC	Richd. Chew.
1661-2	,,	E	,,	,, ,,	1686-7	,,	E	IS	John Smith.
1662-3		F	GM	,, ,, George Mangy.	1687-8	,,	F	IO	John Oliver.
1663-4		G	MB	Marmaduke Best.	1688-9	,,	G	CW	Chris. Whitehill.
1664-5	,,	H	RW	Robt. Williamson.	WM.&MY. 1689-90	,,	H	WB	Wm. Busfield.
1665-6	,,	I	IP	John Plummer.	1690-1		I	RW	Robt. Williamson.
1666-7		K	TM	Thos. Mangy.	1691-2		K	CR	Charles Rhoades.
1667-8	,,	L	MB	Marmaduke Best.	1692-3	,,	L	CW	Chris. Whitehill.
1668-9	,,	M	PM	Philemon Marsh.	1693-4	,,	M	MG	Mark Gill.
1669-70	,,	N	TM	Thomas Mangy.					
1670-1		O	MB	Marmaduke Best.	1694-5		N	WB	Wm. Busfield.
1671-2	,,	P	RK	Roland Kirby.	1695-6		O	CR	Clement Reed.
1672-3		Q	IT	John Thompson.	WM. III. 1696-7	,,	P	WB	Wm. Busfield.
1673-4	,,	R	MB	Marmaduke Best.	1697-8	,	Q	IS	John Smith.
1674-5	,,	S	RW TM	Robt Williamson. Thos. Mangy.	1698-9	,,	R		Wm. Busfield as above.
1675-6	,,	T	WM	Wm Mascall.	1699 1700		S		... ...
1676-7	,,	U	HL	Henry Lee.					
1677-8	,,	V	WB	Wm. Busfield.					
1678-9	,,	W	IP	John Plummer.					
1679-80		X	IT	John Thompson.					
1680-1	,,	Y	WB	Wm. Busfield.					
1681-2	,,	Z	TM	Thos. Mangy.					

	TOWN MARK.	BRITANNIA.	LION'S HEAD ERASED.	DATE LETTER.	MAKER'S MARK.	MAKER'S NAME.
1700-1	✠	🛡	🛡	A	GO	Chas. Goldsborough (probably)
1701-2	✠	🛡	🛡	B	Tu / BE	Danl. Turner. / John Bes..
ANNE. 1702-3	,,	,,	,,	C	Bu	Wm. Busfield.
1703-4	,,	,,	,,	D	LA	John Langwith.
1704-5						
1705-6	,,	,,	,,	F	,,	,, ,,
1706-7	,,	,,	,,	G	RH	Chas. Rhoades.
1707-8					LA	John Langwith.
1708-9	,,	,,	,,		WI	Wm. Williamson.
					wa	
1709-10						
1710-11						
1711-2	,,	,,	,,	U	LA	John Langwith,
1712-3						
1713-4	,,	,,	,,	O	,,	,, ,,
GEO. I. 1714-5						
1715-6						
1716-7						

	Town Mark.	Lion Passant.	Leopard's Head Crowned.	Date Letter.	King's Head.	Maker's Mark.	MAKER'S NAME.
1776-7				A			... ...
1777-8				B			... ...
1778-9				C			... ...
1779-80		🦁	🐆	D		HP	J. Hampston & / J. Prince
1780-1				E			... ...
1781-2	🛡	,,	,,	F		,,	,, ,,
1782-3	,,	,,	.	G		,,	,, ,,
1783-4	,,	,,	,,	H		HP/IP	,, ,,
1784-5	,,	,,	,,	J	👤	,, HaP	,, Hampston & Prince.
1785-6				K			. ...
1786-7				L			... ...

Date	Town Mark	Lion Passant	Leopard's Head Crowned	King's Head	Date Letter	Maker's Mark	Maker's Name
1787-8	⬡	🦁	🐆	👤	A	H·P	J. Hampston & J. Prince.
1788-9					b		... ...
1789-90	,,	,,	,,	,,	c	,,	,, ,,
1790-1	,,	,,	,,	,,	d	,,	,, ,,
1791-2	,,	,,	,,	,,	e	,,	,, ,,
1792-3					f		... ...
1793-4	,,	,,	,,	,,	g	,,	,, ,,
1794-5					h		... ...
1795-6	,,	,,	,,	,,	i	I·H·P	,, ,,
1796-7	,,	,,	,,	👤	K	,,	,, ,,
1797-8					l or L		... .
1798-9	,,	,,	,,	,,	M	HP &Co	H. Prince & Co.
1799 1800	,,	,,	,,	,,	N	,,	,, ,,
1800-1	,,	,,	,,	,,	O	HP&C	,, ,,
1801-2	,,	,,	,,	,,	P	HP &C	,, ,,
1802-3	,,	,,	,,	,,	Q	,,	,, ,,
1803-4	,,	,,	,,	,,	R	,,	,, ,,
1804-5	,,	,,	,,	,,	S	,,	,, ,,
1805-6	,,	,,	,,	,,	T	,,	,, ,,
1806-7					U		
1807-8	,,	,,	,,	,,	V	RC JB	Robt. Cattle & J Barber.
1808-9		,,	,,	,,	W	,,	,, ,,
1809-10		,,	,,	,,	X	,,	,, ,,
1810-1	,,	,,	,,	,,	Y	,,	,, ,,
1811-2					Z		... ,,

Date	Town Mark	Lion Passant	Leopard's Head Crowned	King's Head	Date Letter	Maker's Mark	Maker's Name
*1812-3	⬡	🦁	🐆	👤	a	JB WW	James Barber & Wm. Whitwell
1813-4					b		... ...
1814-5					c		... ,,. ...
1815-6	,,	,,	,,	,,	d	,,	,, ,,
1816-7					e		... ...
1817-8	,,	,,	,,	,,	f	,,	,, ,,
1818-9	,,	,,	,,	,,	g	,,	,, ,,
1819-20					h		.. ..
GEO. IV. 1820-1		,,	,,	,,	i	,,	,, ,,
1821-2		,,	,,	,,	k	,,	,, ,,
1822-3					l		... .
1823-4					m		... ...
1824-5	,,	,,	,,	,,	n	JB &Co	Jas. Barber & Co.
1825-6	,,	,,	,,	,,	o	B·C &N	Jas. Geo. Wm. Barber, Cattle & North
1826-7		,,	,,	,,	p	,,	,, ,,
1827-8					q		... .
1828-9	,,	,,	,,	,,	r	,,	,, ,,
1829-30	,,	,,	,,	,,	s	JB GC WN	,, ,,
WM. IV. 1830-1	🦁	,,	,,	👤	t	JB GC WN	,, ,,
1831-2		,,	,,	,,	u	,,	,, ,,
1832-3					v		.. ..
1833-4					w		
1834-5					x		... ...
1835-6					y		... .
1836 7					z		.. ..

VICT.	TOWN MARK.	LION PASSANT.	LEOPARD'S HEAD CROWNED. TILL 1848	QUEEN'S HEAD.	DATE LETTER.	MAKER'S MARK.	MAKER'S NAME.	
1837-8	(town mark)	(lion)	(leopard's head)	(queen's head)	A	JB WN	Jas.	Barber & Wm. North
1838-9	,,	,,	,,	,,	B	,,	,,	,,
1839-40	,,	,,	,,	,,	C	,,	,,	,,
1840-1	,,	,,	,,	(queen's head)	D	,,	,,	,,
1841-2	,,	,,	,,	,,	E	,,	,,	,,
1842-3	,,	,,	,,	,,	F	,,	,,	,,
1843-4	,,	,,	,,	,,	G	,,	,,	,,
1844-5	,,	,,	,,	,,	H	,,	,,	,,
1845-6	,,	,,	,,	,,	I	,,	,,	,,
1846-7					K		....	... ...
1847-8	,,	,,	,,	,,	L	,,	,,	,,
1848-9	,,	,,		,,	M	JB	James Barber	
1849-50	,,	,,		,,	N	,,	,,	,,
1850-1	,,	,,		,,	O	,,	,,	,,
1851-2					P		... ...	...
1852-3					Q		... ...	...
1853-4					R		.. ..	...
1854-5					S		. ...	...
1855-6					T		... ..	...
1856-7	,,	,,		,,	V	JB	James Barber	

Date	Castle over Lion	Date Letter	Maker's Mark
1565-6		A	
1566-7	,,	B	
1567-8		C	
1568-9		D	
1569-70		E	
1570-1		F	
1571-2	,,	G	
1572-3		H	
1573-4	,,	I	
1574-5	,,	K	
1575-6		L	
1576-7		M	
1577-8		N	
1578-9		O	
1579-80		P	
1580-1		Q	

ROSE CROWNED.

Date	Rose Crowned	Date Letter	Maker's Mark
1581-2		R	
1582-3		S	
1583-4		T	
1584-5		V	

Date (about)	Marks
1590	
1595	
1600-10	
1610	
1620	
,,	
,,	
1620-40	
1624	AH

Date	Castle over Lion	Rose Crowned	Date Letter	Maker's Mark
1624-5			A	
1625-6	,,	,,	B	
1626-7		,,	C	
1627-8	,,	,,	D	
1628-9		,,	E	
1629-30			F	
1630-1	,,		G	
1631-2			H	
1632-3	,,	,,	I	
1633-4	,,	,,	K	
1634-5	,,	,,	L	
1635-6			M	
1636-7			N	
1637-8			O	
1638-9	,,	,,	P	
1639-40			Q	
1640-1	,,	,,	R	
1641-2	,,	,,	S	
1642-3	,,	,,	T	
1643-4			V	

DATE (ABOUT)	MARKS.
1645	(quatrefoil) (castle) (star)
,,	(rose) (rose crowned) (crown) AH
1653	(rose) (crown) (rose) AH
1661	(lion) (crown) (rose) AH
,,	(castle) (crown) (rose) WL
1670	(lion) (crown) (rose) AH
,,	,, ,, (rose) AH
,,	(rose) (crown) (crown) AH
,,	(lion) (crown) AH (rose)
1675	(lion) (crown) (rose) TH★
1676	,, ,, (rose) ,,
1679	,, ,, (rose) ,,
,,	,, ,, ,, (figure)
1680	(lion) (crown) (rose) MH
1685	(crown) (rose) TH★

DATE	ROSE CROWNED.	CASTLE OVER LION.	DATE LETTER.	MAKER'S MARK.	MAKER'S NAME.
1688	(rose crowned)	(castle over lion)	a	EH	... ...
1689	(rose crowned)	(castle over lion)	b	TH	Thomas Havers.
1690			c		... ...
1691	,,	,,	d	,,	Thomas Havers.
1691	,,	,,	,,	DD	James Daniel.
1691	,,	,,	,,	EH	... ...
1691	,,	,,	,,	LG	... ...
1692			E		... ...
1693			F		... ...
1694			G		.. ..
1695			H		....
1696	,,	,,	I	ID	James Daniel.
1697	,,	,,	K	PR	... ...
1697	(rose crowned)	(castle over lion)	,,	EH	... ...

DATE.	MARKS.	MAKER'S NAME.	DATE.	MARKS.	MAKER'S NAME.
e. 1544-98		Richard Hilliard.	1600		Richd. Osborn.
c. 1562 / 1607		Richard Osborne.	,,	HERMAN	R. Herman.
c. 1568-74	NORTH	John North.	,,		No maker's mark.
c. 1570		Henry Hardwicke.	c. 1600		Richd. Osborn.
1570-3	IONS	John Ions (Jones).	1606	OZBORN	,, ,,
,,	IONS	Do. do do.	c. 1610-20		William Bartlett. (1597-1646).
c. 1570 / 1600	MORE	Steven More.	1620	,, ,, ,,	,, ,,
1571	In	John North.	,,	,,	Edward Anthony (1612-67).
,,	IN	Do. do.	,,		,, ,,
,,	IONS	John Jons.	,,		
1572	IW	John Withycombe.	c. 1630	WB WB	Wm. Bartlett (probably).
1575	IONS	John Jons.	,,	T T	Anthony mark, &c.*
,,	,, ,, ,,	Do. do.	c. 1635	IL IL	John Lavers.
,,	I ,, A	Do. do.	,,	IP	I. P.
,,	,, IO ,, ,,	Do. do.	c. 1635-8	IL	John Lavers.
1576	I IONS B	Do. do.	c. 1640		... ...
,,	VI	... ...	,,	HP HP	H. P.
1580	HORWOOD	Wm. Horwood.	,,	RADCLIFF	Jasper Radcliffe.
c. 1580	I YEDS	John Eydes.	,,	LM ,,	L. M.
1582	C ESTON	C. Eston.	,,	R ,, ,,	Jasper Radcliffe.
,,	EASTON	C. Easton.	,,	OSBORN ,,	Richd. Osborn.
1585	BENTLY	— Bently.	,,	IL IL IL	John Lavers.
,,	HERMAN	R. Herman.	,,		No maker's mark.
1590	ESTON N	C. Eston.			
1592	C ESTON P	Do. do.			

DATE.	MARKS.	MAKER'S NAME.
c. 1640-50		{ John Elston / Anthony Tripe
"		P. R.
"		Thomas Bridgeman.
"		Edward Anthony.
"		Do. do.
"		I. F.
c. 1646-98		
c. 1670		Jasper Radcliffe.
1676		M. W.
"		— S.
c. 1680		... ...
"		No maker's mark.
"		I. S.
1690		John Mortimer.
c. 1690		Daniel Slade.
"		Wm. Ekins.
"		Do. do.
"		John Mortimer.
"		.. ..
"		I. P. (See Barnstaple, p. 459 infra).
"		I. P.
1694		Nichs. Browne.
1698		No maker's mark.

DATE.	CASTLE.	BRIT. ANNIA.	LION'S HEAD ERASED.	DATE LETTER.	MAKER'S MARK.	MAKER'S NAME.
1701-2				A		J. Elston.
ANNE. 1702-3		"	"	B	FO	Thos. Foote.
1703-4		"	"	C	Mu / Au	Hy. Muston. / John Audry.
1704-5	"	"	"	D	Br	Wm. Briant.
1705-6	"	"	"	E	FR	Richd. Freeman.
1706-7	"	"	"	F	RE	Thos. Reynolds.
1707-8	"	"	"	G	WI / SA	Richd. Wilcocks. / Thos. Salter.
1708-9		"	"	H	PL	Richd. Plint.
1709-10		"	"	I	FV	Name not traced.†
1710-1	"	"	"	K	Ri	Ed. Richards.
1711-2	"	"	"	L	TR / SW	Geo. Trowbridge. / Ed. Sweet.
1712-3	"	"	"	M	Ri	Ed. Richards.
1713-4		"	"	N	SL	Danl. Slade.
GEO. I. 1714-5	"	"	"	O	To: / Mo	— Tolcher. / John Mortimer.
1715-6	"	"	"	P	TR	Geo. Trowbridge.
1716-7	"	"	"	Q	Sp / Lo	Pent. Symonds. / Ab'm. Lovell.
1717-8	"	"	"	R	SP	Pent. Symonds.
1718-9	"	"	"	S	AR	Peter Arno.
1719-20	"	"	"	T	WO	Andr Worth.
1720-1	"	"	"	V	BL / IE	Saml. Blachford / J. Elston.
1721-2				W	JS	Thos. Sampson.
1722-3				X	SB	Saml. Blachford
1723-4	"	"	"	Y	JE	J. Elston.
1724-5	"	"	"	Z	IW	Jas. Williams.‡

	CASTLE.	LEOPARD'S HEAD CROWNED.	LION PASSANT.	DATE LETTER.	MAKER'S MARK.	MAKER'S NAME.		CASTLE	LEOPARD'S HEAD CROWNED.	LION PASSANT.	DATE LETTER	MAKER'S MARK.	MAKER'S NAME.
1725-6	🏰	🦁	🦁	a	SB	Saml. Blachford.	1749-50	🏰	🦁	🦁	A	TB	Thomas Blake.
1726-7	,,	,,	,,	b	TS	Thos. Sampson.	1750-1	,,	,,	,,	B	,,	,, ,,
GEO. II. 1727-8	,,	,,	,,	c	JC	Joseph Collier.	1751-2	,,	,,	,,	C	,,	,, ,,
					PE	Philip Elliott.							
1728-9	,,	,,	,,	d	JE	John Elston, jr.	1752-3	,,	,,	,,	D	WP	W. Parry.
1729-30	,,	,,	,,	e	{ JS	Do. do. James Strang.	1753-4	,,	,,	,,	E	DC	Danl. Coleman.
1730-1	,,	,,	,,	f	IB	John Burdon.	1754-5	,,	,,	,,	F	WP	W. Parry.
1731-2	,,	,,	,,	g	{ PE	Peter Elliott.	1755-6	,,	,,	,,	G	,,	,, ,,
1732-3	,,	,,	,,	h	JC	Joseph Collier.	1756-7	,,	,,	,,	H	TB	Thomas Blake.
1733-4	,,	,,	,,	i	JE	John Elston, jr.	1757-8	,,	,,	,,	I	,,	,, ,,,
1734-5	,,	,,	,,	k	SB	Sampson Bennett.	1758-9	,,	,,	,,	K		
1735-6	,,	,,	,,	l	PE	Philip Elston.	1759-60	,,	,,	,,	L	SF	Name not traced.
1736-7	,,	,,	,,	m	JS	James Strang.	GEO. III. 1760-1	,,	,,	,,	M		
1737-8	,,	,,	,,	n	PE	Philip Elston.	1761-2	,,	,,	,,	N		
1738-9	,,	,,	,,	o	PS	Pent. Symonds.	1762-3	,,	,,	,,	O	MS	Mat'w Skinner.
1739-40	,,	,,	,,	p	JB	John Burdon.	1763-4	,,	,,	,,	P		
1740-1	,,	,,	,,	q	JB	Do. do.	1764-5	,,	,,	,,	Q		
1741-2	,,	,,	,,	r	Sy	Pent. Symonds.	1765-6	,,	,,	,,	R		
1742-3	,,	,,	,,	s	IF	Name not traced. J. Freeman ?	1766-7	,,	,,	,,	S	RS	Richard Sams.
1743-4	,,	,,	,,	t	JB	John Babbage ?	1767-8	,,	,,	,,	T	,,	,, ,,
1744-5	,,	,,	,,	u	,,	Do. do.	1768-9	,,	,,	,,	U	JH	James Holt.
1745-6	,,	,,	,,	w			1769-70	,,	,,	,,	W	TC	Thomas Coffin.
1746-7	,,	,,	,,	x	PS	Pent. Symonds.	1770-1	,,	,,	,,	X	IF	J. Freeman.
1747-8	,,	,,	,,	y	TB	Thos. Blake.	1771-2	,,	,,	,,	Y	RS	Richard Sams.
1748-9	,,	,,	,,	z	JS	Jas. Strang.	1772-3	,,	,,	,,	Z		... ...

	CASTLE.	LEOPARD'S HEAD CROWNED	LION PASSANT.	DATE LETTER.	MAKER'S MARK.	MAKER'S NAME.		CASTLE.	LION PASSANT.	DATE LETTER.	KING'S HEAD.	MAKER'S MARK.	MAKER'S NAME.
1773-4	castle	leopard	lion	A	RS	Richd. Sams.	1797-8	castle	lion	A	king's head	RF	Richd. Ferris.
1774-5	,,	,,	,,	B			1798-9	,,	,,	B	,,	,,	,, ,,
1775-6	,,	,,	,,	C	{J.E / WW}	Thos. Eustace. William West of Plymouth.	1799 / 1800	,,	,,	C	king's head	JH / WW	Joseph Hicks. W. Welch.
1776-7	,,	,,	,,	D			1800-1	,,	,,	D	,,	JH	Joseph Hicks.
1777-8	,,	,,	,,	E			1801-2	,,	,,	E	,,	,,	,, ,,
1778-9	,,		lion	F	,,	Thos. Eustace.	1802-3	,,	,,	F	,,	,,	,, ,,
1779-80	,,		,,	G	,,	,, ,,	1803-4	,,	,,	G	,,	J.E	Thos. Eustace.
1780-1	,,		,,	H			1804-5	,,	,,	H	,,	RF	Richd. Ferris.
1781-2-3	,,		,,	I	,,	,, ,,	1805-6	castle	lion	I	,,	,,	,, ,,
1783-4	,,	KING'S HEAD	,,	K	W.P	W. Pearse.	1806-7	,,	,,	K	,,	,,	,, ,,
1784-5	,,	(king's head)	,,	L		Thos. Eustace (as 1775-6).	1807-8	,,	,,	L	,,	,,	,, ,,
1785-6	,,	,,	,,	M	TE	Thos. Eustace.	1808-9	,,	,,	M	,,		
1786-7	,,	(king's head)	,,	N	JH	Joseph Hicks.	1809-10	,,	,,	N	,,	J.L	J. Langdon
1787-8	,,	,,	,,	O	,,	,, ,,	1810-1	,,	,,	O	,,	WW	W. Welch.
1788-9	,,	,,	,,	P	,,	,, ,,	1811-2	,,	,,	P	,,	JH	Joseph Hicks.
1789-90	,,	,,	,,	q	JP	J. Pearse.	1812-3	,,	,,	Q	,,	,,	,, ,,
1790-1	,,	,,	,,	r			1813-4	,,	,,	R	,,	GT	G. Turner.
1791-2	,,	,,	,,	f	JH	Joseph Hicks.	1814-5	,,	,,	S	,,	,,	,, ,,
1792-3	,,	,,	,,	t			1815-6	,,	,,	T	,,	,,	,, ,,
1793-4	,,	,,	,,	u			1816-7	,,	,,	U	,,	GF	Geo. Ferris.
1794-5	,,	,,	,,	w									
1795-6	,,	,,	,,	X	RF	Richd. Ferris.							
1796-7	,,	,,	,,	y									

	Castle.	Lion Passant.	Date Letter.	King's Head.	Maker's Mark	Maker's Name.		Castle.	Lion Passant.	Date Letter.	Queen's Head.	Maker's Mark.	Maker's Name.
1817-8	🏰	🦁	a	Q	GF	Geo. Ferris.	VICT. 1837-8	🏰	🦁	A	Q	SOBEY	W. R. Sobey.
1818-9	,,	,,	b	,,	,,	,, ,,	1838-9	,,	,,	B	Q	JO	J. Osmont.
1819-20	,,	,,	c	,,	JH	Joseph Hicks.	1839-40	,,	,,	C	Q	TB	Thos. Byne.
GEO. IV. 1820-1	,,	,,	d	,,	,,	,, ,,	1840-1	,,	,,	D	,,	JS	J. Stone.
1821-2	,,	,,	e	,,	,,	,, ,,	1841-2	🏰	,,	E	,,	RAMSEY	— Ramsey.
1822-3	,,	,,	f	Q	GF	Geo. Ferris.	1842-3	,,	,,	F	,,	SOBEY	W. R. Sobey.
1823-4	,,	,,	g	,,	,,	,, ,,	1843-4	🏰	,,	G	,,	,,	,, ,,
1824-5	,,	,,	h	,,	,,	,, ,,	1844-5	,,	,,	H	,,	WRS	,, ,,
1825-6	,,	,,	i	,,	IE	John Eustace.	1845-6	,,	,,	J	,,	,, / SOBEY	,, ,, / ,, ,,
1826-7	,,	,,	k	,,	GM	Name not traced.	1846-7	,,	,,	K	,,	,,	,, ,,
1827-8	,,	,,	l	,,	JO	J. Osmont.	1847-8	,,	,,	L	,,	WWW	? Williams.
1828-9	,,	,,	m	,,	,,	,, ,,	1848-9	,,	,,	M	,,	JS	J. Stone.
1829-30	,,	,,	n	,,	JH	Joseph Hicks.	1849-50	,,	,,	N	,,	WRS	W. R. Sobey.
WM. IV. 1830-1	,,	,,	o	,,	,,	,, ,,	1850-1	,,	,,	O	,,	,,	,, ,,
1831-2	🏰	🦁	p	Q	WS	W. Sobey.	1851-2	,,	,,	P	,,	JO	J. Osmont.
1832-3	,,	,,	q	,,	JS	John Stone.	1852-3	,,	,,	Q	,,	,,	,, ,,
1833-4	🏰	🦁	r	,,	W-P	Wm. Pope.	1853-4	,,	,,	R	,,	IP	Isaac Parkin.
1834-5	,,	,,	s	Q	JO	J. Osmont.	1854-5	,,	,,	S	,,	,,	,, ,,
1835-6	,,	,,	t	,,	WRS	W. R. Sobey.	1855-6	,,	,,	T	,,	,,	,, ,,
1836-7	,,	,,	u	,,	WW	William Welch.	1856-7	,,	,,	U	,,	JS	J. Stone.

	CASTLE	LION PASSANT	DATE LETTER	QUEEN'S HEAD	MAKER'S MARK	MAKER'S NAME.		CASTLE	LION PASSANT	DATE LETTER	QUEEN'S HEAD	MAKER'S MARK	MAKER'S NAME.
1857-8	🏰	🦁	**A**	👑	**J·S**	J.　　Stone.	1870-1	,,	,,	**O**	,,		..　　..　　...
1858-9	,,	,,	**B**	,,	,,	,,　　　　　,,	1871-2	,,	,,	**P**	,,		...　,　..
1859-60	,,	,,	**C**	,,		.　　..　　..	1872-3	,,	,,	**Q**	,,		.　...　...
1860-1	,,	,,	**D**	,,	**PO**	Name not traced.	1873-4	,,	,,	**R**	,,		.　...　...
1861-2	,,	,,	**E**	,,	**JW**	Jas.　　Williams.	1874-5	,,	,,	**S**	,,		...　...　.
1862-3	,,	,,	**F**	,,		..　　...　　...	1875-6	,,	,,	**T**	,,		...　...　.
1863-4	,,	,,	**G**	,,		..　　...　　..	1876-7	,,	,,	**U**	,,		..　...　...
1864-5	,,	,,	**H**	,,		..　　...　　...	1877-8	🏰	🦁	**A**	👑	**JW&Co**	J. Whipple & Co.
1865-6	,,	,,	**I**	,,		.　　..　　.	1878-9	,,	,,	**B**	,,		...　...　...f
1866-7	,,	,,	**K**	,,		...	1879-80	,,	,,	**C**	,,		..　...　..
1867-8	,,	,,	**L**	,,		.	1880-1	,,	,,	**D**	,,		.　...　...
1868-9	,,	,,	**M**	,,	**H·L**	Henry　Lake.	1881-2	,,	,,	**E**	,,		...　...　...·.
1869-70	,,	,,	**N**	,,		..　　.	1882-3	,,	,,	**F**	,,	**WBFD&T**	Ellis, Depree & } Tucker

SUPPLEMENTARY LIST OF MARKS OF GOLDSMITHS

Impressed at Exeter, but not illustrated in the preceding tables :—

DATE	MARK	NAME	DATE	MARK	NAME
1701	**S·**	Danie　　Slade.	1722	**PS**	Pentecost　Symonds.
c 1706	**PO**	Peter　　Jouett.	1728	**TC**	Thomas　　Coffin.
1707	**S·**	Thos.　　Sampson.	1730	**IR**	John　　Reed
1708	**W**	Richard　Wilcocks.	1732	**TC**	Thomas　　Clarke
1709	**SY**	Pentecost　Symonds.	,,	**IS**	John　　Suger.
1710	**JP**	John　　Pike.	1741	**MM**	Micon　　Melun.
..	**BI**	Joseph　　Bennick.	1771	**R·B**	Richd.　　Birdlake (Plymouth).
1713	**SU**	John　　Suger.	1825	**SL**	Simon　　Lery
1714	**T**	Anthony　Tripe.	1830	**IP**	Isaac　　Parkin.
1717	**W**	Zacariah　Williams.	1835	**GT**	G. Turner & partner (? Son).
1719	**BB**	Joseph　　Bennick.	1845	**JG**	J.　　Golding (Plymouth).
1721	**ER**	Edward　　Richard.	1847	**HE**	Henry　　Ellis.
	IM	John　　March.	1850	**IP GS**	Isaac　Parkin & Geo.　Sobey.

DATE (ABOUT).	MARKS.	MAKER'S NAME.
1658		John Wilkinson.
1664		,, ,,
1668		,, ,,
1670		John Dowthwaite.
1672		,, ,,
,,		Wm. Ramsay.
1675		,, ,,
,,		,, ,,
1680		,, ,,
1684		,, ,,
,,		,, ,,
,,		,, ,,
1685		Wm. Robinson.
,,		,, ,,
1686-7		Eli Bilton.
1686-8		Wm. Robinson.
1690		,, ,,
1692		,, ,,
1694		Robt. Shrive.
,,		Eli Bilton.
,,		,, ,,
1695		Wm. Robinson.
1697		Thos. Hewitson.
1698		,, ,,
1698-9		Eli Bilton.
1700		,, ,,
,,		John Ramsay.
1701		Eli Bilton.

	THREE CASTLES.	BRIT. ANNIA.	LION'S HEAD ERASED.	DATE LETTER.	MAKER'S MARK.	MAKER'S NAME.
ANNE. 1702-3				A	Ra	John Ramsay.
1703-4	,,	,,	,,	B	Ba	Fras. Batty.
1704-5	,,	,,	,,	C	Sh	Robt. Shrive.
1705-6	,,	,,	,,	D	Bi	Eli. Bilton.
1706-7	,,	,,	,,	E	{ Yo	,, ,, John Younghusband.
1707-8		,,	,,	F	{ Yo Fr	,, ,, J'nath'n French.
1708-9	,,	,,	,,	G	By	John Buckle of York.
1709-10	,,	,,	,,	,,	Ki	James Kirkup.
1710-11						
1711-2					Bi	Eli. Bilton.
1712-3				M	Ho	Richd. Hobbs.
1713-4					La	John Langwith.
GEO. I. 1714-5		,,	,,	M	{ Fr Ba Sh	J'nath'n French. Fr. Batty, jr. Nathl. Shaw.
1715-6						
1716-7						
1717-8	,,	,,	,,	P	Bv	Joseph Buckle.
1718-9	,,	,,	,,	Q	Ba	Fras. Batty, as above.
1719-20	,,	,,	,,	D	{ Ki Ma Ba Ca	James Kirkup. R. Makepeace } & F. Batty. John Carnaby.
1720-1	,,	,,	,,	E	Wh	Wm. Whitfield.

Date	Three Castles	Lion Passant	Leopard's Head Crowned	Date Letter	Maker's Mark	Maker's Name
1721-2	▨	⬱	👑	a	FB / IR	Fras. Batty, jr. / John Ramsay, jr.
1722-3	▨	⬱	,,	B	RM / I·K	Robt. Makepeace. / Jas. Kirkup.
1723-4	,,	⬱	,,	C	IF	Jthn. French.
1724-5	,,	,,	,,	D	IC / TP	John Carnaby. / Thos. Partis.
1725-6	▨	⬱	👑	E	IR	Fras. Batty, jr.
1726-7	,,	,,	,,	F	WW / IB	Wm. Whitfield. / John Busfield of York. ?
GEO. II. 1727-8	♥	,,	👑	G	IC	Isaac Cookson.
1728-9	,,	⬱	,,	H	GB / WW / WD	Geo. Bulman. / Wm. Whitfield. / Wm. Dalton.
1729-30	,,	,,	,,	I	GB	Geo. Bulman.
1730-1	,,	,,	,,	K	WD	Wm. Dalton.
1731-2	,,	,,	,,	L	TG / IF	Thos. Gamul ? / Jon. French.
1732-3	,,	,,	,,	M	TM / IB	Thos. Makepeace. / John Busfield of York. ?
1733-4	,,	,,	,,	N	IC	Isaac Cookson.
1734-5	,,	,,	,,	O	TP	Thos. Partis.
1735-6	,,	,,	,,	P	GB	Geo. Bulman.
1736-7	,,	,,	,,	Q	WP	Wm. Partis.*
1737-8	,,	,,	,,	R	IC	Isaac Cookson.†
1738-9	,,	,,	,,	S	WB / IB	Wm. Beilby & Co.
1739-40	,,	,,	,,	T	IC / R·M	Isaac Cookson. / Robt. Makepeace.
1740-1	▨	⬱	👑	A	S·B / I·K	Stephen Buckle. / James Kirkup.
1741-2	,,	,,	,,	B	WB / IB	W. Beilby & Anor. / Perhaps Jno. Busfield (of York.)
1742-3	,,	,,	,,	C	IC	Isaac Cookson.
1743-4	,,	,,	,,	D	TS / WP	Thomas Stoddart. / William Partis.
1744-5	,,	,,	,,	E	FM	F. Martin (probably).
1745-6	,,	,,	👑	F	IB	Thomas Blackett (probably).
1746-7	♥	⬱	👑	G	IC	Isaac Cookson.
1747-8	,,	,,	,,	H	I·W	John Wilkinson of Sheffield (probably).
1748-9	,,	,,	,,	I	TR	? Thos. Reid of York.
1749-50	,,	,,	,,	K	RG / R·M / TP	R. Gillson (of Sunderland). / Robert Makepeace. / Thos. Partis II. (of Sunderland).
1750-1	,,	⬱	👑	L	WB	William Beilby.
1751-2	,,	,,	,,	M	WP	William Partis.
1752-3	,,	,,	,,	N	WD / I·B	William Dalton. / Perhaps John Barrett (of Sunderland).
1753-4	,,	,,	,,	O	IC	Isaac Cookson.
1754-5	,,	,,	,,	P	IL / IG	Langlands & Goodriche.
1755-6	,,	,,	,,	Q	IK	John Kirkup.
1756-7	,,	,,	,,	R	I·L	John Langlands.
1757-8	♥	,,	👑	S	IL / IL	,, ,, / ,, ,,
1758-9				T	R·B	Ralph Beilby.

	THREE CASTLES	LION PASSANT	LEOPARD'S HEAD CROWNED	DATE LETTER	KING'S HEAD	MAKER'S MARK	MAKER'S NAME
1759-60	[castles]	[lion]	[leopard]	A		S·I	Samuel James.
						I·I	Saml. Thompson.
GEO. III. 1760-8	"	"	"	B		I·B	John Barrett of Sunderland.
1769-70	"	[lion]	"	C		S·I / R·P	Saml. James; Robt. Peat.
1770-1	[castles]	"	[leopard]	D		I·K / I·F / I·L	John Kirkup. John Fearny of Sunderland. John Langlands.
1771-2	"	"	"	E		I·C	James Crawford.
1772-3	[castles]	"	"	F		I·I	John Jobson.
1773-4	"	"	"	G		I·H	Jas. Hetherington.
1774-5	"	"	"	H		W·S / I·M	Stalker & Mitchison.
1775-6	"	"	"	I		I·H / H·E	Hetherington & Edwards.
						F·S	Francis Solomon of Whitehaven.
1776-7	"	"	"	K		H&E / J·H	Hetherington & Edwards. James Hetherington
1777-8	"	"	"	L		D·C	David Crawford.
1778-9	"	"	"	M		I·R	Langlands & Robertson.
1779-80	"	[lion]	[leopard]	N		D·C	David Crawford.
1780-1	"	"	"	O		R·P / R·S	Pinkney & Scott.
1781-2	"	"	"	P		I·L / L·R	Langlands & Robertson (as below).
1782-3	"	"	"	Q		I·S / B·D	John Stoddart. Ben. Dryden.
1783-4	"	"	"	R		I·I	John Stoddart.
1784-5	"	"	"	S	[king's head]	R·P / R·S	Pinkney & Scott.
1785-6	"	"	"	T	"	I·M	John Mitchison.
1786-7	"	"	"	U	[king's head]	"	" "
1787-8	"	[lion]	[leopard]	W	"	T·G / L&R	Name not traced. Langlands & Robertson.
1788-9	"	[lion]	"	X	"	C·R	Chrstn. Reid.
1789-90	"	"	"	Y	"	P&S	Pinkney & Scott.
1790-1	"	"	"	Z	"	I·M	John Mitchison.

	LION PASSANT	THREE CASTLES	LEOPARD'S HEAD CROWNED	KING'S HEAD	DATE LETTER	MAKER'S MARK	MAKER'S NAME
1791-2	[lion]	[castles]	[leopard]	[king's head]	A	I·R	Langlands & Robertson.
						R·S	Robert Scott.
1792-3	"	"	"	"	B		
*1793-4	"	"	"	"	C	A·H	Anth. Hedley.
1794-5	"	"	"	"	D	M·A / G·W	Mary Ashworth of Dur. G. Weddell.
1795-6	"	"	"	"	E	I·R / D·D	Robertson & Darling.
1796-7	"	"	"	"	F	T·W / R&D	Thos. Watson. Robertson & Darling.
1797-8	"	"	"	[king's head]	G	G·L / J·W	Geo. Laws & John Walker.
1798-9	"	"	"	"	H	C·R / I·R	Chrstn. Reid. John Robertson.
1799 1800	"	"	"	"	I	I·R	"
						S·C	Sarah Crawford.
1800-1	[lion]	[castles]	[leopard]	[king's head]	K	I·L	John Langlands, jr.
1801-2	"	"	"	"	L	T·W / A·R	Thos. Watson. Ann. Robertson.
1802-3	"	"	"	"	M	D·D / C·R / D·R	David Darling. Chrstn. K. Reid & David Reid.
1803-4	[lion]	"	·	[king's head]	N	A·K	Alexr. Kelty.
1804-5	"	"	"	"	O	I·L	John Langlands, jr.
1805-6	"	"	"	"	P	G·M	George Murray.
1806-7	"	"	"	"	Q	T·W	Thos. Watson.
1807-8	"	"	"	"	R	"	" "
1808-9	"	"	"	"	S	D·D / T·B	Darling & Bell.
1809-10	[lion]	[castles]	[leopard]	[king's head]	T	I·L	John Langlands.†
1810-1	"	"	"	"	U	T·W	Thos. Watson.
1811-2	"	"	"	"	W	D·L / I·R / I·W	Drthy. Langlands. Robertson & Walton.
1812-3	"	"	"	"	X	R·P / M&R	Robert Pinkney. Name not traced.
1813-4	"	"	"	"	Y	C·R / D·R / C·R	Chrstn. Ker Reid, David Reid, & Chrstn. Bruce Reid.
1814-5	"	"	"	"	Z	I·W	John Walton.

Date Letter	King's Head	Lion Passant	Three Castles	Leopard's Head Crowned	Maker's Mark	Maker's Name	King's Head	Lion Passant	Three Castles	Leopard's Head Crowned	Date Letter	Maker's Mark	Maker's Name
1815-6 **A**	(head)	(lion)	(castles)	(leopard)	T·W	Thos. Watson.	1839-40 (head)	(lion)	(castles)	(leopard)	**A**	IW	John Walton.
1816-7 **B**	,,	,,	,,	,,	*TW*	,, ,,	1840-1 ,,	,,	,,	,,	**B**	,,	,, ,,'
1817-8 **C**	,,	,,	,,	,,	C·D	Christ'r. Dinsdale, of Sunderland.	1841-2 (head)	,,	,,	,,	**C**	TW	Thos. Watson,
1818-9 **D**	,,	,,	,,	,,	IR IW	Robertson & Walton.	1842-3 ,,	,,	,,	,,	**D**	,,	,, ,,
1819-20 **E**	,,	,,	,,	,,			1843-4 ,,	,,	,,	,,	**E**		
GEO. IV. 1820-1 **F**	,,	,,	,,	,,	T·W	Thos. Watson.	1844-5 ,,	,,	,,	,,	**F**		Lister & Sons (as 1838-9).
1821-2 **G**	(head O)	,,	,,	,,	,,	,, ,,	1845-6 ,,	,,	,,	,,	**G**		
1822-3 **H**	,,	,,	,,	,,	,,	,, ,,	1846-7 ,,	(lion)	(castles)	(leopard)	**H**	GG	Name not traced.
1823-4 **I**	,,	,,	,,	,,	,,	,, ,,	1847-8 ,,	,,	,,	,,	**I**		
1824-5 **K**	,,	,,	,,	,,	TW	,, ,,	1848-9 ,,	,,	,,	,,	**J**		
1825-6 **L**	,,	,,	,,	,,			1849-50 ,,	,,	,,	,,	**K**		
1826-7 **M**	,,	,,	,,	,,			1850-1 ,,	,,	,,	,,	**L**		
1827-8 **N**	,,	,,	,,	,,			1851-2 ,,	,,	,,	,,	**M**		
1828-9 **O**	,,	,,	,,	,,			1852-3 ,,	,,	,,	,,	**N**		
1829-30 **P**	.	,,	,,	,,			1853-4 ,,	,,	,,	,,	**O**		
WM. IV. 1830-1 **Q**	.	,,	,,	,,			1854-5 ,,	,,	,,	,,	**P**		
1831-2 **R**	..	,,	,,	,,			1855-6 ,,	,,	,,	,,	**Q**		
1832-3 **S**	(head O)	.	,,	.	..	Thos. Watson.	1856-7 ,,	,,	,,	,,	**R**		
1833-4 **T**	..	,,	,,				1857-8 ,,	,,	,,	,,	**S**		
1834-5 **U**	.	..	.	,,	WL	Wm. Lister.	1858-9 ,,	,,	,,	,,	**T**		
1835-6 **W**	..	,,	,,				1859-60 ,,	,,	,,	,,	**U**		
1836-7 **X**	..	,,	,,				1860-1 ,,	,,	,,	,,	**W**		
VICT. 1837-8 **Y**	,,	,,	,,		T·W	Thos Watson.	1861-2 ,,	,,	,,	,,	**X**		
1838-9 **Z**	,,	,,	,,	,,	WL CL WL	Lister & Sons.	1862-3 ,,	,,	,,	,,	**Y**		
							1863-4 ,,	,,	,,	,,	**Z**		

Impressed at Newcastle from c. 1750 to c. 1880, but not illustrated in the preceding tables :—

MARK.	NAME.	MARK.	NAME.	MARK.	NAME.
GL	Name not traced.	L&SONS	Lister & Sons.	I·M	John Miller.
WF	,, ,,	L&S	,, ,,	CD	Cuthbert Dinsdale.
WB	Mr. Bartlett ?	I·B	John Brown.	GL	Geo. Sam. Lewis.
SI	Samuel Jones.	J·B	,, ,,	MY&SONS	M. Young & Sons.
PI	Peter James.	JB	,, ,,	SJ	Simeon Joel.
HI	Name not traced.	WS	Wm. Sherwin.	J.C	John Cook.
FS	{ F. Somerville or Summerville, Sen., and F. S. Junr.	J·D	James Dinsdale.	RD	R. Duncan of Carlisle.
PB	Peter Beatch.	JS	Name not traced.	J&IJ	Joseph and Israel Jacobs.
I·T	Name not traced.	CJR	Chrstn. J. Reid.	J·F	James Foster.
R·D	,, ,,	RR	Robert Rippon.	W&JW	Wm. and Jno. Wilson.
R·W	Robt. Wilson.	JS	John Sutler.	TR	Thos. Ross of Carlisle ?
D&B	Darling & Bell.	J.W	John White.	TALBOT	A. Y. Talbot of Crook, Darlington.
T·H	Thos. Huntingdon.	DR	David Reid.	TS	Thos. Sewill.
H·B	Hugh Brechinridge.	BUXTON	Wm. Buxton of Bishop Auckland.	IR	Name not traced.
PL	Peter Lambert of Berwick.	I·D	John Deas ?	E.J.C	,, ,,
CR DR	Chrstn. K. Reid & David Reid.	OSWALD	Robt. Oswald of Durham.	WR	,, ,,
CAMERON	Alexr Cameron of Dundee.	OY	Oliver Young.	E·O	,, ,,
J·R	John Robertson.	IC	John Cook.	RO	,, ,,
		WW&SONS	W. Wilson & Sons.	I·H HB	,, ,,
		LP	L. Pedrine of Carlisle.		
		A&S	Alder & Sons of Blyth.		

DATE LETTER	
1864-5	a
1865-6	b
1866-7	c
1867-8	d
1868-9	e
1869-70	f
1870-1	g
1871-2	h
1872-3	i
1873-4	k
1874-5	l
1875-6	m
1876-7	n
1877-8	o
1878-9	p
1879-80	q
1880-1	r
1881-2	s
1882-3	t
1883-4	u

DATE.	MAKER'S MARK, TOWN MARK AND DATE-LETTER.	MAKER'S NAME.
1668		George Oulton.
c. 1683	RW STERLING RW	Ralph Walley.
"		Nathanl. Bullen.
c. 1685	NB Sterl:	" "
"		" "
1686-90		Alexand'r Pulford.
"		Peter Edwards.
"		" "
"	RW	Ralph Walley.
1690-2	RW	" "
"	PP " " "	Peter Pemberton.
"		" "
"	PP	" "
c. 1692	PP	"
1692-4	PP STERLING STERLING	" "
1695-1700	BB STERLING BB	Name not traced.
1695	D	… … …
1696	E	… … …
1697	F	… … ..

DATE.	BRITANNIA.	LION'S HEAD ERASED.	DATE LETTER.	TOWN MARK.	MAKER'S MARK.	MAKER'S NAME.
1701-2			A		Ri	Richd. Richardson.
ANNE. 1702-3	"	"	B	"	Bi	John Bingley.
1703-4	"	"	C	"	Bu / Bi	Nath. Bullen. / Chas. Bird.
1704-5	"	"	D	"	Ri	Richd. Richardson,
1705-6	"	"	E	"	Pe / Ho	Peter Pemberton. / Name not traced.
1706-7	"	"	F	"	Ha	" "
1707-8	"	"	G	"	Ro	Thos. Robinson.
1708-9	"	"	H	"	Gi	Name not traced.
1709-10	"	"	I	"	Co	" "
1710-11	"	"	K	"	Ie	" "
1711-2	"	"	L	"	Sa	" "
1712-3	"	"	M	"	Ta	Tarleton.
1713-4	"	"	N	"	Ri	Richd. Richardson.
GEO. I. 1714-5	"	"	O	"	Ri	" "
1715-6	"	"	P	"	Du	Barth. Duke.
1716-7	"	"	Q	"	Ma	Thos. Maddock.
1717-8	"	"	R	"	Ma / Ri	" " / Richd. Richardson.
1718-9	" LION PASSANT.	" LEOP'S HEAD C?	S	"	" "	" "
1719-20			T	.	Ri	" "
1720-1	"	"	U	"	Ma	Thos. Maddock.
1721-2	"	"	V	"	Ri	Richd. Richardson.
1722-3	"	"	W	"	Ri	" "
1723-4	"	"	X	"	Ri	" "
1724-5	"	"	Y	"	Ri	" "
1725-6	"	"	Z	"	JM	John Melling.

	LION PASSANT	LEOPARD'S HEAD CROWNED	TOWN MARK	DATE LETTER	MAKER'S MARK	MAKER'S NAME
1726-7	lion	leopard	town	A	BP	Benj'n Pemberton.
GEO. II. 1727-8	"	"	"	B	BP	" "
1728-9	"	"	"	C	℞℞	Richd. Richardson.
1729-30	"	"	"	D	RP	Richd. Pike.
1730-1	"	"	"	E	WR	Wm. Richardson.
1731-2	"	"	"	F		R.R. conjoined as at 1728 above.
1732-3	"	"	"	G	℞℞	Richd. Richardson.
1733-4	"	"	"	H	RR	" "
1734-5	"	"	"	I	"	" "
1735-6	"	"	"	K	℞℞	" "
1736-7	"	"	"	L	"	" "
1737-8	"	"	"	M	℞℞	" "
1738-9	"	"	"	N	"	" "
1739-40	"	"	"	O	WR	Wm. Richardson.
1740-1	"	"	"	P	BP	Benj'n Pemberton.
1741-2	"	"	"	Q	RR	Richd. Richardson.
1742-3	"	"	"	R	TM	Thos. Maddock.
1743-4	"	"	"	S	RR	Richd. Richardson.
1744-5	"	"	"	T	"	" "
1745-6	"	"	"	U	...	... ...
1746-7	"	"	"	V	...	... ...
1747-8	"	"	"	W		Thos. Maddock as above.
1748-9	"	leopard	"	X	RR	Richd. Richardson.
1749-50	"	"	"	Y	"	" "
1750-1	lion	"	"	Z	RR	" "

	LION PASSANT	LEOPARD'S HEAD CROWNED	TOWN MARK	DATE LETTER	MAKER'S MARK	MAKER'S NAME
1751-2	lion	leopard	town	a	RR	Richd. Richardson.
1752-3	"	"	"	B or b		
1753-4	"	"	"	C	"	" "
1754-5	"	"	"	D or d		
1755-6	"	"	"	e	"	" "
1756-7	"	"	"	F or f		
1757-8	"	"	"	G	RR	" "
1758-9	"	"	"	h	RR	" "
1759-60	"	"	"	I or i		
GEO. III. 1760-1	"	"	"	K or k		
1761-2	"	"	"	L or l		
*1762-3	"	"	"	m	RR RR	" "
1763-4	"	"	"	n	RR	" "
1764-5	"	"	"	O	RR	" "
1765-6	"	"	"	P	"	" "
1766-7	"	"	"	Q or q		
*1767-8	"	"	"	R	RR	" "
1768-9	lion	"	"	S	"	" "
1769-70	"	"	"	T	B&F	Bolton & Fothergill, Birm.
†1771-2	"	"	"	U	I W	Joseph Walley.
1773	"	"	"	V	GW / I·D	Geo. Walker. { James Dixon or Jos. Duke.
1774	"	"	"	W	ID	" "
1775	"	"	"	X	GW	Geo. Walker.
1775-6	"	"	"	Y	RR	Richd. Richardson, jr.

	LION PASSANT.	LEOPARD'S HEAD CROWNED.	TOWN MARK.	DATE LETTER.	KING'S HEAD.	MAKER'S MARK.	MAKER'S NAME.
1776-7	lion	leopard's head	town	a		RR	Richd. Richardson.
1777-8	"	"	"	b		GW	George Walker.
1778-9	"	"	"	c		RR	Richd. Richardson.
1779-80	lion	leopard's head	town	d		IW	Joseph Walley.
1780-1	"	"	"	e		"	" "
1781-2	"	"	"	f		GW	George Walker.
1782-3	"	"	"	g		"	" "
1783-4	"	"	"	h		JA	John Adamson.
1784-5 {	" / lion	" / leopard's head	" / town	i	KING'S HEAD / king's head	RI / RR	Richd. Richardson. / " "
1785-6	"	"	"	k	"	JC	J. Clifton or James Conway. }
1786-7	"	"	"	l	king's head	TP	T. Pierpoint.
1787-8	"	"	"	m	"	RB	Robt. Boulger.
1788-9	"	"	"	n	"	IG / RI	John Gilbert. Robert Jones.
1789-90	"	"	"	o	"	WH	Wm. Hull.
1790-1	"	"	"	p	"	WT / WT	Wm. Tarlton.* / " "
1791-2	"	"	"	q		IB	James Barton.
1792-3	"	"	"	r		EM	E. Maddock.
1793-4	"	"	"	s		TA	Thos. Appleby.
1794-5	"	"	"	t		TH	Thos. Hilsby.
1795-6	"	"	"	u		TM	Thos. Morrow.
1796-7	"	"	"	v		IA&S	John Adamson & Son.

	LION PASSANT.	LEOPARD'S HEAD CROWNED.	TOWN MARK.	DATE LETTER.	KING'S HEAD.	MAKER'S MARK.	MAKER'S NAME.
1797-8	lion	leopard's head	town	A	king's head	GL	George Lowe.
1798-9	"	"	"	B	"	R·I	Robt. Jones.
1799 1800	"	"	"	C	"	RG	Robert Green.
1800-1	"	leopard's head	"	D	"	NC	Nicholas Cunliffe.
1801-2	"	"	"	E	"		Maker's mark indistinct.
1802-3	"	"	"	F	"	GW	George Walker.
1803-4	"	"	"	G	"		" "
1804-5	"	"	"	H	"	D·E	Name not traced.
1805-6				I	"	N·L	Nicholas Lee.
1806-7	"	"	"	K	"		" "
1807-8	"	"	"	L	"	GL	George Lowe.
1808-9	"	"	"	M	"		Mark indistinct.
1809-10	"	"	"	N	"	WJ	Name not traced.
1810-1	"	"	"	O	"	IW	John Walker.
1811-2	"	"	"	P	"	WP	William Pugh (of Birmingham).
1812-3	"	"	"	Q	"	A&I	Abbott & Jones.
1813-4	"	"	"	R	"		" "
1814-5	"	"	"	S	"	JM	Jas. Morton.
1815-6	"	"	"	T	"		" "
1816-7	"	"	"	U	"	H·A	Hugh Adamson.
1817-8	"	"	"	V	"	JA	John Abbott.

	LION PASSANT.	LEOPARD'S HEAD.	TOWN MARK.	DATE LETTER.	KING'S HEAD.	MAKER'S MARK	MAKER'S NAME.		LION PASSANT.	TOWN MARK.	DATE LETTER.	QUEEN'S HEAD.	MAKER'S MARK	MAKER'S NAME.
1818-9	[lion]	[leopard]	[town]	A	[king's head]	J.W	J. Walker	1839-40	[lion]	[town]	A	[queen]	LL HL	J. & Thos. Lowe
1819-20	,,	,,	,,	B	,,	V&R	Vale & Co.	1840-1	,,	,,	B	,,	J&TL	,, ,, ,,
GEO. IV. 1820-1	,,	,,	,,	C	,,	J&R	Jones & Reeves	1841-2	,,	,,	C	,,	HYA	Henry Adamson.
1821-2-3	,,	,,	,,	D	,,	HYA	Hy. Adamson.	1842-3	,,	,,	D	,,	PL	P. Leonard.
1823-4	,,	[leopard]	,,	E	[king's head]	M.H	Mary Huntingdon.	1843-4	,,	,,	E	,,	WS	Wm. Smith.
1824-5	,,	,,	,,	F	,,	JT	John Twemlow.	1844-5	,,	,,	F	,,	RS	Ralph Samuel.
1825-6	,,	,,	,,	G	,,	JM	J. Morton.	1845-6	,,	,,	G	,,	AB WC	Adam Burgess. Wm. Crofton.
1826-7	,,	,,	,,	H	,,	G.L	Geo. Lowe.	1846-7	,,	,,	H	,,	JB	J. Burbidge.
1827-8	,,	,,	,,	I	,,	RB	Robt. Bowers.	1847-8	,,	,,	I	,,	IFW	John F. Wathew.
1828-9	,,	,,	,,	K	,,	TN	Thos. Newton.	1848-9	,,	,,	K	,,	CJ	Christr. Jones.
1829-30	,,	,,	,,	L	,,	JB JH	John Hilsby, L'pool. ,, ,, ,,	1849-50	,,	,,	L	,,	TW	T. Wilson.
WM. IV. 1830-1	,,	,,	,,	M	,,	JC	John Coakley.	1850-1	,,	,,	M	,,	EK	E Kirkman.
1831-2	,,	,,	,,	N	,,	JP	John Parsonage.	1851-2	,,	,,	N	,,	GW	Geo. Ward.
1832-3	,,	,,	,,	O	,,	TW	Thos. Walker or } Thos. Woodfield	1852-3	,,	,,	O	,,	TC	T. Cubbin.
1833-4	,,	,,	,,	P	,,	RL	Robt. Lowe.	1853-4	,,	,,	P	,,	RA GCL	Richard Adamson. G. C. Lowe. (Manchester).
1834-5	,,	,,	,,	Q	,,	RL	Richd. Lucas.	1854-5	,,	,,	Q	,,	TW	Thos. Wooley.
1835-6	,,	,,	,,	R	[king's head]	IW	John Walker.	1855-6	,,	,,	R	,,	AGR	A. G. Rogers.
1836-7	,,	,,	,,	S	,,	ILS	Jos. L. Samuel.	1856-7	,,	,,	S	,,	JL	John Lowe.
VICT. 1837-8	,,	,,	,,	T	,,	JS	John Sutters.	1857-8	,,	,,	T	,,	JM	Joseph Mayer.
1838-9	,,	,,	,,	U	,,	H.C	Henry Close.	1858-9	,,	,,	U	,,	EJ	Edwd. Jones.
								1859-60	,,	,,	V	,,	EN	Elias Nathan.
								1860-1	,,	,,	W	,,	GR	Geo. Roberts.
								1861-2	,,	,,	X	,,	HF	H. Fishwick.
								1862-3	,,	,,	Y	,,	HS	H. J. Stuart.
								1863-4	,,	,,	Z	,,	FB	Francis Butt.

	LION PASSANT.	TOWN MARK.	DATE LETTER.	QUEEN'S HEAD.	MAKER'S MARK.	MAKER'S NAME.
1864-5	🦁	⛨	a	👑	WD	Wm. Dodge.
1865-6	,,	,,	b	,,	JR	John Richards.
1866-7	,,	,,	c	,,	SW	Saml. Ward, Manchester.
1867-8	,,	,,	d	,,	GL	Geo. Lowe, junr.
1868-9	,,	,,	e	,,	HT / HT	Henry Tarlton, Liverpool.
1869-70	,,	,,	f	,,	WR	W. Roskell, Liverpool.
1870-1	,,	,,	g	,,	S.Q	S. Quilliam.
1871-2	,,	,,	h	,,	GR	Geo. Roberts.
1872-3	,,	,,	i	,,	RO	Robt. Over.
1873-4	,,	,,	k	,,	TR	Thos. Russell.
1874-5	,,	,,	l	,,	HG	Hugh Green.
1875-6	,,	,,	m	,,	S&R	Samuel & Rogers.
1876-7	,,	,,	n	,,	AC	A. Cruickshank.
1877-8	,,	,,	o	,,	SQ	S. Quilliam.
1878-9	,,	,,	p	,,	GFW	Geo. F. Wright, Liverpool.
1879-80	,,	,,	q	,,	JK	Joseph Knight, Birmingham.
1880-1	,,	,,	r	,,	TP &S	T. Power & Son, Liverpool.
1881-2	,,	,,	s	,,	B.N	Benge Nathan.
1882-3	,,	,,	t	,,	WS	Wm. Smith, Liverpool.
1883-4	,,	,,	u	,,	AR	A. Rogers, Liverpool.

	LION PASSANT.	TOWN MARK.	DATE LETTER.	QUEEN'S HEAD.	MAKER'S MARK.
1884-5	🦁	⛨	A	👑	NBS
1885-6	,,	,,	B	,,	A.B
1886-7	,,	,,	C	,,	JT&S
1887-8	,,	,,	D	,,	A&M
1888-9	,,	,,	E	,,	W.T
1889-90	,,	,,	F	,,	E.W
1890-1	,,	,,	G		J.W
1891-2	,,	,,	H		T.C
1892-3	,,	,,	I		JH AH
1893-4	,,	,,	K		H.W
1894-5	,,	,,	L		JD WD
1895-6	,,	,,	M		A·M
1896-7	,,	,,	N		W.N
1897-8	,,	,,	O		H.K
1898-9	,,	,,	P		W.A
1899 1900	,,	,,	Q		TPB
1900-1	,,	,,	R		GN RH
EDW. VII. 1901-2	,,	,,	A		J.F
1902-3	,,	,,	B		B.B

MARKS ON CHESTER PLATE. MARKS ON LINCOLN PLATE.

DATE.	LION PASSANT.	TOWN MARK.	DATE-LETTER.
1903-4			C
1904-5	,,	,,	D
1905-6	,,	,,	E
1906-7	,,	,,	F
1907-8	,,	,,	G
1908-9	,,	,,	H
1909-10	,,	,,	I
1910-1	,,	,,	K
1911-2	,,	,,	L
1912-3	,,	,,	M
1913-4	,,	,,	N
1914-5	,,	,,	O
1915-6	,,	,,	P
1916-7	,,	,,	Q
1917-8	,,	,,	R
1918-9	,,	,,	S
1919-20	,,	,,	T
1920-1	,,	,,	U
1921-2	,,	,,	V

DATE (ABOUT).	MARKS.	DATE (ABOUT).	MARKS.
1560		1640-50	
,,		,,	
,,		,,	
1569		1642	
c. 1590		1650	
1617		,,	
1624		1650-6	
1628		1660	
1633		,,	
1639		1686	
1640		1690	
1640-50	,,	,,	
,,		,,	
,,		1706	

	LION PASSANT.	ANCHOR.	DATE LETTER.	KING'S HEAD.	MAKER'S MARK.	MAKER'S NAME.
1773-4	(lion)	(anchor)	A		MB IF	Matthew Boulton & John Fothergill
1774-5	,,	,,	B		,, ,,	{ ,, ,, / ,, ,, }
1775-6	,,	,,	C		CF	Charles Freeth.
1776-7	,,	,,	D		,,	,, ,,
1777-8	,,	,,	E		{ RB CF / MB IF }	Richard Bickley, Charles Freeth. / Boulton & Fothergill.
1778-9	,,	,,	F		,, ,,	,, ,,
1779-80	,,	,,	G		TW	T. Willmore & Alston.
1780-1	,,	,,	H		...	... ...
1781-2	,,	,,	I		...	... ...
1782-3	,,	,,	K		TW	T. Willmore & Alston.
1783-4	,,	,,	L		,,	,, ,, ,,
1784-5	,,	,,	M	KINGS HEAD (head)	SP	Samuel Pemberton.
1785-6	,,	,,	N	,,	HH	Henry Holland.
1786-7	,,	,,	O	(head)	SP	Samuel Pemberton.
1787-8	,,	,,	P	,,	IT	Joseph Taylor.
1788-9	,,	,,	Q	,,	,,	,, ,,
1789-90	,,	,,	R	,,	TW	Thos. Willmore.
1790-1	,,	,,	S	,,	MB	Mathw. Boulton.
1791-2	,,	,,	T	,,	SP	Samuel Pemberton.
1792-3	,,	,,	U	,,	,,	,, ,,
1793-4	,,	,,	V	,,	MB	Mathw. Boulton.
1794-5	,,	,,	W	,,	IT	Joseph Taylor.
1795-6	,,	,,	X	,,	IS	John Shaw.
1796-7	,,	,,	Y	,,	TW	Thos. Willmore.
1797-8	,,	,,	Z	(head)	,,	,, ,,

	LION PASSANT.	ANCHOR.	DATE LETTER.	KING'S HEAD.	MAKER'S MARK.	MAKER'S NAME.
1798-9	(lion)	(anchor)	a	(head)	TW	Willmore & Alston.
1799, 1800	,,	,,	b	,,	SP	Samuel Pemberton.
1800-1	,,	,,	c	,,	F&W	Forrest & Wasdell.
1801-2	,,	,,	d	,,	{ IT / TW }	John Turner? / Thos. Willmore?
1802-3	,,	,,	e	,,	MB	Matthew Boulton.
1803-4	,,	,,	f	,,	IS	John Shaw.
1804-5	,,	,,	g	,,	IT	Joseph Taylor.
1805-6	,,	,,	h	,,	{ ML / WP }	Matthew Linwood. / William Pugh.
1806-7	,,	,,	i	,,	{ JW / C&B }	Joseph Willmore / Cocks & Bettridge.
1807-8	,,	,,	j	,,	WP	William Pugh.
1808-9	,,	,,	k	,,	MB	Matthew Boulton.
1809-10	,,	,,	l	(head)	IS	John Shaw.
1810-1	,,	,,	m	,,	T&T	Thropp & Taylor.
1811-2	,,	,,	n	,,	S&S	T. Simpson & Son.
1812-3	,,	,,	o	(head)	IT	Joseph Taylor.
1813-4	,,	,,	p	,,	C&B	Cocks & Bettridge.
1814-5	,,	,,	q	,,	L&C	W. Lea & Co.
1815-6	,,	,,	r	,,	,,	,, ,,
1816-7	,,	,,	s	,,	{ SP / W&K }	Samuel Pemberton. / Wardell & Kempson.
1817-8	,,	,,	t	,,	E·T	Edward Thomason.
1818-9	,,	,,	u	,,	JW	Joseph Willmore.
1819-20 GEO. IV.	,,	,,	v	,,	,,	,, ,,
1820-1	,,	,,	w	,,	ML	Matthew Linwood & Son.
1821-2	,,	,,	x	,,	L&C	Lea & Clark.
1822-3	,,	,,	y	,,	L&Cº	John Lawrence & Co.
1823-4	,,	,,	z	,,	JW	Joseph Willmore.

LION PASSANT.	ANCHOR.	DATE LETTER.	KING'S HEAD.	MAKER'S MARK.	MAKER'S NAME.
1824-5		A		TP / C·J	T. Pemberton & Son. / Charles Jones.
1825-6	,,	B	,,	LV&W / T·S	Ledsam, Vale & Wheeler. / Thomas Shaw.
1826-7	,,	C		L&C? / NM	John Lawrence & Co. / Nathaniel Mills.
1827-8	,,	D	,,	U&H / MB / J·W	Unite and Hilliard / M. Boulton & Plate Co. / Joseph Willmore.
1828-9	,,	E		ET / WF	Edward Thomason. / William Fowke.
1829-30	,,	F		IB / LV&W	John Bettridge. / Ledsam, Vale & Wheeler.
WM. IV. 1830-1	,,	G		TR&S / MB	Thos. Ryland & Sons. / M. Boulton & Plate Co.
1831-2	,,	H		JW	Joseph Willmore.
1832-3	,,	I	,,	,,	,, ,,
1833-4	,,	K	,,	ES / VR	Edward Smith. / Vale & Ratheram.,
1834-5	,,	L		T&P / WP	Taylor & Perry. / William Phillips.
1835-6	,,	M	,,	GW	Gervase Wheeler.
1836-7	,,	N	,,	FC / J&C?	Francis Clark. / Joseph Jennens & Co.
VICT. 1837-8	,,	O	,,	T·S / R.E.A	Thomas Spicer. / Robinson, Edkins & Aston.
1838-9	,,	P		GU / N·M	George Unite. / Nathaniel Mills.
1839-40	,,	Q	,,	N&R	Neville & Ryland ?
1840-1	,,	R	,,	,,	,, ,,
1841-2	,,	S	,,	... ...
1842-3	,,	T	,,	R.E.A	Robinson, Edkins & Aston.
1843-4	,,	U	,,	ES	Edward Smith.
1844-5	,,	V	,,	N·M	Nathaniel Mills.
1845-6	,,	W	,,	W&ET	Wm. & Ed. Turnpenny.
1846-7	,,	X	,,	Y&W / N·M	Yapp & Woodward. / Nathaniel Mills.
1847-8	,,	Y	,,	,,	,, ,,
1848-9	,,	Z	,,	... ...

LION PASSANT.	ANCHOR.	DATE LETTER.	QUEEN'S HEAD.	MAKER'S MARK.	MAKER'S NAME.
1849-50		A		NM	Nathaniel Mills.
1850-1	,,	B	,,	ES	,, ,, / Edward Smith.
1851-2	,,	C	,,	,,	,, ,,
1852-3	,,	D	,,		Nathl. Mills, as 1849.
1853-4	,,	E	,,		... ...
1854-5	,,	F	,,		... ...
1855-6	,,	G		GU	George Unite.
1856-7	,,	H	,,		... ...
1857-8	,,	I	,,		... ,, ...
1858-9	,,	J	,,		... ...
1859-60	,,	K	,,	GU	George Unite.
1860-1	,,	L	,,		... ...
1861-2	,,	M	,,		... ...
1862-3	,,	N	,,		J. H. & Co., as on page 414.
1863-4	,,	O	,,		... ...
1864-5	,,	P	,,	JM&C?	Names registered after 1850 not disclosed.
1865-6	,,	Q	,,		... ...
1866-7	,,	R	,,		... ...
1867-8	,,	S	,,	JG	... ...
1868-9	,,	T	,,		... ...
1869-70	,,	U	,,		... ...
1870-1	,,	V	,,		... ...
1871-2		W	,,	JT	Crown and 18 instead of lion passant.
1872-3	,,	X	,,		... ...
1873-4	,,	Y	,,		... ...
1874-5	,,	Z	,,		... ...

DATE	LION PASSANT	ANCHOR	DATE LETTER	QUEEN'S HEAD	MAKER'S MARK
1875-6	(lion)	(anchor)	a	(head)	TP&S
1876-7	,,	,,	b	,,	,,
1877-8	,,	,,	c	,,	H&T
1878-9	,,	,,	d	,,	
1879-80	,,	,,	e	,,	
1880-1	,,	,,	f	,,	
1881-2	,,	,,	g	,,	
1882-3	,,	,,	h	,,	H&T
1883-4	,,	,,	i	,,	,,
1884-5	,,	,,	k	,,	
1885-6	,,	,,	l	,,	
1886-7	,,	,,	m	,,	
1887-8	,,	,,	n	,,	
1888-9	,,	,,	o	,,	
1889-90	,,	,,	p	,,	N&H
1890-1	,,	,,	q		T.W.D
1891-2	,,	,,	r		N&H
1892-3	,,	,,	s		J.M.B
1893-4	,,	,,	t		SWS
1894-5	,,	,,	u		L.G
1895-6	,,	,,	v		T.H
1896-7	,,	,,	w		HM
1897-8	,,	,,	x		HH&C JHW
1898-9	,,	,,	y		A&JZ
1899 1900	,,	,,	z		JS SS

DATE	Anchor	Lion Passant	Date Letter	Maker's Mark
1900-1	(anchor)	(lion)	a	E&CoLᴶ
1901-2	,,	,,	b	HWE
1902-3	,,	,,	c	JS 6
1903-4	,,	,,	d	L&Co
1904-5	,,	,,	e	H&F
1905-6	,,	,,	f	
1906-7	,,	,,	g	
1907-8	,,	,,	h	
1908-9	,,	,,	i	
1909-10	,,	,,	k	
1910-1	,,	,,	l	
1911-2	,,	,,	m	
1912-3	,,	,,	n	
1913-4	,,	,,	o	
1914-5	,,	,,	p	
1915-6	,,	,,	q	
1916-7	,,	,,	r	R&TW
1917-8	,,	,,	s	
1918-9	,,	,,	t	
1919-20	,,	,,	u	
1920-1	,,	,,	v	
1921-2	,,	,,	w	
1922-3	,,	,,	x	
1923-4	,,	,,	y	
1924-5	,,	,,	z	

SUPPLEMENTARY LIST OF ADDITIONAL MARKS OF GOLDSMITHS,

Impressed at Birmingham, not illustrated in the preceding tables.

DATE	MARK	MAKER'S NAME
1776-7	JA&S	Jos. Adams & Son.
1778-9	E·S	Edward Sawyer.
1783-4	SP	Samuel Pemberton.
1804-5	W	... ...
1806-7	H&Co.	... ...|
1807-8	M	... ...
1811-2	W	... ...
1814-5	J.L	... ...
1820-1	TN	Thos. Newbold.
1822-3	SP	... ...
1826	T&K	Geo. Tye & Jas. Kilner.
1832-3	GT	Geo. Tye.
1876-7	TT &Co	... ...
1862-3	JH&Co	... ...|
1892-3	HW	... ...

Date	Lion Passant	Crown	Date Letter	King's Head (from 1784)	Maker's Mark	Maker's Name
1773-4	lion	crown	(letter)		R·M & Co / S·R & Co / MF & Co	Rich'd. Morton & Co. / S. Roberts & Co. / Mat'w. Fenton & Co.
1774-5	,,	,,			GA & Co	Geo. Ashforth & Co.
1775-6	,,	,,			IW & Co	John Winter & Co.
1776-7	,,	,,			W·D	Wm. Damant.
1777-8	,,	,,			TT/TL / MF/RC	Tudor and Leader. / Fenton Creswick & Co.
1778-9	,,	,,			I·S	John Smith ?
1779-80	,,	,,			,,	,, ,,
1780-1	,,	,,			NS & Co	Nath'l. Smith & Co.
1781-2	,,	,,			MF/RC	Fenton Creswick & Co.
1782-3	,,	,,			IW & Co	John Winter & Co.
1783-4					DH & Co / IP & Co	Danl. Holy & Co. / John Parsons & Co.
1784-5	,,	,,			,,	,, ,,
1785-6	,,	,,		,,	R·M	Richd. Morton & Co.
1786-7	,,	crown		head	IP & Co	John Parsons & Co.
1787-8	,,	,,		,,	,,	,, ,,
1788-9	,,	,,		,,	ITY & Co	John Younge & Sons.
1789-90	,,	,,		,,	RS	R. Sutcliffe & Co. (?)
1790-1	,,	,,		,,	IP & Co	John Parsons & Co.
1791-2	,,	,,		,,	ITY & Co	John Younge & Sons.
1792-3	lion	crown		,,	IP & Co	John Parsons & Co.
1793-4	,,	,,		,,	TL	Thos. Law.
1794-5	,,	,,		,,	IG & Co	John Green & Co.
1795-6	,,	,,		,,	ITY & Co	John Younge & Sons, as above.
1796-7	,,	,,			GE & Co	Geo. Eadon & Co.
1797-8	,,			head	T·LAW	T. Law.
1798-9	,,	,,		head	SR/GC	Saml. Roberts, jr. } Geo. Cadman & Co.

Date	Lion Passant	Crown	Date Letter	King's Head	Maker's Mark	Maker's Name
1799 / 1800	lion	crown	E	head	IL & Co / IG & Co	John Love & Co. / John Green & Co.
1800-1	,,	,,	N	,,	GA & Co / IG & Co	Geo. Ashforth & Co. / John Green & Co.
1801-2	,,	,,	H	,,	TW & Co	Thos. ,, Watson ,, & Co.
1802-3	,,	,,	M	,,	TL/DL / R·M	Thos. & Danl. Leader. / Richd. Morton & Co.
1803-4	,,	,,	F	,,	NS & Co	Nathan Smith & Co.
1804-5	,,	,,	G	,,	IE & Co	Jas. Ellis & Co.
1805-6	,,	,,	B	,,	AG & Co	Alexr. Goodman & Co.
1806-7	,,	,,	A	,,	ITY & Co	J. T. Younge & Co.
1807-8	,,	,,	S	,,	WT & Co	W. Tucker & Co.
1808-9	,,	,,	P	,,	T·B & Co	Thos. Blagden & Co.
1809-10	,,	,,	K	,,	IR & Co	John Roberts & Co.
1810-1	,,	,,	L	,,	GE & Co	Geo. ,, Eadon ,, & Co.
1811-2	,,	,,	C	head		John Roberts & Co., as 1809-10 above.
1812-3	,,	,,	D	,,	ST/N&H	Smith, Tate & Co. (Nicholson & Holt).
1813-4	,,	,,	R	,,	IK·IW & Co	Kirkby, Waterhouse & Co.
1814-5	,,	,,	W	,,	I·L	John Law
1815-6	,,	,,	O	,,	JE & Co	J. ,, Ellis & Co. (?)
1816-7	,,	,,	T	,,	I.W	John Watson.
1817-8	,,	,,	X	,,	I&T·S·	,, John and Thos. ,, Settle.
1818-9	,,	,,	I	,,	SCY & Co	S. C. Younge & Co.
1819-20	lion	{	V	,,	TIC / IK·IW & Co / GCV & Co	Thos. and Jas. Creswick / Kirkby, Waterhouse & Co. / G. Cooper & Co.
GEO. IV 1820-1	,,	,,	Q	,,	ST/H&T	Smith, Tate, Hoult & Tate.
1821-2	,,	,,	Y	,,	JL	Joseph Law
1822-3	,,	,,	Z	,,	IG & Co	John Green & Co.
1823-4	,,	,,	U	,,	W·B	Wm. Briggs.

	LION PASSANT	CROWN	DATE LETTER	KING'S HEAD	MAKER'S MARK	MAKER'S NAME
1824-5	🦁	👑	a	👤	S.C.Y &Co	S. C. Younge & Co.
					WB&Co	Wm. Blackwell & Co.
1825-6	,,		b	,,	I&I W &Co	Waterhouse, Hodson & Co.
1826-7	,,	,,	c	,,	BH &H	Battie, Howard & Hawksworth.
1827-8	,,		d	,,	TI NC	T. J. & N. Creswick.
1828-9	,,	,,	e	,,	BH &H	Battie, Howard & Hawksworth.
1829-30	,,		f	,,	IS HW	John Settle & Henry Williamson.
WM. IV. 1830-1	,,		g	,,	TI NC	T. J. & N. Creswick.
1831-2	,,	,,	h	👤	JB	Jas. Burbury.
1832-3	,,	,,	k	,,	S&N A&O	Stafford & Newton. Atkin & Oxley.
1833-4	,,		l	,,	TI NC / WALCo	T. J. & N. Creswick. Wm. Allanson & Co.
1834-5	,,		m	,,	I&I W &Co	Waterhouse, Hodson & Co.
1835-6	,,		p	👤	H&H	Howard & Hawksworth.
1836-7 VICT.	,,	,,	q	...		...
1837-8	,,		r	,,	HW &Co	Hy. Wilkinson & Co.
1838-9	,,		s	,,	HW &Co	,, ,, ,,
1839-40	,,	,,	t	,,	SH	Samuel Harwood.
1840-1	,,	,,	u	👤	,,	,, ,,
1841-2	,,		v	,,		...
1842-3	,,		x	,,	HE &Co	Hawksworth, Eyre & Co.
1843-4	,,	,,	z	,,		..

	CROWN	DATE LETTER	LION PASSANT	QUEEN'S HEAD	MAKER'S MARK	MAKER'S NAME
*1844-5	👑	A	🦁	👤	HE &Co	Hawksworth, Eyre Co.
1845-6	,,	B	,,	,,		... .
1846-7	,,	C	,,	,,		... ...
1847-8	,,	D	,,	,,		... ...
1848-9	,,	E	,,	,,		... ...
1849-50	,,	F	,,	,,	,,	Hawksworth, Eyre & Co.
1850-1	,,	G	,,	,,		... ...
1851-2	,,	H	,,	,,		... ...
1852-3	,,	I	,,	,,		... ...
1853-4	,,	K	,,	,,		... ...
1854-5	,,	L	,,	,,		... ...
1855-6	,,	M	,,	,,		... ...
1856-7	,,	N	,,	,,		... ...
1857-8	,,	O	,,	,,		... ...
1858-9	,,	P	,,	,,		... ...
1859-60	,,	R	,,	,,	MH &Co	Martin Hall & Co.
1860-1	,,	S	,,	,,		... ...
1861-2	,,	T	,,	,,		... ...
1862-3	,,	U	,,	,,	HH	Harrison Bros. & Howson.
1863-4	,,	V	,,	,,		... ...
1864-5	,,	W	,,	,,	FBrs	Fenton Bros.
1865-6	,,	X	,,	,,	HA	Hy. Archer & Co.
1866-7	,,	Y	,,	,,	RM EH	Martin Hall & Co., Ltd.
1867-8	,,	Z	,,	,,		... ...

	CROWN.	LION PASSANT.	DATE LETTER.	QUEEN'S HEAD.	MAKER'S MARK.	MAKER'S NAME.		CROWN.	LION PASSANT.	DATE LETTER.	MAKER'S MARK.	MAKER'S NAME.
1868-9	👑	🦁	A	👑	RM EH	Martin Hall & Co., Ltd.	1893-4	👑	🦁	a	J D & S	James Deakin & Sons.
1869-70	,,	,,	B	,,			1894-5	,,	,,	b	JR	John Round & Son, Ltd.
1870-1	,,	,,	C	,,		... .	1895-6	,,	,,	c	JD WD	Jas. Deakin & Sons.
1871-2	,,	,,	D	,,		... ...	1896-7	,,	,,	d	M&W	Mappin & Webb.
1872-3	,,	,,	E	,,		... .	1897-8	,,	,,	e	W.F AF	Fordham & Faulkner.
1873-4	,,	,,	F	,,	IH	John Harrison & Co., Ld.	1898-9	,,	,,	f	HW	Lee & Wigfull.
1874-5	,,	,,	G	,,		... ...	1899 1900	,,	,,	g	HA	Atkin Brothers.
1875-6	,,	,,	H	,,		... ...	1900-1	,,	,,	h	W&H	Walker & Hall.
1876-7	,,	,,	J	,,		... .	EDW. VII. 1901-2	,,	,,	i	R&B	Roberts & Belk.
1877-8	,,	,,	K	,,		... .. .	1902-3	,,	,,	k	GH	Harrison Bros. & Howson.
1878-9	,,	,,	L	,,			1903-4	,,	,,	l		... ...
1879-80	,,	,,	M	,,			1904-5	,,	,,	m		
1880-1	,,	,,	N	,,			1905-6	,,	,,	n		... ...
1881-2	,,	,,	O	,,		.	1906-7	,,	,,	o		.. ..
1882-3	,,	,,	P	,,			1907-8	,,	,,	p		.. . . ..
1883-4	,,	,,	Q	,,		. .. .	1908-9	,,	,,	q		
1884-5	,,	,,	R	,,		. .	1909-10	,,	,,	r		. . ...
1885-6	,,	,,	S	,,		. .	1910-1	,,	,,	s		.
1886-7	,,	,,	T	,,		..	1911-2	,,	,,	t		.. .
1887-8	,,	,,	U	,,		...	1912-3	,,	,,	u		
1888-9	,,	,,	V	,,	J·K·B	Hawksworth, Eyre & Co., Ltd.	1913-4	,,	,,	v		. .
1889-90	,,	,,	W	,,	WB JA	W. Briggs & Co.	1914-5	,,	,,	w		.. ...
1890-1	,,	,,	X	,,	RM EH	Martin Hall & Co., Ltd.	1915-6	,,	,,	x		. ...
1891-2	,,	,,	Y	,,	J·D&S	Jas. Dixon & Sons.	1916-7	,,	,,	y		
1892-3	,,	,,	Z		H·S	Henry Stratford.	1917-8	,,	,,	z		.. ..

SUPPLEMENTARY LIST OF MARKS OF GOLDSMITHS

Impressed at Sheffield, not illustrated in the preceding tables, from 1773 to 1905 :—

DATE.	MARKS.	MAKER'S NAME.	DATE.	MARKS.	MAKER'S NAME.	DATE.	MARKS.	MAKER'S NAME.
1773	W.H I.R	W. Hancock & J. Rowbotham.	1784	T.F&Co	T. Fox & Co.	1822	A.H	A. Hadfield.
"	WB &Co	W. Birks & Co.	1788	P.S	P. Spurr.	1824	CHS	C. Hammond & Co
"	T.L LAW	T. Law.	1789	W.J	W. Jervis.	1825	RG	R. Gainsford.
"		" "	1790	RS	R. Sporle.	1828	GH	G. Hardesty.
"	WB &Co	W. Birks & Co.	1791	I.B	J. Bailey.	1829	D&S	J. Dixon & Son.
"	I.R "	J. Rowbotham ?	"	MF &Co	M. Fenton & Co.	1833	JM	J. Mappin & Son.
"	J.L "	J. Littlewood.	1792	L.P &Co	? Luke, Proctor & Co.	1836	K&W	Kitchen & Walker.
"	SO "	Name not traced.	1796	G.A &Co	G. Ashforth & Co.	1840	L&M	Lee & Middleton.
"	IK&Co	John Kay & Co.	1797	C.P	C. Proctor.	"	WK &Co	Walker, Knowles & Co.
"	J.N W.N	J. Nowill. W. Nowill.	"	E.G	E. Goodwin.	1843	W&S	Waterhouse & Co
1774	I.M	J. Mappin.	"	I.C	J. Creswick.	1844	BW&A	Badger Worrall & Co.
"	W.M &Co	W. Marsden & Co.	"	H.T&Co	Mark of Henry Tudor & Co.	1846	R&S	Roberts & Slater.
"	S.R	S. Roberts.	1798	GG&Co	Goodman, Gainsford & Co.	1847	P.P &Co	Padley, Parkins & Co.
1775	I.R.Co	J. Rowbotham & Co.	"	SK&Co	S. Kirkby & Co.	1853	J.C N.C	J. & N. Creswick.
"	R.K	R. Kippax.	1799	R.J	R. Jewesson.	1856	WS HS	W. & H. Stratford.
"	IM&Co	J. Mappin & Co.	1801	T.P	T. Poynton.	1857	F&A	Fenton & Anderton.
1776	T.H	T. Hoyland.	1804		Name not traced.	1858	WH	W. Hutton.
"	I.T	J. Tibbitts.	"	I.S	J. Staniforth.	"	WS GS	W. & G. Sissons.
1777	I.H Co	J. Hoyland & Co.	1807	W.T&Co	W. Tucker & Co.	1859	MB	Mappin Bros.
"	IH&Co	" "	1808	J.W	J. Watson.	"	EM&Co	Elkington Mason & Co.
1778	S.W	S. Warburton.	1810	G.W	G. Wostenholme	1861	WWH	W. W. Harrison.
"	D.H	D. Holy.	1811	I.S T.S	J. Staniforth & Co.	1862	W&H	Walker & Hall.
1779	M&T	Madin & Trickett	"	R.G	R. Gainsford.	1863	LB	Levesley Bros.
1780	Y.G&H	Young, Greaves & Hoyland.	1813	I.R	J. Rogers.	1864	M&Co	Mappin & Webb.
"	N.S	N. Smith & Co.	1817	R.G	R. Gainsford.	1866	W& MD	W. & M. Dodge.
1781	I.D	J. Dewsnap.	1818	B.R	B. Rooke & Son.	1867	J.H.S	J. Slater & Son.
1783	S.K	S. Kirkby.	"	W.W	W. Wrangham	1868	CL TL	Levesley Bros.
			1820	TJ&NC	T. J. & N. Creswick.	1869	AB	A. Beardshaw.
			1822	T&IS	T. & J. Settle.	1905	IE &S	Name not traced.

HULL

DATE.	TOWN MARK.	MAKER'S MARK.	TOWN MARK.	MAKER'S MARK. (DATE LETTER.)	MAKER'S NAME.
1580	H	PC			Peter Carlille.
1587		I.C	H		James Carlille.
1621	(crown)	IC	RR	HB	„ „ *
1629	H	RR	H		Robt. Robinson.
1635	(crown)	RR	„		„ „
1638	H	CW	H		Chr. Watson.
1651	(crown)	IB	(crown)		James Birkby.
1666	(crown)	EM	(crown)		Edwd. Mangie or Mangy. }
1666-70	(crown)	TG		E	Name not traced.
1670-80	„	„		K	„ „
„	(crown)	EM		A	Edwd. Mangie or Mangy. }
1680	„	M			„ „
„	„	EM	„	D	„ „
1680-97	„	KM	„	E	Kath. Mangy.
„		KM			„ „
„	„	EM	„	F	Edwd. Mangy.
1689	„	TH	„		Thos. Hebden.
1690-7	(crown)	KM	(crown)		Kath. Mangy.
1697	(flower)	KM			„ „
1706	(crown)	AB	„		Abm. Barachin.

SHREWSBURY

DATE.	MARKS.
1530	
1560	
„	

LEWES.

c. 1590		D	
c. 1637		D	

ROCHESTER

DATE.	MARKS.
1560	R R
c. 1640	R

Sandwich.

BARNSTAPLE

DATE (ABOUT).	MARKS.	MAKER'S NAME.
1568-1601		John Coton.
c. 1570-75		Thos. Mathew.
1576		" "
1578		J. Coton.
1580		T. Mathew.
"		*J. Coton.
1584		" "
c. 1650		John Peard
1670-80		" "
1680		" "
1687		" "
1695		" "

TRURO

DATE (ABOUT).	MARKS.
1560-1600	
"	
"	
1600	
1620	
"	
"	
1630	

DEVON AND CORNWALL

DATE. (ABOUT).	MARKS.
1576-80	
"	
1580	
? c. 1600	
c. 1600-30	
"	
"	
"	
"	
"	
1610	
1610-50	
1630	
1641	
1650-1700	
1675	
1680-5	
1690	
1695	
"	
1700	
1715	

TAUNTON

DATE (ABOUT).	MARKS.
1645	
,,	
,,	
1660	
1676-82	
1689	

LEEDS

DATE.	MARKS.
1650 TO 1702	
,,	,, ,,
1660	
1680	,,
1690	
,,	,,

KING'S LYNN

DATE.	MARKS.
1632	
1635	,,
1640	,,

CARLISLE

DATE.	MARKS.
1571	
1630	
,,	
1670	

GATESHEAD

c. 1680	

LEICESTER

DATE.	MARKS.
1540	
1590	
1600	
,,	
1575 to 1600	
1630	
,,	

PLYMOUTH

DATE.	MARKS.
c. 1600	
1690-5	
1695-9	P 𝔐 Brita nnia
,,	𝔐 Star ling
c. 1694	IM Ster ling
1698	Rowe Plm° Britan
to	
1700	Row St Ncʀ Ply

SALISBURY

DATE.	MARKS.
c. 1596	R
,,	
c. 1620	H
,,	JL
c. 1627	IQ
c. 1629	R
,,	CB

COLCHESTER

DATE.	MARKS.
c. 1723	HUTCHINSON R ○ COLCHESTER

JAMAICA

DATE.	MARKS.
c. 1800	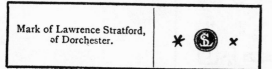

DORCHESTER

Mark of Lawrence Stratford, of Dorchester.	✳ S ✕

SHERBORNE

Mark of Richard Orenge (probably).	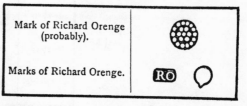
Marks of Richard Orenge.	RŌ

CHANNEL ISLANDS

DATE (ABOUT).	MARKS.
GUERNSEY, c. 1690-1730	
c. 1740	
c. 1750	
,,	
,,	
,,	
JERSEY, c. 1760	
c. 1780	
,,	
c. 1790	
c. 1800	
,,	
,,	
c. 1830	

POOLE.

DATE.	MARKS.
c. 1540	
,,	
c. 1560	
c. 1580	
,,	
c. 1620	

CALCUTTA.

DATE.	MARKS.
c. 1810	
,,	

BRISTOL

DATE.	MARKS.
c. 1730	
c. 1731	
c. 1780-90	

DATE (ABOUT).	MARKS.	DATE (ABOUT).	MARKS.	DATE (ABOUT).	MARKS.
1500		1570-7		1590	
,,		,,		,,	
1510		,,		,,	
1520		,,		1600	
1530		1570-80		,,	
,,		,,		,,	
1550		,,		,,	
,,		,,		,,	
1560		,,		,,	
,,		1576		,,	
1570		1580		,,	
,,		,,		,,	
,,		,,		,,	
1570		,,		,,	
		,,		,,	
		1590		,,	
		,,		,,	
		,,		,,	
		,,		,,	
		,,		,,	
		,,		,,	

DATE (ABOUT).	MARKS.	DATE (ABOUT).	MARKS.	DATE (ABOUT).	MARKS.	DATE (ABOUT).	MARKS.
1600		1620		1630-5		1640	
,,		1623		,,		,,	
,,		1625		,,		,,	
1600-50		1630		,,		,,	
1609		,,		,,		1640-8	
1610		,,		1637		1640-50	
,,		,,		,,		,,	
,,		,,		1638		,,	
,,		,,		1640		,,	
,,		,,		,,		1650	
,,		,,		,,		,,	
,,		,,		,,		,,	
,,		,,		,,		,,	
,,		1630-5		,,		,,	
1620		,,		,,		,,	
,,		,,		,,		,,	
,,		,,		,,		,,	
,,		,,		,,		,,	
,,		,,		,,		,,	
,,		,,		,,		,,	
,,		,,		,,		,,	
,,				,,			

DATE (ABOUT).	MARKS.	DATE (ABOUT).	MARKS.	DATE (ABOUT).	MARKS.
1650		1674		1680	
,,		1675		,,	
,,		,,		,,	
1658		1677		,,	
1660		,,		1680-5	
,,		1680		,,	
,,		,,		,,	
,,		,,		,,	
,,		,,		,,	
,,		,,		,,	
,,		,,		,,	
1660-70		,,		,,	
,,		,,		,,	
1667		,,		,,	
1670		,,		,,	
,,		,,		,,	
1670-4		,,		1682	
,,		,,		1684-5	
1674		,,		,,	
,,		,,		,,	
,,		,,			

DATE (ABOUT).	MARKS.	DATE (ABOUT).	MARKS.	DATE (ABOUT).	MARKS.
1685		1695		1730	
1687		,,		,,	
1690		,,		,,	
,,		,,		,,	
,,		1700		1730-4	
,,		,,		1730-40	
,,		1700-5		,,	
,,		,,		,,	
1690-1		1700-40		,,	
1690-5		1702		,,	
,,		1706-9		,,	
,,		,,		,,	
,,		,,		,,	
,,		1710		1740	
,,		,,		,,	
,,		1720-5		1750	
,,		1720-30		1750-60	
,,		1725-30		c. 1760	
,,		,,			
,,		,,			
1690-9		,,			
,,		1730			
1693					

DATE	MAKER'S NAME	MAKER'S MARK	TOWN MARK CASTLE	DEACON'S MARK	DEACON'S NAME
52-62	Alex. Auchinleck				Thos. Ewing.
63-4	Henry Thompsone (1561)		..		James Cok.
1570	(Mark indistinct.)		..		George Heriot, senr.*
576	Adam Craige				James Mosman.
85-6	John Mosman (1575)		..		John Mosman.
90-1	Adam Allane, jr. (1589)				Geo. Heriot, senr.*
91-2	James Craufuird		,,		Do. do.
91-4	David Gilbert (1590)		..		Wm. Cok (Cokie).
,,	James Craufuird (1591)				Do. do.
596/600	Hugh Lindsay (1587)		..		David Heriot.
09-10	Gilbert Kirkwood (1609)		..		Robert Denneistoun.
11-3	Robert Denneistoun (1597)				David Palmer.
,,	George Craufuird, jr. (1606)		..	..	Do. do.
17-9	Do. do.	..			John Lindsay.
,,	John Lindsay (1605)		..	.,	Do do.
,,	George Robertsone (1616)		..	.,	Do. do.
,,	Thos. Thompson (1617)		..	,,	Do. do.
1617	Hew. Anderson		..		George Craufuird.
13-21	Gilbert Kirkwood (1609)				James Denneistoun.
16-35	George Robertsone (1616)		..		George Craufuird.
633	Adame Lamb (1619)		..	..	Do. do.
,,	Thos. Kirkwood (1631)		..	..	Do. do.
33 (?)	(Mark indistinct.)				Alexr. Reid (probably).

DATE	MAKER'S NAME	MAKER'S MARK	TOWN MARK CASTLE	DEACON'S MARK	DEACON'S NAME
1637-9	Jon Scott Adm. (1621)				Jon Scott.
1640-2	Thos. Clyghorne (1606)				Thos. Clyghorne.
1642	Patrick Borthwick (1642)		..		John Fraser.
1643	Jon Scott (1621)			..	Do. do.
,,	Nicoll Trotter (1635)		..	..	Do. do.
1644-6	George Cleghorne (1641)		..		Adam Lamb.
,,	Andro Denneistoun (1636)		,,	..	Do. do.
,,	Thos. Clyghorne (1606)		..	..	Do. do.
1644	{John Myln or Jas. McAulay}		,,	,,	Do. do.
1649	Andro Burrell (1642)		..		George Cleghorne.
1648-57	Peter Neilsone (1647)		..	..	Do. do.
1650	Thos. Scott (1649)		..	..	Do. do.
1651-9	Robert Gibsoune (1627)		..		James Fairbairne.
1657	John Wardlaw (1642)		..	..	Do. do.
1660	Edwd. Cleghorne (1649)		..		Andro Burrell.
1665-7	Wm. Law (1662)		..		James Symontoun.
,,	Andrew Law (c. 1665)		..	..	Do. do.
1665	Alexr. Reid		..		Do. do.
1669-75	Alexr. Scott (1649)		..		Alexr. Reid (2nd)
1674	James Cockburne (1669)		..	..	Do. do.
1663-81	Alexr. Scott (1649)		..		Edwd. Cleghorne.
1675-7	George Rolland (1675)		..		Wm. Law.
1677	Alexr. Reid (3rd) (1677)		..	..	Do. do.

MAKER'S NAME	DATE	ASSAY MASTER'S NAME
Alexr. Reid (1660) / Edwd. Cleghorne (1649)	1681-2	John Borthwick.
Andrew Law (c. 1665) / Wm. Law (1662)	1682-3	,,
Thos. Yorstoun (1673)	1683-4	,,
John Lawe (1661)	1684-5	,,
James Penman (1673)	1685-6	,,
Do. do.	1686-7	,,
James Cockburne (1669)	1687-8	,,
George Scott (1677)	1688-9 WM. & MY.	,,
Wm. Scott (1686)	1689-90	,,
James Cockburne (1669)	1690-1	,,
Robert Bruce (1687)	1691-2	,,
Robert Inglis (1686)	1692-3	,,
James Sympsone (1687)	1693-4	,,
Geo. Yorstoune (1684)	1694-5 WM. III.	,,
Alexr. Forbes (1692)	1695-6	,,
James Sympsone ? (1687)	1696-7	James Penman.
(Not identified).	1697-8	,,
Thos. Ker (1694)	1698-9	,,
Alexr. Kincaid (1692)	1699 1700	,,
Colin McKenzie (1695)	1700-1	,,
Geo. Scott, jr. (1697)	1701-2 ANNE. 1702-3	,,
Mungo Yorstoun (1702)	1703-4	,,
Thos. Cleghorne (1689)	1704-5	,,
James Sympson (1687)		
Patrick Murray (1701)		

MAKER'S NAME	DATE LETTER	DATE	ASSAY MASTER'S NAME
Patrick Murray (1701) Adm.	A	1705-6	James Penman.
James Tait (1704)			
Walter Scott (1701)	B	1706-7	,,
Wm. Ged (1706)	C	1707-8	Edward Penman.
John Penman, jr. (1703)			
Harry Beathune (1704)	D	1708-9	,,
John Seatoune (1688)	E	1709-10	,,
James Mitchellsone (1706)	F	1710-1	,,
Patrick Turnbull (1689)	G	1711-2	,,
Robert Ker (1705)	H	1712-3	,,
Robert Inglis (1686)	I	1713-4 GEO. I.	,,
Mungo Yorstoun (1702)	K	1714-5	,,
,, ,,			
Thos. Ker (1694)	L	1715-6	,,
Harry Beathune (1704) / John Seatoun (1685)	M	1716-7	,,
Chas. Dickson (as 1721) / Chas. Blair (1707)	N	1717-8	,,
Wm. Ure (1715)	N	,,	,,
James Mitchellsone (1706)	O	1718-9	,,
Mungo Yorstoun (1702) / Alexr. Sympsone (1710)	P	1719-20	,,
Jas. Inglis (1720)	P	,,	,,
,, ,,	¶	1720-1	,,
David Mitchell (1700)			
Chas. Dickson (1719)	R	1721-2	,,
James Clarke (1710)	S	1722-3	,,
Colin Campbell (1714)			
Ken'th McKenzie (1714)	T	1723-4	,,
Chas. Blair (1707)			
Alexr. Edmonstoune (1721)	U	1724-5	,,
Archd. Ure (1715)	V	1725-6	,,
James Taitt (1704)	W	1726-7 GEO. II.	,,
Harry Beathune (1704)	X	1727-8	,,
Patrick Graeme (1725)	Y	1728-9	,,
Wm. Aytoun (1718) / Wm. Jameson (1729)	Z	1729-30	Archibald Ure

MAKER'S NAME	MAKER'S MARK	TOWN MARK CASTLE	ASSAY MASTER'S MARK	DATE LETTER	DATE	ASSAY MASTER'S NAME
...nes Anderson (1729) Adm.	IA	(castle)	AU	A	1730-1	Archibald Ure.
...gh Gordon (1727)	HG	,,	,,	B	1731-2	,,
...orge Forbes (1731)	GF	,,	,,	C	1732-3	,,
...n Main (1729)	IM	,,	,,	D	1733-4	,,
...w'rd Lothian (1731)	E·L	,,	,,	E	1734-5	,,
...n Rollo (1731) (...terwards Lord Rollo).	IR	,,	,,	F	1735-6	,,
...gh Penman (1734)	HP	,,	,,	G	1736-7	,,
...ander Farquharson (1734)	AF	(castle)	,,	H	1737-8	,,
...es Ker (1723)	I·K	,,	,,	I	1738-9	,,
...ugal Ged (1734)	GED					
...es Ker (1723)	I·K	,,	,,	K	1739-40	,,
...,, ,, (1737)	,,	,,	,,			,,
...enr. Oliphant (1737)	EO	,,	GED	L	1740-1	†
...w'ce Oliphant (1737)	LO	,,	,,	M	1741-2	†
...lliam Aytoun (1718)	WA					
...ert Gordon (1741)	RG	,,	E·L	N	1742-3	†
...vd. Lothian (1731)	E·L	,,	,,	O	1743-4	†
...as. Dickson (1738)	CD	(castle)	HG	P	1744-5	Hugh Gordon.
...enr. Oliphant (1737)	EO	,,	,,	Q	1745-6	,,
...n Kincard (1726)	IK	,,	,,	R	1746-7	,,
(Not identified.)	CL	,,	,,	S	1747-8	,,
...liam Gilchrist (1736)	WG	,,	,,	T	1748-9	,,
...ward Lothian (1731)	E·L	,,	,,	U	1749-50	,,
...ert Lowe (1742)	LOW	,,	,,	V	1750-1	,,
...,, ,, ,, enr. Oliphant (1737)	EO	,,	,,	W	1751-2	,,
...es McKenzie (1747)	IM	,,	,,	X	1752-3	,,
...es Weems (1738)	IW					
...a Edmonston (1753)	IE	,,	,,	Y	1753-4	,,
...a. Davie (1740)	WD	,,	,,	Z	1754-5	,,

MAKER'S NAME	MAKER'S MARK	TOWN MARK CASTLE	ASSAY MASTER'S MARK	DATE LETTER	DATE
Ker & Dempster.	K&D	(castle)	HG	A	1755-6
Rbt. Gordon (1741) Adm.	RG	,,	,,	B	1756-7
Wm. Taylor (1753) / John Clark (1751)	WT / CLARK	,,	,,	C	1757-8
Lothian & Robertson. / James Welsh (1746)	L&R / ItW	,,	,, THISTLE	D	1758-9
James Gilsland (1748)	IG	,,	(mark)	E	1759-60
Alexr. Aitchison (1746) / Jas. Somervail (1754)	AIT / I·S	,,	,,	F	GEO. III. 1760-1
John Robertson (1758) / Wm. Dempster (1742)	JR / W·D	,,	,,	G	1761-2
,, ,, / John Welsh (1742)	(mark)	,,	,,	H	1762-3
John Taylor (1760) / James Hill (1746)	IT / JH	,,	,,	I	1763-4
Milne & Campbell?	N&C	,,	,,	K	1764-5
Rbt. Clark (1763) / Wm. Drummond (1760)	RC / WD	,,	,,	L	1765-6
John Stirling? (1757)	IS	,,	,,	M	1766-7
Benjn. Tait (1763) / Gillsland & Ker.	TAIT / G&K	,,	,,	N	1767-8
Patk. Robertson (1751)	PR	,,	,,	O	1768-9
,, Daniel Ker. ,, (1764)	DK	,,	,,	P	1769-70
(not identified.) James Gilsland (1748)	JB / IG	,,	,,	Q	1770-1
Wm. & Jno. Taylor.	WT / T	,,	,,	R	1771-2
Wm. Davie (1740)	WD	,,	,,	S	1772-3
,, ,, Alexr. Gairdner (1754)	AG	,,	,,	T	1773-4
James Welsh (1746)	ItW	,,	,,	U	1774-5
... ...		,,	,,	V	1775-6
Wm. Davie (1740)	WD	,,	,,	W	1776-7
James Dempster (1775)	ID	,,	,,	X	1777-8
Patk. Robertson (1751)	PR	,,	,,	Y	1778-9
James Hewitt (1750)	JH	,,	,,	Z	1779-80

MAKER'S NAME.	MAKER'S MARK.	TOWN MARK CASTLE	THISTLE	DATE LETTER	DATE.
W. & P. Cunningham.	WPC	[castle]	[thistle]	A	1780-1
David Downie (Adm. 1770)	DD	,,	,,	B	1781-2
Fras. Howden (1781)	FH	,,	,,	C	1782-3
Robt. Bowman (1780)	RB	,,	,,	D	1783-4
Alex. Edmonston (1779)	AE	[king's head]	,,	E	1784-5
David Marshall (1782)	DM	,,	,,	F	1785-6
James Dempster (1775)	ID	[king's head]	,,	,,	G	1786-7-8
Thos. Duffus (1780)	TD	,,	,,	,,	H	1788-9
Alex. Gairdner (1754) / James Douglas (1785)	AG / JD	,,	,,	,,	IJ	1789-90
W. & P. Cunningham.	WPC	,,	,,	K	1790-1
Geo. Christie (1791)	GC	,,	,,	L	1791-2
Alex. Zeigler (1782)	AZ	,,	,,	M	1792-3
Peter Mathie (1774)	PM	,,	,,	N	§1793-4
Wm. Robertson (1789)	WR	,,	,,	O	1794-5
Alex. Henderson (1792)	AH	,,	,,	P	1795-6
Geo. Christie (1791) / Alex. Spence (1783)	GC / AS	,,	,,	Q	1796-7
W. & P. Cunningham.	WPC	[king's head]	,,	,,	R	1797-8
Thos. Duffus (1780)	TD	,,	,,	S	1798-9
Alex. Graham & Co.? / W. & P. Cunningham.	AG&C / WPC	[castle]	[thistle]	T	1799 / 1800
John Zeigler (1798)	IZ	,,	,,	U	1800-1
Fras. Howden (1781)	FH	[castle]	,,	V	1801-2
Matt. Craw.	MC	,,	[castle]	,,	W	1802-3
Wm. Auld (1788)	WA	,,	,,	X	1803-4
Simon Cunningham (1800)	SC	,,	,,	Y	1804-5
(Not identified).	M&R	,,	,,	Z	1805-6

MAKER'S NAME.	MAKER'S MARK.	KING'S HEAD	TOWN MARK CASTLE	THISTLE	DATE LETTER	DATE
R. Green or R. Grierson.	RG	[king's head]	[castle]	[thistle]	a	1806-
Cunningham & Simpson. (Not identified).	PC&S / D&M	,,	,,	,,	b	1807-
Do. do. *	IH	,,	,,	,,	c	1808-
George Fenwick. John McDonald.	GF / IMD	,,	[castle]	,,	d	1809-
Robt. Gray & Son (of Glasgow).	RG&S	,,	,,	,,	e	1810-
Math. Craw.	MC	,,	,,	,,	f	1811-
Alexr. Henderson.	AH	,,	,,	,,	g	1812-
J. McKay.	JM	,,	,,	,,	h	1813-
Frs. Howden. R. K. (a Perth maker). Wm. Zeigler.	FH / WZ	,,	,,	,,	i	1814-
					j	1815-
Js. & Wm. Marshall. Chas. Dalgleish.	J&WM / CD	,,	,,	,,	k	1816-
J. McKay. Do. do.	JM	,,	,,	,,	l	1817-
Redpath & Arnot.	R&A	,,	,,	,,	m	1818-
J'n'th'n Millidge?	JM	,,	,,	,,	n	1819-
Frs. Howden.	FH	,,	[castle]	[thistle]	o	GEO. I 1820-
Do. do.	,,	,,	,,	,,	p	1821-
Redpath & Arnot.	R&A	,,	,,	,,	q	1822-
Alexr. Zeigler.	AZ	[king's head]	,,	,,	r	1823-
Marshall & Sons.	M&S	,,	[castle]	,,	s	1824-
J. McKenzie?†	M	,,	,,	,,	t	1825-
J. McKay.	JM	,,	[castle]	,,	u	1826-
Leon'd Urquhart.	LU	,,	,,	,,	v	1827-
(Not identified).	WC	,,	,,	,,	w	1828-
J. McKay.	JM	,,	,,	,,	x	1829-
Do. do.	,,	,,	,,	,,	y	WM. I 1830-
Peter Sutherland.	PS	,,	,,	,,	z	1831-

MAKER'S NAME.	MAKER'S MARK.	KING'S HEAD.	TOWN MARK CASTLE.	THISTLE.	DATE LETTER	DATE.
...rshall & Sons.	M&S	(head)	(castle)	(thistle)	A	1832-3
..., Nasmyth.	JN	,,	,,	,,	B	1833-4
(Not identified).	GB	,,	,,	,,	C	1834-5
...er & Co.	E&Co	,,	,,	,,	D	1835-6
...& R. Keay, of Perth.	R&RK	,,	,,	,,	E	1836-7
...McKay.	JMc	,,	,,	,,	F	VICTORIA. 1837-8
...D. (see the Arbroath Marks).		,,	,,	,,	G	1838-9
..., Howden & Co.	JH&Co	,,	,,	,,	H	1839-40
..., Nasmyth & Co.	JN&C	,, QUEEN'S HEAD	,,	,,	I	1840-1
...o. Jameson, of Aberdeen.	GJ	(Queen's head)	,,	,,	K	1841-2
...rshall & Sons.	M&S	,,	,,	,,	L	1842-3
.. ..		,,	,,	,,	M	1843-4
...McKay.	JM	,,	,,	,,	N	1844-5
... ...		,,	,,	,,	O	1845-6
...G as Canongate c. 1836 (page 514).		,,	,,	,,	P	1846-7
...rshall & Sons.	M&S	,,	,,	,,	Q	1847-8
...Hay.	JH	,,	,,	,,	R	1848-9
...ckay & Chisholm.	M&C	,,	,,	,,	S	1849-50
Do. do.	,,	,,	,,	,,	T	1850-1
.. ..		,,	,,	,,	U	1851-2
.. ..		,,	,,	,,	V	1852-3
.. ..		,,	,,	,,	W	1853-4
...as. Robb.	CR	,,	,,	,,	X	1854-5
...Hay.	JH	,,	,,	,,	Y	1855-6
(Not identified).	RN	,,	,,	,,	Z	1856-7

MAKER'S NAME.	MAKER'S MARK.	QUEEN'S HEAD.	TOWN MARK CASTLE.	THISTLE.	DATE LETTER	DATE.
J. & W. Marshall.	J&WM	(head)	(castle)	(thistle)	A	1857-8
Jonthn. Millidge ?	JM	,,	,,	,,	B	1858-9
(Not identified).	JU	,,	,,	,,	C	1859-60
Alex. Hay.	A-H	,,	,,	,,	D	1860-1
J. Asherheim.	JA	,,	,,	,,	E	1861-2
R. L. Christie. J. E. Vernon.	RLC JEV	,,	,,	,,	F	1862-3
Wm. Crouch.	WC	,,	,,	,,	G	1863-4
D. Blackley. W. J. McDonald.	DB WJM'D RMC	,,	,,	,,	H	1864-5
Wm. Marshall.	WM DM&G	,,	,,	,,	I	1865-6
Elder & Co.	E&C JM	,,	,,	,,	K	1866-7
J. Smith or Scott. D. & J. Sanderson. Cockburn & McDonald.	JS D&JS COCKBURN	,,	,,	,,	L	1867-8
Geo. Edwards & Son.	GE &S	,,	,,	,,	M	1868-9
J. Hamilton & Son.	JHASON GEO. ST	,,	,,	,,	N	1869-70
George Laing. Walter Neil. Wm. Carstairs. Carlisle & Watt. W. Fraser.	GL WN WC C&W WF	,,	,,	,,	O	1870-1
		,,	,,	,,	P	1871-2
Jas. Aitchison.	AITCHISON	,,	,,	,,	Q	1872-3
J. Johnston. Jas. Hamilton.	JJ HAMILTON JH&Co	,,	,,	,,	R	1873-4
John Crichton.	M&GS J.CRICHTON	,,	,,	,,	S	1874-5
M. Crichton.	JH&C MC JG&C	,,	,,	,,	T	1875-6
Robb & Whittet.	R&W J&WM	,,	,,	,,	U	1876-7
C. or J. Gray.	GRAY	,,	,,	,,	V	1877-8
Mackay & Chisholm.	M&C	,,	,,	,,	W	1878-9
J. Crichton.	JC	,,	,,	,,	X	1879 80
Hamilton & Inches.	H&I	,,	,,	,,	Y	1880-1
... ...		,,	,,	,,	Z	1881-2

MAKER'S NAME.	MAKER'S MARK.	QUEEN'S HEAD.	TOWN MARK. CASTLE.	THISTLE.	DATE LETTER.	DATE.
... ...	CS	●	🏰	✾	𝖆	1882-3
Wm. Knaggs.	WK	,,	,,	,,	𝖇	1883-4
Hamilton & Inches.	H&I	,,	,,	,,	𝖈	1884-5
... ...	,,	,,	,,	,,	𝖉	1885-6
Mackay & Chisholm.	M&C	,,	,,	,,	𝖊	1886-7
Jas. Duncan.	JD	,,	,,	,,	𝖋	1887-8
Milne of Aberdeen.	MILNE ABD⁰	,,	,,	,,	𝖌	1888-9
W. Crouch & Sons.	WC&S	,,	,,	,,	𝖍	1889-90
Hamilton & Inches.	H&I		,,	,,	𝖎	1890-1
J. Crichton & Co.	J&C		,,	,,	𝖐	1891-2
Jas. Duncan.	JD					
Brook & Son.	B&S		,,	,,	𝖑	1892-3
J. Crichton & Co.	J&C		,,	,,	𝖒	1893-4
Lewis Cohen.	LC		,,	,,	𝖓	1894-5
Latimer & Sons.	L&SONS					
Jas. Duncan.	JD					
D. Crichton.	D.C		,,	,,	𝖔	1895-6
J. Crichton & Co.	J&Cᵒ		,,	,,	𝖕	1896-7
McDonald & Horne.	M&H					
J. Hardy & Co.	H&C		,,	,,	𝖖	1897-8
	C&K					
W. Crouch & Sons.	WC&S		,,	,,	𝖗	1898-9
W. & J. Milne.	W&JM					
Hamilton & Inches.	H&I		,,	,,	𝖘	1899 1900
Thos. Johnston.	TJ					
Young & Tatton.	Y&T		,,	,,	𝖙	1900-1
Jas. Robertson.	JR		,,	,,	𝖚	EDW. VII. 1901-2
Brook & Son.	B&S		,,	,,	𝖛	1902-3
... ...			,,	,,	𝖜	1903-4
... ...			,,	,,	𝖝	1904-5
... ...			,,	,,	𝖞	1905-6
... ...			,,	,,	𝖟	1906-7

TOWN MARK. CASTLE.	THISTLE.	DATE LETTER.	DATE.
🏰	✾	A	1907-8
,,	,,	B	1908-9
,,	,,	C	1909-10
,,	,,	D	1910-1
,,	,,	E	1911-2
,,	,,	F	1912-3
,,	,,	G	1913-4
,,	,,	H	1914-5
,,	,,	I	1915-6
,,	,,	K	1916-7
,,	,,	L	1917-8
,,	,,	M	1918-9
,,	,,	N	1919-20
,,	,,	O	1920-1
,,	,,	P	1921-2

DATE.	MAKER'S MARK.	TREE, FISH & BELL.	MAKER'S MARK.	DATE LETTER	MAKER'S NAME.
681-2	[TM]	[tree]	[TM]	a	Thos. Moncrur (1665)
682-3				b	... ...
683-4	[RB]	[tree]	[RB]	c	Robt. Brook (1673)
684-5				d	... ...
685-6	,,	,,	,,	e	Robert Brook (1673)
686-7				f	... ...
687-8				g	... .,.
688-9				h	... ...
689-90	[IS]	[tree]	[IS]	i	Jas. Stirling (1686)
690-1	,,	,,	,,	k	Do. Do.
691-2				l	... ...
692-3				m	... ...
693-4				n	... .
694-5	[RB]	[tree]	[RB]	o	Robt. Brook (1673)
695-6				p	... ...
696-7	[RB]	,,	[RB]	q	Robert Brook (1673)
697-8				r	... ...
698-9	[WC]	[tree]	[WC]	s	Wm. Clerk (1693)
1699/1700	[RB]	[tree]	[RB]	t	Robert Brook (1673)
700-1	[IL]	[tree]	[IL]	u	John Luke
701-2	[IL]	,,	[IL]	v	James Luke (1692)
702-3				w	... ...
703-4				x	... ...
704-5	[TC/IL]	,,	[TC/IL]	y	Thos. Cumming (1682) / John Luke, jr. (1699)
705-6	,,	,,	,,	z	Do. do. do.

DATE (ABOUT.)	MAKER'S MARK.	TREE, FISH & BELL.	MAKER'S MARK.	LETTER	MAKER'S MARK.
1706-7				A	... ...
1707-8	[IL]	[tree]	[IL]	B	John Luke, jr. (1699)
	,,	,,	,,	D	Do. do. ,,
1709-10	[WC]	[tree]	[WC]	,,	William Clerk (1693)
1709-20	[IF]	[tree]	[IF]		John Falconer (1709)
,,	[JL]	,,	[JL]		James Lockhart (1707)
1717-49	[IB]	,,	[IB]		Johan Got-helf-Bilsings (1717)
1728-31	,,	,,	,,	S	Do. do. ,,
1725-35	[RL]	,,	[RL]	S	Robert Luke (1721)
1743-52	[IG]	[tree]	[IG]	S	James Glen (1743)
,,	[GLN]	,,	[GLN]	,,	Do. do. ,,
1747-60	[ST]		[ST]	S	Saml. Telfer (1747)
1756-76	[DW]	,,	[DW]	S	David Warnock (1756)
,,		,,		S	(No maker's mark).
1757-80	[IC]	[tree]	[IC]		John Campbell (1757)
,,	[JL]	[tree]	[JL]		(Not identified.)
,,	[J·S]	[tree]	[J·S]	,,	Do. do.
1758-65	[WN]	,,	[WN]		Wm. Napier (1758)
,,	[B&N]	,,	[B&N]	S	Bayne & Napier.

DATE (ABOUT).	MAKER'S MARK.	TREE, FISH & BELL.	MAKER'S MARK.	LETTER.	MAKER'S NAME.
1763-70	AG	(tree/fish/bell)	AG		Adam Graham (1763)
,,	,,	,,	,,	E	Do. do.
,,	,,	,,	,,	F	Do. do.
1773-80	IT	S	IT	S	James Taylor (1773)
1776-80	M&C	(tree/fish/bell)		O	*Milne & Campbell.
,,	M&C	(tree/fish/bell)	M&C	O	*Do. do.
,,	RG	(tree/fish/bell)	RG		Robert Gray (1776)
,,	RG	(tree/fish/bell)	RG	S	Do. do. ,,
1783	T&H	(tree/fish/bell)	T&H		Taylor & Hamilton.
,,	J·Mc	(tree/fish/bell)	J·Mc	,,	James McEwen (1783)
1777-90	WL	,,	WL	,,	Wm. Love (1777)
1782-92	J·W	(tree/fish/bell)	J·W		James Wright (1782)
1785-95	ID	(tree/fish/bell)	ID	S	John Donald (1785)
,,	,,	,,	,,	O	Do. do. ,,
1781 / 1800	MF	(tree)	MF	S	Patrick McFarlane (1781)
		LION RAMPANT.			
1811-3	MF	(lion rampant)			Archibald McFadyen (1811)

DATE.	TREE, FISH & BELL.	LION RAMPANT.	DATE LETTER.	KING'S HEAD.	MAKER'S MARK.	MAKER'S NAME.
1819-20	(mark)	(lion)	A	(head)	B.SCOTT / M&R	B. Scott. (Not identified.)
GEO. IV. 1820-1	(mark)	,,	B	,,	LFN / JD	Luke F. Newlands (1816) / Jas. Downie (1812)
1821-2	,,	,,	C	,,	RG &S	Robt. Gray & Son (1819)
1822-3	,,	,,	D	,,	RD	Robt. Duncan (1813)
1823-4	,,	,,	E	,,	JB	John Bruce (1815)
1824-5	,,	,,	F	,,	M&S	(Not identified.)
1825-6	,,	,,	G	,,	AM	Alexr. Mitchell (1822)
1826-7	,,	,,	H	,,	AMᴰ	Angus McDonald (1824)
1827-8	,,	,,	I	,,	PA	Peter Arthur (1808)
1828-9	,,	,,	J	,,	EB	Edwd. Bell (1827)
1829-30	,,	,,	K	,,	JB CO	Jas. Burrell & Co. (1825)
WM. IV. 1830-1	,,	,,	L	,,	DR	Danl. Robertson (1829)
1831-2	,,	,,	M	,,		John Mitchell ... (as 1835-6 below).
1832-3	,,	,,	N	(head)	RG &S	Robt. Gray & Son (1819)
1833-4	,,	,,	O	,,	PA	Peter Arthur (1808)
1834-5	,,	,,	P	,,	DCR	D. C. Rait (1832)
1835-6	,,	,,	Q	,,	JM	John Mitchell (1834)
1836-7	,,	,,	R	,,	DCR / JW	D. C. Rait (1832) / (Not identified.)
VICT. 1837-8	,,	,,	S	,,	WP	W. Parkins (1835)
1838-9	,,	,,	T	,,	RG &S	Robt. Gray & Son (1819)
1839-40	,,	,,	U	,,	,,	Do. do. ,,
1840-1	,,	,,	V	,,	JM	John Mitchell (1834)
1841-2	,,	,,	W		HM	*Henry Muirhead (1835)
1842-3	,,	,,	X		HD	*Henry Downs (183)
1843-4	,,	,,	Y		DCR	*D. C. Rait (183)
1844-5	,,	,,	Z		CB	*Chas. Bryson (183)

	TREE, FISH & BELL.	LION RAMPANT.	DATE LETTER.	QUEEN'S HEAD.	MAKER'S MARK.
1845-6	🜚	🦁	A	👤	W.B
1846-7	,,	,,	B	,,	R.G &S
1847-8	,,	,,	C	,,	
1848-9	,,	,,	D	,,	J.R
1849-50	,,	,,	E	,,	P.A.Jʀ
1850-1	,,	,,	F	,,	J&WM
1851-2	,,	,,	G	,,	
1852-3	,,	,,	H	,,	R.G&S
1853-4	,,	,,	I	,,	
1854-5	,,	,,	J	,,	A.M
1855-6	,,	,,	K	,,	R.S
1856-7	,,	,,	L	,,	
1857-8	,,	,,	M	,,	A.McᴰD
1858-9	,,	,,	N	,,	W.A&S
1859-60	,,	,,	O	,,	
1860-1	,,	,,	P	,,	
1861-2	,,	,,	Q	,,	
1862-3	,,	,,	R	,,	J.M
1863-4	,,	,,	S	,,	
1864-5	,,	,,	T	,,	
1865-6	,,	,,	U	,,	
1866-7	,,	,,	V	,,	
1867-8	,,	,,	W	,,	
1868-9	,,	,,	X	,,	
1869-70	,,	,,	Y	,,	
1870-1	,,	,,	Z	,,	

	TREE, FISH & BELL.	LION RAMPANT.	DATE LETTER.	QUEEN'S HEAD.
1871-2	🜚	🦁	A	👤
1872-3	,,	,,	B	,,
1873-4	,,	,,	C	,,
1874-5	,,	,,	D	,,
1875-6	,,	,,	E	,,
1876-7	,,	,,	F	,,
1877-8	,,	,,	G	,,
1878-9	,,	,,	H	,,
1879-80	,,	,,	I	,,
1880-1	,,	,,	J	,,
1881-2	,,	,,	K	,,
1882-3	,,	,,	L	,,
1883-4	,,	,,	M	,,
1884-5	,,	,,	N	,,
1885-6	,,	,,	O	,,
1886-7	,,	,,	P	,,
1887-8	,,	,,	Q	,,
1888-9	,,	,,	R	,,
1889-90	,,	,,	S	,,
1890-1	,,	,,	T	
1891-2	,,	,,	U	
1892-3	,,	,,	V	
1893-4	,,	,,	W	
1894-5	,,	,,	X	
1895-6	,,	,,	Y	
1896-7	,,	,,	Z	

	TREE, FISH & BELL.	LION RAMPANT.		DATE LETTER.
1897-8	🜚	🦁		A
1898-9	,,	,,		B
1899 1900	,,	,,		C
1900-1	,,	,,		D
EDW. VII. 1901-2	,,	,,		E
1902-3	,,	,,		F
1903-4	,,	,,		G
1904-5	,,	,,		H
1905-6	,,	,,		I
1906-7	,,	,,		K
1907-8	,,	,,		L
1908-9	,,	,,		M
1909-10	,,	,,		N
1910-1	,,	,,		O
1911-2	,,	,,		P
1912-3	,,	,		Q
1913-4	,,	,,		R
1914-5	,,	,,	🌣	S
1915-6	,,	,,	,,	T
1916-7	,,	,,	,,	U
1917-8	,,	,,	,,	V
1918-9	,,	,,	,,	W
1919-20	,,	,,	,,	X
1920-1	,,	,,	,,	Y
1921-2	,,	,,	,,	

MARK.	NAME.	MARK.	NAME.	MARK.	NAME.
℞	J. Russell.	⌐H⌐	J. Hall.	T.SMITH&SON GLASGOW	T. Smith & Son.
WG	W. Gordon.	J.R.&W.L.	J. R. & W. Laing.	TS&S	Do. do.
VL&C°	V. Levy & Co.	LAING	Do. do.	MF JBM	(Not identified).
SK	D. Sprunt.*	M&M	McIntosh & McCulloch.	A.W.P	A. W. Peden.
JDD	J. D. Davidson.	AB	A. Brown.	R&AA	R. & A. Allen.
M&A	Muirhead & Arthur.	RK	Robt. Kerr.	D.T	D. Todd.
M&A	Do. do.	CCM	C. C. McDonald.	W.S.&C°	W. Scott & Co.
GA	G. Alexander.	H•L	H. Low.	J.W.	J. Wallace.
JB&S	J. Ballantyne & Son.	J.W	Jas. Weir.	T.W.C	T. W. Crawford.
WR	W. Russell.	WEIR	Do. do.	AWA	A. W. Allison.
WC	W. Corbett.	J.E	J. Easton.	W.W	W. Warrington.
A&T	Aird & Thompson.	J.P.C	J. P. Campbell.	MVW	M. V. Wilks.
T.S.&S	T. Smith & Son.	S&M:L	S...... & McLellan.	J·M	J. Moir.
TS&S	Do. do.	JHS	J. H. Storer.	K&P	Kerr & Phillips.
R&WS	R. & W. Sorley.	M.G	Mungo Guthrie.	M&A	Muirhead & Arthur.
R&WS	Do. do.	H&L	Hamilton & Laidlaw.	A.McD	A. McDonald.
DE&GE	Geo. Edward & Son.	W.A	W. Allan.	GJEFFREY	G. Jeffrey.
DF•GE	Do. do.	A.L.B	A. L. Boston.	H&M	Hyslop & Marshall.
P&C°	Parr & Co.	D&M	Duff & Millar.	W.G.T	W. G. Taylor.
GWS	G. W. Stratton.	J.ADAIR DUMFS	John Adair (Dumfries).	T.M	Thos. Mutter.
KELLY DUBLIN	Kelly & Co., Dublin.	L&C°	Lawson & Co.	ALEXR&SN	Alexr. & Son.
HOWELL	A. Howell.	JR	J. Riddoch.	JM	J. Mark.
DS	D. Simpson.	D.T	D. Todd.	F&F	Finlay & Field.
GM	G. Mitchell.	D.F.T	D. F. Turnbull.	WP	W. Paul.
J.E.A.	J. E. Ainsley.	JD	Jas. Douglas.	JP	Jas. Porter.
J.H.&C°	Jos. Haywood & Co.	TF	T. Fyfe.	GMcP	Geo. McPherson.
P.G	(Not identified).	M&C°	Mitchell & Co.	T.S.	Thos. Stewart.
WG	W. Gordon.	R.S	Robt. Scott.	JF	J. Fettes.
K.C.B	(Not identified).	SCOTT	Do. do.	D.F.	Duncn. Ferguson.
G.E.R	G. E. Rattray.	D.C.R.&S	D. C. Rait & Son.	WVJ	W. V. Jackson.
T.C.G.	T. C. Garstang.	DD	David Dow.	G.J.	Geo. Jackson.
D.M.C	D. M. Cameron.	W.J	W. Jenkins.	T.R&S	Thos. Ross & Sons.
DM	D. Munro.	T&W	Thomson & Williamson.	R.T	R. Tennent.
F.&J.S.	F. & J. Smith.	WR	Wm. Russell.	DMcC	D. McCallum.
MF	M. Friedlander.	MACFARLANE PARTICK	—— Macfarlane (of Partick).	J.D	John Donald.
M·F	Do. do.	HG	Hector Gollun.	D.S	Danl. Sutherland.
JR	J. Reid.	MW	Mark Wilks & Co.	J.M	Jas. Myres.
JF	J. Ferrier.	J.C	Jas. Crichton.	JB&S	J. Blond & Son.

MARK.	NAME.	MARK.	NAME.	MARK.	NAME.
W.S	W. Semple.	B & M	Brown & Miller,	J.N	J. Neville.
J.D.R	J. D. Reid.	JS	Jas. Simpson.	D&S	Davis & Son.
WR&S	Wm. Russell & Sons.	J.R	Jas. Ross.	LM&Co	Lorimer, Moyes & Co.
R·Mc·I	R. McInnes.	J&Co	Johnston & Co.	AA	Andrew Allison.
W.&W.LOGAN	W. &. W. Logan.	L&L	Lyle & Lock.	AF	A. Ferrier ?
D&M	Duff & Miller.	J.LYL	J. Lyle.	J.MJR	J. Muir, jr. ?
J.S	Jas. Smith.	J.M.B.&C	J. M. Ballantyne & Co.	H.T	H. Tennant.
J.F	Jas. Forrest.	G.D&Co	Geo. Drummond & Co.	G D	Geo. Drummond.
J.H.G.	*(Not identified.)*	M&T	Miller & Thompson.	W&S	Wilson & Sharp, Edinbro.
J.STEVENSUN	J. Stevenson.	A.T&S	A. Taylor & Son.	M.BROS	Mitchell Bros.
R&F	Ross & Ferrier.	W.M&Co	W. Miller & Co.	F.N	F. Neville.
R.R	Robt. Ross.	H&I	Hamilton&Inches,Edinbro.	L.K	L. King.
WJ	W. Jaffray.	G.W	George White (or Wilson).	RKM	R. K. Muirhead.
W.J	Do. do.	W.M	W. Mitchell.	AAP	Anton Pfaff.
PM	Peter Martin.	J.McA	J. McArthur.	R.L.R	R. L. Rawson.
R.B.F.	R. B. Forrest.	R A	Robt. Arthur.	J&AH	J. & A. Howell.
J&AK	Jas. & Andrew Kelly.	R&G	Reed & Garrick.	G&S	Guthrie & Shear.
T&D	Taylor & Downes.	G.T	Geo. · Thomson.	TLL	T. L. Leck.
JM&S	J. Muirhead & Sons.	G L	*(Not identified.)*	DH	D. Howie.
G.I	Geo. Innes.	R.B	Robt. Buchanan.	S&R	Smith & Rait.
SB GG	Barclay & Goodwin.	J.HERON	J. Heron.	ABA	Alex. B. Arthur.
D.S &Co	Dl. Sutherland & Co.	J.McD	J. McDonald.	AW	Alex. Wotherspoon.
JL	J. Laing.	T.F	T. Finlayson.	H D	Hugh Downs.
J&WM	J. & W. Mitchell.	D.T	David Taylor.	J.B	J. Brown.
W A	W. Allan.	T R	Thos. Ross.	AS	A. Sterling.
YOUNG	—— Young.	W B	Walter Baird.	CCC	Colin C. Campbell.
G&W	Gilmore & Watson.	A.R.S	A. & R. Stewart.	A·L	Alex. Lucas.
L&P	Lindsay & Paisley.	R H	Robt. Hyslop.	MM	M. Michael.
L H	L. Hymens.	L.A	Lawrence Aitchison.	W.N	W. Noble
W.C	Wm. Coghill.	WCM	*(Not identified.)*	J.C.S	*(Not identified)*
J.M·I	J. McInnes.	W&P	Watson & Pozzie.	JAF	John A. Fetter.
W.S	Wm. Sharp.	D.McD	D. McDonald.	J.F	Do. do.
JM·G	J. McGregor.	R D	Robt. Duncan.	R.B.G	*(Not identified.)*
P&Co	Panton & Co.	A C	A. Coghill.	RGL	Do. do.
R L	R. Laing.	T.C	Thos. Chapman.	M&H	Do. do.
T&Co	Tennent & Co.	McK&Co	McKenzie & Co.	GL	Do. do.
J&WB	J. & W. Boyd.	WSR	*(Not identified.)*	W&D	Do. do.
RRK	Robt. Rankin.	L&M	Lorimer & Moyes.	McH&S	Do. do.
J.C	Jas. Crichton.	L.G&Co	Leckie, Graham & Co.	R.W.F	Do. do.
		AMC	*(Not identified.)*	S&R	Smith & Rait.
		G.S.B	Do. do.		

DATE (ABOUT).	MARKS.	MAKER'S NAME.	DATE (ABOUT).	MARKS.	MAKER'S NAME.
1600-25	AB	... ...	1760	BL ... ABD	(Not identified.)
,,	,, ...	... ...	,,	BL ... BL	Do. do.
,,	AB ...	... ...		IG ABD ...	Jas. Gordon (1766)
1650	M ABD M	Thomas Moncrur (1649)	1766-79	IG ABD	Do. do.
,,	M ABD TM	Do. do. ,,		,,	Do. do.
,,	M VM ABD M	Walter Melvil (1650)	1772-7	AT ABD	Alexr. Thompson (1772)
1660-70	AB AB	(Not identified.)		IL ABD ...	Jas. Law (1777)
1670-7	WS VS	Wm. Scott (1666)	1777-8	,, ,,	Do. do.
1672-8	A·G AG	Alexr. Galloway (1671)		LL V ...	Do. do.
1690	AB X	(Not identified.)		IL ... ABD	John Leslie (1782)
1691-7	GW ABD D	Geo. Walker (1685)	1782-96	I·L ABD	Do. do.
1703	GW ABD D	Do. do. ,,		IL V ...	*Do. do.
1708-14	GR ABD GR	Geo. Robertson (1708)		,, ,,	Do. do.
1710-20	GR ... GR G	Do. do. ,,		,, ,, ...	Do. do.
1718-27	IW ... IW ...	John Walker (1713)		J·S ABD	Jas. Smith (1783)
1730	J WALKER	Do. do. ,,	1783-90	JS ABD	Do. do.
,,	GC ... GC P	George Cooper (1728)		... JS ...	Do. do.
,,	AF ... B	Alexr. Forbes (1728)	1785-95	PR ABD	(Not identified.)
,,	GC ...	George Cooper (1728)	1786 to 1818	... NG	Nathl. Gillet (1786)
,,	,, ,, P	Do. do. ,,		,,	Do. do.
1734-51	JA	Jas. Abercrombie (1734)		NG	Do. do.
1748-67	CA ABD	Coline Allan (1748)	1790 to 1800	NG W Z	Do. do.
1750	CA ... ABD	Do. do. ,,		,, ,, N ...	Do. do.
1763-70	IW ... M	James Wildgoose (1763)		E ... AA	James Erskine (1796)
,,	IW ABD	Do. do. ,,		,, ,,	Do. do.
			1796 to 1820	JE ...	*Do. do.
				JE	Do. do.
				R&S A B D	(Not identified.)

DATE (ABOUT).	MARKS.	MAKER'S NAME.
1800	WB [lion]	(Not identified.)
	DOUGLAS [marks] ID	J. Douglas (?)
	JA AB [mark]	John Allan (1797)
	J.A	Do. do.
	ID [shields]	J. Douglas (?)
1800	I·D	Do. do.
TO	GB ABD	(Not identified.)
1830	GB AB GB AB	Do. do.
	G·B ABDN	Do. do.
	WJ ABD WJ	Do. do.
	WJ ABD WJ	Do. do.
	A A A	Do. do.
1820	IB ABD	Do. do.
1830	WJ A B D [mark]	Do. do.
1841	GJ ABDN	Geo. Jamieson
1850	W·W ABDN	(Not identified.)
	WW [mark] ABD WW	Do. do.
1871	GS ABD	Do. do.

DATE (ABOUT).	MARKS.	MAKER'S NAME.
1680	VS ABC	Wm. Scott.
1698	VS BAN D	Do. do.
1720	VS [mark] VS	Wm. Scott, junr.
1725	PS [shield] PS BAN	Patk. Scott.
1732-41	P·G BAF B	Patrick Gordon.
1750	AS BAF AS	Alexr. Shirras.
1775	BA IA	John Argo.
1780	JA BANF	Do. do.
1785	WB BANF	Wm. Byres.
1795	R IK [mark] B	John Keith.
,,	B IK [mark] H	Do. do.
1800-20	[mark] IK F	Do. do.
,,	[mark] IK BANF [mark]	Do. do.
,,	[mark] IK	Do. do.
,,	IK BANF	Do. do.
,,	IK B H	Do. do.
,,	[marks]	Do. do.
,,	S·A [mark]	(Not identified.)
1820	GE B	Geo. Elder.
1835	BA [mark] McQ	John McQueen.
1850	WS H B	Wm. Simpson.
,,	,, ,,	Do. do.

ELGIN

DATE (ABOUT.)	MARKS.	MAKER'S NAME.
1728	WL ELG O	Wm. Livingston.
1730	ER ... ER	E. R.........
1754	IH ELN A	James Humphrey. {(E on its back and LN for Elgin).
1760	H IH	James Humphrey.
1770	JP ELN RS	... ...
	CF ELN	Chas. Fowler.
1790	,, ,,	Do. do.
to		Do. do.
1820	CF ELGIN ,,	W. F.........
	WF ,,	
1830	TS ELN	Thos. Stewart (see Inverness, p. 549).

CANONGATE

DATE (ABOUT).	MARKS.	MAKER'S NAME.
1680	GC XI·D *	... ...
,,	GC KI·D	... ...
,,	MZ MZ	... ...
1696	G·Z G·Z	... ...
1700	P XI ASN	... ...
,,	P XX FIS XI	... ...
1760	CM CM	... ...
1763	WC WC	... ...
1780-90	F GIG GA	... ...
1790	PC PC	... ...
TO	K $	... ...
	K M	M. Hinchsliffe.
1820	e IP	... ...
		... ...
1836	K DG	‡David Greig (?)

GREENOCK

DATE (ABOUT).	MARKS.	MAKER'S NAME.
1750		W. L......)
1765		Jonas Osborne, of Glasgow.
		Do. do.
		Do. do.
		Do. do.
1780		James Taylor, of Glasgow.
		G. B.........
		W. C.........
(")		M. C.
1790		B. C.
"		N. H.
1800		J. H.
"		R. N.
"		P. H.
1800		John Heron.
		Do. do.
		Thos. Davie.
		Do. do.
		John Heron.
1800 TO 1830		J. & G. Heron?
		Do. do.
		W. H. T.........
1820		Do. do.
"		Peterhead and Greenock mark.

MONTROSE

DATE (ABOUT).	MARKS.	MAKER'S NAME.
1670		Wm. Lindsay (probably).
1671		Wm. Lindsay.
		Do. do.
1680-3		Do. do.
1710		... ...
1752		Thos. Johnston.
1788		Benj. Lumsden (admitted 1788).
1811		Wm. Mill (1811)

ARBROATH

DATE (ABOUT).	MARKS.
1830	
1838	
1830-9	
"	

THE ARBROATH BURGH SEAL.

DATE (ABOUT).	MARKS.	MAKER'S NAME.	DATE (ABOUT).	MARKS.	MAKER'S NAME.
1640	[MK] [INS]	M. K......	1800	[J&N] [INS] [symbol]	Jameson & Naughton.
1643	,, ,, [T]	Do. do.	,,	[MAC MAS] ,,	——— Macmas.
1680	[MR] [INS]	M. R......	,,	[DF] [INS]	Donald Fraser.
1708	[M] ,, [M]	M. L......	1810	[C·J] [INS] [animal] [C·J]	Charles Jamieson.
1715	[M] ,, [symbol]	—— M......	,,	,, ,, ,,	Do. do.
1720	[RI] [INS] [A]	R I......	,,	[J·McR] [INS] [symbol]	J. McR.
1730	[IB] [FB] [fleur-de-lis]	John Baillie (and another)	1815	[RN] [INS] [J] [RN]	Robt. Naughton.
,,	[I·B] [FB] [symbol] [A]	Do. do.	,,	[RN] [J] [symbol]	Do. do.
1740	[IB] [INS] [X]	John Baillie	1820	[AM] [INS] [O] [O]	Alexr. MacLeod.
,,	[TB] [animal] [INS]	Thos. Baillie	,,	[AM·L] [INS] [symbols]	Do. do.
1770	[AS] [INS]	Alexr. Stewart	1830	[TS] [INS] [symbol]	Thos. Stewart.
1780	[RA] [animal] [G] [INS]	Robert Anderson	,,	[D·F INS]	Donald Fraser.
1790	[AS] [INS] [O]	Alexr. Stewart, jr.	,,	[AS] [INS] [symbol]	Alexr. Stewart.
,,	[animal] [hand]	(No maker's mark.)	1840	[symbol]	... ...
,,	[H&C°] [animal] [symbol] [A] [^]	Hamilton & Co.	1857	F BROS	Ferguson Brothers.
,,	[JA] ,, [A]	J. A.	1880	[F&M] [animal] [INVS]	Ferguson & MacBean.
,,	[T&C°] [animal] [symbol]	T. & Co.			
,,	[AS] [symbol]	Alexr. Stewart, jr.			
1800	[CJ] [INS]	Chas. Jamieson			

DUNDEE   PERTH

DATE (ABOUT.)	MARKS.	MAKER'S NAME.
1628	AL 🏆 AL	Alexr. Lindsay (1628)
1631	RG 🏆	Robt. Gairdine (mentioned 1683)
1643	RG 🏆 RG	Do. do.
1648	RG 🏆 RG	Do. do.
1667	TL 🏆 TL	Thos. Lindsay (1662)
1722	CD 🏆 CD E	Chas. Dickson (1722)
1730	IS 🏆 IS M	John Steven (mentioned 1764)
1742	AI ,, AI K	Alexr. Johnston (1739)
1764	JS 🏆	John Steven (1764)
1776	WS ,, WS 🏆	Wm. Scott (1776)
,,	,, ,, M	Do. do.
	AC 🏆 C U	Alexr. Cameron (1818)
	EL ,, D ,,	Edwd. Livingstone (1809)
	CAMERON ,, C ,, DUNDEE	Alexr. Cameron (1818)
	RN 🏆 🏆 🏆	Robt. Naughton ? (see Inverness, p. 549)
1800	T.S ,, ,,	Thos. Stewart ? (see Inverness, p. 549)
TO	WC ,, ,,	Wm. Constable (1806)
1840	RH S 👑 🏆 🏆 DUNDEE	(Not identified.)
	EL 🏆 EL M	Edwd. Livingstone (1809)
	WK BUN DEE ✡	(Not identified.)
	DM 🏆 DM	David Manson (1809)
	DM ,, DM	Do. do.
1809	WY 🏆 D 🏆	Wm. Young (1809)

DATE (ABOUT).	MARKS.	MAKER'S NAME.
1675	WM 🐑 B	W. M......
1680	RG 🐎 B	Robert Gardiner (1669)
1687	RG 🐎 RG	Do. do. do.
1710	W·S 🐂 S	William Scott, of Banff
1750	H 🦅 3 🦋	... ...
1772	IC 🦋 IC 🦋	James Cornfute (1772)
1780	TF ,, TF ,,	T. F......
,,	RK 🦋 RK	Robert Keay (1791)
,,	JJ ,,	J. J.
1791	RK 🦋 RK 🦋	Robert Keay (1791)
1800	WR 🦋 WR	William Ritchie (1796)
1810	IS O 🦋 🦋	John Sid (1808)
,,	R&RK ,, R&RK	R. & R. Keay
1815	DG 🦋 DG 🦋	David Greig (c. 1810)
1816	CM 🦋 CM	Charles Murray (1816)
,,	🦋 S ♀	(No maker's mark.)
,,	RMcG ,, RMcG	R. McG.
,,	IH ,, IH	I. H.
1820	RG ,,	Robert Greig (1817)
1830	RK 🦋 RK	Robert Keay, jr. (1825)
,,	AM 🦋 AM	A. M......
,,	P ♀ S 🦋	John Pringle (1827)
,,	,, RK	Robert Keay, jr. (1825)
,,	IP 🦋 IP 🦋	John Pringle (1827)
1830 TO 1850	IK ,, / RD ,,	J. K...... / R. D.....
1856	DG ,,	David Greig, jr.

UNASCRIBED SCOTTISH MARKS

TAIN.

DATE (ABOUT).	MARKS.
1500	IB
1690	DK
1700	IB
,,	HR S&D
1720	G&Mᶜ
1730	AL
1750	JS
,,	GG
,,	IM
,,	IC IC
,,	JB
,,	C&H C&H
1760	S
,,	T.COLGAN
,,	G
1770	INCE
,,	MK

DATE (ABOUT).	MARKS.
1780	JW
,,	CF
1790	R&S
,,	AR
,,	LM
,,	F G
1800	T·H
,,	EW
,,	RR ,,
,,	RB ,,
,,	CM
1816	1816 F.D
1800-20	JG
,,	DI
,,	WV AM

TAIN.

MARKS.
RW ,,
W.I. *TAIN* ,,

ST. ANDREWS.

PG PG

STIRLING.

HL

WICK.

JS WICK

	HARP CROWNED.	DATE LETTER.	MAKER'S MARK.	MAKER'S NAME.
CHAS. I. 1638-9		A		James Vanderbeck,
1639-40		B		John Thornton. / Edwd. Chadsey.
1640-1	,,	C		John Thornton.
1641-2	,,	D		Wm. Cooke.
1642-3		E		... ...
1643-4		F		... ...
1644-5		G		... ...
1645-6		H		... ...
1646-7		I		John Burke (or John Banister).
1647-8		K		.. ..
1648-9		L		.. . ..
COMWTH. 1649-50		M		... .
1650-1		N		... .
1651-2		O		... .
1652-3		P		.. . ..
1653-4		Q		... ...
1654-5		R		.. . ..
1655-6		S		Daniel Bellingham.
1656-7	,,	T		Joseph Stoaker (or John Slicer).
1657-8		U		... ...

	HARP CROWNED.	DATE LETTER.	MAKER'S MARK.	MAKER'S NAME.
1658-9		a		... ...
				Joseph Stoaker.
1659-60		b		Do. do.
CHAS. II. 1660-1		c		... ...
1661-2		d		... ...
1662-3		e		... ...
1663-4		f		Joseph Stoaker.†
1664-5	,,	g		Abel Ram.‡
1665-6		h		... ...
1666-7		i		... ...
1667-8		k		... ...
1668-9		l		... ...
1669-70		m		... ...
1670-1		n		... ...
1671-2		o		Joseph Stoaker.†
1672-3		p		... ...
1673-4		q		... ...
1674-5		r		... .
1675-6		s		... ...
1676-7		t		... ...
1677-8		u		... .

1639-40 George Gallant.

Date	Harp Crowned	Date Letter	Maker's Mark	Maker's Name
1678-9		A		... ...
			[TB]	Timothy Blackwood.‡
1679-80	harp	B	[S·M]	Samuel Marsden.
			[I·K]	James Kelly.
			[AG]	Andrew Gregory.
1680-1	harp	C	"	Do. do.
			[IP]	John Phillips.
			[WL]	Wm. Lucas or Walter Lewis. }
1681-2	"	D	[E·S]	Edwd. Swan.
1682-3	"	E	[IK]	James Kelly.
1683-4		F		... ...
JAS. II. 1685-6 7	"	G	[IF]	John Farmer.
			[IC]	John Cuthbert.
			[RN]	Robert Nevill.
			[IH]	John Humphrys.
1688 to 1692	harp	H	[DK]	David King.
			[RS]	Robt. Smith (warden 1701).
		I		... ...
WM. III. 1693-4-5	harp	K	[IW]	Joseph Walker.
			[WD]	Wm. Drayton.
			[WM]	Wm. Myers.
			[AS]	Ant'ny Stanley.
			[B]	Thos. Bolton.
1696-9	"	L	[IP]	John Phillips.
			[DK]	David King.
			[IW]	Joseph Walker.
			[IH]	John Humphrys.
			[A·S]	Anth'y Stanley.

Date	Harp Crowned	Date Letter	Maker's Mark	Maker's Name
* 1699/1700	harp	M	[EW]	Ant'ny Stanley (as 1693-4-5.) Edward Workman.
1700-1	"	N	[IS]	Alexr. Sinclair.
* 1701-2	harp	O	[IW]	Joseph Walker. ... ...
			[B]	Thomas Boulton.
ANNE. * 1702-3	harp	P	[B]	Do. do.
1703-4	"	Q	"	Do. do.
1704-5-6	harp	R	[HM]	Henry Matthews.
			[IW]	Joseph Walker.
1706-7-8	harp	S	[DK]	David King.
			[EB]	Edward Barrett.
			[B]	Thomas Bolton.
1708-9-0	"	T	"	Do. do. (Maker's mark indistinct)
1710-1-2	harp	U	[DK]	David King. (Maker's mark indistinct)
1712-3-4	harp	W	[EW]	Edward Workman.
			[WA]	Walter Archdall.
			[IC]	John Clifton.
GEO I. 1714-5	"	Y	[WA]	Wm. Archdall.
1715-6	harp	V	[tuite]	John Tuite.+
			[IC]	John Cuthbert, jun.
			[IW]	Joseph Walker. David King (as 1706 above).
1716-7		Z		... ...

HARP CROWNED.	DATE LETTER.	MAKER'S MARK.	MAKER'S NAME.
1717-8	[J]	AW	Joseph Walker.
		CT	Christr. Thompson.
		WC	Wm. Clarke (of Cork).
		IH	John Hamilton.
		Sa	John Savage ?
,,	,,	T.P	Thos. Parker.
1718-9	[C]	EC	Erasm's Cope.
1719-20	[D]	HD	Henry Daniell.
		HC	John Clifton, jr.
,,	[C]	IC	John Clifton, sr.
1720-1	[A]	IH	John Hamilton.
1721-2	[B]	,,	Do. do.
		TS	Thos. Sutton.
1722-3	[C]	AC	John Clifton, sr.
		EB	Edwd. Barrett.
1723-4	[D]	RH	Robert Harrison.
		TW	Thos. Walker.
		WD	Wm. Duggan.
1724-5	[E]	TS	Thos. Slade.
		IT	John Taylor.
		TB	Thos. Bolton.
1725-6	[F]	XXX	Mathw. Walker.
		MH	Michl. Hewitson.,
		XXX	Mathw. Walker.
1726-7	[G]	NV	Noah Vialas.
		PK	Philip Kinnersly.
GEO. II. *1727-8	[H]	RC	Robert Calderwood.
		IK	John King.
		WC	Wm. Clarke (of Cork).
1728-9	[I]	IR	John Robinson.
		BC	Bolton Cormick.
1729-30	[K]	RC	Robert Calderwood.
		IM	John Moore.
		WA	Wm. Archdall.
1730-1	[L]	DK	David King.

HARP CROWNED.	DATE LETTER.	HIBERNIA.	MAKER'S MARK.	MAKER'S NAME.
1731-2	[L]	[O]	EF	Esther Forbes.
			EC	Erasmus Cope ?
1732-3	,,	[B]	AL	Anthony Lefebure.
			JD	James Douglas.
1733-4	,,	[N]	,,	WW	Wm. Williamson.
			CL	Charles Lemaitre.
			IT	John Taylor.
1734-5	[O]		WT	Wm. Townsend.
			CL	Chas. Leslie.†
			TW	Thos. Williamson.
1735-6	,,	[P]	,,	BM	Barth Mosse.
			AB	Alexr. Brown.
1736-7	,,	[Q]	,,	IW	John Williamson.
			IW	John Wilme.
			AG	Andrew Goodwin.
			IT	James Taylor.
1737-8	,,	[R]	,,	DK	David King ?
1738-9	,,	[S]	,,	SW	Samuel Walker.
			MW	Matthew Walker.
			AG	Andrew Goodwin.
1739-40	,,	[T]	,,	FW	Francis Williamson.
			IW	John Walker.
1740-1	,,	[U]	,,	IM	John Moore.
			AR	Alexr. Richards.‡
1741-2-3	[TE] [U]	,,	ID	Isaac D'Olier.
			IL	John Laughlin.
1743-4	,,	[X]	,,	CL	Christr. Locker.
			RH	Robt. Holmes.
			Let	John Letablere.
1745	,,	[Y]	,,	IW	James Whitthorne.§
			M	John Moore.
1746	,,	[Z]	,,	W	Jas. Whitthorne. (see 1745).§

	HIBER-NIA.	DATE LETTER	HARP CROWNED	MAKER'S MARK	MAKER'S NAME		
1747		A		WW	Wm.	Williamson.
				CF	C.	Fox.
1748	,,	B	,,	WW	Will.	Walsh.
				W·B	Will.	Beates.
1749	,,	C		IC	John	Christie.
				IL	John	Laughlin.
1750	,,	D	,,	M·B	Mathias	Brown.
				ID	Isaac	D'Olier.
1751-2	,,	E E		IP	John	Pittar.
				WR	William	Ring.
1752-3	,,	F	,,	MH	Mich'el	Homer.
1753-4	,,	G	,,	W·T	Wm.	Townsend.
				AR	Aléxr.	Richards.
1754-5	,,	H	,,	CS	Christr.	Skinner.
1757	,,	I	,,	A	Matt'w	Alanson.
1758	,,	K		D·P	Daniel	Popkins.
				MS		(Not identified.)
1759	,,	L	,,	SW	Saml.	Walker.
				IP	J'nth'n.	Pasley.
GEO. III. 1760	,,	M	,,	R·C	Robt.	Calderwood.
1761	,,	N		GH	Geo.	Hill.
				TJ	Thos.	Johnston.
					Do.	do.
1762	,,	O		A	Matt'w	Alanson.
1763	,,	P	,,	DP	David	Peter.
1764	,,	Q	,,	WC	Wm.	Currie.
				WH	Wm.	Homer.
1765	,,	R	,,	FI	Francis	Jones.
				IC	Joseph	Cullen.
1766	,,	S	,,	MC IL	{ M. J.	Cormick & Locker. }
				F&K		French & Keating.
1767	,,	T		JW	John	West.
				RW	Richd.	Williams.
1768	,,	U	,,	R·T	Richd.	Tudor.
				ID	Jer'm'h	D'Olier.
1769		W		J·S	John	Shields.
				IG	James	Graham.
1770	,,	X	,,	IL	John	Locker.
				CH	Christr.	Haines.
1771	,,	Y		TK	Thos.	Kinsela.
				L	John	Lloyd.
1772	,,	Z	,,	CT	Chas.	Townsend.
				CM	Chas.	Mullin.

	HIBER-NIA.	DATE LETTER	HARP CROWNED	MAKER'S MARK	MAKER'S NAME		
1773		A		IW	John	Walker.
1774	,,	B	,,	WH	Wm.	Hughes.
				I·C	John	Craig.
1775	,,	C	,,	A·B	Ambrose	Boxwell.
				R·W	Richd.	Williams.
1776	,,	D		CT	Chas.	Townsend.
				MW	Matthew	West.
1777	,,	E	,,	HA	Hay	Andrews.
				DK	Darby	Kehoe.
				SW	Stephen	Walsh.
1778	,,	F	,,	MH	Michael	Homer.
				JP	John	Pittar.
1779	,,	G	,,	I·I	Jos.	Jackson.
				MK	Michael	Keating.
1780	,,	H	,,	MW	Michael	Walsh.
				J·B	John	Bolland.
1781	,,	I	,,	IK	John	Kelly.
				I·I	Jos.	Jackson.
				TJ	Thomas	Jones.
1782	,,	K	,,	WW	Wm.	Ward.
1783	,,	L	,,	L	John	Laughlin, jr.
				RW	Robert	Wyke.
1784	,,	M	,,	W·T	Wm.	Thompson.
				MW	Matthew	Walsh.
1785	,,	N	,,	CH	Christr.	Haines.
				W·S	Wm.	Supple.
1786	,,	O	,,	WJ	Wm.	Johnson.
				L&B		(Not identified.)
1787		P		J·P	John	Pittar.‡
				MW	Matthew	West.
1788	,,	Q	,,	MK	Michael	Keating.
				I·S	John	Stoyte.
1789	,,	R	,,	WL	Wm.	Law.
				RW	Robt.	Williams.
1790	,,	S	,,	AC	Arthur	Clark.
				A·N	Arthur	O'Neill.
1791	,,	T	,,	BT	Benjn.	Tait.
				TJ	Thos.	Jones ?
1792	,,	U	,,	RS	Robt.	Smith.
				WB	Wm.	Bond.
				IK	James	Keating.§
1793	,,	W	,,	MK	Michael	Keating.
				JP	John	Power.
1794		X		GW	George	West.
				L&B		(Not identified.)
1795	,,	Y	,,	IL	John	Laughlin, jr.
				IE	James	England.
1796	,,	Z	,,	GW	Geo.	Wheatley.
				FB	Fredk.	Buck.

	HIBERNIA	DATE LETTER	HARP CROWNED	KING'S HEAD	MAKER'S MARK	MAKER'S NAME
1797	◆	A	harp		J·R	John Rigby / Geo. West (as 1794.)
1798	,,	B	,,		J·K / JD	John Keene / John Daly
1799	,,	C	,,		I·K WEST / IS	James Keating.† / James Scott
1800	,,	D	,,		JK / WP	John Kearns / Walter Peter
1801	,,	E	,,		IC / JP	Jas. Connor / John Power
1802	,,	F	,,		RS / WH	Richd. Sawyer / Wm. Hamey
1803	,,	G	,,		O AN / IB	Arthur O'Neil / J. Brady
1804	,,	H	,,		RB / DE	Robt. Breading / Danl. Egan
1805	,,	I	,,		WD / DM	Wm. Doyle / (Not identified.)
1806	,,	K	,,	KING'S HEAD.	S·N / T&W / W·W	Samuel Neville / Tudor & Whitford / Wm. Ward
1807	,,	L	,,	◆	GB	Gust'v's Byrne
1808	,,	M	,,	,,	CT IW / SN	Terry & Williams (of Cork) / Saml. Neville
1809	,,	N	,,	◆	JJ / RB	Joseph Johnson / Robt. Breading
1810	◆	O	◆	,,	I·L·B / T·R	Jas. Le Bass / (Not identified.)
1811	,,	P	,,	,,	C·S / W·N	Chas. Stewart / W. Nowlan
1812	,,	Q	,,	,,	HAMY R·S / PM	W. Hamy & R. Smith / P Moore
1813	,,	R	,,	,,	WR / J·P	Wm. Rose / John Pittar
1814	,,	S	,,	,,	I·S / LAW / I·N	Jas. Scott / Wm. Law / John Nicklin
1815	,,	T	,,	,,	PG / SB	Phineas Garde (Cork) / S. Bergin
1816	,,	U	,,	,,	DE / RC	Danl. Egan / Randall Cashell
1817	,,	W	,,	,,	J·M / WC / NWB	James Moore / W. Cummins / Sir N.W. Brady
1818	,,	X	,,	,,	T·R / I·B	T. Read / J. Buckton
1819	,,	Y	,,	,,	ILB / IF WEST	Jas. Le Bass / Jas. Fry.†
O. IV. 1820	,,	Z	,,	,,	JS / EM	J. Salter (Cork) / Edwd. Murray

	HIBERNIA	DATE LETTER	HARP CROWNED	KING'S HEAD	MAKER MARK	MAKER'S NAME
1821	◆	A	◆	◆	MW&S / WM	M. West & Sons / Wm. Morgan
1822	,,	B	,,	◆	EC / IB / LAW	E. Crofton / J. Buckton / Wm. Law
1823	,,	C	,,	,,	EP / IF	Edwd. Power / Jas. Fray
1824	,,	D	,,	,,	SN / SB	Saml. Neville / Saml. Beere
1825-6	,,	E e	,,	◆	WT / R·G / W&Co	Wm. Teare? / Richd. Garde (Cork) / Ald'm'n West (& Co.)
1826-7	,,	F	,,	◆	J·S	J. Smith
1827-8	◆	G	◆	◆	CM / I·R	Chas. Marsh / J. Read
1828-9	◆	H	◆	◆	TWY+ / HF	Edwd. Twycross / Hy. Flavelle
1829-30 WM. IV.	◆	I	◆	◆	LN / C·M	L. Nowlan / Chas. Marsh
1830-1	◆	K	◆	◆	& M·G / S&G	D. Moulang & W. Gibson / Smith & Gamble
1831-2	◆	L	◆	◆	E·J / R·S / TF	Edmd. Johnson / Richd. Sawyer, jr. / T. Farnett
1832-3	,,	M	,,	,,	PM / HF	P. Moore / Hy. Flavelle
1833-4	◆	N	◆	,,	TM / EJ	Thos. Meade / Edmd. Johnson
1834-5	◆	O	◆	◆	LN / WS	L. Nowlan? / Wm. Sherwin
1835-6	,,	P	,,	,,	PW / I·M	P. Weeks? / J. Moore
1836-7	,,	Q	,,	,,	WS / R·G	Wm. Sherwin / Richd. Garde (Cork)
VICT. 1837-8	,,	R	,,	,,	IL / S&G	Josiah Low / Smith & Gamble
1838-9	,,	S	,,	◆	H&F	Hughes & Francis
1839-40	◆	T	◆	,,	PW	Peter Walsh
1840-1	,,	U	,,	,,	E&JJ / LN	E. & J. Johnson / L. Nowlan
1841-2	,,	V	,,	,,	GA	G. Alcock
1842-3	◆	W	◆	,,	IW / I·L·B	John Warren / Jas. Le Bass
1843-4	,,	X	,,	,,	IF / GW	J. Francis / Geo. West?
1844-5	◆	Y	◆	,,	MN	Michl. Nowlan
1845-6	◆	Z	◆	◆	JG / 1120	J. Gamble / † Joseph Johnson

HIBER-NIA.	DATE LETTER.	HARP CROWNED.	QUEEN'S HEAD.	MAKER'S MARK.	MAKER'S NAME.
1846-7	a			JJ	Joseph Johnson.
1847-8	b	,,	,,	JM / TM	J. Mahoney. / Thos. Mason.
1848-9	c	,,	,,	CC / WL / RS	C. Cummins, jr. / Wm. Lawson. / R. Samuel.
1849-50	d	,,	,,	D&W	Donegan & Co.
1850-1	e	,,	,,	JG / HF	J. Gamble. / Henry Flavelle.
1851-2	f	,,	,,	IN / AC	Joseph Needham, / Ann Cummins.
1852-3	g	,,	,,	GARDNER / JS	— Gardner. / J. Smyth.
1853-4	h	,,	,,	RS / T&W	R. Sherwin. / Topham & White.
1854-5	j	,,	,,	MK	Michael Keating.
1855-6	k	,,	,,	CC	C. Cummins.
1856-7	l	,,	,,	WA	W. Atcheson.
1857-8	m	,,	,,	D&W / AJ	Donegan & Co. / Arthur Johnson.
1858-9	n	,,	,,	JRN / NEILL	J. R. Neill. / Do. do.
1859-60	o	,,	,,	SLB	Samuel Le Bass.
1860-1	p	,,	,,	WP / W&IP	Wm. Percival. / W. & I. Percival.
1861-2	q	,,	,,	EP	E. Powell.
1862-3	r	,,	,,	JK / EJ&JJ	J. Keating. / E. & J. Johnson.
1863-4	s	,,	,,	JS	John Smyth.
1864-5	t	,,	,,	IS / RYAN&O	J. Scriber. / Ryan & Co.
1865-6	u	,,	,,	I.W / WATERHOUSE	Jas. West. / Waterhouse & Co.
1866-7	v	,,	,,	FM / AH / BRUNKER DUBLIN	Francis Martin. / A. Hutton. / Thos. Brunker.
1867-8	w	,,	,,	PD / WL	Patk. Donegan. / Wm. Lawson.
1868-9	x	,,	,,	EJ / MT	Edmd. Johnson, jr. / Mars. Trench.
1869-70	y	,,	,,	WL	Wm. Lawson.
1870-1	z	,,	,,	TDB	T. D. Bryce.

DATE.	MARKS.	MAKER'S NAME.
1663-4		Abel Ram.
1708-10		Philip Tough.
1715-6		Wm. Archdall.
1731		—— Sutton ?
1739		Robert Holmes.
1740		Will. Walsh. / Jane Daniell.†
,,	,, ,, ,, Su	—— Sutton ?
c. 1750		

1660	Æ	Andrew Edwards.
1704	A	Abraham Voisin.
,,	RS	Robert Smith.

1704	IG	John Garrett.
,,	IW	James Walker.

	HIBERNIA.	DATE LETTER.	HARP CROWNED.	QUEEN'S HEAD.	MAKER'S MARK.	MAKER'S NAME AND DATE OF REGISTRATION OF MARK.		
1871-2	⬢	A	⬢	⬢	J.W. W.&R.	J. Weir	Wickham. & Rogers.	(1871). "
1872-3	,,	B	,,	,,	J.D	John	Donegan.	(1872).
1873-4	,,	C	,,	,,	EGAN CORK	Wm.	Egan & Son (of Cork).	"
1874-5	,,	D	,,	,,	I.C	Ignatius	Cummins.	(1874).
1875-6	,,	E	,,	,,	McD.BS	McDowell	Bros.	(1875).
1876-7	,,	F	,,	,,	M'DB	Do.	do.	,,
1877-8	,,	G	,,	,,	W&S	West	& Son.	(1877).
1878-9	,,	H	,,	,,	J.R	J.	Redmond.	(1876).
1879-80	,,	I	,,	,,	W&S	West	& Son.	(1879).
1880-1	,,	K	,,	,,	O.C &D	O'Connor	& Dillon.	(1880).
1881-2	,,	L	,,	,,	E.JOHNSON E.J	Edmond Do.	Johnson. do.	(1881). (1882).
1882-3	,,	M	,,	,,	W.C H.H	Wm. Henry	Carty. Hopkins.	(1881). (1883).
1883-4	,,	N	,,	,,	D.M	Danl.	Moulang.	,,,
1884-5	,,	O	,,	,,	W&L	Winder	& Lamb.	,,,
1885-6	,,	P	,,	,,	F.BS	Frengley	Bros.	(1885).
1886-7	,,	Q	,,	,,	A&C?	Austin	& Co.	(1886).
1887-8	,,	R	,,	,,	M.A J.E.P	M. Jas. E.	Anderson. Pim.	(1887). ,,
1888-9	,,	S	,,	,,	T.B F.H	Thomas Fredk.	Barton. Hill.	(1871). (1889).
1889-90	,,	T	,,	,,	W.Q J.F	Wm. Joseph	Quinlan. Fray.	(1888). (1889).
1890-1	,,	U	,,		H.L.S	Henry L.	Stewart (of Limerick).	,,
1891-2	,,	V	,,		S.D.NEILL	Sharman D.	Neill (of Belfast).	(1890).
1892-3	,,	W	,,		H&H MOSLEY	Hopkins Jas.	& Hopkins. Mosley (Waterford).	(1883). (1892).
1893-4	,,	X	,,		C.H E.J	C. Edmond	Harris (Coventry). Johnson.	(1893). ,,
1894-5	,,	Y	,,		C.H.L K&G R.D	Chas. Howard Lawson. Kane Richard	& Gunning Dillon (Waterford).	(1894). ,, ,,
1895-6	,,	Z	,,		C.L C&S	Charles Chancellor	Lamb. & Son.	(1893). (1895).

	HIBER-NIA.	DATE LETTER.	HARP CROWNED.	MAKER'S MARK.	MAKER'S NAME AND DATE OF REGISTRATION OF MARK.		
1896-7		A		R&W / J·M	Richards	& Walsh.	(1895).
					John	Morton.	(1896).
1897-8	,,	B	,,	G LTD	Gibson,	Ltd. (Belfast).	(1897).
1898-9	,,	C	,,	R·K / M&C / RV	Robert	Knaggs.	(1898).
					Moore	& Co.	,,
					Robert	Valentine.	,,
1899	,,	D	,,	W.J·G / LAWSON DUBLIN	W. J.	Gethings.	,,
1900					Chas. Howard	Lawson.	(1900).
1900-1	,,	E	,,	L·A·W	Langley Archer	West.	,,
EDW. VII. 1901-2	,,	F	,,	H&T / M·C·&·D	Henderson	& Thompson (Belfast).	,,
					McCutcheon	& Donaldson (Belfast).	(1901).
1902-3	,,	G	,,	W&S	West	& Son.	(1902).
1903-4		H		JEB	J. E.	Byrne (Belfast).	(1909).
1904-5	,,	I	,,	JAMESON	——	Jameson.	,,
1905-6	,,	K	,,	R LTD	Russell	Ltd. (Manchester).	,,
1906-7	,,	L	,,	A.DUFFNER TIPPERARY	A.	Duffner (Tipperary).	(1907).
1907-8	,,	M	,,	F·S·LD	Finnegans	Ltd. (Manchester).	(1912).
1908-9	,,	N	,,	E&C	Elkington	& Co. (Birmingham).	,,
1909-10	,,	O	,,	W.E.&SNS LTD	W. Egan	& Sons (Cork).	(1910).
1910-1	,,	P	,,	N	——	Neill (Belfast).	(1906).
1911-2	,,	Q	,,	Y·A·M	Youghal Art Metal Works Co.		,,
1912-3	,,	R	,,	FALLER GALWAY	——	Faller (Galway).	,,
1913-4	,,	S	,,	J·M·D	J.	McDowell.	,,
1914-5	,,	T	,,	C.CROMER LIMERICK	C.	Cromer (Limerick).	(1907).
1915-6	,,	U	,,	& W/W	Wakeley	& Wheeler (London).	(1909).

	HIBER-NIA.	DATE LETTER.	HARP CROWNED.	MAKER'S MARK.	MAKER'S NAME AND DATE OF REGISTRATION OF MARK.		
1916-7		A		W·S	Will	Stokes.	(1910).
1917-8	,,	b	,,	WALDRON SKIBBEREEN	M.	Waldron (Skibbereen).	,,
1918-9	,,	C	,,	JR	Jas.	Ramsay (Dundee).	(1912).
1919-20	,,	D	,,	RS	R.	Sharman.	(1908).
1920-1	,,	e	,,	L·A·C	Crichton	Bros. (London).	(1912).

SUPPLEMENTARY LIST OF MARKS OF GOLDSMITHS,

impressed at Dublin but not illustrated in the preceding tables.

DATE.	MARK.	MAKER'S NAME.	DATE.	MARK.	MAKER'S NAME.	DATE.	MARK.	NAME OF MAKER.
1636	IW	John Woodcocke.	1706	B	Thos. Bolton.	1725-6	MB	Mary Barrett.
1663-4	FC	Francis Coffee or Clifton.	1710	HS	Henry Sherwin.	"	TW	Thòs. Wheeler.
1679	E·S	Edward Swan.	1710-2	TB	Thos. Bolton?	1726-7	PR	Peter Racine.
1680	E·S	" "	"		J. Pennyfather or J. Palet?	1728-9	S+C	... ...
"	LS	Lawrence Salmon.	1712-4	ED	... ...	1729	EF	Esther Forbes.
"	I·S	John Seager.	1715	GS	Geo. Smart.	"	US	Thos. Sutton.
1685	I·P	John Phillips.	"	E+D	Ed. Dowdall.	1730-1	GC	George Cross.
1685-7	IC	John Cuthbert.	1715-6	M	Mark Twelves.	"	GC	Geo. Cartwright.
1696-7	DM	(Not identified.)	1716-7	Z IW	... ...	"	D·M	Dorothy Monjoy.
1698	AS	A. Stanley?	1717-8	WB	W. Bell.	1731	A	Matthew Alanson.
1699	CM P	Cyriac Mallory.	1718-9	TW	Thos. Walker.	1732-3	EC	Erasmus Cope.
"	GL	George Lyng.	1719-20	AW	Arthur Weldon.	1734	I·G	John Gumly.
1700	AM	Alexr. Mackay.	1720	JR	Thos. Racine.	1735	D	Isaac D'Olier.
1701-2	T·S	Thos. Sumpner.	1722-3	E·F	Ed. Fitzgerald.	1736-7	TM	Thos. Maculla?
"	AS	.. ..	1723-4	D WS	... .	"	A	Anthony Lefebure.
1702-3	EB	Edward Barrett.	1724-5	PK	Phillip Kinnersly.	"	R·W	Ralph Woodhouse.
"	H	Thos. Hartwell.	1725-6	SA	John Sale.	"	D S	... ...
1703-4	D	... ...	"	RP	Robt. Pilkington.	1737-8	I·F	John Freebough.
"	K	David King.	"	MC	Matt. Copeland.			
1706	RF	Robt. Forbes.						

SUPPLEMENTARY LIST OF MARKS OF GOLDSMITHS

DATE.	MARK.	NAME OF MAKER.	DATE.	MARK.	MAKER'S NAME.	DATE.	MARK	MAKER'S NAME.
1737-8	TD	Thos. de Limarest.	1752	ER	Edward Raper.	1780	HO	Hugh O'Hanlon or Owen Hart?
1740-1	PD	Peter Desenard.	1754	R·C	Robt. Calderwood or Cope.	c. 1780	O·C	Owen Cassidy.
"	MR	... ...	"	H★W	Hy. Waldron.	"	AB	Alex. Barry?
"	I·C	Jas. Champion?	1757	M·F	Michael Fowler.	1780-5	BD	Barnaby Delahoyde?
"	PD	... ...	1758	WW	Wm. Williamson.	1785	D·E	Dan. Egan?
"	I·L	John Letablere.	"	CS	Christr. Skinner.	1792	MH	Michael Homer?
"	T·B	Thos. Burton.	c. 1760	H★W	See 1754 above.	1795	JASK	J. R. Ash.
"	SU	Thos. Sutton.	1762	I·M	John Moore, Jr.	c. 1795	I·W	... ...
c. 1740	II	? Henry Jago.	1764	ID	John Dawson.	c. 1797	TT	Thos. Tudor.
1743-4	WB	Wm. Bonynge.	"	FI	... ...	1798	IB	John Brooks?
"	R·C	Robt. Calderwood.	1766	RV	Ralph Vizard?	1800	S·T	Saml. Teare.
1745	G·B	George Beere.	1767	W★F	Wm. French.	1800-1	JB	John Bolland.
"	R·G	Robt. Glanville.	c. 1767	WT	Wm. Townsend.	"	G&PW	... ...
1746	I·H	John Hamilton?	1768	IW	Jno. Williamson.	1802	JD	John Daly?
"	W·F	Wm. Faucett?	"	B·W	Benj. Wilson.	1807	C&W	Clarke & West.
"	B·S	Bart'mew Stokes.	"	A·T	Abraham Tuppy.	"	ÆR	Æneas Ryan.
"	WW	Wm. Walsh.	1769	W·T MC	... ...	1810	RS	Richard Sawyer.
c. 1750	IT	Joseph Taafe.	"	GH	George Hall.	"	IT	John Teare.
1751	NM	Nathan Murray.	1770	KAR	John Karr.	1811	JK RF	... .
"	I★P	J. Pittar.	1776	I·B	... ...	1812	JH	J. Henzell?
"	WB	Wm. Betagh.	1779	IL	John Locker?	"	JK	... ...
			"	MS	... ...	1815	R·W	Richard Whitford.

The marks illustrated below are reproduced from a plate of pewter preserved at the Dublin Assay Office, in which marks in use at various dates, from about 1765 to 1812, have been stamped. The plate contains a number of other marks which it is unnecessary to illustrate here, as they appear in the preceding tables.

MARK.	NAME.	MARK.	NAME.	MARK.	NAME.
RA	Robt. Atkinson?	JSB		WG	
ET		EB		I·T	
RID	Richard & Jeremiah } D'Olier.	C·F		W·S	Will. Stafford?
GM		IN	Joseph Nixon.	I·E	John Ebbs.
JA	John Austin.	RB	Robert Breading.	TA	
JC	John Clarke.	RH		EC BC	
T·F	Thos. Farley.	IE	Joshua Emerson.	GN	George Nangle.
II	Joseph Jackson.	SR	Saml. Reily (Cork).	IH	James Hadmill.
TS		R·L		G·ALLEY	Geo. Alley.
W·D	Will. Digby?	G·T	Geo. Thompson.	IK	James Kenzie.
JK	John Keene.	J·J	James Jones.	IA	Jerome Alley?
G&B		PM		I·D	John Dalrymple.
TW	Thos. Williamson.	M·CL	Mark M'Cloughlin.	WS	
WB	Will Beere.	WFG	Wm. Fitzgerald (Limerick).	PS	
TP		HL		T M	Thos. Martin.
JC	John Coleman.	IN		WJ	Will. Johnson.
MB	Michael Byrne.	AN	Ambr'se Nicklin.	AT	Alex. Ticknell.
WP	Walter Peter.	O M·N		IO	John Osborne.
CD	Chas. Dowdall.	HM		HN	Henry Nicholson.
T·C	Thos. Cooksey.	NICOLSON	J. Nicolson (Cork).	RT	
J·J	James Jones.	JA		W·S	
IP		WK	Wm. Keene.	S·R	Saml. Reily (Cork).
GW		JJ	James Jones?	H&H	Hopper & Hannay.
CC	Christr. Clarke?	IN		JG	
I·W	Jacob West.	LM	La'rence Martin (Kilkenny).	TH	Thos. Hunt?
I·M		C·G		GN	George Nangle.
L·A				PF	

DUBLIN GOLDSMITHS' MARKS, 1765 TO 1812—

MARK.	NAME.	MARK.	NAME.	MARK.	NAME.
LH		WW		FB	Fredk. Buck.
WH	Will. Hughes?	BT	Benjn. Tait.	ST	Samuel Taylor.
CK		PW	Peter Wingfield.	RC	Randall Cashell?
WG	Will. Gethin?	TA	Thos. Adams.	WH	Wm. Hannay?
IT	John Tweedie?	HM		IC	
RS	Robt. O'Shaughnessy (Limerick).	TR	Thos. Rourke.	JL	John Lloyd.
IH	James Hewitt?	DP		E&B	
IW	John West?	RC	Randall Cashell?	WF	Will French.
JR	J'n'th'n Robinson?	GIBSON	Joseph Gibson (Cork).	WW	Will Ward.
SLY	Thos. Sly.	GR		AM	Arthur Murphy.
G&PW		JJ	Joseph Johnson.	WL	
MS		JC	James Campbell?	RD	
TE		DP		BP	
IM	James Mills?	ID	Isaac Davis?	JT	
WL	Wm. Law?	MW&S	Matt. West & Son.	IG	
WH	Will. Hamey?	IC	Jas. Connor?	WH	
TB	Thos. Baker?	BB		IB	John Bolland?
WF		SINGLETON	—— Singleton.	TSW	
FR		TT	Thomas Townsend.		

THE FOLLOWING MARKS, WHICH ARE STAMPED ON A COPPER-PLATE OF LATER DATE, RANGE FROM ABOUT 1813 TO ABOUT 1850.

MARK.	NAME.	MARK.	NAME	MARK.	NAME.
WG		GF		LK	
TK JF		TT		GW WM	
TK		CM		GA	
HL	Henry Lazarus.	IH		JT	John Townsend.
DM		WHT	Wm. H. Townsend.	WN	Wm. Nelson.
S&W		SB	S. Bergin.	K&F	
JM EM		J·MOORE	James Moore.	RE	
IM	J. Moore.	WC		TO	
BOYLE	—— Boyle.	FM&S		GRAYS	—— Grays.
EM	Edwd. Murphy.	LEE		PG	
		RWS	R. W. Smith.	IS	

DATE.	MARKS.	MAKER'S NAME.
1662		James Ridge.
1663		(Not identified).
1670		Walter Burnett.
1673		James Ridge.
1679		Richard Smart.
1680		Samuel Pantaine.
,,		Walter Burnett.
,,		(Both marks repeated).
,,		John Hawkins.
1691		Do. do.
1683		Robert Goble.
1686		Do. do.
1690		Do. do.
1692		Caleb Webb.
,,		Robert Goble.
1696		Do. do.
,,		Walter Burnett.
,,		Robert Goble.
,,		Do. do.
1697		Charles Bekegle.
1700		Robert Goble.
,,		Anthony Semirot.
1705		Robert Goble.
1709		William Clarke.

DATE.	MARKS.	MAKER'S NAME.
1709		Adam Billon.
1702-29		George Brumley.
1709		John Wigmore.(?)
1710		Wm. Clarke.
,,		Robert Goble.
1710-20		John Rickotts
1712		Robert Goble.
1715-25		Robert Goble, Junr
,,		,, ,,
,,		William Clarke
,,		,, ,,
1719		Caleb Rotheram
,,		William Clarke.
1720		,, ,,
,,		Bernald Baldwin.
,,		
1720-30		
,,		} Wm. Newenham
,,		Edward Dunsterfield.
1720-34		William Newenham
,,		,, ,,
,,		(Not identified—perhaps not Cork).
1722		... ...

DATE.	MARKS.	MAKER'S NAME.
1724	THO·LILLY STERLING	} Thomas Lilly.
1725-6	RM STERLING	Reuben Millard.
1730	WN STERLING	Wm. Newenham.
,,	WN STERLING	,, ,,
1730-40	W★B STERLING	William Bennett.
,,	IH STERLING IH	John Harding ?
,,	CR STERLING CR	Caleb Rotheram.
,,	STERLING I·H	John Harding ?
,,	R·G	Robt. Goble, jr. ?
,,	CP CP CP	Christr. Parker.
1720-37	W·MARTIN	William Martin.
,,	W·MARTIN	Do. do.
,,	W·M	Do. do.
,,	R·M	Reuben Millard.
1730-40	WB STERLING WB	William Bennett or Wm. Bentley.
1731	T.BULL	Thomas Bull.
1740	G·H STERLING	George Hodder.
,,	G·H ✠ G·H	Do. do.
,,	WB WB	William Bennett or Wm. Bentley.
1740-50	RA	,, ,,
,,	AS STERLING	} Anthony Semirot.
1745-70	STARLING G✠H	George Hodder.
,,	GH STERLING GH	Do. do.
,,	STARLING GH	} Do. do.
,,	G★H GH GH G‡H	Do. do.

DATE.	MARKS.	MAKER'S NAME.
c. 1750	STERLING SB	} Stephen Broughton.
1750-70	R·P STERLING	Robt. Potter.
,,	II IRISH II	John Irish.
,,	II STERLING	Do. do. (?)
1757-80	MD DERMOTT	Michael McDermott.
,,	MD STER	Do. do.
,,	MD STERLING MD	Do. do.
,,	WR ,,	William Reynolds.
,,	WR ,,	Do. do.
,,	WR	Do. do.
,,	WR ☘ STER·NG	Do. do.
,,	,, STERLING	Do. do.
,,	WR	Do. do.
,,	WR WR	Do. do.
,,	WR WR	Do. do.
,,	McD STERLING	Michael McDermott.
,,	MD ,,	Do. do.
1760	L★R STARLING L·R	... ...
,,	IA STERLING IA	... ...
1760-80	WALSH SW STERLING	} Stephen Walsh.
,,	C·B STERLING	Croker Barrington.
,,	SW WALSH STERLING	} Stephen Walsh.
,,	SW STERLING	Do. do.
,,	WALSH STERLING	} Do. do.
,,	SW WALSH STERLING	Do. do.
,,	SW ,,	Do. do.
,,	SM ,,	Stephen Mackrill.

DATE.	MARKS.	MAKER'S NAME.
1760-80	STERLING DMC	} Daniel McCarthy?
,,	DMC STER	Do. do.
,,	STARLING C·B	Croker Barrington.
,,	C·B DOLLAR	Do. do.
1760-85	IH STERLING	John Hillery
1765-95	CT ,, CT	Carden Terry.
1770	IRH STER	John Irish.
,,	TA STERLING TA	... ...
,,	McD Sterling	Michael McDermott.
,,	MD STERLING	Do. do.
1770-88	STER JWS STER	} John Whitney (free 1775).
1770-99	IN STERLING	John Nicolson.
,,	IN STERLING	Do. do.
,,	JN ,,	Do. do.
,,	,, NICOLSON	Do. do.
1777-1820	PW STERLING	Peter Wills.
1780	C·T STERLING	Carden Terry.
,,	IH STERLING IH	John Humphreys
,,	I·H ,,	Do. do.
,,	JK STERLING	Joseph Kinselagh.
,,	I·H STERLING	John Hillery.
,,	CT STERLING	Carden Terry.
,,	SC STERLING	(Not identified.)
,,	SR ,,	Samuel Reily.
,,	JSN ,,	Jno. & Sam. Nicolson.
,,	TC STIRLING	} Thomas Cumming.

DATE.	MARKS.	MAKER'S NAME.
1770-80	WM STERᴳ	W. Morrisey.
1770-99	NICOLSON STERLING	John Nicolson.
1777-1810	S·R STERLING	Samuel Reily.
,,	S·R STERLING	Do. do.
,,	SR STERLᴳ	Do. do.
,,	REILY STERLING	Do. do.
1783-95	W·ROE STERLING	} William Roe.
,,	TG STERLING TG	... ...
1786-95	TH STERLING	Thos. Harman.
1787-95	TC STERLᴳ TC	Tim. Conway.
1787	TD STERLING	Thomas Donnallan.
1787-95	JS ,,	John Sheehan.
,,	IG STERLING	Joseph Gibson.
1787-99	R·S STERLING	Richard Stevens.
,,	R·S STERLING	Do. do.
,,	I·S ,, I·S	John Sheehan.
,,	STERLING SHEEHAN	Do. do.
,,	SHEEHAN STERᴳ	Do. do.
,,	SHEEHAN STERLING	} Do. do.
,,	R·S STERLING	} Richard Stevens.
1790-1800	JMᶜN STERLING	} (Not identified.)
,,	RI STERLING	} Do. do.
1795	WT STERLᵍ	Wm. Teulon.
,,	W.T STERLINᴳ	Do. do.
,,	WT STERLINᴳ	Do. do.
,,	,, STERLᵍ	Do. do.

DATE.	MARKS.	MAKER'S NAME.
1795		John Supple.
,,	WT [crown] STERLING	William Teulon.
,,	WT STERLING	Do. do.
,,	HSM STERLING	(Not identified.)
,,	WT ,,	William Teulon.
,,	TJB STERLING	(Not identified.)
1791	IW ,,	John Warner
1780-99	,, STIRLING	Do. do.
1795	IW STERLING	John Williams.
,,	I.W STER	James Warner.
,,	I.W STERLING	Do. do.
,,	I.W STERLG	Do. do.
,,	{ STERLING / TOLLAND / STERLING }	—— Tolland.
1796	I.H STERLING	James Heyland.
,,	RD STERLING	... ...
,,	HEYLAND [crown] STERLING	} James Heyland.
,,	J.K STERLING	Jos. Kinselagh.
,,	JMd	... ...' ...
1800	IT TOLEKEN	John Toleken.
,,	IWM STERLING	(Not identified.)
1800-20	{ GIBSON / STERLING / GIBSON }	Joseph Gibson.
,,	WHELPLEY STERLING	John Whelpley.
,,	,, WHELPLY	Do. do.
,,	X ,, WHELPLY	Do. do.

DATE.	MARKS.	MAKER'S NAME.
1800-20	GIBSON STERLING	Joseph Gibson.
,,	HEYLAND ,,	William Heyland.
,,	,, TOLEKFN	John Toleken.
1795 / 1807	T&W ,,	{ Carden Terry & John Williams. }
1805	SG STIRLING	Samuel Green.
1805-14	SG / STERLING / SG	} Do. do.
,,	C.T I.W STERLING	Terry & Williams.
,,	T.MONTJOY ,,	Thomas Montjoy.
,,	IN NN ,,	John & Nicholas } Nicolson.
1807-21	C.T I.W STERLING	{ Carden Jane Terry & Williams }
1808-20	CORBETT STERLING	Daniel Corbett.
1809-30	JS STERLING	James Salter.
,,	R.G ,,	Richard Garde.
1810	T.MONTJOY STERLING	Thos. Montjoy.
,,	CONWAY STERLING	} James Conway.
,,	IE STERLING	John Egan.
,,	P.W STERLING	Peter Wills.
1810-20	WS STERLING	—— Steele ?
,,	1 SOLOMON STERLING	Isaac Solomon.
,,	IS STERLING	John Seymour.
,,	I.SOLOMON ,,	Isaac Solomon.
,,	F.S ,,	(Not identified.)
,,	PG STERLING	Phineas Garde.
1810-40	IS ,,	{ Isaac Solomon, or John Seymour. }
1812	GARDE STERLING	Phineas Garde.
1820	SEYMOUR STERLING	John Seymour.
1820-40	KM ,,	Kean Mahony.
,,	EH ,,	Edward Hawkesworth.
1824	O.BRIEN STERLING	Francis O'Brien'
,,	MAHONY STERLING	} Kean Mahony.
1838	M&B STERLING	(Not identified.)

YOUGHAL

DATE (ABOUT).	MARKS.	MAKER'S NAME.
1620		Morrish Lawless.
,,		John Sharpe.
1644		John Green.
1650		Do. do.
1683		Bartholomew Fallon of Galway.
1702		(*Not identified*, but possibly Bartholomew Fallon as above.)
1712		Edward Gillett.
1720	,,	Austin Beere.

BELFAST

APPROXIMATE DATE.	MARKS.	MAKER'S NAME.
1780		... ...
,,		... ...
1790		*Matthew Bellew ?
1800		... ...
,,		... ...

GALWAY

DATE (ABOUT).	MARKS.	MAKER'S NAME.
1648		R. Joyes, sen. (?)
1666-1684		. . . .
1695		Richard Joyes.
1700		Do. do.
,,		... ...
,,		.. ...
1720		.. ...
1725		Richard Joyes.
1730		Mark Fallon.
,,		Do. do.
1743-5		... ...

DATE (ABOUT).	MARKS.	MAKER'S NAME.	DATE (ABOUT).	MARKS.	MAKER'S NAME.
1710	[castle shield] I·B [castle shield] I·B	J. Buck, senr. (?)	1784	P·C STER P·C	Patrick Connell.
1718	AB	Adam Buck.	"	" STERLING "	• Do. do.
1730-40	I·B / STERLING	Jonathan Buck. (free 1731)	"	MFG " MFG	Maurice Fitzgerald.
"	STERLING / IB	Do. do.	"	MFG MFG MFG	Do. do.
1730-62	[animal] STERLING [animal] / IB	Do. do.	"	MFG STERLING	Do. do.
"	.. IB ..	Do. do.	"	STER TB STER	Thomas Burke.
"	[animal] STERLING IB	Do. do.	"	TB STERLING TB	Do. do.
"	[animal] / STERLING / IB	Do. do.	"	TB STER TB	Do. do.
1730-75	[mark] STERLING [mark]	Joseph Johns.	"	TB STERLING [fleur]	Do. do.
"	[mark] STERLIN	Do. do.	"	TB STERLING	Do. do.
"	..	Do. do.	"	MW STERLING	Matt. Walsh.
1749-50	I·I [heart]	? Joseph Johns.	"	MW STERLING	Do. do.
1750	S.J / STARLING	Samuel Johns.	1786	DL STERLING DL	Daniel Lysaght.
1760-85	GM STERLING	George Moore.	"	DL STERLING	Do. do.
"	GM STARLING	Do. do.	"	DL "	Do. do.
1768-80	GFG STERLING GFG	Garret Fitzgerald.	1798	WW STER WW	Wm. Ward.
1770	GM	George Moore.	1800	WFG STERLING WFG	Wm. Fitzgerald.
1780	TW [cross]	(Not identified.)	"	WFG [cross] STERLING	Do. do.
[,,]	TW STERLING	Do. do.	"	R°S [cross] R°S	Robt. O'Shaughnessy.
1784	P.C Ster P.C	Patrick Connell.	"	R°S STERLS	Do. do.
"	P.C STER P.C	Do. do.	"	WW [cross] WW	Will. Ward.
			"	WW STERLING	Do. do.
			"	M [anchor] C	... ...
			1810-20	S★P STERLING	Samuel Purdon.
			"	" [fleur]	Do. do.
			1800-13	IP [marks] [crown]	John Purcell.

UNASCRIBED IRISH PROVINCIAL MARKS.

UNASCRIBED MARKS

DATE (ABOUT).	MARKS.	DATE (ABOUT).	MARKS.
1611		1574	
1650			
1652		1590	COK
1666			
		1660	
1673			
1680		1680	
"		"	
1682			
"		1700	
1690			
1700		"	
1705		1730	
1710			
"		1740-50	
1720			
1720-40		"	
1726		1770	
"		1780	
1750			
1756		1800	
1760			
"			
1780			
"			
"			

INDEX

ENGLISH, SCOTTISH AND IRISH MARKS

Name of Firm.	Maker's Marks.	Date.
Ashforth G. & Co. ...		1784
Fox T. & Co.	FOX.PROCTOR PASMORE.& Cº	1784
Green W. & Co.	W.GREEN &Cº	1784
Holy D., Wilkinson & Co.	DANˠHOLY WILKINSON & Cº	1784
Law T. & Co. ..., ...	THOˢLAW & Cˢ	1784
Parsons J. & Co.	IOHN PARSONS &Cº	1784
Smith N. & Co.	N·SMITH & Cº	1784
Staniforth, Parkin & Co.	STANIFORTH PARKIN&Cº	1784
Sykes & Co.	SYKES &Cº	1784
Tudor, Leader & Nicholson	TUDOR&Cº	1784
Boulton M. & Co. ...	BOULTON	1784
Dixon T. & Co.	DIXON&Cº	1784
Holland H. & Co. ...	HOLLAND&Cº	1784
Moore J.	Moore MOORE §	1784
Smith & Co.	SMITH&Cº	1784

Name of Firm.	Maker's Marks.	Date.	Name of Firm.	Maker's Marks.	Date.
Beldon, Hoyland & Co.		1785	Newbould W. & Son		1804
Brittain, Wilkinson & Brownill		1785	Drabble I. & Co.		1805
Deakin, Smith & Co.		1785	Coldwell W.		1806
Love J. & Co. (Love, Silverside, Darby & Co.)		1785	Hill D. & Co.		1806
Morton R. & Co.		1785	Law J. & Son		1807
Roberts, Cadman & Co.		1785	Butts T.		1807
Roberts J. & S.		1786	Green J.		1807
Sutcliffe R. & Co.		1786	Hutton W.		1807
Bingley W.		1787	Law R.		1807
Madin F. & Co.		1788	Linwood J.		1807
Jervis W.		1789	Linwood W.		1807
Colmore S.		1790	Meredith H.		1807
Goodwin E.		1794	Peake		1807
Watson, Fenton & Bradbury		1795	Ryland W. & Son		1807
Froggatt, Coldwell & Lean		1797	Scot W		1807
Green J. & Co.		1799	Silkirk W		1807
Goodman, Gainsford & Fairbairn		1800	Thomason E. & Dowler		1807
Ellerby W		1803			
Garnett W.		1803			
Holy D., Parker & Co.		1804	Tonks Samuel		1807

Name of Firm.	Maker's Marks.	Date.
Waterhouse & Co. ...	WATERHOUSE&Cᵒ	1807
Wilmore Joseph ...	J W / PATENT / WILMORE & MILNES	1807
Gainsford R.	GAINSFORD / GA	1808
Hatfield A.	A H H	1808
Banister W.	BANI STER	1808
Gibbs G.	GIBBS / GIBB / GBB / GIBB	1808
Hipkiss J.	HIPKISS	1808
Horton D.	D·HORTON	1808
Lea A. C.	A·CLEA	1808
Linwood M & Sons ...	LIN WOOD	1808
Nicholds J	J·NICHOLDS	1808
Beldon G.	BEL DON 8	1809
Wright J. & Fairbairn G.	WRIGHT FAIRBAIRN	1809
Cheston T	Ches ton	1809
Harrison J	HARRI SON	1809
Hipwood W	WHIP WOOD	1809
Horton J	HOR TON	1809
Silk R.	S I L K	1809
Howard S. & T.	S H & Cᵒ / How ard	1809
Smith, Tate, Nicholson & Hoult	SMITH&Cᵒ	1810
Dunn G B	DUNN	1810

Name of Firm.	Maker's Marks.	Date.
Hanson M.	HAN SON	1810
Pimley S.		1810
Creswick T. & J.	T C T C	1811
Stot B.	Stot	1811
Watson, Pass & Co. (late J. Watson)	WATSON PASS&Cᵒ	1811
Lees G.	I I I / LEES	1811
Pearson R.	PEAR SON	1811
White J. (White & All-good)	WHITE	1811
Kirkby S.	KIRKBY FOR·USE	1812
Allgood J	ALL GOOD	1812
Allport E	All port All port	1812
Gilbert J	G PS / Gil bert / Gil	1812
Hinks J.	HINKS	1812
Johnson J	JOHN SON	1812
Small T . ..	SMALL	1812
Smith W	SM ITH	1812
Younge S. & C & Co. ...	S.C.YOUNGE &Cᵒ	1813
Thomas S.	THO MAS	1813
Tyndall J	TYN DALL	1813
Best H.	B E S T	1814
Cracknall J.	CRACK NALL	1814
Jordan T.	JOR DAN Jor dan	1814

Name of Firm.	Maker's Marks.	Date.
Woodward W.		1814
Lilly John		1815
Best & Wastidge ...		1816
Ashley		1816
Davis J.		1816
Evans S.		1816
Freeth H.		1816
Harwood T.		1816
Lilly Joseph		1816
Turley S.		1816
Cope C. G.		1817
Pemberton & Mitchell ...		1817
Shephard J.		1817
Markland W.		1818
Corn J. & J. Sheppard...		1819
Rogers J.		1819
Hall W.		1820 §
Moore F.		1820
Turton J.		1820

Name of Firm.	Maker's Marks.	Date.
Blagden, Hodgson & Co.		1821
Holy D. & G. ..., ...		1821
Needham C.		1821
Sansom T. & Sons ...		1821
Child T.		1821
Smith l.		1821
Worton S.		1821
Rodgers J. & Sons ...		1822
Bradshaw J.		1822
Briggs W.		1823
Harrison G.		1823
Smallwood J.		1823
Causer J. F.		1824
Jones		1824
Tonks & Co.		1824
Roberts, Smith & Co. ...		1828
Smith J. & Son		1828
Askew		1828
Hall Henry		1829
Hobday J.		1829
Watson J. & Son ...		1830

Name of Firm.	Maker's Marks.	Date.
Bishop Thomas.... ...		1830
Hutton W.		1831
Atkin Henry		1833
Waterhouse I. & I. & Co.		1833
Watson W. ...., ...	W WATSON MAKER SHEFFIELD	1833
Dixon J. & Sons		1835
Smith J. ... , ...	JOSEPHUS SMITH	1836
Waterhouse, Hatfield & Co.		1836
Wilkinson H. & Co. ...		1836
Hutton W.		1837
Hutton W.	H & S T	1839
Prime J.		1839
Walker, Knowles & Co.		1840
Waterhouse George & Co.	W 8 Co S	1842
Smith, Sissons & Co. ...		1848
Padley, Parkin & Co. ...		1849

Name of Firm.	Maker's Marks.	Date.
Hutton W.	W H & S T	1849
Mappin Bros.		1850
Oldham T.	T OLDHAM MAKER NOTTINGHAM	1860
Roberts & Briggs ...	R & B X	1860

MISCELLANEOUS MARKS WHICH HAVE NOT BEEN TRACED.

Maker's Marks.	Approximate date of manufacture.
	1780-1790
BEST PLATE	1790
DEVER	1790
ALWH CA IH EE	1790-1800
Do.	1790-1800
R. JEWESSON MIDLETON & Co *	1800-1810
W.B. PINE 352 STRAND	1815-1825
	1815 1825
WILSON	1815-1825
GILBERT LONDON	1840
REGISTERED BY MAPPLEBECK&LOWE JAN.Y.27.1840.N.223	1840
RW&W	1840
PAT ENT XD PAT ENT	1840
	1850
SALT	1850
	1850
	1850

One date indicates the period, two dates the birth and death.

A

RON, JOSEPH
hiladelphia, Pa. 1798

BOTT, JOHN W.
ortsmouth, N.H. ....1839 · JABBOTT

KERMAN, DAVID
ew York, N.Y. 1818

KLEY, FRANCIS M.
ew York, N.Y. ....1797 · F.ACKLEY

ON, GEORGE
ew York, N.Y. 1795

AM, I.
exandria, Va. ....1800 · *H* *GH* *I.Adam* *I.ADAM*

AM, JOHN B.
ew Orleans, La, ...1822

AM, JOHN
exandria, Va. 1829

AMS, JONATHAN
hiladelphia, Pa. ....1785 · *I.ADAM* *I.Adams*

AMS, PYGAN
ew London, Conn. ..1712-1776 · *P·A* *PA* *PA*

AMS, WM. L.
ew York, N.Y. ....1842 · W.ADAMS NEWYORK

DISON, GEORGE M.
altimore, Md. 1804

GATE, WM.
orwich, Conn. 1767

RIANCE, E.
Louis, Mo. ....1820 · E.ADRIANCE ST.LOUIS

EN, GEORGE
altimore, Md. ....1765-1832 · G·A *G.Aiken* *G.Aiken* G.Aiken AIKEN GAIKEN

SWORTH, MICHAEL
redericksburg Co., Va. ...1755

KEN, JOHN
hiladelphia, Pa. ....1785 · *I.Aitken* IAITKEN

KINS, W.
altimore, Md. 1802

N, JOHN B.
anville, Ky. ....1850 · JOHN B.AKIN DANVILLE KY

DIS, CHARLES
ew York, N.Y. .... 1814 · CALDIS

XANDER, A.
iladelphia, Pa. 1802

XANDER, S. & SIMMONS, A.
iladelphia, Pa. 1800

XANDER, SAMUEL
iladelphia, Pa. .... 1808 · S.ALEXANDER

ORD, SAMUEL
iladelphia, Pa. 1840

ORD, THOMAS
iladelphia, Pa. 1762

COCK & ALLEN
ew York, N.Y. .... 1820 · ALLCOCK+ALLEN

ALLEN, CHARLES
Boston, Mass. ....1760 · C·ALLEN

ALLEN & EDWARDS
Boston, Mass. ....1700 · IA IE

ALLEN, JAMES
Philadelphia, Pa. 1720

ALLEN, JOEL
Middletown, Conn. 1787

ALLEN, JOHN
Philadelphia, Pa, ...1814 · IA IA IA

ALLEN, JOHN
Boston, Mass. ...,....1691-1760

ALLEN, RICHARD
Philadelphia, Pa. 1816

ALLEN, ROBERT
Philadelphia, Pa. ...,....1776

ALLEN, THOMAS
Boston, Mass. ...,......1758

ALLISON, PETER
New York, N.Y. 1791

ALSTYNE, JEROMIMUS
New York, N.Y. ....1787 · *Alstyne* IA IA

ANDERSON, WM.
New York, N.Y. ....1746 · WA WA

ANDRAS & CO.
New York, N.Y. ....1800 · ANDRAS&CO

ANDRAS & RICHARD
New York, N.Y. ....1797 · A&R

ANDRAS, WM.
New York, N.Y ....1795 · ANDRAS

ANDREAS, ABRAHAM
Bethlehem, Pa. 1780

ANDREW, JOHN
Salem, Mass. ....1747-1791 · IANDREW

ANDREWS, ABRAHAM
Philadelphia, Pa. 1795

ANDREWS, H.
Boston, Mass. 1830

ANDREWS, HENRY
Philadelphia, Pa. ...,....1795 · HA

ANDREWS, JEREMIAH
Philadelphia, Pa. 1776

ANDREWS, JOSEPH
Norfolk, Va. ...... .1800 · J.ANDREWS IANDREWS NORFOLK *J.Andrews*

ANDREWS, JR.
Philadelphia, Pa. .... .1746

ANTHONY, ISAAC
Newport, R. I.
Swansea, Mass.
.... 1690-1773 · IA

ANTHONY, J.
Philadelphia, Pa. 1770

ANTHONY, JOSEPH
Philadelphia, Pa. .... .1783 · J.A J·A

ANTHONY, JOSEPH, JR.
Philadelphia, Pa. 1783-1814

ANTHONY, JOSEPH & SONS
Philadelphia, Pa. 1810

ANTHONY, L. D.
Providence, R. I. 1805

ANTHONY, M. H. & T.
Philadelphia, Pa. 1814

ANTHONY, MICHAEL H.
Philadelphia, Pa. 1810

ANTHONY, THOMAS
Philadelphia, Pa. 1810

ANTHONY, WM.
New York, N. Y. 1800

ANWYL, KENRICK
Baltimore, Md. 1780

APPLETON, GEORGE B.
New York, N. Y. 1820

ARCHIE, JOHN
New York, N. Y. 1759

ARMS, T. N.
Albany, New York 1849

ARMSTRONG, ALLEN
Philadelphia, Pa. 1806

ARMSTRONG, JOHN
Philadelphia, Pa. 1810

ARMSTRONG, WM.
Philadelphia, Pa. 1756

ARNOLD, THOMAS
Newport, R. I. ....,..1739-1828

ARNOLD, THOMAS
Philadelphia, Pa. 1760

ASHMEAD, WM.
Philadelphia, Pa. 1797

ATHERTON, NATHAN
Philadelphia, Pa. 1825

ATKINSON, ISAAC
Philadelphia, Pa. 1825

ATLEE, CHARLES
Philadelphia, Pa. 1837

ATTERBURY, J.
New Haven, Conn. 1799

AUSTEN, DAVID
Philadelphia, Pa. 1837

AUSTIN, BENJAMIN
Portsmouth, N. H. 1775

AUSTIN & BOYER
Boston, Mass. 1770

AUSTIN, EBENEZER
Hartford, Conn. 1782

AUSTIN, EBENEZER J.
Boston, Mass. 1790

AUSTIN, JAMES
Charlestown, Mass. 1780

AUSTIN, JOHN
Philadelphia, Pa. 1802

AUSTIN, JOSEPH
Hartford, Conn. 1740

AUSTIN, JOSIAH
Charlestown, Mass. 1718-1780

AUSTIN, NATHANIEL
Boston, Mass. 1734-1818

AVERY, JOHN
Preston, Conn. .....,..1732-1794

AVERY, JOHN, JR..
Preston, Conn. 1776

AVERY, ROBERT STAUNTON..
Preston, Conn. 1792

AVERY, SAMUEL
Preston, Conn. 1760-1836

AVERY, WM.
Preston, Conn. 1786

AVERY, WILLIS & BILLIS
Salisbury, N. Y. 1820

AYRES, S.
Lexington, Ky. 1805

AYRES, T.
Unknown 1800

B

BABCOCK, SAMUEL
Middletown, Conn. 1788-1857

BACALL, THOMAS
Boston, Mass. 1836

BACHMAN, A.
New York, N. Y. 1848

BACKUS, DELUCINE
New York, N. Y. 1792

BAIELLE, LEWIS
Baltimore, Md. 1799

BAILEY, BENJAMIN
Boston, Mass. 1820

BAILEY, B. M.
Ludlow, Vt. 1824-1913

BAILEY & CO.
Philadelphia, Pa. 1850

BAILEY, EDWARD
Baltimore, Md. 1779

BAILEY, E. E. & S. C.
Portland, Me. 1825

BAILEY, HENRY
Boston, Mass. 1780

BAILEY, JOHN
New York, N. Y. ..,......1762

BAILEY & KITCHEN
Philadelphia, Pa. 1853

ILEY, LORING Hingham, Mass. 1780	L·B	
ILEY, ROBERT H. Woodstock, Vt. 1825	R.H.BAILEY	
ILEY, SIMEON A. New York, N.Y. 1789		
ILEY, JOHN Philadelphia, Pa. 1762		
ILY, WM. New York, N.Y. 1820	WBAILY	
KER Boston, Mass. 1765		
KER, ANSON New York, N.Y. 1821		
KER, E. New York, N.Y. 1740-1790	E.BAKER	
KER, GEORGE Providence, R. I. 1825	G.BAKER G.BAKER	
KER, S. New York, N.Y. 1787-1858	S.BAKER	
LCH, EBENEZER Hartford, Conn. 1744	E.BALCH	
LCH & FRYER Albany, N.Y. 1784		
LDWIN & BAKER Providence, R. I. 1817		
LDWIN & CO. Newark, N.J. 1830	BALDWIN&CO NEWARK	
LDWIN, EBENEZER Hartford, Conn. 1723-1808	BALDWIN BALDWIN.	
LDWIN, JABEZ Boston, Mass. 1808	BALDWIN	
LDWIN, J. C. Boston, Mass. 1815	J.C.BALDWIN	
LDWIN, JEDEDIAH Portsmouth, N. H. 1793	J.BALDWIN	
LDWIN & JONES Boston, Mass. 1813	BALDWIN & JONES BALDWIN & JONES	
LDWIN, STANLEY-S New York, N.Y. 1820	STANLEY.S.BALDWIN	
LL, BLACK & CO. New York, N.Y. 1850	BALL.BLACK&CO	
LL & HEALD Baltimore, Md. 1810	BALL&HEALD	
LL, HENRY New York, N.Y. 1833		
LL, JOHN Boston, Mass. 1765	JOHN BALL. JOHN BALL.	
LL, S. S. Boston, Mass. 1838	J·BALL	
LL, THOMPKINS & BLACK New York, N.Y. 1839	BALL.TOMPKINS&BLACK	

BALL, TRUE M. Boston, Mass. 1815-1890	W·B W·BALL W·BALL W·BALL
BALL, W. Baltimore, Md. 1802	
BALL, WM. Philadelphia, Pa. 1752	WB W·Ball BALL BALL W·BALL WBALL
BANCKER, ADRIEN New York, N.Y. 1703-1772	AB AB
BANGS, JOHN Cincinnati, O. 1825	
BARBERET, THEON New Orleans, La. 1822	
BARBIER, PETER Philadelphia, Pa. 1823	
BARD, CONRAD Philadelphia, Pa. 1825	C.BARD 205 ARCH ST.
BARD, C. & SON Philadelphia, Pa. ....,.....1850	
BARD & HOFFMAN Philadelphia, Pa. 1837	
BARD, J. Philadelphia, Pa. 1800	
BARD & LAMONT Philadelphia, Pa. 1841	BARD & LAMONT
BARDEER, CONNARD Philadelphia, Pa. 1831	
BARDICK, GEORGE Philadelphia, Pa. 1790	G·B
BARDICK, JOHN Philadelphia, Pa. 1805	
BARDON, STEPHEN Philadelphia, Pa. 1785	
BARIA, WM. New York, N.Y. 1805	
BARNES, ABRAHAM Boston, Mass. 1716	
BARRET, JAMES Norwich, Conn. 1717	
BARRETT, JAMES New York, N.Y. 1805	J·B
BARRETT, S. Nantucket, Mass. 1800	★ S.BARRETT ★
BARRIER, DAVID Baltimore, Md. 1810	D.BARRIER
BARRINGTON & DAVENPORT Philadelphia, Pa. 1806	B&D
BARROWS, JAMES MADISON Tolland, Conn. 1809	J.M.BARROWS
BARRY, STANDISH Baltimore, Md. 1763-1844	SB SB SB BARRY Standish Barry Standish Barry Barry 1792
BARTHOLOMEW, JOSEPH Philadelphia, Pa. ..,......1833	

BARTHOLOMEW, LE ROUX
New York, N. Y. 1688-1713

BARTHOLOMEW, ROSWELL
Hartford, Conn.......1781-1830

BARTLETT, EDWARD
Philadelphia, Pa. 1833

BARTLETT, NATHANIEL
Concord, Mass. 1760

BARTLETT, SAMUEL
Boston, Mass. 1750-1821

BARTON, ERASTUS
New York, N. Y. 1810

BARTON, ERASTUS & CO.
New York, N. Y. 1821

BARTRAM, WM.
Philadelphia, Pa. 1769

BASSET, FRANCIS
New York, N. Y. 1774

BATCHELLOR, N.
New York, N. Y. 1825

BATTELS, A. T.
Utica, N. Y. 1847

BAY, A. S.
New York, N. Y. 1786

BAYLEY, ALEXANDER
New York, N. Y. 1790

BAYLEY & DOUGLAS
New York, N. Y. 1789

BAYLEY, S. & A.
New York, N. Y. 1790

BAYLEY, S. H.
New York, N. Y. 1790

BAYLEY, SIMON A.
New York, N. Y. 1789

BAYLY, JOHN
Philadelphia, Pa. 1755

BAYSSET, JOSEPH
New Orleans, La. 1822

BEACH, A.
Hartford, Conn.......... .1823

BEACH, ISAAC
New Milford, Conn. 1788

BEACH, IVES & CO.
New York, N. Y. 1820

BEACH, MILES
Litchfield, Conn. 1743-1828

BEACH & SANFORD
Hartford, Conn. 1785-1788

BEACH & WARD
Hartford, Conn. 1789-1795

BEAL, CALEB
Boston, Mass. 1796

BEAM, JACOB C.
Philadelphia, Pa. 1818

BEAUVAIS, RENO
St. Louis, Mo. 1850

BECHAM
Unknown ....c 1740

BECK, THOMAS
Philadelphia, Pa. 1773

BECKER, FREDERICK
New York, N. Y. 1736

BECKER, PHILIP
Lancaster, Pa. 1764

BEDFORD, JOHN
Fishkill, N. Y. 1781

BEEBE, J. W. & CO.
New York, N. Y. 1844

BEEBE, JAMES W.
New York, N. Y. 1835

BEEBE, STANTON
Providence, R. I. 1824

BEEBE, WILLIAM
New York, N. Y. 1850

BEECHER, CLEMENT
Berlin, Conn. 1778-1869

BEECHER, C. & CO.
Meriden, Conn. 1820

BELIN, LEWIS
Philadelphia, Pa. 1818

BELKNAP, SAMUEL
Boston, Mass. 1789

BELLIARD, FRANCOIS
New Orleans, La. 1822

BELLONI, LOUIS J.
New York, N. Y. 1835

BELLONI, & DURANDEAU
New York, N. Y. 1835

BENEDICT, A. C.
New York, N. Y. 1840

BENEDICT, J.
New York, N. Y. 1830

BENEDICT & SON
New York, N. Y. 1840

BENEDICT & SQUIRE
New York, N. Y. 1825

BENJAMIN, BARZILLAI
New Haven, Conn. 1799

BENJAMIN, BENJAMIN
New York, N. Y. 1825

BENJAMIN, EVERERD
New Haven, Conn. 1807-1874

BENJAMIN, JOHN
Stratford, Conn. 1731-1796

NJAMIN, SAMUEL C.
New Haven, Conn. . . . 1819

NJAMIN, SOLOMON
altimore, Md. 1817

NNET, JAMES
New York, N. Y. 1773

NNETT, JACOB
hiladelphia, Pa. 1839

NTLEY, THOMAS
oston, Mass. . . . . . 1762-1800 (T·B) (BENTLEY)

NTSON, PETER
hiladelphia, Pa. 1718

RARD, ANDREW
hiladelphia, Pa. 1797

RARD, E.
hiladelphia, Pa. . . . . . . 1800 (E·BERARD)

RKENBUSH, CHAS. H.
ew York, N. Y. 1825

RRY, WM.
ew York, N. Y. 1805

SLEY, THAUVET
ew York, N. Y. . . . . . 1727 B

SSELIEVRE, THOMAS
hiladelphia, Pa. 1831

ST, JOSEPH
hiladelphia, Pa. . . . 1723

VAN, RICHARD
altimore, Md. 1804

RSHING, HENRY
agerstown, Md. . . . . . 1815 (H·B)

GELOW & BROS.
oston, Mass. . . . . . 1840 (BIGELOW & BROTHERS)

GELOW BROS. & KENNARD
oston, Mass. . . . . . 1845 (BIGELOW BROS & KENNARD)

GELOW, JOHN
oston, Mass. . . . . . 1830 (JOHN BIGELOW)

GGS, JOSEPH
New York, N. Y. . . . 1830

GOTUT, S.
New York, N. Y. . . . 1800

JOTAL, SILVIAN A.
New York, N. Y. . . . 1795

LLING, A.
roy, N. Y. . . . . 1780 (A·BILLING) (AB) ★

LLINGS, A.
reston, Conn. . . . 1780 (A·B) (A·BILLINGS) (A·BILLINGS)

LLINGS, DANIEL
reston, Conn. . . 1795 (D. Billings)

LLON, CHARLES
t. Louis, Mo. . . . . . . 1821 (C·BILLON)

NGHAM, JOHN
ewark, N. J. 1664

BINNEAU, THEODORE
Philadelphia, Pa. . . 1820

BIRD, CONARD
Philadelphia, Pa. 1831

BISSBROWN, THOMAS
Albany, N. Y. 1790

BLACK, JAMES
Philadelphia, Pa. . . . . . . 1795 (J.B)

BLACK, JAMES
Philadelphia, Pa. . . . . . 1811 (JB) (JB)

BLACK, JOHN
Philadelphia, Pa. 1819

BLACK, WM.
New York, N. Y. 1833

BLACKMAN, FRED'S. S. & CO.
Danbury, Conn. 1811-1898

BLACKMAN, FRED'K STARR
Danbury, Conn. . . . . . 1811-1898 (F.S.BLACKMAN.) (F·S·B&Co)

BLACKMAN, JOHN C.
Danbury, Conn. 1829

BLACKMAN, JOHN STARR
Danbury, Conn. . . . 1777-1851 (J.S.B)

BLAKSLEE, WM.
Newtown, Conn. 1820

BLAKSLEE, ZIBA
Newtown, Conn. . . . . . . 1790 (A.BLANCHARD) (A.BLANCHARD)

BLANCHARD, ASA
Lexington, Ky. 1810

BLAUVELT, JOHN W.
New York, N. Y. 1835

BLEASOM & REED
Portsmouth, N. H. . . . . 1830 .BLEASOM&REED NASSAU

BLISS, JONATHAN
Middletown, Conn. 1800

BLONDELL, ANTHONY
Philadelphia, Pa. 1797

BLONDELL & DESCURET
Philadelphia, Pa. . . 1798

BLOWERS, JOHN
Boston, Mass. . . . 1710-1748 (Blowers) (BLOWERS)

BOEHLER, ANDREAS W.
New York, N. Y. . . . 1784

BOEHME, CHARLES L.
Baltimore, Md. . . . 1774-1868 (C·L·B) (C L B) (C.L.Boehme) (C Boehme) (C.L.BOEHME)

BOELEN, HENRICUS
New York, N. Y. . . 1684-1755 (HB) (HB) (HB) (HB)

BOELEN, JACOB
New York, N. Y. . . . 1773 (IB) (IB) (IB)

BOELEN, JAMES
New York, N. Y. . . 1659-1729 (IB) (IB) (IB) (IB)

BOEMPER, ABRAHAM
Bethlehem, Pa. . . . 1780

BOGARDUS, EVERARDUS
New York, N. Y. . . . . 1698 (EB)

BOGERT, ALBERT
New York, N. Y. 1815

BOGERT, NICHOLAS J.
New York, N. Y. 1801   `N·BOGERT`   `N.J.BOGERT`

BOLTON, JAMES
New York, N. Y. 1789

BOND, W.
Unknown ....C 1765   `WBond`

BONJEAN, VICTOR
New Orleans, La. 1822

BONTECOU, TIMOTHY
New Haven, Conn. 1693-1784   **T.B. TB.**

BONTECOU, TIMOTHY, JR.
New Haven, Conn. 1723-1789   `TB`

BOONE, JEREMIAH
Philadelphia, Pa. 1791   `BOONE`

BORDEAUX, AUGUSTINE
Philadelphia, Pa. 1798

BORHEK, E.
Philadelphia, Pa. 1835   `E.BORHEK` `STANDARD`

BOSS & KINDELL
New York, N.Y. 1794

BOSTWICK, ZALMON
New York, N. Y. 1846   `Z·BOSTWICK`

BOSWORTH, SAMUEL
Buffalo, N. Y. ... .,1835   `BOSWORTH`

BOTSFORD, GIDEON B.
Woodbury, Conn. 1776-1866   `G.B.BOTSFORD`

BOUDAR, JOSEPH
New York, N. Y. 1800

BOUDINOT, ELIAS
Philadelphia, Pa. 1706-1770   `EB` `BOUDINOT` `BOUDINOT`

BOUDO, LOUIS
Charleston, S. C. ... 1825   `LfBOUDO`

BOULLIEN, MOUSIER
Philadelphia, Pa. 1811

BOURDETT, STEPHAN
New York, N. Y. 1730   `SB`

BOUTIER, JOHN
New York, N. Y. 1805   `J.BOUTIER`

BOUTELLE, JAMES
Worcester, Mass. 1787

BOUVAR, JOSEPH
Philadelphia, Pa. 1797

BOWER, C.
Philadelphia, Pa. 1831

BOWNE, SAMUEL
New York, N. Y. 1778   `S:Bowne` `SBowne`

BOYCE, GERADUS
New York, N. Y. 1814   `G.B` `G:Boyce` `G.BOYCE`

BOYCE & JONES
New York, N. Y. . 1825   `B&J` `BOYCE&JONES`

BOYCE, JARED
New York, N. Y. 1820

BOYCE, JOHN
New York, N. Y. 1801   `J.B`

BOYD & HOYT
Albany, New York 1830

BOYD, JOSEPH W.
New York, N. Y. 1820   `J.W.B`

BOYD & MULFORD
Albany, N. Y. 1840   `BOYD&MULFORD`

BOYD, WM.
Albany, N. Y. 1800

BOYER, DANIEL
Boston, Mass. ... 1726-1779   `DB` `DB` `BOYER` `Boyer` `BOYER`

BOYER, JAMES
Boston, Mass. 1700-1741

BOYLSTON E.
Stockbridge, Mass. 1789

BRABANT, ISAAC
Savannah, Ga. 1750

BRACKETT, JEFFREY R.
Boston, Mass. ..../.....1840   `JEFFREY R.BRACKE`

BRADBURY, THEOPHILUS
Newburyport, Mass. 1815   `BRADBURY` `Bradb`

BRADBURY & BROTHER
Newburyport, Mass. .... .1810

BRADFORD, CHARLES H.
Westerly, R. I. ....Unknown

BRADLEY, ABNER
New Haven, Conn. 1753-1824   `A.BRADLEY`

BRADLEY & BUNCE
Hartford, Conn. ....,.1830

BRADLEY, LUTHER
New Haven, Conn. ...1772-1830   `LB`

BRADLEY & MERRIMAN
New Haven, Conn. 1826   `B&M`

BRADLEY, PHINEAS
New Haven, Conn. . .1745-1797   `PB` `PB`

BRADLEY, RICHARD
Hartford, Conn. 1825

BRADLEY, ZEBUL
New Haven, Conn. ..1780-1859   `Z.BRADLEY`

BRADY, E.
New York, N. Y. 1825   `BRADY` `E.BRADY`

BRADY, WM. V.
New York, N. Y. 1835

BRAINERD, CHARLES
Hartford, Conn. 1809

BRAMHALL, S.
Plymouth, Mass. 1800   `S.BRAMHALL`

BRANDT, A. & C.
Philadelphia, Pa. 1800   `A&CBRANDT`

BRASHER, A.
New York, N. Y. 1790   `A.BRASHER`

ASHER & ALEXANDER
New York, N. Y. 1800

ASHER, E. & CO.
New York, N. Y. 1790

ASHER, EPHRIAM
New York, N. Y. 1766

ASIER, A.
Unknown ...... Unknown

AY, HENRY
Philadelphia, Pa. 1799

EED, JOHN
Colchester, Conn. 1773

EED, WM.
Boston, Mass. 1750

ENTON, BENJAMIN
New York, N. Y. 1825

EVOORT, JOHN
New York, N. Y. ... 1715-1775

EWER, CHARLES
Middletown, Conn. .. 1778-1860

EWER & CO.
Middletown, Conn. 1810

EWER & MANN
Middletown, Conn. ... .1803

EWSTER, ABEL
Norwalk, Conn. 1797

DGE, JOHN
Boston, Mass. 1723

DGE, JOHN
Boston, Mass. 1751

GDEN, C.
Boston, Mass. 1770

GDEN, TIMOTHY
Albany, N. Y. 1813

GDEN, ZACHARIAH
Boston, Mass. 1734-1787

GHT, ANTHONY
Philadelphia, Pa. ... .1739

NKLEY, WM.
New York, N. Y. 1802

NTON, GORDON & QUIRK
Boston, Mass. 1780

TTON, ISAAC
Philadelphia, Pa. 1811

TTON, JACOB
Philadelphia, Pa. 1807

ADHURST, SAMUEL
New York, N. Y. 1724

CK, JOHN
New York, N. Y. 1833

CK, L.
New York, N. Y. 1830

BROOKHOUSE, ROBERT
Salem, Mass. 1750

BROOKS, SAMUEL
Philadelphia, Pa. 1793

BROTHEARS, MICHAEL
Philadelphia, Pa. 1772

BROWER & RUSHER
New York, N. Y. 1834

BROWER, S. & B.
Albany, N. Y. 1810

BROWER, S. D.
Albany, N. Y. 1834

BROWER, WALTER S.
Albany, N. Y. 1850

BROWN, ALEXANDER
Philadelphia, Pa. 1840

BROWN, D.
Philadelphia, Pa. 1811

BROWN, ELNATHAN C.
Westerly, R. I. ......Unknown

BROWN, EBENEZER
Boston, Mass. 1793

BROWN, HENRY
Philadelphia, Pa. 1777

BROWN & HOULTON
Baltimore, Md. 1799

BROWN, JAMES
Philadelphia, Pa. 1785

BROWN, JESSE
Philadelphia, Pa. 1813

BROWN, JOHN
Philadelphia, Pa. 1785

BROWN, LIBERTY
Philadelphia, Pa. 1801

BROWN, ROBERT
Baltimore, Md. 1830

BROWN, SAMUEL C.
New York, N. Y. 1850

BROWN, WM.
Albany, N. Y. 1849

BROWN & SON, R.
Baltimore, Md. 1830

BROWNE & KIRBY
Philadelphia, Pa. 1825

BROWNE & SEAL
Philadelphia, Pa. 1810

BRUFF, CHARLES OLIVER
New York, N. Y. 1763

BRUFF, JOSEPH
Easton, Maryland 1790

BRUFF, JOSEPH
Easton, Maryland ...1730-1785

BRUFF, THOMAS
Easton, Maryland 1790   [T.BRUFF] [T.BRUFF]

BRUSH, EDWARD
New York, N.Y, ...1774

BRYAN, PHILLIP
Philadelphia, Pa. 1802   [BRYAN]

BUCHE, PETER
New York, N.Y. 1795

BUCHOZ, I. R.
New York, N.Y. 1835

BUCKLEY & ANDERSON
Philadelphia, Pa. 1804

BUCKLEY, J. B.
Philadelphia, Pa. 1807   [BUCKLEY]

BUDDY, DANIEL
Philadelphia, Pa. 1769

BUEL, ABEL
New Haven, Conn. 1742-1825   [AB] [AB] [BUEL]

BUEL, ADRIEN
New Haven, Conn. 1742-1825

BUEL, D. H.
Hartford, Conn. 1825

BUEL & GREENLEAF
New Haven, Conn. 1798

BUEL, JOHN
New Haven, Conn. 1789

BUEL & MIX
New Haven, Conn. 1783

BUEL, SAMUEL
Middletown, Conn. 1742-1819   [S·B]

BUICHLE, LEWIS
Baltimore, Md. 1798   [LB] [LB] [L.B] [L.Buichle]

BULL, CALEB
Hartford, Conn. 1840

BULL, EPAPHRAS
Boston, Mass. 1813

BULL, G. W.
East Hartford, Conn. 1840   [G.W.BULL]

BULL, MARTIN
Farmington, Conn. 1775

BULL & MORRISON
Hartford, Conn. 1780

BUMM, PETER
Philadelphia, Pa. 1814

BUMM & SHIPPER
Philadelphia, Pa. 1819

BUNKER, BENJAMIN
Providence, R. I. 1810

BURDICK, WILLIAM S.
New Haven, Conn. 1810

BURDOCK, GEORGE
Philadelphia, Pa. 1791

BURDOCK, NICHOLAS
Philadelphia, Pa. 1797   [N·B]

BURGALIE, J. P.
New York, N.Y. 1799

BURGER, DAVID I.
New York, New York 1805   [D·I·Burger]

BURGER, JOHN
New York, New York ...1786   [I·B] [Burger] [Burger]

BURGER, JOHN
New York, New York 1767   [Burger] [N Y°] [Burger] [NYork] [Burger] [NYork]

BURGER, THOMAS
New York. New York 1805

BURNAP, DANIEL
East Windsor, Conn. ...1791

BURNETT, CHARLES A.
Alexandria, Va. 1793   [C.A.B] [C.A.BURNETT]

BURNETT & RYDER
Philadelphia, Pa. 1795   [B.R]

BURNHAM, ROBERT
New York, New York ...1790

BURKLOE, SAMUEL
Philadelphia, Pa. 1795

BURNET, SAMUEL
Newark, N. J. 1796

BURNET & RYDER
Philadelphia, Pa. 1795

BURNETT, CHARLES A.
Alexandria, Va, ...1793

BURNS, ANTHONY
Philadelphia, Pa. 1785

BURNS, JAMES
Philadelphia, Pa. 1810

BURNS, JOHN H.
New York, New York 1835

BUROT, ANDREW
Baltimore, Md. 1819

BURR, A. C.
Providence, R. I. 1815   [A.C.BURR]

BURR, CHRISTIAN A.
Providence, R. I. 1810   [C.A.BURR]

BURR, C. A. & CO.
Providence, R. I. 1820

BURR, E. & W.
Providence, R. I. 1793

BURR, EZEKIEL
Providence, R. I. 1764-1846   [EB] [EB] [EB] [EB] [E·BURR] [EBURR]

BURR & LEE
Providence, R.I. 1815

BURR, NATHANIEL
Fairfield, Conn. ......1698-1784.   [NB]

BURR, WILLIAM
Providence, R. I. 1793

BURRILL, JOSEPH
Boston, Mass. 1823

URRILL, SAMUEL
Boston, Mass. 1733

URRILL, SAMUEL, JR.
Boston, Mass. . . . 1829

RRILL, THEOPHILUS
New London, Conn. . . . 1736

RROWS, WILLIAM
Philadelphia, Pa. . . 1831

RT, BENJAMIN
Boston, Mass. . . . 1691-1745

RT, BENJAMIN
Boston, Mass. . . . 1729-1803

RT, JOHN
Boston, Mass. 1691-1745

USHNELL, PHINEAS
Guilford, Conn. 1762

RT, WILLIAM
Boston, Mass. . . . 1726-1752

RTON, JACOB
Philadelphia, Pa. 1839

RT, SAMUEL
Boston, Mass. 1724-1754

SSEY, BENJAMIN
Dedham, Mass. 1757-1842

SSEY, THOMAS
Baltimore, Maryland 1799

SWELL, JASON
Portsmouth, N. H. 1839

TLER, HENRY W.
Philadelphia, Pa. 1833

TLER, JAMES
Boston, Mass. 1713-1776

TLER, JOHN
Portland, Me. 1765

TLER, N.
Utica, New York 1800

TLER, N. H.
Philadelphia, Pa. 1837

TLER & LITTLE
Portland, Me. 1759

TLER & McCARTHY
Philadelphia, Pa. 1850

TLER WISE AND CO.
Philadelphia, Pa. 1845

ZELL, J. L.
Unknown . . . . C 1750

YNE, JAMES
New York, New York . . . 1789

RNE, JAMES
Philadelphia, Pa. 1784

C

DY, SAMUEL
New York, New York 1792

CADY AND BACKUS
New York, New York 1792

CALDER AND COMPANY
Albany, New York 1830

CALDWELL, E.
New York, New York 1800

CAMERON, ALEXANDER
Albany, New York 1813

CAMMAN, ALEXANDER
Albany, New York . . .1813

CAMOIN
Philadelphia, Pa. 1797

CAMP, ELIAS
Bridgeport, Conn. 1825

CAMPBELL, CHRISTOPHER
New York, N.Y. 1808

CAMPBELL, JOHN W.
New York, New York . .1814

CAMPBELL, R.
Baltimore, Md. 1824

CAMPBELL, R. & A.
Baltimore, Md. 1835

CAMPBELL, ROBERT
Baltimore, Md. 1819

CAMPBELL, R.
Baltimore, Md. 1824

CAMPBELL, THOMAS
New York, New York 1770

CAMPBELL, W.
Philadelphia, Pa. 1765

CANAVILLO, ANTONIO
New York, New York 1825

CANAVILLO, S.
New York, New York 1825

CANDEE & COMPANY, L. B.
Woodbury, Conn. 1830

CANDEE, LEWIS B.
Woodbury, Conn. 1825

CANDELL, CHARLES
New York, New York 1795

CANFIELD AND BROTHER
Baltimore, Md. 1830

CANFIELD AND FOOT
Middletown, Conn. 1798

CANFIELD AND HALL
New York, New York 1805

CANFIELD, SAMUEL
Middletown, Conn. 1780-1800

CANFIELD, SAMUEL
Lansingburg, N.Y. 1801

CANFIELD BROTHERS & CO.
Baltimore, Md. 1850

CANN, JOHN
New York, New York . 1835

CANON. GEORGE
Warwick, R. I. . 1800   GC GCANON

CANT, GODFREY
New York, N.Y. 1796

CAPELLE, J.
Stt. Louis, Mo. 1850   CAPELLE ST.LOUIS

CARALIN, PIERCE
New York, N.Y. 1804

CARBIN, THEODORE
Philadelphia, Pa. .1758

CARGILL   (Noted)

CARIO, MICHAEL
New York, N.Y. 1728

CARIO, WILLIAM
New York, N.Y. 1721   W.CARIO W.CARIO

CARIOLLE
New Orleans, La. 1822

CARLETON, GEORGE
New York, N.Y. 1810   CARLETON

CARLISLE, ABRAHAM
Philadelphia, Pa. .....1791 A.Carlile

CARMAN, JOHN
Philadelphia, Pa. 1771   IC

CARMAN, JOHN
New York, N.Y. 1800

CARMAN, SAMUEL
New York, N.Y, ...1807

CARPENTER, CHARLES
Boston, Mass. 1807

CARPENTER, JOSEPH
Norwich, Conn. .....1747-1804 I·C I·C

CARREL, DANIEL
Philadelphia, Pa. 1806

CARRELL, JOHN & DANIEL
Philadelphia, Pa. ....1785 CARREL

CARRIBEC, PETER
Philadelphia, Pa. ...,....1795

CARROL, JAMES
Albany, N.Y. 1834

CARROLL, JAMES
New York, N.Y. 1825

CARSON, DAVID
Albany, N.Y. 1849

CARSON, THOMAS
Albany, N.Y. 1815   TC

CARSON & HALL
Albany, N.Y. 1813

CARY, LEWIS
Boston, Mass. 1820   L.CARY

CASE, GEORGE
East Hartford, Conn. 1779

CASEY, GIDEON
South Kingston, R.I. ..1753

CASEY, GIDEON
Providence, R.I. .1726-1786   G:CASEY

CASEY, SAMUEL
South Kingston, R.I. 1724-1773 SC S:CASEY S:CASEY

CASHELL, RANDALL. H.
Philadelphia, Pa. 1807

CASSEDY, ANDREW
Philadelphia, Pa. 1840

CASTON, FRANCOISE
New York, N.Y. 1804

CERNEAU, JOHN
New York, N.Y. 1823

CERNEAU. JOSEPH
New York, N.Y. .... :1807

CERNEAU & CO.
New York, N.Y. . 1811

CHADWICK, THOMAS
Philadelphia, Pa. .. 1809

CHALMERS, JAMES, Sr.
Annapolis, Md. ... 1749   IC IC

CHALMERS, JOHN
Annapolis, Md. 1770   IC

CHAMBERLAIN, WILSON
Portsmouth, N.H. 1839

CHAMPLIN, JOHN
New London, Conn. ..1745-1800 IC

CHANDLER, STEPHEN
New York, N.Y. 1812   CHANDLER

CHANDLESS, WILLIAM
New York, N.Y. 1846

CHAPIN, AARON
Hartford, Conn. 1790

CHAPIN, ALEXANDER
Hartford, Conn. 1838

CHARTERS, JAMES
New York, N.Y. 1844

CHARTERS, CANN & DUNN
New York,, N.Y. 1850   CC&D

CHASE, J. D.
New York, N.Y. 1820

CHASE & EASTON
Brooklyn, N.Y. 1837

CHASLEY
Boston, Mass. 1764

CHAT, EASTON
Philadelphia, Pa. 1793

CHAT, LE SIEUR
New York, N.Y. 1790

CHAUDRONS & RASCH
Philadelphia, Pa. ....1812 CHAUDRONS&RASCH STERN.

CHAUDRONS, SIMON
Philadelphia, Pa. 1798

MAUDRONS, SIMON & CO. Philadelphia, Pa. 1807	SC&Co	
ENE, DANIEL New York, N.Y. 1786		
ERRY, JAMES Philadelphia, Pa. 1824		
EVALIER, CLEMENT E. Philadelphia, Pa. 1816		
EVALIER & TANGUAY Philadelphia, Pa. 1816		
ILDS, GEORGE H. Philadelphia, Pa. 1828		
ILDS, GEORGE K. Philadelphia, Pa. 1837		
ITRY, PETER New York, N.Y. 1814	P.Chitry P.Chitry	
ITTEN, EBENEZER New Haven, Conn. 1747	EC EC E.CHITTENDEN	
ITTENDEN, BERIAH New Haven, Conn. 1787		
ITTENDEN, EBENEZER New Haven, Conn. ...1726-1812		
URCH, JOSEPH New Haven, Com. 1818		
URCH, JOSEPH Hartford, Conn. 1794-1876		
URCH, RALPH Buffalo, N.Y. 1832		
URCH & ROGERS Hartford, Conn. 1825	CHURCH & ROGERS	
URCHILL, JESSE Boston, Mass. 1773-1819	I.CHURCHILL CHURCHILL	
URCHILL & TREADWELL Boston, Mass. 1805	CHURCHILL & Treadwell	
URCHWELL, CHARLES Philadelphia, Pa. 1781		
APP, A. L. New York, N.Y. 1802	A.L.CLAPP	
APP, PHILIP New York, N.Y. 1802		
APP & RIKER New York, N.Y. . 1802		
ARK & ANTHONY New York. N.Y. 1790	CLARK & ANTHONY	
ARK, ANDREW New York, N.Y. 1744		
ARK & BRO. Norwalk, Conn. . 1825	CLARK & BRO. NORWALK.	
ARK, C. & G. Boston, Mass. 1833		
ARK, CHARLES Boston, Mass. 1798		
ARK & COIT Norwich, Conn. 1820		

CLARK, CURTIS New York, N.Y. 1823		
CLARK, GABRIEL D. Providence, R.I. 1824	G.D.CLARK	
CLARK, GEORGE, C. Providence, R.I. 1824	G.C.CLARK	
CLARK, GEORGE D. Baltimore, Md. .... .1826	G.D.CLARK	
CLARK, HENRY Philadelphia, Pa. 1813		
CLARK, I. Boston, Mass. 1754	I·C I.CLARK J.:CLARK I.CLARK CLARK	
CLARK, I. & H. New York, N.Y. 1812	I.&H·CLARK	
CLARK, J. H. New York, N.Y. 1812	J.H.CLARK	
CLARK, JOSEPH Danbury, Conn. 1791	JC J.:CLARK	
CLARK, LEVI Norwalk, Conn. 1801-1875	CLARK NORWALK	
CLARK, METCALF B. Boston, Mass. 1835		
CLARK, PETER G. New Haven, Conn. 1810		
CLARK, RICHARD New York, N.Y. ....,.1795		
CLARK, SAMUEL Boston, Mass. 1681		
CLARK, THOMAS Boston, Mass. .,1783	T.Clark T.Clark	
CLARK, WILLIAM New Milford, Conn. 1774	WC WC	
CLARKE, JAMES Newport, R.I. 1734		
CLARKE, JONATHAN Newport, R.I. 1734	IC IC J.Clarke J.:CLARKE I.CLARKE	
CLEVELAND, AARON Norwich, Conn. 1820	AC A·CLEVELAND	
CLEVELAND, BENJAMIN Norwich, Conn. 1760	B·CLEVELAND	
CLEVELAND & POST Norwich, Conn. 1815	C&P C&P	
CLEVELAND, WILLIAM Norwich, Conn. . .1770-1837	WC Cleveland	
CLEVELAND, WILLIAM New London. Conn. ..1770-1837	WC WC	
CLINE. CHARLES Philadelphia, Pa. . .. 1829		
CLUSTER, ISAAC D. St. Louis, Mo. . 1850	I.D.CLUSTER ST.LOUIS.M	
COAN, DANIEL B. New York, N.Y. 1789	D·C	

COBB, EPHRAIM
Boston, Mass. ......1708-1777 [EC] [ECobb] [E.Cobb]

COBURN, JOHN
Boston, Mass. ....1765 [J.COBURN] [IC] [IC]

COBURN, JOHN
Boston, Mass. ....1725-1803 [IC] [I.C] [J.COBURN]

CODDINGTON, JOHN
Newport, R.I. 1690-1743

CODMAN, WILLARD
Boston, Mass. 1839

CODNER, JOHN
Boston, Mass. 1754-1782

COE & UPTON
New York, N.Y. ....1840 [COE & UPTON] [H.L.SAWYER]

COEN, DANIEL BLOOM
New York, N.Y. ......1787 [D.COEN]

COFFMAN, WILLIAM
Philadelphia, Pa. 1839

COGSWELL, H.
Boston, Mass. ....1760 [H.COGSWELL]

COHEN, BARROW A.
New York, N.Y. 1825

COHEN, WILLIAM
Alexandria, Va., D.C. 1833

COIGNARD, LOUIS
New York, N.Y. 1805

COIT, E.
Norwich, Conn. ....1839 [E.COIT]

COIT & MANSFIELD
Norwich, Conn. ....1816 [C&M] [C&M]

COIT, THOMAS CHESTER
Norwich, Conn. ....1812 [T.C.C.]

COLE, ALBERT
New York, N.Y. 1844

COLE, EBENEZER
New York, N.Y. 1818

COLE, JACOB
Philadelphia, Pa. 1785

COLE, JOHN
Boston, Mass. 1686

COLEMAN, B.
Burlington, N.J. ....1785 [B.COLEMAN]

COLEMAN, C. C.
Burlington, N.J. 1835

COLEMAN, JOHN
New York, N.Y. 1814

COLEMAN, NATHANIEL
Burlington, N.J. ....1776 [NC] [N.COLEMAN]

COLEMAN, S.
Burlington, N.J. ....1805 [S.COLEMAN]

COLES, JOHN A.
New York, N.Y. ....1830 [C]

COLEY, SIMEON
New York, N.Y. ....1767 [S.Coley]

COLEY, WILLIAM
New York, N.Y. ....1801 [W.Coley]

COLLET, J. B.
New York, N.Y. 1805

COLLETTE, LAMBERT
Buffalo, N.Y. 1835

COLLINS, ARNOLD
Newport, R.I. ....1690 [AC] [AC] [AC]

COLLINS & J. W. FORBES
New York, N.Y. ....1825 [C&I.W.FORBES]

COLLINS, S.
Utica, N.Y. ....1840 [S.COLLINS] [UTICA]

COLLINS, W. & L.
New York, N.Y. 1830

COLNER, JOHN
New York, N.Y. 1818

COLONEL, JOHN
Philadelphia, Pa. 1804

COLTON & BALDWIN
New York, N.Y. 1819

COLTON & COLLINS
New York, N.Y. 1832

COLTON, LEVI
New York, N.Y. 1825

COLTON, OREN
New York, N.Y. 1818

COLWELL & LAWRENCE
Albany, N.Y. 1850

CONEY, JOHN
Boston, Mass. ....1655-1722 [IC] [IC] [IC] [IC] [IC]

CONNELL, M.
Philadelphia, Pa. ....1800 [M:CONNELL]

CONNING, J.
New York, N.Y. ....1840 [J.CONNING]

CONNOR, JOHN H.
New York, N.Y. ....1812 [J.H.CONNOR]

CONNOR, JOHN W.
Norwalk, Conn. ....1836 [J.H.CONNOR] [J.H.CONNOR]

CONYERS, JOSEPH
Boston, Mass. ....1708 [RC]

CONYERS, RICHARD
Boston, Mass. 1688

COOK, JOHN
New York, N.Y. ....1795 [J.COOK] [COOK] [ICOOK] [JCOOK]

COOK, JOHN
New York, N.Y. 1797-1805

COOK & COMPANY
New York, N.Y. 1797

COOKE, JOSEPH
Philadelphia, Pa. 1785

COOKE & COMPANY
Philadelphia, Pa. 1785

OLIDGE, JOSEPH, Jr.
oston, Mass. . . . 1770

OPER
hiladelphia, Pa. 1816

OPER, B.
ew York, N.Y. 1814

OPER, B. & J.
ew York, N.Y. 1810

OPER, FRANCIS W.
ew York, N.Y. 1846

OPER, JOHN
ew York, N.Y. 1814

OPER, JOSEPH
ew York, N.Y. 1770

PP, JOSEPH
ew London, Conn. 1757

PP, NATHANIEL P.
lbany, N.Y. 1834

RLEY, WILLIAM
ew York, N.Y. 1811

RNELISON, CORNELIUS
ew York, N.Y. 1711

RNELIUS, CHRISTIAN
hiladelphia, Pa. 1810

RNWELL, N.
anbury, Conn. . . . 1776-1837

RNELL, WALTER
rovidence, R.I. 1780

RRIN, JOSIAH
hiladelphia, Pa. 1823

URCELLE, HILAIRE
ew Orleans, La. 1822

VERTIE, LOUIS
ew Orleans, La. 1822

ERLY, THOMAS
ewport, R.I. 1765

ERLY, THOMAS
ewburyport, Mass. . .1730-1800

VAN, WILLIAM D.
hiladelphia, Pa. 1808

WELL, WM.
oston, Mass. 1682-1736

WELL, WILLIAM J.
oston, Mass. 1736

WELL, WILLIAM, Jr.
oston, Mass. 1713-1761

VLES, RALPH
leveland, Ohio 1850

X, J. & I.
ew York, N.Y. 1844

X, JOHN
hiladelphia, Pa. 1818

CRAFT, STEPHEN
New York, N.Y. 1811

CRAIG, JAMES
Williamsburg, Va. 1750

CRANDALL, BENJAMIN
Providence, R.I. 1824

CRANDALL, BENJAMIN
Portsmouth, N.H. 1839

CRANE, STEPHEN M.
New York, N.Y. 1813

CRANSTON, SAMUEL
Newport, R.I. 1684

CRAWFORD, JOHN
New York, N.Y. 1820

CRAWFORD, JOHN
New York, N.Y. 1815

CREW, J. T.
Albany, N.Y. 1849

CRITTENDEN, NEWTON E.
Cleveland, Ohio 1839

CRONE, HENRY
Cleveland, Ohio 1780

CROSBY, JONATHAN
Boston, Mass. 1743-1769

CROSBY, SAMUEL T.
Boston, Mass. 1850

CROSS, WILLIAM
Boston, Mass. 1712

CROUCKESHANKS, ALEX.
Boston, Mass. 1768

CUMMINGS, DAVID B.
Philadelphia, Pa. 1811

CURRIER & TROTT
Boston, Mass. 1836

CURRIN, JOSEPH
Philadelphia, Pa. 1829

CURRY, JOHN
Philadelphia, Pa. 1831

CURRY & PRESTON
Philadelphia, Pa. 1831

CURTIS, CANDEE & STILES
Woodbury, Conn. 1831

CURTIS, DANIEL
Woodbury, Conn. 1831

CURTIS, JOEL
Wolcott, Conn. 1810

CURTIS, LEWIS
Farmington, Conn. 1797

CURTIS, THOMAS
New York, N.Y. 1835

CURTIS & CANDEE
Woodbury, Conn. 1826

CURTISS, CANDEE & STILES
Woodbury, Conn. 1825

CURTISS & DUNING
Woodbury, Conn. 1828

CURTISS & STILES
Woodbury, Conn. 1835

CUSHMAN, ISAAC
Boston, Mass. 1823

CUTLER, A.
Boston, Mass. 1820

CUTLER, E.
New Haven, Conn. 1820

CUTLER, J. N.
Albany, N.Y. 1849

CUTLER, RICHARD
New Haven, Conn. 1760

CUTLER, RICHARD, Jr.
New Haven, Conn. 1800

CUTLER, RICHARD & SONS
New Haven, Conn. 1800

CUTLER, SILLIMAN, WARD
New Haven, Conn. 1767

CUTLER, WILLIAM
New Haven, Conn. 1806

CUTTER WILLIAM
Portland, Me. 1823

D

DAGGETT, HENRY
New Haven, Conn. 1763

DALLON, JOHN
Philadelphia, Pa. 1791

DALLY, PHILLIP
New York, N.Y. 1779

DALLY & HALSEY
New York, N.Y. 1787

DANE, THOMAS
Boston, Mass. 1723-1796

DANIEL, PERRY O.
Unknown 1830

DANIELS, CHARLES W.
Troy, N.Y. 1836

DARGEE, JOHN
New York, N.Y. 1810

DARROW, DAVID
New York, N.Y. 1825

DAUBAYSON, VICTOIRE
Philadelphia, Pa. 1820

DAUCE, SIMON
Philadelphia, Pa. 1798

DAVENPORT, JONATHAN
Baltimore, Md. 1789-1801

DAVENPORT, ROBERT
Philadelphia, Pa. 1808

DAVENPORT, SAMUEL
Milton, Mass. 1741

DAVERNE, JOHN
Baltimore, Md. 1799

DAVID & DUPUY
Philadelphia, Pa. 1792

DAVID, JOHN
Philadelphia, Pa. 1736-1794

DAVID, JOHN, Jr.
Philadelphia, Pa. 1792

DAVID, LEWIS A.
Philadelphia, Pa. 1825

DAVID, PETER
Philadelphia, Pa. ...1707-1755

DAVIS & BABBITT
Providence, R.I. 1820

DAVIS & BROWN
Boston, Mass. .....,......1802

DAVIS, E.
Newburyport, Mass. 1775

DAVIS, JOSHUA, G.
Boston, Mass. 1796

DAVIS, PALMER & CO.
Boston, Mass. 1841

DAVIS, SAMUEL
Providence, R.I. ....,....1801

DAVIS, SAMUEL
Boston, Mass. 1813

DAVIS, T. A.
Boston, Mass. 1824

DAVIS & WATSON
Boston, Mass. 1815

DAVIS, WILLIAM
Boston, Mass. 1823

DAVISON, BRAZILLIA
Norwich, Conn. 1765

DAVISON, CHARLES
Norwich, Conn. 1805

DAVY, ADAM
Philadelphia, Pa. 1795

DAWES, WILLIAM
Boston, Mass. 1766

DAWS, R.
Unknown 1800

DAWSON, JOHN
New York, N.Y. 1769

DAWSON, WILLIAM
Philadelphia, Pa. 1763

DEANE, JAMES
New York, N.Y. 1760

DEAS, DAVID
Philadelphia, Pa. 1831

DECKER, J. New York, N.Y. 1830	J.DECKER	DESQUET & TANGUY Philadelphia, Pa. 1805	
DELAGROW, ANDREW Philadelphia, Pa. 1795		DESURET, LEWIS Philadelphia, Pa. 1799	
DELANO, JABEZ New Bedford, Mass. 1784		DEVERELL, JOHN Boston, Mass. 1764-1813	Deverell
DE LAROUX, JOHN New Orleans, La. 1822	✳ *la rue* ✳	DEVERELL, JOHN Boston, Mass. 1785	
DELAUNEY, JEAN New York, N.Y. 1805		DEXTER, JOHN Marboro, Mass. 1756	
DEMILT, ANDREW New York, N.Y. 1805	DEMILT	DE YOUNG, MICHAEL Baltimore, Md. 1816	M·DEYOUNG
DEMMOCK, JOHN Boston, Mass. 1798		DICKERSON, H. & CO. Philadelphia, Pa. 1815	
DEMORSY, JEAN New Orleans, La. 1822		DICKERSON, JOHN Morristown, Mass. 1778	
DEMORT, JOHN New York, N.Y. 1810		DICKINSON, JONATHAN Philadelphia, Pa. 1794	
DEMORT, LUCIEN New York, N.Y. 1810		DICKINSON & ROBINSON Philadelphia, Pa. 1796	
DENISE, JOHN New York, N.Y. 1798	J:D JD	DIMMOCK, JOHN New York, N.Y. 1801	
DENISE, JOHN Philadelphia, Pa. 1698	IN	DIMOND, ISAAC M. New York, N.Y. 1830	
DENISE, JOHN & TUNIS South Kingtson, R.I. 1770	J&TD J&T.D	DISBROW, G. E. New York, N.Y. 1825	GEDISBROW NEWYORK
DENISON, T. Uknown 1790	T·DENISON	DIXWELL, BASIL Boston, Mass. 1732	
DENNIS, EBENEZER Hartford, Conn. 1757		DIXWELL, JOHN Boston, Mass. 1680-1725	ID
DENNIS & FITCH Troy, N.Y. 1836		DOANE, JOSHUA Providence, R. I. 1753	DOANE DOANE
DENNIS, GEORGE, Jr. Norwich, Conn. 1770		DOBBS New York, N.Y. 1788	
DE PARISIEN, OTTO PAUL New York, N.Y. 1763	OP OPDP	DOBLEMAN, FREDERICK Philadelphia, Pa. 1813	
DE PERRIZANG, OTTO New York, N.Y. 1786		DOBLEMAN, F. F. G. Philadelphia, Pa. 1810	
DE PEYSTER, WILLIAM New York, N.Y. 1732		DODGE, BENJAMIN Boston, Mass. 1836	
DE RIEMER, CORNELIUS B. Ithaca, N.Y. 1804		DODGE, EZEKIEL New York, N.Y. 1792	
DE RIEMER, JACOB R. New York, N.Y. 1830		DODGE, EZRA New London, Conn. 1787	
DE RIEMER & MEAD Ithaca, N.Y. 1831		DODGE, JOHN New York, N.Y. 1790	J·DODGE
DE RIEMER, PETER New York, N.Y. 1738-1814	PDR	DODGE, NEHEMIAH Providence, R.I. 1795	N·DODGE
DESHON, DANIEL New London, Conn. ..1697-1781	DD	DODGE, SERIL Providence, R.I. 1765-1803	☆ S·DODGE ☆
DE SPIEGEL, JACOBUS VAN New York, N.Y. 1668-1708	IVS IVS IVS	DOLE, D. N. Portsmouth, N.H. 1805	D·N·DOLE

DOLE, E. G.
Portsmouth, N.H. ....1820 [EGDole]

DOLER, DANIEL
Boston, Mass. 1765

DONALON, JOHN W.
Boston, Mass. 1823

DONOVAN, WILLIAM
Philadelphia, Pa. ....1784 [W DONOVAN]

DONTREMEI, C.
Philadelphia, Pa. 1805

DOOLITTLE, AMOS
New Haven, Conn. ...1754-1832 [AD] [AD]

DOOLITTLE, ENOS
Hartford, Conn. 1781

DORAN, JOHN
Cincinnati, Ohio 1826

DORGY, PETER
Philadelphia, Pa. 1816

DORSEY, JOSHUA
Philadelphia, Pa. ....1796 [I·DORSEY]

DORSEY, SAMUEL
Philadelphia, Pa. 1804

DORSEY, SIMON
Philadelphia, Pa. 1820

DORSON, JOSHUA
Philadelphia, Pa. 1802

DOSTER, MICHAEL
Philadelphia, Pa. 1831

DOUGLAS, ALEXANDER
New York, N.Y. 1792

DOUGLAS, CANTWELL
Baltimore, Md. 1799

DOUGLAS, JAMES, W.
Philadelphia, Pa. 1791

DOUGLAS, ROBERT
New London, Conn. ....1776 [RD] [RD] [R.D]

DOUGLASS & HECKMAN
Philadelphia, Pa. 1837

DOUGLASS, JAMES
New York, N.Y. ....1800 [JDouglas]

DOUGLASS, JEREMOTT W.
Philadelphia, Pa. ....1790 [JDouglass]

DOUGLASS, JOHN
Philadelphia, Pa. 1840

DOUTIEMER, CULE
Philadelphia, Pa. 1791

DOWIG, CHRISTOPHER
Philadelphia, Pa. 1765

DOWIG, GEORGE
Baltimore, Md. ....1724-1807 [G·D]

DOWIG, GEORGE
Philadelphia, Pa. ....1770 [GD] [GD] [GD]

DOWNES, J.
Philadelphia, Pa. ....1770 [J.Downes] [J.DOWNES] [J.Downes]

DOWNING, G. R.
New York, N.Y. ....1810 [GRD] [N·YORK]

DOWNING & PHELPS
New York, N.Y. ....1810 [D&P] [DOWNING&PHELPS]

DRAPER, J.
Wilmington, Del. ....1816 [J.DRAPER]

DREWRY, GEORGE
Philadelphia, Pa. ....1763 [GD]

DRINKER, JOHN
New York, N.Y. 1835

DROWN, T. P.
Boston, Mass. ....1790 [T.P.DROWN] [T P DROWN]

DROWNE, BENJAMIN
Portsmouth, N.H. 1800

DROWNE, SAMUEL
Portsmouth, N.H. .....1749-1815 [S×D] [S×Drowne]

DROWNE, SHEM
Boston, Mass. ....1749 [SD]

DRUMONT, ANTOINE
New York, N.Y. 1808

DUBOIS, ABRAHAM
Philadelphia, Pa. ....1777 [AD] [A DUBOIS] [A·DUBOI]

DUBOIS, A., Sr. & Jr.
New York, N.Y. 1803

DUBOIS, JOSEPH
New York, N.Y. ....1790 [J·DUBOIS] [I·DUBOIS]

DUBOIS, TUNIS, D.
New York, N.Y. ....1799 [T·D·D] [▨] [▨] [T·D·DUBOIS]

DUBOIS & CO.
New York, N.Y. 1803

DUCHE, RENE
New York, N.Y. 1795

DUCHE & DONARD
Philadelphia, Pa. 1820

DUDLEY, BENJAMIN
Birmingham, Ga. 1768

DUFFEL, JAMES
New York, N.Y. ....1801 [I·DUFFEL]

DUHME & CO.
St. Louis, Mo. ....1850 [DUHME]

DUMMER, JEREMIAH
Boston, Mass. ....1645-1718 [ID] [ID]

DU MORTE, JOHN
Philadelphia, Pa. 1796

DUMOURIER, JOSEPH
Philadelphia, Pa. 1816

DUMOUTET, JOHN BAPTISTE
Philadelphia, Pa. ....1793 [DUMOUTET] [DUMOUTE]

DUNDAS, PRATT
Philadelphia, Pa. 1837

DUNKERLY, JOSEPH
Boston, Mass. 1787

DUNLEVY, ROBERT
Philadelphia, Pa. 1831

DUNN, CARY
New York, N.Y. 1764

DUNN, DAVID
New York, N.Y. 1835

DUNN & SON
New York, N.Y. 1787

DUNSCOMB, DENNIS
New York, N.Y. 1765

DUON, H.
Baltimore, Md. 1819

DUPUY, DANIEL
Philadelphia, Pa. 1719-1807

DUPUY, DANIEL, Jr.
Philadelphia, Pa. 1782

DUPUY, JOHN
Philadelphia, Pa. 1770

DUPUY, JOHN & DANIEL, Jr.
Philadelphia, Pa. 1783

DUPUY & SONS
Philadelphia, Pa. 1784

DURAND, JOHN
New York, N.Y. 1835

DURANDEAU, JOHN
New York, N.Y. 1835

DURGIN, WILLIAM B.
Concord, N.H. 1850

DUSENBERRY, W. C.
New York, N.Y. 1830

DUTEUS, CHARLES J.
Philadelphia, Pa. 1751

DUTEUS & HARPER
Philadelphia, Pa. 1755

DUVALIER
Unknown ....c. 1800

DUYCKINCK, DANIEL
New York, N.Y. 1798

DWIGHT, TIMOTHY
Boston, Mass. 1645-1691

E

EAGLES & MORRIS
New York, N.Y. 1799

EAMES, JOSHUA
Boston, Mass. 1828

EASTON. J.
Nantucket, Mass. 1828

EASTON. NATHANIEL
Nantucket, Mass. 1780

EASTON & SANFORD
Nantucket, Mass. 1830

EASTWICK, THOMAS
Boston, Mass. 1743

EATON, TIMOTHY
Philadelphia, Pa. 1793

EAYRES, THOMAS S.
Boston, Mass. 1760-1803

EDGAR, JOHN
New York, N.Y. 1807

EDMECHAT, CLAUDE
New York, N.Y. 1790

EDWARDS, ABRAHAM
Ashby, Mass. 1763

EDWARDS, ANDREW
Boston, Mass. 1796

EDWARDS, CALVIN
Ashby, Mass. 1710

EDWARDS, JOHN
Boston, Mass. 1700

EDWARDS, JOSEPH, Jr.
Boston, Mass. 1707-1777

EDWARDS, SAMUEL
Boston, Mass. 1705-1762

EDWARDS, SAMUEL
Natick, Mass. 1726-1783

EDWARDS, THOMAS
Boston, Mass. 1701-1755

EDWARDS, THOMAS
New York, N.Y. 1731

EMBREE
Unknown ....c. 1790

ELDERKIN, ALFRED
Killingsworth, Conn. 1792

ELDERKIN, ELISHA
New Haven, Conn. 1777

ELDERKIN & STANIFORD
Windom, Conn. 1790

ELLIOTT, JOHN A.
Sharon, Conn. 1815

ELLIOTT, JOSEPH
New Castle, Delaware 1768

ELLIS, LEWIS W.
Philadelphia, Pa. 1837

ELLISON, PETER
New York, N.Y. 1792

ELLSWORTH, DAVID
Windsor, Conn. 1772

ELTONHEAD. THOMAS
Baltimore, Md. 1835

EMERY, STEPHEN
Boston, Mass. 1746-1789

EMERY, STEPHEN
Boston, Mass. 1725-1801

EMERY, THOMAS KNOX Boston, Mass. 1781-1815	T·Emery TKE T·K·EMERY· T·Emery
EMERY & COMPANY New York, N.Y. 1798	
ENGLAND, GEORGE New York, N.Y. 1800	
ENGLAND, WILLIAM Philadelphia, Pa. 1717	
ENSIGN Unknown ....c. 1800	ENSIGN
EOFF & CONNOR New York, N.Y. 1833	J.H.CONNOR & G.EOFF
EOFF, EDGAR W. New York, N.Y. 1785-1858	EME
EOFF, GARRET New York, N.Y. 1785-1858	G·EOFF G.Eoff
EOFF & HOWELL New York, N.Y. 1805	EOFF&HOWELL
EOFF & MOORE New York, N.Y. 1835	G.EOFF J.C.MOORE
EOFF & PHYFE New York, N.Y. 1844	E&P
EOFF & SHEPARD New York, N.Y. 1825	E&S
EOLLES & DAY Hartford, Conn. 1825	EOLLES & DAY HARTFORD
EPPS, ELLERY Boston, Mass. 1808	
EQUER & AQUIMAC New York, N.Y. 1816	
ERWIN, ANDREW Philadelphia, Pa. 1837	
ERWIN, HENRY Philadelphia, Pa. 1817	H·ERWIN H.ERWIN
ERWIN, JOHN New York, N.Y. 1815	J.ERWIN
ESTEVA, HAYACINTH New York, N.Y. 1804	
ETTER, B. Unknown ....c. 1780	B·ETTER
ETTING, BENJAMIN New York, N.Y. 1769	
EVANS, HENRY New York, N.Y. ...1820	HENRY EVANS
EVANS, JOHN New York, N.Y. 1830	EVANS
EVANS, ROBERT Boston, Mass. 1768-1812	RE R·E R.EVANS EVANS EVANS
EVERITT, JESSE New York, N.Y. 1811	
EVERSTEN, JOHN Albany, N.Y. 1813	

EWAN, JOHN Charleston, S.C. 1800	J.EWAN
F	
FABER, WILLIAM Philadelphia, Pa. 1837	
FABER & HOOVER Philadelphia, Pa. 1837	
FAGALER, GEORGE M. Philadelphia, Pa. 1808	
FAIRCHILD, JAMES L. New York, N.Y. 1830	
FAIRCHILD, JOSEPH New Haven, Conn. 1824	
FAIRCHILD, ROBERT Durham, Conn. 1703-1794	R&F R.FAIRCHILD RF RF R·FAIRCHILD
FARIS, CHARLES Boston, Mass. 1790	Cs Faris Chas Faris Chas Faris Cs Faris
FARIS, WILLIAM Annapolis, Md. 1728-1804	W·F W·F W.F.
FARLEY, CHARLES Portland, Me. 1812	C.FARLEY FARLEY.
FARNAM, HENRY Boston, Mass. 1799	H·FARNAM
FARNAM, R. & H. Boston, Mass. 1807	R&H·FARNAM
FARNAM, RUFUS Boston, Mass. 1796	R.FARNAM
FARNAM, THOMAS Boston, Mass. 1836	Th:Farnam
FARNUM & WARD Boston, Mass. 1810	FARNAM&WARD
FARNHAM & OWEN Unknown 1810	
FARR, JOHN C. Boston, Mass. 1812	J.C.FARR JOHN C.FARR
FARRINGTON & HUNNEWELL Boston, Mass. 1830	F&H FARRINGTON & HUNNEWELL
FARRINGTON, JOHN Boston, Mass. 1826	
FAULKNER, J. W. New York, N.Y. 1835	JWF J.W.FAULKNER 371 B'd'y
FELLOWS, ABRAHAM Newport, R.I. 1826	FELLOWS
FELLOWS & GREEN Maine 1825	FELLOWS & GREEN
FELLOWS, JOHN F. Portsmouth, N.H. 1824	
FELLOWS & STORM Albany, N.Y. 1839	FELLOWS & STORM
FENNO, J. Unknown 1825	J.Fenno
FERGUSON, JOHN Philadelphia, Pa. 1802	

FERRIER, JOHN
New Orleans, La. 1802

FERRIS, BENJAMIN
New York, N.Y. 1816

FESSENDEN
Newport, R.I. 1845   [FESSENDEN] [PURE SILVER]

FEURT, JETER
New York, N.Y. 1731   [PF]

FIELDING, GEORGE
New York, N.Y. 1731   [GF]

FIELDS, SAMUEL
Philadelphia, Pa. 1816

FIFIELD, JOHN S.
Westerly, R.I.

FINCH, HIRAM
Albany, N.Y. 1840

FINEWELL, SAMUEL
New York, N.Y. 1835

FIRENG, J. P.
Burlington, N.J. 1810   [J.P.FIRENG] [BURLINGTON N.J]

FISHER, JAMES
New York, N.Y. 1821

FISHER, THOMAS
Philadelphia, Pa. 1797   [T.Fisher] [T.FISHER] [TFisher]

FITCH, ALLEN
New Haven, Conn. 1808

FITCH, D. M.
New Haven, Conn. 1840   [D.M.FITCH]

FITCH & HOBART
New Haven, Conn. 1811

FITCH, JOHN
Trenton, N.J. 1769-1875   [J.FITCH] [●] [●]

FITE, JOHN
Baltimore, Md. 1810   [I·FITE]

FLAGG, JOSIAH
Boston, Mass. 1765

FLAGG, JOSIAH, Jr.
Boston, Mass. 1810

FLETCHER & BENNETT
Philadelphia, Pa. 1837

FLETCHER, CHARLES
Philadelphia, Pa. 1817

FLETCHER & BARDINER
Philadelphia, Pa. 1812   [F.&G.] [F.&G.]

FLETCHER, THOMAS
Philadelphia, Pa. 1813   **T.FLETCHER PHILAD·**

FLING, GEORGE
Philadelphia, Pa. 1749

FLOTT, LEWIS
Baltimore, Md. 1817

FOLLOPPE, A. A.
Boston, Mass. 1806

FOLSOM, JOHN
Albany, N.Y. 1781

FOOTE, WILLIAM
Middletown, Conn.
East Haddam, Conn. 1796

FORBES, ABRAHAM G.
New York, N.Y. 1769   [AGF] [AF] [N.YORK]

FORBES, BENJAMIN G.
New York, N.Y. 1817

FORBES, COLLINS V. G.
New York, N.Y. 1816   [CVGF]

FORBES, C. V. G. & SON
New York, N.Y. 1835   [FORBES&SON]

FORBES, G.
New York, N.Y. 1816

FORBES, G. & J. W.
New York, N.Y. 1810

FORBES, GARRET
New York, N.Y. 1808   [G.FORBES]

FORBES, I. W.
New York, N.Y. 1805

FORBES, JOHN W.
New York, N.Y. 1805   [IWF] [IWF] [IWFORBES] [NY] [NY] [I.W.FORBES]

FORBES & SON, C. V. G.
New York, N.Y. 1835   [WF] [●] [NEW YORK]

FORBES, WILLIAM
New York, N.Y. 1830   [W·FORBES] [NY] [N.YORK]

FORBES, WILLIAM G.
New York, N.Y. 1773   [W.FORBES] [W.G.Forbes] [WGForbes] [WGForbes] [W.G.FORBES] [N.YORK]

FORCE, JABEZ W.
New York, N.Y. 1819   [J.W.FORCE]

FORD, SAMUEL
Philadelphia, Pa. 1797   [SF]

FOREST, ALEXANDER
Baltimore, Md. 1802

FORMAN, BENONI B.
Albany, N.Y. 1813

FORREST, ALEXANDER
Baltimore, Md. 1802

FORTUNE, ANTHONY
Philadelphia, Pa. 1767

FOSTER, ABRAHAM
Philadelphia, Pa. 1816

FOSTER, G.
Salem, Mass. 1838

FOSTER, I.
Unknown 1761

FOSTER, JOHN
New York, N.Y. 1811   [J.FOSTER] [●] [●]

FOSTER, JOSEPH
Boston, Mass. 1760-1839   [FOSTER] [I·FOSTER]

FOSTER, N. & J.
Newburyport, R.I. 1823

FOSTER & RICHARDS
New York, N. Y. 1815

FOSTER, SAMUEL
Boston, Mass. 1676-1702

FOSTER, THOMAS
Newburyport, Mass.......1823

FOURNIQUET, LOUIS
New York, N. Y. 1795

FOURNIQUET & WHEATLEY
New York, N. Y. 1817

FOWLER, GILBERT
New York, N. Y. 1825

FRADGLEY, THOMAS
New York, N. Y. 1797

FRANCIS, JULIUS C.
Middletown, Conn. 1807

FRANCIS, NATHANIEL
New York, N. Y. 1804

FRANCIS, NATHANIEL
New York, N. Y. 1819

FRANCISCUS, GEORGE
Baltimore, Md. 1776

FRANK, JACOB
Philadelphia, Pa. 1793

FRANKS, WILLIAM
Philadelphia, Pa. 1839

FRASER, WILLIAM
Philadelphia, Pa. 1735

FREEBORN, N.
Unknown ....C 1800

FREEMAN, WILLIAM
Philadelphia, Pa. 1839

FREEMANS, J. M. & CO.
Unknown ....C 1800

FRINTH, JAMES
Philadelphia, Pa. 1840

FROBISHER, BENJAMIN C.
Boston, Mass. 1836

FROST & MUMFORD
Providence, R. I. 1810

FROTHERINGHAM, EBENEZER
Boston, Mass. 1756-1814

FRYER, JOHN W.
Albany, N. Y. 1784

FUETER, DANIEL C.
New York, N. Y. 1756

FUETER, DAVID
New York, N. Y. 1789

FUETER, LEWIS
New York, N. Y. 1775

FULLER, ALEXANDER
New York, N. Y. 1811

FURIS, LEWIS
New York, N. Y. 1810

G

GADLEY & JOHNSON
Albany, N. Y. 1849

GAFKINS, J.
Providence, R. I. 1832

GAITHER, GREENBERG
District of Columbia 1834

GALE & HAYDEN
New York, N. Y. 1846

GALE, JOHN
New York, N. Y. 1816

GALE, JOHN
New York, N. Y. 1819

GALE, JOHN S.
New York, N. Y. 1820

GALE & MOSELY
New York, N. Y. 1830

GALE & STICKLER
New York, N. Y. 1823

GALE, WILLIAM
New York, N. Y. 1816

GALE, WILLIAM, JR.
New York, N. Y. 1823

GALE & SON, WM.
New York, N. Y. 1823

GALE & WILLIS
New York, N. Y. 1840

GALE, WOOD & HUGHES
New York, N. Y. 1835

GALLOP, CHRISTOPHER
Ledyard, Conn. 1790

GALT, SAMUEL
Williamsburg, Va. 1749

GARDINER, B.
New York, N. Y. 1829

GARDINER, BALDWIN
Philadelphia, Pa. 1814

GARDINER & CO.
New York, N. Y. 1836

GARDINER, JOHN
New London, Conn. ...1734-1776

GARDINER, SIDNEY
Philadelphia, Pa. 1810

GARDINER, JOHN J.
Boston, Mass. 1730-1776

GARLLOW, SHAVELIER
Philadelphia, Pa. 1813

GARNER, JOHN
Cincinnati, Ohio 1825

GARRE, S.
New York, N. Y. 1825

GERREN, ANTHONY Philadelphia, Pa. 1813		
GARRETT, P. Philadelphia, Pa. 1811	P.GARRETT	
GARRETT, T. C. Philadelphia, Pa. 1815		
GARRETT, T. C. & CO. Philadelphia, Pa. 1815	T.C.GARRETT & CO	
GARRISON, JOHN New York, N.Y. 1825		
GARROW & DORSEY Baltimore, Md. 1800		
GASKINS, J. Unknown 1760		
GASKINS, W. W. Providence, R. I. .,.....1830	WWG	
GATHAM, WILLIAM Philadelphia, Pa. ..,....1802		
GAY, CHARLES Baltimore, Md. ..-...-.....1779		
GAY, NATHANIEL Boston, Mass. 1664		
GEE, JOSEPH Philadelphia, Pa. 1785		
GEFFROY, NICHOLAS Newport, R.I. 1761-1839	N GEFFROY. GEFFROY N.GEFFROY	
GELEY, PETER Philadelphia, Pa. 1793		
GELSTON & CO. New York, N.Y. 1837	GELSTON&CO	
GELSTON, GEORGE S. New York, N.Y. 1833	G.S.GELSTON	
GELSTON & GOULD Baltimore, Md. 1819		
GELSTON, HUGH Baltimore, Md. 1794-1873	HU.GELSTON GELSTON	
GELSTON, LADD & CO. New York, N.Y. 1836	GELSTON LADD & CO	
GELSTON & TREADWELL New York, N.Y. 1836		
GEORGEON, BERNARD Philadelphia, Pa. 1797		
GERMON, J. D. Philadelphia, Pa. 1819		
GERMON, JOHN D. Philadelphia, Pa. 1782	I.G	
GERRISH & PEARSON New York, N.Y. ,.......1800	Gerrish&Pearson	
GERRISH, TIMOTHY Portsmouth, N. H. ..1753-1813	TG J.Gerrish GERRISH J.Gerrish	
GETHEN, JOHN Philadelphia, Pa. 1811		

GETHEN, WILLIAM Philadelphia, Pa. 1797	W.GETHEN	
GETTY, JAMES Williamsburg, Va 1772		
GETZ, PETER Lancaster, Pa. 1792	P.Getz	
GHISELIN, CESAR Philadelphia, Pa. 1695	CG CG CG	
GHISELIN, WILLIAM Philadelphia, Pa. 1751	WG GHISELIN	
GIBBS, DANIEL Boston, Mass. 1716		
GIBBS, JOHN Providence, R.I. 1798	J GIBBS	
GIBBS, JOHN F. Providence, R.I. 1803		
GIBSON, WILLIAM Philadelphia, Pa. 1845	GIBSON	
GIFFING, CHRISTOPHER New York, N.Y. ...,...1816	C.Gifing.N.Y	
GILBERT, SAMUEL Hebron, Conn. 1798	SG SG	
GILBERT, WILLIAM W. New York, N.Y. 1767	WG N.YORK GILBERT W.Gilbert Gilbert N.York	
GILBERT & CUNNINGHAM New York, N.Y. 1839		
GILL, CALEB Boston, Mass. .,..,...1774-1855	GILL	
GILL, LEAVITT Hingham, Mass. 1810		
GILLEY, PETER Philadelphia, Pa. 1797		
GILMAN, BENJAMIN CLARK Exeter, N. H. 1763-1835	BCG	
GILMAN, JOHN WARD New York, N.Y. ...... :1792	I·W·G	
GIQUEL, JOHN B. F. New Orleans, La. ... .1822		
GIRARD, FRANCIS Philadelphia, Pa. 1817		
GIRAUD, HENRY New York, N.Y. 1805		
GIRRAD, HENRY New York, N.Y. 1805		
GIRREAUN, STEPHEN Philadelphia, Pa. 1785		
GIVEN, A. Albany, N.Y. 1849		
GLIDDEN, JOSEPH Boston, Mass. 1607-1780		
GODDARD D. & SON Worcester, Mass. 1845	D.GODDARD & SON	

GOELET, PHILIP New York, N. Y. 1731	PG PG PG	
GOFORTH, JEREMIAH Philadelphia, Pa . . .1700		
GOLDTHWAITE, JOSEPH Boston, Mass. ... 1706-1780	I·G I·G IG	
GOMBACH, JOHN Philadelphia, Pa. 1802		
GOODHUE, D. T. Boston, Mass. 1840	DTG ☒ DT GOODHUE	
GOODHUE, JOHN Salem, Mass. 1840	J.GOODHUE	
GOODING, HENRY Boston, Mass. ...., 1833	GOODING GOODING	
GOODING, JOSEPH Boston, Mass. 1815		
GOODING, JOSIAH Unknown 1810	Josiah Gooding Joys Building	
GOODWIN, ALLYN Hartford, Conn. 1811		
GOODWIN, BENJAMIN Boston, Mass. 1756	B.Goodwin	
GOODWIN & DODD Hartford, Conn. . . 1812	G&D	
GOODWIN, H. & A. Hartford, Conn. . .. 1811		
GOODWIN, HORACE Hartford, Conn. 1811		
GOODWIN, HORACE & ALLYN Hartford, Conn, ... 1811	GOODWIN	
GOODWIN, RALPH Hartford, Conn. 1828		
GORDON, A. & J. New York, N. Y. 1798		
GORDON, ALEXANDER S. New York, N. Y. 1795	GORDON	
GORDON, ANDREW New York, N. Y. .. 1796		
GORDON & COMPANY Boston, Mass. 1849		
GORDON, G. New York, N. Y. 1800	G.Gordon	
GORDON, JAMES New York, N. Y. 1795		
GORDON, JAMES S. Philadelphia, Pa. 1769		
GORHAM, JABEZ Providence, R. I. 1792	J.GORHAM	
GORHAM, JABEZ & SON Providence, R.I........ 1842	J.GORHAM&SON	
GORHAM, JOHN New Haven, Conn. 1814		

GORHAM, MILES New Haven, Conn. ..1757-1847	M.G M.GORHAM	
GORHAM, RICHARD New Haven, Conn. 1799		
GORHAM & THURBER Providence, R. I. ..... .1850	Gorham & Thurbe.	
GORHAM & WEBSTER New York, N. Y. 1831	Gorham & Webster	
GOUGH, JAMES New York, N. Y. 1769	IG	
GOULD, J. Baltimore, Md. 1795-1874		
GOULD, JAMES Baltimore, Md. 1816-1868	J·GOULD J·GOULD 10-1	
GOULD, JOHN Philadelphia, Pa: 1840		
GOULD, STOWELL & WARD Baltimore, Md. 1840		
GOULD & WARD Baltimore, Md. ..... .1850	GOULD & WARD	
GOVERT, JAMES Philadelphia, Pa. 1802		
GOWEN, WILLIAM Medford, Mass. ...,......1772	WG W·GOWEN	
GRAHAM, DANIEL West Suffield, Conn. .. .1789		
GRANT, THOMAS Marblehead, Mass. 1754	T·GRANT	
GRANT, WILLIAM, JR. Philadelphia, Pa. . . 1785		
GRAVELLE, RENE S. Philadelphia, Pa. . 1813		
GRAVES, THOMAS Cincinatti, Ohio 1828		
GRAVIER, NICHOLAS New Orleans, La. 1822		
GRAY, G. Portsmouth, N. H. 1839	G.GRAY	
GRAY, JOHN New London, Conn. 1692-1720	I.G IG	
GRAY, ROBERT Portsmouth, N. H. 1850	ROBT GRAY R·Gray ROBT GRAY	
GRAY, SAMUEL New London, Conn. 1684-1713	S:GRAY GRAY	
GRAY, SAMUEL Boston, Mass. . 1732	S:GRAY	
GREEN, BENJAMIN Boston, Mass. 1712-1748	B:GREEN	
GREEN, JAMES New York, N. Y. 1805		
GREGG, HAYDEN & CO. New York, N. Y. 1850	GREGG.HAYDEN & CO	

GREENE, RUFUS
Boston, Mass. 1707-1777

GREENE, WM. & CO.
Providence, R. I. 1815

GREENLEAF, DAVID
Norwich, Conn. 1737-1800

GREENLEAF, DAVID, Jr.
Hartford, Conn. 1766

GREENLEAF, JOSEPH
New London, Conn. ...1779-1798

GREFFIN, PETER
Philadelphia, Pa. 1801

GRIFFEN & HOYT
Albany, N. Y. 1830

GRIFFEN, P.
Albany, N. Y. 1825

GRIFFING, CHRISTOPHER
New York, N. Y. 1816

GRIFITH, DAVID
Boston, Mass. 1789

GRIGG, WM.
New York, N. Y. 1765

GRIGNON, BENJAMIN
Boston, Mass. 1685

GRIGNON, RENE
Norwich, Conn. 1715

GRIMKE, JOHN P.
Charleston, S. C. 1744

GRISCOM, GEORGE
Philadelphia, Pa. 1791

GRISELM, CAESAR
Philadelphia, Pa. 1700

GRISWOLD, GILBERT
Middletown, Conn. 1825

GRISWOLD, WILLIAM
Middletown, Conn. 1820

GROEN, JACOB MARIUS
(Morrisgreen)
New York, N. Y. 1701

GUERCY, DOMINICK
New York, N. Y. 1795

GUERIN, ANTHONY
Philadelphia, Pa. 1791

GUILLE, NOAH
Boston, Mass. 1701

GUIRNA, ANTHONY
Philadelphia, Pa. 1796

GUNN, ENOS
Waterbury, Conn. 1792

GURLEY, WILLIAM
Norwich, Conn. 1804

GURNEE, BENJAMIN
New York, N. Y. 1820

GURNEE, B. & S.
New York, N. Y. 1833

GURNEE & COMPANY
New York, N. Y. 1820

H

HACKLE, WILLIAM
Baltimore, Md. 1776

HADDOCK & ANDREWS
Boston, Mass. 1838

HADDOCK, HENRY
Boston, Mass. 1836

HADWEN, WILLIAM
Nantucket, Mass. 1816

HAGGENMACHER, J. H. & CO.
Philadelphia, Pa. 1836

HAINES, ABRAHAM
New York, N. Y. 1801

HALL, ABIJAH
Albany, N. Y. 1813

HALL & BROWER
Albany, N. Y. 1830

HALL, BROWER & CO.
Albany, N. Y. 1836

HALL, CHARLES
Lancaster, Pa. 1755

HALL, DAVID
Philadelphia, Pa. 1760-1779

HALL, DREW
New York, N. Y. 1789

HALL, GREEN
Albany, N. Y. 1813

HALL & HEWSON
Albany, N. Y. 1819

HALL, HEWSON &
MERRIFIELD
Albany, N. Y. 1814

HALL, IVORY
Concord, N. H. 1781

HALL & MERRIMAN
New Haven, Conn. 1825

HALL & MERRIMAN
Albany, N. Y. 1825

HALLAM, JOHN
New London, Conn. 1773

HALSEY, JABEZ
New York, N. Y. 1762-1820

HALSTED, BENJAMIN
New York, N. Y. 1764

HALSTED & SON
New York, N. Y. 1790

HALSTRICK, J.
Boston, Mass. 1846

HAM, GEORGE
Portsmouth, N. H. 1810

HAMILL & COMPANY
New York, N. Y. 1817

HAMILL, JAMES
New York, N. Y. 1816   `J·HAMILL·N.Y.`

HAMILTON, JAMES
Annapolis, Md. 1766

HAMILTON, JOHN
New York, N. Y. 1798

HAMLIN, CYRUS
Portland, Me. 1831

HAMLIN, WILLIAM
Middletown, Conn. 1761   `W.H` `WH` `HAMLIN`

HAMMERSLEY, THOMAS
New York, N. Y. ...:...1727-1781   `GH` `T·H` `TH`

HANCOCK, JOHN
Boston, Mass. 1732-1772   `J·HANCOCK` `J·HANCOCK` `J·HANCOCK`

HANDLE, JOHN
Philadelphia, Pa. 1839

HANKS, BENJAMIN
Wyndham, Conn. 1777

HANNAH, W. W.
New York, N. Y. 1840   **W.W.HANNAH**

HANNERS, GEORGE
Boston, Mass. 1697-1740   `GH` `G·HANNERS`

HANNERS, GEORGE, JR.
Boston, Mass. 1721-1760   `GH` `G.H`

HANSELL, ROBERT
Boston, Mass. 1823

HARACHE, PIERRE
Williamsburg, Va. 1691

HARDING, N. & C.
New York, N. Y. 1830

HARDING & CO. N.
Boston, Mass. 1830   `N.H&CO`

HARDING, NEWELL
Boston, Mass. 1822   `N.Harding` `NHarding` `N.HARDING` `N.H&CO` `N.Harding&Co`

HARDWOOD, JOHN
Philadelphia, Pa. ...·.....1816

HARDY, STEPHEN
Portsmouth, N. H. 1781-1843   `HARDY` `HARDY`

HARLAND, THOMAS
Norwich, Conn. .....:1735-1807   `HARLAND`

HARLAND, THOMAS, JR.
Norwich, Conn. ......:...1777

HARPEL, THOMAS W.
Philadelphia, Pa. 1813

HARPER, ALEXANDER
Philadelphia, Pa. ....:.

HARPER, DAVID
Philadelphia, Pa ....

HARPER, THOMAS W.
Philadelphia, Pa. .... .1813

HARRIS, GEORGE
New York, N. Y. 1802

HARRIS, H.
Albany, N. Y. ...·.......1820

HARRIS & STANWOOD
Boston, Mass. 1835   `HARRIS & STANWOO`

HARRIS & WILCOX
Albany, N. Y. 1844   `HARRIS & WILCOX`

HART & BLISS
Middletown, Conn. 1803

HART & BREWER
Middletown, Conn. 1800-1803   `H&B`

HART, ELIPHAZ
Norwich, Conn. ...1789-1866   `EH` `E.HART`

HART, JOHN
Philadelphia, Pa. 1776

HART, JOHN J.
New York, N. Y. 1820

HART, JUDAH
Middletown, Conn. 1777-1824   `J.HART` `JHart` `JHART`

HART & SMITH
Baltimore, Md. 1816   `H&S`

HART & WILCOX
Norwich, Conn. 1805-1807   `H♥W`

HART, WILLIAM
Philadelphia, Pa. 1818   `W.HART.`

HARTFORD, GEORGE
Philadelphia, Pa. 1794

HARTIN & BARGI
Bound Brook, N. J. 1766

HARTLEY, SAMUEL
Philadelphia, Pa. 1818

HARTMAN, PHILIP
Philadelphia, Pa. 1813

HARVEY, LEWIS
Philadelphia, Pa. 1811   `HARVEY.LEWIS`

HASCY, ALEXANDER
Albany, N. Y. 1849

HASCY, NELSON
Albany, N. Y. 1849

HASKELL, BARNABUS
Boston, Mass. 1833

HASTIER, JOHN
New York, N. Y. 1726   `IH` `IH` `IH` `IH` `J·`

HASTIER, MARQUERIETTE
New York, N. Y. 1771   `MH`

HASTINGS, B. B.
Cleveland, Ohio 1835   `HASTINGS`

HASTINGS, H.
New York, N. Y. 1815   `H·HASTINGS`

HAUGH, SAMUEL Boston, Mass. 1675-1717	**SH**	
HAVERSTICK, WILLIAM Philadelphia, Pa. 1781	**WH**	
HAWLEY, NOAH New York, N.Y. 1816		
HAWS, JOHN Philadelphia, Pa. 1837		
HAYDEN & GREGG New York, N.Y. 1840	**HAYDEN&GREGG**	
HAYES & COLTON Newark, N.J. 1831		
HAYES, W. Connecticut 1780	**WH** **W.Hayes**	
HAYS, ANDREW Newark, N.J. 1769		
HAYS & MYERS New York, N.Y. 1770	**H&M**	
HEAD, JOSEPH Philadelphia, Pa. 1798		
HEALD, J.S. Baltimore, Md. 1810	**J.S.HEALD** **IP**	
HEALY Boston, Mass. 1773		
HEATH, JOHN New York, N.Y. 1761	**J·HEATH**	
HEBBERD New York, N.Y. 1847		
HECK, LUDWIG Lancaster, Pa. 1760	**LH**	
HEDGES, DANIEL Unknown ....C 1830	**HEDGES**	
HEDGES, DANIEL, JR. East Hampton, N.Y. ..1779-1856		
HEGUENBURG, CHARLES, JR. New Haven, Conn. 1809		
HELME, NATHANIEL South Kingston, R.I. .1761-1789	**HELME** **HELME** **NH**	
HEMPSTED & CHADLER New York, N.Y. 1811		
HENCHMAN, DANIEL Boston, Mass. 1730-1775	**D·H** **Henchman**	
HENDERSON, A.A. Philadelphia, Pa. 1837	**HENDERSON**	
HENDRICKS, AHASUERUS New York, N.Y. 1676	**AH** **A·H**	
HENRY, FELIX New York, N.Y. 1815		
HEOUENBOURG, CHARLES, Jr. New Haven, Conn. ... 1760-1851	**CH** **C.HEQUEMBOURG.JR**	
HERBERT, TIMOTHY B. New York, N.Y. 1816		

HERILS, FRANCIS Philadelphia, Pa. 1804	
HERON, ISAAC New York, N.Y. 1768	
HEURTIN, WILLIAM New York, N.Y. 1731	
HEWS, ABRAHAM, JR. Boston, Mass. 1823	**A.HEWS.JR**
HEWSON, JOHN D. Albany, N.Y. 1815	
HEYDORN & IMLAY Hartford, Conn. 1810	**H&I**
HEYER & CALE New York, N.Y. 1807	**W.B.HEYER & J.CALE**
HEYER, WILLIAM B. New York, N.Y. 1798	**W.B.HEYER** **W.B.Heyer** **W.B.Heyer** **H&NJ**
HIGBIE & CROSBY Boston, Mass. 1820	**HIGBIE & CROSBY**
HILDEBUR Philadelphia, Pa. 1790	
HILL, JAMES Boston, Mass. 1770	
HILL & WADDILL Petersburgh, Va. 1780	
HILLDRUP, THOMAS Hartford, Conn. 1774	
HILLER, BENJAMIN Boston, Mass. 1687	**BH** **BH** **BH**
HILLER, JOSEPH Boston, Mass. 1745	
HILLDRAUP, THOMAS Hartford, Conn. 1772	
HILTON, WM. Philadelphia, Pa. 1814	
HIND, JOHN Philadelphia, Pa. 1760	
HINSDALE & ATKIN New York, N.Y. 1830	**HINSDALE&ATKIN**
HINSDALE, EPAPHRAS New York, N.Y. 1797	**HINSDALE**
HINSDALE, H. New York, N.Y. 1831	
HITCHBORN, DANIEL Boston, Mass. 1773	
HITCHBORN, SAMUEL Boston, Mass. 1752	
HITCHCOCK, ELIAKIM Boston, Mass. 1752	**E+H** **EH**
HOBARTH, JOSHUA New Haven, Conn. 1811	**J·HOBART**
HOBBS, NATHAN Boston, Mass. 1792-1868	**HOBBS** **N.Hobbs**

HODGE, JOHN
Hadley, Mass. . . . . . . 1775 [J.HODGE] [HADLEY]

HOFFMAN, FREDERICK
Philadelphia, Pa. . . . 1819

HOFFMAN, JAMES M.
Philadelphia, Pa. . . 1820 [J.M.HOFFMAN]

HOLLAND, LITTLETON
Baltimore, Md. . . . . 1804 [L&C] [L.Holland] [L·HOLLAND] [HOLLAND] [Holland]

HOLLINGSHEAD, JOHN
Philadelphia, Pa. . . 1768

HOLLINGSHEAD, WILLIAM
Philadelphia, Pa. . . 1770 [WH] [WH]

HOLMES, ADRIAN B.
New York, N. Y. . . . 1801 [A.HOLMES]

HOLMES, ISRAEL
Waterbury, Conn. . . 1793

HOLMES, J.
New York, N. Y. 1816

HOLMES, WILLIAM
New York, N. Y. 1801

HOLSEY, E.
Philadelphia, Pa. . . . . . 1820 [E·HOLSEY] [E]

HOLTON, DAVID
Baltimore, Md. 1804

HOLTON, JOHN
Philadelphia, Pa. 1794

HOLYOKE, EDWARD
Boston, Mass. . . . . 1817 [HOLYOKE]

HOMES, WILLIAM
Boston, Mass. . . . . . . 1717-1783 [WH] [WH] [HOMES] [W·HOmes]

HOMES, WILLIAM, JR.
New York, N. Y. . . . . 1742-1825 [WH] [WH] [HOMES]

HOOD & TOBY
Albany, N. Y. . . . . 1849 [HOOD & TOBEY]

HOOKEY, WILLIAM
Newport, R. I. 1750

HOOVER, HENRY
Philadelphia, Pa. 1816

HOOVER, JOSEPH E.
Philadelphia, Pa. 1837

HOPKINS, JESSE
Waterbury, Conn. 1787

HOPKINS, JOSEPH
Waterbury, Conn. . . . 1730-1801 [HOPKINS]

HOPKINS, STEPHEN
Waterbury, Conn. . . . 1721-1796 [SH]

HOPPER, SAMUEL
Philadelphia, Pa. 1835

HORN, E. B.
Boston, Mass. 1847

HOSFORD, HARLEY
New York, N. Y. . . . . . . 1820 [HOSFORD]

HOTCHKISS, HEZEKIAH
New Haven, Conn. 1754

HOUGH, SAMUEL
Boston, Mass. . . . . 1675-1717 [SH]

HOULTON, JOHN
Philadelphia, Pa. . . . . 1797 [HOULTON]

HOUTZELL, JACOB
Philadelphia, Pa. 1801

HOW, DAVID
Boston, Mass. 1790

HOWARD, ABRAHAM
Salem, Mass. 1810

HOWARD, JOHN
Philadelphia, Pa. . . . 1819

HOWARD, THOMAS
Philadelphia, Pa. . . . 1620

HOWARD, WILLIAM
Boston, Mass. 1800

HOWE, GEORGE C.
New York, N. Y. . . . . 1810 [GEORGE C.HOWE]

HOWE, OTIS
Boston, Mass. 1788

HOWELL & ARNOLD
Albany, N.Y. 1797

HOWELL, G. W.
Unknown . . . . 1790 [G·W·Howell]

HOWELL, JAMES
Philadelphia, Pa. . . . . . 1802 [J.Howell] [Howell] [J·Howell·]

HOWELL, PAUL
New York, N. Y. . . . . . 1812 [P.HOWELL]

HOWELL, SILAS W.
Albany, N. Y. . . . . . . 1798 [S·W·Howell] [S·W·Howell]

HOYT, GEORGE B.
Albany, N. Y. . . . . . . 1827 [GEO.B.HOYT]

HOYT, HENRY E.
New York, N. Y. . . . . 1820 [HENRY HOYT]

HOYT, S.
New York, N. Y. . . . . 1840 [S·HOYT]

HUBBAL
Washington, D. C. 1834

HUERTIN, WILLIAM
New York, N. Y. . . . 1731-1771 [WH] [WH] [WH]

HUGHES & BLISS
Middletown, Conn. 1806

HUGHES, CHRISTOPHER
Baltimore, Md. . . . 1744-1824 [CH] [CH]

HUGHES & FRANCIS
Middletown, Conn. 1807

HUGHES, HENRY
Baltimore, Md. 1781

HUGHES, J.
Middletown, Conn. . . . . 1798 [J.HUGHES] [✦] [STERL]

GHES, JEREMIAH
annapolis, Md. .... 1805 — J·HUGHES

GHES, WILLIAM
altimore, Md. ......1785-1791 — W.H

LBEART, PHILIP
Philadelphia, Pa. 1761

LL, JOHN
oston, Mass. 1624-1683

LL & SANDERSON
oston, Mass. 1652

MBERT, AUGUSTUS
New York, N.Y. 1818

MPHREYS, RICHARD
Philadelphia, Pa. 1772

MPHREYS, THOMAS
Philadelphia, Pa. 1814

NLOCK, BOUMAN
Philadelphia, Pa. 1752

NNEWELL, GEORGE W.
oston, Mass. 1836

NT, EDWARD
oston, Mass. 1717

NT, WILLIAM
oston, Mass. 1819

NTINGTON, PHILIP
orwich, Conn. ......1770-1825 — PH Huntington

NTINGTON, ROSWELL
orwich, Conn. 1763

NTINGTON, S.
Maine ....1850 — S·HUNTINGTON

RD, BENJAMIN
oston, Mass. ......1739-1781 — B·H

RD, ISAAC
Roxbury, Mass. 1754

RD, JACOB
oston, Mass. 1702-1758

RD, NATHANIEL
Boston, Mass. ......1730-1777 — N·Hurd N·Hurd N·Hurd

RLBEART, PHILLIP
Philadelphia, Pa. ...1761 — PH

RST, HENRY
Boston, Mass .....1665-1717 — HH H·H

RTIN & BURGI
Bound Brook, N.J. 1766

SBAND, JOHN
Philadelphia, Pa. 1796

SSEY, STEPHEN
Maryland .... 1818 — S·HUSSEY

USTON, JAMES
Baltimore, Md. 1799

UTCHINS, JACOB
New York, N.Y. ....1774 — HUTCHINS

HUTCHINS, NICHOLAS
Baltimore, Md. 1777-1845

HUTTON, GEORGE
Albany, N.Y. 1799

HUTTON, I & G.
Albany, N.Y. 1799

HUTTON, ISAAC
Albany, N.Y. 1767-1855 — HUTTON ALBANY

HUTTON, JOHN
New York, N.Y. .....1720 — H·I I·H

HUTTON, JOHN S.
New York, N.Y. ... 1684

HYDE
Newport, R.I. .... 1730 — HYDE

HYDE & GOODRICH
New Orleans, N.Y. .. 1810 — HYDE & GOODWICH N.O.

HYDE & NEVINS
New York, N.Y. .....1798 — Hyde & Nevins

I

IAGO, HENRY
New York, N.Y. 1745

INCH, JOHN
Annapolis, Md. 1720-1763

INGRAHAM, JOSEPH
Portland, Me. 1785

INMAN, BENJAMIN
Philadelphia, Pa. 1816

ISAACKS, MICHAEL
New York, N.Y. 1765

IVERS, B.
Unknown ....C 1800 — B·Ivers

J

JACCARD & COMPANY
St. Louis, Mo. ....1850 — JACCARD & CO ST LOUIS

JACKS, JAMES
Charleston, S.C. 1795

JACKS, WILLIAM
Philadelphia, Pa. 1798

JACKSON, DANIEL
New York, N.Y. ....1782 — DJ DJACKSON

JACKSON, JAMES
Baltimore, Md. 1775

JACKSON, JOHN
New York, N.Y. ....1731 — JACKSON

JACKSON, JOSEPH
Baltimore, Md. 1803 — J Jackson J Jackson

JACOB, GEORGE
Baltimore, Md. ......1802 — G.JACOB

JACOB, MOSES
Philadelphia, Pa. 1775

JACOBS, ABEL
Philadelphia, Pa. ....1816 — A.JACOBS

JACOBS & CO. A. Philadelphia, Pa. 1820	`A·J·&·Cº`		JONES, JOHN Boston, Mass. 1810	`J.JONES`	
JANVIER, LOUIS Charleston, S. C. ,.,.,.:...1744			JONES, JOHN B. Boston, Mass. 1782-1854	`J.B.Jones`	
JARVIS, MUNSON Stamford, Conn. 1742-1824	`MJ` `MJ`		JONES, JOHN B. & COL. Boston, Mass. 1813	`J.B.JONES&CO`	
JENCKES, JOHN C. Providence, R.I. 1798	`JJENCKES` `JCJENCKES`		JONES, LOWS & BALL Boston, Mass. 1850		
JENCKES & COMPANY Providence, R. I. 1798			JONES & WARD Boston, Mass. 1815	`JONES&WARD`	
JENKINS, JOHN Philadelphia, Pa. 1777	`H`		JONES, WILLIAM Marblehead, Mass. 1694-1730	`W·I`	
JENNINGS, JACOB Norwalk, Conn. 1739-1817	`I·I`		JONES, WILLIAM New York, N.Y. 1820		
JENNINGS, JACOB, JR. New London, Conn. 1800			JORDAN, PETER Philadelphia, Pa. 1823		
JESSE, DAVID Boston, Mass. 1670-1705	`D I` `D·I`		JOUBERT, P. Philadelphia, Pa. 1807		
JOHANNES, JOHN M. Baltimore, Md. 1835			JUDAH New York, N.Y. 1774		
JOHN Unknown ....C 1760			KAY, AMOS Boston, Mass. 1725	`AK`	
JOHNSON & BALL Baltimore, Md. 1785	`J&B`		KEDZIE, J. Philadelphia, Pa. 1830	`J.KEDZIE` ⬤ `R` `W`	
JOHNSON, C. Albany, N.Y. 1828			KEELER, A. Norwalk, Conn. 1800-	`KEELER`	
JOHNSON & GODLEY Albany, N.Y. 1847			KEELER, JOSEPH Norwalk, Conn. 1786-1824	`JK` `IK` `KEELER`	
JOHNSON, JOHN Pittsburg, Pa. 1815			KEELER, THADDEUS New York, N.Y. 1805	`T.KEELER`	
JOHNSON, MAYCOCK W. Albany, N.Y. 1815	`M.W.JOHNSON`		KEIFF, JOSEPH Philadelphia, Pa. 1831		
JOHNSON & REAT Baltimore, Md. 1786	`JOHNSON & REAT` `JOHNSON&REAT`		KEITH, T. & W. New York, N.Y. 1805	`T.&W.KEITH`	
JOHNSON & RILEY Baltimore, Md. 1786	`J&R`		KELEY, GRAEL Boston, Mass. 1823		
JOHNSON, SAMUEL New York, N.Y. 1780	`S·J` `S·J`		KELLEY, ALLEN Providence, R.I. 1810		
JOHNSON, SAMUEL New York, N.Y. ....,1796	`JOHNSON`		KELLEY, E. G. & J. H. Providence, R.I. 1820		
JOHNSTON, A. Philadelphia, Pa. 1830	`A·JOHNSTON` `STER`		KENDLE, CHARLES New York, N.Y. 1807		
JOHONNOT, WILLIAM B. Middletown, Conn. 1766-1849	⬤ `WJ` ⬤		KENDRICK, WILLIAM Louisville, Ky. 1840	`W.KENDRICK.Louisvi`	
JONES, BALL & POOR Boston, Mass...........1840	`JONES.BALL&POOR`		KENNEDY, MATHEW Philadelphia, Pa. 1825		
JONES, E. Baltimore, Md. 1820			KENRICK, ANWYL Maryland 1775		
JONES, GEORGE B. Boston, Mass. 1839			KEPLINGER, SAMUEL Baltimore, Md. 1770-1849	`SKEPLINGER` `C`	
JONES, JAMES Philadelphia, Pa. 1815			KETCHAM, JAMES New York, N.Y. 1814	`I.KETCHAM`	

TELL, THOMAS arlestown, Mass. 1781	T·K	KRIDER & BIDDLE Philadelphia, Pa. 1830	K/B
WORTH, ROBERT shington, D.C. 1831	R·KEYWORTH	KRIDER, PETER L. Philadelphia, Pa. 1850	P·L·K
NEY, CANN & JOHNSON w York, N.Y. 1850	K.C.& J.	KUCHER, JACOB Philadelphia, Pa. 1813	I·KUCHER
NEY & DUNN w York, N.Y. 1844	K&D K&D	KUMBEL, WILLIAM New York, N.Y. 1780	
RSTEADE, CORNELIUS w York, N.Y. 1753	CK CK	**L**	
RSTEADE, CORNELIUS w Haven, Conn. 1722		LACHAISE, PETER New York, N.Y. 1794	
BERLY, WILLIAM w York, N.Y. 1792	WK Kimberly	LADD, WILLIAM F. New York, N.Y. 1830	Wᵐ·F.LADD NEW·YORK
, JOSEPH dletown, Conn. 1770		LAFORME, ANTOINE Boston, Mass. 1836	
, THOMAS R. timore, Md. 1819	TRKING	LAFORME, BERNARD Boston, Mass. 1836	
GSTON, JOHN w York, N.Y. 1775		LAFORME, F. J. Boston, Mass. 1835	
NEY, THOMAS wich, Conn. 1786-1824	TK T·K	LAFORME, VINCENT Boston, Mass. 1850	V.LAFORME
SEY, DAVID cinatti, Ohio 1850	DKINSEY	LAINECOURT, STEPHEN New York, N.Y. 1800	
SEY, E. & D. cinnati, Ohio 1845	E.&D.KINSEY	LAKEMAN, E. K. New York, N.Y. 1800	E.K.LAKEMAN
BENJAMIN w York, N.Y. 1702		LAMAR, BENJAMIN Philadelphia, Pa. 1785	BL LAMAR
EN, GEORGE dgeport, Conn. 1820	G·KIPPEN	LAMAR, MATHIAS Philadelphia, Pa. 1796	ML
Y, WILLIAM w York, N.Y. 1783		LAMESIERE, PETER Philadelphia, Pa. 1811	
, SAMUEL timore, Md. 1792-1872	S.K S.Kirk Kirk S·KIRK KIRK S·KIRK SAM·KIRK	LAMOTHE, JOHN New Orleans, La. 1822	
& SMITH timore, Md. 1815	KIRK&SMITH	LAMOTHE, PIERRE New Orleans, La. 1822	Lamothe Lamothe
WOOD, PETER apolis, Md. 1799	PK	LAMPE, JOHN Baltimore, Md. 1787	
WOOD, PETER stertown, Md. 1790		LAMSON, J. Unknown 1790	J·LAMSON J·L
LAND, JOSEPH P. dletown, Conn. 1796		LANE, AARON Elizabeth, N.J. 1780	AL
HEN, ANDREW adelphia, Pa. 1835		LANG, EDWARD Salem, Mass. 1742-1830	EL LANG
E, BARTHOLOMEW adelphia, Pa. 1837		LANG, JEFFERY Salem, Mass. 1708-1758	I·LANG LANG I·LANG
E, B. & CO. adelphia, Pa. 1837		LANG, RICHARD Salem, Mass. 1733-1810	R·LANG
ELAND, JOSEPH ton, Mass. 1698-1760	I·Kneeland	LANGE, WILLIAM New York, N.Y. 1844	LANGE·
USE, JOHN S. hlehem, Pa. 1805		LANGER, JOSEPH Philadelphia, Pa. 1811	
		LANSING, JACOB G. Albany, N.Y. 1736	IGL

LAPEROUSE, JOHN B.
New Orleans, La. 1832

LAROUSSEBIERRE, PETER
New York, N.Y. 1797

LASHING, PETER
New York, N.Y. 1805

LATHROP, RUFUS
Norwich, Conn. 1755

LATRUIT, JOHN P.
Washington, D.C. 1833

LAWRENCE, JOSIAH H.
Philadelphia, Pa. 1817

LAWRIE, ROBERT O.
Philadelphia, Pa. 1840

LEA, SAMUEL J
Baltimore, Md. 1814

LEACH, CHARLES
Boston, Mass. 1765-1814

LEACH, JOHN
Boston, Mass. 1780

LEACH, NATHANIEL
Boston, Mass. 1789

LEACH, SAMUEL
Philadelphia, Pa. 1741

LEACH & BRADLEY
Philadelphia, Pa. 1832

LEACOCK, JOHN
Philadelphia, Pa. 1751

LAYCOCK, PETER
Philadelphia, Pa. 1750

LE BLANC, LEWIS
Philadelphia, Pa. 1815

LEDELL, JOSEPH
Philadelphia, Pa. 1797

LE DORC
Philadelphia, Pa. 1797

LEE, SAMUEL J.
Baltimore, Md. 1815

LEE, S. W.
Providence, R.I. 1815

LEFEVRE, F.
Philadelphia, Pa. 1818

LEFEVRE & GRAVELLE
Philadelphia, Pa. 1811

LEFEVRE, JOHN F.
Philadelphia, Pa. 1806

LEGARE, DANIEL
Boston, Mass. 1688-1724

LEGARE, FRANCIS
Boston, Mass. 1657

LEMAIRE, BAPTISTE
Philadelphia, Pa. 1804

LEMAIRE, MATHIAS
Philadelphia, Pa. 1781

LENCH, PETER
New York, N.Y. 1805

LENDIGREE, M.
New York, N.Y. 1814

LENT, JOHN
New York, N.Y. 1787

LEONARD, S.
New York, N.Y. 1830

LEONARD, SAMUEL
Baltimore, Md. 1786-1848

LEONARD & WILSON
Philadelphia, Pa. 1847

LERET, PETER
Baltimore, Md. 1787

LE ROUX, BARTHOLOMEW
New York, N.Y. 1700

LE ROUX, CHARLES
New York, N.Y. 1689-1745

LE ROUX, JOHN
New York, N.Y. 1723

LESCURE, EDWARD
Philadelphia, Pa. 1822

LE TELIER, JOHN
Philadelphia, Pa. 1770

LETOURNEAUX
New York, N.Y. 1797

LEVELY
Baltimore, Md. 1788

LEVERETT, KNIGHT
Boston, Mass. 1736

LEWYN, GABRIEL
Baltimore, Md. 1771

LEWIS, WILLIAM
Philadelphia, Pa. 1810

LEWIS, HARVEY
Philadelphia, Pa. 1811

LEWIS, ISAAC
Huntington, Conn. 1796

LEWIS & SMITH
Philadelphia, Pa. 1805

LEWIS, TUNIS
New York, N.Y. 1805

LIBBY, J. G. L.
Boston, Mass. 1830

LIDDEN, JOHN
St. Louis, Mo. 1850

LIGHTFOOT, JAMES
New York, N.Y. 1749

LINCH, PETER
New York, N.Y. 1805

COLN, A. L. Louis, Mo. 1850	A.L.Lincoln	
COLN, ELIJAH ston, Mass. 1794-1861	E.Lincoln	
COLN & FOSS ston, Mass. 1829	LINCOLN&FOSS	
COLN & GREEN ston, Mass. 1810	L&G	
COLN & READ ston, Mass. 1835	LINCOLN&READ	
ONER, GEORGE ladelphia, Pa. 1837		
GLEY, HENRY w York, N.Y. 1810		
K, PETER iladelphia, Pa. 1811		
TOT w York, N.Y. 1762		
LE, PAUL rtland, Me. 1760		
LE, WILLIAM wburyport, Mass. 1775	W·L WL	
KWOOD, A. w York, N.Y. 1810	A·LOCKWOOD	
KWOOD, F. w York, N.Y. 1845	F.LOCKWOOD	
KWOOD, JAMES w York, N.Y. 1799	Lockwood	
LAND, PURNEL iladelphia, Pa. 1810		
AN, ADAM w York, N.Y. 1803	A·LOGAN	
AN, JAMES iladelphia, Pa. 1810		
G, ANDREW iladelphia, Pa. . 1837		
G, WILLIAM iladelphia, Pa. . 1807		
GLEY, HENRY w York, N.Y. 1810	H.Longley Longley	
MIS, G. & CO. ie, Pa. 1850	G.LOOMIS&CO ERIE	
D, BENJAMIN ttsfield, Mass. 1786		
D, JABEZ C. w York, N.Y. 1835	J.LORD	
D, JOSEPH iladelphia, Pa. 1815		
D & SMITH w York, N.Y. 1823		
RING, ELIJAH arnstable, Mass. 1744-1782	E.Loring. E.Loring	

LORING, HENRY Boston, Mass. 1773-1818	HL		
LORING, JOSEPH Boston, Mass. 1743-1815	J·L J.Loring J·Loring J.Loring J.Loring I.Loring		
LOUS, ASA Hartford, Conn. 1792			
LOW, BALL & COMPANY Boston, Mass. 1840			
LOW, FRANCIS Boston, Mass. 1827			
LOW, JOHN J. & COMPANY Boston, Mass. 1828	J.J.LOW&CO		
LOW, JOHN S. Salem, Mass. 1821			
LOWER, JOSEPH Philadelphia, Pa. 1803	LOWER		
LOWNER, JACOB Philadelphia, Pa. 1833			
LOWNER, WILLIAM Philadelphia, Pa. 1833			
LOWNES, EDWARD Philadelphia, Pa. 1817	E.LOWNES E.LOWNES		
LOWNES & ERWIN Philadelphia, Pa. 1816			
LOWNES, J. & J. H. Philadelphia, Pa. 1816			
LOWNES, JOSEPH Philadelphia, Pa. 1780	J·L J.Lownes		
LOWNES, JOSIAH H. Philadelphia, Pa. 1822	IHL JHL		
LOYER, ADRIAN Savannah, Ga. 1860			
LUCET, JAMES New York, N.Y. 1802			
LULIS, LAMBERT New York, N.Y. 1804			
LUPP, HENRY New Brunswick, N.J. .. 1783	H.Lupp		
LUPP, PETER New Brunswick, N.J. 1797-1827	PL		
LUPP, S. V. New Brunswick, N.J. 1815	SV.LUPP		
LUSADA, BENJAMIN New York, N.Y. 1797			
LUSCOMB, JOHN G. Boston, Mass. 1823			
LUSSAUR, JOHN New York, N.Y. 1791			
LUZERDER, BENJAMIN New York, N.Y. .. 1796			
LYELL, DAVID New York, N.Y. 1699			

LYNCH, JOHN
Baltimore, Md. 1761-1848

LYNDE, THOMAS
Worcester, Mass. 1748-1812

LYNG, JOHN
Philadelphia, Pa. 1734

LYNG, JOHN BURT
New York, N. Y. 1759

LYNN, ADAM
District of Columbia 1796

LYTLE, R. A.
Baltimore, Md. 1825

M

MABRID & COMPANY
New York, N. Y. 1787

MACHON, AUSTIN
Philadelphia, Pa. 1759

MAIN, DAVID
Stonington, Conn. 1773

MAINWARING, THOS.
West New Jersey 1664

MARIOT, JEAN C.
New Orleans, La. 1822

MANN, ALEXANDER
Middletown, Conn. 1804

MANNERBACK, W.
Reading, Pa. 1825

MANNING, DANIEL
Boston, Mass. 1823

MANNING, JOSEPH
New York, N. Y. 1823

MANNING, SAMUEL
Boston, Mass. 1823

MANSFIELD, ELISHA H.
Norwich, Conn. 1816

MANSFIELD, JOHN
Charlestown, Mass. 1634

MANSFIELD, THOMAS
Philadelphia, Pa. 1804

MARBLE, SIMEON
New Haven, Conn. 1777-1856

MARCHAND, EVARISTE
New Orleans, La. 1822

MARQUAND & BROTHER
New York, N. Y. 1825

MARQUAND & COMPANY
New York, N. Y. 1810

MARQUAND, FREDERICK
New York, N. Y. 1823

MARQUARD, ISAAC
New York, N. Y. 1810

MARS, S.
Unknown ....C 1770

MARSH, T. K.
Paris, Kentucky 1830

MARSHALL, JOSEPH
Philadelphia, Pa. 1818

MARSHALL & TEMPEST
Philadelphia, Pa. 1813

MARSHALL, THOMAS
Troy, N.Y. 1839

MARTIN, ABRAHAM W.
New York, N. Y. 1835

MARTIN, PETER
New York, N. Y. 1756

MARTIN, V.
Boston, Mass. 1859

MASI, SERAPHIM
Washington, D. C. 1832

MASON, J. D.
Philadelphia, Pa. 1830

MATHER & NORTH
New Britain, Conn. 1827

MATLACK, WILLIAM
Philadelphia, Pa. 1828

MAVERICK, D.
New York, N. Y. 1828

MAVERICK, PETER R.
New York, N. Y. 1780

MAYSENHOEDER, C.
Philadelphia, Pa. 1824

MEAD & ADRIANCE
St. Louis, Mo. 1835

MEAD, EDMUND
St. Louis, Mo. 1850

MEADOWS & CO.
Philadelphia, Pa. 1831

MECOM, JOHN
New York, N. Y. 1770

MECOM, GEORGE
Boston, Mass. 1836

MERCHANT, J.
New York, N. Y. 1795

MEREDITH, JOSEPH P.
Baltimore, Md. 1824

MERKLER, JOHN H.
New York, N. Y. 1780

MERRIFIELD, THOMAS V. Z.
Albany, N.Y. 1840

MERRIMAN & BRADLEY
New Haven, Conn. 1817

MERRIMAN, C.
New York, N. Y. 1825

MERRIMAN, MARCUS
New Haven, Conn. 1762-1850

RRIMAN, MARCUS & CO. ew Haven, Conn. 1817	M.M.&Co
RRIMAN, REUBEN tchfield, Conn. 1783-1866	R.MERRIMAN PureCoin RM
RRIMAN, SAMUEL ew Haven, Conn. .. 1769-1805	S.Merriman
RRIMAN, SILAS ew Haven, Conn. ......- 1760	
RRIMAN & TUTTLE ew Haven, Conn. 1802	
RROW, NATHAN ast Hartford, Conn. ..../1783	
HAELS, JAMES ew York, N.Y. 1820	
KSCH, JOHN MATHEW ethlehem, Pa. 1775	I·M·MIKSCH
ES, JOHN hiladelphia, Pa. 1785	
HE, STEPHEN hiladelphia, Pa. 1780	
LAR, JAMES oston, Mass. 1832	
LARD, GEORGE hiladelphia, Pa. 1816	
LER, D. B. oston, Mass. 1850	D.B.MILLER
LER, I. R. hiladelphia, Pa. 1810	I.RMILLER
LER, P. hiladelphia, Pa. 1810	P.MILLER P.MILLER
LER, WILLIAM hiladelphia, Pa. 1814	MILLER MILLER
LER & SON hiladelphia, Pa. 1833	
LNER, THOMAS oston, Mass. 1690-1745	TM TM
NE, EDMUND hiladelphia, Pa. 1757	EM EM E·MILNE
NE, F. ew York, N.Y. 1800	
NE, THOMAS ew York, N.Y. 1795	
LON, PETER ew York, N.Y. 1820	
LOUDON, PHILLIPPE hiladelphia, Pa. 1811	
LS, EDMUND hiladelphia, Pa. 1785	
LS, EDWARD hiladelphia, Pa. 1794	
LS, JOHN hiladelphia, Pa. ..-.....1793	

MINOTT & AUSTIN Boston, Mass. .1765-1769	Minott Minott I·A I·Auſtin
MINOTT, SAMUEL Boston, Mass. 1732-1803	S·M M S·M M·Minott Minott Minott
MINOTT & SIMPKINS Boston, Mass. 1769	WS Minott
MINSHALL, WILLIAM Philadelphia, Pa. 1773	
MITCHELL, HARRY Philadelphia, Pa. 1844	MITCHELL
MITCHELL, PHINEAS Boston, Mass. ... 1812	
MITCHELL, WILLIAM Boston, Mass. 1820	W.MITCHELL.
MIX, JAMES Albany, N.Y. 1817	
MIX, VISSCHER Albany, N.Y.___........:.1849	
MOBBS, WILLIAM Buffalo, N.Y. 1835	
MOFFAT, CHARLES H. New York, N.Y. 1830	
MOFFAT, J. L. New York, N.Y. 1815	J·L·MOFFAT
MOHLER, JACOB Baltimore, Md. 1744-1773	I·M
MUNROE, JAMES Barnstable, Mass. 1806	
MONTIETH, J. & R. Baltimore, Md. 1814	MONTEITH
MONTIETH, ROBERT Baltimore, Md. 1814	.RM
MOOD, J. & P. Charleston, S. C. 1806	J.&P.MOOD
MOOD, JOSEPH Charleston, S. C. 1806	I MOOD IMOOD J MOOD J.&P.MOOD
MOOD, P. Charleston, S. C. 1806	P.M
MOORE & BREWER New York, N.Y. 1835	
MOORE & BROWN New York, N.Y. ...._.....1833	
MOORE, CHARLES Philadelphia, Pa. 1804	
MOORE, & FERGUSON Philadelphia, Pa. 1804	MOORE & FERGUSON
MOORE, JOHN C. New York, N.Y. 1844	J.C.M.
MOORE, JOHN L. New York, N.Y. 1835	J.L.MOORE
MOORE, ROBERT , Maryland 1778	

MOORE, THOMAS
Philadelphia, Pa. 1805

MORGAN, E.
Poughkeepsie, N. Y. 1810   E.MORGAN   POUGHKEEPSIE

MORGAN, JOHN
Philadelphia, Pa. 1813

MORMAGEA, MICHAEL
Philadelphia, Pa. 1816

MORRIS, JOHN
New York, N. Y. 1796

MORRIS, SYLVESTER
New York, N. Y. 1709-1783   SM

MORRIS, WILLIAM H.
New York, N. Y. 1759

MORRISON, ISRAEL
Philadelphia, Pa. ..:......1823

MORSE, DAVID
Boston, Mass. ....,1798

MORSE, HAZEN
Boston, Mass. ....-...1815

MORSE, J. H.
Boston, Mass. 1792   J.H.MORSE

MORSE, MOSES
Boston, Mass. 1816   M.MORSE

MORSE, NATHANIEL
Boston, Mass. 1709   NM   NM   NM

MORSE, STEPHEN
Boston, Mass. 1764   MORSE

MOSELEY, DAVID
Boston, Mass. 1753-1812   DM   DMoseley   D.Moseley

MOSELEY, JOSEPH
New York, N. Y. 1830

MOSES, JACOB
Birmingham, Ala. 1768   MOSES

MOSES, M.
Boston, Mass. 1830

MOSES, ISAAC N.
Derby, Conn. 1781

MOTT, J. S.
New York, N. Y. 1790   J.MOTT   JMOTT   J.S.MOTT

MOTT, JOHN & WILLIAM
New York, N. Y. 1789

MOTT, W. & J.
New York, N. Y. 1789   MOTT'S

MOULINAR, JOHN
New York, N. Y. 1744   I.M   IM

MOULTON, ABEL
Newburyport, Mass. 1815   A.MOULTON

MOULTON & BRADBURY
Newburyport, Mass. 1796   MOULTON   B

MOULTON & DAVIS
Newburyport, Mass. 1824

MOULTON, EBENEZER S.
Boston, Mass. 1796   E.S.MOULTON   E.S.Moulton

MOULTON, ENOCH
Portland, Me. 1801   E.MOULTON

MOULTON, JOSEPH, I
Newburyport, Mass. 1680   J·M

MOULTON, JOSEPH, II
Newburyport, Mass. 1757   J·M   J·M   IM   I·MOULTON

MOULTON, JOSEPH, III
Newburyport, Mass. 1814   J.MOULTON.   J.MOULTON

MOULTON, WILLIAM, I
Newburyport, Mass. 1710

MOULTON, WILLIAM, II
Newburyport, Mass.·......1720

MOULTON, WILLIAM, III
Newburyport, Mass. 1772   W·M   W.MOULTO   MOULTON   MOULT

MULFORD, JOHN H.
Albany, N. Y. 1835

MULFORD & WENDELL
Albany, N. Y. 1842   MULFORD&WENDELL

MULLIGAN, H.
Philadelphia, Pa. 1840   H.MULLIGAN 415 21ST ST PHILA

MUMFORD, H. G.
Providence, R. I. 1813

MUNROE, JAMES
Barnstable, Mass. 1784-1879   JamesMunroe   Purel   I.MUNROE   I.MUNR   JamesMunroe

MUNROE, NATHANIEL
Baltimore, Md. 1777-1861   N.MUNROE   N.MUNR

MUNSON, AMOS
New Haven, Conn. 1776

MUNSON, CORNELIUS
Wallingford, Conn. 1742

MURDOCK, JAMES
Philadelphia, Pa. 1779   I.M   J.Murdock

MURPHY, JAMES
Philadelphia, Pa. 1823   J.MURPHY

MUSGRAVE, JAMES
Philadelphia, Pa. 1795   Musgrave

MYER, H. B.
New York, N. Y. 1810   HBMyer

MYERS, ALBERT
Philadelphia, Pa. 1837

MYERS & JACOB
Philadelphia, Pa. 1839

MYERS, JOHN
Philadelphia, Pa. 1773   I·MYERS   JMye

MYERS, MYER
New York, N. Y. 1723-1795   MM   M·M   Myers   Myers

MYGATT, COMFORT
Danbury, Conn. 1763-1823

MYGATT, DAVID
Danbury, Conn. 1777-1822   DM   D.MYGATT   D.MYGATT

WYGATT, ELY
Danbury, Conn. 1742-1807

WYSENDHENDER
Philadelphia, Pa. 1813

Mc

McCLYMON, JOHN C.
New York, N.Y. 1805

McCONNEL, HUGH
Philadelphia, Pa. 1813

McCONNELLY, H.
Philadelphia, Pa. 1811

McCORMICK, JOHN
Philadelphia, Pa. 1837

McCREA, ROBERT
Philadelphia, Pa. 1785

McDANIEL, PETER
New York, N.Y. 1743

McDONALD, DANIEL
Philadelphia, Pa. 1828

McDONNOUGH, PATRICK
Philadelphia, Pa. 1811

McDONNOUGH, JOHN
Philadelphia, Pa. 1775

M'FADDEN, J. B.
Pittsburgh, Pa. 1840

McFARLANE, JOHN
Boston, Mass. 1796

McFEE, JOHN
Philadelphia, Pa. 1793

McFEE, M.
Philadelphia, Pa. 1769

McFEE & REEDER
Philadelphia, Pa. 1796

McGRAW, DANIEL
Chester, Pa. 1772

McHARG, ALEXANDER
Albany, N.Y. 1849

McINTIRE, JAMES
Philadelphia, Pa. 1840

McINTOSH, JOHN
Ft. Stanwix, Pa. 1761

McKEEN, HENRY
Philadelphia, Pa. 1823

McKLIMENT, JOHN
New York, N.Y. 1804

McLAWRENCE, JOHN
New York, N.Y. 1818

McMAHON, JOHN
Philadelphia, Pa. 1804

McMASTER, HUGH A.
Philadelphia, Pa. 1839

McMULLEN, JAMES
Philadelphia, Pa. 1814

McMULLEN, WILLIAM
Philadelphia, Pa. .....,....1791

McMULLIN & BLACK
Philadelphia, Pa. 1813

McMULLIN, JOHN
Philadelphia, Pa. 1765-1843

McPARLIN, WILLIAM
Maryland 1780-1850

McPHERSON, ROBERT
Philadelphia, Pa. 1831

N

NAGLES, JOHN
Philadelphia, Pa. 1748

NEEDELS, WILLIAM
Easton, Md. 1798

NEVILL, RICHARD
Boston, Mass. 1674

NEUSS, JAN
Philadelphia, Pa. 1698

NEVILL R.ICHARD
Boston, Mass. 1764

NEWBERRY, EDWIN C.
Mansfield, Conn. 1828

NEWHALL, DUDLEY
Salem, Mass. 1730

NEWKIRKE, JOHN VAN
New York, N.Y. 1716

NEWMAN, TIMOTHY H.
New York, N.Y. 1799

NICHOLAS, WILLIAM S.
Newport, R.I. 1785-1871

NICHOLS, BASSET
Providence, R.I. 1815

NICHOLS, WILLIAM S.
Newport, R.I. 1808

NICHERSON, BATY
Harwich, Mass. 1825

NIXON, RICHARD
Philadelphia, Pa. 1820

NOBLE, JOSEPH
Portland, Maine 1823

NORCROSS, NEHEMIAH
Boston, Mass. 1796

NORRIS, GEORGE
Philadelphia, Pa. 1779

NORTH, W. B. & CO.
New York, N.Y. 1823

NORTH, WILLIAM B.
New York, N.Y. 1787-1838

NORTHEE, DAVID I.
Salem, Mass. 1788

NORTHEY, ABIJAH
Salem, Mass. 1775

NORTON, ANDREW
Goshen, Conn. 1787

NORTON, BENJAMIN
Boston, Mass. 1810

NORTON, C. C.
Hartford, Conn. ....1820 | C.C.NORTON

NORTON, SAMUEL
Hingham, Mass. 1795

NORTON, THOMAS
Farmington, Conn. ...1796-1806 | TN TN

NORTON & PITKIN
Hartford, Conn. ....1825 | C.C.NORTON & W.PITKIN

NORWOOD, RICHARD
New York, N.Y. 1774

NOXON
Unknown ....c 1800 | NOXON

NOYES, JOHN
Boston, Mass. ....1695 | IN IN IN

NOYES, JOSEPH
Philadelphia, Pa. ....1719 | IN IP

NOYES, SAMUEL
Norwich, Conn. 1770

NUSZ, FREDERICK
Frederick, Md. ....1819 | F.NUSZ.

NUTTALL, JOSEPH
Maryland 1778

NYS, JOHANNIS
Philadelphia, Pa. ....1695 | IN IN IN

O

OAKES, FREDERICK
Hartford, Conn. ....1825 | OAKES OAKES

OAKES & SOENCER
Hartford, Conn. ....1814 | O&S

OBRIHIM, JOSEPH
Annapolis, Md. 1784

ODELL, LAWRENCE
New York, N.Y. 1830

OERTELT, CHARLES E.
Philadelphia, Pa. 1831

OGIER, JOHN
New York, N.Y. 1791

OGILVIE, GABRIEL
New York, N.Y. 1791

OLIVER, ANDREW
Boston, Mass. ....1722 | A·OLIVER

OLIVER, DANIEL
Philadelphia, Pa. ....1805 | D.OLIVER

OLIVER, PETER
Boston, Mass. ....1709 | PO PO

OLIVIER, PETER
Philadelphia, Pa. ....1797 | P.O

OLMSTED, NATHANIEL
Farmington, Conn. ....1808 | N.OLMSTED P

OLMSTED, N. & SON
Farmington, Conn. ....1847 | N.OLMSTED & SON P S

ONCLEBAGH, GARRETT
New York, N.Y. ....1698 | B GO

OSGOOD, J.
Salem, Mass. ....1817 | J:OSGOOD

OSTHOFF, ANDREW
Baltimore, Md. ....1810 | OSTHOFF

OTIS, JOHN
Barnstable, Mass. 1703

OTIS, JONATHAN
Newport, R.I. ....1723-1791 | I·O J.Otis Otis J.Otis OTIS J·OT

OTT, DANIEL
New York, N.Y. 1792

OTT, GEORGE
Norfolk, Va. ....1806 | J.Ott Ott.

OVERIN, RICHARD
New York, N.Y. 1702

OWEN, JESSE
Philadelphia, Pa. ....1794 | OWEN J.&OWEN

OWEN, JOHN
Philadelphia, Pa. ....1802 | I·OWEN

Philadelphia, Pa.   1804

P

PADDY, SAMUEL
Boston, Mass. 1659

PAINTER, JOHN
Philadelphia, Pa. 1735

PALMER & BACHLADER
Boston, Mass.   1815 | PALMER & BACHLADER

PALMER & CLAPP
New York, N.Y. 1823

PALMER & HINSDALE
New York, N.Y. 1815

PALMER, JAMES
New York, N.Y. 1815

PANCOAST, SAMUEL
Philadelphia, Pa. 1785

PANGBORN & BRINSMAID
Burlington, Vermont 1833

PARADICE, WILLIAM A.
Philadelphia, Pa. 1799

PARASET, WILLIAM
Philadelphia, Pa. 1811

PARHAM, WILLIAM
Philadelphia, Pa. 1785

PARIE, JOSEPH
Philadelphia, Pa.   1811

PARISEN, OTTO
New York, N.Y. ....1763 | PARISIEN

PARISIEN, O & SON
New York, N.Y. ....1789 | OPDP

RISIEN, OTTO W. ew York, N.Y. 1791		
RKER, DANIEL oston, Mass. 1726-1785	D:P D:PARKER D.PARKER	
RKER, GEORGE altimore, Md. 1804	G.PARKER	
RKER, ISAAC eerfield, Mass. 1780	I·PARKER	
RKER, RICHARD hiladelphia, Pa. .:......1785		
RKER, WILLIAM H. ew York, N.Y. 1835		
RKMAN, C. oston, Mass. 1790	C·PARKMAN	
RKMAN, JOHN oston, Mass. 1738	PARKMAN	
RKMAN, THOMAS oston, Mass. 1793	T·PARKMAN	
RKS, JOHN ew York, N.Y. 1791		
RMELE, JAMES urham, Conn. 1763-1828		
RMELEE, SAMUEL uilford, Conn. 1737-1803	SP SP S·Parmele SP S·Parmele	
RROTT, T. nknown 1760	T·PARROTT	
RSONS nknown 1750	PARSONS	
RRY, MARTIN ortsmouth, N.H. 1737-1807	PARRY	
RRY & MUSGRAVE hiladelphia, Pa. 1793	P&M	
RRY, ROWLAND hiladelphia, Pa. 1819	R·PARRY	
RSONS, JOHN oston, Mass. 1780	I·PARSONS	
SCAL, WILLIAM hiladelphia, Pa. 1765		
TTERSON, GEORGE ew York, N.Y. 1835		
TON, A. oston, Mass. 1850		
TTERSON, JOHN nnapolis, Md. 1751	I·P	
TTIT, THOMAS ew York, N.Y. 1796		
TTON, THOMAS hiladelphia, Pa. 1824		
ULGREEN, OUOM hiladelphia, Pa. 1798		
XSON JOHN A. hiladelphia, Pa. 1810		

PEABODY, JOHN Enfield, Conn. 1799	J.PEABODY	
PEALE, CHARLES W. Philadelphia, Pa. 1765		
PEAR, EDWARD Boston, Mass. ....:..1836	E P E.P.	
PEAR & BACALL Boston, Mass. ....,...1850		
PEARCE, WILLIAM Norfolk, Va. ....:1820	W.PEARCE VA. NORFOLK	W.PEARCE VA NORFOLK
PEARSE. SAMUEL New York, N.Y. 1783		
PEARSON, JOHN New York, N.Y. 1791	IP J.Pearson J.Pearson	
PECK, B. Connecticut 1820	B·PECK	
PECK, LAWRENCE M. Philadelphia, Pa. 1837		
PECK, TIMOTHY Middletown, Conn. 1786		
PEDASY, S. Philadelphia, Pa. 1810		
PEIRCE, JOHN Boston, Mass. 1810	PEIRCE	
PEIRI, JOSEPH Philadelphia, Pa. 1811		
PELLETREAU, ELIAS Southampton, N.Y. .. 1726-1810	EP	
PELLETREAU. JOHN Southampton, L.I. .:......1785		
PELLETREAU, MALTBY New York, N.Y. 1813		
PELLETREAU & RICHARDS New York, N.Y. 1825	WSP TR	
PELLETREAU & UPSON New York, N.Y. ....,....1818	P&U	
PELLETREAU & VAN WYCK New York, N.Y. 1815	WSPELLETREAU SVANWYCK	
PELLETREAU, W. SMITH Southampton, N.Y. ...1786-1842		
PEPPER. HENRY I. Philadelphia, Pa. 1766	H.I.PEPPER HIPEPPER H.J.PEPPER	
PERKINS. HAUGHTON Boston, Mass. ....:.1762		
PERKINS. ISAAC Charlestown, Mass. 1707	IP	
PERKINS, JACOB Newburyport, Mass. ..1766-1849	I·P J·PERKINS IP	
PERKINS. JOSEPH Little Rest. R.I. 1770	J:PERKINS	
PERKINS. T. Boston, Mass. 1810	T·PERKINS	

PERPIGNAN, PETER
Philadelphia, Pa. 1809

PERPIGNAN & VARNIER
Philadelphia, Pa. 1800

PERRET & SANDOR
New York, N.Y. 1810

PERREAUX, PETER
Philadelphia, Pa. 1797   P·P   PP

PERRET, AUGUSTA
New York, N.Y. 1801

PERRY, THOMAS
Westerly, R.I.

PETERS, JAMES
Philadelphia, Pa. 1821

PETERS, R.
Philadelphia, Pa. 1807

PETIT, MATTHEW
New York, N.Y. 1811   M·P

PETTIT, THOMAS
New York, N.Y. 1791

PHELPS, CHARLES H.
Bainbridge, N.Y. 1825   CH.PHELPS

PHELPS, JEDEDIAH
Great Barrington, Vt. 1781

PHILIP & YVER
Philadelphia, Pa. 1796

PHILIPS, JASPER D.
Cincinatti, Ohio 1820   JA&D.PHILIPS

PHILLIPE, JOSEPH
Baltimore, Md. 1796   J.P

PHILLIPS, JAMES D.
Cleveland, Ohio 1829

PHILLIPS, SAMUEL
Salem, Mass. 1680   SP

PHINNEY & MEAD
Unknown 1825   P&M

PHYFE, WILLIAM
Boston, Mass. 1830

PICKERING, CHARLES
Philadelphia, Pa. 1683

PIERCE, HART
New York, N.Y. 1835

PIERCE, JOHN
Boston, Mass. 1810   PIERCE

PIERCE, O.
Boston, Mass. 1821   O.PIERCE

PIERPONT, BENJAMIN H.
Boston, Mass. 1730-1797   B·P   BP   B.P   B·PIERPONT   PIERPONT   PIERPONT   B·PIERPONT

PIERSON, PHILLIP
New York, N.Y. 1798

PINCHIN, WILLIAM
Philadelphia, Pa. 1779

PINTO, JOSEPH
New York, N.Y. 1758

PITKIN, HENRY
East Hartford, Conn. 1834   HP

PITKIN, HORACE E.
Hartford, Conn. 1832

PITKIN, JAMES F.
East Hartford, Conn. 1834

PITKIN, JOHN O.
East Hartford, Conn. .1803-1891   PITKIN

PITKIN, J. O. & W.
East Hartford, Conn. 1826   J.O&W.PITKIN

PITKIN & NORTON
Hartford, Conn. 1825   W.PITKIN   C.C.NOR

PITKIN, WALTER
East Hartford, Conn. .1808-1885   W.PITKIN

PITKIN, WILLIAM J.
East Hartford, Conn. 1820   WM.J.PITKIN

PITKIN, WILLIAM L.
East Hartford, Conn. 1825   WmL.PITKIN

PITKINS, JAMES
Hartford, Conn. 1812

PITMAN, BENJAMIN
Providence, R.I. 1810   B.PITMAN

PITMAN & DORRANCE
Providence, R.I. 1795

PITMAN & DODGE
Providence, R.I. 1796

PITMAN, JOHN K.
Providence, R.I. 1805

PITMAN, SANDERS
Providence, R.I. 1760

PITMAN, WILLIAM R.
New Bedford, Mass. 1835   Pitman   PITM

PITT, RICHARD
Philadelphia, Pa. 1741

PITTMAN, I.
Unknown 1785   I.Pittman

PITTS, A.
Philadelphia, Pa. 1790

PITTS, RICHARD
Philadelphia, Pa. 1741   Pitts

PLAIN, EDWARD
New York, N.Y. 1835

PLANQUET, GREGORY
New York, N.Y. 1797

PLATT & BROTHER
New York, N.Y. 1820   PLATT&BRO   PLATT&BROTHER

PLATT, GEORGE W.
New York, N.Y. 1820

PLATT, G. W. & N. C.
New York, N.Y. 1820   G.W.&N.C.PLATT   PLATT&BROTHER

ATT, JAMES
New York, N.Y. 1835

ATT, M. C.
New York, N.Y. 1820

INCIGNON, FRANCIS
Philadelphia, Pa. 1796

INCY, PETER
Philadelphia, Pa. 1813

INTE, JAMES
Philadelphia, Pa. 1813

INTE & TANGUY
Philadelphia, Pa. 1818

ISSENOT, N. J.
Philadelphia, Pa. 1806

ISSONIER, FRANCIS
Philadelphia, Pa. 1795

LAND, P.
Philadelphia, Pa. 1837

LGRAIN, QUOM
Philadelphia, Pa. 1797

LHAMUS, J.
New York, N.Y. 1802

LLARD. WILLIAM
Boston, Mass. 1711

NCET, LEWIS
Baltimore, Md. 1800

NS. THOMAS
Boston, Mass. 1789

OR, NATHANIEL
Boston, Mass. 1829

RTER, F. W.
New York, N.Y. 1820

RTER. HENRY C.
New York, N.Y. 1820

RTER & CO., HENRY C.
New York, N.Y. 1830

RTER, I. S.
New York, N.Y. 1850

RTRAM, ABRAHAM
New York, N.Y. 1727

SEY, FREDERICK J.
Hagerstown, Md. 1820-1850

ST, SAMUEL
New London, Conn. 1783

TTER, NILES
Westerly, R.I.

TTER, J. O. & J. R.
Providence, R.I. 1824

TWINE, JOHN
Boston, Mass. 1737

TWINE & WHITING
Hartford, Conn. 1761

POUPARD, JAMES
Boston, Mass. 1751

POUTREAU, ABRAHAM·
New York, N.Y. 1726

POWELL, C. F.
Boston, Mass. 1746

POWELSON, CHARLES
Albany, N.Y. 1840

PRATT, HENRY
Philadelphia, Pa. 1730

PRATT, NATHAN
Essex, Conn. 1792

PRATT, PHINEAS
Lyme, Conn. 1747-1813

PRATT, SETH
Lyme, Conn. 1754

PRESTON, S. L.
Philadelphia, Pa. 1830

PRICE, BENJAMIN
Boston, Mass. 1767

PRICE, HENRY P.
Philadelphia, Pa. 1810

PRICE, JOHN
Lancaster, Pa. 1764

PRIE, P.
Unknown 1780

PRINCE. JOB
Milford, Conn. .. 1680-1704

PURSELL, HENRY
New York, N.Y. 1775

PUTNAM. EDWARD
Salem, Mass. . . . 1710

PUTNAM & LOW
Boston, Mass. 1822

PUTNAM, RUFUS
Albany, N.Y. 1814

Q

QUARITUS. FREDERICK
New York, N.Y. 1835

QUINCY, DANIEL
Braintree, Mass. . . . 1651

QUINTARD. PETER
New York, N.Y. 1731
Norwalk, Conn. 1737

R

RABETH, JAMES
New York, N.Y. . . . 1835

RAIT, DAVID
New York, N.Y. 1835

RAIT, ROBERT
New York, N.Y. . 1830

RASCH, ANTHONY
Philadelphia, Pa. 1807

RASCH, ANTHONY & CO. Philadelphia, Pa. 1820	A.RASCH&CO
RASCH, W. A. New Orleans, La. 1830	W.A.RASCH NEWORLEANS
RASCH & WILLIG Philadelphia, Pa. 1819	
RAVEE, XAVIER Philadelphia, Pa. 1796	
RAYMOND, JOHN Boston, Mass. 1775	
REED, A. G. & CO. Nassau, N.H. 1835	
REED, ISAAC Stamford, Conn. 1776	
REED, ISAAC & SON Stamford, Conn. 1810	IR&S I.REED&SON
REED, JONATHAN Boston, Mass. 1725-1740	IR
REED, LEWIS New York, N.Y. 1810	
REED, O. & CO. Philadelphia, Pa. 1841	O.REED&CO.
REED, OSMAN Philadelphia, Pa. 1840	O.REED PHILA
REED, STEPHEN Philadelphia, Pa. 1840	SREED S.REED
REEDER, ABNER Philadelphia, Pa. 1797	A.REEDER
REEDER, JOHN Philadelphia, Pa. 1835	
REEVE, G. Unknown 1825	G.REEVE
REEVE, I. New York, N.Y. 1790	I.Reeve
REEVES, ENOS Charleston, S.C. 1746-1807	REEVES
REEVES, STEPHEN Burlington, N.J. 1767	S.Reeves
REVERE, EDWARD Boston, Mass. 1796	
REVERE, J. W. Boston, Mass. 1798	
REVERE, PAUL Boston, Mass. 1735-1818	PR PR PR REVERE ·REVERE REVERE ·REVERE
REVERE, PAUL, Sr. Boston, Mass. 1702-1754	PR P.Revere P.REVERE
REVERE, PAUL, III Boston, Mass. 1795	PR
REVERE & SON Boston, Mass. 1796	
REVERE, THOMAS Boston, Mass. 1789	TR

REYNOLDS, JOHN Hagerstown, Md. 1790-1832	IR JR Jn Reynolds
REYNOLDS, THEODORE J. Philadelphia, Pa. 1835	
RICE Unknown ....c. 1780	Rice
RICE, HENRY P. Albany, N.Y. 1815	
RICE, JOSEPH Baltimore, Md. 1784	I.RICE
RICE, JOSEPH T. Baltimore, Md. 1785	I.RICE
RICE, JOSEPH T. Albany, N.Y. 1835	Joseph T.Rice Albar J.T.RICE Albany
RICH, OBADIAH Boston, Mass. 1836	O.RICH O.RICH ☆ BOSTON ☆ BOSTON
RICHARD, AUGUSTA Philadelphia, Pa. 1818	
RICHARD, STEPHEN New York, N.Y. 1828	S.Richard RICHAR S.RICHARD S.RICHA
RICHARDS, SAMUEL New York, N.Y. 1828	
RICHARDS, SAMUEL Philadelphia, Pa. 1770	S.RICHARDS S.Richards
RICHARDS, SAMUEL R., Jr. Philadelphia, Pa. 1793	SR S.Richards
RICHARDS, STEPHEN Cohansey Bridge, N.J. 1767	S.RICHARDS S.RICHAR
RICHARDS, T. Unknown ....c. 1800	T.RICHARDS
RICHARDS, THOMAS New York, N.Y. 1815	T.RICHARDS
RICHARDS, W. Philadelphia, Pa. 1813	
RICHARDS, W. & S. R. Philadelphia, Pa. 1818	
RICHARDS, & WILLIAMSON Philadelphia, Pa. 1797	RICHARDS& WILLIAMSON S.Richards S·W
RICHARDSON, FRANCIS Philadelphia, Pa. ... 1718	FR
RICHARDSON, JOSEPH Philadelphia, Pa. ... 1711-1784	IR IR IR JR
RICHARDSON, JOSEPH, Jr. Philadelphia, Pa. ... 1777	J·R
RICHARDSON, JOSEPH & **NATHANIEL** Philadelphia, Pa. 1785	I·NR
RICHARDSON, RICHARD Philadelphia, Pa. ... 1793	
RICHMOND, FRANKLIN Providence, R.I. 1815	F.RICHMOND
RICHMOND, G. & A. Providence, R.I. 1815	

DGEWAY, JAMES
Boston, Mass. 1789

DGEWAY, JOHN
Boston, Mass. ....1813 **J·RIDGWAY**

DOUT, GEORGE
New York, N.Y. ....1745 **GR**

ED, JOHAN
Philadelphia, Pa. 1810

LLY, BERNARD
New York, N.Y. 1835

GGS, GEORGE W.
Georgetown, D.C. ....1805-1810 **GR** *Riggs* **RIGGS**
Baltimore, Md. ......1810-1840 **RIGGS**

GS AND GRIFFITH
Baltimore, Md. ....1816 **R&G**

GS, RICHARD
Philadelphia, Pa. .... 1819 **RR** *Riggs*

ER, PETER
New York, N.Y. ....1802 **P·RIKER**

ER & ALEXANDER
New York, N.Y. 1800

TER, MICHAEL
New York, N.Y. 1786

ATH, ROSWELL W.
Norwich, Conn. 1826

BINS, ELISHA
Philadelphia, Pa. 1831

BS
New York, N.Y. 1788

ERT, CHRISTOPHER
New York, N.Y. ......1708-1783 **CR**

ERTS, FREDERICK
Boston, Mass. 1770

ERTS & LEE
Boston, Mass. ....1775 **R·L**

ERTS, MICHAEL
New York, N.Y. 1786

ERTSON, ALEXANDER
Philadelphia, Pa. 1740

ERTSON, ANTHONY W.
Philadelphia, Pa. 1798

ERTSON, ROBERT
Philadelphia, Pa. 1777

INSON, ANTHONY W.
Philadelphia, Pa. ....1798 **A·ROBINSON**

NSON, BENJAMIN
Philadelphia, Pa. 1818

NSON, E.
Unknown ....1820 **E·ROBINSON**

NSON, ISREAL
Philadelphia, Pa. 1840

NSON, & HARWOOD
Philadelphia, Pa. 1814

ROBINSON, O.
New Haven, Conn. ....1800 **O·ROBINSON**

ROCKWELL, EDWARD
New York, N.Y. ....1825 **ROCKWELL** **ROCKWELL**

ROCKWELL, S. D.
New York, N.Y. ....1830 **S.D.ROCKWELL** **NEW YORK**

ROCKWELL, THOMAS
New London, Conn. ......1795 *Rockwell*

RODIER, PETER G.
New York, N.Y. 1825

ROE, WILLIAM
Kingston, N.Y. ....1805 **W·ROE** **W·ROE**

ROE, W. & STOLLENWERCK
New York, N.Y. ....1800 **W·ROE & STOLLENWERCK**

ROFF
New York, N.Y. 1813

ROGERS, AUGUSTUS
Boston, Mass. 1818

ROGERS, DANIEL
Newport, R.I. ....1792 **D·R** **DR** **D·R** **D·ROGERS**

ROGERS, DANIEL
New York, N.Y. 1835

ROGERS, JOSEPH
Hartford, Conn. ....1808 **I·R** **JR** **I·R** **I·R**

ROGERS & WENDT
Boston, Mass. 1850

ROGERS, WILLIAM
Hartford, Conn. ......1801-1873 **Wm ROGERS** **Wm ROGERS** **HARTFORD**

ROGERS, WILLIAM & SON
Hartford, Conn. ....1850 **WM.ROGERS & S**

ROHR, JOHN A.
Philadelphia, Pa. ....1807 **I·ROHR**

ROLLINGSON, WILLIAM
New York, N.Y. 1783

ROMNEY, JOHN
New York, N.Y. 1770

ROOSEVELT, NICHOLAS
New York, N.Y. ...1745-1769 **N·R** **VR**

ROOT, W. N. & BRO.
New Haven, Conn. ....1850 **W.N.ROOT & BROTHER**

ROSE, ANTHONY
New York, N.Y. 1755

ROSHORE, JOHN
New York, N.Y. 1792

ROSHORE, & PRIME
New York, N.Y. 1825

ROSS, JOHN
Baltimore, Md. ......1756-1798 **I·R** **I·R**

ROSS, ROBERT
Frederika, Delaware 1789

ROUND, JOHN
Portsmouth, N.H. 1634

ROUSE, ANTHONY
Philadelphia, Pa. 1807

ROUSE, MICHAEL
Boston, Mass. 1711

ROUSE, WILLIAM
Boston, Mass. 1639-1705

ROYALSTON, JOHN
Boston, Mass. 1770

RULE
Massachusetts 1780

RUSSEL, DANIEL
Newport, R.I. 1792

RUSSEL, JONATHAN
Ashford, Conn. 1770-1804

RUSSELL, GEORGE
Philadelphia, Pa. 1831

RUSSELL, JOHN H.
New York, N.Y. 1794-1798

RUSSEL, MOODY
Barnstable, Mass. 1694

RUSSELIER, PETER
New York, N.Y. 1794

RUTTER, RICHARD
Baltimore, Maryland 1790

RYERSON, LOW
York, Pa. 1760

S

SACHEVERELL, JOHN
Philadelphia, Pa. 1732

SACKETT & WILLARD
Providence, R.I. 1815

SADD, HARVEY
New Hartford, Conn. .1776-1840

SADTLER, P. B. & SON
Baltimore, Md. 1850

SADTLER, PHILIP B.
Baltimore, Md. 1771-1860

SADTLER, PHILLIP P.
Baltimore, Md. 1819

SAINT MARTIN, ANTHONY
Philadelphia, Pa. 1796

SANBORN, A.
Lowell, Mass. 1850

SANDELL, EDWARD
Baltimore, Md. 1816

SANDERSON, BENJAMIN
Boston, Mass. 1649-1678

SANDERSON, ROBERT
Boston, Mass. 1693

SANDERSON, ROBERT, Jr.
Boston, Mass. 1638

SANDERSON, WILLIAM
New York, N.Y. 1799

SANDFORD, ISAAC
Hartford, Conn. 1793

SANFORD, F. S.
Nantucket, Mass. ..,......1828

SANFORD, WILLIAM
Nantucket, Mass. 1817

SANDOZ & BROTHER
New York, N.Y. 1811

SANDOZ, PHILIP A.
Philadelphia, Pa. 1814

SANDS, STEPHEN
New York, N.Y. 1774

SANFORD, ISAAC
Hartford, Conn. 1785

SARDO, MICHAEL
Baltimore, Md.........- ..1817

SARGANT, ENSIGN
Boston, Mass. 1820

SARGEANT, JACOB
Hartford, Conn. 1761-1843

SAVAGE, EDWARD
Philadelphia, Pa. 1794

SAVAGE, THOMAS
Boston, Mass. 1689

SAVAGE, THOMAS, Jr.
Boston, Mass. 1719

SAWIN, SILAS
Boston, Mass. 1823

SAWIN, SILAS W.
New York, N.Y. 1835

SAWYER, H. L.
New York, N.Y. 1840

SAYRE, JOEL
New York, N.Y. 1778-1818

SAYRE, JOHN
New York, N.Y. 1771-1852

SAYRE & RICHARDS
New York, N.Y. 1802

SCARRET, JOSEPH
Philadelphia, Pa. 1797

SCHAATS, BARTHOLOMEW
New York, N.Y. 1683-1758

SCHAFFIELD, JEREMIAH
Philadelphia, Pa. 1785

SCHANK, GARRET
New York, N.Y. 1791

SCHANK, JOHN A.
New York, N.Y. 1792

SCHOFIELD, SOLOMON
Albany, New York 1815

COT, I.
Albany, N.Y. 1750   `SCOT`

COTT, J. B.
New York, N.Y. 1820   `J.Scott` `J.SCOTT`

OVIL & KINSEY
Cincinatti, Ohio 1830   `SCOVIL&KINSEY CINCINNATI`

RYMAGEOUR, JAMES
New York, N.Y. 1835

WIND, JOHN
New York, N.Y. 1790

AL, WILLIAM
Philadelphia, Pa. 1817   `W.SEAL`

ARS, MATTHEW
New York, N.Y. 1835

EBASTIEN, JEANNE L.
New York, N.Y. 1814

GN, GEORGE
Philadelphia, Pa. 1820

LKIRK, WILLIAM
New York, N.Y. 1817

LL, J.
New York, N.Y. 1800

ENEMAND, JOHN B.
Philadelphia, Pa. 1798

EVEIGNES, JACQUES
New Orleans, La. 1822

VRIN, LEWIS
Philadelphia, Pa. 1837

EXNINE, SIMON
New York, N.Y. 1722   `SS`

EYMOUR & HOLLISTER
Hartford, Conn. 1845   `SEYMOUR&HOLLISTER`

EYMOUR, JOSEPH
New York, N.Y. 1835

EYMOUR, OLIVER D.
Hartford, Conn. 1843   `O.D.Seymour`

HARP, W.
Philadelphia, Pa. 1835

HARP, W. & G.
Philadelphia, Pa. 1848   `W.&G.SHARP`

HAW, I. A.
Unknown 1800   `I·A·SHAW` `J.SHAW`

HARRARD, J. S.
Shelbyville, Ky. 1850   `J.S.SHARRARD`

HAW & DUNLEVY
Philadelphia, Pa. 1833   `SHAW&DUNLEVEY PHILA`

HAW, EDWARD, G.
Philadelphia, Pa. 1825

HAW, JOHN A.
Newport, R.I. 1819

HEETS
Henrico, Va. 1697

SHEPHERD & BOYD
Albany, N.Y. 1810   `S&B` `SHEPHERD&BOYD`

SHEPHERD, ROBERT
Albany, N.Y. 1805   `SHEPHERD` `R.Shepherd`

SHEPPER, JOHN D.
Philadelphia, Pa. 1818

SHETHAR, SAMUEL
Litchfield, Conn. 1801

SHETHAR & GORHAM
New Haven, Conn. 1806

SHETHAR & THOMPSON
Litchfield, Conn. 1801

SHEILDS, CALEB
Baltimore, Md. 1773   `C·S`

SHIELDS, THOMAS
Philadelphia, Pa. 1771   `T·S` `T·S`

SHIPMAN, NATHANIEL
Norwich, Conn. 1764-1853   `N·S` `N·SHIPMAN`

SHIVING, GODFREY
Philadelphia, Pa. 1779

SHOEMAKER, CHARLES
New York, N.Y. 1825

SHOEMAKER, JOSEPH
Philadelphia, Pa. 1798   `J.SHOEMAKER`

SHONNARD, GEORGE
New York, N.Y. 1797

SHOPSHIRE, ROBERT
Baltimore, Md. 1778

SHREVE, BENJAMIN
Boston, Mass. 1834

SIBLEY, CLARK
New Haven, Conn. ...1778-1808   `SIBLEY`

SIBLEY, JOHN
New Haven, Conn. 1810   `J.SIBLEY`

SIBLEY & MARBLE
New Haven, Conn. ...1801-1806   `S&M`

SILLIMAN, HEZEKIAH
New Haven, Conn. ...1739-1804

SIME & MOSES
Birmingham, Ga. 1768

SIME, WILLIAM
Birmingham, Ga. 1768

SIMES, WILLIAM
Portsmouth, N.H. 1773-1824   `W·S` `W·SIMES` `W·SIMES`

SIMMONS & ALEXANDER
Philadelphia, Pa. 1798   `SIMMONS& ALEXANDER.`

SIMMONS, ANDREW
Philadelphia, Pa. 1796

SIMMONS, ANTHONY
Philadelphia, Pa. 1797   `A.S.` `A.S.` `A·SIMMONS` `A·SIMMONS`

SIMMONS, J.
Philadelphia, Pa. 1810   `J.Simmons`

SIMMONS, J. & A.
New York, N.Y. 1805   `J.&A.S.` `J.&A.SIMMONS`

SIMMONS, JAMES
New York, N.Y. 1815   `J.Simmons`

SIMMONS, JOSEPH
Philadelphia, Pa. 1828

SIMMONS, PETER
New York, N.Y. 1816

SIMMONS, S.
Philadelphia, Pa. 1797   `S.SIMMONS`

SIMPKINS. THOS. BARTON
Boston, Mass. 1728-1804   `T.B.Simpkins`

SIMPKINS, WILLIAM
Boston, Mass. 1704-1780   `WS` `WS` `Simpkins`
                                  `W.SIMPKINS`
SIMPSON & BECKEL   `W.Simpkins`
Albany, N.Y. 1849
                                  `WSIMPKINS`
SINGLETON & YOUNG
New York, N.Y. 1800

SIXTE, JOSEPH A.
Philadelphia, Pa. 1837

SIXTE, VINCENT B.
Philadelphia, Pa. 1837

SKATTS, BARTHOLOMEW
Freeman, N.Y. 1784

SKERRET, JOSEPH
Philadelphia, Pa. 1797

SKERRY, GEORGE W.
Boston, Mass. 1837

SKINNER, ABRAHAM
New York, N.Y. 1756   `Skinner`

SKINNER, ELIZER
Hartford, Conn.

SKINNER, MATT
Philadelphia, Pa. 1752   `MATT SKINNER`

SKINNER, THOMAS
New York, N.Y. 1712-1761   `TS`

SLIDELL, JOSHUA
New York, N.Y. 1765   `SLIDELL` `NYORK`

SLOAN, WILLIAM
Hartford, Conn.. 1794

SMITH, DAVID
Philadelphia, Pa. 1778   `D.SMITH`

SMITH, CHRISTIAN
Philadelphia, Pa. 1820

SMITH, EBENEZER
Brookfield, Conn. 1775

SMITH, GEORGE
Philadelphia, Pa. 1831

SMITH, GEORGE O.
New York, N.Y. 1825

SMITH, I.
Boston, Mass. 1742-1789   `IS` `IS`

SMITH & GRANT
St. Louis, Mo. 1850   `Smith & Grant`

SMITH, JACOB
Philadelphia, Pa. 1809

SMITH, JAMES
New York, N.Y. 1794

SMITH, JAMES
Philadelphia, Pa. 1807

SMITH, JOHN
Philadelphia, Pa. 1819   `I·SMITH`

SMITH, JOHN & THOMAS
Baltimore, Md. 1817

SMITH, JOSEPH
Boston, Mass. 1742-1789   `I·S` `I·SMITH`

SMITH, JOSEPH
Philadelphia, Pa. 1804

SMITH, J. & T.
Baltimore, Md. 1817

SMITH, LEVIN H.
Philadelphia, Pa. 1837

SMITH, ROBERT E.
Philadelphia, Pa. 1820   `R.E.SMITH`

SMITH, SAMUEL
Philadelphia, Pa. 1785

SMITH, WILLIAM
New York, N.Y. 1770

SMITH, ZEBULON
Maine 1786-1865   `ZSMITH`

SOMERBY, ROBERT
Mass. 1794-1821

SNOW, J.
Unknown 1750   `I.SNOW` `J:SNOW`

SNYDER, GEORGE
Philadelphia, Pa. 1816

SOLOMON, SAMUEL
Philadelphia, Pa. 1811

SONNIER, JOSEPH
Philadelphia, Pa. 1811

SOUMAIEN, SAMUEL
Philadelphia, Pa. 1754   `SS`

SOUMAIN, SIMEON
New York, N.Y. 1685-1750   `SS` `SS`

SOQUE, MICHAEL
New York, N.Y. 1794

SOWERLT, ANTHONY
Philadelphia, Pa. 1823

SPARROW, HENRY
Philadelphia, Pa. 1811

SPARROW, THOMAS
Annapolis, Md. 1764-1784   `TS`

SPEAR, ISAAC
Boston, Mass. 1836

NCER, GEORGE
ssex, Conn. ....:1810

NCER, JAMES
artford, Conn. 1793

IRE & BROTHER
ew York, N.Y. ....1846 SQUIRE & BROTHER OF COIN

IRE & LANDER
ew York, N.Y. ....1840 SQUIRE & LANDER

IRE, S. P.
ew York, N.Y. ....1835 S.P.SQUIRE

CY, P.
oston, Mass. ....:1819 P.STACY

LL, JOSEPH
altimore, Md. 1804

NIFORD, JOHN
indham, Conn. ....1737-1811 JS Staniford

NTON, DANIEL
onington, Conn. ....1755-1781 D.Stanton

NTON, ENOC
onington, Conn. 1745

NTON, ZEBULON
onington, Conn. ....1753-1828 ZS STANTON

NWOOD & HALSTRICK
oston, Mass. 1850

NWOOD, HENRY B.
oston, Mass. ....1818-1869 HenryB.Stanwood

NWOOD, J. E.
hiladelphia, Pa. ....1850 J.E.STANWOOD

NWOOD, JAMES D.
oston, Mass. 1846

PLES, JOHN J.
ew York, N.Y. ....1788 IIS J.J.S.

PLES, JOHN J., Jr.
ew York, N.Y. 1788

CYR., S. L.
ew Orleans, La. 1822

RR, R.
nknown ....1800 R·STARR

RR, RICHARD
hiladelphia, Pa. ..,......1813 R·STARR

EBBINS & CO. E.
ew York, N.Y. ....1810 E.STEBBINS ¥CO

EBBINS & HOWE
ew York, N.Y. ....1815 STEBBINS & HOWE

EBBINS, T. E.
ew York, N.Y. ....1810 STEBBINS T.STEBBINS

EDMAN, ALEXANDER
hiladelphia, Pa. 1793

EELE, JOHN
nnapolis, Md. 1710

EELE, T. & CO.
artford, Conn. ....1805 T.Steele & Co

STEELE, T. S.
Hartford, Conn. ....1790 T.Steele

STEPHANIS, GOTHELF
New York, N.Y. 1791

STEPHEN, THOMAS H.
Philadelphia, Pa. .... .1839

STEPHENS, GEORGE
New York, N.Y. ....:1790 G.S

STEPHENSON, THOMAS
Buffalo, N.Y. ....1840 STEPHENSON

STEVEN, GEORGE
New York, N.Y. 1719

STEVENS & LAKEMAN
Salem, Mass. ....1825 STEVENS ¥LAKEMAN

STEWART C. W.
Lexington, Ky. ....1850 C.W.STEWART LEX.KT.

STEWART, JOHN
New York, N.Y. 1791

STICKLER, JOHN
New York, N.Y. 1823

STICKNEY, JONATHAN, Jr.
Newburyport, Mass. ......1798 I·STICKNEY

STICKNEY, M. P.
Newburyport, Mass. ....1820 M.P.STICKNEY

STILES, BENJAMIN
Woodbury, Conn. 1831

STILLMAN, ALEXANDER
Philadelphia, Pa. 1806

STILLMAN, BARTON
Westerly, R.I.

STILLMAN, E.
Stonington, Conn. ....1825 E.Stillman E.Stillman

STILLMAN, PAUL
Westerly, R.I.

STILLMAN, RICHARD
Philadelphia, Pa. ....1805 R.STILLMAN

STILMAN, WILLIAM
Hopkington, R.I. 1788

STINSON, WILLIAM
New York, N.Y. .... .1813

STOCKMAN & PEPPER
Philadelphia, Pa. ....1840 STOCKERMAN & PEPPER

STOCKMAN, JACOB
Philadelphia, Pa. 1828

STODDER & FROBISHER
Boston, Mass. ....1817 STODDER & FROBISHER

STOLLENWRECK
New York, N.Y. ....1800 Stollenwerck FB

STOLLENWERCK & BROS.
New York, N.Y. . ...1805 Stollenwerck&Bros

STOLLENWERCK & CO.
New York, N.Y. 1800

STONE, ADAM
Baltimore, Md.

STONE & OSBORN
New York, N.Y. 1796

STORM, A. G.
Albany, N.Y. 1830   A.G.STORM

STORM, A. G. & SON
Albany, N.Y. 1835

STORRS & COOLEY
New York, N.Y. 1832   S&C

STORRS, N.
New York, N.Y. 1825   N.STORRS

STOUT, J. D.
New York, N.Y. 1850   J.D.STOUT

STOUT, SAMUEL
Princeton, N.J. 1779

STOW, JOHN
Wilmington, Del. 1772

STOUTENBURGH, TOBIAS
New York, N.Y. ...1700-1759   TSB TSB

STOWELL, A., Jr.
Baltimore, Md. 1855   A.STOWELL JR

STRONG, JOHN
Maryland 1778   IS Stuart * Stuart *

STRONG, WILLIAM
Philadelphia, Pa. 1807

STUART, H.
New York, N.Y. 1808

STUART, JOHN
Providence, R.I. 1737

STUCKERT, ISAAC
Philadelphia, Pa. 1809

STUDLEY, D. F.
Unknown 1830   D.F.STUDLEY.

SULLIVAN, C. D.
St. Louis, Mo. 1850   CDSULLIVAN

SULLIVAN, D. & CO.
New York, N.Y. 1820   D.SULLIVAN&Co.

SUPPLEE, JACOB
Philadelphia, Pa. 1791

SUTHERLAND, GEORGE
Boston, Mass. 1810

SUTTON, ROBERT
Boston, Mass. 1820   R.SWAN   R.SWAN

SWAN, B.
Unknown 1825   B.SWAN

SWAN, CALEB
Boston, Mass. 1775

SWAN, ROBERT
Philadelphia, Pa. 1824

SWAN, ROBERT
Philadelphia, Pa. 1799   R SWAN   R.SWAN
                              R:SWAN

SWAN, WILLIAM
Worcester, Mass. 1715-1774   WS W:WAN Sivan SWAN

SWEETER, HENRY P.
Worcester, Mass. 1768

SYMMES, JOHN
Boston, Mass. 1766

SYNG, DANIEL
Lancaster, Pa.

SYNG, PHILIP
Philadelphia, Pa. 1703-1789   PS PS

SYNG, PHILIP, Jr.
Philadelphia, Pa. 1676-1739   PS * PS PS *

T

TABER, WILLIAM
Philadelphia, Pa. 1835

TANGUY, J. & P.
Philadelphia, Pa. 1808

TANGUY, JOHN
Philadelphia, Pa. 1818   I.TANGUY I.TANG
                           J.TANGUY

TANGUY, PETER
Philadelphia, Pa. ...._1810

TANGUY, REPITON
Philadelphia, Pa. ...._1806

TANNER, JOHN
Newport, R.I. 1740   IT

TANNER, P. G.
Newport, R.I. .... :1800   PGTANNER

TARBELL, E.
Unknown .... c. 1830

TARGEE, JOHN
New York, N.Y. 1799   I.T. V

TARGEE, JOHN & PETER
New York, N.Y. 1811   I♥PT I&P.TARGE

TARGEE, PETER
New York, N.Y. 1811

TARGEE, WILLIAM
New York, N.Y. 1807

TAYLOR, GEORGE W.
Philadelphia, Pa, ... 1824

TAYLOR & HINSDALE
New York, N.Y. .... :1801   T&H t

TAYLOR, JOHN
New York, N.Y. 1801

TAYLOR & LAWRIE
Philadelphia, Pa. 1841   TAYLOR&LAWRIE

TAYLOR, NAJAH
New York, N.Y. 1793

TAYLOR, N. & CO.
New York, N.Y. 1825   N.TAYLOR&CO

TAYLOR, THOMAS
Providence, R.I. 1727

AYLOR, WILLIAM
Philadelphia, Pa. 1772

AYLOR & LAWRIE
Philadelphia, Pa. 1837

EMPEST, ROBERT
Philadelphia, Pa. 1814

EN EYCK, JACOB
Albany, N.Y. 1704-1793

EN EYCK, KOENRAET
New York, N.Y. 1678-1753

ENNEY, WILLIAM I.
New York, N.Y. 1840

ERRY, GEER
Enfield, Conn. 1775-1858

ERRY, JOHN
New York, N.Y. 1820

ERRY, L. B.
Enfield, Conn. 1810

ERRY, WILBERT
Enfield, Conn. 1810

ERRY, WILLIAM
Enfield, Conn. 1785

HAXTER, JOSEPH B.
Highham, Mass. 1815

HEOFILE, WILLIAM
New Orleans, La. 1822

HIBAULT & BROS.
Philadelphia, Pa. 1810

HIBAULT & COMPANY
Philadelphia, Pa. 1797

HIBAULT, FELIX
Philadelphia, Pa. 1814

HIBAULT, FRANCIS
Philadelphia, Pa. 1800

HIBAULT, FRANCIS & FELIX
Philadelphia, Pa. 1807

HIBAULT, FREDERICK
Philadelphia, Pa. 1818

HIBAULT, FREDERICK &
FELIX
Philadelphia, Pa. 1813

HOMAS, CARSON & HALL
Albany, N.Y. 1818

HOMAS, THOMAS
New York, N.Y. 1784

HOMAS, WALTER
New York, N.Y. 1769

HOMAS, WILLIAM
Trenton, N.J. 1775

THOMISON, PETER
Boston, Mass. 1817

THOMPSON, D. B.
Litchfield, Conn. 1825

THOMPSON, WILLIAM
Maryland 1762-1774

THOMSON, ISAAC
Litchfield, Conn. 1801

THOMSON, JAMES
New York, N.Y. 1834

THOMSON, PETER
Philadelphia, Pa. 1835

THOMSON, JAMES
New York, N.Y. 1834

THOMSON, WILLIAM
New York, N.Y. 1810

THORNTON HENRY
Providence, R.I. 1824

TILEY, JAMES
Hartford, Conn. 1740-1792

TINGLEY, SAMUEL
New York, N.Y. 1767

TISDALE, B. H.
Providence, R.I. 1824

TITCOMB, FRANCIS
Newburyport, Mass. 1813

TOMPKINS, EDMUND
Waterbury, Conn. 1779

TOUZELL, JOHN
Salem, Mass. 1756

TOWNSHENDT, THOMAS
Boston, Mass. 1727

TOWNSEND, S.
Unknown 1775

TOWSON, OBADIAH W.
Philadelphia, Pa. 1819

TOWZELL, JOHN
Salem, Mass. 1726-1785

TOY, ISAAC NICHOLAS
Maryland 1771-1834

TOY, JOSEPH
Abingdon, Md. 1748-1826

TRACY, ERASTUS
Norwich, Conn. 1791

TRACY, GORDON
Norwich, Conn. 1767-1792

TRAUX, HENRY R.
Albany, N.Y. 1815

TRIPLER, CHRISTIAN
New York, N.Y. 1794

TROLL, WILLIAM
Philadelphia, Pa. 1810

TROTH, JAMES
Pittsburgh, Pa. 1800

TROTT & BROOKS
New London, Conn. 1798

TROTT & CLEVELAND
New London, Conn. ..1792-1794

TROTT, GEORGE
Boston, Mass. 1765

TROTT, J. P.
New London, Conn. 1769

TROTT, J. P. & SON
New London, Conn. 1820

TROTT, J. PROCTOR
New London, Conn. 1799

TROTT, JOHN PROCTOR
New London, Conn. 1792

TROTT, JONATHAN
Boston, Mass. 1771

TROTT, JONATHAN, Jr.
New London, Conn. 1800

TROTT & SON, JOHN P.
New London, Conn. 1820

TROTT, THOMAS
Boston, Mass. 1701-1777

TRUAX, HENRY, R.
Albany, N.Y. 1815

TRUMBUL, RICHARD
Boston, Mass. 1767

TUCKER, DANIEL
Portland, Me. 1781

TUCKER, J. W.
New York, N.Y. 1803

TURNER, JAMES
Boston, Mass. 1759

TUTHILL, CHRISTOPHER
Philadelphia, Pa. 1731

TUTTLE, BETHUEL
New Haven, Conn. 1802

TUTTLE, WILLIAM
New Haven, Conn. 1821

TYLER, ANDREW
Boston, Mass. 1692-1741

TYLER & CO., JOHN H.
Boston, Mass. 1840

TYLER, DAVID
Boston, Mass. 1760-1804

TYLER, D. M.
Boston, Mass. 1810

TYLER, GEORGE
Boston, Mass. 1740-1785

U

UBELIN, FREDERICK
Philadelphia, Pa. 1773

UFFORD, & BURDICK
New Haven, Conn 1814

UNDERHILL, ANDREW
New York, N.Y. 1780

UNDERHILL, THOMAS
New York, N.Y. 1779

UNDERHILL & VERNON
New York, N.Y. 1787

UNDERWOOD, JOHN
Philadelphia, Pa. 1797

V

VAIL, ELIJAH
Troy, N.Y. 1836

VAISSIERE, VICTOR
New York, N.Y. 1816

VALET, PETER
New York, N.Y. 1787

VALLEE, ANTOINE
New Orleans, La. 1822

VAN BERGEN, JOHN
Albany, N.Y. 1813

VAN BEUREN, PETER
New York, N.Y. 1798

VAN BEUREN, WILLIAM
New York, N.Y. 1790

VANDERBURGH, CORNELIUS
New York, N.Y. 1677

VANDERHAN, J.
Philadelphia, Pa. 1740

VANDERHAUL
Philadelphia, Pa. 1740

VANDERSPIEGEL
New York, N.Y. 1701

VANDERSPIEGEL, JACOBUS
New York, N.Y. 1702

VANDERSPIEGEL, JOHANNIS
New York, N.Y. 1687

VAN DYKE, PETER
New York, N.Y. 1684-1750

N DYKE, RICHARD
ew York, N.Y. 1717-1770

N HORN, DAVID
hiladelphia, Pa. 1801

N INBURGH, PETER
New York, N.Y. 1689-1740

N NESS, & WATERMAN
ew York, N.Y. 1835

N RIPER, TUNIS
ew York, N.Y. 1813

N SCHAICK, G.
nknown 1840

N VEGHTEN, HENRY
bany, N.Y. 1760

N VLEIT, B.V.
oughkeepsie, N.Y. 1840

N VOORHIS, DANIEL
ew York, N.Y. 1779

N VOORHIS & COOLEY
ew York, N.Y. 1786

N VOORHIS & SCHANCK
ew York, N.Y. 1791

N VOORHIS & SON
ew York, N.Y. ....,1798

N WYCK & PELLETREAU
ew York, N.Y. 1815

N WYCK, S.
ew York, N.Y. 1810

RNEY, JOHN
hiladelphia, Pa. ....,.1795

ZIE, JOSEPH
ovidence, R.I. 1815

GEREAU, PETER
w York, N.Y. 1700-1755

NON, J. & CO.
York, N.Y. 1798

NON, JOHN
ew York, N.Y. 1793

NON, N. & CO.
arleston S.C. 1800

NON, NATHANIEL
arleston, S.C. 1777-1843

NON, SAMUEL
ewport, R.I. ......,1683-1735

NON & PARK
ttsburg, Pa. 1815

ANT, WILLIAM
hiladelphia, Pa. 1725

VILLARD, R. H. L.
Georgetown, D.C. 1833

VINCENT, RICHARD
Baltimore, Md. 1799

VINTON, DAVID
Providence, R.I. 1790

VIRGIN, W. M.
Unknown 1830

VOORHIS, DANIEL VAN
New York, N.Y. 1769

W

WACHNER, F. W.
New York, N.Y. 1819

WADDILL, NOEL
Petersburg, Va. 1778

WAGLIN, THOMAS
Philadelphia, Pa. 1837

WAGSTAFF, THOMAS
New York, N.Y. 1791

WAGSTER, ISAIAH
Baltimore, Md. 1776-1793

WAIT & WRIGHT
Philadelphia, Pa. 1837

WAITE, JOHN
Kingstown, R.I. 1770

WAITE, JOHN
New York, N.Y. 1798

WAITE, W.
Unknown 1770

WAITE, WILLIAM
Kingstown, R.I. 1760

WALDRON, D.
New York, N.Y. 1789

WALKER, GEORGE
Philadelphia, Pa. 1797

WALKER, HANNAH
Philadelphia, Pa. 1816

WALKER, JOHN, Jr.
Philadelphia, Pa. 1798

WALKER, L.
Boston, Mass. 1825

WALKER, WILLIAM
Philadelphia, Pa. 1793

WALKER, W. & S.
Phialdelphia, Pa. 1795

WALLACE, WILLIAM F.
Westerly, R.I.

WALLER, JOHN
Philadelphia, Pa. 1804

WALLIS, THOMAS
Philadelphia, Pa. 1804

WALRAVEN, JOHN
Baltimore, Md. 1771-1814

WALTER, JACOB
Baltimore, Md. ... 1782-1865

WALTON, DANIEL
Philadelphia, Pa. 1808

WALWORTH, DANIEL
Middletown, Conn. ... 1785

WARD, AMBROSE
New Haven, Conn. 1767

WARD & BARTHOLOMEW
Hartford, Conn. 1804

WARD, BARTHOLOMEW &
BRAINARD
Hartford, Conn. 1809

WARD, BILLIOUS
Guilford, Conn. 1729-1777

WARD & COX
Hartford, Conn. 1811

WARD & GAVETT
Hartford, Conn. 1813

WARD & HUGHES
Middletown, Conn. 1805

WARD, JAMES
Hartford, Conn. 1768-1856

WARD, JOHN
Philadelphia, Pa. ... .. .1808

WARD, JOHN
Middletown, Conn. 1805

WARD & MILLER
Philadelphia, Pa. 1822

WARD & RICH
Boston, Mass. 1830

WARD, RICHARD
Boston, Mass. 1815

WARD, SAMUEL L.
Boston, Mass. 1830

WARD, TIMOTHY
Middletown, Conn. 1776

WARD, WILLIAM, Jr.
Guilford, Conn. 1705-1761

WARD, WILLIAM
Litchfield, Conn. .. 1742-1828

WARDIN, DANIEL
Bridgeport, Conn. 1811

WARNER, A. E. & T. H.
Baltimore, Md. 1805

WARNER, ANDREW E.
Baltimore, Md. 1786-1870

WARNER, ANDREW E., Jr.
Baltimore, Md. 1805

WARNER, CALEB
Portsmouth, N.H. 1784-1861

WARNER, C. & J.
Baltimore, Md. 1825

WARNER, D.
Ipswich, Mass. 1810

WARNER & FELLOWS
Portsmouth, N.H. 1824

WARNER, JOSEPH
Philadelphia, Pa. 1811

WARNER, JOSEPH
Wilmington, Del. 1768

WARNER, JOSEPH P.
Baltimore, Md. ....,1811-1862

WARNER, SAMUEL
Philadelphia, Pa. 1797

WARNER, THOMAS & A. E.
Baltimore, Md. 1805

WARNER, THOMAS H.
Baltimore, Md. 1780-1828

WARREN, BENJAMIN
Philadelphia, Pa. 1809

WATERMAN, GEORGE
Albany, N.Y. 1849

WATERS, SAMUEL
Philadelphia, Pa. 1790

WATKINS, JAMES
New York, N.Y. 1819

WATLING, JAMES
Philadelphia, Pa. 1837

WATSON & BROWN
Philadelphia, Pa. 1830

WATSON, EDWARD
Boston, Mass. 1821

WATSON, JAMES
Philadelphia, Pa. 1830

WATTS, J. & W.
Philadelphia, Pa. 1829

WATTS, JAMES
Philadelphia, Pa. 1835

WATTS, JOHN W.
New York, N.Y. 1794

WAYNES, RICHARD
Philadelphia, Pa. 1750

WEATHERS, MICHAEL
New York, N.Y. 1794

WEAVER, EMMOR T.
Philadelphia, Pa. 1808

WEAVER, JOSHUA
Westchester, Pa. 1815

WEBB, BARNEBUS
Boston, Bass. 1762

WEBB & BOON
Philadelphia, Pa. 1785

WEBB, CHARLES
Philadelphia, Pa. 1738

WEBB, EDWARD
Boston, Mass. 1718

WEBB, GEORGE W.
Baltimore, Md. 1812-1890

WEBB, JAMES
Baltimore, Md. 1788-1844

WEBB, ROBERT
Philadelphia, Pa. 1798

WEBSTER, HENRY L.
Providence, R.I. 1831

WEBSTER, HENRY L. & CO.
Providence, R.I. 1842

WEDGE, S.
Baltimore, Md. 1804

WEDGE, SIMON, Sr.
Baltimore, Md. 1774-1823

WEEDER, PELEG
North Kingstown, R.I.

WELCH, JOHN
Boston, Mass.

WELLES, A. & G.
Boston, Mass. 1830

WELLES, ANDREW
Hebron, Conn. 1804

WELLES & CO.
Boston, Mass. 1810

WELLES & GELSTON
New York, N.Y. 1840

WELLES, GEORGE
Hebron, Conn. 1784
Boston, Mass. 1827

WELLES, GEORGE I.
Boston, Mass. 1784-1823

WELLES, JAMES M.
New York, N.Y. . 1835

WELLS, L. & C.
New York, N.Y. 1798

WELLS, L. & H.
New York, N.Y. 1794

WELLS, LEMUEL
New York, N.Y. . 1791

WELLS, LEMUEL & CO.
New York, N.Y. 1794

WELLS, WILLIAM
Hartford, Conn. 1828

WENDOVER, JOHN
New York, N.Y. 1694

WENNAM, BARNARD
New York, N.Y. 1789

WENTWORTH & CO.
New York, N.Y. 1850

WEST, BENJAMIN
Boston, Mass. . 1770

WEST, CHARLES
Boston, Mass. 1830

WEST, JOSEPH
Philadelphia, Pa. ... 1797

WESTERVELL, JOHN L.
Newburgh, N.Y. 1845

WESTON, BENJAMIN
Philadelphia, Pa. 1797

WESTPAHL, CHARLES W.
Philadelphia, Pa. 1802

WHARTENBY & BUNN
Philadelphia, Pa. 1816

WHARTENBY, JOHN
Philadelphia, Pa. 1829

WHARTENBY, THOMAS
Philadelphia, Pa. 1811

WHARTENBY, THOMAS & CO.
Philadelphia, Pa. 1850

WHEATLEY, FREDERICK G.
New York, N.Y. 1805

WHEATON, CALEB
Providence, R.I. 1784-1827

WHEATON, CALVIN
Providence, R.I. 1791

WHETCROFT, WILLIAM
Baltimore, Md. .. .1735-1799

WHITAKER & GREENE
Providence, R.I. 1825

WHIPPLE, ARNOLD
Providence, R.I. .. .. .1825

WHITE, ALFRED
Boston, Mass. 1807

WHITE, AMOS
East Haddam, Conn. ..1745-1825   `A.WHITE` `WHITE`

WHITE, EDWARD
Ulster County, N.Y. 1757   `E:WHITE`

WHITE, GEORGE L.
Cincinnati, Ohio 1822

WHITE, PEREGINE
Woodstock, Conn. 1774   `P.WHITE`

WHITE, PETER
Norwalk, Conn. 1738

WHITE, SAMUEL
New York, N.Y. 1805

WHITE, SILAS
New York, N.Y. 1792   `S.WHITE`

WHITE, STEPHEN
New York, N.Y. 1805

WHITE, WILLIAM
Philadelphia, Pa. 1805   `W.W.WHITE`

WHITE, WILLIAM J.
New York, N.Y. 1835

WHITE, WILLIAM W.
New York, N.Y. 1835   `W.W.WHITE`

WHITEMAN, IRA
New York, N.Y. 1761

WHITING, B.
Norwich, Conn. 1755   `B:WHITING`

WHITING, CHARLES
Norwich, Conn. 1725-1765   `CW` `WHITING`

WHITING, S.
New York, N.Y. 1700

WHITLOCK, THOMAS
New York, N.Y. ..,......1796

WHITLOCK, THOMAS B.
New York, N.Y. 1805   `Whitlock`

WHITLOCK, WILLIAM H.
New York, N.Y. 1805   `Wm.H.WHITLOCK`

WHITON, EBED
Boston, Mass. 1826   `E.WHITNEY.` `Whitney`

WHITTEMORE
Unknown 1736

WHITNEY, AMOS
New York, N.Y. 1800   `A.WHITNEY`

WHITNEY, E.
New York, N.Y. 1805

WHITNEY, M.
Unknown 1823   `M.WHITNEY`

WHITNEY & HOYT
New York, N.Y. 1808   `WHITNEY&HOY`

WHITON, EBED
Boston, Mass. 1813-1879   `E.Whiton.` `E.Whiton`

WHITTAKER & GREEN
Providence, R.I. 1825

WHITTEMORE, WILLIAM
Portsmouth, N.H. 1710-1770   `Whittemore` `Whittmore`

WICKHAM, DANIEL H.
New York, N.Y. 1835

WILCOX, MICHAEL
Maryland 1772-1799   `XXXX`

WILLARD, A.
Utica, N.Y. 1810   `A.WILLARD` `Utica`

WILLARD, JAMES
East Windsor, Conn. 1815   `WILLARD`

WILLCOX, ALVAN
New Haven, Conn. 1805

WILLCOX, CYPRIAN
New Haven, Conn. 1827

WILLEY, B.
Unknown 1790   `B.WILLEY`

WILLIAMS, A. WILLIAM
Washington, D.C. 1829   `W.A.WILLIAMS`

WILLIAMS, ALEXANDER
Philadelphia, Pa. ../......1807

WILLIAMS, CHARLES M.
New York, N.Y. 1825

WILLIAMS, DEODAT
Hartford, Conn. 1776

WILLIAMS, JOHN
Philadelphia, Pa. 1793

WILLIAMS, STEPHEN
Providence, R.I. 1799

WILLIAMS, W. A.
Washington, D.C. 1829

WILLIAMS, W. W.
Washington, D.C. 1829

WILLIAMSON, SAMUEL
Philadelphia, Pa. 1794

ILLIG, GEORGE
Philadelphia, Pa. 1819

ILIS, J.
Boston, Mass. 1820

ILLIS, STILLMAN
Boston, Mass. 1823

ILLIS, WILLIAM S.
Boston, Mass. 1825

ILLS, HENRY
New York, N.Y. 1774

ILMOT, SAMUEL
New Haven, Conn...1777-1846

ILMOT, SAMUEL, Jr.
New Haven, Conn. ...1808-1846

ILMOT & STILLMAN
New Haven, Conn. 1800

ILMOT, T. T.
New Haven, Conn. 1810

ILSON, ALBERT
Troy, N.Y. 1834

ILSON, GEORGE
Philadelphia, Pa. 1850

ILSON, H. & CO.
Philadelphia, Pa. 1815

ILSON, HOSEA
Philadelphia, Pa. 1812

ILSON, HOSEA & CO.
Baltimore, Md. 1814-1816

ILSON, JAMES
Trenton, N.J. 1769

ILSON, JOHN
Philadelphia, Pa. 1770

ILSON, R. & W.
Philadelphia, Pa. 1825

ILSON, ROBERT
New York, N.Y. 1816

ILSON, S.
Philadelphia, Pa. 1805

ILSON, S. & S.
Philadelphia, Pa. 1797

ILSON, THOMAS
Philadelphia, Pa. 1837

WILSON, WILLIAM
Philadelphia, Pa. 1829

WILTBERGER & ALEXANDER
Philadelphia, Pa. 1797

WILTBERGER, CHRISTIAN
Philadelphia, Pa. 1770-1851

WINDOVER, JOHN
New York, N.Y. 1694

WINSLOW, EDWARD
Boston, Mass. 1669-1753

WINSOR, WILLIAM
Boston, Mass. 1759

WISHART, ALEXANDER
New York, N.Y. 1808

WISHART, DANIEL
New York, N.Y. ....,1825

WISHART. HUGH
New York, N.Y. 1784

WISHART, WILLIAM
New York, N.Y. 1800

WOLCOTT & GELSTON
Boston, Mass. 1824

WOLF, JAMES G.
Philadelphia, Pa. 1831

WOLFE, FRANCIS H.
Philadelphia, Pa. 1829

WOLFE & WRIGGINS
Philadelphia, Pa. 1837

WOOD, A. & W.
New York, N.Y. 1850

WOOD, ALFRED
Unknown 1800

WOOD, BENJAMIN B.
New York, N.Y. 1805

WOOD & HUGHES
New York, N.Y. 1846

WOOD, J. E.
New York, N.Y. 1845

WOODCOCK, BANCROFT
Wilmington, Del. 1754

WOODRUFF, ENOS
Cincinnati, Ohio 1820

WOODRUFF & WHITE
Cincinnati, Ohio 1829

WOODS, FREEMAN
New York, N.Y. 1791

WOODWARD, ANTIPAS
Middletown, Conn. 1791

WOODWARD, CHARLES
New York, N.Y. 1825

WOODWARD, ELI
Boston, Mass. 1812

WOODWARD & GROSJEAN
Boston, Mass. 1847

WOODWORTH, E.
Unknown 1800

WOOL, JEREMIAH W.
New York, N.Y. 1791

WRIGGIN & CO.
Philadelphia, Pa. 1831

WRIGGINS, THOMAS
Philadelphia, Pa. 1837

WRIGHT, ALEXANDER
Maryland 1776

WRIGHT, JOHN F.
Philadelphia, Pa. 1831

WRIGHT, W.
Unknown 1800

WYATT, JOSEPH
Philadelphia, Pa. 1797

WYER, ELEAZER
Portland, Me. 1768-1848

WYER, ELEAZER, Jr.
Boston, Mass. 1773

WYER & FARLEY
Portland, Me.........1828-1832

WYER & NOBLE
Portland, Me. 1823

WYNKOOP, BENJAMIN
New York, N.Y. 1675-1751

WYNKOOP, CORNELIUS
New York, N.Y. 1724

WYNKOOP, JACOBUS
New York, N.Y. 1765

WYNN, CHRISTOPHER
Baltimore, Md. 1795-1883

Y

YATES, S.
Albany, N.Y. 1810

YATES, S.
Unknown ....c. 1825

YEOMANS, ELIJAH
Hadley, Mass. 1771

YETTONS, RANDELL
Philadelphia, Pa. 1739

YOU, DANIEL
Charleston, S.C. 1744

YOU, THOMAS
Charleston, S.C. 1756

YOUNG, ALEXANDER
Camden, S.C. 1800

YOUNG, EBENEZER
Hebron, Conn. 1778

YOUNG, LEVI
Bridgeport, Conn. 1827

YOUNG, S. E.
Laconia, N.H. 1840

YOUNG, WILLIAM
Philadelphia, Pa. 1761

Z

ZAHM, G. M.
Lancaster, Pa. 1840

ZAHM & JACKSON
New York, N.Y. 1830

NOTE: Most town marks have variable date letters. A mark identical to one shown except for the letter will represent the same town, but a different year.

A

Aix; charge mark; 1781-Revolution.

Paris; charge mark; 1789.

Paris; charge mark; 1681-1684.

Paris; charge mark; 1677-1680.

Paris; charge mark; 1687-1691.

Paris; charge mark; 1684-1687.

Paris; charge mark; 1684-1687.

Paris; charge mark; 1691-1698.

Paris; charge mark; 1672-1677.

Paris; charge mark; 1698-1703.

Paris; charge mark; 1703-1708.

Paris; charge mark; 1708-1715.

Paris; charge mark; 1726-1732.

Arras; town mark.

Paris; charge mark; 1744-1750.

Paris; charge mark; 1715-1717.

Paris; charge mark; 1732-1738.

Paris; charge mark; 1756-1762.

Vicinity of Paris; charge mark; 1781.

Paris; charge mark; 1768-1774.

Paris; charge mark; 1762-1768.

Paris; charge mark; 1738-1744.

Paris; charge mark; 1717-1722.

Vicinity of Paris; charge mark; 1672-1768.

Paris; charge mark; 1750-1756.

Paris; charge mark; 1774-1780.

Paris; charge mark; 1780-1782.

Paris; charge mark; 1782-1789.

Apt; town mark.

Paris; discharge mark; 1687-1691.

Metz; charge mark; 1775-1781.

Metz; charge mark; 1781-Revolution.

Bayonne; town mark.

Paris; Bailly, Antoine; 1748-1756.

Paris; Bertin, Antoine; 1700.

Paris; Boullier, Antoine; 1775.

Paris; Bourgeois, Antoine; 1708.

Paris; Brigal, Antoine; 1746.

Abbeville; town mark.

Makers mark; after 1797.

Paris; Dutry, Antoine; 1767.

Paris; Deroussy, Alexandre; 1758.

Paris; Fillassier, Antoine; 1704.

Paris; Fillassier, Antoine-Philippe; 1720-1739.

Paris; Loret, Antoine-Gaspard; 1769.

Paris; Haudry, Antoine; 1718.

Paris; Joubert, Aimé; 1703.

Aix; town mark.

Paris; Masse, Ange-Jacques; 1780.

Paris; Jan de Villeclair, Antoine; 1750.

Paris; Loir, Alexis; 1733.

Paris; Lucas, Antoine; 1770.

Paris; Cassé, André-Louis; 1763.

Paris; charge mark; 1722-1726.

Strasbourg; makers mark.

Alais; town mark.

Amiens; town mark.

Amiens; charge mark; 1775-1781.

Paris; Maillet, Claude-Antoine; 1781.

Paris; Marsillac, Antoine; 1777.

Paris; Micallef, Alexis; 1756.

Paris; Raveché, Antoine-Martin; 1772.

Paris; Cousinet, Ambroise-Nicolas; 1745.

Angers; town mark; 18th century.

Angers; town mark; after 1750.

Arles; town mark.

Amiens; charge mark; 1781-Revolution.

Paris; Durand, Antoine-Sébastien; 1740.

Paris; Saint-Nicolas, Antoine; 1714.

Temporary admission mark; 1911.

Paris; Vachette, André-Maximilien; 1779.

Bayonne; town mark?

Aix; charge mark; 1775-1781.

B

Bourges; charge mark; 1781-Revolution.

Bordeaux; charge mark; 1781 Revolution.

Besancon; town mark; 18th cent

Troyes; town mark.

Saint-Germain-en-Laye; town mark.

Paris; town marks; 1765.

Besancon; town mark; 18th cent.

Paris; town mark, 1695.

Rouen; charge mark; 1768-1775.

Rouen; charge mark; 1775-1781.

Rouen; charge mark; 1781-Revolution.

Versailles; charge mark; 1780.

Bagnols; town mark.

Bayonne; town mark.

Paris; Charlié, Brice; 1704.

Beaucaire; town mark.

Bordeaux; charge mark; 1775-1781.

Béziers; town mark.

Bourges; charge mark; 1775-1781.

Bordeaux; town mark.

Bordeaux; town mark.

Bayonne; charge mark; 1775-1781.

Bordeaux; town mark.

Bordeaux; town mark.

Bordeaux; town mark.

Béziers; town mark.

Makers mark; after 1797.

Béziers; town mark.

Béziers; town mark.

C

Reims; charge mark; 1781-Revolution.

Paris; town mark; 1743.

Lunéville; town mark; after 1773.

Caen; charge mark; 1744-1750.

Strasbourg; town mark.

Caen; charge mark; 1775-1781.

Caen; charge mark; 1781-Revolution.

Caen; charge mark; 1781-Revolution.

Paris; Aubry, Claude-Auguste; 1758.

Paris; Bouillerot, Charles-Alexandre; 1769.

Paris; Charvet, Claude-Antoine; 1757.

Paris; Crozé, Georges-Antoine; 1777.

Cahors; town mark.

Paris; Robert, Claude-Alexis; 1761.

Carcassonne; town mark.

Castres; town mark.

Paris; Ballin, Claude; 1688.

Besancon; town mark; 18th cent.

Besancon; town mark; 18th cent.

Dole; town mark; 18th cent.

Paris; Charvet, Claude; 1728.

Paris; Crozé, Charles-Francois; 1712.

Makers mark; after 1797.

Paris; Haudry, Charles-César; 1732.

Paris; Donze, Charles; 1756.

Paris; Duvivier, Claude; 1720.

Paris; Dardet, Claude-Gabriel; 1715.

Caen; charge mark; 1775-1781.

Paris; Favier, Claude-Eustache; 1732.

Paris; Girard, Charles; 1722.

Chatellerault; town mark; after 1760.

Paris; Bourgoin, Claude-Isaac; 1779.

Paris; Lebastier, Charles; 1754.

Paris; Delanoy, Claude-Nicolas; 1766.

Paris; Souchet, Claude-Hyacinthe-Nicolas; 1777.

Paris; Petit, Charles; 1659.

Paris; Deville, Claude-Pierre; 1769.

Paris; Spriman, Charles-Louis-Auguste; 1775.

Paris; Viardot, Charles; 1723.

D

Dijon; charge mark; 1781-Revolution.

Douai; town mark.

Lyon; charge mark; 1762-1768.

Lyon; charge mark; 1768-1775.

Lyon; charge mark; 1775-1781.

Lyon; charge mark; 1781-Revolution.

Paris; André, David; 1703.

Paris; Colombier, Denis; 1776.

Paris; Frankson, Denis; 1765-1773.

Dijon; charge mark; 1775-1781.

328 FRENCH HALLMARKS

E

 Dole; town mark; 18th cent.

 Paris; town mark; 1673.

 Paris; town mark; 1721.

 Tours; charge mark; 1775-1781.

 Tours; charge mark; 1781-Revolution.

 Strasbourg; town mark; after 1752.

 Paris; Godin, Edme-Francois; 1747.

 Paris; Gondouin, Etienne; 1778-1786.

 Paris; Guérin, Eloy; 1727.

 Paris; Pollet, Etienne; 1747.

 Paris; Balzac, Edme-Pierre; 1739.

 Import mark; 1864.

 Import mark; 1864.

 Import mark; 1864.

 Import mark; 1864.

 Makers mark; after 1797.

 Makers mark; 1819.

 Foreign mark; 1797/1809.

 Export mark; 1884.

F

 Strasbourg; town mark; after 1752.

 Paris; town mark; 1674.

 Angers; town mark; 18th cent.

 Paris; Caron, Francois-Alexis; 1777.

 Paris; Corbie, Francois; 1777.

 Paris; Jacob, Francois; 1637.

 Paris; Aubert, Francois-Joachim; 1747.

Paris; Joubert, Francois; 1749.

G

 Paris; Riel, Francois; 1769.

 Makers mark; after 1797.

 Paris; Germain, Francois-Thomas; 1748.

 Fontenay-le-Comte; town mark.

 Grenoble; charge mark; 1781-Revolution.

 Paris; town mark; 1675.

 Poitiers; charge mark; 1775-1781.

 Poitiers; charge mark; 1781-Revolution.

 Strasbourg; town mark; after 1752.

 Paris; Chayé, Germain; 1755.

 Paris; Gouel, Gilles-Claude; 1727.

 Paris; Egée, Guillaume; 1716.

 Paris; Roland, Guillaume Francois; 1777.

 Paris; Gouffé, Guillaume-Jean-Baptiste; 1775.

 Makers mark; after 1797.

 Paris; Loir, Guillaume; 1716.

 Paris; Lucas, Guillaume; 1665.

 Grenoble; charge mark; 1775-1781.

 Paris; Pigeron, Guillaume; 1762.

 Vicinity of Paris; charge mark; 1781.

H

 Salins; town mark.

 Paris; town mark; 1771.

 La Rochelle; charge mark; 1775-1781.

 La Rochelle; charge mark; 1781-Revolution.

Saint-Omer; town mark.

 Paris; Adnet, Henri; 1712.

 Paris; Allain, Henri; 1745.

 Paris; Auguste, Henri; 1785.

 Paris; Debrie, Henri-Nicolas; 1758.

I

 Joinville; town mark.

 Limoges; charge mark; 1775-1781.

 Limoges; charge mark; 1781-Revolution.

 Valenciennes; town mark.

 Paris; Bouillerot, Joseph; 1759.

 Paris; Deharchies, Jean; 1720.

 Paris; Fillassier, Jacques; 1718.

 Commercy; town mark.

 Paris; Josset, Julien; 1767.

 Paris; Bastin, Jean-Nicolas; 1774.

 Paris; Picard, Jean; 1652.

 Paris; Roettiers, Jacques; 1733.

J

 Paris; Anthiaume, Jacques; 1758.

 Paris; Bonhomme, Jacques-Antoine; 1777.

Paris; Bernier, Jacques; 1781.

Paris; Besnier, Jacques; 1720.

Paris; Chéret, Jean-Baptiste-Francois; 1759.

Paris; Lange, Jean-Baptiste; 1716.

Paris; Odiot, Jean-Baptiste-Gaspard; 1720.

Paris; Petit, Julien-Boulogne; 1765.

Paris; S a u r i n, Jean-Baptiste; 1774.

Paris; Boudou, Jean-Charles-Marie; 1783.

 Paris; Ducrollay, Jean-Charles; 1755.

 Paris; Morée, Jacques-Charles; 1754.

 Paris; Roquillé-Desnoyers, Jean-Charles; 1772.

 Paris; Ducrollay, Jean; 1734.

 Paris; Debrie, Jacques; 1777.

 Paris; Dubois, Jacques; 1779.

 Paris; Ecosse, Jean; 1705.

 Paris; Famechon, Jacques; 1770.

 Paris; Formey, Jean; 1754.

 Paris; Balzac, Jean-Francois; 1749.

 Paris; Balzac, Jean-Francois, 1755.

 Makers mark; after 1797.

 Paris; Caron, Jean-Francois-Nicolas; 1775.

 Paris; Genu, Jean-Francois; 1754.

 Paris; Garand, Jean-Francois; 1748.

 Paris; Georges, Jean; 1752.

 Paris; Gouel, Jean; 1728.

 Paris; Barriere, Jean-Joseph; 1763.

 Paris; Baudet, Jean-Joseph; 1782.

 Paris; Moillet, Jacques-Joseph; 1742.

 Paris; O u t r e b o n, Jean-Louis-Dieudonné; 1772.

 Paris; Mauzié, Jean; 1723.

 Paris; Quin, Jean-Malquis le; 1735.

 Paris; Roettiers, Jacques-Nicolas; 1765.

 Paris; Pigeon, Jerome; 1705.

 Paris; Charpenat, Jean-Pierre; 1782.

Saumur; town mark.

Paris; Pontaneau, Jean-Simon; 1776.

Paris; Van Conwenberghe, Joseph-Théodore; 1770.

 Paris; Valot, Jean; 1742.

 Paris; Huguet, Jean-Vincent; 1745.

K

 Paris; town mark; 1726.

 Bordeaux; town mark.

 Bordeaux; town mark.

 Bordeaux; town mark.

 Bordeaux; town mark.

 Bordeaux; town mark.

 Bordeaux; town mark.

 Bordeaux; charge mark; 1775-1781.

 Bordeaux; charge mark; 1781-Revolution.

 Lille; town mark.

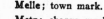 Strasbourg; makers mark.

L

 Lyon; charge mark; 1781-Revolution.

 Vesoul; town mark.

 Paris; town mark; 1752.

 Bayonne; charge mark; 1775-1781.

 Paris; Antoine, Léopold; 1706.

 Paris; Taillepied, Louis-Antoine; 1760.

 Paris; Charonnat, Louis; 1748.

 Lucon; town mark.

 Paris; Gabriel, Louis-Emmanuel; 1773.

 Limoges; charge mark; 1781-Revolution.

 Paris; Anthiaume, Louis-Julien; 1779.

 Paris; Gresset, Louis-Joseph; 1781.

 Paris; Prion, Lambert-Joseph; 1770.

 Paris; charge mark; 1780-1782.

 Paris; charge mark; 1782-1789.

 Paris; discharge mark; 1715-1717.

 Versailles; charge mark; 1780.

 Paris; Lenhendrick, Louis-Joseph; 1747.

 Paris; Loir, Louis; 1696.

 Limoges; charge mark; 1775-1781.

 Lunel; town mark.

 La Rochelle; charge mark; 1775-1781.

 La Rochelle; charge mark; 1781-Revolution.

 Paris; Regnard, Louis; 1733.

 Lyon; charge mark; 1775-1781.

M

 Melle; town mark.

 Metz; charge mark; 1781-Revolution.

Paris; town mark; 1775.

Saint-Malo; charge mark; about 1707.

 Toulouse; charge mark; no date established.

Toulouse; charge mark; no date established.

 Toulouse; charge mark; no date established.

 Toulouse; charge mark; 1775-1781.

 Toulouse; charge mark; 1781-Revolution.

 Paris; Leroy, Marc-Antoine, Noel; 1769.

Paris; Berthe, Martin; 1712.

Mende; town mark.

Paris; Janety, Marc-Etienne; 1777.

 Paris; Georges, Marie-Gabriel; 1745.

FRENCH HALLMARKS 331

Paris; Machy, Mathieu de; 1770.

Millau; town mark.

Orléans; charge mark; 1781-Revolution.

Montauban; town mark.

Montpellier; charge mark; 1781-Revolution.

Montpellier; charge mark; 1775-1781.

Paris; Delapierre, Michel; 1737.

Montpellier; town mark.

Montpellier; town mark.

Meaux; town mark.

Metz; charge mark; 1775-1781.

N

Bourg-en-Bresse; makers mark.

Béziers; charge mark; 1689.

Paris; town mark; 1682.

Montpellier; charge mark; 1775-1781.

Montpellier; charge mark; 1781-Revolution.

Nantes; charge mark; 1762.

Narbonne; town mark.

Paris; Besnier, Nicolas; 1714.

Paris; Crochet, Nicolas; 1720.

Paris; Dandrieux, Nicolas; 1716.

Paris; Delacroix, Noel; 1560.

Paris; Gonthier, Nicolas; 1768.

Niort; town mark.

Paris; Lefevre, Nicolas; 1759.

Paris; Langlois, Nicolas-Martin; 1750.

Paris; Outrebon, Nicolas; 1735.

Paris; Vial, Nicolas; 1781.

O

Paris; town mark; 1707.

Riom; charge mark; 1775-1781.

Riom; charge mark; 1781-Revolution.

Orléans; charge mark; 1775-1781.

P

Périgueux; makers mark.

Poitiers; charge mark; 1781-Revolution.

Dijon; charge mark; no date established.

Dijon; charge mark; no date established.

Dijon; charge mark; no date established.

Nantes; charge mark; 1746.

Dijon; charge mark; no date established.

Dijon; charge mark; 1775-1781.

Dijon; charge mark; 1781-Revolution.

Paris; town mark; 1784.

Paris; town mark; 1785.

Paris; town mark; 1786.

Paris; town mark; 1787.

Paris; town mark; 1788.

Paris; town mark; 1789.

Paris; Delaunay, Pierre-Antoine; 1770.

Perpignan; makers mark.

Paris; charge mark; 1774-1780.

Pau; town mark; 18th cent.

Paris; Bourlier, Philippe; 1769.

Paris; Clément, Pierre; 1694.

Paris; Delions, Pierre; 1720-1722.

Paris; Buron, Pierre-Etienne; 1735.

Paris; Garbe, Philippe-Emmanuel; 1748.

Paris; Goguely, Pierre-Francois; 1768,

Paris; Germain, Pierre; 1744.

Paris; Sallot, Pierre-Guillaume; 1750.

Parthenay; town mark.

Paris; Hannier, Pierre; 1716.

Paris; Jarrin, Pierre; 1712.

Paris; Beaulieu, Pierre-Francois-Mathis; 1768.

Paris; Sommé, Pierre-Nicolas; 1768.

Poitiers; town mark.

Paris; Soulaine, Paul; 1720.

Poitiers; charge mark; 1775-1781.

Paris; Valliere, Pierre; 1776.

Pézenas; town mark.

Pézenas; town mark.

Q

Perpignan; town mark.

Paris; town mark; 1709.

R

Riom; charge mark; 1781-Revolution.

Rennes; charge mark; 1781-Revolution.

Paris; town mark; 1733.

Orléans; charge mark; no date established.

Orléans; charge mark; no date established.

Orléans; charge mark; no date established.

Orléans; charge mark; 1775-1781.

Orléans; charge mark; 1781-Revolution.

Arras; town mark.

Vicinity of Orléans; charge mark; 1768-1775.

Paris; Chatria, Rémi; 1724.

Rouen; charge mark; 1775-1781.

Import mark; 1893.

Paris; Auguste, Robert-Joseph; 1757.

Paris; Dany, Roch-Louis; 1779.

Rennes; charge mark; 1775-1781.

Rouen; charge mark; 1781-Revolution.

Riom; charge mark; 1775-1781.

La Rochelle; town mark.

La Rochelle; town mark.

Paris; Ferrier, René-Pierre; 1775.

Reims; charge mark; 1775-1781.

Paris; Turpin, Robert; 1704.

S

Lille; town mark.

Reims; charge mark; 1768-1775.

Vicinity of Chalons; charge mark; 1775-1781.

Vicinity of Chalons; charge mark; 1781-Revolution.

Paris; Boulanger, Simon; 1691.

Paris; Bourguet, Simon; 1740.

Saint-Germain-en-Laye; charge mark; 1780.

Saint-Germain-en-Laye; charge mark; 1780.

Paris; Leblond, Sébastien; 1675.

Saint-Omer; town mark.

Saint-Omer; town mark.

Paris; Parisy, Séverin; 1771.

Soissons; town mark.

T

T   Toul; town mark.
Thouars; town mark.

Tours; charge mark; 1781-Revolution.

Dinan; charge mark; 1759.

Nantes; charge mark; 1744.

Dunkerque; town mark.

TAR   Tarascon; town mark.

Paris; Germain, Thomas; 1720.

Toulouse; charge mark; 1775-1781.

Toulouse; charge mark; 1781-Revolution.

Toulouse; town mark; 17th cent.

Toulouse; town mark; 17th cent.

Toulouse; town mark; 18th cent.

Paris; Breton, Thomas-Pierre; 1739.

Tours; charge mark; 1775-1781.

U

Paris; town mark; 1783.

V

Verdun; town mark.

Nantes; charge mark; no date established.

Troyes; charge mark; 1768-1774.

Uzes; town mark.

Paris; Bréant, Vincent; 1754.

Le Vigan; town mark.

Versailles; town mark.

Wassy; town mark.

X

Paris; town mark; 1690.

Paris; town mark; 1714.

Amiens; charge mark; 1775-1781.

Amiens; charge mark; 1781-Revolution.

Amiens; charge mark; 1768-1775.

Vicinity of Soissons; charge mark; 1768-1774.

Y

Paris; town mark; 1692.

Bourges; charge mark; 1775-1781.

Bourges; charge mark; 1781-Revolution.

Bourges; charge mark; 1768-1775.

Z

Grenoble; charge mark; end of 17th cent.

Grenoble; charge mark; 1775-1781.

Grenoble; charge mark; 1781-Revolution.

&

Foreign mark; 1819.

Aix; charge mark; 1775-1781.

Aix; charge mark; 1781-Revolution.

NUMBERS

Rennes; charge mark; no date established.

Rennes; charge mark; about 1680.

Rennes; charge mark; no date established.

334 FRENCH HALLMARKS

 Rennes; charge mark; no date established.

 Rennes; charge mark; no date established.

 Rennes; charge mark; no date established.

 Rennes; charge mark; about 1725.

 Rennes; charge mark; about 1730.

 Saint-Malo; charge mark; about 1740.

 Rennes; charge mark; 1775-1781.

 Rennes; charge mark; 1781-Revolution.

 Vesoul; town mark.

 Strasbourg; town mark; 1681-Revolution.

 Strasbourg; town mark; 1681-Revolution.

 Strasbourg; town mark; 1567-1681.

 Strasbourg; town mark; 1681-Revolution.

 Strasbourg; town mark; 1681-Revolution.

CONSTELLATIONS

 Saint-Germain-en-Laye; charge mark; 1768-1774.

 Lorient; town mark.

 Senlis; town mark.

 Paris; discharge mark; 1722-1726.

 Chaumont-en-Bassigny; town mark.

 Lunéville; makers mark.

HUMAN FACES AND PARTS OF THE HUMAN BODY

 Beaune; makers mark.

 Saint-Quentin; town mark.

 Vicinity of Orléans; discharge mark; 1781-Revolution.

 Orléans; town mark; after 1784.

 Toul; town mark; after 1784.

 Rouen; discharge mark; 1781-Revolution.

 Departments; recense mark; 1819.

 Export mark; 1840.

 Export mark; 1840.

 Export mark; 1879.

 Export mark; 1879.

 Export mark; 1879

 Export mark; 1879.

 Export mark; 1879.

 Export mark; 1879.

 Export mark; 1879.

 Departments; standard mark; 1819-1838.

 Metz; discharge mark; 1775-1781.

 Paris; discharge mark; 1780-1782.

 Paris; standard mark; 1819.

 1st standard mark; 1838.

 2nd standard mark; 1838.

 Paris; recense mark; 1819.

 Paris; standard mark; 1819-1838.

Paris; standard mark gold; 1819-1838.

Paris; discharge mark; 1780-1782.

Vicinity of Chalons; discharge mark; 1781-Revolution.

Paris; recense mark; 1798-1809.

Departments; r e c e n s e mark; 1798-1809.

Paris; recense mark; 1798-1809.

Departments; r e c e n s e mark; 1798-1809.

Caen; discharge mark; 1775-1781.

Departments; 2nd standard mark; 1819-1838.

Paris; 1st standard mark; 1819-1838.

Paris; 2nd standard mark; 1819-1838.

Vannes; town mark; after 1784.

Sens; discharge mark; 1768-1774.

Dijon; discharge mark; 1781-Revolution.

Orléans; discharge mark; 1768-1775.

Blois; discharge mark; 1768-1775.

Lyon; discharge mark; 1762-1768.

Amiens; discharge mark; 1775-1781.

Paris; garantie mark; 1798-1809.

Departments; g a r a n t i e mark; 1798-1809.

Paris; garantie mark; 1798-1809.

Departments; g a r a n t i e mark; 1798-1809.

Departments; g a r a n t i e mark; 1819.

Meaux; discharge mark; 1672-1768.

Reims; discharge mark; 1768-1774.

Export mark; 1912.

Paris; discharge mark; 1756-1762.

Paris; discharge mark; 1768-1774.

Paris; discharge mark; 1782-1786.

Departments; 1st standard mark; 1819-1838.

Paris; discharge mark; 1768-1774.

Vicinity of Orléans; discharge mark; 1781-Revolution.

Paris; garantie mark; 1819.

Departments; g a r a n t i e mark; 1819.

Uzes; town mark; after 1784.

Paris, foreign mark; 1819-1838.

Export mark; 1884.

Export mark; 1884.

1st standard mark gold; 1838.

2nd standard mark gold; 1838.

3rd standard mark gold; 1838.

Toulon; town mark; after 1784.

Paris; foreign mark; 1819-1838.

Poitiers; discharge mark; 1781-Revolution.

Bordeaux; discharge mark; 1775-1781.

Paris; garantie mark; 1819-1838.

Departments; g a r a n t i e mark gold; 1819-1838.

Import mark; 1912.

Import mark; 1926.

Maubeuge; town mark; after 1784.

Departments; recense mark; 1819.

Paris; discharge mark; 1789.

Lyon; discharge mark; 1775-1781.

Tours; discharge mark; 1781-Revolution.

Melle; town mark; after 1784.

Paris; recense mark; 1819.

Saint-Lo; town mark; after 1784.

Senlis; charge mark; 1768-1774.

Versailles; charge mark; 1768-1774.

Saint-Germain-en-Laye; c h a r g e mark; 1768-1774.

Montpellier; charge mark; no date established.

Macon; town mark; after 1784.

Departments; g a r a n t i e mark gold; 1819.

Besancon; makers mark; 15th cent.

Paris; recense mark; 1819.

Vicinity of Orléans; discharge mark; 1775-1781.

Bourges; discharge mark; 1775-1781.

Paris; charge mark; 1744-1750.

Paris; charge mark; 1738-1744.

Riom; discharge mark; 1775-1781.

Tours; discharge mark; 1775-1781.

Bayonne; discharge mark; 1775-1781.

MAMMALS

Paris; discharge mark; 1738-1744.

Paris; discharge mark; 1774-1780.

Avallon; town mark; after 1784.

Rennes; discharge mark; 1781-Revolution.

La Rochelle; discharge mark; 1775-1781.

Gold watch mark; 1819-1838.

Paris; 3rd gold standard mark; 1819-1838.

Pau; town mark; after 1784.

Caen; discharge mark; 1781-Revolution.

Bourges; town mark; after 1784.

Paris; garantie mark; 1819-1838.

Les Sables; town mark; after 1784.

Amiens; discharge mark; 1781-Revolution.

Bourges; discharge mark; 1775-1781.

Rouen; makers mark; 15th and 16th centuries.

Rouen; makers mark; 17th and 18th centuries.

Poitiers; discharge mark; 1775-1781.

Compiegne; town mark; after 1784.

Nantes; discharge mark; 1746.

Metz; discharge mark; 1775-1781.

Recense mark; 1838.

Paris; discharge mark; 1732-1738.

Caen; discharge mark; 1781-Revolution.

Lyon; discharge mark; 1775-1781.

Limoges; discharge mark; 1781-Revolution.

Cambrai; town mark; after 1784.

Gold garantie mark; 1838.

Angouleme; town mark; after 1784.

Riom; discharge mark; 1781-Revolution.

Sedan; town mark; after 1784.

Sedan; makers mark.

Paris; discharge mark; 1750-1756.

Toulouse; discharge mark; 1781-Revolution.

Paris; garantie mark; 1838.

Paris; gold chain mark; 1838.

Departments; gold chain mark; 1838.

Paris; gold mark; 1847.

Alloy mark; 1905.

Departments; 2nd gold standard marks; 1819-1838.

Angers; charge mark; 18th cent.

Valenciennes; town mark.

Caen; discharge mark; 1744-1750.

Lyon; town mark.

Lyon; discharge mark; 1762-1768.

Lyon; discharge mark; 1781-Revolution.

Paris; gold garantie mark; 1819.

Lyon; town mark; after 1784.

Grenoble; discharge mark; 1775-1781.

Montpellier; charge mark; no established date.

Caen; makers mark.

Laval; makers mark.

Poitiers; discharge mark; 1775-1781.

Meaux; town mark; after 1784.

Cahors; town mark; after 1784.

Montargis; discharge mark; 1768-1775.

Paris; discharge mark; 1732-1738.

Paris; discharge mark; 1762-1768.

Paris; discharge mark; 1782-1789.

Saint-Germain-en-Laye; discharge mark; 1780.

Platinum mark; 1912.

Recense mark; 1838.

Salins; town mark; after 1784.

Paris; discharge mark; 1744-1750.

Paris; 1st gold standard mark; 1819-1838.

Departments; recense mark; 1819-1838.

Departments; 1st gold standard mark; 1819-1838.

Lyon; discharge mark; 1768-1775.

Limoges; discharge mark; 1781-Revolution.

Amiens; discharge mark; 1775-1781.

Vesoul; town mark; after 1784.

Paris; discharge mark; 1738-1744.

Nantes; charge mark; no date established.

Nantes; charge mark; middle of the 18th cent.

Mirecourt; makers mark.

Morlaix; town mark.

Morlaix; town mark.

Rennes; town mark.

Rennes; town mark.

Rennes; town mark.

Rennes; town mark; after 1784.

Paris; discharge mark; 1774-1780.

Nimes; town mark; after 1784.

Central France; garantie mark; 1819-1838.

Paris; garantie mark; 1819-1838.

Export mark; 1888.

Export mark; 1888.

Saint-Germain-en-Laye; town mark; after 1784.

La Rochelle; discharge mark; 1775-1781.

Vicinity of Orléans; discharge mark; 1775-1781.

Perpignan; town mark; after 1784.

Arras; town mark.

Arras; town mark.

Arras; town mark.

Arras; town mark.

Tours; discharge mark; 1775-1781.

BIRDS

Toulouse; discharge mark; 1781-Revolution.

Departments; recense mark; 1819.

1st gold standard mark; 1919.

2nd gold standard mark; 1919.

3rd gold standard mark; 1919.

Paris; gold garantie mark; 1838.

Paris; gold garantie mark; 1847.

Nancy; makers mark.

 Briey; town mark.

 Bouquemont; town mark.

 Commercy; town mark.

 Dieuze; town mark.

 Etain; town mark.

 Forbach; town mark.

 Mirecourt; town mark.

 Neufchateau; town mark.

 Pont-a-Mousson; town mark.

 Rosieres-aux-Salines; town mark.

 Saint-Mihiel; town mark.

 Saint-Nicolas-du-Port; town mark.

 Sarreguemines; town mark.

 Vézelise; town mark.

 Lunéville; town mark; before 1773.

 Charmes; town mark.

 Darney; town mark.

 Epinal; town mark.

 Rambervillers; town mark.

 Remiremont; town mark.

 Saint-Dié; town mark.

 Besancon; makers mark; 18th cent.

Brest; town mark; about 1770.

Alencon; makers mark.

 Import mark; 1893.

 Chateau-Thierry; town mark; after 1784.

 Paris; discharge mark; 1708-1715.

 Soissons; discharge mark; 1768-1774.

Beauvais; discharge mark; 1768-1774.

Montpellier; charge mark; no date established.

 Paris; 1st gold standard mark; 1798-1809.

 Paris; 2nd gold standard mark; 1798-1809.

 Paris; 3rd gold standard mark; 1798-1809.

 Departments; 1st gold standard mark; 1798-1809.

 Departments; 2nd gold standard mark; 1798-1809.

 Departments; 3rd gold standard mark; 1798-1809.

 Paris; 1st standard mark; 1798-1809.

 Paris; 2nd standard mark; 1798-1809.

 Departments; 1st standard mark; 1798-1809.

 Departments; 2nd standard mark; 1798-1809.

 Paris; 1st gold standard mark; 1819.

 Paris; 2nd gold standard mark; 1819.

 Paris; 3rd gold standard mark; 1819.

 Departments; 1st gold standard mark; 1819.

 Departments; 2nd gold standard mark; 1819.

 Departments; 3rd gold standard mark; 1819.

 Paris; 1st standard mark; 1819.

Paris; 2nd standard mark; 1819.

 Departments; 1st standard mark; 1819.

 Departments; 2nd standard mark; 1819.

 Paris; discharge mark; 1750-1756.

 Vicinity of Paris; discharge mark; 1781.

 Paris; gold garantie mark; 1798-1809.

 Departments: gold garantie mark; 1798-1809.

 Paris; gold garantie mark; 1819.

 Paris; gold garantie mark; 1819.

 Departments; gold garantie mark; 1819.

 Departments; gold garantie mark; 1819.

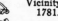 Metz; town mark; after 1784.

 Vicinity of Paris; discharge mark; 1781.

 Versailles; discharge mark; 1768-1774.

 Import mark; 1893.

 Montpellier; charge mark; no date established.

 Morlaix; town mark; about 1740.

 Chartres; town mark; after 1784.

 Toulouse; discharge mark; 1775-1781.

 Lille; town mark; after 1784.

 Trévoux; town mark; after 1784.

 Beaumont-sur-Oise; discharge mark; 1768-1774.

 Paris; discharge mark; 1786-1789.

 Import mark; 1893.

 Aix; discharge mark; 1775-1781.

Saint-Martin-de-Ré; town mark; after 1784.

Saint-Esprit; town mark; after 1784.

 Paris; discharge mark; 1726-1732.

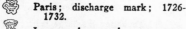 Laon; makers mark.

Angers; charge mark; 18th. cent.

 Aix; town mark; after 1784.

Laon; discharge mark; 1768-1774.

Pontoise; discharge mark; 1672-1768.

FISH

 Bar-le-Duc; town mark; after 1784.

 Beauvais; town mark; after 1784.
Dieppe; town mark; after 1784.

 Southern France; 800 mark; 1819-1838.

 Parthenay; town mark; after 1784.

 Northwest France; 800 mark; 1819-1838.

 Melun; town mark; after 1784.

 Grenoble; town mark; after 1784.

 Paris; discharge mark; 1744-1750.

 Bray-sur-Seine; discharge mark; 1768-1774.

 La Rochelle; discharge mark; 1781-Revolution.

 Dunkerque; town mark.

 Grenoble; town mark.

 Grenoble; town mark.

 Grenoble; town mark.

 Gisors; town mark; after 1784.

AMPHIBIANS AND REPTILES

 Laval; town mark; after 1784.

 Southwest France; 800 mark; 1819-1838.

 Le Havre; makers mark.

Vitry-le-Francois; town mark.

Nimes; town mark.

Nimes; town mark.

INVERTEBRATES

 Abbeville; town mark; after 1784.

 Rennes; discharge mark; about 1730.

Sainte-Ménehould; town mark; after 1784.

 Compiegne; discharge mark; 1768-1774.

Metz; discharge mark; 1781-Revolution.

Mende; town mark; after 1784.

Northern France; 800 mark; 1819-1838.

Gien; discharge mark; 1768-1775.

Departments; g a r a n t i e mark; 1838.

Lyon; discharge mark; 1768-1775.

Etampes; town mark; after 1784.

Watch mark; 1819-1838.

Rouen; discharge mark; 1768-1775.

Northeastern France; 800 mark; 1819-1838.

Périgueux; town mark; after 1784.

Western France; 800 mark; 1819-1838.

Etampes; discharge mark; 1768-1774.

Central France; 750 gold standard mark; 1832-1838.

Import mark; 1838.

Import mark; 1838.

Import mark; 1864.

Import mark; 1864.

Import mark; 1893.

Import mark; 1893.

Alencon; town mark; after 1784.

Southeastern France; 800 mark; 1819-1838.

Paris; discharge mark; 1756-1762.

Bordeaux; discharge mark; 1781-Revolution.

Eastern France; 800 mark; 1819-1838.

Rouen; discharge mark; 1768-1775.

Provins; discharge mark; 1768-1774.

Dijon; discharge mark; 1775-1781.

Marennes; town mark; after 1784.

Morlaix; town mark; about 1740.

MYTHICAL ANIMALS

 Departments; 3rd gold standard mark; 1819-1838.

 Paris; 2nd gold standard mark; 1819-1838.

 Bordeaux; town mark; after 1784.

 Import mark; 1838.

 Import mark; 1838.

 La Rochelle; town mark; after 1784.

 Liesse; discharge mark; 1768-1774.

 Paris; charge mark; 1732-1738.

PLANTS

 Clermont-Ferrand; town mark; after 1784.

 Amiens; discharge mark; 1781-Revolution.

 Alais; town mark; after 1784.

 Draguignan; town mark; after 1784.

 Vicinity of Chalons; discharge mark; 1775-1781.

 Valognes; makers mark.

 Payrat; town mark; after 1784.

 Riom; discharge mark; 1781-Revolution.

 Thiers; town mark; after 1784.

 Rouen; town mark; after 1784.

 Rouen; discharge mark; 1781-Revolution.

 Rouen; discharge mark; 1775-1781.

 Verdun; town mark; after 1784.

 Grenoble; discharge mark; 1781-Revolution.

 Montpellier; charge mark; no date established.

 Paris; discharge mark; 1726-1732.

 Reims; town mark; after 1784.

 Dijon; discharge mark; 1781-Revolution.

 Troyes; town mark; after 1784.

 Vicinity of Chalons; discharge mark; 1781-Revolution.

 Toulouse; discharge mark; 1775-1781.

 Paris; discharge mark; 1789.

 Laon; town mark; after 1784.

Soissons; town mark; after 1784.

Saint-Germain-en-Laye; discharge mark; 1780.

Issoire; town mark; after 1784.

Departments; foreign mark; 1819-1838.

Lunel; town mark; after 1784.

Montpellier; discharge mark; 1775-1781.

Departments; foreign mark; 1819-1838.

Montpellier; discharge mark; 1781-Revolution.

Versailles; discharge mark; 1780.

Provins; town mark; after 1784.

Aix; discharge mark; 1781-Revolution.

Paris; discharge mark; 1762-1768.

Dreux; discharge mark; 1768-1774.

Toulouse; discharge mark; no date established.

Paris; charge mark; 1768-1774.

Versailles; charge mark; 1780.

Paris; recense mark; 1819-1838.

Paris; recense mark; 1819-1838.

Orléans; town mark.

Orléans; makers mark.

La Fere; town mark; after 1784.

Pons; town mark; after 1784.

Mantes; discharge mark; 1768-1774.

Grenoble; discharge mark; 1781-Revolution.

Millau; town mark; after 1784.

Le Mans; town mark; after 1784.

Valognes; town mark; after 1784.

Montpellier; discharge mark; 1781-Revolution.

Liesse; discharge mark; 1768-1774.

Clermont; discharge mark; 1768-1774.

Melun; discharge mark; 1768-1774.

Crépy; discharge mark; 1768-1774.

Nancy; town mark.

Nancy; town mark.

Paris; charge mark; 1762-1768.

Montpellier; discharge mark; 1775-1781.

Versailles; discharge mark; 1768-1774.

Rennes; discharge mark; 1775-1781.

Dunkerque; town mark; after 1784.

ARTICLES OF CLOTHING

Eastern France; gold 750 mark; 1819-1838.

Bordeaux; discharge mark; 1775-1781.

Limoges; discharge mark; 1775-1781.

Senlis; discharge mark; 1768-1774.

Arles; town mark; after 1784.

Dijon; discharge mark; 1775-1781.

Boulogne-sur-Mer; discharge mark; after 1784.

Bourges; discharge mark; 1781-Revolution.

Poitiers; town mark; after 1784.

Riom; discharge mark; 1775-1781.

Tarascon; town mark; after 1784.

La Rochelle; discharge mark; 1781-Revolution.

Western France; gold 750 mark; 1819-1838.

Strasbourg; town mark; after 1784.

Grenoble; discharge mark; 1775-1781.

Aix; discharge mark; 1781-Revolution.

Southern France; gold 750 mark; 1819-1838.

Vitry-le-Francois; town mark; after 1784.

Marseille; town mark; after 1784.

Rennes; discharge mark; 1775-1781.

Lyon; discharge mark; 1781-Revolution.

Saintes; town mark; after 1784.

Bayonne; discharge mark; 1775-1781.

Bourg-en-Bresse; t o w n mark; after 1784.

Colmar; town mark; after 1784.

Aurillac; town mark; after 1784.

Abbeville; discharge mark; 1768-1775.

Autun; town mark; after 1784.

Metz; discharge mark; 1781-Revolution.

Calais; town mark; after 1784.

ARMS

Saint-Germain-en-Laye; discharge mark; 1768-1774.

Saumur; town mark; after 1784.

Northeastern France; gold 750 mark; 1819-1838.

Gien; town mark; after 1784.

Lyon; town mark.

Angers; makers mark.

Amiens; town mark; 1748.

Rethel; town mark; after 1784.

Cognac; town mark; after 1784.

Nantes; town mark; after 1784.

Hasard mark; 1798-1809.

Liesse; town mark; after 1784.

Paris; garantie mark; 1798-1809.

Departments; g a r a n t i e mark; 1798-1809.

Paris; garantie mark; 1819.

Departments; g a r a n t i e mark; 1819.

Vicinity of Chalons; discharge mark; 1775-1781.

Mézieres; town mark; after 1784.

Marle and Vervins; discharge mark; 1768-1774.

Guise; town mark; after 1784.

Le Havre; town mark; after 1784.

Caen; discharge mark; 1744-1750.

VASES

Poitiers; discharge mark; 1781-Revolution.

Rennes; discharge mark; 1781-Revolution.

Semur; town mark; after 1784.

Western France; recense mark; 1819-1838.

Saint Quentin; discharge mark; 1768-1775.

Rodez; town mark; after 1784.

Limoges; discharge mark; 1775-1781.

Blois; town mark; after 1784.

Péronne; discharge mark; 1768-1775.

Beaune; town mark; after 1784.

Carcassonne; town mark; after 1784.

Eastern France; recense mark; 1819-1838.

Rouen; charge mark; 1768-1775.

Issoudun; town mark; after 1784.

Southeastern France; m a k e r s mark; 1819-1838.

Riez; town mark; after 1784.

Roye; discharge mark; 1768-1775.

D'Aligre (Marans); town mark; after 1784.

Noyon; town mark; after 1784.

Beaucaire; town mark; after 1784.

Northern France; makers mark; 1819-1838.

Niort; town mark; after 1784.

Nevers; town mark; after 1784.

LAMPS

Le Mans; makers mark.

Auxerre; town mark; after 1784.

Lons-le-Saunier; t o w n m a r k ; after 1784.

La Fere; discharge mark; 1768-1774.

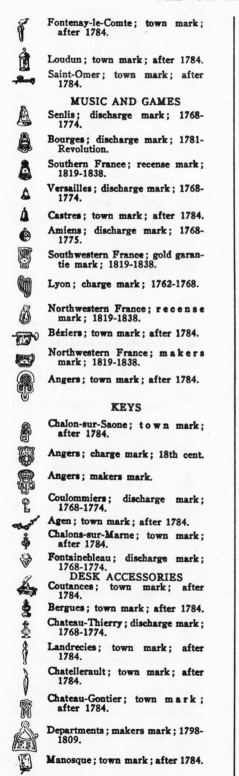

Fontenay-le-Comte; town mark; after 1784.

Loudun; town mark; after 1784.

Saint-Omer; town mark; after 1784.

MUSIC AND GAMES

Senlis; discharge mark; 1768-1774.

Bourges; discharge mark; 1781-Revolution.

Southern France; recense mark; 1819-1838.

Versailles; discharge mark; 1768-1774.

Castres; town mark; after 1784.

Amiens; discharge mark; 1768-1775.

Southwestern France; gold garantie mark; 1819-1838.

Lyon; charge mark; 1762-1768.

Northwestern France; r e c e n s e mark; 1819-1838.

Béziers; town mark; after 1784.

Northwestern France; m a k e r s mark; 1819-1838.

Angers; town mark; after 1784.

KEYS

Chalon-sur-Saone; t o w n mark; after 1784.

Angers; charge mark; 18th cent.

Angers; makers mark.

Coulommiers; discharge mark; 1768-1774.

Agen; town mark; after 1784.

Chalons-sur-Marne; town mark; after 1784.

Fontainebleau; discharge mark; 1768-1774.

DESK ACCESSORIES

Coutances; town mark; after 1784.

Bergues; town mark; after 1784.

Chateau-Thierry; discharge mark; 1768-1774.

Landrecies; town mark; after 1784.

Chatellerault; town mark; after 1784.

Chateau-Gontier; town m a r k; after 1784.

Departments; makers mark; 1798-1809.

Manosque; town mark; after 1784.

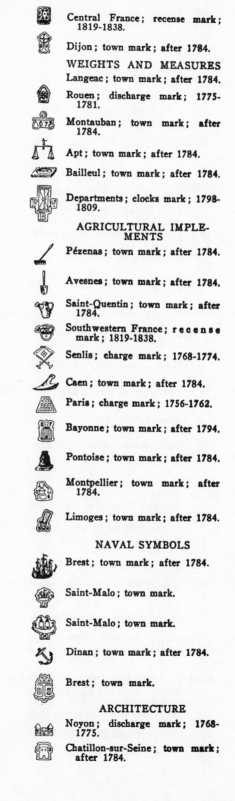

Central France; recense mark; 1819-1838.

Dijon; town mark; after 1784.

WEIGHTS AND MEASURES

Langeac; town mark; after 1784.

Rouen; discharge mark; 1775-1781.

Montauban; town mark; after 1784.

Apt; town mark; after 1784.

Bailleul; town mark; after 1784.

Departments; clocks mark; 1798-1809.

AGRICULTURAL IMPLEMENTS

Pézenas; town mark; after 1784.

Avesnes; town mark; after 1784.

Saint-Quentin; town mark; after 1784.

Southwestern France; r e c e n s e mark; 1819-1838.

Senlis; charge mark; 1768-1774.

Caen; town mark; after 1784.

Paris; charge mark; 1756-1762.

Bayonne; town mark; after 1794.

Pontoise; town mark; after 1784.

Montpellier; town mark; after 1784.

Limoges; town mark; after 1784.

NAVAL SYMBOLS

Brest; town mark; after 1784.

Saint-Malo; town mark.

Saint-Malo; town mark.

Dinan; town mark; after 1784.

Brest; town mark.

ARCHITECTURE

Noyon; discharge mark; 1768-1775.

Chatillon-sur-Seine; town mark; after 1784.

Tours; discharge mark; 1781-Revolution.

Northeastern France; recense mark; 1819-1838.

Tours; town mark.

Dinan; town mark.

Honfleur; makers mark.

Caen; discharge mark; 1775-1781.

Morlaix; town mark; after 1784.

Aix; discharge mark; 1775-1781.

Calais; discharge mark; 1768-1775.

Joinville and Wassy; town mark; after 1784.

Moulins; town mark; after 1784.

Le Puy; town mark; after 1784.

MISCELLANEOUS

La Charité; town mark; after 1784.

Langres; town mark; after 1784.

Falaise; town mark; after 1784.

Thouars; town mark; after 1784.

Caen; charge mark; 1744-1750.

Southeastern France; gold 750 mark; 1819-1838.

Montargis; town mark; after 1784.

Montereau; discharge mark; 1768-1774.

Luçon; town mark; after 1784.

Valenciennes; town mark; after 1784.

Narbonne; town mark; after 1784.

Grasse; town mark; after 1784.

Besancon; town mark; after 1784.

Guise; discharge mark; 1768-1774.

Dole; town mark; after 1784.

Le Vigan; town mark; after 1784.

Montdidier; discharge mark; 1768-1775.

Montreuil; discharge mark; 1768-1775.

Quimper; town mark; after 1784.

Arras; town mark; after 1784.

Antibes; town mark; after 1784.

Tours; town mark; after 1784.

Saint-Maixent; town mark; after 1784.

Toulouse; town mark; after 1784.

Northern France; gold 750 mark; 1819-1838.

Fécamp; town mark; after 1784.

Bar-sur-Aube; town mark; after 1784.

Saint-Jean-d'Angély; town mark; after 1784.

Rochefort; town mark; after 1784.

Saint-Germain-en-Laye; discharge mark; 1768-1774.

Sens; town mark; after 1784.

Bordeaux; discharge mark; 1781-Revolution.

Paris; discharge mark; 1722-1726.

Lisieux; town mark; after 1784.

Saint-Malo; town mark; after 1784.

Mantes; town mark; after 1784.

Lyon; charge mark; 1768-1775.

Longwy; town mark; after 1784.

FLEURS-DE-LIS. CROWNS. CRUCIFIXES

Versailles; town mark; after 1784.

Central France; gold 750 mark; 1819-1832.

Paris; charge mark; 1680-1681.

Paris; discharge mark; 1717-1722.

Lille; town mark.

Lille; town mark.

Lille; town mark.

Montpellier; charge mark; no date established.

Calais; town mark.

FRENCH HALLMARKS

345

Bolbec; makers mark.

Languedoc; charge mark; 1700.

Paris; discharge mark; 1717-1722.

Paris; discharge mark; 1717-1722.

Morlaix; town mark; about 1725.

Paris; discharge mark; 1691-1698.

Paris; discharge mark; 1687-1691.

Paris; discharge mark; 1703-1708.

Paris; discharge mark; 1681-1684.

Paris; discharge mark; 1681-1684.

Paris; discharge mark; 1684-1687.

Paris; discharge mark; 1684-1687.

Paris; discharge mark; 1698-1703.

Brest; town mark; about 1720.

Morlaix; town mark; about 1725.

Riom; town mark; after 1784.

Boulogne; discharge mark; 1768-1775.

Neufchateau; town mark.

Pont-a-Mousson; town mark.

Rosieres-aux-Salines; town mark.

Saint-Mihiel; town mark.

Saint-Nicholas-du-Port; town mark.

Sarreguemines; town mark.

Vézelise; town mark.

Lunéville; town mark; before 1773.

Lunéville; town mark; after 1773.

Charmes; town mark.

Darney; town mark.

Epinal; town mark.

Rambervillers; town mark.

Remiremont; town mark.

Saint-Dié; town mark.

Nancy; makers mark.

Briey · town mark.

Bouquemont; town mark.

Commercy; town mark.

Dieuze; town mark.

Etain; town mark.

Forbach; town mark.

Mirecourt; town mark.

COATS-OF-ARMS

Strasbourg; town mark; 1472-1534.

Strasbourg; town mark; 1434-1567.

Strasbourg; town mark; 1567-1681.

Salins; town mark.

Lons-le-Saunier; town mark.

Dijon; makers mark.

Dijon; makers mark.

Chalon-sur-Saone; makers mark.

Clermont-Ferrand; makers mark.

Toulouse; discharge mark; no date established.

Trévoux; town mark.

Trévoux; town mark.

Montauban; town mark.

Montauban ; town mark.

 Langres ; makers mark

 Tours : makers mark.

 Metz ; town mark.

 Metz ; town mark.

 Autun ; makers mark.

 Dole ; makers mark.

 Vesoul ; town mark.

 Vesoul ; makers mark.

 Bourg-en-Bresse ; makers mark

 Toulon ; town mark.

 Marseille ; town mark

A

73	550	840 „AP"	433	932
27 „A"	948 „A FS"	1447	1436	584
89 „A"	947	380	805	412
1293 „A"	989 AG	1040	920	1202
110	643 AG	1325 „AR"	540	1425
1166	1005 AG	501	781	827
1377	508 AH	1313	1433
1154	1400	381	520	1332 „C NH"
306	1312	54 „AS"	641	1467 „CO W"
185	55 „AK"	970 AS		731
278	1334	661 AS	**B**	1466
238	642 AL	448	307 „B"	59
108	492 AL	362	1294 „B"	1411
65	51 „AM"	1324	1355 „B"	454
66	90 „AM"	516	1459 „B"	1446
67	675 AM	1389	1085	633
	522	1388	1106	1131
	452 AN		1088	

| 110 | 1065 | 1064 | 62 „AB" | 579 AB | 443 | 1146 | 580 AB | 1001 „A BM" | 20 „ACH" | 21 „ACH" | 982 ACH | 18 ACH | 1012 „AC W" | 936 AD | 597 AD |

B (second section)

1090 B	1096 B	84 BO	**C**	38 „CF"	1393 „ES"
1089 B	1103 B	484 BE	1295 „C"	649 CF	803 ES
693 B	1097 B	707 BE	1380	70 CFH	1119 ES
1091 B	1235	1448 BH	1155	68 CFS	764 EW
1095 B	1238	903 BH	240	1030 CFT	626 „E W"
1356 B	239	1039	281	1037 CGS	
1473 „B"	1320 „B IB"		602 CH	**F**
1379 B	315	1315 BK	308	1438 CH	1298 „F"
1230	279	432	76	1126 CH	421 F
1092	280	377 BL	109 CB	429 CH	705 F
1460	1474 „B"	474 BL	453 CB	623	777 F
1461	375	1180 BO	944 CB	933 „C IS"	1167
1378 B	1309 BB	679 BS	1404	58 „CK"	1382
1084	566	891 BS	1417 „CD"	682 „CK"	1156
1086	1317	386	987 CD	1451 CK	1158
1098	587	538 „B W"	885 CD	949 CKM	284
	378	537	366	974 CL	
			398	839 CL	
				585 CL	

1127 CS, 768 CS, 1004 CSB, 1445 SG, 1220 CV, 1434 CW, 763 CW, 1139, 1440, 1016 CXS

243, 370 „DA", 370 DA, 370 „D·A·F", 753 „DB", 1470 „DF", 485 DF, 1353, 1171 DM, 467, 468, 1409 DI, 802 DN, 628 DF, 1415, 34, 1077 „DS", 788 DS, 801, 360, 640 DW

D

1296 „D", 1381 D, 282, 309, 241, 242

439 PW, 1464, 496 DZ

E

310 „E", 1297 „E", 86 „E", 31, 1142, 1157, 283, 246, 245, 244, 75, 809 EA

810 EA, 811 EB, 663 EB, 1217 „ECH", 1453 „E CS", 835 ED, 938 ED, 507, 506, 1432 EG, 1147, 1221 EGE, 1011 EGM, 608 „EH", 502 „EL", 1398, 1178 „ERF"

311, 249, 248, 247, 498, 940 „FAB", 858 FAB, 999 FAG, 981 „FA L", 81 FAL, 83 FAL, 847 „FB", 1314 „FB", 899 FCM, 928 FCM, 1047 FD, 1452 FG

100, 1429, 751, 1007 „FI M", 878 „F IS", 1051 „FK", 1414 FN, 917 „FR L", 1482 „FS", 646 FS, 853 „FS", 1135 FS, 1248 „FT I", 869, 1416, 594 „F W", 1179 FW

G

28 „G", 1384 G, 1383 G, 285, 251, 312, 250, 78 G, 22 ACH, 829 GAS, 1125, 729 GB, 909 GB, 1144 GB

931 GCD, 1054 GCN, 683 GE, 527 GE, 1321, 1322, 1323, 988 GBO, 736 „GF", 737 GF, 1022 GFG, 1021, 1335 „GG B", 1426 GH, 1408 GH

359, 687, 1435, 1330, 975, 995 "GIK", 1430, 1449, 1443, 543, 524, 541, 441, 837 GLG, 812 "GM", 836, 1117

1418, 394, 620, 1170, 968, 371, 494, 983 "GW", 684, H, 1299 "H", 1265 "H?", 437 "H", 87 "H", 1385, 1392

1159, 252, 286, 313, 390, 879, 404, 536, 658, 1419, 770, 376, 555, 616, 910, 790

791, 459, 632, 542, 635, 1026, 464, 1327, 1129, 636, 353, 396, 972 "HI", 1421, 793 "HI", 473, 1175

441, 441, 531, 615, 749, 504, 464, 654, 1333, 695, 368 "HK", 417 "HK", 517, 653, 486, 407, 774, 40 "HM", 656, 1017 "HM"

609 "ICH", 63 "ICHS", 1190 "ICL", 816, 61 "ICM", 918 "ICM", 696, 1019, 782 "ICP", 924, 710 "ICR", 967, 1075, 1337 "ICS", 776, 906 "ICS"

914, 908 "ICS", 907 "ICS", 922, 1255, 862, 1003, 373, 704, 919, 514, 1444, 939 "ID", 551, 676, 715, 1025, 798 "IDO", 748, 760 "IDS"

799, 462, 814, 1130 "IEP", 1032, 373, 513, 732, 871, 69, 828, 874, 817, 1247, 104, 1036 "IFF"

868 "IFH", 792, 1053 "IFN", 926 "IFS", 780, 47 "IG", 888 "IG", 521, 1048 "IG", 1176, 1049, 1203 "IGH", 950, 72 "IGK", 951, 1177 "IGP", 1008 "IGS"

972 "IH", 793 "IH", 1402, 472, 775 "IH", 36, 941, 896, 102, 1308, 598, 886, 1423, 1002 "IHS", 1243, 716, 821

611, 769 "HM", 1469, 915, 364, 1462, 451, 500, 773, 511, 545, 426, 699 "HO", 586, 629, 528, 1422

458 "HP", 1121, 1143, 787, 401, 401', 612, 634 "HPS", 603, 53, 510, 350, 1399, 461, 625, 56 "H.S.Z.", 969

1413, 489, 408, I, 314 "I", 1160, 253, 287, 1361, 509, 631 "IA", 1145, 1033, 1257 "IAF", 1223 IAG, 893

1010 "IAO", 943 "IAR", 1018 IAS, 980 "IAW", 1245, 664, 525, 965, 718, 1076 "I:B", 785, 103, 582, 758, 934, 655 IBE

824 "IBE", 957 "IBH", 576, 1210 IBM, 1336, 1014 "IBS", 1015 "IBS", 971 ICB, 900 "ICB", 990 "ICB", 991, 973 "ICB", 1028, 867 ICD, 960 "ICD", 927 ICE, 925 "ICG", 898 "ICH"

750, 766, 771, 621, 622, 60 "IIA", 956, 844, 986 "IIB", 901, 583, 650, 786, 1000 "IIM", 820, 895

894, 795, 1006, 730 "IK", 674, 1034, 414 "JKF", 415 "JKF", 890, 759, 845, 565, 911 ILA, 574, 573, 1339 "ILM", 1128

1200, 779, 850 "LS", 806, 592, 469, 1024, 403, 1059, 953, 665, 666, 667, 823, 82, 954, 872

866, 735, 784, 942, 992 "IMS", 1450, 887 "IMZ", 1044, 937, 1045 "INS", 993 "IOG", 833 "IOM", 599, 881, 30, 1050

1138 "IPH", 955, 998 "IPH", 897, 852, 813, 1123, 875 "IPS", 734, 562, 996 "IR", 563 "IR", 560, 561, 1050 IRH, 119 "IS", 610, 686

873   963 „IWG"   80 KM   815 „LK"   291   37 „PIS"   264   706 „S"   52 „SH"   754

685 ISA   964 „IWG"   415 „LKI"   345   652 PK   946 „S"   106   865

1046 ISA   **L**   1405 M   422   671 „PLD"   265   1134   1027 SHB

1052   1023 IWK   547 L   495 N   822 MAE   1401   266   S   471   **I**

719 „ISP"   447 „IZ"   1168 L   772 LR   723 MB   800 PR   849   530   298 „T"

(1174 JSW   756 IZ   316 L   1029 LR   711 MB   765 PR   297   1305 „T"

880 „IT"   **K**   289   727   383 MB   1211 PRW   268   1241   1387 T

994 ITH   1300 K   256   877 „LS"   **R**   648 „PS"   296 „R"   460 „SA"   405   270

1485   598 K   290   424 LS   384 MB   322 „R"   1246 SAb   1242   269

977 „IVG"   457 K   570 „LB"   1326 LS   553 MB   670 PS   1303 „R"   997 „SB"   419   218

830 IVG   1161   930 LB   702 LW   505 MB   778 PS   1116 „R"   324

689 IW   288   843 LB   794 „MDW"   834 ST   681 R   1311 SB   1120   725 „TB"

385 IW   254   577 LB   **M**   861 „PV"   267 R   1035 „SC"   708 TB

1319 „IW"   255   569 LB   26 „M"   1352 ME   613 PW   1340 „RGS"   1124 SC   1182 SM   709 T·B

688   315   568 LB   317 „M"   1136 SW   1132 RW   1407 S   714 SM   1442

860   423 KE   85 „LE"   672   668 MG   912 SD   724 SI   497

958 IWD   32   1483 „LF"   870 „M"   478 MG   **Q**   **S**   673 SF   929 ST   832 TD

959   717 KLD   402 LH   700   1329 „MGE"   321 „Q"   323 „S"   1410   382   1060 „TDI"

  593   1316   692 „M:H"   1302 „Q"   1304 „S"   1386 S   1189 SG   660 SS

  549   257   601 MH   677   1133 S   783 SGK   761 SW

  295   590

---

721 MI   662 „MP"   1463 NK   98   262   923   **V**   **W**   1222 „WB"   **Y**

730   1437 „MPB"   430 NL   33   74   1427 TGW   301 „V"   302 „W"   966 „WD"   304 „Y"

1465 MI   369 MR   431 NL   1396   1041 „PAG"   1428 TK   326 „V"   327 „W"   490 WD   329

789 MM   529 MS   519 NN   1185 OM   945 „PCS"   515 TK   25   627 „W"   1331 „WG"   276 Y

1412 MI   491 MS   738 NO   41   857 PD   481 TL   271 V   1371 „W"   119 „YS 1549"

698 MM   1056 „MU"   372 NI   1391   819 PG   984 „TM"   272   1368 W   411

826 „MK"   1441 MW   703 PG   694 „VB"   1366 V   39 „WH"   **Z**

1057 „ML"   726   319 „O"   902 „PH"   1431 P   1365 W   638 WI   330 „Z"

591 MM   **N**   293   **P**   1328 PH   1193 TR   436 VB   1367 W   848 „Z"

105 H·M   318 „N"   261   320 „P"   410 PH   1187 R   374 VH   1370 W   518   913 Z

882 „MM"   1162   1301 „P"   595 PH   1439 TS   113   1369 W   1354 WM   277

690 MM   292   260   512 P   552 PH   916 TVG   808 „V·I"   463 W   728 „WS"   305

691 MM   258   230   392 P   647 PD   373   1406 K   1169 W   1318 „ZB"

639 MM   259   96   393 P   1115 PH   1390   767   420

924 „MM"   564 NF   99   1164 P   1420 VM   274   **X**   413 Z L

488 „MN"   863 NF   95   294   713 PHI   **U**   328 „X"   413 „Z.L.F."

35 „MO"   477 VK   97   263   637 PIS   325 „U"   440   273   275 X   332 Z

  722 PID   299 U   556 „VS"   1338 „ZUZ"

  300 U   859 „VSI"   892 „W"   303

Heavenly Bodies

1	499	2	1165	338
1234 Halb-mond	526	5	370	336
1358	807	3	358	797
35	234	4	337	

Man

46	548	1373	1376	50
				733
831	1372	1375	49	796

Lions

1479 Löwe	1282	1288	1291	1279
1290				
1292	1281	1278	1285	1280
1277	1276	1287	1284	1283

1286	1099	1101	1105	1094
1289	1102	1104	89ᴬ Löwe	1394
1087	1093	1100	588	

Miscellaneous Mammals

1148	1152	1236	1260	353
1149	1153	1240 / 1479 Pferd	1262	851
1150	1239	367 / 701 Ein Lamm	1263	607
1151	1237	921 Lamm	1261	651

Eagles and Miscellaneous Birds

107 „Adler" / 1483 „Adler"	16	1478	442	712
18	13	1232	669	864 Eule
22	14	1231	657	438
17	15	1233	755	101
			614	

Water

445	93	94	92

Plants

428	644	137	153	169
213	122	138	154	170
355	123	139	155	171
356	124	140	156	172
357	125	141	157	173
842	126	142	158	174
	127	143	159	175
532	128	144	160	176
503	129	145	161	177
697	130	146	162	178
533	131	147	163	179
889	132	148	164	180
450	133	149	165	181
449	134	150	166	182
361	135	151	167	183
757	136	152	168	

184	194	203	212	224
186	194ᵇ	204	214	225
187	195	205	215	226
188	196	206	216	227
189	197	207	217	228
190	198	208	219	229
191	199	209	220	231
192	200	210	221	235
193	201	211	222	523
194	202		223	

Scepters and Arms

1253 / 1483 Szepter	456	1254	479	352

Utensils

605	1360 / 1359	1350	1349	1351
233	1345	1348	1344	1347
232	1346	1341	1342	739

45	1484	744	1457	1472
618	546	743	1456	363
600	544	741	645	1480
883	434	746	720 Hift-horn	818
630	401	742	589	539
619	346	747	856	606
	745	1458	855	935

Architecture

| 465 | 427 | 71 Drei Türme | 1140 | 1141 |

Crosses

| 1468 | 487 | | | |

Trade Marks

1264 Haus marke	344	389	534	1306
349	435	397	343	
678	446	354	342	1310

554	444	341	604	400
1307	1395	409	119	387
	339	1362		493
	388			1476
455	476	395	399	

Shields

| 1068 | 1069 | 1070 | 1071 | 365 |
| | | 1072 | | |

Numbers

| 1163 | 237 | 1107 | 1109 |
| 236 | 1110 | 29 | 1108 |

A

1687 „A"-„Z"
1851 „A" „Z"
1934 „A" „Z"
3362 „A" „Z"
1696 „A"
2834
2835
3017
1687
3013
2513
1706
2822
2697
2357
2146
2148
3062

3523 „A B"
2392 „A B"
1966
3531
2090
1828
1967
1827
2450
3559 „A FS"
1970
1986
2462
2464
2324
1578
1898
2877

2878
3052 „AIR"
3117
3038
1786 „AK D"
2759
1588
2326
2102
1862
3225 „AN L"
3513
3515 „A P"
3514 „A P"
2746

2099
3043
1743 „AS"
2779 „AS"
3558 „AS"
3084
1636
2494
3557 „AS"
3489
1646
2833
1852
2477
2322
2241 „AW"
1649
2238
2239

2240
1612
2247

B

2505 „B"
2617 „B"
2766 „B"
2539 „B"
1526
1899
2833
1852
2514
1527
2206 „B"
2823

2698
2923 B8
2455 „Bad"
1504 BB
1569 BC
2124 „BF"
2129
1565
1897 „BH"
2499
2932
2963 „BK"
2867 BK 07
2866 BK 86
3057 „BL" „1670"
3058 BL

3585 „BM"
2402
3306
3496
1615 „BR"
2566
3064
2756 „B W"
2754
2755
2045

2955 „C"
2950
2956
2951
3255
2308
1697
2824
2683
3014
1721
2699
2358
2370

C

2683 „C"
3255 „C"
1882
3051
2038 CB
2101 CB

2985 CB
2063 CB
2842
3410 „CB"
3059 CB
3183
1566 CBH
1680
2873
2727
1805
1806
1808
1807
1865
2980 CH
1638
1864 CH A

2274
2876
2790 CF
2927 „CF"
2868
2882 CFH
1792
2057 „CFI"
2988 „CFR"
1787
1790 CGI
1800
2793

1916 „CH"
1502 CH
1590 CH
3274
2508
1798
1799
1568
3104
2064 „CHM"
1822 CHR
1981
2497 CI
1542
3027

1971 „CK"
2316
3097
2880 CL
2879 CL
3398
3278
2075
3055 „CM"
3087 „CM"
2409 „CM"
1913
3119 „CM"
2381 CM
3056 CM
1992
2776
1973 „CP" 3614
1549

3184 „CR"
2041
2296 CR
2192
2670 „CS"
3209 „CS"
3288 „CS"
2175 CS
1556
2780 „C.S."
3122
3525 „CST"
1532
1510 CT
2391
2418
1853
1755 „CW"

2204 „CW"
3026
2315 „CW"
1797 CWK
2787

D

1659 „D"
3299 „D"
1896
1658
1659
1622
1650 „D"
1651 „D"
1621
1623
2825
1625

1624
1626
2263
2309
3022
1722
1620
1620 „D"
2504
2700
1663
1661
1664
1681
1673
1678
1674

1660
1675
1683
1672
1662
1667
1680
1677
1676
1668
1679
1684
1685

1669
1671
1682
2359
3289
2860
2503
2861
3216
1908
1909
1991
1911
1915

2473 DI
3356 „DIW"
1747 „DK"
1748 „DK"
1748 „DK"
„1629"
1744
3203
1745 „1613"
1746 „DKF" „1617"
2517
1583 „DM"
2404 DM
3342
2893 „DS"
3221 „DS"
1912 DS
1910 DS
2388
2851

2044
2074
2657
1937
2765 „D W"
2093
„D CW"
1925
1926
1933
1948
1956
1525
2532
3256
1955

E

1954
1949
1950
1952
1951
1953
1518
1519
3005
2813
2830
2618
1874
1937
1942

2761 „E A"	1962 EW	1528	2015	2190	
3213 „E AM"	1961 EW	2284 F	2373	3086 FGM	
1928 EC		1523	3018 „FAO"	2131 „FH"	
2125		F	2826 F	3284 „FAR"	2530
1524 EE	2118 „F" Kreuz?	2814 F	2478 „FHV"		
2668 E E	2310 „F"	1698 F	2941 FAW	2940 FIK	
	3114 „F"	3006 7	2294 FB	2269 „FI M"	
3363	2080 F	1723 f	2777 FB	3336 „FK"	
1757 EG	2078 F	2152 F	3528 „FC" 1492 „FCM"	3507 FK	
3082 „EH"	2079 F	2010	1491 FCT	3508 FK	
2401 HH	2082 F	2013	3078 FCS	1753 FK	
3573 „EI"	2081 F	2619	2751 FD	3553 „FL"	
1555 EK	1982 „F"		2741 „FE"	1647 FL	
1554 E·K	2083 F	2084	2774 FE	2527 FL	
1929 B	2106 F	2086	2384 „FF"	2297 FLR	
3035 EO	3257 F	2085	2395 F	2472 N	
3060 ER	2197 F	2360	3046 FF	3504 FO 3568 „FP"	
2070 „E.S.&Co."	1983 „F"		1990 „FG" 3592 „FG"	3526 FP	

	H	2049 HAS	3199 HD	2538 „HH"	Ao: 1585
1522 „H"	3218 „HAS" Totenschädel	1732	1875 „HH"	1733	
1508 H	2394 „HB"	2139 „HE"	3505 „HH"		
3212 „H"	3414 „HB"	2138		3103	
3174 H	2534 HB	1548 HE	2926		
3597 H	3067 HB	2407 „HE"	3617 „HHO"	2742 „HL"	
1531 H	3598 „HB"	2922	3188 „HL"		
1707 H		2140 „HF"	1979 „HI"	2378 „HL"	
2815 H	3598	2389 „HF"	2730 HI	2953 HL	
2264 H	2445 Hammer „HB"	2476 „HF"	1903	1964 HL	
2311 H		1917	3269 „HI"	2410 HL	
1725 h	1546 „H C"	3307 HG	3223 „HI B"	2417 H	
3276	3068 HB	3493 „HG"	2939 HB	2397 „HL"	
3173 „H"	2669 „HCH"		2127 „HIH"		
	2068 „H. & Co."	2638 HCG	3175 „H"	2565	
2363	3364 HGW	3287 HG	1936	2422	
2368 H	2981 „HD(?)"	3206 „HH"	2040 HS	2423	
2230	3608 „HD"	3049 H	2662 „HK"		
2564	1900 „HD"	3047 H	3102 „HK"	1969 HLH	
	1901	3048 H			

1813 FRS	2174 G	2361 HG	3292	1836 „GR"	
	2236 G	2218	2625 „G H"	3500 „GR" 3090 „GS"	
2930 FS	2235 G	2217	1545 „GH"	3053 GS	
3407 FS	3484 G	2321 „GA W"	2626 GH	3063 GS	
2203 FS	3300 G	1834 „GB"	2029 G	3551 GS	
2161 „F SH"	3018 G	2935 CB	3032 G	2627 GS	
2760 FW	3007 G	2223 GL	2286 „GK"	2849 GS	
2438 FW	3469	1957 GB	3525 „GST" 3587 „GST"		
2529	1724	2518 GB	3405 GLU	1592 G·V	
2143 FXC	2170	2525 „GD"	2396 G	2555 „GW" 1594 GW	
3495 FZ	2620	2749 GD	3497 C	2938 GW	
	2285 GE	2098 „GL K"	2541 „GWR"		
	2234	2674 GE	1740 GM	2059 GWS	
	1815	1739 GM	3576 „GZ"		
G	2162 G	1818 GTB			
1688 „G"		2954 GE	1817	3479	
2249 „G"	2233	3349 „GG"			
2252 „G"	2216 G	1593 „GG"	8305 GO		
3115 „G"	2215 G	3080 GGB	3377 „GP" „1692"		
3259					

2426 „H·L·P"	2033	2771 HSI	2663 IA		
1795 HLS	2250 „HP"	2495 HSI	2198 IA		
2453 HM	3600 „HP"	3477	1965 HJ	2054 IAB	
2433 „HM"	2533 HP		2231 IAJ		
2856 HM	2435 HP	1741 IV	„I ? M"		
2857 HM	3603 HP	3399	3406 „IAR"		
2850 M	2862 PA	1635 HW			
2888 HM 72	3030 HR	3081 HW	2943		
2042 M	3031 HR	2406 HX	3121 „IB"		
2199 HN	3482	3304 MB	3286 „IB"		
2036 NB	3483 „HR"	2557 „HS"	2200 HZ	2221 IB	
2039 RB	3030 HR	3211 „HS"	3041 IB		
	3270 HR	2507 HS	I	2630 IB	
1557 HH	1904 „HS"	3185 „I"	3079 IB		
2412 H	3418 HS	2836 I	1863 IB		
	1641 HR	3011 I	2429 IB		
3194 Turm „HO"	2493 HR	2768 HB	2799 ·J·	2624 IB	
1582 HL	2733 HR	3499 HSI	2346	2871 IB 94	
		3045 HSI			

No.	Mark		No.	Mark
2872	IB		2942	ICL
3547	IBC		1639	ICR
1571	IBH		1637	ICR
1553	IBM		2664	ICS
2576	IBW		3076	ICS
3616	"IC?"		2665	ICS
3310	"J.C.B."		2595	ICS
3089	ICB		3536	ICS
3095	ICB		3535	ICS
1640	ICB		2076	ICST
3092	ICB		3098	ICV
1515	ICD		2875	ICWP
2239	"ICF"		3096	ID
2242	ICF		2763	ID
1505	ICH		3215	ID
2680	"I.C.H. 1761"		2169	IDA
1572	ICK			

No.	Mark		No.	Mark
2052	IDG		2194	IF
2053	IDG		2195	(mark)
2058	IDK		2454	"IFB"
2628	"IDS"		1778	IFB
2870	IDT		3546	IFC
1923	"IE"		1618	"IFF"
2202	"IE"		3094	"IFL"
1963	IE		3083	"IFM"
2270	IEC		3350	IFS
1619	IEF		2449	IFS
3365	IEH		2982	IFS
1567	(mark)		2269	(mark)
3577	"I ES"		2444	"IFW"
2160	"JF"		2605	IFW
2773	"IF"		2205	IG
2925	IF		3533	IG
3345	IF		3388	"IG"
			3502	"IG"

No.	Mark		No.	Mark
3534	IG		2778	"IR"
3032	"IGB"		2623	(mark)
3543	GB		2424	(mark)
2104	"IGG"		2425	(mark)
3309	"IGG"		2594	IRG
2096	"IGG"		3549	"I RZ"
1802	IGG		1614	"IS"
2104	"I.G.H."		2955	"IS"
1570	IGH		3509	"IS"
1597	IGIOD		3571	"IS"
1974	IGK		3093	"ITN"
2269	IGM		3072	IS
3516	IGO		1861	IS
1918	IGP		1540	IS
2246	"JGR"		2934	IS
2173	IGR		2420	IS
			2631	IS
			2750	"IS"
			3522	IS

No.	Mark		No.	Mark
3563	"IS"		3569	"IW"
3352	IS		1756	IW
1655	(mark)		1634	IW
3527	"IW"		3196	K
3394	"IW"		1613	K
2144	"ISK"		2839	K
2141	ISK		2640	"K"
3524	"IZ"		1718	K
1877	"ISM"		2050	IZ
3066	(mark)		2874	"IZ"
1869	IT		2641	"K"
1906	"JZ"			
3540	"IV"		2621	(mark)
2604	IVE		2362	(mark)
3538	"I VH"			
2528	IVHK		2640	"K"
2637	"IW"		3261	K
2965	"IW"		2671	K
3217	"IW"			
3510	"IW"			

No.	Mark		No.	Mark
2155	K		3260	L
2672	K		2990	L
			2992	L
			2995	L
1785	"IWM"		2991	L
			2993	L
			2994	L
1760	KF		3135	"L"
1761	F		1511	L
1762	F		1517	L
2030	KI		2827	L
2575	K		1854	L
2531	K		3021	L
2719	(mark)		1520	L
			1521	L
			2830	"I"
			1708	1

No.	Mark		No.	Mark
1810	"IGS"		3224	"IHS"
3554	"IGS"		2769	II
1784	IGS		3567	IF
1819	IGSN		2061	IIH
3544	IGV		1771	(mark)
3511	"IGZ"		1779	IIS
2962	"IH"		2968	"JJS"
3520	"IH"		1734	"IK"
3120	IH		3313	IK
3204	"IH"		2948	
2448	IH		3550	"ILW"
2432	IH		3542	"IM"
3226	"IHK"		1984	"IM"?
3290	IHK		2961	"IM"
1803	IH		1562	IK
2786	IHM		2936	IK
2474	IHP		3054	IK
2037	IRB		2268	"IKB 17 18"
1796	IHS		2220	"IL"
			2639	"IL"

No.	Mark		No.	Mark
3033	"IL"		3201	IMF
3347	IL		3601	"JP"
3346	IL		3539	"IMI"
2506	IL		2577	"IMK"
2447	ILD		3562	IMM
2885	ILK		3621	"JMO"
2886	"ILK 12"		3548	"IMR"
2887	(mark)		2055	IMS
2509	ILS		2065	IMS
3542	"IM"		1774	IMW
1867	IM		1773	IMW
1868	IM		2062	IN
2784	"J.M.C."		2468	IN
3517	"IME"		3396	IN
3532	IME		3397	(mark)
2442	IM		1617	IMW
			1591	(mark)
			2678	
			3070	IOM

No.	Mark		No.	Mark
3065	"IP"		2622	(mark)
1872	IP		3003	(mark)
1742	IP		2998	(mark)
2748	IP		2996	(mark)
3604			2997	(mark)
	IP		3001	(mark)
3344	"IPK"		2999	(mark)
3094	"IPL"		3002	(mark)
1581	"IPR"		3000	(mark)
2318	"IPS"		3004	(mark)
3351	"IR"		2989	(mark)
3116	IR		1628	(mark)
2130	"IR"		1627	(mark)
2767	IR			
1489	IR			
2157	IR			
3564	IR			
1575	IR			
	IR			

No.	Mark		No.	Mark
1629	IL		3572	LR
3348	LB		2427	LRW
1501	LD		2770	"LS"
3208	"LD"		3589	"L.S."
2881	LEO		1940	LH
3301	IF		1689	"M"
2966	"LH"		3413	"M"
2967	LH		3384	"M"
2855	LH		3409	M
3283	LH		2540	"M"
2295	LHB		3355	"M"
2854	LH		1503	M
2060	LS		2726	M
1539	LK		2831	M
3118	LK		1699	M
2639	"LL"		1709	M
3545	"LP"		1573	m
			1716	m
			1968	MW
			2219	MF

No.	Mark		No.	Mark
2364	(mark)		2593	M
2846	M		3537	"MFK"
1544	M		2267	"MG"
3530	"MA"		2843	MC
2043	MB		2792	"MH"
3609	"MB"		2592	"MH"
1749	MB		1763	MH
1737	MB		2320	MH
1738	MB		3123	"MHB"
2869	MCH		2775	"MHR"
1589	MD		2791	"MI"
3355	MD		3566	"MI"
3555	MD		1563	M
3610	MD		2376	MH
3579	"ME"		1632	M
3501	ME		2783	"M.I.R."
	ME		2984	MS
			3205	"MK"

No.	No.	No.	No.	No.
2673	1768	1586	3012 q	3220 „P HK"
2526	2658	1584	3008 q	1558
3039	2399 „NF"	2682 „NW"	1642	3285 „PHM"
2377	2403	1616	2681	2046
1766 „MR"	2772 „NH"		2629	2047 13 PHS
2323 „MS"	2463 „NH"	1701 O	2548 P.B.&C.	3069
3512 „MS"	1902	2072	3222 „PB VA"	2659
2196	2666 „NIT"	2721	1574	1781
2983	2782 „NK I"	3167	2788	2325
1780 „MS"	1947	2864	2847	2568 „PI S"
3516 „MV"	1769 „NM"	2865	2848	2567
3518 „MV"	3282		3088	2838 „PH"
3200 „MvB"	2056		3085	2667 „P·I W"
3472 „MZ"	1576		2661	2789
	1577		2379	2451 „P·K."
N	1561	**P**	2863	1727
1690 N	1559 „NPI"	1894		
1700 N	1585	3599		
3015 N		2071 „P"		
2369		2816 P		

No.	No.	No.	No.	No.
2762	3016 T	2266	1731	1506
	1711 J		2443	1537
3073	3096 „TB"	3498	2440	2844
1533	2023 „TB.fe"		2929	3552 „W"
1536	1514	2722	3480	2408
2553 „SV"	2405	2723	2978	1535
1794 „SW"	2764	3124 „TW"	3413 „VS"	2726
3506	2222	**U**	3519	2088
3521	1941	1717 u	3519	2821
2537 „SZ"	1767 „TL"	1726	1726	3611 „W"
2944	1552	2366	2094	3187 Hausmarke
„ZS"	2757 „TN"	2371	3471	„W"
2945	3182	**III. V**	2201	3181 „W"
„ZS"	2758	3470		3277
	2158 „TS"	1719 V		3170
I		2372	1693 „W"	1804 „WB"
1692 „T"	1655	1516	2128 „W"	3207 „WB"
3202		2937 „VE"	2165	2134
2312 T	2747	3312 „VG"	1656 „W"	3091 „WH"
2820 T	1914			

No.	No.	No.	No.	No.
2025	1550	1509	3272	1750
2858	3042	1550 „R"	2105	
2027	1755 „PZ"	2166 „R"		1551
3303	2496	2818	1512	3214 „SFS"
2156 „PP"		3020	1513	2103
2319		2798 „R"	3611	3219 Anker „SH"
1560	1691 „Q"	2028	2828	1770
1580	1507	1905	1530	2069 S.H.&Co.
2237 „P·S·"	2817	2437 „RG"	1710	3180 „SI"
3077	1702	1633	1769	2745
3074	3019	2920	3529 „S"	2097
3071	3343	2732	2924	3029
2859		3386 „RT"	2051	3044
	R	2717	2126	2095
3575 „P ST"	3195 „R"		1811 „S.BS."	2928 „SL"
3061 „PT"	1547	**S**	1788	1587
3541 „PV"	3075	1538 „S"	2852	2554 „S OW"
3341	1534	1821 „S"	2853	1490
		2819 „S"		
		2428		

No.	No.	No.	No.
1938	1978 „WV"	3578 „XB"	**Z**
2434	3040 „WZ"	1924 „XE"	1695 „Z"
1564		3561	3357
		3560	
3308	1703 „X"		2829
3620 „WO"	2832	**Y**	1715
3503 „WR"	3009	1704	1720
2785	1712 X	1705	3010
3280	1855 X	1713	1714
	1694 x	2367	

No.
1758 „ZR"
1907
1758 „ZR" „ZB"
2944 „ZS"
2945 „ZS"
1751
1752
1764

Heavenly Bodies

Man

Lions

Misc. Mammals

Griffins, Eagles, Misc. Birds

2560	2563	2573	3298	2108
2559	2891 Ein Schwan	2574	1876 Flug	2117
2948	2841	2073	1878 Flug „IO"	2110
2562 Adler 49	2383	3186	1878 Flug „12"	2114
2561 Adler 16 45	2393	1541	2111 Raben-kopf	2115
	2382	2471	2118 Raben-kopf	2116
	2441	2352	2107	2113
			2109	2112

Marine Life and Water

| 2397 Schlange „PO" | 2167 Salm | 1529 / 2947 Krebs | 2283 | 2375 |

Plants

1860 Baum	2643	2648	2651	3179
3192 Baum-strunk	2647	2644	2650	2800 Klee-blatt
2606	2646	2481	2419 Klee-blatt
2290	2649	2481	2958 Dreiblatt 8
2653	2654	2652	2289	2489
	2645			

2491	2488	3487	2374	3165
2490	3279	2515	3172	2288
2492	2612	1644	2430	2293
2483	2613	1645	2744	2292
2484	2615	1643	3166 Rosette 2164	2168 Frucht
2485	2614	2213	3193	2031
2486	2616	1858	2163	1859
2487			3275	

Crowns, Scepters, and Arms

2713 Krone	2314	2380	2712	2974
1782	2713 Krone 13	2696	3416 Szepter	2971
2677	2691	2705	3263	2976
2676	2693	2704	3265	2972
2675	2692	2711	2970 Ritter-helm	2973
2313	2694	2701	2975	2969 3 Helme
	2695	2708		

| 1977 | 1666 | 1670 | 1665 | 3037 |

Implements

2398 Becher (?)	3163	2261	1841	2457
3159	3330	2258	1838	3417
2552 „Gekreuzte Äbtstäbe"	3325	2259	1837	2482 Sichel / 2445 Hammer „HB"
2986 Gekreuzte Schlüssel	3324	2260	1844	2193
3111 Gekreuzte Schlüssel	3326	2262	1843	3340 Schere
3107	3327			
3108	3335	3360	1842	3189 Hift-horn
3109	3331	3361	3398 Anker „CL"	3191 Hift-horn
3110	3328	2257	3219 Anker „SH"	3190 Post-horn
3112 Gekreuzte Schlüssel 12	3332		2414	2680 Hufeisen / 3034 Hufeisen, 1920
3337	3168	2892 Kessel-haken	1486	3380
3169	3359	3164 Anker	1488	1921
3339	3358	1840	1487	3160
	2256	1839	3157 Faß	

Architecture

1975 Architektur-marke	2335	2331	2328	2345
3194 Turm „HO"	2334	2336	2341	2356
2987 Tor-turm	2344	2329	2519	2340
3099	3373	2343	2339	2365
3100	2327	2342	2350	2355
3101	3376	2348	2351	2353
2600 Tor	2347	2349	3375	2354
1985	2330	2338	3374	

Crosses

2118 „F" Kreuz?	2159	2906	2145	2800
1943 Andreas-kreuz?	2905	3230	2147	2801
3402	2911	3229	2459	2804
3404	2908	2960	Kreuz	2802
1980	2914	2800	Krone	
3463 Kreuz	2904	2191	2810	2807

Trade Marks

Shields and Geometrical Forms

A

No.	Code		No.	Code		No.	Code		No.	Code		No.	Code
3638	„A"		4675	AK		4100	AR		4802	B		4952	„BW"
4410	A		4677	AL		3978	AS		4884	B		4391	BW
3772	A		4149	AL		4189	AS		3632	„B"		4950	„B W"
3631	„A"		4150	AL		4456	AI		3980	B		4450	BZ
3637	„a"		4660	„AM"		3656	„ASZ"		3797				
4540			4165			4050			3756				**C**
4438			4062	AP		4051			3971	„BG"		3774	C
4187	„AA"		4448			4164			3972	„BG"		3633	„C"
4535	ABE		4164			4112	BH					4698	„?C"
4228			3944			3907	A		4853	„BK"			C
4229			3924	A R		3982	AV		4021	BK		3839	
3644	„AD"		4065	A R		4487	„AV"		4445	B		4147	B
4697	„AG"		3925	„AR"		4637	XX		4792	BM		4567	CB
4531	AH		4903	„AR"		3920	IV		4339			4888	
	AI		4480	AR			**B**		4226	BF		4163	„CD"
3838			4778	AR		4582	„B"		3653			4347	
			4212	AR		4411	B		4770	BS		4471	„CDH"
			4099	AR		3773	B		4951	„B W"			

No.	Code		No.	Code		No.	Code		No.	Code		No.	Code
4916	CDH		4699			4066	„CS"		4403	B			(IIII)
4168	CE		4076	„CK"		4961	GS		3634	„D"		4542	
4804	„CE O"		4791	CK		4067	CS		3798				
4334	CFR		3929			4600	„CV"		4588	DB		4674	
3646	CGB		4596	„CK"		4361	CV		4700			4587	EB
4592	GG		4286	„CK"		4595	„CV"		3997			4308	F·F
4412	GG KEL		4079	„CL"		3861			3998			4500	EC P
3673	„CH"		4813	„CL W"		4975	„CW"		4490			4679	EE
4266	CH B		4532	CM		4331			4458	„D MB"		4074	„EH"
4117	GHc		4788	CM		4251			4033			3994	EK
4267	CH		4796	CM		3999			4467			3910	„EL"
4639			4330			4260	„CW"		4598	DS		4678	EL
4915			4192			4245			3984	„DS"		3951	EL
4324			4928			4261			4270	„DW"		4767	
4233	CK		4201			4648	CY			Vogel		4183	EM D
4259	C·K		4646			4982	„CZ"			**E**		4351	EP
			4386				**D**		3776	E		4654	ES
						3639	„D"		4620			4460	S·S
						3775	D						

F

No.	Code		No.	Code		No.	Code		No.	Code		No.	Code
3777	F		4309	FS		4284	„GDW"		3855	GP		3889	
3799	F		4421	FW		4918			4908	„GP"		4176	HA
4871			4420	FW		3647	GFS		4787	GP		4083	HDB
4599	„FB"		4419	FW		4314	CH		4262	GR		4085	HADR
4390	FDS		4422	HW		4313	CH		4049	„GS"		4084	HADE
3947			4870	„FWL"		4870			4819	„GS"		4929	HB
4854	„F.H."		4872			4166	„GHB"		4611	CS		3876	HB
4244	FH			**G**		4783	GB		4569	GS		4089	HB
4017	FH		4913	„G"		4932	„G"		3875	¢		4090	HB
3980	FH		4932	„G"		3875			4954	„GS D"		4091	HB
4458	FI		3778	G		3662	„G IN"					4092	HB
3660	FH		3662			3879				**H**		4917	
4175			4442						4493	„H"		4096	HB
4287	FIW		4333	GK					3779	H		4093	HB
4862	„FK"		4443						4435	„H"		4095	HB
4416	„FM"		4319	G					3835	H		4094	HB
4793	FM		4444									4056	H
4248	P		3922	„GB"								4774	HB
4931	„GC C"		4200	„GB"								3853	
4063			4202	GB									
4064	FF		4346	„GB"									
			4721	GM									
			4303	„G CG"		4293	GNB		4758				

No.	Code		No.	Code		No.	Code		No.	Code		No.	Code
3890	HB		4178	HG		4132	HL		4289	HN		4919	„HS"
4682	4HB		4350			4781	HZ		4371	HN		4111	„HS"
4057	HB					4782	HK					3685	„HS"
3995	BK					4645	„HM"		3655	B		4447	
4108	„HC"		4268	HH		4019	HM		4852	„HP"		4642	
4225	HC		4359	HH		3811	„HM"		4608			3969	ISI
4717	K					4644	„HM"		4638	HP		4937	„HT"
4282	HGH		4047	HH			HM					4059	H
4647	HK		4934	„HIB"		3862	„HM"		4354	HP		4060	H
4340	HP		4436	„HIK"		4643	HM		4861	PK		4223	„HV"
3645	HR		4491	HK		4534	HM		3932	HR		4058	HV
4185	HK		4454	HK		4694	M		4126	HR		4352	HV
4140	„HD"		4780	HK		4927	M		4137	„HR"		3641	H
4128	HD		4256	HL		4145	M		3955	HR		4655	Hul
3987	HE		3859	HL		4762	M		4133	HR		4138	HW
4187	HE		3942	HM					4156	„HR"		3811	M
4453	HF		4511	MR		4134	HR		4139	„HW"			
4221	HF		3981	M		4136	HR		4043	HW			
3905	H		4461	HMS		4720			4216	HWH			
4098	HG		4459	HMS									

No.	Mark	No.	Mark	No.	Mark	No.	Mark	No.	Mark
4041	HZ	4272		4905	„IE"	4288		4519	IMF
4018	HZ	4613	„IC"	4211	„I·F"	4288		4805	IMW
3931		4311		4304		4680	IHS	3672	JNB"
	I	4205	IC	4725		4273		4814	INP"
4309	„I"	4300	ICB	4107		4301		4298	INW
4672	„I"	4948	ICP	4306		4651		4574	IOS
3780		4501	„IFL"	4181	„IK"				
3836		4947	ICP	4364	IFSI	4120	JK	4143	IP
4552		4389		4193	IFT	4946	„IK"	4641	IP
4302	IAH	4650	ICS	4462	„IG"	4182	IK	4640	I·P
4859	IAK	4279	ICW	3926	G	4585	„JKOR"	4551	IP
4723	IAS	4122	ID	4935	Stern „IG"	3958	JL	3950	IP
4722	IAS	4962	ID	4291		3959	„IL"	4518	IP
4695	„IB"	4949		3659	„IGP"	4800	IA	4257	IP
3967	I B	4285		4533		4277		4785	IIK	4265	IPH
4789	IB	4553	IDS	3960	IH	4653	ILW	3904	„IR"
4795	IB	3991	IE	4360	„IH"	4469	„IM"	4806	IR
4597	„IB"	3992	IE	4238	IH	4464		4217	IR
3968	IB								

No.	Mark	No.	Mark	No.	Mark	No.	Mark	No.	Mark
4151	MM		N	3764	N	4356	O	4208	PB
3975	MM	3684		3758	N	4357	O	3952	PF
3976	MM			3768	„N"	4358		4110	PF
4008	„MN"	3686		3757	N	4318	OF	4790	PH
4505	„MP"	3687		3769		4214	OH	4862	„PK"?
4797	MR			3770		4029	NE	4863	PK
3962	MR			4014	IH	4372		4327		3863	„PL"
4981	R	3756		4075	NJ	4363		4242	„PM"
4129	RI	3784	„N"	3939	R	3756		3669	
3654	MR	3736	N	4106	NR	4842		4203	PR
4039	MS	3759		4759	NR		P	4449	
3652	MT	3763		3822	N	3786	„P"	4069	PS
4612	MV	3765	N	4014	ISI	4375	„P"	4070	PS
4610	MX	3761	N	4652	NTH	4393	„P"	4071	PS
4973	XX	3767	N					4478	
4973	„MWA"	3766	N	3785	„O"	3913		3933	
4280		3760	N	4914	„O"	3912		3934	
		3762		4355	O	4455		3935	
						4451	„PA"	4877	„PTS"

No.	Mark	No.	Mark	No.	Mark	No.	Mark	No.	Mark
4153	IR	4724	„ISS"	3813		4034	„LO"	3849	
4218	IR	3917		4271	K	4408	12LO	4148	MB
4086	IR	4798		4271	K	4179	LR	3804	·M·B·
3661	IR	4362	IV	3909		4142	„LT"	3806	MB
		4719				4177	LT	3993	MB
4665		4609	W	3782	„L"	3963		4097	MD
4154	IR	4799		3810		4186	IV	3744	„ME"
4307	IRK	4353	IWV	4328			M	3979	ME
4974	IS	4299	„IWW"	4329		3783	„M"	3979	„ME"
3986	IS			4505	„12L"	4659	„M"	3949	MF
3974	IS	3678	IZ	4310	LA	3658	M	3949	„MF"
4073	IS		K	4936	„LB"	4841	M	4463	MF
3985		4673	„K"	4476	„LD"	4812		4489	MF
4976	„ISB"	3781	K	4818		4760	M	4109	MH
4466	„ISG"	4666	K	4028	IH	4562	M	4488	MH
4465		4784	K	4885	LI	3846	„M"		
4963	ISM	4004	K	3668		4775		4452	
3643		3856	KB	3668	LK	3845		4037	MK
		3857	KB	4909					

No.	Mark	No.	Mark	No.	Mark	No.	Mark	No.	Mark
4061		3814		4275		3989	SR	4171	„TW"
4119		4387	„RZ"	3928		4657		4121	
			S	4118	SG	4930			
3787	„Q"	3789	„S"	4938	„SI"				U
4580	Q	4536	„S"	4104		3870		3791	„U"
		4537	„S"		I				
4629		4538	„S"	3790	„T"				V
		4509	„S"	4082		4670	T	3792	„V"
	R	4527		4105		4671	T	4481	„V"
4483		4803	S	3918	T	4794	V		
4484		4622		4470	„SIA"	4180	ID	4816	V
4482		4617		3943	SK	4417	„TE"	4432	
		4222		3756		4174	„TH"	4728	
4485		4526	S12	4676		4209	FJ	4731	
3788	„R"	4525	S12	3756		4933	„THD"	4733	
4020	„R"	4498	„SA"			4082	„TL"	4732	
		4236	„SB"	4446	SP	4246	„TR"	4735	
4702	R	4904	„SB"	3936		4081	S		
4232	RR	4227	SBF	3961	S	4207	S	4487	VA

4372 „VH"	4851	4881 „W 12"	4044	4960	
3906 „VK"		4022 WZ		4964	
4953 „VPT"	4801	4876 „13 W"			
4457	3635 „W"	4943	4024 WZ	3800	
	4517	4539 „WD"	4026 „WZ"	4768	
W					
3793 „W"	4253 „W"	3988	X	4769 Ž	
4870 „W"	4312	4206 ЭC			
4878 „W"	3670	4294 „W IW(?)"	3794 „X"	4958	
4169 „W"					
4332	3832	3966 WZ	Y	4965	
4955	4807	4428	3795 „Y"	4966	
	4188	3854	Z		
4855	3965	4305 „WS"	3796 „Z"	4255 „ZH"	
4867		4388 WS	3636 „Z"	4023 ZM	
		4402 „WV"	4959	4195 „Z M"	
4868	4584			4025	
4001	3956	4401	4957	4027 „Z M"	

Misc. Mammals

4437 Tier?	4630	4627	4901	4269				
4727	3964	4624		4516				
4379 Wolf	4701		4894	4515				
4383		4911	4900	4159				
	4510			4969				
4384	4625	4912	4897	4237				
4385	4618			4087				
4590	4615	4619	4899	4231				
4080	4616	4910	4898	4323				
4243	4623	4880 Stier-kopf	4219 Schaf	4365				
3824	4628	4902	4002	4263				
4321 Hirsch-stangen	4621		4895	4887				
4631	4626		4003					

Heavenly Bodies

4892 Halb-mond	4696	4197	3681	3880	
4508 Stern, Mond	4690	4220	3680	3884	
Ringe	3841	4718	3682	3818	
4509 Rose Halb-mond	4131	4040	3882		
	4130	4278	3880		
4006	3888	4250	3881	HICKEN	

Man

4283	4667	3828	

Lions

3665 Löwe?	4381	4315	4869	3921	
4376	4382	4821	4146	4968	
4337 Löwe					
4499	4856 Löwe	4504	3834	3675 Tatze	

Griffins, Eagles, Misc Birds

4486 Greif	4714	4710	4424	4326 Hahn	
4475 Adler		4705		3957	
4891 Adler	4716		4425		
4320 Adler		4708		4196	
4322 Adler	4715	4707	4336 Adler	4141	
4838		4706	4427	4247	
4522	4712		4882	4577	
4839	4523	4406	4971	4579	
4704	4713		4972	4578	
3677	4711	4407	4687 Schwanen-hals		
4524	4709	4423	4295	3871	

Marine Life

4101	4703	4492 Fische	4687 Muschel	3945	
4591		4167	4160	4005	

Plants

4235	4530	3817	3864	3927	
4135	4757	4756	3865		

Crosses

Trade Marks

Crowns, Scepters, and Arms

Implements

Shields and Geometrical Forms

Numbers

Architecture

411. Hans Waidely, 1606 or H. Waidli, 1603
412. Christoph Lencker, 1583-1613
419. Heinrich Winterstein, 1585-1634
423. Cornelius Erb from Genova, 1586-1618
428. Mathaeus Wallbaum from Kiel, 1590-1632
433. Bartholme Lotter, 1590-1606
434. Jeremias Nathan (Nathen), 1623
441. Georg Lang the older, 1620
442. perhaps Balthasar Grill, 1617
456. Johannes Lencker, 1616-1637 ?
464. Hans Jacob Bair, 1604-1628
465. perhaps David Eckirch, 1604-1613
477. Nicolaus Kolb, 1582-1621
479. Philipp (Jacob) Benner, 1615-1634
481. Tobias Leuckhardt, 1615-1632
484. Benedikt Engelschalk, 1623 or Bernhart Elsesser, 1634
492. perhaps Abraham Lotter, 1626
493. perhaps Tobias Kramer, 1634
494. Gabriel Schmidt, 1643
495. Lucas Neisser, 1657
499. Hans Andreas Anthoni, 1630 ?
503. Melchior Gelb, 1617
524. Gregor Leider (Linderer), 1673
526. Hans Peters, 1672 ? or Hans Christoff Petters, 1677
548. Johannes Mair, 1687
566. Johann Baptist Biller, 1683
584. Christoph Leipziger, 1678
586. Hans Ott(o), 1678 ?
587. David Bessmann, 1677 ?
589. David Jäger, 1661 ?
592. Johannes Miller, 1624 ?
595. Paul Höschel, 1664
597. Abraham Drentwett, 1666 ?
599. Joh. Pepfenhauser, 1681 or Joh. Priester, 1694
603. Heinrich Rott (Roth), 1683 or Hans Ramminger, 1676
606. Hohleisen, late 17. cent.
610. Johannes Scheppich, 1701
611. Heinrich Mannlich, 1659-1698
613. Peter Winter, 1651-1703
620. Georg Reischli, 1700
621. Johann (Hans) Jäger, 1669 or Jacob Jäger, 1674
632. Heinrich Eichler, 1708 ?

633. Caspar Riss von Rissenfels, 1712 ?
636. Hans Heinrich Hering, 1696 ?
638. Wolfgang John, 1685
639. Moritz Mittnacht, 1690 ?
641. Abraham Waremberger, 1704 ?
643. Adolf Gaap, 1695 ?
644. Heckel ?
651. Christoph Drentwett, 1705 ?
652. Philipp Kuesel, 1700
654. Hans Jacob Schech, 1692
655. Joh. Babtist Ernst, 1697
656. Hans Jacob Ernst, 1703
660. Samuel Schneeweiss, 1697 ?
685. Joh. Sigmund Schuch, 1715
689. Johann Wagner, 1725 ?
690-691. Michael Mayr, 1714
695. Hans Jacob Wildt, 1733
704. Johann Christoph Treffler, 1722
722. Philipp Jacob Drentwett, 1712 ?
726. Mattheus or Markus Wolff, 1716 ?
727. Ludwig Schneider, 1729 ?
729. Gottlieb Bauer, 1735 or Gabriel Besmann, 1735
731. Cornelius Poppe, 1723
732. perhaps Johannes Fassnacht, 1726
734. Joh. Phil. Schuch, 1733
756. Johann Zeckel, 1728
761. Samuel Wolffgang, 1737 ?
765. Peter Rams, 1737
773. Johann Heinrich Mannlich, about 1700
778. Philipp Stenglin, 1744
779. Johann Lukas Sigel, 1745
781. Andreas Wickhardt, 1728
784. Johann Matthäus Rem, 1707
788. Dominikus Saler, 1718
795. Johann Jacob Vogelhund, 1745
799. Johann David Schoap, 1751
801. Daniel Schaeffler, 1727
809-810. Elias Adam, 1745
814. Johannes Engelgrecht, 1748
816. Johann Christoph Laminet, **1705-1753**
817. Joh. Friedr. Bräuer, 1706-1753
836. Gottlieb Mentzel, 1709-1757
844. Joh. Jac. Bruglocher, 1710-1752
845. Jakob Lutz, 1747
860. Johann Wagenknecht, 1716-1752 ?
862. Joh. Erhard Heuglin 2nd, 1717-1757

867. Joh, Christoph Drentwett, 1749-1763
869. Franz Thaddaeus Lang, 1748-1773
872. Phil. Jakob Drentwett, 1718-1754
894. Joh. Ignaz Saler, 1727-1764
895. Johann Jabok Schoap, 1732-1766 ?
899. Franz Christoph Mäderl, 1747-1765
901. Joh. Jak. Baur, 1745-1774 ?
910. Bernhard Heinrich Weye, 1753-1782
911. Johann Leonhart Allmann, 1733-1775
912. Salomon Dreyer, 1761-1762
920. Abraham Winkler, 1736-1768
928. Friedr. Conrad Mittnacht, 1788
934-935. Johann Bartermann, 1741-1782 or Johann Busch, 1748-1794
936. Abraham Drentwett, 1741-1785 ?
941. Johannes Hübner, 1743-1776
950. Johann Georg Jaser, 1746-1760
955. Joh. Ph. Heckenauer, 1765-1794
956. Joh. Jacob Adam, 1762-1792
958-959. Johann Wilhelm Dammann, 1773-1784
965. probably Johann Becker, 1749-1761
967. Johann Christian Reinhardt, 1750-1772
968. Gottlieb Satzger, 1750-1783
971. Johann Karl Burger, 1750-1795
975-976. Georg Ignatius Bauer, 1764-1790
987. Christian Drentwett the younger, about 1800
994. Joseph Tobias He(r)zebik, 1788
1016. Caspar Xaver Stippeldey, 1766-1809
1018. Jos. Ant. Seethaler, 1788-1813 ?
1029. Lukas Römer, 1797-1819
1030. Karl Ferdinand Tautenhahn, 1781-1810 ?
1032. Johann Esaias Niggus, 1782-1818

AURICH

1064. 16. cent.
1065. 19. cent.

BADEN-BADEN

1068. 16. cent.
1069. 16.-17. cent.
1070. 17. cent.
1071. 10.-19. cent.
1072. 19. cent.

BAMBERG

1084. 16.-16. cent.
1085. about 1600

1086. 1618
1087. 1626
1088. 1639
1089-1092. 17.-18. cent.
1093. 18. cent.
1094. 18. cent.
1095-1096. beginning of 18. cent.
1097-1098. middle of 18 cent.
1099. end of 18. cent.
1100-1101. 18.-19. cent.
1102-1105. 18.-19. cent.
1106. 1830
1107-1108. 18. cent.
1109-1110. early 19. cent.

BAUTZEN

1140-1141. 18. cent.

BERLIN

1148. second half 17. cent.
1149-1150. first half 18. cent.
1151-1152. since 1735 or earlier ?
1153. since 1735 or earlier ?
1154-1158. second half 18. cent.
1159-1160. 18.-19. cent.
1161-1162. 19. cent.
1163-1164. 18.-19. cent., changing with the years or masters
1165-1169. 18.-19. cent., changing with the years or masters
1171. Daniel Männlich, 1676-1701
1199. Christian Lieberkühn, 1738-1764

BEUTHEN/ODER

1230. about 1732
1231-1232. about 1736-1770
1233. about 1775

BIBERACH

1235-1236. 17. cent.
1237. middle of 18. cent.
1238. middle of 18. cent.
1239-1240. 18.-19. cent.

BRAUNSBERG

1260. about 1684
1261-1262. about 1740
1236. late 18. cent.

BRAUNSCHWEIG

1276. end of 16. cent.
1277. 16.-17. cent.
1278. 17. cent.
1279. second half 17. cent.
1280. about 1680-1690
1281. end of 17. cent.
1282. about 1690
1283. about 1695
1284-1285. about 1695-1700
1286. about 1705
1287-1288. beginning of 18. cent.
1289-1290. about 1750
1291-1292. about 1790-1800
1313. Adam Wagner, 1675-1681

1315. Berendt Knop(f), 1686
1324. Andreas Seitz, 1692-1709 ?
1327. Herman Georg Mirus, 1699
1330. Gottfried Johann Boden, 1709

BREMEN

1342. 17. cent.
1343. about 1650
1344-1345. about 1690
1346. 17.-18. ? cent.
1347. about 1700
1348. about 1720
1349. about 1750
1350. about 1800
1351. 19. cent.
1358. M. H. Wilkens, founder of the business M. H. Wilkens & Sons, 1782-1869

BRESLAU

1365. from 1542 till 1553
1366. from 1553 till early 17. cent.
1367. early 17. cent.
1368. middle of 17. cent.
1369. second half of 17. cent., till after 1721
1370. from before 1737 till about 1740
1372. with 19 different variations, end of 17. cent., till 1842
1373. since about 1710
1375-1376. since 1843
1377. 1710-1712
1378. 1712-1721
1379. 1721-about 1727
1380. about 1727-1737
1381. 1737-1745
1382. 1746-1758
1383. after 1758-about 1760
1384. about 1761-1776
1385. 1776-about 1791
1386. 1839-1849
1387. 1849-1861
1391. Oswald Rothe, 1503-1522
1392. Andreas Heidecker, 1509-1533
1399. Hans Schönaw, 1567-1608 or Hans Strich, 1582-1616
1400. Augustin Heyne, 1571-1601
1401. Paul Nitsch, 1573-1609
1402. Joachim Hiller, 1573-1613
1404. Caspar Bendel, 1575-1599
1406. Veit Koch, 1580-1619
1407. Christoph Stimmel, 1584-1627
1408. Georg Hoffmann, 1586-1609
1410. Friedrich Schoenau, 1598-1627
1411. Caspar Pfister, 1598-1635
1413. Hans Volgnadt, 1605-1622

1414. Fabian Nitsch, 1602-1630
1421. Hans Jachmann, 1638-1685
1425. Christian Mentzel, 1668-1699
1426. Gottfried Heintze, 1673-1707
1428. Thomas Kuntze, 1683-1716
1429. Gottfried Heyner, 1682-1716
1430. Gottfried Körner, 1685-1722
1434. Christian Winckler, 1690-1706
1435. Gottfried Ihme, 1691-1737
1438. Christian Heintze, 1701-1732
1439. Tobias Schier, 1702-1733
1440. Carl Wilhelm Hartman, 1706-1729
1441. Michael Wissmar, 1715-1746
1442. Thomas Beyl, 1719-1758
1444. Johann Christoph Vogel, 1722-about 1742
1448. Benjamin Hentschel, 1732-1774
1449. George Kahlert the younger, 1732-1772
1451. Christian Kretschmer, 1734-1758
1455. Karl Friedrich Korok, 1835-1858

BRIEG (SILESIA)

1456. end of 16. cent.
1457. 16.-17. cent.
1458. 17. cent.
1459. since 1685 and 18. cent.
1460. about 1740
1461. about 1745
1463. Nickel Knobloch, 1578-after 1596

BRUSHSAL (BADEN)

1448. 17. and 18. cent.

BÜTZOW (MECKLENBURG-SCHWERIN)

1472. 16. cent.
1473. 17. and 18. cent.
1474. 19. cent.

BUNZLAU (SILESIA)

1478. about 1750

CHAM (BAVARIA)

1480. end of 17. cent.

CRAILSHEIM (WUERTTEMBERG)

1484. 17. cent.

DAGEBUELL

1486-1487. 17. cent.
1488. 17.-18. cent.

DANZIG (Free State)

1494. 17. cent.
1495. 17. cent.
1496. 17. cent.
1497. second half of 17. cent.
1498. 17.-18. cent.
1499-1500. 17. and early 18. cent.

INSPECTION MASTERS

1501. 1730, 38, 44
1502. 1731, 37
1503. 1732, 41
1504. 1734, 43, 47, 53
1505. 1735
1506. 1737 or 42, 46, 54
1507. 1740
1508. 1745, 49, 59
1509. 1748, 56, 62, 66
1510. 1752, 58, 64
1511. 1755, 61
1512-1213. 1757, 65, 69
1514. 1758, 64
1515. 1760.
1516. 1763, 67
1517. 1768, 72, 86, 90
1518. 1770, 74
1519. 1770, 74
1520-1521. 1771, 75, 79
1522. 1773, 77
1523. 1778, 82, 84
1524-1525. 1781, 85, 91, 95
1526-1527. 1789, 93, 97
1528-1529. 1792, 96, 1800, 04, 08
1530. 1799, 1803
1531. 1801, 05
1532-1533. 1814, 18, 19
1534. 1829-33, 36
1535. 1834, 35, 37-39
1536. 1840, 45, 50, 51
1537. 1841-44, 46-49
1549. Christian Paulsen I, 1630-1650
1556. Christian Schubert, 1644-1651
1557. Hans O p h a g e n, 1648-1701
1560. Peter Rohde 2nd, 1654-1677
1567. Ernst Kadau(w) 2nd, 1674-1690
1571. Jacob Beckhausen, 1678-1704
1572. Conrad Jacob Keseberg, 1679-1722
1594. Christian Pichgiel, 1681-1700
1575. Johann Rohde 2nd, 1684-1720
1578-1579. A n d r e a s Haidt, 1686-1721
1580. Peter Rohde 3rd, 1688-1717
1584-1586. Nathanael Schlaubitz, 1690-1726
1587. Siegfried Oernster, 1691-1735
1596. J o h a n n Gottfried Sclaubitz, 1 7 3 3 - 1766

DARMSTADT

1601. (16. till) 17. cent.
1602-1603. 17.-18. cent.
1604. about 1700
1605. about 1800
1606. 18.-19. cent.

1607-1608. 19. cent.
1609-1611. 18.-19. cent.

DEMMIN (POMMERN)

1620. "D with crown"

DESSAU (ANHALT)

1621. 17. cent.
1622-1623. 18. cent.
1624-1625. 18.-19. cent.
1626. 19. cent.
1627. 18. cent.
1628-1629. 18.-19. cent.
1630-1631. 19. cent.

DILLINGEN

1643-1644. first half of 18. cent.
1645. second half of 18. cent.
1646. Anton Simon Lang, 1723-1753
1647. Franz Lang, 1753-1785

DINGOLFING

1648. end of 17. cent.

DONAUWOERTH (BAVARIA)

1653-1653a. 16.-17. cent.
1654. 18. cent.

DRESDEN

1658. 16.-17. cent.
1659. 17. cent.
1660-1662. first quarter of the 18. cent.
1663-1664. 1722-1725
1665. 1730
1666. 1737
1676. 1739
1668-1670. middle of 18. cent.
1672-1678. third quarter of 18. cent.
1679-1680. end of 18. cent.
1681-1686. 19. cent.

DATE LETTERS

1687. 1702
1688. 1708.
1689. 1713.
1690. 1714.
1691. 1717.
1692. 1720.
1693. 1722
1694. 1723 or 1747
1695. 1725
1696. 1726
1697. 1728
1698. 1731
1699. 1737
1700. 1738
1701. 1739
1702. 1741
1703. 1747
1704-1705. 1748
1706. 1750
1707. 1757 ?
1708. 1760 ?
1709. 1761
1710. 1767
1711. 1768
1712. 1771
1713. 1772
1714. 1773

1715. 1773 ?
1716. 1785
1717. 1793
1718. 1808
1719. 1818
1720. 1822
1721. 1825
1722. 1826
1723. 1828
1724. 1829
1725. 1830
1739. Georg Mond, 1599-1623 ?
1751-1752. Zacharias Schlosser, 1624-1654 ?
1756. Jakob W a t z k y, 1641-1679 ?
1764. Zacharias Schlosser, 1646-1676 ?
1768. Niclas Bille, 1676-1687 ?
1773-1774. Johann M i c h a e l W i n c k e l - mann, 1690-1724 or Johann Michael Wecker, 1716-1749
1788-1789. Samuel Gaudig(ch), 1717-1759
1790. Christian Gottlieb Irminger, 1719-1749
1800. Carl Gottlieb Ingermann, 1 7 3 6 - 1774
1805-1808. Carl David Schrödel, about 1762
1812-1813. Friedrich Reinhard Schrödel, 1 7 5 6 - 1796
1814. J o h a n n Christian Neuber, 1752-1808
1815-1816. brothers Schrödel, about 1770
1817-1818. Gotthelf M o r i t z Hauptvogel, 1768-1810 ?

DUESSELDORF

1837-1838. 17. cent.
1839-1844. 17.-18. cent.
1845-1851. 18. cent.

DATE LETTERS

1852-1853. beginning of 18. cent.
1854-1855. 18. cent.

EINBECK

1874. first half 17. cent.

ELBERFELD

1880. end of 19. cent.

ELBING

1885. 1647-end of 17. cent.
1886. a b o u t 1657-1728, perhaps-1772
1887. 1698-1705
1888. 1705
1889. 1708-1744
1890. 1742
1891. 1743-1753
1892. 1792-1797, perhaps 1777-1811
1893. beginning of 19. cent.

1908-1912. Daniel Herrmann, 1730-1740

ELLWANGEN

1920-1921. 18. cent.

EMDEN

1925. 1474 ?
1926. 16. cent.
1927. about 1601, seems to be a spread eagle
1928. in connection with annual letter "C," 1603
1929. 1612
1930. 1632
1931. 1634
1932. 1645
1933. 1820

ENGEN

1946. 17. cent.

ERFURT

1948. 16. cent.
1949-1950. 16.-17. cent.
1951-1952. first half of 17. cent.
1953. second half of 17. cent.
1954. 17.-18. cent.
1955. first half of 18. cent.
1956. second half of 18. cent.
1960-1962. Erasmus Wagner, 1606-1645

ESSENS (HANNOVER)

1976. inspection mark

ESSEN (RHINE)

1977. 17. cent.

EUTIN

1980. 1623

FLENSBURG

1982. 1673
1983. 18. cent.

FRANKENSTEIN

1987. beginning of 18. cent.

FRANKENTHAL

1989. 17. cent.

FRANKFURT A/MAIN

1995. about 1500
1996-1999. 16.-17. cent.
2000-2002. 17. cent.
2003-2004. 17.-18. cent.
2005-2007. early 18. cent.
2008-2015. middle of 18. cent.
2016. end of 18. cent.
2017-2018. 1850-1860
2029. Georg (Jörg) Haas, 1588-1605
2031. Paul Birckenholtz, 1559-1633

2038. Caspar Birckenholtz, 1661-1689 ?
2046-2047. Philipp Heinrich Schonling, 1696-1755
2052-2053. Joh. David Griebel, 1705-1744

FRANKFURT / ODER

2072. 17.-18. cent.
2073. 1772

FREIBERG (SILESIA)

2078. 1562
2079. end of 16. and beginning of 17. cent.
2080. 1654
2081. 1658
2082. 1660-1667
2083. 1668
2084. 18. cent.
2085. middle of 18. cent.
2086. 18.-19. cent.
2097. Samuel Klemm, 1644-1678

FREIBURG (BREISGAU)

2106. 1466
2107. about 1528
2108-2110. 16. cent.
2112. 1607
2113. 1609
2114. 17. cent.
2115-2116. 17.-18. cent.
2117. 18. cent.
2119. 19. cent.
2134. Wilhelm Feuerstein, 1883 with standardmark 13

FREISING

2136. end of 17. cent.
2137. 18. cent.

FRIEDEBERG near AUGSBURG

2145. 16. cent.
2147. 16. cent.

FUERTH

2151. 16. cent.
2152. 18. cent.
2153. 19. cent.
2154. control mark
2157. J. Rimonim, first half of 18. cent. ?

FULDA

2159. beginning of 18. cent.

GANDERSHEIM

2162. second half of 18. cent.

GEISLINGEN

2163. 17.-18. cent.
2164. middle of 18. cent.

GIENGEN

2170. 1745

GLATZ

2172. 18. cent.

GLOGAU

2174. 17. cent.

SCHWAEBISCH-GMUEND

2177. 16.-early 18. cent.
2178-2179. about 1720-about 1788
2180. about 1740
2181. about 1762-1786.
2182. about 1791
2183-2186. beginning-middle of 19. cent.
2187-2190. 18.-19. cent.
2195. Joseph Fischer, 1699-1728

GNOIEN

2213. 18. cent.

GOERLITZ

2215. 16. cent.
2216. 17. cent.
2217-2218. 18. cent.

GOSLAR

2228. till 1782
2229. after 1782

GOTHA

2233. 17. cent.
2234. about 1688
2235. about 1689
2236. about 1701

GRABOW

2248. inspection mark

GREIFFENBERG

2251. 1794

GUESTROW

2252. end of 17. till middle of 18. cent.
2253. second half of 18. cent.

GUTTSTADT

2255. 18. cent.

HALBERSTADT

2256. middle of 17. cent.
2257. 1697
2258-2260. early 18. cent.
2261-2262. middle of 18. cent.
2263-2264. date letters late 17.-18. cent.
2266. master mark with changing annual letter
2267. master mark, 1697
2269. master mark
2273. master mark, 1709

SCHWAEBISCH HALL

2275. second half of 16. cent.
2276-2279. 17. cent.

2803. 1754-1761
2804. 1760-1772
2805. 1760-1770
2806. 1780-1790
2807. 1784-1786
2808. 1788-1800
2809. 1800-about 1830
2810. for more than 6 oz. silver, only 1815
2811. about 1830-1860
2812. 19. cent.

Annual letters

2813. 1693
2814. 1694
2815. 1696
2816. 1703
2817. 1704
2818. 1705
2819. 1706
2820. 1707
2821. 1709
2822. 1713
2823. 1714
2824. 1715
2825. 1740
2826. 1742
2827. 1747
2828. 1754
2829. 1761
2830. 1766 or 1772
2831. 1773
2832. 1784
2833. 1788
2834. 1818
2835. 1843
2846. Andreas Meyer from Nuremberg, 1608-1647
2847-2848. Paul Eckloff, 1612-1646
2854-2855. Lorenz Hoffmann from Nuremberg, 1659-about 1684
2856-2857. Johann (Hans) Meyer, 1662-1688
2858-2859. Peter Schoenermark, 1665-1703
2860-2861. David Doehring, 1670-1696
2862-2863. Peter Andreas Haendel (Hendel), 1671-1699
2863-2865. Otto Schwerdtfeger, 1685-1713
2868. Christian Friedrichs, 1688-1708
2869. Michael Christian Hetsch 1st, 1695-1721
2870. Johann Daniel Tamnau 1st, 1696-1732
2877-2878. Andreas Junge 1st, 1710-1757
2879-2881. Christian Leo, 1734-1771
2884. Christoph Philipp Hartung, about 1777-1800
2885-2888. Johann Leopold Kaewerstein, 1790-1812

KONSTANZ

2900. about 1557
2901-2905. 16.-17. cent.
2906-2909. early 17. cent.
2910-2911. middle of 17. cent.
2912-2913. end of 17. cent.

2914-2917. 18. cent.
2918-2919. 19. cent.

KULMBACH

2950-2951. 16.-17. cent.

LANDSBERG

2960. 17.-18. cent.

LANDESHUT

2966-2967. 18. cent.

LANDSHUT

2969. 15. cent.
2970. middle of 16. cent.
2971. 16. cent.
2973. 1723
2973. 1751
2974-2975. middle of 18. cent.
2976. end of 18. cent.
2982. Joseph Ferdinand Schmid (1), 1741-1790
2983-2984. Martin Spitzelberger, end of 18. cent.
2985. Caspar Bettinger (Pettinger), 1780-1794

LAUBAN

2986. inspection mark

LEER (EAST FRESLAND)

2989. end of 18. cent.

LEIPZIG

2990-2991. 16. cent.
2992. 16. perhaps 17. century too
2994-2996. 17. perhaps 18. century too
2997. 17.-18. cent.
2998-2999. early 18. cent.
3000-3003. 18. cent.
3004. end of 18. cent.

DATE LETTERS

3005. 1587-89
3006. 1588-90
3007. 1589-91
3008. 1597-99
3009. 1626-28
3010. 1627-29
3011. 1635-37
3012. 1641-43
3013. 1650-52
3014. 1656-58
3015. 1662-64
3016. 1668-71
3017. 1675-77
3018. 1682-84
3019. 1692-94
3020. 1693-95
3021. about 1711
3022. about 1725
3032. Elias Geier, 1589
3038. Andreas Kauxdorf, 1618-1669
3039. Melchior Lauch, 1622-1665
3042. perhaps Peter Richter, 1633

3043. Augustus Richter, 1633
3044. Sebald Krumbholz, 1634-1656
3045. Hans Scholler, 1642
3049. master mark, 1800
3053. Gottfried Schmidt, 1667-1681
3054. Joachim Krumbholz, 1669
3066. Johann Paul Schmidt, 1683-1703
3084. perhaps Andreas Schroeder, 1700
3085. Paul Gottfried Haussmann, 1732

LEUTKIRCH

3099. 16. cent.
3100-3101. 17. cent.

LIEGNITZ

3107. 16. and 17. cent.
3108. early 17. cent.
3109-3110. end of 17. cent.
3111. 17.-18. century (crossed keys in a square)
3112. about 1720 (crossed keys with 12)

ANNUAL LETTERS

3113. 1729 ?
3114. 1730
3115. 1731

LUDWIGSBURG

3129-3130. 19. cent.
3131. 19. cent.
3132. date letter

LUDWIGSLUST

3135. 19. cent.

LUEBECK

3137. 15. cent.
3139. 1501
3140. 1507
3141. early 16. cent.
3142. 1540
3143. middle of 16. cent.
3144. second half of 16. cent.
3145. 16.-17. cent.
3146. 1622
3147. 1631
3148-3151. middle of 17. cent.
3152-3153. 18. cent.
3154. 1828-1831
3155. 1831-1834

LUENEBURG

3232-3234. 15.-16. cent.
3235-3238. first half of 16. cent.
3239. middle of 16. cent.
3240. second half of 16. cent.
3241-3244. second half of 16. cent.
3245-3248. 16.-17. cent.
3249-3250. about 1650
3251. beginning of 17. cent.

3252-3254. beginning of 19. cent.
3255. 1790-1828
3256-3257. 19. cent.

MAGDEBURG

3293. 1622
3294. 1666.
3295. 1667
3296. end of 17. cent.
3297. early 18. cent.
3298. 17.-18. cent.
3299-3300. end of 17. cent.

MAINZ

3324-3325. 16. cent.
3326. 17. cent.
3327. late 17. cent.
3328. early 18. cent.
3329-3330. 1761 and later.
3331. 1765-1769
3332. 19. cent.
3333-3334. 19. cent.
3335. mark of the arch-bishop

MANNHEIM

3357. 17.-18. cent.
3358. 1717
3359. 1727
3360. 1737-1766
3361. 1775

MARIENBURG

3373. 17. cent.
3374. 17.-18. cent.
3375. 17. cent. ?
3376. 19. cent.

MARIENWERDER

3380. 18. cent.

MARKDORF

3381. 17. cent.

MEININGEN

3384. 1688

MEISSEN

3387. inspection mark

MEMMINGEN

3389-3390. middle of 16. cent. perhaps earlier
3391-3392. 17. cent.

MERGENTHEIM

3402. inspection mark, time not sure
3403. about 1700
3404. late 18. cent.

MERSEBURG

3408. 1661
3409. 18. cent.

MUEHLHAUSEN

3417. 1618

MUENCHEN

3439. 15.-16. cent.
3440. 16.-17. cent.

3441-3443. second half of 17. cent.
3444-3447. about 1700
3448-3452. early 18. cent.
3453. 1742
3454. 1752
3455. 1754
3456. 1760
3457. 1762
3458. 1769
3459. 1773
3460. 1784
3461. 1795
3462. 1800-1820
3463. 1815-1822
3465. 1820-1835
3467. 1835-1850
3468. 1840-1860
3507. Franz Kessler, 1664-1717
3516. Johann Georg Oxner (1), 1677-1712
3533-3534. Joseph Grossauer, 1718-1755, perhaps Ignaz Gruenewaldt, 1745-1764
3567. Ignaz Franzowitz, 1765-1813

MUENSTER

3593-3594. 16. cent.
3595-3596. 17. cent.

NAUMBURG

3623. 16.-17. cent.
3624-3625. 17. cent.
3626. 1684
3627-3630. 18. cent.

ANNUAL LETTERS

3631. A 1700
3632. B 1701
3633. C 1702
3634. D 1703
3635. W 1720
3636. Z 1723
3637. 1724
3638. 1748
3639. 1749

NEISSE

3648. 1604
3649. 1610-1614
3650. about 1700
3651. 1742

NEUSTADT on the HARDT

3666. 18. cent.
3667. 19. cent.

NEUSTADT on the SAALE

3671. about 1750

NOERDLINGEN

3677. 17. cent.

NORDEN
(PROVINCE HANNOVER)

3680-3681. 18.-19. cent.
3682. 19. cent.
3683. 19. cent.

NORDHEIM

3684. 1660

OLD-NUREMBERG

3686. inspection mark
3678. about 1600

NUREMBERG

3757. 1550-1600
3758-3759. 1550-1650
3760. 1600-1660
3761. 1600-1700
3762-3763. 1600-1700
3764. 1640-1675
3765-3766. 1650-1700
3767. 1700-1750
3769. 19 cent., earlier
3770. 19. cent., later
3771. 19. cent.

Assayer marks

3772. 1766-perhaps 1769
3773. 1769-1773 ?
3774. 1773-1776 ?
3775. 1776-1780 ?
3776. 1780-1783 ?
3777. 1783-1787 ?
3778. 1787-1790 ?
3779. 1790-1794 ?
3780. 1794-1797 ?
3781. 1797-1800 ?
3782. 1800-1804 ?
3783. 1804-1808
3784. 1808
3785. 1808-1811 ?
3786-3796. early 19. cent.
3797-3800. middle of 19. century and perhaps also later
3801. 19. cent.
3839. Christoph Jamnitzer, 1592-1618
3856-3857. Kaspar Bauch, 1541-1583
3878. Christoph Lindenberger, 1546-1580
3880. Christoff Ritter (le) 1st, 1547-1598
3881. Christoff Ritter (le), 2nd, 1577-1616
3882. Jeremias Ritter, 1605-1646
3899-3900. master mark, 17. cent.
3912-3913. Paulus Dulner, 1552-1596
3919. Caspar Widmann, 1554-1590
3923. Jacob Froehlich, 1555-1579
3928. Erhard Scherl, 1556-1593
3962. Martin Rehlein, 1566-1613
3966. Wolff Loescher, 1568-1591
3969. Hannss Straub, 1568-1610
4002-4003. Hans Petzold, 1578-1633
4004. Heinrich Jonas, 1579-1605
4017. Friedrich Hillebrandts, 1580-1608
4029. Nicolaus Emmerling, 1582-1606
4031-4032. Hans Keller, 1582-1609
4033. Eustachius Hohman, 1682-1612
4054-4055. Hannss Beutmueller, 1588-1622
4070-4071. Peter Sigmundt, 1608-1624

STADTAMHOF
4573. 1767

STETTIN
4577. 16.-17. cent.
4578. 18. cent.
4579. gold 18. cent.
4580. 18. cent.

WERNIGERODE and STOLBERG
4590-4591. 18. cent. (stag for Stolberg, fish for W.)

STRALSUND
4593-4594. 17. cent.

STRAUBING (BAVARIA)
4602. tin (1614)
4603-4606. second half of 16. cent.
4607. middle of 18. cent.

STUTTGART
4615. end of 16. cent.
4616. middle of 17. cent.
4617. end of 17. cent.
4618-4619. about 1700
4620-4621. about 1700-1760
4623-4624. 18.-19. cent.
4625-4629. 19. cent.
4632-4635. 19. cent.

SUHL
4657-4658. 17.-18. cent.

TILSIT
4663. 18. cent.
4664. beginning of 19. cent.

TORGAU
4670. 16.-17. cent.
4671. 17. cent.
4672-4673. 17. cent.

TREBNITZ
4681. 17. cent.

TUEBINGEN (WUERTTEMBERG)
4690. 16.-17. cent.
4691. beginning of 17. cent.
4692. 17. cent.
4693. 18. cent.

TUTTLINGEN (WUERTTEMBERG)
4701. about 1660
4702. about 1660

UEBERLINGEN (BADEN)
Inspection marks
4704-4706. end of 16. cent.
4707-4709. 16.-17. cent.
4710-4713. 17. cent.
4714-4716. 18. cent.

ULM
Inspection marks
4728-4729. 16. cent.
4730. 16.-17. cent.
4731-4736. 17. cent.
4737-4744. 17.-18. cent.
4745-4752. 18. cent.
4784. Johann Adam Keinlin the older, 1651-1691 ?
4787. Georg Preg, 1658-1691

URACH
4816. about 1700
4817. 17.-18. cent.

VELBURG
4821. 18.-19. cent.

VERDEN
4823. 17. cent.

VILLINGEN
4838. 15. to 16. cent.
4839. 18. cent.
4840. 18. cent.

WAREN
4851. 18. cent.

WEILHEIM
4857. 17.-18. cent.
4858. 18. cent.

WEIMAR
4867-4868. 17. cent.
4869. end of 17. cent.

WERTHEIM
4882. about 1660
4883. 19. cent.

WESEL
4887. 16. and also 17. cent.

WISMAR
4893. end of 16. cent.
4894. beginning of 17. cent.

4895. 1694, probably since 1686
4869. end of 17. cent.
4897. beginning of 18. cent.
4898. about 1730-1748
4899. about 1736-1746
4900. middle of 18. cent.
4901. end of 18.-beginning of 19. cent.
4902. 19. cent.

WITTENBERG
4906. middle of 17. cent.

WOLFENBUETTEL
4910. 1668.
4911. 17. cent.
4912. 17.-18. cent.
4913. 1707
4914. 1714.

WORMS
4921-4922. 16.-17. cent.
4923. 17. cent.
4924-4925. 17. to 18. cent.

WUERZBURG
4939. early 18. cent.
4940-4942. 18. cent.
4943. early 18. cent.

WURZEN
4955. 18. cent.

ZERBST
4957. 1696
4958. about 1700
4959. 1723
4960. 1752

ZITTAU
4964. 1710
4965. 1731
4966. about 1750

ZWEIBRUECKEN
4968. 18. cent.

ZWICKAU
4971. 16.-17. cent.
4972. 17. cent.

FRAUSTADT
4979-4980. 17.-18. cent.

A

5257 „A"
8176
8181
8319 „A"
8321
8333
8340
9520
9115
5007
5006
5363
9597 „A"
7217
7877
7880
7863
5100
9500

5060
9534
8710
6016
5968
7501
8592
7111
7175
7187
7201
7219
7220
8763 „A" x

6086 „A"
6128 „A"
6174 „A"
6791 „A"
6453
6455
7633
6290 „A"
6449
6459
6461
6463
9454
6027 „A"

6353 „A"
5805
8722
6527
6357
6538
6383
6511
6396
6521
5553
5961
6470
6502
5160

6369
6544
6527
6538
6511
6521
6472
6423
6490

6474
6495
6451
6515
6534
6506
6479
6499
5161 „A"
6292 „A"
7859

7860
7861
7862
6555
7963 „AI"
7962 „AI"
5004
5005
7873
9240 „A 6"
9241 „A 6"
9264 „A 7"
9265 „A 7"
9306 „A 8"
9307 „A 8"
9382 „A10"

5960 „A" 87-
6084 „AA"
9154
6236
6232
7246
7892
6084 „AB"
8621 „AB"
9585 AB
5733 „AB"
7770
7233
7420
6686
6026

6969
7084 ABD
9063
7085
ABD
9499
8883
7518
7075
6629 „AC"
9094
6096
5792 „ACB"
5788 „ACR"
7358 „A R C"
7950

5495 „AD"
7959
5785 „AD"
5811 „AD"
7918
5417
5468 „A D"
7945
DOMANEK
6704
5642 „AE"
5440
8032
„A" „Ev(O)RA" „7"
7293
8808 „AF"
5415 „AF"
6781 „AF"

5531 „A F"
7930
9386 „AF K"
5451 „AG"
7351 „AH"
9507 AH
8824 „AH"
7636
8366 1722
5815 „AI"
7961 „AI"
7675
6666
9248 „AI A"
6628 a) „AIV"
6693

8798 „AK"
7818 AK
9450 AK
9331
8609
8671
ÂKERMAN
7768
7767
8397 AL
9079
5169
5975 „AM" „G"
8845 „A MOLL"
5679 1769
5720 „A N"
5080
9154
6487
8659 ALM
9157 Â Lopcz

6278
8846 AM
5768 „AM"
8623
5979
5974 „AM"
7336
A: MANZ
5958
5577
5682 „AR 84"
5832| 8876|
6687 „ANC"
5991|-5992|„ANGERS"

8820 „Annoni"
8653 „AO"
5692 „AP"
8709
7405 AP 82
9176 Â PE EZ
7337
7281
AQVS
8710 y

7421
7236
5983
8718 ASB
6668 A S N
8672 „A. STAFHELL"
8676 „ÂSTRÖM"
9528
8710 „AT"
5646 „AT"
5472
7887
7082 „AΘΕΝΑΙ"

B

7889
7890
7891
7283
7711
7711
7721
9463
7893
7894
6759
6760
6458
7895
6760
8644
7819

8364
6277 AW/I
5964
8182
8188
8341 „B"
6344
5548
7107
7194
5242
7167
7164

5362 B
5554 B
8343 B
7502 B
5366 B
6063
6076
7176
7161
5549
7215
7341 „B"
8748 „B"
8843 „B"
9327 „B"
9328 „B"
5295 „B"
7749 „B"
6041 „B"
8027 „B"

8026 „B"
9530 B
6397
6859
6855
6424
5174
5172
5176
6054 „B"
5194 „B?"
5202 „Bet..."
6770
9234
6340

6042 „B"
8789
8790
8791
8783
8784
8785
8786
8787
8788
7481
9429
7569
9323

C

D

E

9324 · 5535 „B D" · 9075 BNB · 9403 C · 5273 · 6319 · 6757 · 6744 · 8593 · 6938

7836 „B 4" · 5654 „D B H" 1708 · 7841 · „C" · 5637 · 7205 · 6698 · 7949 · 9523 · 6139 · 6425

5376 „BA" · 9135 BER · 6055 BOR · „C" · 8220 8222 8228 · 7049 „C" · 9599 · CLE · 9473 · 7504 D · 9263 „D 1"

9101 BA · 8684 „BERGS" · 7478 „B P?" · 8271 „C" · 7070 „C" · 5607 CL MW · 9196 · 6223 6268 „D" · 9305 „D 2"

9100 BR · 7361 „BERS" · 7784 BP · 8383 · 7834 „C" · 5779 „CM" · 5105 · 6850 „D" 7986 · 9381 „D 4"

9104 BR · 8654 „BFR" · 9538 BP · 8390 „C" · 7837 „C" · 5134 · 5678 · 7989 „D" · 7359 „DA"

9102 BA · 6072 · 7470 · 9325 „C" · 8749 „C" · 7511 CM · „C.WER" · 8750 „D" · 5656 „D B" 1688

9105 BAR · 8838 · 7573 BHP · 7195 · 9326 „C" · 7470 CHM · 7362 „COZ" · 9477 CZ LTD · 6939 · 5663 „D B" 1708

9103 ✠BAR · 8951 „BH" · 7771 BRE VIG · 6005 SH G · 5715 „C P" · 7254 „CP" · 6315 „D" ·

9098 · 9246 BI · 9456 · 5364 C · 6291 „C" · 5778 „CMF" · 7617 CP · **D** · 6356 · 6974 DB

BARDA · 8606 BI · 6250 · 7739 C · 7776 „C" · 5776 CM · 8726 „C·P·A" · „D" · · 5410 „D B"

9096 ✠BAROK · 5133 BK · 9123 · 5056 C · 7777 „C" · 7019 „C R" · 6678 „D" ·

„BARK NONA" · 6084 „BI" · · 6972 C · 8031 „C" · 5777 CMF · 5509 CR · 5635 „D" · 5319 · 8082

9097 · 6768 · 9090 BV · 6109 · 8227 8393 „C" · 9577 C · 5331 „C R" · 5272 · 5507 · 5404 „DC"

7479 BB · 5132 „BK" · 9371 BW · 8390 · · 9088 „CM K" · 5571 CR · 7160 · · 6399 · 8915 „DCC"

7470b · 6034 „BK" · · 5550 · 6384 · 9575 CMM · 9483 · 7170 D · 5071 · 7958 DD

7477 „BC" · 5401 „BM" · 7765 B W · 5097 C · 6398 · 6252 CMPL · 7280 CR · 9239 „D" · 9909 „DD"

6059 · 8885 „BM" · · 9440 „C" · 6094 · 8074 CMV · 5638 CRO · 7600 D · 5075 · 5773 „DE"

7503 C · · 7939 CN · 7729 C3 · 6956 · 6206 · 8604

9324 ... 5551 D · 6202 · 8349

6090 · 9131 CASTE · 8221 „CC" 8385 · 9133 CERD · 7179 · 5402 DFL · 7938 · 7810 „E" · 7206 · 7051

5200 · 9330 u. 7894 · 6045 „OC" · 9181 SBD · 7743 · 9288 DG · 7285 DL · 8189 bis 8192 „E" · 5505 · 6946

8392 · · 6044 „OC" · 9180 SBS HUC · 8018 CIB · 9497 · 5736 „DO" · 8322 8347 8352 · 7188 · 6412

8393A · 8895 CB · 8384 · · 6628 · 7411 D.G. · „DOUBLE" · · 9404 E · 6426

5277 O · 8435 ✱CB✱ · 6044 · 8388 „CG" · 6279 CI M · 8350 DH · 5134 „DP" 5675 „DP" 1747 · 7211 · 5973 6010 „E" ·

6293 „C" · 8939 · 6152 · 6669 CG · 8984 CG · 6986 · 5659 DSK 1720 · 5002 · 6050 „E" 6194 · 7567

9276 · 7248 CB · · 5734 CGB · 5752 „CK" · 6987 · 5660 „DSK" 1720 · 5367 · 6245 „E" 6828 · 7811

6804 „C 5" · 8358 B · 5821 „C.C.T" · 9548 CGM · 9513 CK · 8617 · 5406 „DT" · 7976 „E" · 7977 7978 · 7971

6192 „C 6." · · 6674 „CD" · 5681 „C H" · 9550 CL · 9073 DWV · 5636 DUC · 7640 · 6947 · 7344 „E 1"

9252 „C 7" · 7476 · 8922 CD · 7527 CH · 8013 CL · 6991 DTH · 7522 DVH · 8034 „E" · 7789 „E 3"

9253 „C 7" · 7289 CB · 9054 CD · 7921 CH · 8014 CL · 6992 · 6124 DW · 5052 E · 5072 · 9581 EA

7775 CG · 6650 · 8944 CD · 9050 „CH" · 7773 · 6993 · 8836 DW · 7168 E · 5552 · 9446 EB

7876 „CA" · · 7526 CDEY · 7288 CH · 7581 · 5676 DH 1742 · 6122 DW · 7505 E · · 7383

9130 CAPO · 8610 CB · 6092 · 9088 · 9525 · 5482 „D I" · 7845 DW · 5523 E · 6400 · 7387

9187 CAMPOS · 8375 · 9142 · 9072 CLOD · 9588 · 6135 · 9126 „DX" · 5845 · 5771 „EG"

6710 · 6779 „CC" · CB RONA · 7635 · 9281 · 5197 DJC · **E** · 5046 · 6947 · 7290 EG

5843 6442 „E" · 7763 DK · „E" · 7216 · 7055 · 8953 „E? GO"

7937 · 9522 C

No.	Mark / Label
5324	„EH"
6120	EH
8351	
8840	
8841	„EK"
8812	„EL"
5384	„EM"
8998	EMG
9195	EN 3150
6019	
6015	
6684	EPB
6117	„ES"
8625	„ES"
9256	„ES"
7330	
9095	ESTOR GA
9514	
5842 / 6442 / 7414	„ET"
8098	„ET"
6614	ET
6958 A / 6958 B	„ET"
5908	ET
5909	ET
6957	„ETR"
8033	EV
9193	
8839	„EW"
8344	EW
8665	„EWS"
5889	„EXP" 583 M
	F
	„F"
	„F"
	„F"
5614	F
5365	F
6002	F
9468	F
7218	F
5610	
5609	
5553	
5611	
5612	
8420	F
8394	F
6401	
5472 A	
5066	
6413	
8597	
9304	„F 1"
7364 A / 7988	„F"
8751	„F"
9238	„F"
9242	„F"
9243	„F"
6955	
6954	
5399	„F"
6346	„F"
9553	
6370	
6360	
7368	F
9308	„F 1"
9380	
9391	„F 3"
9262	„F 4"
8650	„FB"
8796	„FB"
8884	„FB"
9089	
7302	„F·B N·D"
6669	„FC?"
6709	„FC"
6153	

No.	Mark / Label
6799	
6795	
8036	
6427	
8872	„G" Schlüsselbart(?)
8775	„G" Schlüsselring
9598	
7823	„G 2"
7824	„G 2"
9216	„G 3"
9217	„G 3"
7356	„GA"
6737	„GA G"
5831	Garni
5661	„GB"
7310	GB
7389	
7408	GBAC
7388	G.B.S.
7242	GC
5396	„GC"
7943	GCM
7807	„GD"
8941	
5387	„GL"
5394	„GD"
5388	„GD B"
7410	GDB
7407	GC
7392 / 7356	„GM"
7469 B	
6663	G+M
8924	
6536	„GP"
7470 B	
9132	
7925	G
5123	
8950	
8983	„GI S"
7307	GK
9481	
6189	
5409	
5408	„GL"
6158	
6971	
7746	„GR KEUR"
8858	
6771	„GRM"
8641	GS
9595	GS
7935	GS
7847	
7868 / 7869	
9311	
8954	
8795	GT
7480	GV
8787	
5662	„GVH"
5746	GH
7791	„H"
7099	„H"
7812	„H"
8206 / 8213 / 8215 / 8367 / 8371 / 8372 / 8374	„H"
6001	H
7196	H
7212	H
7574	H
8369	HH
5437	H
5425	H
8370	„H"
8587	H
8594	H
8360 B	H

No.	Mark / Label
6629	FC
5714	„FCF"
5719	„FCM"
5718	FCI
7347	„FF"
8796	„FF"
5664	FF 1719
5198	„FG"
6482	„FH"
5324	„FH"
5721	„FH G"
8645	„FHK"
9569	F·K
9124	„F(I)"
6691	FJ
5288	
8855	„F?IB?"
8965	„FIR"
9374	FK
5381	F·K
7286	FK
7924	FL
7271	FL
7301	FLHB
5389	„FM"
9587	„FM"
7940	FO
9197	
5666	F OW
5667	F OW 173?
7425	FP
6681	FPH
8071	
	„F.P.H."
7885	FR
7886	FR
9127	„FRA SID"
8969	„FRT"
8628	FS
7418	F·T
6658	FGT
5534	„FV"
7927	FV
	G
7799	„G"
7967	„G"
8356	„G"
8198 / 8203	„G"
7601	G
7687	
6276	G
8037	„G"
7801	„G"
5053	
7169	G
7109	G
9551	G
9487	G
6162	G
5472	G
5492	G
7174	G
7802 A	„G"
7802 B	„G"
8752 / 8778	„G"
8753	„g"
7797	
7801	„G"
8359	„G"
6347	
8204	„G"
5269	
6358	
5073	
5271	
6371	
5067	

No.	Mark / Label
7162	h
8216	„h"
8214	„h"
6033 / 6101 / 6167 / 6806 / 6879 / 6962 / 7800 / 7803 / 7805	„H"
5226	
6372	H
6385	H
6361	H
6402	H
5074	H
7263	H
6842	
6838	
6428	
7816	„H 1"
7790	„H1"
7817 A	„H 1"
7345	„H 2"
7346	„H 2"
9259	
6674	„HA"
6767	„HA"
6766	„HA"
7266	
6685	
6674 B	
7267	H·A
5818	„HA"
8363	HAB
7624	„HAD?"
5820	„HB"
9070	HB
8084	HB
5135	
8016	HCB
7623	HCB V
5329	„HD"
5122	HD
9466	
8988	H·EH
7993	HFISIG
5880	„HF"
6153	„HF"
8837	
	HF
7261	HG
7309	HH
5787	„HHG"
9603	HM
5232	
9049	H
9048	H
9505	H
8821	HF
9052	HIH
8952	H
5743	HIS
8685	„HK"
9298	HK
8615	HK
6040	HK
8800	„HL"
9515	HL
5582	„HLH"
9556	HLS
8611	„HM"
6240	„HM"
7514	HM
9495	HM
9335	HR
8433	„HN"

Upper-left section

No.	Mark	No.	Mark	No.	Mark	No.	Mark	No.	Mark
8637	„HN"	7250	HS	7740	—	6348	—	6717	IAR
5148	—	9384	„HT"	8218	„I"	6354	—	7350	I·A·W
9125	„HONDA"	8935	HV	7207	I	6403	—	5653	„JB"
8651	„HP"	9475	M	7663	I	6386	—	8643	„JB" I·A·B
8636	„HP"	7677	HVB	9428	—	6187	—	6815	—
9552	HP	8096	„HW"	7554	I	6183	—	8801	IB
9332	—	9385	„H W"	8588	I	6414	—	8811	IB
9554	HR	8663	HW	9405	I	6429	J	8802	IB
5658	„HR 04"	7228	HW	5988/6082/6144/6297/7821/7825/8758	„I" „I" „I" „J" „J" „J"	7568	—	8639	IB
8999	HR			7115	i	5774	„IA"	8620	„JB"
8817	HS		—		„I"	5187	IA	9536	JB
9373	HS	6626	„I"	7189	i	9605	AB	8642	JB
9485	HSI	7817	„I"	8598	i	8856	IAC	9606	B
8099	HSI	7213	—	5063	—	7423	JAG	6716	„JB"
9035	HS	8217/8378	„J"			8060	JAR	6254	—
8989	IS							6705	—

Upper-right section

No.	Mark	No.	Mark	No.	Mark	No.	Mark	No.	Mark
5378	„IH" B	6027	—	5657	„IK" 1697	7234	IM	6674	„JOR" A
5812	„IH"	6715	—	7593/7594	„IL"	7252	IMFB	5403	„IP"
7349	„IH"	6752	—	8632	„JL"	7956	„IM H"	6180	„IP"
7225	IH	8866	—	5807	„JL"			6714	„IP" b)
7229	IH			5119	—	7313	IM & ISH	8445	„JP"
7295	—	8925	IM	7533	—	9249	„I MK"	9412	IP
5665	JH 723	5795	„IIO"	7516	—	5668	IM L29	9408	—
9051	—	5680	„IIS"					7730	IP
5120	IK	7524	—	7004	IM LIN			7299	JP
		7957	—	7005	IM LIN			5405	„IP"
5785	„I HR"	7946	IW	5458	—	8616	IN	6662	—
		5391	„IK"	9591	IM			5260	JAP
7314	—	8437	„IK"	5686	„IM"	5669	INR	7244	—
5588	„IHS"	5650	„IK"	7948	IM	7101	„INS"		
		9593	—	5131	IM	7101	„INVS"	5325	„IP"
6630	IHS	6121	IK	9383	IM	5471	„IO"	8432	IPB
5688	II	5769	„IK"			6994	O	7300	PAC
8017	—	6180	—	7257	IM	5786	„I OM"	6180	„IPK"

Lower-left section

No.	Mark	No.	Mark	No.	Mark	No.	Mark	No.	Mark
7519	—	6683	—	8380	„IE"	7015	—	6808	IG B
8805	—	9503	IC8	6147	„IE"	7014	—	5766	„IG"
6765	—	7531	ICH	6985	—	7235	—	7235	—
8857	IBC	6999	ICR	7247	IE	6689	—	6536	—
6708	—	5418	„ID"	7954	—			6697	—
5687	„IBD"	8337	ID	9517	„J.E."	6231	IFD	6996	IGB
9179	„I BENA BENTE"	8373	ID	6148	„IE"	6771	JFF	5791	„I GD"
6652	—	9461	—	9566	IEB	6695	—	5790	„IGD"
8901	I·BOSSARD	6701	—	6724	„IE B"	6699	—	7521	„IGE"
6716	„JB P"	5188	„IDC"	5753	„IE K"	6735	—	7520	IGE
7444	„IC"	5793	„IDK"	7308	IET	7010	—	7844	IGG
5677	„IC"	8862	„ID M"	5705	„J. F"	5257	„JFS"	6275	IGH
6196	IC	9338	„ID P"			9583	IFS	9337	„IG L"
8016	ICB	7529	—	8822	—	8612	—	5685	„IGS"
		7528	—	8813	„IFB"	8336	—	9372	—
7534	IC B	5651	—	6722	„JF B"	5114/6147/6280	„IG" „IG" „IG"	9527	IGZ
				7012	IF B	8657	IG	3147	IH

Lower-right section

No.	Mark	No.	Mark	No.	Mark	No.	Mark	No.	Mark
8962	„I PR *"	8635	„IS"	5749	„IVH"	7822	„K"	6941	—
7952	„IR"	7278	IS	9560	IVR	7197	—	5825	—
7530	IR	6734	—	8966	„IW"	7214	—	8652	„K"
5716	IR	5416	IS	7348	IW	7181	K	6349	B
6680	—	7279	JS	7249	—	5480	K	5586	—
7243	IR	5649	„IS"	5413	„IW"	8934	K	5590	—
5783	„IR(?)S"	5648	„IS"	5199	IW	9521	K		
8634	„IS"	7312	ISH	8640	IVVH	7806	—	7653	—
8662	„JS"				K	7744	—	5590	—
9388	IS	9531	IR		„K"	8589	K	6373	—
9290	IS	7523	IST	5589	„K"				
8794	IS			7824	„K"	7190	K	5068	—
7951	IS	7953	—	8219/8223	„K"				
7304	JS	5398	„IT"	8226/8229	„K"	7208	K	6057	—
7305	JS	9188	IU ORI CO	8232/8379		7191	k	6061	—
7253	IS	8823	—	8391 / 8381	„K"	6851/9214/9218	„K" „K" „K"	6940	—

Top-left quadrant

No.	No.	No.	No.	No.
6430	5048	6374	6179 „l.d."	6547
7282	7182	8042	7042	6688 „LL"
7287	7689	8038	9155 „Icon"	7073
9420 „KB"	9273	6431	9158 „13 LEONI"	6653
5371 „K" / „D"	5361	5399 / 5402	5471 „L·F"	5386 „LM"
7510	6208	8040	8809 „LF"	6227 „L.M."
6180 „KI"	8595	8044	7040 „L GUI TOU"	8816
8137 KIOV	7741	8041	7674 „LH"	6176
6180 „KIP"	6017	9602	6218	5823 „LM"
7016 KIRSTEIN	8243 „I"	7275	6761	8399
7008 KRUG	8239 „I"	5400 „L AD"	8422	9136
L	7462 „L" / 7465 „L" / 8754 „L"	5332 „LB"	6646	
„L"	6953	9213 „13 Adler LB"	6541	6714 „LR"
9215 „L"	8045 „L"	5081	6546	8996 „LR"
8233 / 8238 / 8240 / 8241 / 8242 / 8244 / 8401 / 8403 / 8405 / 8406 / 8408 „L"	5426	5470 „L·D"		

Top-right quadrant

No.	No.	No.	No.	No.
7356 C / 7394 „MDA"	6185	6259	5049	6405
7589 „ME"	5587 „MM"	8059	5613	6376
8701	5673 „MM" 175?	9573	8618 „N"	
8605	8835 MN	5377 „MS"	5317	5069
6756	5250 „MO"	7393 „MS"	7171	6257
9501	8252 „MO"	7470 E	7209	6261
8073	8062		5054	9299
9255	6323	5748	8335	
8688 „MHB"	6249	5149 A	9406	7985
5737 „MHH"	ŌP	9161 MVNOZ 1712		7398 B „NA"
5745 „M I"	6250	8834	5998 „N" / 8755 „N" / 8756 „N" / 8916 „N"	7409 N·A·C
	ŌP	6234		7404
6770 „M JG G"	5459 „MP"	N	7406 B	7402
7582 MK	7809 „MP"	„N"	9223 „N 2"	7399
9310 „MK"	7764 MP	7963 B „N"	7024 B	7403
7515	8613	8255 bis / 8263 bis / 8426 / 8430 / 8436 B / 8439 „N"		7401 NAP 762
7944 h) „ML"	6263	5064		
	7486 M·P			

Bottom-left quadrant

No.	No.	No.	No.	No.
5819 „LR"	6204	5180 M	6387	7315 MA
7917	6844	7466 „M"		7416 MA·C
	6021	6230	6404	9164 „MAIO RCA"
6679	5229	5192 B „M"	5075 B	9166 MAI ORaa
6714	8043	5521	6359	9165
7970 „LT"	7512 M	5275		8022
5395 „LT"	M	8590 M	7052	9116
7447 LV	„M"	6238	7036	7032 MARTIN
9137 LVIS	5450 „M"	8596	6432	8608 „MB"
7933 LW	5744 „M" / 6342 „M" / 8624 „M" / 8842 „M"	6225 „M" / 6307 „M" / 7467 „M" / 7578 „M" / 5322 „M?"	7044	8607 MB
7931 LW				9254
7932	8245 bis / 8251 bis / 8253 / 8254 / 8424 „M"	9601	6216 1260	6665 M#B
5411 „LW" A	7379 B „M"	8991 „M"	5576 „M"	7808 „MB H"
7006		9590	8602 M3	5249
5747	7198	6350	9225 „M 5" / 9224 „M 5"	5412 M·D
9177 LZUA	5615 M	6375	6220 „MA"	5781 „MD"
6840				

Bottom-right quadrant

No.	No.	No.	No.	No.
7400 NAP	5696 NE	8434 NO	5525 „NV?"	7691
	6288	8918	8919	7610 S.XVII .7608
7398 B NAP	5695 NE	8920		7774 „O"
7398	5697 „NEV"	6284 NAP		7576
8614	5671 NF	6979 NR		6888
8398 NB	7884 R	6980 NR	„O"	6406
	6846 „NG"	6981 NR	5011	
5128	7926	6982 NR	5008	7541
6667	5382 „NG"		5010	
7397 h „NIC"		8963	8264 / 8323 bis / 8328 bis / 8440 „O"	5224
9189 „?NCA (L)AD?"	6726 N·G	NR D"		6830
	6725	7638		
6285	8997 „NHM"	9544 NS	7178 O	6834
5414	8666 NL	7292	7210 O	6415
6627	5491	7412 „NSC"	7656	7632
8409 „N.Dahl"	8923	7374 NT	7192 O	8851
		9464 N8	7733	7659

6772	7992	7122	6407	9296 "P 3"	6797	Q	8266 "R"	5062	6857	
5009	9174	7120	6389	9297 "P 3"	6178 "P. t."	"Q"	7184	6390	6130 Lilie	
8395	8345	5443	5427	9342 "P 4"	9540	7183	5151	6317	6131 "RF"	
9121	P		5433	9343 "P 4"	7705 "PV 1610"	7692	6975	6321	7311	
	"P"	6801	6133	8103 "P10"	7706 "P.V.1611"	8685	5057	6417	8814 "RH"	
8365	9401 "P"	7604	6137	9221 "P11"	7707 "P.V.1612"	7670	6836	6434	5616	
8690 "OHB"	7199	9434	6433	9430 PA	7697 "P V"	8599	6823	6975	9074	
6994	7180	8757 "P"	6416	7273 PA	7698 "P V 1606"	5070	6975	9415 "R 4"	6703	
9511	9489	9402 "P"	6436	8648 "P·A·H"	7700 "P V 1607"	6408	5233	9416 "R 4"	7230 "RL"	
8415 "O:L"	8265 "P"	6950	6439 40	5959	7699	9272 "R"	5001	9286 "R 6"	5704 RM	
8416 OLD	9312	8068 "P"	6441	6529	7701 "P V 1608"	6363	6355 "R"	7232 RB	6671 R★M	
8414 OLA	8066			5251 "PB"	7726		5707	7269 RC	6819	
6988	8067	5061	7011	5252 "PB"		R	6377	7738 RD	6861	
9118 "OO"	7764	8729	6973	8807 PB	7704 1610	"R"	6409	6675 "RDC"	6832	
8065	9313		9421 "P1"	8622 PB	8719 PW	9271 "R"			R	
6310	5424	6362	9368 "P2"	8674 "PB" Halbmond	5772 PWP	5000	6364	7303 "R D H H"	6815 O A	
			9369 "P2"		8267 "R"				7440 "ROMA"	

6729	6690	9564	5106 "PM"	6786 "PP .EYA"	6023	7827 "S"	7172	7785	8975	
5653 JB 1688	9400	8633 "PIZ"	6743 "PMB"	8844 "PR"	9125 "RONDA"	7848 "S"	8167	6435	8976	
5390 "PC"	5374 "PF"	9247 "PI W"	6721 "PM B"	8660 "PR"	S.307 "RS"	7828	8170	6942	8977	
6730 "PC"	6674	9274 PK		5094 PR	6105		7829	6103	5708 "SA"	
5292 "PC"	5452 "PG"	7627 CK	6740 6741		5152	7780			9043 SA	
6758	6659 "PG"	7455 PL	5822 "PM G"	5093	7251 RS	7831	8279 "J"	6107	5644	
7417 PD	6655 "PG"	7276 PL	6253 MPL	8063	7030	7830	8284 "J"	5397 "S"	7043 SAMSON	
9413 PD	7769 PGA	7272 PL	9275 "PN"	9444 P9R	9122 "RS A??"	7833	7693	5397 "S"	7045 SAMSON	
8891	8689 "PH"		5608	8083	S		5482 "S" 7050 "S" 8759 "S"	8075		
6712	5689 PH	7277	6983 PC	8669 "PS"	"S"	7832	6943	9365	8658 "SAUTER"	
	9452 PI	6197	7356 "PP"	7306 PS	S.121 "S"	7177		9366	8061 SB	
6645 PDN	9546 PH	6880 "PLS"	7356 7395 "PP" 7934	6977 PS	7836 "S"		S.191 "S"		7297 S·C	
7702 "PDVF 1608"	8630 PH	7041	6786 "PP"	5088 "PS"	8949 "S"	5050	5225	9367	7296	
9119 PGDRO	8723	6198	6852	7607 "PS"	5767 "S"	7781		9504	S·C	
9120	7265	6622 "PM"	7356 "PPA"	5780	8268 8273 8275 8277 8280 8281 8283 8285 8288 8291 "S"	5142	6378	8972	9427	
PBDIO	6673 "PJB"	5407 "PM"	7298 PPAM	6998 PSAM	8442 8443 8694	7202 7203	6391 5318	8973 8974	8931 "SCH" 6774	

9555

9012		9022		6020		5966	
9008		7960		6422		5962	
9033		9390		6352		„ʒ“	
9027						5228	
9015		8427	„Z“	7734			

5546

_Z_

„Z“

7669		9029		7621		9058		8282 / 8286	Σ
5051		9028		7424		8196	Φ
9014		9030		5824		8030	„Z CIO PRA“	8110	
9013		9032		6368		8955	„ZCT“	8112	
9031		9024		6154				8115	
9026		9021		6382		8338		8114	
9011		9023		6395				8113	
9010		9018		6156		7941		8105	
9009		9017							
9016		9025		6160		6611			
9019						5903			

8108	8109	8270 / 8272		6440		6439	
8106	8111	8278 / 8287		6438		5563	
		5144					
8107	8269 / 8276	5563		6437		7478	
		7381					

Heavenly Bodies

7327		S.491	Halb-mond	8138		7658		7629	
8039		7227						7630	
5164	Globus	8942		8441		6118			

5130		9053		6289	Stern	6976		7614	
				5989	Stern	7342			
8699		5529	Halb-monde	5280	Stern	7343		5618	
8699		7525		5456	Stern			5619	
6132	Globus	9561		5286	Stern	8987		5620	
5126	Sonne	7606		7657		8986		5621	
5291	Sonne	8961		9046		8956		7760	
6486		7876				8957		5622	
7031		6949		9476				7782	
6288	Mond	6217		9496		8958			
8649	Halb-mond			5327	Stern D	7628		5623	

5624		5626		7762		5630		7759	
5625		5627				5632		S. 214 Weitere Monats-zeichen
7761		5628		5629		5631		

Man

8135	7146	8122	8150	9071	
8136	7147	9066	8148	8696	Brust-bild
8695 Figur	7123	5634		5344	
5139 Figur?	7148	5723	8149	5244	Kopf
6251 Madonna	7149	7779	8151	7605	Männer-kopf
7379 hl.Ambrosius	7145	8004 Jungfrau		5482	Männer-kopf
8887 St.Fridolin	9171		8152	S.491	Kopf
9319 Wenzel		8160		6618	Merkur-kopf
	5219		9050	Mann CH	5466	
8404 Bischof	5221		9038	Mann	Beginen-kopf?
8404	8340		8428		5291	Mohren-kopf
7112	8159	8153	9041	5864	

7547 8379 7119 7126 7113
8382 7544 7133 7128 7154
7339 7545 7132 7114 7152
8161 9572 7118   7124
5350 7646 7131 7130
      8130 7134 7129 7151
7867 5706 8407 7108 6545
7548 7088 5243 7127 7552
7795 5154 Löwen, 9204 7106 6209
7798 7666 9205   7543
9520 Löwe 17 76 7667 8407 8871 Löwenkopf 5175
9432 7324 7485 7150 5171
9543 7125 7422 7153 5171

9261 5879 6528 9229 9418
      4998   6097
8736 9206 6498 5186 8374
      7468 Stier 6841 5581 6798
8745 7468 Stier 5955 5582 Pferd Baum 6875 Hund
8746 6577 8048 5578 Lamm 6522
6839   8050 6852 Lamm 6503
6320 8990 Stierkopf 8797 Schweinskopf 6853 6872
5453 Pferd 7967 Stierkopf 6837 7320 6516
6497 7991 8052   6530
5297   8054 6852 6564
8870 Pferdekopf 6619 Ochsenkopf 6597 6852 5897 6606
6095 5923 7037   5892
4999 7476 6509 8797 Lammskopf 7865
6205 7556 6073 5837 7867
6561 7475 6078 Widderkopf 5984 9228
6188 5826 6591 9419 6155
      6824

6584 9209 7899 6201 Löwenkopf 6157

6796 6003 6500 6531 7724
6787 Ratte 6496 6496 5108 Tierkopf
9062 6505 6505 7492 9186 Hermelin
6000 6507 6763 7493 6084 Anker

Misc Mammals

6634 8156 8830 5978 8848
      8832 6190 8849
7896 6052 Leoparden kopf 8739 7637 8947
7897 5893 6601 8740 5241 8945
7898 5858 8829 5240 8946
9203 6575 8828 7732 8948
6620 6621 Nashorn 8131 5289 Hirschkopf 6816 Affe
5925 8761 9160 4997 5110
7904 8762 8967 Bär 7223 7728
7793 4992 8827 6233 9227
7983 8733 8826 9036 5922
7792 8831 9309 8847 6594
                  9260 Igel

Mythical Animals, Eagles, and Other Birds

6056 Einhorn 8429 Greif
5860 8134 9292 8332 9300
      9436 9510 8332 7474
8019 6576 9291 8910 7473
7379 dragon 7982 9537 8912 7396
6617 Chimäre 8714 9592 8911 7426
5912 8714 8330 8047 5360
5912 5091 Adler 8331 8049 4991
4990 9474 8440 9449 9210
6846 Greif 9470 9594 9301 9302
      9472

Crowns Scepters Weapons

Implements

Column group 1 (top-left)

5307	8874 Schlüssel- stiel(?) „G"	7998	6111 Uhrschlüssel	9387
5308	5732 Schwert Schlüssel	7644	6856	5246 Rost
9506	8694	7433	6272	6513
	5730	7434	6273	6153 Sensen
5750	5731	7436	6271	5230
5751	9431	7432	6270	9040
5994 Schlüssel		7431	9034	5256 Striegel
		7499	7490	9443
5312	8968	7500	7491	9453
	7997	7498	9600	9069
5314	8930	7496	5293	5433
8720	8412	7497	8704	8021
5316	8411	7495	8703	8436
8721	8412	7494 7435	8705	7086 7443

Column group 2 (top-right)

6006 Stuhl	7238	7025 Triumph- wagen	6089 Pflug- schar	5456
6181 Trag- korb		6256 Destillier- Apparat	6696	5472
6028 Vogel- bauer		5930	9580	
		7380		

Architecture

5200 B Haus	9445		7750	7535	7371
5195 Haus					
7093	7090		7751	5514	9398
	7056		9397	5370	8101
8727	8133				
8728	9194		9395	5441	9399
6029 Turm				5442	8025
7316 Turm	5513		9394		
8005 Turm				7369	7340 Türme
6287 Turm	5472		9396		
5278 Turm			7749 B Turm	5515	9451
5935	7753				9482
9480			9316	7372	
8438 H	7752		8438 A	7373	9253

Column group 3 (bottom-left)

8146	5113	7579	9280	6207
8145	5810	5449	5290 Post- horn	6820
8143	5579	5279 Hammer	7643	8125
8141	7488	5136	7922	7843
8142	7091	8940 8441 Hämmer	5936	9067 Ringe
9144	5838	9364	8158	5158 Brillen- zeichen
6085 Drei- master	5840	8921	6553	5159
5711	5839 5841	7059 Maurer- kelle	6794 Turban	5165 Brillenz.
5713	4993	8843	6077	5157
8711	6240 Baß- geige	5103	6833 6186	6022
5712	5095	7846	6136	5939
7994	5490	5166	6146	5956
7326	7329		6119 Hand- schuh	5993 Ball- schläger
7089	7580	8341	5834 6219 Schleife	6046 Kork- zieher / 9045

Column group 4 (bottom-right)

5589 Türme	8859		5603	8377 Türme	9317 Stadtmauer
7083 Türme		Drei Türme			
8418 Türme	5705 Türme			8089 Tor	9038 Gitter
7317	9219		5604	8012	9277 „Pyra- mides"
7097	9568		5596	8090	8126
9567			5593	9156	9257
	5598		5594	8091	9278
8367					9279
7981	5597		5592	9340	5509
7982	5599		5595	9341	9314 Staut- mauer
8418	5601		5606	5585	9604
9339	5600		5605		7972
8124			5591	9318 Staut- mauer	7973
5439	5602		5576	9315	9516
8860		8011 Stadttor		9417	7815

Crosses

Trade Marks

Shields and Geometrical Forms

Numbers

6911	7758 [20]	6165 42	6295 63	6008 76
	7878	6327 43	6790 64	6877 76
6906	8173 ..20 K..	5997 47	7068 64*	6788 77
		6114 49	5444 64	6959 78
6903	6936 20 K	6812 49		6125 79
		6325 50	5162 ..64..	6031 79
6907	8650 ..21 K..	5555 ..50..	5168	6211 80
			6961 ..65..	6780 ..80..
6904	6049 23	5255 ..51..	5077 [6]	5524 81
	8172 ..23 K..	5556 ..51..	6127 ..66..	6789 81
9582	6047 24	5227 [mark]	6242	6805 81
	6048 25		5257 ..67..	6193 82
7975	6086 27	6296 52	6213 67	6960 82
	7048 29	6326 52	6304 68	5446 82
8421	6086 30	7069 53	6171 69	
6098 14	6067 31	5995 55	6243 69	6126 ..83..
6099 14	6086 31	6244 55	6305 71	8023 [84]
6280 15	6267 32	6306 56	5163 [71]	5079 [84]
8603	6827 33	6112 56(57)?	5169	8157 [84*]
[15 Löö]	7046 33	6810 56*(?)	5320 ..72..	5276 ..85..
	7047 34	5996 57	6172 ..72..	5294 ..85..
6849 16	6065 35	6173 57	7079	5212 ..85..
6081 17	7062 35	6803 59	5078 [72]	7755 [87]
6847 17	7375 [mark]	5256 ..60..	5321 ..73..	5524 87
6848 17	6066 36	6009 60	6007 73	
6079 18	6166 36	6113 60	6865 73	7077 87
6080 18	6265 37	6294 60	6876 73 (?)	6863 88
8174 ..18 K..	6266 38	6811 60*	5987 75	5985 90
6935 18/6	6825 38	6878 60*	6030 75(?)	5428 ..96..
6143 19	6826 39	5468 61	5445 76	5437
6141 20	7060 40	7067 61*(?)		
6142 20	6164 41	6032 62*		
	7061 41	5147 ..63..		

7385 91·	7078 94	6927 [Xld 12g]	9293 [17 36]	7872
	6864 95		5257 1760	[A798]
5447 91	6191 96	6928 [Xld 12g]	5703 [1763]	7464 [1805]
	5986 98		7870 [1774]	7874 [1824]
5429 [91]	7756 [99]	6929 [IId 12g]	7958 [795]	8902 ..1891
5437	6926 [Xld 12g]			

Note that the marks shown on pages 373-387 are of all European countries except Germany. They have been classified according to character only, no distinction being made as to locality. However, they have been numbered according to locality and indexed accordingly, so that the marks of any locality may be ascertained by consulting the index first and then referring to the marks.

Numbers 5823-7081 are French marks and 7083-7324 are English marks. These are more completely and more specifically listed in the special tables for those countries.

BELGIUM

4990-4992. Gold, 1831-1869
4993-4994. Silver, 1831-1869
4995-4996. 1831-1869 silver
4997-4999. 1831-1869 gold
    5002. import 1831-1869
5004-5005. silver since 1869
5006-5007. silver since 1869
5008-5009. gold since 1869
5010-5011. gold since 1869

ALOST (AELST)
5013. about 1730
5013. middle of 18. cent.

ANTWERP
5015. so or similar 1507-08, 58-59, 63-64
5016. 1524-25
5017. 1527
5018. so or similar 1537-38, 1566-67
5019. 1539-40

5020. 1544-45 or 1552-53
5051. 1550-51 or 1558-59
5022. so or similar 1565-66 or 1581-82
5023. 1574-75
5024. 1588-89
5025. 1602-03
5026. 1606-07
5027. 1610-11 or 1611-12
5028-5029. after 1620
5030. 1627-28
5031. 1641-42

TONGRES

5509a-5509b. about 1759
5510. another comark to the inspection mark about 1764-1783

TOURNAI

5513. about 1528, if not much older
5514. 16.-17. cent.
5515-5516. 1627
5517-5518. middle of 17. cent.
5519-5520. about 1766 and 1781
5521. about 1606
5522. about 1615
5523. 1624 or 1627
5524a. 1781
5524b. 1787

VIRTON

5536. 1733

YPRES

5541. about 1525
5542-5543. second half of 17. cent.
5544-5545. end of 17. cent.
5546. 1701-1713
5547. 1750
5548. about 1526
5549. perhaps 1684-85
5550. 1701
5551. 1702
5552. 1703
5553. 1714
5554. 1750-51
5555-5556. 1750 and 1751

DENMARK

AALBORG, JUTLAND

5576a. 1686

AARHUS, JUTLAND

5577. inspection mark

HELSINGOER, SEELAND

5579. 1741

HOLBAEK, SEELAND

5580. 19. cent.

HORSENS, JUTLAND

5581. inspection mark

KALUNDBORG, SEELAND

5585. 17. cent.

COPENHAGEN

Inspection marks
5591. 1608
5592. 1610
5593. 1639
5594. 1645
5595. 1663
5596. 1707
5597. 1721
5598. 1725
5599. 1733
5600. 1736
5601. 1743

5602. 1747
5603. 1769
5604. 1783
5605. 1841
5606. 1851
5607. Conrad Ludolf, mint-assayer 1679-1729
5608. Pet. Nicolai von Haven, assayer, 1729-1749
5609. Christopher Fabritius, assayer 1749-1787
5610-5612. Frederik Fabritius, assayer 1787-1823
5613. Christian Peter Naeboe, assayer 1823-1827
5614. Jacob Greg. Graah-Fabritius, assayer 1827-1831
5615. Christian Olsen Möller, assayer 1831-1840
5616. Pter Reimer Hinnerup, assayer 1840-1863
5617. Sim. Chr. Sch. Groth, assayer 1863-1904

MONTH MARKS

5618. January
5619-5620. February
5621. March
5622. April
5623. May
5624. June
5625. July
5626. August
5627. September
5628. October
5629-5630. November
5631. December
5632. December
5633. June
5634. November
5635. gold since 1685
5636. gold, 18. cent.
5637. gold since 1685
5638. 18 carat gold

NAESTVED, SEELAND

5693. 1608
5694-5696. 17.-18. cent.
5697. middle of 17. cent.

ODENSE, FUENEN

5701. 1625, 1763
5702. of 18. cent.
5703. 1763

RANDERS, JUTLAND

5705. 18. cent.

RIPEN (RIBE), JUTLAND

5706. 18.-19. cent.

ROSKILDE, ZEALAND

5707. inspection mark

STEGE, ZEALAND

5710. 1750

TONDERN, SOUTH JUTLAND

5711-5712. 17. cent.
5713. 17.-18. cent.

VIBORG, JUTLAND

5723. 17.-18. cent.
5724. 1800-

ESTLAND DORPAT

5730. 17. cent.
5731. 18. cent.
5732. 18. cent.

NARVA

5738-5739. 17. cent.
5740. about 1700
5741. 17.-18. cent.
5742. 18. cent.

PERNAU

5750-5751. 18. cent.

REVAL (TALLINN)

5754. middle of 16. cent.
5755. late 17. cent.
5756. about 1690
5757. middle of 18. cent.
5758. end of 18. cent.
5759-5760. about 1780
5761. about 1716
5762. about 1796

FINLAND

FINLAND (SUOMEN TASAVALTA)

5798. 1759-1782
5799. 1783-1808
5800. 1807-1809 (10?)
5801. 1810/11-1833/34
5802. 1834/35-1857/58
5803. 1858/59
5804. since 1810

ABO

5805. 1822

HELSINGFORS

5810. inspection mark

NYSTAD

5813. inspection mark

WASA

5814. 18. and 19. cent.

WIBORG

5816. silver 18. cent.
5817. gold 18.-19. cent.

ITALY

7326-7327. 1810-1872
7328-7329. 1810-1872
7330. import mark
7331. 1818-1872
7333-7335. since 1873

AQUILA (ABRUZZI)

7336. early 15. cent.
7337. early 16. cent.

BOLOGNA

7339. 18. cent.
7340. 1811-1817
7341. inspection mark Vatican City since 1817

BOLZANO

7342. 1708
7343. middle of 18. cent.
7344. 1824-1866
7345. 1866-1872
7346. since 1872

FERRARA

7364a. 17.(?) cent.
7364b. 1815

FLORENCE

7366. 16. cent.
7367. 17.-18. cent.
7368. 18. cent.

GENOA

7369. 16. cent.
7370. 17.-18. cent.
7371. (1)720-(1)768.
7372. end of 18. cent.

LUCCA

7378. 17. cent.

MILAN

7379b. beginning of 16. cent.
7379c. middle of 16. cent.
7379d. 17.-18. cent.
7380. 1810
7381. control mark
7382-7386. master marks with comarks

MANTUA

7391. 17. cent.

MODENA

7396. 17. cent.

NAPLES

7379a. silver since 1380
7379b. gold since 1380
7398a. about 1400
7398b. 16. cent.
7399. 17. cent.
7400. 17??
7401. 1702
7402. 1716
7403. 1720
7404. 1736
7405. 1782
7406a-7406b. probably also Naples 17.-18. cent.

ASSAYER MARKS

7407. about 1700 ?
7408. about 1702
7409. about 1716
7410. about 1720
7411. about 1736
7412. about 1742

PALERMO

7426. 17. cent.

PARMA

7427. 17. cent.

ROME

7431. 17. cent.
7432-7433. end of 17. cent.
7434. 17.-18. cent.
7435. 18.-19. cent.
7436. 18.-19. cent. for gold
7437-7438. sterling, 1358-1398
7439. Bolognese standard 1508
7440. Caroline-silver 1508

SULMONA

7451. 13. and 14. cent.
7452. 14. cent. till 1406
7453. 1406-middle of 15. cent.
7454. middle of 15. cent. till ??

TRIESTE

7457-7459. 18. cent.
7460. 1805
7461. 1805
7462. 1807/09 and 1824/66
7463-7464. gold 1805
7465. 1806/07
7466. 1866-1872
7467. since 1872

TURIN

Inspection marks
7468a. 1597
7468b. 1597
7469a. since 1678
7469b. 17. cent.
7470a-7470e. 18. cent.
7471-7472. 18. cent.
7473a-7476a. about 1750
7476b. 18. cent.

VENICE

7484. 15.? cent.
7485. 17.-18. cent.
7486. 16.-18. cent.
7487a. silver since 1805
7487b. silver since 1805
7488. since 1810

LATVIA

BAUSKA

7489. inspection mark 18. cent.

GOLDINGEN

7490. 18. cent.
7491. 18.-19. cent.

MITAU

7492-7493. 17. cent.

RIGA

7494. 16. cent.
7495-7496. about 1600
7497-7498. 16.-17. cent.
7499-7500. 18. eent.

7501. 1749-56
7502. 1756-60.
7503. 1760-64
7504. 1764-68
7505. 1768-80
7514. Heinrich Meyer, 1654-1694
7516. Juergen Linden, 1674-1688
7517. Heinrich von Koelln (Kollen, Coeln), 1679-1693
7520. Joh. Georg Eben, 1703-1710
7524. Johann Abrahamsohn Lamoureux (Lamore), 1719-1744
7526. Christoffer Dey, 1729-1748
7528-7529. Johann Dietr. Rehwald, 1738-1759
7531. Joh. Christian Henck, 1750
7532. Michael Kresner the younger, 1758
7533. Joh. Friedrich Lamoureux, 1763-1797
7534. Joh. Christoph Barrowsky, 1771-1790

MEMEL

7535. mark 18. cent.

NETHERLANDS

7542. silver, since 1852
7543. gold, since 1852
7544. silver standard
7545. silver standard
7546. silver standard
7547. gold standard
7548. gold standard
7549. gold standard
7550. gold standard
7551. gold standard
7552. gold standard
7553. taxes mark till 1909
7554. inland
7555. import till 1909
7556. import till 1909
7557. since 1909
7558. export
7559. gold

AMSTERDAM

7561. about 1566
7562. 16.-17. cent.
7563. about 1606
7564. about 1608
7565. 1655
7566. about 1694
7567-7569. 18. cent.

ANNUAL LETTERS

7570. 1566
7571. 1608
7572. 1609
7573. 1655
7574. 1694
7575. 1696 and later
7576. old mark 1807

BOLSWARD

7595. mark 1725

BREDA
7598. 15.-16. cent.
7599. 16.-17. cent.
7600. 1595 or 1694

DORDRECHT
7608-7610. inspection marks with annual letters

ENKHUIZEN
7611-7613. inspection marks with annual letters

GOUDA
7614. 16. cent.

GRONINGEN
7616-7617. Cornelis Papinck,
7618-7619. master marks

THE HAGUE
7620. inspection mark
7621. inspection mark with annual letter
7622. 17. cent.

HAARLEM
7628. about 1700
7629-7630. 18. cent.
7631. middle of 18. cent.
7632. 1807

HERZOGENBUSCH
7639-7641. Aert van Muers, 1607

HOORN
7643. about 1640

LEIDEN
7644. 17. cent.

LEEUWARDEN
7645. 17.-18. cent.
7646. 1695
7652a-7652b. Johannes Lelij, 1695
7654-7656. Garbijnus van der Lelij, 1731

MAASTRICHT
7657. end of 18. cent.
7658. end of 18. cent. with annual letter

MIDDELBURG
7659. 1726
7660. middle of 18. cent.
7661-7664. inspection marks

ROTTERDAM
7665-7667. 18. cent.
7668-7669. 18. cent.
7670. 18.-19. cent.
7671. 18. cent.
7672. 18.-19. cent.

SNEEK (PROVINCE FRIESLAND)
7679. about 1770

UTRECHT
7681. about 1614
7682. 17. cent.
7683. about 1710
7684-7686. 18. cent.
7687. 1602
7688. 1614
7689. about 1650
7690. 1733 ?
7691. 1748 ?
7692. 1775 ?
7693. 1775 ? or 1802 ?

VLISSINGEN (PROVINCE ZEALAND)
7731. inspection mark

ZIERIKZEE
7734. 1600
7735. 1700

ZWOLLE
7736. 17. cent.
7737. 1721
7738. about 1726 and later
7739. 17. cent.
7740. about 1721
7741. about 1726

NORWAY

BERGEN
inspection marks
7750. 1784
7751. 1799
7752. 1812
7753. 1820
7754. 1844 (seven dots without the tower)

ANNUAL LETTERS
7755. 1787
7756. 1799
7757. 1812
7758. 1820
7759-7762. monthly marks
7763. Dimar Kahs, assayer 1763-1789
7764a-7764b. Mathias Pettersen, assayer 1796-1812
7765. Peter Michael Blytt, assayer 1812-1821

BREVIK
7771. 1779

FREDRIKSSTAD
7772. about 1687

LARVIK
7773. about 1746

OSLO (formerly CHRISTIANIA)
7774. end of 16. cent.-1624
7775. 1624
7776. 1712 ?-1781
7777. 1782-after 1814
7778. since about 1820

7779-7781. assayer mark second half of 19. cent.
7782. monthly mark April-May

SKIEN
7785. about 1781

STAVANGER
7786. first half of 18. cent.

TRONDKJEM
7787. 1746

AUSTRIA

BREGENZ
7788. about 1732
7789. since 1824
7790. 1866-68, as Vienna
7791. since 1868

GRAZ
7792. end of 16. cent.
7793. 1678
7794-7795. 1732 and 1743
7796. 1764
7797. 1778
7798. 1800
7799. 1778-1800
7800. 1807-1866
7801. 1866-1872
7802a. since 1872
7802b. since 1922
7804. 1807-1824
7805. 1810-1824

HALL (TIROL)
7810. since 1809
7811. 1809 ? 1824-1866
7812. 1866-1868

INNSBRUCK
7814. end of 17. cent.
7815. 17.-18. cent.
7816. 1868-1872
7817a. since 1872
7817b. since 1922

KLAGENFURT
7820. 1801
7821. 1807-1866
7822. 1866/67
7823. 1868-1872
7824a. since 1872
7824b. since 1922, law 1921
7825. 1806/07
7826. 1811-1824

SALZBURG
7827. 1494
7828. 16. cent.
7829. end of 16. cent.
7830. 1638
7831. 1662
7832-7833. 16.-17. cent.
7834. 1807/09
7835. 1866-72
7836a. since 1872
7836b. since 1922
7837. since 1806/07

SCHAERDING

7846. about 1600
7848. since 1781

VIENNA

Inspection marks
7849. 1524
7850. middle of 16. cent.
7851. end of 16. cent.-1674
7852. 16.-17. cent.
7853. 1675-1696
7854. 1675-1696
7855. 1699 till 1736
7856. silver 1737-1806
7858. silver 1764-1795
7859. silver 1807-1810
7860-7861. silver 1810-1866
7862. silver with changing annual letters 1819-1866
7863. 1866-1872
7864-7865. 1866-1872
7866-7867. since 1872
7868-7869. for all Austria-Hungary
7870. gold from 1774
7871-7872. gold 1791-1824
7873-7874. gold 1824-1866
7875-7877. silver
7878-7880. gold
7881-7882. 1807-24
7884-7886. 1809-10
7887. 1810-1824
7888. 1810-1824
7889. import 1866-68
7890. import 1868-1872
7891. import gold 1868-1872
7892. import since 1872
7893. import gold since 1872
7894. import silver 1902-1921
7895. import gold 1902-1921
7896-7904. standard mark
7905-7915. import

WIENER—NEUSTADT

7960. 1807-1866
7962. 1866-1872
7963a. 1872-
7963b. since 1922

POLAND

GRAUDENZ

7967a. 17. cent.
7967b. 18. cent.

KRAKOW

7971. 1807-09
7972-7973. 1809-1835
7974. 1835-1866
7975. 1859
7976. 1866-1872
7977. since 1872
7978. 1806-07
7979-7980. standard mark

LEMBERG (LWOW)

7983. 1694
7984. 18. cent.
7985. 1787-1806
7986. 1807-1866

7987. 1866-1872
7988. since 1872
7989. 1806-07
7990. 1811-1824

LISSA (LESZNO)

7991. second half of 18. cent.

LOMSHA

7994. 1781

POSEN (POZNAN)

7997-7998. 17.-18. cent.

THORN (TORUN)

8007-8009. 17. cent.
8010. 18. cent.
8012. 1760-1780
8017. Jakob Jenny, 1704-1749
8018. Johann Christian Broellmann, 1700-1719

WILNA (WILNO)

8025. 16.-17. cent.

PORTUGAL

BEJA

8026. 18. ?-19. cent.

BRAGA

8027. 1800-1881

COIMBRA

8031. 17. cent.

EVORA

8033. 1740
8034. 18.-19. ?

GUIMARAES

8036. 1790
8037. 19. cent.

LISBON

8038. 1688
8039. 1700
8040. 17.-18. cent.
8041-8042. 18. cent.
8043. 1780
8044. 18, cent.
8045. 19. cent.
8047-8050. on bigger implements
8051-8054. on smaller implements
8055. for ancient implements
8056-8057. export since 1891

PORTO

8065. about 1600
8066-8067. 17. cent.

ROUMANIA

SIBIU

8080. since 1872

CLUJ

8089. 16. cent.
8090. 16.-17. cent.
8091. 1833
8092. 1866-1872
8093. since 1872

KRONSTADT

8094. 1866-1872
8095. since 1872

TEMESVAR

8101. 1838
8102. 1866-1872
8103. since 1872

RUSSIA

8105-8110. about 1700
8116-8121. 1727-1740
8122-8126. 1741-1762

ASTRACHAN

8129. 1771

IRKUTSK OR TOBOSK

8130. 1774, 1776

JAROSSLAWL

8131. 1756, 1767

KALUGA

8132. 1797, 1799

KAMJENEZ-PODOLSK

8133. 1857-61

KASAN

8134. 1763, 1797

KIEV

8135. about 1794
8136-8137. 19. cent.

KOSTROMA

8138. 1834-1878

LENINGRAD (ST. PETERSBURG)

Inspection mark
8139-8140. about 1730-40
8141. about 1740-50.
8142. about 1760-80
8143. about 1780-1800
8144. 1808
8145. about 1810-1820
8146. about 1820-1880

MOSCOW

8147. 1734-41
8148. 1747
8149. 1751
8150. 1778

8151. 1780
8152. about 1782-1787
8153. about 1790-1801
8154. 1816-1843
8155. beginning of 19. cent.

PSKOW (PLESKAU)
8156. 1771, 1791

TULA
8157. 19. cent.

TWER
8158. 18. ? cent.

WELIKI-USTJUG
8159. beginning of 19. cent.

WITEBSK
8160. 1873

WLADIMIR
8161. 1763

WOLOGDA
8162. 18. and 19. cent.

SWEDEN
8165. s i n c e 1752, but since 1912 only for gold
8166-8167. silver since 1912
8168. import mark since 1912 only for gold
8169-8170. import mark since 1912 for silver
8176-8328. Town Marks

ARBOGA
8330-8332a. 17.-18. cent.
8332b. about 1771
8333. since 1860 ?
8334. 1733/34, 1757/58
8335. 1771

ASKERSUND
8340a. about 1742-1765
8340b. since 1860

BORAS
8341a. 18. cent.
8341b. since 1860 ?
8342. 1694, 1718, 1742
8343. 1743 ? 1760 ?

EKSJOE
8346a. 17. cent.
8346b. 18. cent.
8347. since 1860 ?
8348. 1730, 1773

ENGELHOLM
8351. 1722-1775
8352. 1860 ?

FALKENBURG
8353. 1809-1825
8354. 1860 ?

FALUN
8355a. about 1768
8355b. since 1860 ?

GAEVLE
8356. 17.-19. cent.

GOETEBORG
8358. first half of 18. cent.
8359. since 1812
8360a. 1693 and 1717
8360b. 1724
8361. 1735
8362. 1737

HAELSINGBORG
8367a. 1702-1739
8367b. 1860 ?

HAERNOESAND
8369-8370. 18. and 18.-19. cent.

HALMSTAD
8371a. 17.-18. cent.
8371b. since 1860 ?

HEDEMORA
8372a. 18. cent.
8372b. since 1860 ?

HUDIKSVALL
8374a. 18. cent.
8374b. since 1860 ?

KALMAR
8379a. 17.-18. cent.
8379b. since 1860 ?

KARLSHAMN
8381. about 1714
8382a. end of 18. cent.
8382b. 18.-19. cent.
8383. since 1860 ?

KARLSKRONA
8384. 17. and 18. cent.
8385. since 1860 ?
8386. 1733 ?

KARLSTAD
8390a. m i d d l e of 18. cent.
8390b. since 1860 ?

KOEPING
8391a. m i d d l e of 17. cent.
8391b. since 1860 ?

KRISTIANSTAD
8392. 17. and 18. cent.
8393a. 18. and 19. cent.
8393b. since 1860 ?
8394. 1764

8395. 1820
8396. 1826

LAHOLM
8400. 17.-18. cent.
8401. since 1860 ?
8405. since 1860 ?

LIDKOEPING
8404a. beginning of 18. cent.
8404b. 18. and 19. cent.

LINDESBERG
8406a. 18. cent.
8406b. since 1860 ?

LINKOEPING
8407a-8407b. end of 18. cent.
8408. since 1860 ?

LULEA
8411. middle of 18. cent.
8412a-8412b. beginning of 19. cent.
8413. since 1860 ?

LUND
8418a. 18. cent.
8418b. 18. and 19. cent.
8419. since 1860 ?
8420. 1764
8421. about 1764

MALMOE
8423. 17.-18. cent.
8424. since 1860 ?

NORA
8425a. about 1760
8425b. about 1840-1850
8426. since 1860 ?

NORRKOEPING
8427. 17.-18. cent.
8428. 18. cent.
8429. 17. (?) and 18. cent.
8430. since 1860 ?
8431a. 1754
8431b. since 1759

NORRTAELJE
8436a. early 19. cent.
8436b. since 1860 ?

NYKOEPING
8438a. 18. cent., after 1730
8438b. early 19. cent.
8439. since 1860 ?

OEREBRO
8440a. after 1750
8440b. since 1860 ?

SALA

8441. beginning of 18. cent.
8441b. about 1760
8442. since 1860 ?

SOEDERHAMN

8443a. 18. cent.
8443b. since 1860 ?

STOCKHOLM

8446. 16.-17. cent.
8447. first half of 17. cent.
8448. middle of 17. cent.
8449. 1650
8450. 1674
8451. second half of 17. cent.
8452-8453. end of 17. cent.
8454. 1707
8455. 1713
8456. 1716
8457. 1720
8458. 1723
8459. 1724
8460. 1745
8461. 1752
8462. 1756
8463. 1797
8464. 1850
8464-8586. annual letters for Stockholm 1689, for all Sweden 1759
8587. 1696
8588. 1697
8589. 1698
8590. 1700
8591. 1707
8592. 1713
8593. 1716
8594. 1720
8595. 1723
8596. 1724
8597. 1742
8598. 1745
8599. 1752
8600. 1756
8601. 1757
8602. 1818

STRAENGNAES

8694a. about 1787, in changing sizes 18. and 19. cent.
8694b. since 1860 ?

TORSHAELLA

8696b. since 1860 ?

ULRICEHAMN

8697a. early 19. cent.
8697b. since 1860 ?

UPSALA

8699a. 18. cent.
8699b. 17.-19. cent.
8700. since 1860 ?

VADSTENA

8702a. about 1760
8702b. since 1860 ?

VAE

8713-8705. 16.-17. cent.

VAESTERAS

8710a. 17. cent.
8710b. since 1860 ?

VAESTERVIK

8711a. 18. cent.
8711b. since 1860 ?

VAEXJOE

8712a. about 1700 till now
8712b. since 1860 ?

VISBY

8713a. about 1600 till now
8713b. since 1860 ?

YSTAD

8714a. 18.-19. cent.
8714b. 19. cent.
8715. since 1860 ?
8716. 1738
8717. 1850

SWITZERLAND

8733-8734. 1882-1892
8735-8736. gold, (18 and 14 carat), 1882-1892
8739-8740. various
8741-8746. various
8747. BERN
8748. BIEL (BIENNE)
8749. LA CHAUX-DE-FONDS
8750. Délémont
8751. FLEURIER
8752. GENOVA
8753. GRANGES-SOLEURE
8754. LE LOCLE
8755. NEUCHATEL
8756. LE NOIRMONT
8757. PORRENTRUY
8758. SAINT-IMIER
8759. SCHAFF-HAUSEN
8760. TRAMELAN
8761-8763. import since 1917

BADEN in the ARGOVIA

8766-8767. 16.-17. cent.
8768-8769. early 17. cent.
8770. 17.-18. cent.

BASLE

8780. since 16. cent.
8781. middle of 17. cent.
8782. middle of 17. cent.
8783-8784. 17. cent.
8785. about 1678
8786. 17. cent.
8787-8788. 17.-18. cent.
8789-8790. 18. cent.
8791-8793. 18. cent.
8803-8804. Sebastian Fechter the older, 1633-1692, Sebastian Fechter the younger, 1673-1687

8818. Johann Ulrich Fechter 2nd, 1702-1747
8823. Johann Ulrich Fechter 3rd, 1741-1765

BERN

8826-8830. 16. cent.
8831. about 1690
8832. about 1800
8833. since 1893

BIEL (BIENNE)

8843. 18. cent.

CHUR

8847-8849. 16.-17. cent.

EINSIEDELN CANTON SCHWYZ

8853. 17.-18. cent.
8854. 18. cent.

FRIBOURG

8859. about 1630
8860. about 1700
8861. about 1750

GENOVA

8865-8866. 18. cent.
8867. 18. cent.
8869. standard for silver
8870. standard for silver
8871. standard for silver
8872. standard for gold
8873. guarantee for silver
8874. guarantee for gold
8876. gilded silver
8878. since 1881
8883. with standard mark

LAUSANNE

8889. 18. cent.

LUCERNE

8894. 16. cent.
8896-8903. J. Bossart and Karl Bossart

MORAT CANTON FREIBURG

8908. late 18. cent.

NEUCHATEL

8910-8912. 17.-18. cent.
8913. 1820-1866
8914. 1797-1881
8916b. since 1893

NEUVEVILLE

8930. 17. cent.

PAYERNE

8932-8933. 16. and 17. cent.

RAPPERSVIL (CANTON ZURICH)

8936-8937. 16.-17. cent.
8938. 18. cent.

SCHAFFHAUSEN

8945. 16. cent.
8946. 17.-18. cent.
8947-8948. 18. cent.
8949. since 1893

SION

8956. 16. cent.
8957. 17. cent.
8958. 18. cent.

STANS (CANTON UNTERWALDEN)

8968-8969. F r a n z Remigius Trachser, 1724-1752

SURSEE CANTON (LUCERNE)

8970-8971. 17. and 18. cent.
8972. beginning of 17. cent.
8973-8975. 17.-18. cent.
8976. about 1680
8977. 1707

THUN

8986-8987. 17. cent.

URI

8990. inspection mark

VEVEY

8992. 16. and 17. cent.
8993-8994. 18. cent.
8995. 18. cent.

WINTERTHUR

9002. 18. cent.

ZOFINGEN, CANTON ARGAU

9005. 18. cent.

ZURICH

9007. 1545
9008. 1563
9009. 1563, 1564, 1565
9010. 1608
9011. 1621
9012-9013. early 17. cent.
9014. about 1629
9015. 1631
9016. 1633
9017. 1638
9018. 1642
9019-9029. 17. and 18. cent.
9030. 1667
9031. 1674
9032. 1752
9033. 1779
9037. Abraham Gessner, 1571-1613
9051-9052. Hans Jacob Holzhalb, 1634-1657

ZUG

9080. 1584
9081. 1620
9082. 17. cent.
9083-9084. 18. cent.

SPAIN

9092-9093. since 1881

AGUILAR, PROVINCE CORDOBA

9094. 17. cent.

ASTORGA

9095. 16. cent.

BARCELONA

9096. 14.-16. ? cent.
9097. 15. cent.
9098. 15. cent.
9099-9100. 15.-16. cent.
9101. 16. cent.
9102. late 16. cent.
9103. 16. (also 17. ?) cent.
9104-9105. 16. (also 17. ?) cent.

CERVANTES, PROVINCE LUGO, or CERVERA, PROVINCE LERIDA

9133. 15.-17. cent. ?

CORDOBA

9134. 15. cent.

MADRID

9160. 18. cent.

PALMA MALLORCA

9164. 15. cent.
9165. 15.-16. cent.
9166. 16. cent.

TOLEDO

9173. 16. cent.
9174. about 1600
9175. 17. cent.

VALENCIA

9178. 16. cent.

VALLADOLID

9179. Juan de Benavente, 1565-1609

ZARAGOZA

9180. 14. and 15. cent.
9181-9182. 16. cent.

JUGOSLAVIA

ZAGREB

9198. 1866-1872
9199. since 1872

BELGRADE

9200-9203. gold 1882-1919
9204-9207. silver 1882-1919
9208. import gold
9209. import silver

LAIBACH (LJUBLJANA)

9210. 18. cent.
9211. 1802
9212. 1806
9213. 19. cent.
9214. 1807/08 and 1824-66.
9215. 1866/68
9216. 1868/72
9217. since 1872

NEUSATZ (NUVI SAD)

9219. inspection mark
9220. 1866-1872
9221. since 1872

RAGUSA (DUBROVNIK)

9222. 17. or 18. cent.
9223. 1866/67
9224. 1868/72
9225. since 1872

CZECHOSLOVAKIA

9226. standard mark 1-4
9227-9229. standard marks
9230. import mark silver

ALTSOHL (ZVOLEN)

9231. 1657

BRUNN (BRNO)

9233-9234. till 1646
9235. 1683
9236. 1769
9237. 1806
Official marks
9238. 1807-1866
9239. 1866-1868
9240. 1869-1872
9241. since 1872
9242. 1806/07
9243. 1810-1824
9244. 1811-1824

EGER (CHEB)

9250. 17.-18. cent.
9251. beginning of 18. cent.
9252. 1868-1872
9253. since 1872

HOTZENPLOTZ (OSOBLAHA)

9257. 1769

(HUNGARIAN) HRADISCH

9258. 1608
9259. 1769

IGLAU (JIHLAVA)

9260. 1548-beginning of 18. cent.
9261. 1769 (-1776).
9262. 1807-1866
9263. 1866-1868
9264. 1869-1872
9265. since 1872

KASCHAU (KOSICE)

9267. 16. cent.
9268. 17.-18. cent.

9269-9270. 1799-1866
9271. 1866-1872
9272. since 1872

KREMNITZ (KREMNICA)

9276. inspection mark

KREMSIER (KROMERIZ)

9277. 1689
9278-9279. 1769
9280. 1769

LEUTSCHAU (LEVOCA)

9281. 1664
9282-9285. 17. cent.
9286. since 1872

MORAVIAN TRUBAU

9294. 17. cent. to 19.
cent.
9295. 1813
9296. 1866-1872
9297. since 1872

NIKOLSBURG (MIKULOV)

9299. 1769

OLMUTZ (OLOMOUC)

9300. 1593, 1599
9301. 17. cent.
9302. 1755
9303. 1769-1776

Official marks

9304. 1807-1866
9305. 1866-1868
9306. 1869-1872
9307. since 1872
9308. 1810-1824 in the
free mark

PRAGUE (PRAHA)

9312. 16. cent.
9313. 17. cent.

9314. second half of 17.
cent.
9315-9316. 1673
9317. beginning of 18.
cent.
9318. middle of 18. cent.
9319. end of 17. cent. till
second half of 18.
cent.
9320. since 1776
9321. 1795
9322. 1800

Official marks

9323. 1807-1813
9324. 1814-1866
9325. 1866-1872
9326. since 1872
9327. 1806/07
9328. 1810-1824
9330a. 1776-1806
9330b. import silver
1902-21

PRESSBURG
(BRATISLAVA)

9364. 1576
9365. 17. cent.
9366. 17.-18. cent.
9367. 18. cent.
9368. 1866-1872
9369. since 1872

ROSENAU (ROZNAVA)

9363. 19. cent.

SCHEMNITZ

Inspection marks

9364. 1576
9365. 17. cent.
9366. 17.-18. cent.
9367. 18. cent.
9368. 1866-1872
9369. since 1872

TROPPAU (OPAVA)

9376. 16.-17. cent.
9377. 1674
9378. 1759
9379. 1789-1806

Official marks

9380. 1807-1866
9381. 1866-1868
9382. since 1872

TYRNAU (TRNAVA)
9387. 18. cent.

ZNAIM (ZNOJMO)

9389. 1727
9390. 1769
9391. official mark 1807
1866

HUNGARY

BUDAPEST

Inspection marks

9394. 17.-18. cent.
9395. 18. cent.
9396-9397. 18.-19. cent.
9398-9399. 1808, 1866
9401. 1866-1872
9402. since 1872
9403-9404. 17.-18. cent.
9405-9406. 18.-19. cent.

GRAN (ESZTERGOM)

9419. 18.-19. cent.

KECSKEMET

9418. 16. cent.

MISKOLCZ

9421. since 1872

BIBLIOGRAPHY

"English Goldsmiths and Their Marks"—Sir Charles James Jackson. Macmillan and Co. Ltd. London, 1921.

"History of Old Sheffield Plate"—Frederick Bradbury. Macmillan. 1912.

"Der Goldschmiede Merkzeichen"—Marc Rosenberg. Berlin, 1928.

"American Silversmiths and Their Marks"—Stephen G. C. Ensko. New York, 1927.

"Les Poinçons de L'Orfèvrerie Française"—Louis Carré. Paris, 1928.

"Guide de L'Amatur d'Orfèvrerie Française"—Louis Carré. Paris, 1929.

"Domestic Silver of Great Britain and Ireland"—Edward Wenham. Oxford University Press. London, 1931.

"Old English Silver"—William W. Watts. E. Benn, Ltd. London, 1924.

"Old Silver of Europe and America"—Edward Alfred Jones. B. T. Batsford, Ltd. London, 1928.

"Chats on Old Silver"—Arthur Hayden. T. F. Unwin Ltd. London, 1915.

"English Domestic Silver"—Charles C. Oman. A. C. Black Ltd. London, 1934.

"Matthew Boulton"—H. W. Dickinson. Cambridge University Press. London, 1937.

"Paul de Lamerie"—P. A. S. Phillips. B. T. Batsford, Ltd. London, 1935.

"American Silversmiths and Their Marks II"—Stephen G. C. Ensko. New York, 1937.

"Early American Silvermarks"—James Graham Jr. New York, 1936.

"American Church Silver"—Museum of Fine Arts. Boston, Mass., 1911.

"American Silver"—Introduction. R. T. H. Halsey. Museum of Fine Arts. Boston, Mass., 1906.

"American Collector"—New York, 1936 and 1937. Various.

GENERAL INDEX